Studies in the History of Medieval Religion

VOLUME IX

WESTMINSTER ABBEY AND ITS PEOPLE

c.1050–c.1216

This book surveys the monastic community at Westminster from the time when Edward the Confessor (1042–1066) adopted it as his burial church to the end of the reign of King John, tracing its history and development and studying its most notable personalities in detail.

Originating according to legend during the Roman occupation, the West Minster was converted from a little collegiate church into a Benedictine monastery around 970. However, the growth of its significance largely dates from its endowment by King Edward, who commissioned a lavish rebuilding of the abbey church, a focal point in his programme of monarchical propaganda. In the period between the deaths of Edward and John, one of comparative tranquillity, the abbey grew substantially in power and influence.

Dr Mason covers every aspect of the abbey community. She examines the careers of the abbots, including the scholarly Gilbert Crispin and King Stephen's son Gervase, the victim of Angevin hostility; and priors, such as the ambitious and confrontational Osbert de Clare, twice sent into monastic exile. Other lesser figures are not neglected: monks, scribes, craftsmen, lay servants, clerics in the monastic churches, personnel of the royal court associated with the abbey, visiting legates and other prelates – and the laity who frequented the abbey. The author also considers the community's dealings with the growing ecclesiastical bureaucracy; the management of its properties, including its parochial churches; its relationship with other religious houses; and its promotion of cults and festivals.

Dr EMMA MASON is Reader in Medieval History at Birkbeck College, London.

Studies in the History of Medieval Religion

ISSN 0955–2480

General Editor Christopher Harper-Bill

I

Dedications of Monastic Houses in England and Wales 1066–1216
Alison Binns

II

The Early Charters of the Augustinian Canons of
Waltham Abbey, Essex, 1062–1230
Edited by Rosalind Ransford

III

Religious Belief and Ecclesiastical Careers in Late Medieval England
Edited by Christopher Harper-Bill

IV

The Rule of the Templars: the French text of the Rule of
the Order of the Knights Templar
Translated and introduced by J. M. Upton-Ward

V

The Collegiate Church of Wimborne Minster
Patricia H. Coulstock

VI

William Waynflete: Bishop and Educationalist
Virginia Davis

VII

Medieval Ecclesiastical Studies in honour of Dorothy M. Owen
Edited by M. J. Franklin and Christopher Harper-Bill

VIII

A Brotherhood of Canons Serving God: English Secular
Cathedrals in the Later Middle Ages
David Lepine

X

Gilds in the Medieval Countryside: Social and
Religious Change in Cambridgeshire c.1350–1558
Virginia R. Bainbridge

WESTMINSTER ABBEY AND ITS PEOPLE

c.1050–c.1216

EMMA MASON

THE BOYDELL PRESS

First published 1996
The Boydell Press, Woodbridge

ISBN 0 85115 396 8

The Boydell Press is an imprint of Boydell & Brewer Ltd
PO Box 9, Woodbridge, Suffolk IP12 3DF, UK
and of Boydell & Brewer Inc.
PO Box 41026, Rochester, NY 14604–4126, USA

British Library Cataloguing in Publication Data

Mason, Emma
Westminster Abbey and its people, c.1050–c.1216. – (Studies in the history of medieval religion ; v. 9)
1. Westminster Abbey – History 2. Monastic and religious life – History – Middle Ages 3. England – Church history – 1066–1485
I. Title
255.1'00942132
ISBN 0851153968

Library of Congress Cataloging-in-Publication Data

Mason, Emma.
Westminster Abbey and its people, c.1050–c.1216 / Emma Mason.
p. cm. – (Studies in the history of medieval religion, ISSN 0955–2480 ; v. 9)
Includes bibliographical references and index.
ISBN 0–85115–396–8 (alk. paper)
1. Westminster Abbey – History. 2. Monasticism and religious orders – England – History – Middle Ages, 600–1500. 3. Westminster (London, England) – Church history. I. Title. II. Series.
BX2595.W47M37 1996
271'.1042132 – dc20 96–13652

This publication is printed on acid-free paper

Printed in Great Britain by
St Edmundsbury Press Ltd, Bury St Edmunds, Suffolk

Contents

In Memoriam

Jennifer Bray
1947–1987

Acknowledgements

My thanks are offered to all those bodies which granted financial support to successive stages of my work on the eleventh- and twelfth-century charters of Westminster abbey which formed the basis of the present study. The Leverhulme Trust awarded me a Research Fellowship in 1983 and extended it in 1984, the Nuffield Foundation awarded a grant in 1985, and subsequently the British Academy made me a most generous Personal Award.

For permission to reproduce the articles published as appendices to this study, I am grateful to the following: Cambridge University Press, in respect of 'Westminster Abbey and the Monarchy between the Reigns of William I and John (1066–1216)', which was published in *The Journal of Ecclesiastical History*, vol. 41 (1990), pp. 199–216; the Ecclesiastical History Society, in respect of ' "The Site of King-Making and Consecration": Westminster Abbey and the Crown in the Eleventh and Twelfth Centuries', published in Diana Wood, ed., *The Church and Sovereignty c.590–1918: Essays in Honour of Michael Wilks*, Studies in Church History, Subsidia 9 (Oxford, 1991), pp. 57–76; Medieval Institute Publications, Western Michigan University, in respect of 'The Donors of Westminster Abbey Charters c.1066–1240', originally published in *Medieval Prosopography*, vol. 8, no. 2 (Autumn 1987), pp. 23–39; Headstart History, in respect of 'Westminster Abbey and its Parish Churches', first published in *Monastic Studies: the Continuity of Tradition*, II, ed. Judith Loades (Bangor, 1991), pp. 43–65. The maps are reproduced from Barbara Harvey, *Westminster Abbey and its Estates in the Middle Ages* (1977), by permission of Oxford University Press.

Over a long period of time, much invaluable advice and practical help was given to me by the staff of Westminster Abbey Library and Muniment Room, including the late Nicholas MacMichael, Keeper of the Muniments, and the late Howard Nixon, Librarian; by Enid Nixon, formerly Assistant Librarian; Christine Reynolds, Assistant Keeper of the Muniments; and Richard Mortimer, Keeper of the Muniments. My thanks are also offered to the staff of the British Library Students' Room; and to those of the College of Arms, London; Corpus Christi College, Cambridge; the Round Room of the Public Record Office, Chancery Lane, London; the Archives Department of St Bartholomew's Hospital; and the Department of Manuscripts of the Guildhall Library.

My understanding of the charters owes much to the generous advice of Barbara Harvey, in particular, and also to that of Diana Greenway, Jane Sayers and David Bates. Those who have advised on points of detail include David Carpenter, Stephen Church, Vanessa Harding, Brian Kemp, Patrick McGurk, Ian Short, David Sullivan, and Pamela Taylor, who also commented on a draft of Chapter One. Peter Kidson kindly allowed me to cite his unpublished lecture on the Imperial churches. Students of the History Department of Birkbeck College provided stimulating comment on several aspects of life in medieval Westminster.

Preparation of the copy for the press owes much to the meticulous care taken by Jane Dobson. Christopher Harper-Bill first encouraged me to offer the study for inclusion in this series, and Richard Barber and Caroline Palmer were encouraging and understanding when its completion was delayed by other constraints upon my time.

My greatest obligation is to the late Jennifer Bray, whose assistance was financed by the grant-awarding bodies named above. Her enthusiasm and commitment to the project went far beyond what would reasonably be expected of a research assistant, the more so in that latterly her health was failing rapidly. The dedication of this volume is offered in tribute to the memory of a supportive friend, an exemplary assistant and a fine historian in her own right.

2 July 1995 Emma Mason

Preface

My interest in Westminster Abbey dates back to the time when I was editing the charters of the Mauduit chamberlains of the Exchequer, who accumulated tenements in the vill of Westminster around the end of the twelfth century. Occasionally I exchanged information with Desmond Murphy, who was editing a selection of Westminster charters, and, like me, was working under the supervision of R.R. Darlington. After Mr Murphy's untimely death, his widow Phyllis, at the suggestion of Darlington, kindly invited me to continue his work. In due course a volume of Westminster's charters was published, and it is this corpus, ranging in date from the accession of William I to the last years of John's reign, which forms the basis of the present study. Its range has been extended both by an introductory chapter on the early history of the West Minster, down to the time of its endowment by King Edward and its reconsecration on 28 December 1065, and also by consideration of developments in some areas during the abbacy of William de Humez, 1214–22.

The great wealth and variety of the abbey's muniments ensures that any number of historians may be working on them simultaneously without treading on one-another's toes. Such is the volume of detailed documentation available that any one writer, after selecting a chronological span, still has to choose some clearly defined aspect of the abbey's activities. The focus of the present study, the abbey and its people, examines working relationships among inmates of the great church, and those pertaining between the monks and their neighbours, tenants and other associates. While the geographical balance of interests depicted in the surviving muniments ensures that attention is largely focused on Westminster abbey and its neighbouring vill, on the City of London and on Westminster's estates in the home counties, the diverse interests of the abbot and convent also encompassed lands and tenants within an outer radius touching both the West Midlands and Lincolnshire, and also led to correspondence with Continental clerics. Missions to the papal court, and unavoidable involvement in political developments in England add further layers to this depiction of the activities of the abbots and monks.

Given the writer's second main research interest, in the cathedral and diocese of Worcester, it was a particular pleasure to chart ongoing contacts between these two great churches and those connected with them. Abbots of Westminster regularly visited their broad acres in south-west Mercia, while former members of the communities of Worcester or Great Malvern came to the abbey for refuge. In a dramatic role-reversal, the formidable sheriff Urse de Abetot, depicted by the Worcester monk Hemming as a persecutor, is found at Westminster making restitution of wrongfully-alienated lands, in an urgent attempt to retrieve the spiritual prospects of his dying brother.

Westminster is famous – or notorious – for its output of forged charters, a corpus initiated under the auspices of Prior Osbert de Clare, but augmented at intervals well into the thirteenth century. This initiative was firmly grounded in the need to exploit to the full the potential of all properties by claiming for them wide-ranging fiscal and franchisal rights. It is conjectural whether such creative skills were ever made available, at a price, to benefactors. The forged charters which the Mauduit chamberlains commissioned could equally well have been drawn up by their Exchequer clerks, who certainly acted for them in a private capacity. On the other hand, when the dependent cell of Hurley embarked on the production of forgeries, inspiration and probably also instruction came from the mother-house. The monks of Westminster, far from seeing anything morally wrong in this activity, would hold it to be an essential adjunct to the maximizing of returns on their property, a duty which was owed by the custodians of the lands of St Peter.

1

Westminster from its Origins to the Reign of King Edward

Romano-British origins were claimed for the church of Westminster by the fifteenth-century monk-historian of the abbey, John Flete. He dated the foundation of the first church on the site to A.D. 184 when, he related, the British King Lucius designated his new foundation as the place of royal burial and the depository of the regalia.[1] Lucius, 'a king of Britain', was briefly mentioned by the Venerable Bede in his *Ecclesiastical History of the English People*, completed in A.D. 731. Bede told how Lucius wrote to Pope Eleutherius (c.174–89), requesting his help in converting to Christianity.[2] In fact, Bede's story derives from a mis-application of an episode relating to Lucius, king of Edessa, which occurs in the *Liber Pontificalis*, a work of the mid-sixth century.[3] Bede's brief account was expanded, with much circumstantial detail, by Geoffrey of Monmouth in *The History of the Kings of Britain*, completed shortly before January 1139.[4] Neither Bede nor Geoffrey associated Lucius with the foundation of the first church of Westminster, although the work of one, or both, of these writers presumably inspired the 'first foundation' narrative of John Flete. He related that this first church was subsequently desecrated, and its site was occupied by a temple of Apollo, during the reign of the Emperor Diocletian, but that the British ruler, Ambrosius Aurelianus, restored the church 'in 488'.[5] Flete cited 'a certain very ancient

1 John Flete, *The History of Westminster Abbey*, ed. J. Armitage Robinson (Cambridge, 1909), p. 34.

2 *Bede's Ecclesiastical History of the English People*, ed. B. Colgrave and R.A.B. Mynors (Oxford, 1969), pp. 24–5.

3 *Ibid.*, p. 24, n. 2. See also J.N.D. Kelly, *The Oxford Dictionary of Popes* (Oxford, 1986), pp. 11–12.

4 Geoffrey of Monmouth, *The History of the Kings of Britain*, transl. and introd. L. Thorpe (Harmondsworth, 1966), pp. 124–6. Geoffrey gives Lucius's death as A.D. 156 (*ibid.*, p. 126). On the date of Geoffrey's work, see J. Gillingham, 'The Context and Purposes of Geoffrey of Monmouth's *History of the Kings of Britain*', in Marjorie Chibnall, ed., *Anglo-Norman Studies*, XIII, *Proceedings of the Battle Conference 1990* (Woodbridge, 1991), p. 100 and n. 5.

5 Flete, *The History of Westminster Abbey*, pp. 34–5, 63, 76–7.

book of chronicles written in the old language of the English or the Saxons',[6] but his source has not been traced. Probably Flete wanted to boost Westminster's claims to precedence over the ancient church of Glastonbury, an issue which had topical relevance at the time when he was writing.[7] Classical antecedents would also enable Westminster to upstage the cathedral church of St Paul, which allegedly stood on the site of a temple of Diana, and Flete's claims on behalf of his own church were perhaps inspired by the discovery of Roman artifacts on or near the monastic site.[8] The eleventh-century monks, in contrast, ascribed the origins of their house to the impact of the mission led by St Augustine of Canterbury, who was sent by Pope Gregory I (590–604) to convert Britain.

Sulcard, monk of Westminster, writing in the time of Abbot Vitalis (1076–c.1085), stated that the house was founded by King Æthelbert of Kent (560–616). Having honoured St Paul by founding a church dedicated to him in London, he wanted to honour St Peter in the same way, and encouraged a rich Londoner and his wife to build a church with this dedication on Thorney Island. Later legend identified the couple as Sæberht of the East Saxons and his wife Æthelgoda, who were reputedly buried in their new church early in the seventh century. According to this tradition, St Peter's church was known as the West Minster (*occidentale monasterium*) 'whether from the prevailing wind or because of its location to the west of the city [of London]'.[9]

Its site was chosen to give it some natural protection. The river Tyburn divided as it entered the Thames, some two miles west of the city of London. Marshes formed around its branches, isolating a little gravel island in their midst.[10] On this was built the first church of St Peter. Its Petrine dedication, documented initially in sources dating from some centuries after the original foundation, was by far the most popular one for English religious houses in

6 *Ibid.*, p. 34.

7 Barbara Harvey, *Westminster Abbey and its Estates in the Middle Ages* (Oxford, 1977), p. 17 and n. 1.

8 G. Rosser, *Mediaeval Westminster 1200–1540* (Oxford, 1989), pp. 12–13. Archaeological evidence indicates that there was a major Roman temple on, or near, the site of St Paul's cathedral, although its dedication is uncertain: D. Perring, *Roman London* (London, 1991), pp. 1, 60–1, 93, 95, 106. Westminster has been tentatively identified as the original site where Watling Street crossed the Thames: *ibid.*, pp. 1, 3, 5. See also R. Merrifield, 'The Contribution of Archaeology to our Understanding of Pre-Norman London, 1973–1988', in Lindy Grant, ed., *Mediaeval Art, Architecture and Archaeology in London*, Conference Transactions for the year 1984, British Archaeological Association (London, 1990), pp. 5; 14 n. 23.

9 B.W. Scholz, 'Sulcard of Westminster: "Prologus de Construccione Westmonasterii" ', *Traditio*, 20 (1964), pp. 59, 64–5, 85; Flete, *The History of Westminster Abbey*, pp. 40, 42, 63, 83. However, there is no genuine evidence to support the tradition that Saberht was buried at Westminster. Harvey, *Westminster Abbey and its Estates*, p. 372. On Saberht, see also S. Bassett, *The Origins of Anglo-Saxon Kingdoms* (Leicester, 1989), pp. 113, 120, 136, 138.

10 Rosser, *Mediaeval Westminster*, p. 9.

the seventh and eighth centuries, when it was fostered by kings and nobles making the pilgrimage to Rome, and by other high-level contacts with the papacy.[11]

Sulcard related a memorable story of how, when St Peter's was completed, a high tide prevented the bishop of London, Mellitus (604–c.617), from crossing to the island to dedicate the church. As night fell, a fisherman was hailed by a stranger, who asked to be ferried over to the island. On landing, he struck the ground twice, producing two springs of water (rendering the site habitable), before entering the building, which then became radiant with light, while a heavenly choir burst into song. The stranger was St Peter himself, who proceeded to consecrate the church, and then told the fisherman to notify Bishop Mellitus that the ceremony was completed. St Peter promised the fisherman, as recompense for his help, a large catch of fish, but warned him that he must never again go fishing on Sundays, as he had been doing that night. Sure enough, when Bishop Mellitus eventually reached the island, he found that the marks of consecration were already on the walls. Since there was now no need for him to dedicate the church, he simply preached, and celebrated mass.[12] Differing interpretations can be placed on Sulcard's story, but most likely it was intended to highlight Westminster's claim to be exempt from the authority of the bishop of London, an issue which was contested with great intensity from the late eleventh century well into the twelfth.

Leaving aside the legendary origins of the church, it is arguable that it owed its origins to an East Saxon initiative, to underline the political presence of this dynasty in the area, and promoting the Christian religion in territory where missionaries had at best a precarious foothold.[13] The bleak location of this first church is underlined by its early name of Thorn Island (*Torneia* or *Torneie*), 'that terrible place which is called Thorney by the inhabitants'. The name of Thorney, together with that of Westminster, is recorded in documents which, with varying degrees of credibility, purport to date from between the late eighth century and the late tenth.[14] The first priests who moved into this minster church were not in monastic orders and may well have been married men with families. Their task was to pray for the rulers of the East Saxons, while simultaneously serving as a visible reminder of their political hold over the area.[15]

The royal house of the East Saxons was established with Kentish help not

11 Alison Binns, *Dedications of Monastic Houses in England and Wales 1066–1216* (Woodbridge, 1989), pp. 20–21.

12 Scholz, 'Sulcard of Westminster', pp. 83–5.

13 On the activities of Saberht and his successors, see Barbara Yorke, 'The Kingdom of the East Saxons', *Anglo-Saxon England*, 14 (1985), pp. 1–36, esp. pp. 1–2, 16–18.

14 J.E.B. Gover, A. Mawer and F.M. Stenton, with S.J. Madge, *The Place-Names of Middlesex*, English Place-Name Society, XVIII (Cambridge, 1942), p. 165.

15 On the staffing and function of early minsters, see John Blair, 'From Minster to Parish Church', in John Blair, ed., *Minsters and Parish Churches: the Local Church in Transition*

long before Sæberht attained power. King Æthelbert of Kent was his maternal uncle,[16] which supports the foundation story depicting Sæberht acting on the prompting of this more powerful ruler. The geographical extent of the East Saxon kingdom varied throughout its history. In the early seventh century, it probably included what later became known as Essex, Middlesex (whose inhabitants had been absorbed some time earlier), and part of Hertfordshire. Surrey, 'the southern region', was a buffer zone over which rulers of several rival kingdoms contended.[17] Throughout its existence, the kingdom of the East Saxons was usually subject to more powerful rulers, who reinforced their dominance by attempts to convert its pagan people. When, in A.D. 604, Sæberht was converted to Christianity, he and his kingdom were currently under the control of King Æthelbert of Kent, a fact underlined by the latter's foundation of St Paul's in London. Within a year of the death of Æthelbert, which occurred in 616, Sæberht himself was dead, possibly killed in an ensuing pagan reaction. Sæberht's sons promptly expelled Bishop Mellitus from London. After his death in 624, there was an interval of some thirty years before any successor was established in the see. It is doubtful whether the early church on Thorney survived for any length of time during the troubled period which followed Sæberht's death. Even though there was a virtual continuity of succession in the see of London from the time of Bishop Cedd (c.653–664), the East Saxon kingdom continued to experience unrest and instability throughout much of the seventh century.[18]

Later Westminster tradition claimed that the church was eventually restored by Offa of the East Saxons, who was the reputed donor of Blechenham, in Hendon (Middx).[19] He was an under-king, subject to more powerful kinsmen. His name, an unusual one in his dynasty, is associated with the royal house of Mercia, to which the East Saxons were subordinated from the latter part of the seventh century.[20] Offa came to power in 694 or later. If he really did restore or (re-) found the West Minster, this would reinforce his political presence in the area around London, within which he probably occupied a royal palace at Aldermanbury. Sites for minster-churches were often founded by rulers on estates near their residences, and were chosen for their historical associations, which enabled the rulers to enhance their legitimacy.[21] In view of the chequered history of the East Saxon dynasty throughout the seventh century, Offa would welcome an opportunity to associate

950–1200, Oxford University Committee for Archaeology, Monograph no. 17, 1988, pp. 1–2.

16 Yorke, 'The Kingdom of the East Saxons', p. 16.

17 *Ibid.*, pp. 27–30.

18 *Ibid.*, pp. 18, 31–2.

19 Scholz, 'Sulcard of Westminster', p. 66. On Blechenham, see Harvey, *Westminster Abbey and its Estates*, p. 21.

20 Yorke, 'The Kingdom of the East Saxons', pp. 22, 25–7.

21 Rosser, *Mediaeval Westminster*, p. 12. On the political potential of minsters, see J. Blair, 'Minsters in the Landscape', in D. Hooke, ed., *Anglo-Saxon Settlements* (Oxford, 1988),

himself with a church alleged to have been founded by one of his more reputable predecessors. Offa's support, though, did not fully guarantee Westminster's survival, owing to the constraints of Mercian overlordship, which had been asserted by King Wulfhere, from A.D. 664.[22] His successor, Æthelred of Mercia (675–704), is known to have been actively involved in East Saxon affairs, from c.688, and it was most likely in his time that London became an important trading outlet for Mercia.[23] On Æthelred's relinquishing the throne for a life of religious retirement at Bardney, his nephew Cenred succeeded as king of Mercia and overlord of London and Middlesex, but his reign was a short one. Arguably it was the influence of his uncle which caused him to abdicate in turn, to leave the way clear for the accession of Æthelred's son Ceolred, in 709. Cenred went off to Rome, taking with him the East Saxon Offa.[24] Any ensuing patronage for the West Minster must therefore come from the Mercian royal house.

Ceolred's successor, Æthelbald (716–57), finally detached London and Middlesex from the control of the East Saxons and incorporated the region into Mercia.[25] Mercian hegemony opened up new prospects for Westminster, thanks to the growing trading wealth of London, or rather, of its suburb to the west of its walls. The walled city itself was essentially a fortified enclave, sheltering the bishop, with his cathedral and its clerical staff, together with the royal palace, fully occupied only when the Mercian king visited London. The trading area, in contrast, was centred on the present-day Aldwych (the 'old *wic*' or trading-post) and the Strand. In fact the residential area stretched as far as the present-day district of Westminster.[26]

King Offa (757–96) is recorded as having granted to the West Minster the Hertfordshire manor of Aldenham.[27] While the fall of dynasties, and of kingdoms, might destabilize such endowments as the minster accumulated in this period, yet its Petrine dedication and its geographical location were assets which would appeal to newcomers. Incoming kings would assume the role of benefactor in order to enlist spiritual support for their rule; a territorial 'presence' near to the increasingly-important London, and a recognition of

pp. 35–58; E. Ewig, 'Résidence et capitale pendant le Haut Moyen Age', *Revue Historique*, 230 (1963), pp. 25–72.

22 Yorke, 'The Kingdom of the East Saxons', p. 31.

23 *Ibid*., p. 33. On the importance to ecclesiastical proprietors of commercial activities in the port of London, see Susan Kelly, 'Trading privileges from eighth-century England', *Early Mediaeval Europe*, 1 (1992), pp. 3–28.

24 Yorke, 'The Kingdom of the East Saxons', p. 34.

25 *Ibid*., p. 35.

26 Merrifield, 'The Contribution of Archaeology to our Understanding of Pre-Norman London', pp. 11–12; Kelly, 'Trading Privileges from Eighth-century England', p. 3.

27 *Cartularium Saxonicum*, ed. W. de Gray Birch, 3 vols and index (London, 1885–93), I (1885), no. 245, pp. 339–40. The text of this grant, as it now survives, is of doubtful authenticity: P.H. Sawyer, *Anglo-Saxon Charters: an Annotated List and Bibliography* (London, 1968), no. 124. Aldenham was, however, an early possession of Westminster's: Harvey, *Westminster Abbey and its Estates*, pp. 21, 345.

the legitimacy of their authority. Given these priorities, the real surprise about Offa's patronage is that it was so limited, and that he preferred St Alban's abbey as his religious base in the region. Coenwulf of Mercia (796–821) was of a rival dynasty to that of Offa, but he too is documented as having perceived the advantages deriving from his becoming a benefactor of Westminster.[28] Reputed benefactions of the Mercian kings must be discussed cautiously though, since all such early grants are known only from suspect documents. The West Minster perhaps derived more stable benefits from the expansion of suburban settlement, up the north bank of the Thames, virtually to Thorney, and the continuous survival of this suburb throughout the later Anglo-Saxon period.[29] Minster churches had pastoral oversight of the neighbouring laity, and consequently one frequent source of income was church scot, which was often imposed for their benefit by rulers.[30] Some such steady income was certainly needed in the ninth century, when Mercian supremacy gave way to that of the West Saxons, whose king, Egbert, conquered the East Saxons in A.D. 825. The London region was drawn into the West Saxon orbit, and the bishops of London began to attest the charters of its rulers.[31]

By the middle decades of the ninth century, the dwindling of royal patronage was the least of the West Minster's problems. Once the Danish invasions were under way, London suffered major assaults in 842 and 851, and was occupied in 872.[32] The ravaging of the Danish fleet and army in its hinterland probably led to the looting of Westminster and the damaging of its property, but the silence of the sources indicates its relatively low place in the hierarchy of minsters which were attacked at this time. In 886 came a much-needed respite, when Alfred, king of the West Saxons, seized London and entrusted it to Æthelred of Mercia.[33] West Saxon sources consistently styled him ealdorman, indicating his subordination to Alfred, while the Mercians, and their Celtic neighbours, regarded him as having royal status.[34] This revival of Mercian control over London and its hinterland finally lapsed

28 His benefaction is confirmed in a charter of King Edgar, *Cartularium Saxonicum*, III, no. 1050.

29 Rosser, *Mediaeval Westminster*, pp. 9–12; Merrifield, 'The Contribution of Archaeology', p. 12.

30 M.J. Franklin, 'The Identification of Minsters in the Midlands', in R. Allen Brown, ed., *Anglo-Norman Studies, VII, Proceedings of the Battle Conference 1984* (Woodbridge, 1985), pp. 70–71.

31 Yorke, 'The Kingdom of the East Saxons', p. 36.

32 *The Anglo-Saxon Chronicle*, transl. and ed. Dorothy Whitelock, with D.C. Douglas and Susie I. Tucker (London, 1961), *sub an.* 842, 851, 872; *Alfred the Great: Asser's Life of King Alfred and other contemporary sources*, transl. and introd. S. Keynes and M. Lapidge (Harmondsworth, 1983), pp. 43, 68, 81.

33 *Anglo-Saxon Chronicle*, *sub an.* 887, *Alfred the Great*, pp. 43–4, 97–8.

34 E.B. Fryde, D.E. Greenway, S. Porter and I. Roy (eds), *Handbook of British Chronology*, 3rd edn (London, 1986), p. 17. See also *Alfred the Great*, pp. 190 (read with p. 336, n. 16); p. 256 n. 145; p. 323 n. 19.

on Æthelred's death in 911, when the city was acquired by the West Saxon King Edward 'the Elder'.[35]

The growing power of the kings of his line, and the gradual extension of their power over the whole of England, had the effect of marginalizing any status which the West Minster had accrued in earlier centuries through its usefulness to successive rulers, whether as a source of spiritual support; as a symbol of their political presence, or as a supplier of practical services of the kinds required of many minsters at that period.[36] Even the survival of some form of communal life at the West Minster between the mid-ninth century and the mid-tenth is debatable. Any continuous religious activity on the site is likely to have been on a very small scale. One outcome of the Danish invasions was that the victorious West Saxon dynasty absorbed into the royal fisc the lands of many of those minsters which had been devastated during the attacks. These lands comprised a valuable resource for the expanding monarchy. Occasionally the kings of the house of Wessex used estates to endow royal officials, but many remained in royal hands until the monastic revival of the mid-tenth century was well under way. The lands of some former minsters were then granted – or sold – to the reformers, to enable them to establish religious houses.[37] In this way, the site of the West Minster was acquired from King Edgar by Dunstan.[38] Westminster tradition dates the appointment of Wulfsige, the first known abbot, to 958, which would imply that Dunstan acted while he was briefly bishop of London (c.957–959) but the textual evidence for the date of the foundation is late, and decidedly suspect. The actual date was probably 970, when Dunstan was archbishop of Canterbury.[39] In later times, the community of Westminster depicted Dunstan as the prime mover in re-establishing their house, although in fact this re-foundation was one of many which occurred c.970, as part of a programme

35 *Anglo-Saxon Chronicle*, *sub an*. 911 (912, C, D).

36 Certain Hwiccian minsters, for instance, were required to stable the king's horses: Blair, 'From Minster to Parish Church', p. 3.

37 Robin Fleming, 'Monastic Lands and England's Defence in the Viking Age', *English Historical Review*, 100 (1985), pp. 241–65, see esp. pp. 247–51, 257, 265. Asser, the biographer of King Alfred, was one official recompensed with the land of former religious houses: *Alfred the Great*, pp. 97 and 264, n. 192. However, on the extent to which monastic lands were diverted to such uses see D.N. Dumville, 'Ecclesiastical Lands and the Defence of Wessex in the First Viking Age', in his *Wessex and England from Alfred to Edgar* (Woodbridge, 1992), pp. 29–54, esp. pp. 30, 53.

38 *Cartularium Saxonicum*, III, 1048; Sawyer, *Anglo-Saxon Charters*, no. 670; Harvey, *Westminster Abbey and its Estates*, pp. 22–3; Flete, *The History of Westminster*, pp. 12–13, 50–51.

39 The Westminster tradition is followed by William of Malmesbury, *Gesta Pontificum Anglorum*, ed. N.E.S.A. Hamilton, Rolls Series (London, 1870), p. 178; Flete, *The History of Westminster*, pp. 13, 45, 79–80; Scholz, 'Sulcard of Westminster', pp. 66–7, 86–7. See also N. Banton, 'Monastic Reform and the Unification of Tenth-Century England', in S. Mews, ed., *Religion and National Identity*, Studies in Church History, 18 (Oxford, 1982), pp. 76–7 and n. 35.

by which King Edgar reinforced his hegemony over territories acquired by his dynasty in recent generations.[40]

The monastic church continued to be known as Westminster, even though it now housed monks, rather than secular clerks, as minsters did. King Edgar guaranteed the establishment of this new monastery, and the stability of its new territorial endowment, but the costs of securing this endowment were met by Archbishop Dunstan. His efforts on behalf of Westminster can be deduced to some extent from the text of the *Telligraphus*, a twelfth-century charter spurious in its present form, but perhaps drawing on reliable tradition. This document states that Dunstan gave 120 *mancuses* of gold to King Edgar to obtain the church.[41] The late-eleventh century Westminster writer, Sulcard, names the price of its restoration as a gold ewer worth fifty *sicli*.[42] Dunstan's outlay on lands for Westminster's endowment, comprising those granted or restored by King Edgar, and those acquired from private individuals, totalled over £200.[43] King Edgar confirmed several estates: Fanton and Ham (in East Ham) in Essex; Aldenham in Hertfordshire (reputedly a benefaction of King Offa of Mercia); Paddington in Middlesex and Morden in Surrey.[44] Their geographical spread is consonant with the landholding of a small minster formerly subject to the kings of the East Saxons. Edgar made new grants of land in Datchworth with Watton, and in Holwell, Hertfordshire, additionally granting, or restoring, lands around Westminster itself. The estates acquired from King Edgar perhaps brought in an annual income of £60 in 1066, although the income of Paddington cannot be determined with certainty before 1535.[45] St Dunstan's own donations to Westminster strengthened its holdings in Middlesex, with estates at Cowley Peachley; Hanwell; Hendon; Shepperton; and Sunbury, which by 1066 had a total annual value of £35. In addition, he granted the reversion of Parham in Sussex, worth £4 in 1086.[46] Further benefactions augmented the Middlesex holdings in the next reign. King Æthelred (Unraed) donated the manor of Hampstead, worth £5 annually, besides re-confirming the manor of Paddington. In his reign, too, benefactions made by private individuals added to the pre-existing holdings in Essex, when Leofwine son of Wulfstan granted an estate at Kelvedon, and in Hertfordshire, where Ælfhelm Polga, a former

40 Banton, 'Monastic Reform and the Unification of Tenth-Century England', pp. 71–85.

41 Harvey, *Westminster Abbey and its Estates*, p. 22. Large donations were frequently valued in *mancuses* of gold in tenth-century texts.

42 Scholz, 'Sulcard of Westminster', p. 86. The *siclus* was originally a Hebrew gold or silver coin, mentioned in several German and Anglo-Saxon texts, and the equivalent of two silver *denarii*: *ibid.*, n. 1. By the time Sulcard wrote, it was no longer in use but he perhaps deemed that an archaic coin equated with the biblical *shekel* was appropriate in his foundation-narrative.

43 Harvey, *Westminster Abbey and its Estates*, p. 23.

44 *Ibid.*, pp. 341, 342, 345, 353, 358.

45 *Ibid.*, pp. 346, 354–5.

46 *Ibid.*, pp. 350, 352, 354, 359.

minister of King Edgar, granted land in Brickendon. Subsequent additions to the abbey's lands brought their annual value up to about £80 by 1042. This was a comfortable income, although not equal to that of the richest monasteries.[47] It supported a community of about twelve monks.[48]

The accumulation of estates in Middlesex during the later tenth century and the early eleventh included what has been likened to a 'corridor' of properties stretching north-west from the rural area around Westminster to northern Hendon, many of these lands abutting directly upon Watling Street. One consequence of this build-up was that Westminster's 'corridor' bordered on the substantial estates held by the bishop of London and the canons of St Paul's.[49] It is unlikely, though, that there was any intention of establishing the new abbey as a territorial counterpoise to the older secular church.[50] More probably, the 'Westminster Corridor' simply composed the only properties still available for monastic endowment in the south-east during the late tenth century, and may be compared to other swathes of ecclesiastical lands radiating from the area around London. These included the lands of St Paul's; the substantial Middlesex estates of the archbishop of Canterbury; the lands of Chertsey to the south-west and, further afield, those of St Albans, to the north-west.[51] The 'corridor' theory though does raise the possibility that a strategic design perhaps lay behind the endowment of Westminster, over the thirty years or so from its re-foundation. The lands which it accumulated in this period aligned with three routeways, each of major strategic significance. Westminster's lands bordered the north-west and westerly roads converging on London, together with the route on, and bordering, the Thames to the south-west. The Westminster 'presence' along Watling Street, the north-westerly route into the City, can be plotted in its estates stretching through Hendon, Hampstead and Paddington, approximately aligned with the present Edgware Road, then making a turn to the east, along the southern side of the Watling Street extension now represented by Oxford Street and High Holborn, as far as the gates of the City. Towards the Holborn end, Westminster's properties included land on the northern side of the road. Westminster's 'presence' on the westerly approaches centred on its lands in Hanwell, running across the routes from Bath and Oxford, which in turn merged with Watling Street in the vicinity of the present Marble Arch. The properties around Hanwell also bordered the River Brent, and fronted the River Thames around its important ford at Brentford. Moreover, Westminster's lands in Sunbury and Shepperton ran

47 *Ibid.*, pp. 23–4, 352–3.

48 William of Malmesbury, *Gesta Pontificum Anglorum*, p. 178.

49 D. Sullivan, *The Westminster Corridor* (London, 1994), pp. 64–7, 69–71, and Map A.

50 On the estates held by St Paul's in the tenth and eleventh centuries, see Pamela Taylor, 'The Endowment and Military Obligations of the See of London: a Reassessment of Three Sources', in Marjorie Chibnall, ed., *Anglo-Norman Studies, XIV, Proceedings of the Battle Conference 1991* (Woodbridge, 1992), pp. 287–312.

51 Pamela Taylor, in a personal communication.

along a stretch of the road between Staines and Kingston, and fronting the Thames.[52]

But while the location of Westminster's growing estates had strategic potential (much as did the concentrated holdings of St Paul's on the other side of the City),[53] yet the late Anglo-Saxon kings did not permit these ecclesiastical landholders to pose a political threat to the stability of London, with its economic and strategic importance. Neither the cathedral nor the abbey, nor, for that matter, any other landholder, was permitted to retain a private hundred in Middlesex.[54]

In the later part of Ethelred's reign, the resumption of Danish incursions brought renewed danger to London and its hinterland, first in 994, then in 1009, when the marauders 'lived off the shires on both sides of the Thames', in 1013 and finally in 1016, in which year Ethelred's son Edmund Ironside won a victory at Brentford.[55] This repeated foraging and trampling of armies would cause short-term depreciation of Westminster's estates, but no long-term losses are known.

Edmund's brief reign in southern England ended with his death late in 1016. Cnut was now acknowledged as king of all England, and set about eliminating surviving English magnates.[56] Religious houses had long been required to serve the secular interests of their royal patrons, and Westminster now became a temporary prison for the infant sons of the late King Edmund, before Cnut had them shipped abroad, with the intention of having them killed overseas.[57] A late source records Cnut as having been a benefactor of the abbey. Certainly he donated prestigious relics, including an arm of St Cyriacus, covered in gold and silver; relics of King Edward the Martyr, a finger and other bones of St George, and a finger of St Ælfheah.[58] Veneration of Edward the Martyr's cult was perhaps intended to raise Cnut's standing at the expense of Ethelred II, whose followers were blamed for Edward's death, while veneration of the murdered Archbishop Ælfheah would be intended to mollify anti-Danish feelings.[59] The Petrine dedication of Westminster

52 Sullivan, *The Westminster Corridor*, p. 70.

53 Taylor, 'The Endowment and Military Obligations of the See of London', esp. pp. 304–11.

54 *Ibid.*, p. 302.

55 *Anglo-Saxon Chronicle*, C (D, E), *sub an.* 994; 1009; 1013; 1016.

56 *Ibid.*, C (D, E), *sub an.* 1016; 1017.

57 *L'estoire des Engleis by Geffrei Gaimar*, ed. A. Bell, Anglo-Norman Text Society, 14–16 (Oxford, 1960), lines 4491–2, 4507. See also *The Chronicle of John of Worcester, II, 450–1066*, ed. R.R. Darlington and P.M. McGurk, Oxford Mediaeval Texts (Oxford, 1995), pp. 502–3, for Cnut's treatment of the children, although Westminster is not mentioned.

58 *Ricardi de Cirencestria Speculum Historiale de Gestis Regum Angliae*, ed. J.E.B. Mayor, Rolls Series, 2 vols (London, 1863–9), II, p. 185; Flete, *The History of Westminster Abbey*, p. 70.

59 M.K. Lawson, *Cnut. The Danes in England in the Early Eleventh Century* (London, 1993), pp. 139–42.

perhaps appealed to Cnut, who made a pilgrimage (perhaps even two) to Rome.[60]

Cnut perhaps also began the process by which Westminster became the hub of secular government. The old royal palace at Aldermanbury, within the city of London, dated from the time of the Mercian hegemony.[61] No doubt it appeared somewhat antiquated by the eleventh century, and there are tentative grounds for suggesting that it was Cnut who founded a new royal residence next to the abbey church, on Thorn Island.[62] It is usually King Edward who is credited with making the move to more salubrious and spacious surroundings, building a new royal palace, the West Hall, on this site,[63] but the location already had some significance for King Harold (I) Harefoot, one of Cnut's sons, who died in 1040. The circumstances of his burial occasioned the first mention of Westminster in the *Anglo-Saxon Chronicle*. According to both the E-text of the *Chronicle*, and also William of Malmesbury, Harold died in Oxford, but was buried at Westminster,[64] an indication that the dying king, or his entourage, acknowledged some special claim on the part of the abbey. The other versions of the *Chronicle* make no mention of where Harold died, but the twelfth-century Worcester chronicler, who agrees that the king was buried at Westminster, stated that he died in London.[65] In either case, it is remarkable that the suburban abbey was chosen for his burial, rather than St Paul's cathedral, where Ethelred II had been buried,[66] or else Winchester, where King Cnut had been buried,[67] as had members of the English royal line.

Even if Harold wanted to rest under the protection of the Prince of the Apostles, St Peter was among the dedicatees of both the Old Minster and the New Minster of Winchester.[68] It was customary to transport the bodies of

60 *Anglo-Saxon Chronicle*, *sub an.* 1031 D (E, F) for 1027. See also Frank Barlow, 'Two Notes: Cnut's Second Pilgrimage and Queen Emma's Disgrace in 1043', *English Historical Review*, 73 (1958), pp. 649–56; reprinted in F. Barlow, *The Norman Conquest and Beyond* (London, 1983), pp. 649–56.

61 J. Clark, *Saxon and Norman London* (London, 1989), p. 14 and maps on pp. 18, 25.

62 *The Carmen de Hastingae Proelio of Guy, Bishop of Amiens*, ed. Catherine Morton and Hope Muntz (Oxford, 1972), pp. xli and n. 1, 42–3 and nn. 3–4. On the debate concerning the date of this poem (and hence the extent to which its factual content may be balanced against poetic licence), see R.H.C. Davis, 'The Carmen de Hastingae Proelio', in R.H.C. Davis, *From Alfred the Great to Stephen* (London, 1991), pp. 79–100, and the publications listed in the Postscript to that article.

63 *The Life of King Edward who Rests at Westminster, Attributed to a Monk of Saint-Bertin*, ed. and transl. F. Barlow, 2nd edn (Oxford, 1992), pp. xlvi, 100, 102.

64 *Anglo-Saxon Chronicle* (E), *sub an.* 1039. William of Malmesbury gives Harold's death as April 1040: William of Malmesbury, *De Gestis Regum Anglorum*, ed. W. Stubbs, Rolls Series, 2 vols (London, 1887, 1889), I, p. 228.

65 *The Chronicle of John of Worcester, II, 450–1066*, pp. 528–9.

66 *Ibid.*, pp. 484–5.

67 *The Anglo-Saxon Chronicle* states that Cnut died at Shaftesbury and was buried at Winchester: C (D) *sub an.* 1035; E (F) *sub an.* 1036.

68 Binns, *Dedications of Monastic Houses in England and Wales*, p. 90.

kings over considerable distances to an appropriate burial church, but the choice of Westminster for Harold's burial is logical only if this church already had royal associations – that it was in the vicinity of a royal residence. If in fact he died in Oxford, and not in London, then the case for Westminster's perceived significance is heightened. By burying him at a site of symbolic importance for the monarchy, his advisors demonstrated their belief that they had served a legitimate king, not a usurper. The existence of a royal palace adjacent to a monastery, on the Continental model, and indeed, that of Winchester, would readily account for Harold's burial at Westminster.

There was perhaps a dawning awareness that the old royal 'capital', if such an anachronistic term may be used for Winchester, was inadequate as the hub of government for a king whose territories encompassed virtually the whole of England and, in theory, Denmark, too. The underlying significance of Harold's burial-place was highlighted with the arrival in England, some three months later, of his half-brother Harthacnut. He ordered that the dead king's body should be dug up and thrown into 'the fen', that is, the marshland surrounding Thorn Island. The disinterment was a public act, carried out by Ælfric Puttoc, archbishop of York (1023–51); Earl Godwin; Stir, the master of the royal household; Eadric, the royal steward; Thrond, the executioner, and an accompanying posse.[69] To the new regime, Harold was a usurper, to be obliterated from public memory. King Harthcnut (1040–42) had no recorded interest in Westminster abbey, and, like his father, he was buried at Winchester,[70] an act which symbolized the legitimacy of this line.

Harthacnut's successor, his uterine brother Edward, also regarded Harold as a usurper, and would not have acknowledged any precedent which the latter had set in the choice of a burial church. What did attract Edward, however, was the proximity of Westminster to London, with its strategic and economic importance, even though the monastery itself was still largely surrounded by fertile lands and green fields.[71] On deciding to have the abbey rebuilt as his burial church, he committed large sums to the project. His first *Life* claims that he assigned 'the tithes of all his revenues'. There was to be no counting of the cost, so long as the finished building was deemed worthy of God and St Peter. Both in its scale and in its architectural arrangements, the church was intended to be spectacular.[72] Probably the building work did make substantial ongoing demands on the royal revenues, as indicated in the first *Life*, which is the earliest relevant narrative, and one produced in court circles. Certainly, given the scale of the work, ongoing funding from the

69 Harold's body was retrieved by a fisherman and buried by the Danes in their cemetery in London: *The Chronicle of John of Worcester, II, 450–1066*, pp. 530–1; *Anglo-Saxon Chronicle* C (D), *sub an.* 1040. See also William of Malmesbury, *De Gestis Regum Anglorum*, I, p. 228.

70 *Anglo-Saxon Chronicle*, E (F), *sub an.* 1041; *The Chronicle of John of Worcester, II, 450–1066*, pp. 534–5, *s.a.* 1042.

71 *The Life of King Edward who Rests at Westminster*, pp. 66–8.

72 *Ibid.*, p. 68.

annual royal revenues is a more likely source than that indicated by the monk Sulcard – namely the funds which the king had intended to support a pilgrimage to Rome, which his magnates dissuaded him from making.[73]

As to when Edward began his project, the documentation is unclear. Two relevant writs, now surviving only in unauthentic forms, appear to date from 1042x1044, but others more certainly show that work had started by 1051, and perhaps a little earlier.[74] Progress was slow, though. Work was still under way on the abbey church in September 1065, when the queen's rival rebuilding project, the church of Wilton nunnery, was dedicated.[75] The new church of Westminster was sited some distance to the east of the older one, enabling the monks to remain in that, performing their essential task of celebrating the Divine Office without disruption, until work on the last stages of the nave of the new church necessitated the dismantling of the old one.[76] This occurred only during the abbacy of Vitalis (1076–c.1085).[77]

The great scale of King Edward's new church far outclassed any other building in England at that time. Its internal length has been calculated at 98.2 metres (322 feet), markedly bigger than the contemporary great churches being built in Normandy – both La Trinité and St Etienne in Caen; Jumièges, or Rouen cathedral, or even Chartres in France. In size, King Edward's Westminster more nearly matched Mainz and Speyer, great churches constructed under imperial patronage in the Rhineland.[78] The style of Westminster, on the other hand, most closely resembled Jumièges in Normandy, even though there were also parallells with various other contemporary Continental churches.[79] The rebuilding of Jumièges started in 1040, under the direction of its abbot, Robert Champart. He continued to support this work financially after 1044, when he moved to England, to become bishop of London. Most probably it was his influence which accounted for the stylistic resemblance between Jumièges and Westminster, even though the Norman abbey was itself far from complete when Robert returned to it in 1052.[80] The new church of Westminster far outshone Robert's cathedral of St Paul's, where no rebuilding project is known until after the devastating fire of 1087.[81]

King Edward's intentions in rebuilding Westminster on the scale which he

73 Scholz, 'Sulcard of Westminster', pp. 69–71; 90–91.

74 R.D.H. Gem, 'The Romanesque Rebuilding of Westminster Abbey (with a reconstruction by W.T. Ball)', in R. Allen Brown, ed., *Proceedings of the Battle Conference on Anglo-Norman Studies, III, 1980* (Woodbridge, 1981), p. 34. See also *Anglo-Saxon Writs*, ed. Florence E. Harmer, 2nd edn (Stamford, 1989), nos 73, 75 (1042–44) and nos 77–9.

75 *The Life of King Edward who Rests at Westminster*, pp. 70–74.

76 *Ibid.*, pp. 68–70; Gem, 'The Romanesque Rebuilding of Westminster Abbey', pp. 35–6.

77 Gem, 'The Romanesque Rebuilding of Westminster Abbey', p. 38.

78 *Ibid.*, pp. 44–6.

79 *Ibid.*, pp. 46, 50.

80 *Ibid.*, p. 54.

81 R.D.H. Gem, 'The Romanesque Architecture of Old St Paul's Cathedral and its Late

employed reflect the Continental influences which he had imbibed during his long years of exile. Most likely further influences reached him through the Continental clerics, Lotharingian as well as French, whom he recruited after his accession to the throne.[82] During his long years of exile, between 1016 and 1041, Edward would have witnessed the earlier phase of the monastic revival in Normandy from his privileged position in the ducal household.[83] Particular significance lies in his attestation of charters granted by Duke Robert to the abbey of Fécamp.[84] The abbey of the Trinity, Fécamp, was protected within the enclosure which also surrounded the ducal palace, a favourite residence of the rulers of Normandy from the mid tenth century to the late eleventh. Duke Richard II (996–1026) wanted to make the site a great centre – not only political and religious, but also economic and intellectual. The dukes preferred to hold their great and solemn Easter courts there, and both Duke Richard I and Richard II were buried on the outside of the basilica.[85] The young Edward would learn to appreciate the advantages of such a multi-purpose site, and most likely he was influenced by it when he conceived his plans for rebuilding Westminster.

On the other hand, the initial inspiration for putting Thorn Island to such a combination of uses perhaps lay with his predecessors, Cnut and Harold Harefoot. As has been indicated above, the former probably established a new palace there, while the latter was buried in the adjacent church. Both would probably have known of the layout of Fécamp, even if neither of them visited it. Although Cnut had arrived in England as a conquering Viking, once he became king he aspired to be accepted as an equal by his Continental contemporaries.[86] It would not be surprising if he decided to emulate Duke Richard's palatial residence, choosing a site which was more appropriate to his wide political horizons than was the old royal palace closely bordering on Winchester cathedral.

Another probable influence on Westminster emanating from northern

Eleventh-century Context', in Grant, ed., *Mediaeval Art, Architecture and Archaeology in London*, pp. 51, 53.

82 On the recruitment of men of Continental origin to the ranks of the higher clergy in Edward's reign, see F. Barlow, *The English Church 1000–1066*, 2nd edn (London, 1979), pp. 30–86.

83 F. Barlow, *Edward the Confessor* (London, 1970), pp. 36–47; S. Keynes, 'The Æthelings in Normandy', in Marjorie Chibnall, ed., *Anglo-Norman Studies, XIII, 1990* (Woodbridge 1991), pp. 173–205.

84 Keynes, 'The Æthelings in Normandy', pp. 187–90, 203.

85 Annie Renoux, 'Fouilles sur le site du château ducal de Fécamp (Xe- XIIe siècle): Bilan provisoire', in R. Allen Brown, ed., *Proceedings of the Battle Conference on Anglo-Norman Studies, IV, 1981* (Woodbridge, 1982), pp. 133–52 and 221–3. See also Annie Renoux, *Fécamp: du palais ducal au palais de Dieu* (Paris, 1991).

86 Cnut's pride in his honourable reception at the Easter Synod of 1027 by Pope John XIX, the Emperor Conrad and other western-European leaders is evident in a letter which he subsequently sent to his English subjects: Dorothy Whitelock, ed., *English Historical Documents c.500–1042*, 2nd edn (London, 1979), no. 53, cap. 5, p. 477.

France was the French royal burial church of St Denis, just outside Paris.[87] By Edward's time, this abbey already had long-established and mutually-beneficial links with the Capetian dynasty.[88] Relics of St Denis had been acquired by Abingdon and Glastonbury. King Edgar's daughter Edith was a devotee of the cult of St Denis, and dedicated to him the church which she built at Wilton. Here a later Edith, King Edward's wife, was educated. The king's physician, Baldwin, was a former monk of the abbey of St Denis, to which Edward granted the church of Deerhurst.[89] The significance for the French monarchy of the cult and its associated abbey would not be lost on King Edward, so that the abbey of St Denis, as well as the abbatial-palatial complex at Fécamp, most likely contributed to his concept of the role to be played by the rebuilt Westminster abbey.

Equally, however, German models can be cited. There, a series of royal burial churches, including Magdeburg and Bamburg, culminated, by Edward's day, with the magnificent Speyer, in the Franconian heartland, a location more suited to spectacular display than the earlier mausolea sited in frontier territories. At Speyer liturgical practice combined with the visual impact of the great church to project an aura of majesty.[90] King Edward's clerics included those born in Lotharingia or educated there, as was Leofric of Exeter. Indeed, high-ranking Englishmen such as Ealdred of Worcester, who had travelled in the German-speaking lands,[91] would have been aware of Speyer's role, whether or not they had actually seen the great church for themselves. While attention has been drawn to the probable French influences on King Edward, not only in respect of Westminster, but also on his concept of monarchy,[92] German influences should not be underestimated. Acquiring the throne as he did, after long years of exile, he would want to promote an image of invincible majesty. Viewed in this light his plans for Westminster can be fitted into a wider context, along with his issue of an innovatory coin type which depicted him enthroned; his (thwarted) plans for the remodelling of the crown jewels, and, above all, a seal which copied that of the Ottonian rulers of Germany, in depicting him enthroned with orb and sceptre. The depiction of enthronement put his official image on a par with those of the French and German rulers, while in his two-sided seal, he competed with the

87 Veronica Ortenberg, *The English Church and the Continent in the Tenth and Eleventh Centuries: Cultural, Spiritual and Artistic Exchanges* (Oxford, 1992), p. 86.

88 Gabrielle M. Spiegel, 'The Cult of St Denis and Capetian Kingship', *Journal of Mediaeval History*, 1 (1975), pp. 43–69.

89 Ortenberg, *The English Church and the Continent*, pp. 246–7.

90 P. Kidson, 'The Cathedral of Speyer and the Salian Dynasty', paper delivered to the London Society for Mediaeval Studies, Institute of Historical Research, 12 November, 1991; Elizabeth M. Hallam, 'Royal Burial and the Cult of Kingship in France and England 1060–1330', *Journal of Mediaeval History*, 8 (1982), pp. 360, 364.

91 Barlow, *The English Church 1000–1066*, pp. 83–4, 87–9; F. Barlow, 'Leofric and his Times', in his *The Norman Conquest and Beyond* (London, 1983), pp. 113–28.

92 For instance Ortenberg, *The English Church and the Continent*, p. 86. See, however, Barlow, 'The King's Evil', in *The Norman Conquest and Beyond*, esp. pp. 37–8.

bullae of the German emperor, with his Byzantine counterpart and with the Pope himself.[93]

So far as the rebuilt Westminster was concerned, therefore, Edward was primarily concerned with what the abbey could do for his kingly image and authority, rather than with what he could do for the monastic community. It is unlikely that he accorded it the privileges claimed by its subsequent publicists, of being in a special position with regard to the bishop of London, or of being directly commended to the see of Rome.[94]

On the other hand, in order to ensure that the abbey and its inmates would perform the role which he intended, Edward greatly enlarged its endowment. At his accession, rather more than half of its income of about £80 per annum derived from estates in Middlesex, with smaller amounts accruing from properties in Essex, Hertfordshire, Surrey and Sussex.[95] The first *Life* of King Edward, intending to maximize the impact of his benefactions, described the abbey as poor and insignificant at the outset of his reign, whereas in fact its income rendered it a middle-ranking house.[96] His own benefactions contributed about £270 per annum, from estates scattered over Berkshire, Gloucestershire, Hampshire, Hertfordshire, Middlesex, Northamptonshire, Oxfordshire, Staffordshire and Worcestershire.[97]

Some of his intended benefactions, which were supposed to pass to the monks on the death of Queen Edith, did not do so because King William I had other plans. In particular the monks failed to acquire the wapentake of Martinsley in Rutland, and eventually gained Islip (Oxfordshire) only in the reign of King John. Windsor, which they did gain in King Edward's lifetime, was taken from them by William I.[98] This expropriation, a preliminary to the afforestation of Windsor, operated to the monks' advantage, since they were given in exchange two (and probably three) estates in Surrey and a further two (and probably three) in Essex. As a result of this exchange, the abbey was raised to being among the richest English religious houses, with an income of over £515 per annum.[99] While King Edward's endowments accounted for most of this income, a small proportion (£38 in 1066; £55 10s in 1086) derived from private benefactions, mostly from King Edward's thegns.[100] In his reign, non-royal donors contributed to Westminster manors in Buckinghamshire, Essex, Lincolnshire, Middlesex and Surrey, while in the reign of King Harold II Godwinson further manors in Essex and Surrey were acquired

93 G. Zarnecki, J. Holt and T. Holland, *English Romanesque Art 1066– 1200* (London, 1984), p. 301, no. 328; pp. 324–5, nos 380–81.

94 Harvey, *Westminster Abbey and its Estates*, pp. 24–5.

95 *Ibid*., pp. 24, 341ff.

96 *The Life of King Edward who Rests at Westminster*, p. 66; see also Harvey, *Westminster Abbey and its Estates*, p. 24.

97 Harvey, *Westminster Abbey and its Estates*, p. 27 and n. 1.

98 *Ibid*., and notes 2–3.

99 *Ibid*., pp. 27–8.

100 *Ibid*., pp. 36–7.

from people of comparable standing.[101] Harold II himself is not recorded as a benefactor.

Notwithstanding the territorial losses which resulted from the Norman Conquest, most of King Edward's endowment remained theoretically at least, in Westminster's possession. In practice, however, control weakened in some areas, due to extensive subinfeudation. The imposition of knight service on ecclesiastical estates, led to the establishment of individual fees, while the granting out of land 'at farm' often resulted in a further weakening of control.[102] Westminster faced depredations of this nature, but conversely gained two further manors in Middlesex from private benefactors in the late eleventh century.[103] Thereafter, new landed endowments were rare before King Henry III took an interest in the abbey. In 1086 there were at most about 80 monks, supported by a net income of perhaps £511. The abbey also employed considerable numbers of servants, despite paying for the as yet uncompleted building works and routine maintenance of the great church and its precincts.[104]

Some tenuous evidence indicates that by the end of Edward's reign, Westminster was one of the locations for solemn crown-wearings.[105] These ceremonies added to the prestige of the abbey and perhaps earned it a handsome donation from the king, although the evidence for this is late.[106]

By Christmas 1065 the new great church of Westminster was ready to be dedicated, but King Edward became ill on Christmas Eve. He managed to appear in public before his magnates on Christmas Day, but the effort proved too much and it was clear that the dedication would have to proceed without him. Queen Edith supervised the last minute preparations and the dedication took place on 28 December, in the presence of the bishops and nobles.[107] When King Edward died, on 5 January, he was conveyed from the palace of Westminster into his new church, and buried before the altar of St Peter.[108]

The king's lack of any direct heir rendered the political situation precarious, but the throne was immediately claimed by Harold Godwinson, earl of

101 *Ibid.*, pp. 36–7, 338–59; A. Ayton and V. Davis, 'Ecclesiastical Wealth in England in 1086', in W.J. Sheils and D. Wood (eds), *The Church and Wealth*, Studies in Church History, 24 (Oxford, 1987), p. 48.

102 Harvey, *Westminster Abbey and its Estates*, pp. 1, 55; Ayton and Davis, 'Ecclesiastical Wealth in England', pp. 48–50.

103 Harvey, *Westminster Abbey and its Estates*, pp. 349–50.

104 *Ibid.*, pp. 1–2, 27, 55–7.

105 M. Biddle, 'Seasonal Festivals and Residence: Winchester, Westminster and Gloucester in the Tenth to Twelfth Centuries', in R. Allen Brown, ed., *Anglo-Norman Studies, VIII, Proceedings of the Battle Conference 1985* (Woodbridge, 1986), pp. 56, 59. *The Life of King Edward who Rests at Westminster*, p. 102.

106 *Westminster Abbey Charters 1066–c.1214*, ed. Emma Mason, assisted by the late Jennifer Bray, continuing the work of the late D.J. Murphy, London Record Society 25 (London, 1988), no. 58.

107 *The Life of King Edward who Rests at Westminster*, pp. 110–12.

108 *Ibid.*, p. 124

Wessex, the brother of Queen Edith. His coronation took place in the abbey on 6 January.[109] While Edward had intended the abbey to become his new royal burial church, he had not anticipated that it should also become the site of king-making, but the association of the great church with Edward was an advantage which neither of his immediate successors could overlook, since both Harold II and William I claimed to be Edward's designated and lawful heir.[110] Consequently their decision to receive unction and coronation at Westminster established a definitive role for the abbey which it has upheld for some nine hundred years. Its initial role of royal burial church, however, had a more chequered history. Although King Edward's widow, Edith, was buried in the abbey, as was his kinswoman Edith Matilda, the first wife of Henry I, subsequent kings usually designated a burial church elsewhere.[111] The original role of the abbey was revived only by King Henry III, whose exalted concept of kingship had much to gain by utilizing the cult of Edward. At the time of his canonization in 1161, Edward had been declared a Confessor, someone who had lived a model Christian life, and was to be venerated as a saint.[112]

109 *Anglo-Saxon Chronicle* (E), *sub. an.* 1066; *The Chronicle of John of Worcester, II, 450–1066*, pp. 600–601; Barlow, *Edward the Confessor*, pp. 251–5.

110 On the claims made by Harold Godwinson and William of Normandy to the English throne, see Ann Williams, 'Some Notes and Considerations on Problems Connected with the English Royal Succession 866–1066', in R. Allen Brown, ed., *Proceedings of the Battle Conference on Anglo-Norman Studies, I, 1978* (Woodbridge, 1979), pp. 144–67, esp. pp. 165–7.

111 Emma Mason, '*Pro Statu et Incolumnitate Regni Mei*: Royal Monastic Patronage 1066–1154', in S. Mews, ed., *Religion and National Identity*, Studies in Church History, 18 (Oxford, 1982), pp. 99–117.

112 S.H. Wander, 'The Westminster Abbey Sanctuary Pavement', *Traditio*, 34 (1978), pp. 137–56, esp. p. 153.

2

The Early Abbots c.970–c.1136

The early heads of the religious community at the West Minster are extremely shadowy figures. Before Benedictine monasticism was introduced there in the wake of the Tenth Century Reform, these heads of the little community would not have been abbots in a technical sense, although they were known as such in the later historiography of the house. Its fifteenth-century monk-historian, John Flete, named seven such 'abbots': Siward, Ordbritht, Ælfwig, Ælfgar, Adymer, Ælfnoth and Ælfric. He cited 'the muniments of very ancient books' for their existence, although he did not claim to know their terms of office, beyond the fact that Ordbritht is mentioned in a charter of King Offa of Mercia.[1] Flete's belief that Ordbritht became bishop of Selsey is based on his confusing him with a later Ordbritht, abbot of Chertsey. The charter of King Offa in which Ordbritht (of the West Minster) occurs is dated 785, and there is some tenuous evidence to indicate that he died in 797.[2] According to Flete, both Ælfwy and Ælfnoth were also elevated to the episcopate. Flete naturally wanted to depict the early heads of his house in the best possible light, but in fact there are no earlier sources which list these early 'abbots'. Strong circumstantial evidence suggests that the 'very ancient books' were compiled not long before Flete wrote, and were probably his own work. It is suggested by Barbara Harvey that a didactic purpose underlay the list compiled by Flete, who wanted his readers to note the contrast between the English names of these early abbots and the Continental names of those who attained office in the generations after the Norman Conquest.[3] Efforts by other scholars to support or amend Flete's list produced no concrete evidence.[4]

1 John Flete, *The History of Westminster Abbey*, ed. J. Armitage Robinson (Cambridge, 1909), p. 78.

2 *Anglo-Saxon Writs*, ed. Florence E. Harmer, 2nd edn (Stamford, 1989), no. 78, and pp. 500–501; 568–9.

3 Barbara Harvey, *Westminster Abbey and its Estates in the Middle Ages* (Oxford, 1977), pp. 17–18; cf. Flete, *The History of Westminster Abbey*, pp. 79–81.

4 *Anglo-Saxon Writs*, ed. Harmer, p. 548; D. Knowles, C.N.L. Brooke and V.C.M. London, *The Heads of Religious Houses, England and Wales 940–1216* (Cambridge, 1972), p. 76.

The increasing volume of documentation generated by the Tenth Century Reform ensures that the abbots of Westminster from the later tenth century onwards can be discussed at least in outline, and on the basis of more reliable sources.

Wulfsige was the first head of the reformed house. He is believed to have been appointed in 958, and continued to hold this office for some time after he was appointed bishop of Sherborne c.993. He resigned the abbacy by 997, but held Sherborne until his death on 8 January 1002.[5] As the man who was to preside over the introduction of the Benedictine Rule to Westminster, he was brought in by Dunstan.[6] He enjoyed a good reputation at Sherborne for his holy life – although his efforts to reform his diocese were not remembered for long. Within a few years of his death he was acclaimed as a saint by Archbishop Ælfheah and the Witan, and his elevation was marked by the solemn Translation of his body.[7] His cult was observed at Sherborne in the decades after his death and in the mid eleventh century his *Life*, the *Vita Wlsini*, was written by the hagiographer Goscelin of St Bertin.[8]

While Wulfsige held Westminster in plurality with Sherborne, it is likely that he employed a coadjutor in the abbey. There is some evidence that Ælfwig II acted in this capacity, before becoming abbot on Wulfsige's resignation before 997. His term of office is uncertain, but he died c.1020.[9]

Wulfnoth then succeeded to the abbacy and held office to his death on 19 October 1049.[10] Flete wrote that Wulfnoth obtained his appointment 'through the mediation of King Cnut'.[11] This seems likely, given the location of the abbey and the increasing wealth of its endowment. Flete added that Wulfnoth was an adviser to Cnut, who often took his advice because he was truthful in speech.[12] There is no Westminster source earlier than Flete himself for this statement, although it is clear that Cnut was a benefactor of the abbey.[13] Wulfnoth's term of office encompassed most of Cnut's reign, those of two of his sons, Harold I Harefoot and Harthacnut, and the early years of Harthacnut's half-brother Edward. The abbot, as a figure of some consequence, attested royal charters on occasion.[14]

Edwin (Eadwine), the last of the Anglo-Saxon abbots, held office from

5 Knowles, Brooke and London, *Heads of Religious Houses*, p. 76. The date of his appointment to Sherborne is corrected in E.B. Fryde, D.E. Greenway, S. Porter and I. Roy, eds, *Handbook of British Chronology*, 3rd edn (London, 1986), p. 222.

6 Flete, *The History of Westminster Abbey*, p. 45.

7 F. Barlow, *The English Church 1000–1066*, 2nd edn (London, 1979), pp. 65, 70, 222.

8 *Ibid.*, pp. 24; 242. See also Antonia Gransden, *Historical Writing in England c.550 to c.1307* (London, 1974), p. 108 and n. 15.

9 Knowles, Brooke and London, *Heads of Religious Houses*, p. 76.

10 *Ibid.*, p. 76.

11 Flete, *The History of Westminster Abbey*, p. 81.

12 *Ibid.*, p. 81.

13 *Ibid.*, p. 81; Harvey, *Westminster Abbey and its Estates*, p. 18.

14 D. Matthew, *The Norman Monasteries and their English Possessions* (Oxford, 1962; reprinted Westport, CT, 1979), pp. 143–4.

c.1049 to his death on 12 June 1068.[15] According to Flete, Edwin had earlier been a monk of the house, and owed his appointment to King Edward. Flete stated that it was due to Edwin's sanctity, and his prudent advice, that King Edward endowed Westminster so generously, increased its privileges, and decided to be buried there.[16]

In fact, Edward's interest in the potential of Westminster may have prompted his appointment of Edwin. As shown in the previous chapter, firm evidence for the king's augmentation of the endowment dates from 1051 and most likely from a year or two earlier, in other words, coincidental with Abbot Edwin's appointment. The king's plans for the development of the abbey would prompt him, when looking for a successor to Wulfnoth, to select a man of proven managerial and presentational skills. Edwin, presumably occupying some conspicuous post in the monastery, was in the right place at the right time. Firm evidence for Edwin's activities in King Edward's reign is hard to establish, since, although texts survive of numerous charters in his name issued for the benefit of Westminster, these are all suspect, to a greater or lesser degree. When Abbot Edwin is named, there is the possibility that this is the work of a later scribe seeking to add evidence of authenticity.[17]

Edwin survived in office for almost two years after the Norman Conquest, and had the task of ensuring that the abbey retained its endowment in the wake of the Norman settlement. A number of early writs of William I were issued for the benefit of Westminster, presumably in response to petitions on the part of Edwin.[18] Most of these confirmed existing properties, although there was one new grant, of land in Battersea and Pyrford, formerly held by Harold Godwinson. Edwin was evidently trusted by the new régime, since this site was one of strategic importance.[19] Edwin's success in securing the abbey's endowments, and his part in negotiating the profitable exchange of Windsor (required by the king) in return for Battersea and Wandsworth in Surrey, and Feering and Ockendon in Essex,[20] ensured his later reputation at the abbey and, inevitably, his appearance in several charters which were later forged at Westminster in order to reinforce more questionable claims.[21] Flete reported that Edwin used to visit the tomb of King Edward daily.[22] Flete would naturally want to establish an early date for the foundation of Edward's

15 Knowles, Brooke and London, *Heads of Religious Houses*, p. 76.

16 Flete, *The History of Westminster Abbey*, pp. 82–3.

17 For example, *Anglo-Saxon Writs*, ed. Harmer, nos 79, 81.

18 *Westminster Abbey Charters*, ed. Emma Mason, assisted by the late Jennifer Bray, continuing the work of the late D.J. Murphy, London Record Society, 25 (London, 1988), nos 4–10.

19 *Ibid*., no. 6 and note.

20 *Ibid*., nos 9–10. On the relative value of the lands exchanged, see Harvey, *Westminster Abbey and its Estates*, pp. 27–8, 338, 341, 343, 357–8.

21 For example, *Westminster Abbey Charters*, nos 1–3, 13; *Anglo-Saxon Writs*, ed. Harmer, p. 291.

22 Flete, *The History of Westminster Abbey*, p. 82.

cult, but it is also possible that Abbot Edwin himself saw its potential as a means of assisting him in his efforts to secure the abbey's recent lucrative endowments. Since William I claimed to rule as Edward's rightful heir, it might be hoped that the fostering of Edward's cult would prompt the new dynasty to take a beneficial interest in his burial-church.

Edwin's death in June 1068 spared him from the trauma of witnessing the removal of many eminent English clerics in 1070. This was effected by papal legates, overtly on disciplinary grounds, but several of the clerics were really ousted to suite the king's political interests.[23] Edwin, as head of the community which presided over the coronation church, would probably not have found himself on the hit-list: the success of his petitions over the abbey's endowments argues against it.

The vacancy caused by his death nevertheless paved the way for the introduction of a French-speaking head of house. This was Geoffrey, formerly abbot of St Peter of Jumièges in Normandy. The high status of his former appointment would have rendered him a suitable candidate for Westminster, but in fact he proved a total disaster. The abbey's scribes subsequently did such a thorough job of editing him out of their records that even his term of office is uncertain. Probably there was a vacancy of two or three years before his appointment. It can only be said that he was in office for four years, more or less, and that he was certainly in post towards the end of May 1072.[24] Flete reports of Geoffrey that he did not walk rightly in the ways of his fathers. In the fourth year of his abbacy, King William and Archbishop Lanfranc admonished him 'on certain true and legitimate grounds', and he was then deposed. 'And so he returned in great shame to his monastery in Normandy from which he had come. He died there. May God have mercy on his soul. Amen.'[25] The reason for Geoffrey's dismissal is conjectural. When later abbots earned a poor reputation, this was usually either because their actions in some way threatened the stability of Westminster's endowment, or, more often, because they adopted an arbitrary managerial style, administering directly estates which contributed to the maintenance of the monastic chapter. But in the mid 1070s, most of the monks would still be Englishmen, and it is doubtful whether they would have had enough influence to lobby the archbishop and the king to secure the removal of an unpopular new abbot, simply because he was treating their property in a high-handed way. Around the time of his removal one matter which preoccupied both king and archbishop was the rebellion of 1075, but Geoffrey is not known to have been implicated in this. A more likely hypothesis, at which Flete appears to hint, is that there were grave shortcomings in his personal life, but if the in-house writers knew any scandalous details, they were not revealing them. No surviving royal charter for Westminster is addressed to Geoffrey, which creates a

23 F. Barlow, *The English Church 1066–1154* (London, 1979), p. 57.

24 Knowles, Brooke and London, *Heads of Religious Houses*, p. 76.

25 Flete, *The History of Westminster Abbey*, p. 84.

superficial impression that he failed in the basic responsibility of obtaining royal support for the house. Many of the early charters of the house now survive only as entries in Westminster's cartularies and it would be easy for any copyist to omit mention of Geoffrey, or even to substitute the name of some more reputable eleventh-century abbot, since texts of this period rarely carried a precise date. Perhaps by such means, and for whatever reason, Geoffrey became a non-person.

Following his dismissal, King William is recorded as saying that he gave 'long and careful thought' to the question of who should become the next abbot. He consulted Archbishop Lanfranc and his barons, and on their advice he compelled the reluctant Abbot Vitalis of Bernay to accept the post, since he had done so much to improve the condition of Bernay. This sequence of events is described in a letter written in the king's name to Abbot John of Fécamp (the mother-house of Bernay), requesting his approval of Vitalis's promotion, and also of his request that Vitalis's brother, Osbern, should be allowed to succeed him as abbot of Bernay. This letter can be dated to 1076.[26]

Vitalis, as a former monk of Fécamp, would know what was expected of the abbot of a monastery which had a special relationship with the ruling dynasty. William was a visitor there in 1066, and returned to Fécamp at Easter 1067 for ceremonies which marked his recent victory in England.[27] Vitalis was well-experienced in running a monastery, having been abbot of Bernay since c.1055.[28]

At Westminster, Vitalis certainly came up to expectations. He earned commendations from contemporary writers, both for his continuation of the building work at the abbey[29] and also for his effective supervision of the ongoing work on the royal palace nearby.[30] Vitalis also commissioned the monk Sulcard to write his *Prologus de Construccione Westmonasterii*, a tract which outlines the history of the church from (he claimed) the time of Æthelbert of Kent to King Edward. Sulcard dedicated this work to Vitalis. The abbot would find it useful to have an outline history of his new abbey,

26 *Regesta Regum Anglo-Normannorum, I 1066–1100*, ed. H.W.C. Davis with the assistance of R.J. Whitwell (Oxford, 1913), no. 91. See also D. Bates, 'The Earliest Norman Writs', *English Historical Review*, 100 (1985), pp. 267–8.

27 D. Bates, *Bishop Remigius of Lincoln, 1067–92* (Lincoln, 1992), p. 3. The close relationship between Fécamp and the ducal dynasty is discussed by Annie Renoux, *Fécamp: du palais ducal au palais de Dieu* (Paris, 1991).

28 J. Decaens, 'La datation de l'abbatiale de Bernay: quelques observations architecturales et résultats des fouilles récentes', in R. Allen Brown, ed., *Anglo-Norman Studies, V, Proceedings of the Battle Conference 1982* (Woodbridge, 1983), p. 114.

29 R.D.H. Gem, 'The Romanesque Rebuilding of Westminster Abbey (with a reconstruction by W.T. Ball)', in R. Allen Brown, ed., *Proceedings of the Battle Conference on Anglo-Norman Studies, III, 1980* (Woodbridge, 1981), p. 38.

30 B.W. Scholz, 'Sulcard of Westminster: "*Prologus de Construccione Westmonasterii*" ', *Traditio*, 20 (1964), p. 60.

and particularly wanted a work which would serve the cult of its patron, St Peter.[31]

The late-eleventh century charters of Westminster reflect Vitalis's energetic pursuit of the community's territorial endowments. Four royal writs for Westminster specifically name the abbot, [32] and he is a likely recipient of some of the less precisely addressed late-eleventh century writs.[33] Additionally he is the named beneficiary of a further seven writs, which are rendered spurious in their present form, by the addition either of unauthentic attestations or of clauses conferring extensive judicial privileges.[34] Yet these documents all contain an underlying stratum of fact, and it can be assumed that Vitalis petitioned the king for the original grants on which the dubious texts are based. Of the two surviving charters issued in his name, one records a grant, made jointly with the brethren, of a property called *Vuerc* in the City of London to a certain Gerald and his heirs,[35] while the other is a confraternity agreement made between Vitalis and the brethren, on the one hand, and, on the other, William of St Calais, bishop of Durham, and the monks of his cathedral priory.[36] Vitalis ruled for some nine years, and died on 19 June (1085).[37]

He was succeeded, perhaps in 1085, by Gilbert Crispin, who was abbot for upwards of thirty years, until his death on 6 December 1117 (or 1118).[38] Gilbert's father, William Crispin, was lord of a castle on the frontier between Normandy and France. It was later believed at Westminster that William's family were close advisors of the dukes of Normandy. Gilbert's mother Eva, when she was left a widow, lived a religious life at Bec, in company with two other women. She is said to have regarded the monks as her sons.[39] Gilbert himself was presented to Bec as a child oblate, c.1055. By that time, the lifestyle of Bec had relaxed from its early strictness, and the monastery had a good intellectual reputation, thanks to the activities of Lanfranc, who was teaching there.[40] Lanfranc became archbishop of Canterbury in 1070. Some years later, in the winter of 1073, he wrote to Gilbert, at that time still at Bec, concerning the conduct there of his nephew, another Lanfranc. This young

31 *Ibid.*, pp. 61–2.
32 *Westminster Abbey Charters*, nos 19, 22, 26, 31.
33 *Ibid.*, nos 23, 27, 29, 32, 37.
34 *Ibid.*, nos 20, 21, 24, 25, 30, 35, 36.
35 *Ibid.*, no. 234.
36 *Ibid.*, no. 235.
37 Flete, *The History of Westminster Abbey*, pp. 84, 141; Knowles, Brooke and London, *Heads of Religious Houses*, p. 76.
38 Knowles, Brooke and London, *Heads of Religious Houses*, p. 77.
39 Flete, *The History of Westminster Abbey*, p. 85; J. Armitage Robinson, *Gilbert Crispin, Abbot of Westminster* (Cambridge, 1911), pp. 7, 15. See also D. Bates, *Normandy before 1066* (London, 1982), p. 177, 187 note 110.
40 Flete, *The History of Westminster Abbey*, p. 85; Margaret Gibson, *Lanfranc of Bec* (Oxford, 1978), pp. 23, 25, 34.

man had been entrusted to Gilbert's care, but was presenting problems.[41] Seemingly Gilbert handled the situation with some credit, since Archbishop Lanfranc summoned him to Canterbury about 1080, when Gilbert was perhaps thirty-four years old.[42]

Gilbert did not hold a major office at Canterbury but was reputedly close to the centre of its more enterprising administrative activities. In 1086 there was a renewal of the struggle between Canterbury and York, with Canterbury basing its case on a forged charter, which had been sealed with the king's seal, fraudulently obtained for this purpose. A York writer gave his highly-charged account of what followed. He alleged that William I denied the authenticity of the charter, and said that if God willed that he returned from Normandy he would himself judge the dispute between the two archbishops. The king's words were heard by those around him, including Ranulf Flambard and Gilbert Crispin. They both spread word of what they had heard, adding that they were prepared to swear that the Canterbury charter had been fraudulently confirmed, and giving details of the king's reply. It was also claimed at York that William I ordered Gilbert Crispin to bear testimony to the church of York, whatever might happen to the king himself.[43] As matters transpired, this proved to be the king's last Channel crossing, and he did not return to give his verdict in the dispute. The testimony of the bystanders became crucial to the Chapter of York, but it comes as a surprise to read that Gilbert, who had only just been promoted from Canterbury to Westminster (or, as the York writer maintained, was still at Canterbury at this point), was prepared to speak out in this way. According to the York writer, when the issue blew up again in 1109, Archbishop Thomas II requested Henry I to compel Ranulf Flambard and Gilbert Crispin to declare the facts known to them. This, according to the York writer, was something on which they were competent to speak since, at the time when the false charter was created, Gilbert was a monk of Lanfranc's *familia*, while Ranulf was keeper of the royal seal. Henry I replied indignantly that neither was a credible witness in the case, beyond orders given (directly) to themselves.[44] With hindsight, it can be suggested that neither in fact witnessed the earlier dispute, but that they were cited both because of their respective positions in the mid 1080s, when they 'could have' known of the alleged forgery, and because of their eminence by 1109, when Ranulf was bishop of Durham and Gilbert was the well-entrenched abbot of Westminster. Both may have known of a forgery made in the 1080s, but their career prospects at that time depended on their discretion. If the earlier events are substantially true, then York's narrative might

41 *The Letters of Lanfranc, Archbishop of Canterbury*, ed. and transl. Helen Clover and Margaret Gibson (Oxford, 1979), nos 18, 20.

42 Armitage Robinson, *Gilbert Crispin*, p. 9.

43 Hugh the Chantor, *The History of the Church of York 1066–1127*, transl. and introd. C. Johnson (London, 1961), p. 6.

44 *Ibid.*, p. 26.

be reinterpreted by suggesting that they started to gossip, and that York's supporters then put pressure on them to confirm publicly their 'leaks from well-placed sources'. Even after his promotion to Westminster, Gilbert remained in the circle of Archbishop Lanfranc, and as abbot, witnessed the record of the archbishop's judgement of a dispute between Bishop Gundulf of Rochester and his vassal, Gilbert 'of Tonbridge', *alias* Gilbert Fitz Richard de Clare.[45]

Gilbert Crispin's social background would be an asset in his new position. His immediate family remained in Normandy. His father became a monk during his last illness, and died at Bec in 1074. Gilbert's mother died there in 1099, repenting her frivolity in maintaining 'little dogs and such'.[46] Gilbert had a well-placed kinsman in England, where his cousin Miles Crispin was a substantial landholder. The bulk of his estates lay in Oxfordshire, and he was sometimes styled Miles 'of Wallingford' from the *caput* of his barony.[47] Miles and Gilbert derived their cognomen from the shock of hair, standing up on end, which was inherited by generations of their family.[48]

At Westminster, Gilbert proved an active abbot. The long-running building programme was probably still in progress in his time, although Gilbert's projects are undocumented.[49] However, certain decorative features found in the abbey precincts resemble work at Westminster Hall, on which work was in progress in 1097.[50] Specific projects at Westminster abbey which have been ascribed to Gilbert are the building of the abbot's *camera*, or of his *capella*, or perhaps both, over the locutory which formed the entrance to the cloister at its south-west angle.[51]

When it came to the imposition of monastic discipline, there are hints in the letters of Anselm to Gilbert that some individuals among the monks of Westminster were proving difficult to manage, but no details of any troubles are known. It has been suggested that later, towards the end of Gilbert's long abbacy, some relaxation of his grip on the administration of the estates contributed to the problems which faced his successor, but that is purely conjectural.[52] More positively, it can be demonstrated that he brought to Westminster the *Monastic Constitutions of Lanfranc*, since sections of these are re-used in the *Customary* authorized by Abbot Richard Ware (1258–1283).[53]

45 Barlow, *The English Church 1066–1154*, p. 174, citing *Textus Roffensis*, ed. T. Hearne (Oxford, 1720), p. 149.

46 *Ibid.*, pp. 15–16.

47 I.J. Sanders, *English Baronies: a Study of their Origin and Descent 1086–1327* (Oxford, 1960), p. 93.

48 Armitage Robinson, *Gilbert Crispin*, p. 13.

49 Gem, 'The Romanesque Rebuilding of Westminster Abbey', p. 38.

50 *Ibid.*, p. 60.

51 Armitage Robinson, *Gilbert Crispin*, p. 36.

52 E. Carpenter, *A House of Kings: the History of Westminster Abbey* (London, 1966), p. 15.

53 Armitage Robinson, *Gilbert Crispin*, p. 28. See also *Customary of the Benedictine Monas-*

Their introduction and regular use would do much to ensure the smooth conduct of the monastic life.

Firm documentation exists for Gilbert's promoting the cult of King Edward. While this cult is discussed in more detail in a later chapter, it is relevant to note here that Gilbert presided over the opening of the king's tomb in 1102,[54] and issued, seemingly over a period of several years, a series of writs which specifically associate the tomb with the abbey's status as a privileged sanctuary.[55]

Two of these writs were written in English, which by Gilbert's time in office had become an anachronistic language for use in official documents.[56] Its employment in these writs may suggest that surviving English *seniores* in the chapter took the lead in promoting the cult,[57] although Gilbert perhaps considered the use of the English language appropriate when promoting the claims of an English king. His own perspective, as a historian and one of the leading monastic intellectuals of his day, might prompt him to encourage the linguistic initiative, even if it was not his own. As an abbot zealous for the prestige of his house, and as a first-generation Norman immigrant working in a close-knit community which still held a large English presence, he would appreciate the value of the cult from a practical standpoint. Gilbert was zealous in furthering Westminster's interest by enlisting royal support. He obtained at least four royal charters between his own appointment, c.1085, and the death of William I two years later.[58] A fifth charter in that king's name probably contains a genuine core, although it is suspect in its present form.[59]

Over the thirteen-year reign of King William Rufus, Westminster obtained at least nine royal charters,[60] and a tenth which is perhaps, but not necessarily, of doubtful authenticity.[61] This king did not earn a posthumous reputation as a major benefactor of the abbey. However, as Frank Barlow pointed out in his biography of the king, Westminster recorded one major benefaction of his in visual form. This record was made on the faces of a capital which was probably designed for an arcade in the cloister. In successive 'scenes', first, the enthroned king, and secondly Abbot Gilbert, flanked by two of his monks, is depicted holding a long parchment roll, most likely a *pancarte*, listing, and then confirming, all the properties held by

teries of St Augustine, Canterbury, and St Peter, Westminster, ed. E. Maunde Thompson, Henry Bradshaw Society, XXIII and XXVIII (1902, 1904).

54 Armitage Robinson, *Gilbert Crispin*, p. 24.

55 *Westminster Abbey Charters*, nos 238–40.

56 *Ibid.*, nos 238–9.

57 Carpenter, *A House of Kings*, p. 15.

58 *Westminster Abbey Charters*, nos 41–5.

59 *Ibid.*, no. 40.

60 *Ibid.*, nos 48–56.

61 *Ibid.*, no. 47. Suspect charters are discussed below, in the chapter on scribes.

Westminster at the time this record was made.[62] Probably it would include some new royal benefaction, but most importantly, it would guarantee the abbey's title to its many scattered possessions. The third recorded scene (the fourth is missing) shows Abbot Gilbert officiating, with his service book open at the words 'I am (the Good Shepherd).' The running heading to the whole capital can be reconstructed to read 'Praise, under Abbot Gilbert and King William the Second, to the founders and other holy men.'[63]

The abbot who had secured this valuable confirmation, and the king who had granted it, naturally deserved more prominent mention than past donors. The capital showing Abbot Gilbert with his service book can be interpreted in three ways. In its obvious Scriptural sense, the abbot is reminding his monks that Christ is the Good Shepherd, who provides for His people.[64] Secondly, there is a strong hint that Gilbert, in his pastoral capacity as abbot, is providing for the needs of his monks by enlisting royal support, and thirdly, perhaps at the prompting of English *seniores*, there is an echo of the tenth century monastic code, the *Regularis Concordia*, in which the term 'The Good Shepherd' is applied to the king who, as patron of the reformed monasteries, guaranteed their endowments. He protected the monasteries and the monks in turn prayed intensively for him.[65] Professor Barlow suggested that the scenes commemorated some sort of 'founders' day'.[66] On such an occasion, a sermon on the three-fold implications of the Scriptural texts on 'The Good Shepherd' would be especially appropriate. While Westminster's archives have survived remarkably well over the centuries, they contain no document purporting to be this *pancarte*. The most likely hypothesis is that it was used as the basis of one or more of the spurious royal charters of confirmation which were created in the late 1120s or the 1130s, when they were all ascribed to King William I.[67]

Over the last seventeen or so years of his abbacy, which coincided with the earlier part of the reign of Henry I, Abbot Gilbert continued to obtain royal charters, of a less spectacular kind. Eleven appear to date from this period,[68] and a further four are all more or less suspect in their present form.[69] Additionally, Abbot Gilbert obtained one grant from Henry I's first wife, Edith Matilda.[70] The texts survive of seven documents issued in the name of Abbot Gilbert, including the three writs, discussed above, relating to Westminster's

62 F. Barlow, *William Rufus* (London, 1983), pp. 113, 114 and note; Plate 12 facing p. 331.

63 *Ibid.*, p. 114 and note; Plate 12.

64 John 10: 11–16.

65 *Regularis Concordia: The Monastic Agreement*, transl. and ed. T. Symons (London, 1953). See esp. p. 2; and also pp. 3–4, 16, 21–3.

66 Barlow, *William Rufus*, p. 114.

67 *Westminster Abbey Charters*, nos 1, 14, 15, 33, 43. These charters are discussed further in the chapter on scribes, below.

68 *Ibid.*, nos 58–61, 65–69, 71–2.

69 *Ibid.*, nos 62–4, 70.

70 *Ibid.*, no. 97.

privileged sanctuary.[71] The remaining four documents are all grants to tenants: land was granted to William Baynard for one knight's fee, in the berwick of Tothill in Westminster;[72] Robert, son of Sweyn of Essex, was granted land in Wheatley, Essex, donated to the abbey by his late father, to hold at an annual rent;[73] Gunter and his heir were granted the manor of Hendon, Middlesex, in return for one week's fee-farm each year;[74] and William of Buckland was granted a collection of estates in Buckinghamshire, Huntingdonshire and Middlesex, each on specified conditions at various rents.[75]

Some details of Abbot Gilbert's administration are known only from indirect sources. The *Customary* of Abbot Richard Ware noted Gilbert's assignment to the Chamber, or central finance office, of sufficient revenues to provide the clothing and shoes of eighty monks, while he himself received from the chamberlain an allowance of ten marks yearly, in lieu of the provision of clothing.[76] Gilbert not only presided over a sizable community, but also witnessed the expansion of Westminster's influence through the creation of its daughter-houses. Gilbert was certainly abbot when Hurley (Berks.) was founded by Geoffrey de Mandeville;[77] was probably abbot when Great Malvern (Worcs.) was secured as a cell of Westminster;[78] and when the little cell of St Bartholomew's, Sudbury, was established.[79] Properties granted to Great Malvern by Abbot Gilbert and the convent are recorded in a confirmation made to the priory by Henry I in c.1127.[80] Elsewhere in Worcestershire, Pershore Abbey received a grant from Abbot Gilbert and his monks of tithes and other payments due to it as the local mother-church. Once again, the original charter is now lost, but is known from Archbishop Theobald's confirmation.[81]

Gilbert, in his early years at Bec, was a pupil of Anselm.[82] After the

71 *Ibid.*, nos 238–40.
72 *Ibid.*, no. 236.
73 *Ibid.*, no. 237.
74 *Ibid.*, no. 241.
75 *Ibid.*, no. 242.
76 *Customary of the Benedictine Monasteries of St Augustine, Canterbury, and St Peter, Westminster*, II, pp. 149, 150; *Documents Illustrating the Rule of Walter de Wenlok, Abbot of Westminster 1283–1307*, ed. Barbara F. Harvey, Camden Fourth Series, II (1965), pp. 19, 217 note 2.
77 *Westminster Abbey Charters*, no. 462.
78 *Ibid.*, no. 243 note; *The Cartulary of Worcester Cathedral Priory (Register I)*, ed. R.R. Darlington, Pipe Roll Society, new series XXXVIII (1968), no. 300 and note; *The Vita Wulfstani of William of Malmesbury*, ed. R.R. Darlington, Camden Third Series, XL (1928), pp. xli–xlii, 26.
79 *Westminster Abbey Charters*, no. 72; Armitage Robinson, *Gilbert Crispin*, p. 34.
80 W. Dugdale, *Monasticon Anglicanum*, revised H. Caley, H. Ellis and B. Bandinel, 6 vols in 8 (London, 1817–1830), III, no. 447; *Regesta Regum Anglo-Normannorum, II: 1100–1135*, ed. C. Johnson and H.A. Cronne (Oxford, 1956), no. 490.
81 A. Saltman, *Theobald, Archbishop of Canterbury* (London, 1955; reprinted New York, 1969), no. 199.
82 R.W. Southern, *Saint Anselm and his Biographer* (Cambridge, 1966), p. 205.

Norman Conquest, when Gilbert was a young adult member of the community, he would have been as grateful as his fellow-monks when Bec, like many other Continental religious houses, received substantial endowments in England. It did not concern him at that period of his life that some of these estates, in Essex, Surrey and other shires, adjoined properties held by Westminster abbey.[83] Disputes arose between the two religious houses, seemingly because Westminster's tenants were harassed by those who were in charge of adjoining Bec lands. Abbot Vitalis appealed to King William I, who ordered his sheriffs, especially those of Essex and Surrey, to see that Westminster's lands were left in peace. Moreover, Abbot Vitalis was to have justice against Abbot Anselm of Bec.[84] In 1086, Abbot Anselm paid a lengthy visit to his former pupil, the recently-appointed abbot of Westminster.[85] It is unlikely that their conversation was confined to purely academic matters.

Anselm was again in England in the autumn of 1092, when circumstantial evidence based on their respective works does indicate some theological discussions between them.[86] Other business did not grind to a halt, however. Abbot Gilbert successfully petitioned King William II for a confirmation of the manor of Feering in Essex, with the customary rights enjoyed by Abbot Vitalis and their English predecessors. Abbot Anselm was enlisted as chief witness.[87] His attestation reflected both his own standing in the Anglo-Norman church, and also his role as a close acquaintance of Abbot Gilbert, while the other interested parties perhaps thought it advisable to secure his ratification of Westminster's rights in a shire in which the representatives of Westminster and Bec had recently been in dispute. Anselm's visit to England over the winter of 1092–93 culminated in his appointment as archbishop of Canterbury.[88] The zealous stand which he took on church-state relations during his term of office was not supported with any marked enthusiasm by his erstwhile pupil. Gilbert's views were perhaps naturally more moderate, and in any case, a prime duty of any responsible abbot, in the eyes of his convent, was to further the territorial interests of his house. This could not be achieved by an abbot who was seen to support an archbishop who antagonized successive kings. Moreover, since collective monastic memories were long, there were doubtless those among his chapter who were ready to

83 Marjorie Morgan, *The English Lands of the Abbey of Bec* (London, 1946), map facing p. 41; cf. Harvey, *Westminster Abbey and its Estates*, Map 1, p. 471.

84 *Westminster Abbey Charters*, no. 26; cf. *ibid*., no. 21. See also *Select Documents of the English Lands of the Abbey of Bec*, ed. Marjorie Chibnall, Camden Third Series, LXXIII (1951).

85 R.W. Southern, *Saint Anselm: A Portrait in a Landscape* (Cambridge, 1990), p. 167, note.

86 *Ibid*., p. 198.

87 *Westminster Abbey Charters*, no. 50.

88 Eadmer, *The Life of St Anselm, Archbishop of Canterbury*, ed. and transl. R.W. Southern (1962), pp. 63–5 and notes; R.W. Southern, 'St Anselm and Gilbert Crispin, Abbot of Westminster', in *Medieval and Renaissance Studies*, ed. R.W. Hunt and R. Klibansky, III (1954), pp. 78–115.

remind Gilbert that it was not worth stepping out of line for the sake of the former abbot of the rapacious Bec. The steady support which Westminster received from the two kings embroiled in the conflict with Archbishop Anselm proved, if proof were needed, that moderation was the best policy.

The abbot of Westminster would be required to attend the royal court *ex-officio*, no matter what the prevailing circumstances there or elsewhere. In 1100, for instance, Gilbert attended the Easter court at Winchester. The Pentecost court convened at Westminster which was also the venue, on 5 August, for the hurried coronation of Henry I. Traumatic political change was matched by equally emotive clerical gatherings for which Westminster provided a convenient location.[89] At Michaelmas 1102, during the respite between his two periods of exile, Anselm held a reforming council there, at which several abbots were deposed for simony and other offences.[90] When Anselm went back into exile, Gilbert addressed him in a set of verses, arguing that the archbishop's place was in England, where his flock was harried by ravening wolves.[91] Gilbert implies that the pastoral needs of Anselm's archdiocese far outweighed any technical objections which there might be to the continued practice of lay investiture.[92] Gilbert's known moderate stance led to his employment as a go-between after the archbishop's eventual return. Hugh, the abbot of St Augustine's, Canterbury, demanded to be consecrated in his own abbey church, which Anselm flatly refused. Gilbert was the one delegate who was not of episcopal rank in a party sent by Henry I to lobby on Hugh's behalf, a mission which proved unsuccessful.[93] Gilbert's enlistment in the mission presumably reflected his known long acquaintance with Anselm even more than it did his status in the clerical hierarchy.

In the intervals between his monastic duties and his public activities, Gilbert found time to produce a number of scholarly works besides the verses to Anselm mentioned above.[94] His best known theological work is his Disputation with a Jew (a work surviving in many manuscripts). This evidently arose from the arrival in London, from Mainz, of some learned Jewish scholars with whom Gilbert debated the doctrine of the Incarnation.[95] Gilbert's response to their arguments perhaps influenced Anselm's formulation of his own work, the *Cur Deus Homo* – Why God Became Man.[96] A second of Gilbert's treatises which takes the dialogue form is his *Debate between a*

89 Armitage Robinson, *Gilbert Crispin*, pp. 20–21.
90 *Ibid.*, pp. 20–21.
91 *Ibid.*, pp. 22, 83.
92 Carpenter, *A House of Kings*, p. 92.
93 Armitage Robinson, *Gilbert Crispin*, p. 23.
94 *Ibid.*, p. 58. For a detailed discussion of Gilbert's writings, see *The Works of Gilbert Crispin, Abbot of Westminster*, ed. A.S. Abulafia and G.R. Evans, Auctores Britannici Medii Aevi, VIII (1986).
95 Armitage Robinson, *Gilbert Crispin*, pp. 60–67.
96 Southern, *Saint Anselm: a Portrait in a Landscape*, p. 198; Eadmer, *The Life of St Anselm*, p. 63, n. 2; p. 107, n. 2.

Christian and a Pagan Philosopher, which is a less successful work.[97] Of his minor treatises, *On Simoniacs* adopts a definite reforming stance – but a moderate one.[98] His *De Anima* – On the Soul, discusses a subject on which Anselm had been reflecting at the time of his death,[99] while other short works include his *On the Holy Spirit*, *On the Fall of the Devil* and his *Sermon on Palm Sunday*.[100]

Gilbert's reputation as a theologian lasted for little more than a generation, but he was approvingly mentioned at Rheims in 1148, by those who objected to Abbot Bernard of Clairvaux's browbeating of the eminent churchmen who were assembled to debate the theological errors alleged against Gilbert de la Porrée, bishop of Poitiers.[101] Sir Richard Southern's verdict on Gilbert Crispin as a theologian was that he was a man of judicious and solid learning, rather than of more brilliant gifts of intellect.[102] From Westminster's viewpoint, however, sober judgement outweighed brilliance. The head of a monastic community had to look to the interests of his house, and the monks of Christchurch, Canterbury, felt that Anselm had not acted in their best interests, despite all his theological brilliance.[103]

Gilbert Crispin's best-known work now is his *Life of Herluin*.[104] As a distinguished intellectual, Gilbert could appreciate the scholarly attainments of Lanfranc and Anselm, yet his highest admiration was for Herluin, the former knight who founded Bec, and whose life embodied all that was best in the Norman monastic revival of the earlier eleventh century.[105] Gilbert wrote this work more than fifty years after his own entry to Bec and his portrayal contains an element of idealization, but he seems to have truly valued Herluin's achievement. Indeed, it is entirely due to Gilbert, writing directly from his own experiences, that so much is known about the foundation and early history of Bec.[106] Gilbert died on 6 December, probably in 1117, but possibly in 1118.[107]

Following the death of Abbot Gilbert, there was an interval of more than

97 Armitage Robinson, *Gilbert Crispin*, pp. 58, 73–5; Southern, *Saint Anselm and his Biographer*, pp. 205–6.

98 Armitage Robinson, *Gilbert Crispin*, pp. 111–24; Carpenter, *A House of Kings*, p. 14.

99 Armitage Robinson, *Gilbert Crispin*, pp. 58, 72–3; Southern, *Saint Anselm and his Biographer*, p. 206.

100 Armitage Robinson, *Gilbert Crispin*, pp. 58, 70–73.

101 *Ibid.*, p. 51; John of Salisbury, *Memoirs of the Papal Court*, transl. and introd. Marjorie Chibnall (London, 1956), pp. 18–19.

102 Southern, *Saint Anselm and his Biographer*, p. 206.

103 Eadmer, *The Life of Saint Anselm*, p. 130 note; Southern, *Saint Anselm and his Biographer*, pp. 306–7.

104 Armitage Robinson, *Gilbert Crispin*, pp. 87–110.

105 Barlow, *The English Church 1066–1154*, p. 192.

106 Gibson, *Lanfranc of Bec*, pp. 23–5, 195, 198; Armitage Robinson, *Gilbert Crispin*, pp. 58–60.

107 Flete, *The History of Westminster Abbey*, p. 87; Knowles, Brooke and London, *Heads of Religious Houses*, p. 77.

two years (three, if Gilbert did in fact die in 1117). This interregnum was to prove disastrous for Westminster, since it presented an opportunity for various unscrupulous (but generally nameless) individuals to treat properties of the abbey as though these were their own. Additionally, Henry I would assert his regalian right, appointing a *custos* to administer the estates of the abbey for the benefit of the crown, and simply making an allocation from the revenues for the support of the monks.[108] This situation was entirely to the king's benefit, and was concluded only in January 1121 with the appointment of Abbot Herbert.[109] The ending of the interregnum at this time, within a few weeks of the death of the king's heir, was perhaps intended as an act of reparation, one manifestation of the remorse which the king was believed to have expressed in consequence of his harsh government.

Abbot Herbert was said to have been of Norman birth,[110] and was formerly monk, and almoner, of Westminster.[111] His immediate task was to secure the return of those lands which had been lost during the interregnum. Within two years of his accession, he had successfully petitioned for nine royal charters,[112] of which four ordered either the restoration of wrongfully alienated properties, or else the cessation of injustices inflicted on Westminster.[113]

A further twelve royal charters, at most, may be dated to the latter part of Herbert's abbacy.[114] In this batch, too, there are repeated references to losses of one sort and another incurred by Westminster.[115] Intensive lobbying at the royal court was the surest way of recovering lost lands, but unfortunately it was also expensive. Plaintiffs, monastic as well as lay, were always expected to pay in order to obtain the intervention of the king.[116] If it was not possible to pay up immediately, then debts were usually allowed to run on for years. The extent of Westminster's indebtedness to the Crown is revealed in the Pipe Roll of Michaelmas 1130, where it was noted that the abbot of Westminster accounted for one thousand marks of silver (£666 13s 4d) for the restitution of the goods of his church which had been unjustly dispersed, and that, once

108 On royal intrusion into monasteries during abbatial vacancies, see Margaret Howell, 'Abbatial Vacancies and the Divided Mensa in Medieval England', *Journal of Ecclesiastical History*, 33 (1982), pp. 173–92.

109 Eadmer, *Historia Novarum in Anglia*, ed. M. Rule, Rolls Series (1884), p. 291.

110 Flete, *The History of Westminster Abbey*, p. 87.

111 Knowles, Brooke and London, *Heads of Religious Houses*, p. 77.

112 *Westminster Abbey Charters*, nos 73, 75–82.

113 *Ibid.*, nos 73, 75, 81, 82. A tenth charter, designed to appear to date from this period of Herbert's abbacy, is a forgery: *ibid.*, no. 74.

114 *Ibid.*, nos 84–92, 94–96. Two of this group may in fact have been issued in response to Abbot Gilbert's petitions (nos 84–5). Two further charters may be forgeries (nos 83, 93).

115 *Ibid.*, nos 84, 92, 94, 96.

116 This is evident from the Pipe Rolls, which survive on a regular basis from the early years of Henry II's reign. For the practice in the eleventh century, see Emma Mason, *St Wulfstan of Worcester c.1008–1095* (Oxford, 1990), p. 91.

restored, they might be safeguarded. Herbert had actually paid off only 50 marks; by a writ issued on 24 June (year unspecified), the king had cancelled a further 50 marks; a pardon issued on the authority of Roger, bishop of Salisbury, and Geoffrey Rufus the chancellor cancelled a further 900 marks, and the abbot still owed 100 marks.[117] This entry does not necessarily relate to a debt incurred by Herbert in the financial year 1129–30. More likely the figure of 1000 marks represented the aggregated fines which he had promised in return for the various writs of restitution and of protection which he had obtained over a number of years, while trying to make good the losses of the interregnum. The remissions, made at some indeterminate date but possibly in 1130, indicate the recognition by the king and his senior officers that Westminster's cash flow was completely inadequate to pay off this debt.

Their readiness to shrug off this bad debt was perhaps triggered by the recent litigation between Abbot Herbert and his men and some Jewish moneylenders. Most probably an attempt was made to pay off the debt to the Crown by borrowing elsewhere, again seemingly without the wherewithal to reimburse the new lenders.[118] Herbert accounted for a further 20 marks at the Exchequer at Michaelmas 1130, an amercement resulting from a plea at which William d'Aubigny had presided. It appears as though the abbot was required to answer for a breach (and more likely several) of the forest laws, committed by tenants on his estates in Essex. Herbert paid 10 marks of this; the balance was carried over.[119]

The financial crisis, and the failure to remedy it, caused much ill-feeling among the monastic community at Westminster. While administration, on a large scale, was perhaps not Herbert's strong point, matters were made worse by the antagonistic attitude adopted towards him by Prior Osbert de Clare who, in a particularly forceful letter, pointed out the disciplinary and tenurial consequences of a long period of poor management.[120] Osbert's confrontational stance eventually overshot the mark, and he was banished to Ely.[121]

Heavy financial outgoings were involved in petitioning the papal curia, as well as the royal court. During Herbert's abbacy, the monks of Westminster increasingly resisted the jurisdiction of the bishop of London. When in 1133 Bishop Gilbert (the Universal, 1127–34) arrived at the abbey on the feasts of SS Peter and Paul (29 June) and proceeded to celebrate Mass, this was seen as the last straw. An indignant embassy to Pope Innocent II, then at Pisa, resulted in the dispatch of a bull to King Henry I authorizing him to take the abbey under his protection, and excluding it from the control of the bishop of London. From now on, Westminster was to be deemed a 'special daughter' of

117 *The Great Roll of the Pipe for the Thirty-First Year of the Reign of Henry I (Michaelmas 1130)*, ed. J. Hunter (Record Comm., London, 1833), p. 150.

118 *Ibid*., pp. 146, 150.

119 *Ibid*., p. 56.

120 *The Letters of Osbert de Clare, Prior of Westminster*, ed. E.W. Williamson; introd. J. Armitage Robinson (London, 1929), no. 2, p. 51.

121 *Ibid*., pp. 2–11.

the papal see.[122] The financial outlay involved in securing this bull, at a time of financial crisis, is some gauge of the intensity of feeling on the matter at Westminster. Rather less expensive, but still no doubt necessitating a financial outlay, were the indulgences which, from Abbot Herbert's time, were requested from visiting papal legates. Two indulgences, of dubious authenticity, survive in the name of the legate Peter Pierleoni. Purporting to date from the period June–September 1121, within a few months of Herbert's becoming abbot, they were designed to foster attendance at the abbey on the feast of SS Peter and Paul, and, in one bull, on that of St Peter's Chains.[123] A third, genuine, indulgence, granted in the late summer of 1125 by John of Crema, at the request of Abbot Herbert and the convent, was also designed to encourage attendance on the feast of SS Peter and Paul.[124]

At the petition, and with the assent, of the monks, Herbert assigned specified revenues for the service of the High Altar;[125] three charters survive in his name concerning tenancy arrangements, one concerning land in Hendon (Middx),[126] and two concerning properties in Essex;[127] and there is one writ surviving in his name concerning the abbey's right to offer sanctuary.[128]

Several of Herbert's charters reflect dealings with religious houses. Two concern the establishment and endowment of the little nunnery of Kilburn;[129] the abbey's dependent priory of Great Malvern was granted the manor of Powick at farm,[130] and a letter written in the names of Herbert and Prior Edwy concerns the return of a runaway monk of Great Malvern to Worcester cathedral priory, where he had been working on a missal for that house.[131] Herbert and the convent gave lands to their cell of Hurley, and the stability of this grant was reinforced by a successful petition to Henry I to notify his officers in Oxfordshire about it.[132]

The benefactions of King Edward had included much of the estates of Pershore (Worcs.), which were transferred to Westminster.[133] The tenants on these remote lands tried to evade rendering tithes and alms which they continued to owe to Pershore abbey, as the 'mother church' of the area. Presumably a formal complaint was sent by Pershore to Westminster, since

122 *Westminster Abbey Charters*, no. 155; *Papsturkunden in England*, ed. W. Holtzmann, 3 vols, Abhandlungen der Gesellschaft der Wissenschaften in Göttingen, phil.-hist. Klasse, Berlin, Göttingen (I = neue Folge XXV, 1930–31; II = 3. Folge XIV–XV, 1935–6; III = Folge XXXIII, 1952), I, no. 17.
123 *Westminster Abbey Charters*, nos 187–8.
124 *Ibid*., no. 189.
125 *Ibid*., no. 244.
126 *Ibid*., no. 245.
127 *Ibid*., nos 246–7.
128 *Ibid*., no. 248.
129 *Ibid*., nos 249–50.
130 *Ibid*., no. 243.
131 *Ibid*., no. 248a.
132 T. Madox, *Baronia Anglica* (London, 1736), p. 252n; calendared *Regesta*, II, no. 1838.
133 Harvey, *Westminster Abbey and its Estates*, pp. 27, 363 and n. 3.

Herbert wrote a strong letter to the tenants, ordering them to render tithes, alms and other services, without any contradiction or causing agitation.[134]

Herbert died on 3 September, perhaps in 1136, but possibly as late as 1138.[135] If he did die in the earlier year, then Westminster experienced a further two-year vacancy, which compounded the financial and tenurial problems accumulating from before his own accession.

134 B.R. Kemp, 'The Mother Church of Thatcham', *Berkshire Archaeological Journal*, LXIII (1967–68), p. 21, n. 32; P. Chaplais, 'The Original Charters of Herbert and Gervase, Abbots of Westminster (1121–1157)', in his *Essays in Medieval Diplomacy and Administration* (London, 1981), pp. XVIII, 89–110, at pp. Addendum.

135 Knowles, Brooke and London, *Heads of Religious Houses*, p. 77.

3

The Abbots, c.1138–1173

Gervase de Blois, abbot of Westminster c.1138–c.1157, earned a bad reputation at the abbey from the time of his successor onwards. His notoriety was accepted without question throughout the rest of the Middle Ages, and indeed well into the twentieth century. The allegations about his shortcomings were then carefully investigated by H.G. Richardson and G.O. Sayles, who concluded that in most respects the charges made against him were unfounded.[1] A further detailed examination of his tenurial policy, the most contentious aspect of his activities, was made by Barbara Harvey, who concluded that, except in perhaps three individual cases, his dealings with tenants were perfectly above-board.[2] These stages in the rehabilitation of Gervase will be examined below, in their appropriate context.

The crucial fact that he was a son of King Stephen both earned Gervase his abbacy at an early age, and also ensured that he later lost it. Gervase and, probably, his brothers Ralph and Amalric[3] were sons of King Stephen and his mistress Damette (the Little Lady).[4] Although illegitimacy was a technical bar to a clerical career, dispensations could be obtained, and the later criticism of Gervase did not focus on this point. Equally, it was normal to provide high-ranking clerical posts for kinsmen of the king. There were no recorded protests at Gervase's appointment to Westminster, and the most likely reaction among the chapter would be a belief that, with the king's son as abbot, their financial difficulties would soon fade into oblivion.

Gervase's appointment probably dates from the latter part of 1138. There is uncertainty on this point, because the first that is known of it is a note of his blessing, by the visiting papal legate, on 17 December 1138.[5] Given that

1 H.G. Richardson and G.O. Sayles, *The Governance of Medieval England from the Conquest to Magna Carta* (Edinburgh, 1963), pp. 413–21.

2 Barbara Harvey, 'Abbot Gervase de Blois and the Fee-Farms of Westminster Abbey', *Bulletin of the Institute of Historical Research*, 40 (1967), pp. 127–41.

3 *Westminster Abbey Charters, 1066–c.1216*, ed. Emma Mason, assisted by the late Jennifer Bray, continuing the work of the late Desmond J. Murphy, London Record Society, 25 (London, 1988), nos 258, 263, 269.

4 *Ibid.*, nos 109, 262.

5 *The Chronicle of John of Worcester, 1118–1140*, ed. J.R.H. Weaver, Anecdota Oxoniensia, Medieval and Modern Series, XIII (Oxford, 1908), p. 53.

the archbishopric of Canterbury had been vacant since 21 November 1136, and that the archbishop of York was dying, it may be that the blessing postdated the appointment by nearly two years.[6] The status of Anselm, bishop of London (1136–38) was doubtful,[7] and in any case his involvement in the ceremony of blessing would have outraged the chapter of Westminster. On the other hand, Gervase was a young abbot even in 1138. His father's date of birth is itself uncertain, but occurred perhaps c.1090x1096.[8] Gervase would barely have reached the canonical age to be made a priest even by the time of his blessing, and it is unlikely that his appointment antedated that ceremony by long. In December 1138, the legate Alberic, cardinal-bishop of Ostia, held a general council which convened at Westminster, and at which three abbots were deposed.[9] In theory, at least, he could also have voiced any objections which were deemed to debar Gervase from his abbacy, but in practice it is likely that an understanding had been reached with the king before Gervase was blessed on 17 December.[10]

It is arguable that Gervase was one of the four abbots from the province of Canterbury who attended the Second Lateran Council, which opened on 3 April 1139, since those clergy who did attend took the opportunity of petitioning for privileges for their churches.[11] Westminster certainly obtained two bulls dated 22 April 1139. In one of these Pope Innocent II notified Gervase that he had taken the abbey under his protection, and that he confirmed its privileges and possessions.[12] By the second, the pope notified Gervase that, at the request of Henry (of Blois), bishop of Winchester, he took under his protection lands held by Gilbert of Hendon, a tenant of the abbey.[13]

One item on the agenda of the Lateran Council was a debate on the rival claims of King Stephen and the Empress Matilda to the English throne. Arnulf (of Lisieux) was Stephen's chief spokesman, supported by Roger de Clinton, bishop of Coventry, and Lupellus, a clerk of the late archbishop of Canterbury. Technical rulings rather than a verdict as such operated to the

6 F. Barlow, *The English Church 1066–1154* (London, 1979), p. 93.

7 John Le Neve, *Fasti Ecclesiae Anglicanae 1066–1300. I. St Paul's, London*, compiled Diana E. Greenway (London, 1968), p. 1.

8 King Stephen is thought to have been born c.1096: R.H.C. Davis, *King Stephen 1135–1154*, 3rd edn (Harlow, 1990), pp. 1 and note 1; 7 and note 15. See, however, A. Morey and C.N.L. Brooke, *Gilbert Foliot and his Letters* (Cambridge, 1965), p. 78, where it is suggested that Stephen's younger brother, Henry, was himself born c.1090–92, or perhaps even a few years earlier.

9 Barlow, *The English Church 1066–1154*, p. 93.

10 D. Knowles, C.N.L. Brooke and Vera C.M. London, *The Heads of Religious Houses England and Wales 940–1216* (Cambridge, 1972), p. 77.

11 A. Saltman, *Theobald, Archbishop of Canterbury* (London, 1955; reprinted New York, 1969), pp. 137–9; Richardson and Sayles, *The Governance of Medieval England*, p. 418.

12 *Papsturkunden in England*, ed. W. Holtzmann, 3 vols (Berlin and Göttingen, 1930–31, 1935–6, 1952), I, no. 21; *Westminster Abbey Charters*, no. 156.

13 *Papsturkunden in England*, I, no. 20; *Westminster Abbey Charters*, no. 157.

advantage of the *de facto* king, so that Stephen effectively won his case.[14] One way and another, the proceedings would prove most instructive to any young abbot, quite apart from presenting him with an opportunity to meet many of the most eminent clergy from all over western and central Europe.

The appointment of Gervase to Westminster afforded an opportunity for recalling Prior Osbert from his exile.[15] In the course of 1139, they appear to have co-operated in preparing a petition for the canonization of King Edward. While Osbert was the prime mover, it would clearly be to Gervase's advantage to preside over a church which housed the relics of a newly-canonized saint, and he was able to enlist the support of his father, and in a rather perfunctory fashion, that of his uncle Henry of Blois, bishop of Winchester.[16]

Osbert's mission to the *Curia* took place in the late autumn of 1139 and its outcome is recorded in a series of bulls dated from the Lateran on 9 December. The two aims of the prior's mission, to secure King Edward's canonization and to ensure the integrity of Westminster's endowment, are both reflected in one of these bulls. In this, addressed to Abbot Gervase and the monks, Innocent II announced that the canonization of King Edward would require more evidence than had been offered. Further evidence, and the petition for canonization, should be presented by the whole realm (of England). However he, Innocent, had written to the legate, Henry (of Blois), bishop of Winchester, ordering the restitution to the abbey of those lands which had been misappropriated.[17]

The pope's letter to the bishop is the second of the bulls dated 9 December 1139. In it, Innocent II stated that he had learned from Prior Osbert of the complaint of the monks of Westminster that many people had wrongfully seized, and violently detained their property. The pope ordered Henry to hear this complaint; to render justice to the monks, and to prevent anyone from doing them further injury or harm.[18]

A third bull was addressed to David I, king of Scots, requesting him to confirm to the abbey the land which provided his annual donation of £1 10s, which supported the commemoration of the death of his late sister, Queen Matilda.[19]

These three bulls are straightforward in their content, and all reflect the monks' anxiety over their endowment. Clearly they had incurred considerable

14 Saltman, *Theobald, Archbishop of Canterbury*, pp. 140–41.

15 *The Letters of Osbert de Clare, Prior of Westminster*, ed. E.W. Williamson; introd. J. Armitage Robinson (London, 1929), p. 16.

16 F. Barlow, *Edward the Confessor* (London, 1970), p. 275; *English Episcopal Acta VIII. Winchester 1070–1204*, ed. M.J. Franklin (Oxford, 1993), pp. 214–15.

17 *Letters of Osbert de Clare*, pp. 87–8, no.19; *Westminster Abbey Charters*, no. 158.

18 *Letters of Osbert de Clare*, p. 88, no. 20; *Westminster Abbey Charters*, no. 159.

19 *Papsturkunden in England*, I, no. 25; *The Acts of Malcolm IV, King of Scots 1153–1165*, ed. G.W.S. Barrow (Edinburgh, 1960), pp. 290–91, no. 319; *Westminster Abbey Charters*, no. 160.

losses, not only in the interregnum preceding Herbert's abbacy, but perhaps also both during his time and in the interval between Herbert's death and the appointment of Gervase. With civil unrest now mounting in England, the resident papal legate was perhaps the man who might most effectively secure restitution. In the event of full-scale civil war, King David, it would be presumed, would support his niece the empress and, since the outcome was unpredictable, the chapter of Westminster would be eager to secure his earlier endowment during this window of opportunity. David's initial grant had been made in his capacity as earl of Huntingdon[20] and now that he was king it was desirable to ensure that he confirmed his donation. He did so while he was in London in June 1141.[21]

The fourth bull of Pope Innocent II for Westminster is a much more contentious document.[22] Until recent times it was accepted as genuine, and was cited as conclusive evidence that Gervase personally was responsible for the declining standards of estate management at Westminster, and that he had been acting on bad advice from people whom he consulted from outside the community.[23] A more recent commentary made on it, while still assuming that the bull is genuine, believed it to have been issued in response to an initiative by Gervase himself, in his efforts to recover lands lost in the time of Abbot Herbert, a conjecture which is supported by the instructions contained in the bull issued to Henry of Blois in his capacity as legate.[24] The bull instructed Gervase to reassemble the lands and rents which had been administered by individual monks, and to manage both the internal and the external property of the abbey with the advice of the chapter. He was further instructed to recover the churches and tithes which had been dispersed without the consent of the brethren. The monks professed in the abbey were to be his collaborators and colleagues; advice was not to be taken from monks from elsewhere, nor were they to be consulted about confidential matters. Essentially, these points required Gervase to correct irregularities which had developed in the administration during the time of Herbert.[25] A bull incorporating some, at least, of these instructions would have strengthened Gervase's hand against entrenched obedientiaries, who were perhaps responsible for the alienation of property. Such a document was perhaps requested by the young abbot himself, rather than by the confrontational Prior Osbert,

20 *The Acts of Malcolm IV*, p. 134, no. 6; *Westminster Abbey Charters*, no. 99.

21 *The Acts of Malcolm IV*, pp. 140–41, nos 13–14; *Westminster Abbey Charters*, nos 100–101.

22 *Papsturkunden in England*, I, no. 24; *Westminster Abbey Charters*, no. 161.

23 The bull was accepted as genuine by P. Chaplais, 'The Original Charters of Herbert and Gervase, Abbots of Westminster (1121–1157)', in P.M. Barnes and C.F. Slade, eds, *A Medieval Miscellany for Doris Mary Stenton*, Pipe Roll Soc., new series, XXXVI (1960), pp. 89–110, at p. 91; reprinted in P. Chaplais, *Essays in Medieval Government and Administration* (London, 1981), pp. XVIII, 89–110, at p. 91.

24 Richardson and Sayles, *The Governance of Medieval England*, p. 416.

25 *Ibid.*, p. 417.

wanting to wrong-foot the new abbot in the eyes of the chapter. The eventual wording of the bull, however, might owe much to Osbert's verbal representations at Rome. The administrative chaos which awaited Gervase in 1138 was comparable with that later prevailing at Bury St Edmunds in the period before the election of Abbot Samson in 1182.[26] Whereas Samson was already experienced in monastic administration at the time he became abbot, Gervase is not known to have had this advantage, and might welcome papal backing, in the form of instructions which he could cite, when he faced up to *seniores* accustomed to running things as they pleased. Moreover, when Prior Osbert later went into exile, he did not write reprovingly to Gervase as he had done to Herbert.[27] There are subsequent indications that Gervase was regarded favourably at Rome. During the 1140s, the papal curia became increasingly biased towards the empress and against King Stephen. While Henry of Blois came in for occasional sniping,[28] Gervase was able to obtain from Pope Eugenius III in 1146 and again in 1151 bulls granting privileges to Westminster.[29] Seemingly Gervase was a perfectly acceptable abbot.

There is, however, one passage in Innocent II's bull on the abbey's administration which has given rise to suspicion, and these suspicions in turn prompted a closer analysis of the rest of its contents. In her article on Gervase's administration of the abbey's properties, Barbara Harvey noted that the charges of mismanagement later brought against him rest primarily on this one papal bull, and on the comments of John Flete, the fifteenth-century chronicler.[30] Like Richardson and Sayles, she considers that in December 1139, when Gervase had been abbot for scarcely a year, he could not have caused such cumulative damage to the abbey's property as to earn a papal rebuke.[31] What chiefly prompted her suspicions, though, was that the bull, known only from cartulary copies, contains a passage in which the monks are instructed to ensure the safety of King Edward's regalia. These objects (vestments and communion vessels used at the coronation) are also mentioned as being rightfully in the custody of the monks in one of Prior Osbert's major forgeries, the so-called Third Charter of King Edward, and in another of his products, a spurious bull of Pope Paschal II. By inference, then, Prior Osbert also had a hand in the 'critical' bull of Innocent II. This probability is heightened in that the injunction that the abbot should administer Westminster's property according to the advice of the monks is reminiscent of a passage in Edward's First Charter, yet another of Osbert's products, in which the abbot was forbidden to alienate monastic property. Barbara Harvey

26 *The Chronicle of Jocelin of Brakelond*, transl. and ed. H.E. Butler (London, 1949, reprinted 1951), pp. 1–13.
27 Richardson and Sayles, *The Governance of Medieval England*, p. 420.
28 John of Salisbury, *Historia Pontificalis: Memoirs of the Papal Court*, transl. and introd. Marjorie Chibnall (London, 1956), pp. 78–80.
29 *Papsturkunden in England*, I, pp. 286–8, no. 47; *Westminster Abbey Charters*, nos 162–3.
30 Harvey, 'Abbot Gervase de Blois and the Fee-Farms of Westminster Abbey', p. 127.
31 Harvey, 'Fee Farms', p. 128.

concluded that, since the papal style and address appear authentic, Osbert used a simpler bull, one of the batch entrusted to him when he left Rome in December 1139, as the basis for the document as it now survives, which consequently cannot be used as proof of the allegations which were made against Gervase.[32]

The later criticisms of Gervase by John Flete rested largely on a series of grants of land in fee-farm, which he alleged were made by Gervase to the detriment of the abbey.[33] In fact, only seven of the twelve grants listed by Flete[34] were made by Gervase, as Barbara Harvey demonstrated, when she considered these grants in fee-farms in the wider context of his tenurial policy.[35] As she pointed out, only two basic questions need to be asked of each of his grants: first, whether its terms were reasonable under the circumstances in which they were made; and secondly, whether the grant was made with the assent of the convent. The one grant which clearly did not meet these conditions was Gervase's grant of the manor of Chelsea, in fee and inheritance, to his mother Damette. Two others which were possibly made without the consent of the convent as a whole were his grant of a plot of land in London to his clerk, Elias son of Goldwin, and his grant of the land of Endiff (near Charing in Westminster) to Gerin, the king's minister.[36] However, Prior Elias witnessed the grant to Gerin, while three monks, albeit including one novice, witnessed that to Elias, whose rent was to contribute towards providing clothes for the monks.[37] The grant to Damette was the one most likely to provoke criticism. Whereas she was to render £4 annually, the annual rent of Chelsea had been £9 in 1086, when the overlord had been Edward of Salisbury.[38] On the other hand, Abbot Gilbert Crispin had leased Chelsea to William of Buckland, c.1115x1117, at an annual rent of £4, although he was also liable to pay geld and scutage.[39]

Since Damette and her heirs were to hold Chelsea in fee, she and they were presumably also liable to pay scutage, and any incoming heir would be liable to pay the normal feudal relief. Moreover, when Damette received Chelsea, she rendered an additional 40 shillings, together with a pall worth £5. These latter payments represent the entry-fine, which was levied to take account of current market values, whereas the annual rent was usually fixed by custom. It was twenty years or more since the rent of Chelsea had been

32 Harvey, 'Fee-Farms', pp. 128–9.

33 J. Flete, *The History of Westminster Abbey*, ed. J. Armitage Robinson (Cambridge, 1909), pp. 89–91.

34 J. Flete, *The History of Westminster Abbey*, p. 89.

35 Harvey, 'Fee-Farms', esp. pp. 129–30.

36 Harvey, 'Fee-Farms', esp. p. 138. For the texts, see *Westminster Abbey Charters*, nos 258, 261–2.

37 Harvey, 'Fee-Farms', p. 138.

38 See Richardson and Sayles, *The Governance of Medieval England*, p. 415, n. 5, for discussion of the identity of this estate and its value.

39 *Westminster Abbey Charters*, no. 242.

fixed at £4, and custom, once established, could not easily be overturned. On economic grounds, therefore, Gervase's grant to his mother was not unreasonable. As Richardson and Sayles pointed out, the grant of Chelsea was perhaps perceived as a scandal because it established the king's mistress in a Westminster manor which was readily accessible from the royal palace.[40] If, as is likely, King Stephen instructed Gervase to provide Damette with a suitable home, this would account for the lack of any recorded discussion with the chapter.

Royal charters granted to Westminster during Gervase's abbacy are fewer in number than might be expected, once the forgeries have been eliminated.[41] King Stephen, in a charter which probably dates from immediately after Gervase's blessing as abbot, ordered the justice, sheriff, barons and officers of London to guard the lands and tenements of his son Abbot Gervase as they would the royal demesne. They were to enable him to have his rents and dues, and especially St Mary Newchurch.[42] Another writ from early in Stephen's reign, but perhaps issued before the beginning of Gervase's abbacy, ordered that the men in the soke of St Peter were to be quit of the Hustings and Folkmoot, as their charter attested.[43] Similarly a writ granting exemption from 'the sheriff's aid called justice-aid' on Westminster's lands in Essex, although issued no earlier than the latter part of 1138, may pre-date Gervase's consecration.[44] Much the same applies to writs which, respectively, grant assarts in Kelvedon, Essex, and confirm the manor of Doddington, Lincs., although in these cases the possible date-span is more open-ended.[45]

Of the remaining charters, one gave an interim verdict, largely in Westminster's favour, in a dispute between this abbey and Chertsey;[46] a second confirmed Westminster's title to Parham (Sussex) and Mapelfort (Middx),[47] and a third granted geld exemption on six and a half hides in the manor of Westminster 'since the royal court and palace, and the infirmary of St Giles, are established there'.[48] Of the forgeries, two are all-embracing confirmations of lands and privileges, purportedly dating respectively from 13 December 1138 and January to June 1139.[49] The remaining forgeries comprise a complex series of grants of geld exemption for the manor of Westminster; the

40 Richardson and Sayles, *The Governance of Medieval England*, p. 415.

41 Charters forged in the name of King Stephen, and purportedly dating from Gervase's abbacy, include *Regesta Regum Anglo-Normannorum III. 1135–1154*, ed. H.A. Cronne and R.H.C. Davis (Oxford, 1968), nos 928, 929, 937, 939, 940, 941. See also *Westminster Abbey Charters*, nos 106, 110–11, 119–21.

42 *Regesta III*, no. 930; *Westminster Abbey Charters*, no. 109.

43 *Regesta III*, no. 927; *Westminster Abbey Charters*, no. 112.

44 *Regesta III*, no. 931; *Westminster Abbey Charters*, no. 113.

45 *Regesta III*, nos 932–3; *Westminster Abbey Charters*, nos 114–15.

46 *Regesta III*, no. 934; *Westminster Abbey Charters*, no. 116.

47 *Regesta III*, no. 935; *Westminster Abbey Charters*, no. 117.

48 *Regesta III*, no. 938; *Westminster Abbey Charters*, no. 118.

49 *Regesta III*, nos 928–9; *Westminster Abbey Charters*, nos 110–11.

manor of Battersea; and finally for both together, with quittance of secular service on a virgate in Hanwell.[50]

As a king's son, Gervase might have expected to obtain more for his abbey, but, given that civil war and unrest prevailed for much of his father's reign, he perhaps obtained all that could be expected. Conversely, one of Westminster's tenants in the West Midlands, William of Darnford, even succeeded in obtaining the empress's confirmation of a charter in which Gervase and the convent had confirmed to him the manor of Deerhurst.[51]

Following the two Westminster delegations to the papal *curia* in April and December 1139, there was a lull in such activities until 8 March 1146, when, at Trastevere, Pope Eugenius III confirmed to Gervase and his successors papal, royal and other privileges granted to the abbey.[52] Five years later, on 27 March 1151, at Ferentino, Pope Eugenius confirmed to Gervase and his successors the privileges granted by earlier popes, kings, Archbishop Dunstan and other magnates.[53] It is not known that the abbot travelled to Rome himself in order to obtain either bull. It is possible that they were obtained directly, by a Westminster deputation, although their generalized terms may indicate that on each occasion someone attending the *curia* on other business slipped in a petition for some papal privilege for Westminster. One kinsman of Gervase who did travel to Rome, towards the end of 1145, was William Fitz Herbert, hoping to obtain his pallium as archbishop of York. Although a number of cardinals supported him, he eventually left the *curia* without it.[54] The privilege granted for the benefit of his cousin Gervase may represent the reward of lobbying on the part of someone in William's entourage, perhaps a clerk of Gervase, or a monk of Westminster, who had been incorporated into the retinue as William headed for the Channel.

The second of Eugenius III's bulls for Gervase may, in contrast, have been obtained by a lobbyist in the party of William's rival for York, the Cistercian Henry Murdac, consecrated as archbishop by the pope on 7 December 1147.[55] Following his eventual reconciliation with King Stephen, he acted on the king's behalf in a diplomatic mission to Rome in 1151,[56] arriving in time to celebrate Easter, which fell on 8 April.[57] The archbishop was unsuccessful, however, in his mission to secure papal recognition for Eustace as heir

50 *Regesta III*, nos 939–41; *Westminster Abbey Charters*, nos 119–21.

51 *Regesta III*, no. 259; *Westminster Abbey Charters*, no. 98.

52 *Westminster Abbey Charters*, no. 162.

53 *Papsturkunden in England*, I, no. 47; *Westminster Abbey Charters*, no. 163.

54 *English Episcopal Acta V. York 1070–1154*, ed. Janet Burton (Oxford, 1988), p. xxxi; H.A. Cronne, *The Reign of Stephen 1135–1154. Anarchy in England* (London, 1970), p. 59.

55 *English Episcopa Acta* V, p. xxxii.

56 *Ibid.*, p. xxxii.

57 Cronne, *The Reign of Stephen*, p. 63. Cf. C.R. Cheney, ed., *Handbook of Dates for Students of English History* (London, 1948), Table 18.

to the throne.[58] It is conjectural whether a subsidiary task had been to obtain a privilege for Westminster, and it is more likely that a subordinate of Gervase was enabled to join the archbishop's party. Westminster's geographical location rendered it well placed to serve as a stopover for clerical delegations travelling to and from the *Curia*, and hence to profit from contact with parties moving in both directions.

Pope Eugenius III evidently regarded Gervase as an acceptable abbot of Westminster, despite the worsening relations between the papal see and King Stephen. The privilege granted in 1151 may in a sense have underlined his personal standing, even though the pope had rejected his candidature for the see of Lincoln in 1148. Early in 1148, King Stephen prohibited all clergy except for a hand-picked trio of bishops from attending the General Council which the pope summoned to meet at Rheims on 2 March. In consequence, Stephen narrowly escaped excommunication, and his refusal to allow Archbishop Theobald to return to England after secretly making his way to the Council greatly damaged relations between king and pope.[59] This confrontation coincided with a vacancy in the see of Lincoln, and the king and his brother, Henry bishop of Winchester, prepared a short-list comprising Gervase, together with their nephews Henry de Sully, abbot of Fécamp, and Hugh, abbot of St Benet's, Holme. All three were rejected by Pope Eugenius, evidently because of their kinship to King Stephen. The approved candidate, Robert de Chesney, was formally elected in the monastic chapter at Westminster, in the presence of the king and queen and other dignitaries, a scene which was perhaps mortifying for Gervase, his father and uncle.[60] That personal factors did not enter into the rejection of Gervase and his cousins is indicated by Hugh's subsequent monastic career as abbot of Chertsey, Surrey, and then of Lagny-sur-Marne;[61] and Henry's tenure of Fécamp to 1187; as well as by the papal privilege granted to Gervase in 1151.

There was an interval of some years before Gervase again petitioned the papal court. On this occasion he was chiefly concerned to assert Westminster's control over Great Malvern and its other dependent cells. Pope Adrian IV, on 25 May 1157, confirmed to Gervase and the convent jurisdiction over Great Malvern.[62] The Westminster delegation petitioned for two further privileges, which were granted on 1 June 1157. One of these confirmed control over Hurley (Berks.) and Sudbury (Suffolk), as well as over Great

58 Cronne, *The Reign of Stephen*, p. 63.

59 Saltman, *Theobald, Archbishop of Canterbury*, pp. 25–8; Cronne, *The Reign of Stephen*, pp. 60–61.

60 *English Episcopal Acta I. Lincoln, 1067–1185*, ed. D.M. Smith (Oxford, 1980), p. xxxv; Saltman, *Theobald, Archbishop of Canterbury*, pp. 106–7; *The Letters and Charters of Gilbert Foliot*, ed. Z.N. Brooke, A. Morey and C.N.L. Brooke (Cambridge, 1967), no. 75.

61 Knowles, Brooke and London, *Heads of Religious Houses*, pp. 38, 68.

62 *Papsturkunden in England*, I, no. 68; *Westminster Abbey Charters*, no. 164.

Malvern, together with the abbey's churches and chapels;[63] and the other was an all-embracing confirmation of the abbey's privileges, exemptions and lands.[64]

Within England, Gervase evidently maintained a good reputation among his fellow-prelates. In 1145 he attended the legatine Council held by Cardinal Imar of Tusculum.[65] Archbishop Theobald energetically supported Gervase's efforts to retain control over Great Malvern. He was supported in this by Gilbert Foliot, bishop of Hereford (a kinsman of Robert de Chesney), by the abbots of Gloucester and Pershore, and by others.[66] A strongly supportive letter which Theobald wrote to the pope on Gervase's behalf no doubt carried weight when Adrian IV was petitioned to reassert Westminster's control over Great Malvern.[67] Given the stance taken by Theobald, and by Gilbert Foliot, as relations between king and pope worsened in the later years of Stephen's reign, their support for his son Gervase indicates that they viewed him as a reputable cleric. It is even more remarkable that Theobald continued his support of Gervase in the early years of Henry II, when support of the late king's son might be thought courageous. There are rulings by Theobald in favour of Gervase's rights in the manor of Kelvedon and the advowson of Ockendon[68] and he granted an indulgence to those visiting the abbey on certain feast days.[69] Gervase, for his part, in 1156 or 1157, witnessed a ruling by Theobald on tithes disputed between the monks of Belvoir and those of Thetford.[70] Theobald, as a defender of the rights of the clerical order, might instinctively rally to Gervase's support if he believed him to be threatened by the accession of Henry II, but there is no reason to believe that the archbishop was supporting an abbot who had failed to meet the requirements of his office.

In fact, Gervase is shown to have been a diligent abbot. Two of his surviving *acta* specify rents to be paid towards the expenses of the monks' clothing;[71] two more specified annual payments towards lights for the high altar;[72] and one granted to the precentor annually tithes from Roding, Essex, for the repair of books.[73]

63 *Papsturkunden in England*, I, no. 70; *Westminster Abbey Charters*, no. 166.
64 *Papsturkunden in England*, I, no. 69; *Westminster Abbey Charters*, no. 165.
65 Saltman, *Theobald, Archbishop of Canterbury*, p. 450, no. 233; Richardson and Sayles, *The Governance of Medieval England*, p. 419 and note.
66 Saltman, *Theobald, Archbishop of Canterbury*, pp. 88–9.
67 *The Letters of John of Salisbury I. The Early Letters (1153–1161)*, ed. W.J. Millor and H.E. Butler, revised by C.N.L. Brooke (London, 1953), no. 45.
68 Saltman, *Theobald, Archbishop of Canterbury*, pp. 507–9, nos 276, 278; *Westminster Abbey Charters*, nos 198–9.
69 Saltman, *Theobald, Archbishop of Canterbury*, p. 509, no. 279; *Westminster Abbey Charters*, no. 200.
70 Saltman, *Theobald, Archbishop of Canterbury*, p. 246, no. 16.
71 Harvey, 'Fee Farms', pp. 138–9; *Westminster Abbey Charters*, nos 255, 258.
72 *Westminster Abbey Charters*, nos 252–3.
73 *Ibid.*, no. 251.

Dealings with, or on behalf of, other religious houses include provision of pannage for the dependent cell of Hurley priory,[74] the confirmation of certain corrodies to the nuns of Kilburn, besides a confirmation of land in the manor of Knightsbridge,[75] and an exchange of land with Merton priory to facilitate the construction of mills.[76] Those of his *acta* which concern lands or other property rights, apart from the fee-farms discussed above, appear to be straightforward confirmations, made with the consent of the convent, to beneficiaries whose forebears had held the property in question.[77] There is also a series of writs in his name concerning the flight of outlaws to the sanctuary, one addressed to the sheriff of Middlesex, and one to the sheriff of Sussex.[78]

Throughout his abbacy, Gervase cannot have known much peace of mind. He had inherited from his predecessor a confrontational relationship with Prior Osbert. Even though Osbert did not attack him in a directly-addressed letter, as he did to Herbert, yet the forged papal bull was equally damaging, if its contents became widely known. On the wider clerical stage, and in addition to Gervase's disappointment over the Lincoln election, there was the on-going tense relationship between his father, King Stephen, and his clerical superior, Archbishop Theobald, while the civil unrest which was endemic virtually throughout Stephen's reign endangered Westminster's lands, particularly those further afield. The estates in the West Midlands were harried by Earl Robert and his men.[79] In the East Midlands estates whose revenues supported the convent were seized, variously, by John de Stuteville and Robert Foliot, while Alice de Condet, a sister of Ranulf earl of Chester, 'violently' withheld a rent which normally contributed to the monks' clothing allowance.[80] When the forces of the Empress Matilda set out for London in the early summer of 1141, Westminster stood directly in their line of march, while the counter-attack by Stephen's wife involved the deliberate wasting of the lands encircling London.[81] One way and another, Westminster's estates probably suffered much damage as a result of the political situation, but that was no reflection on the abbot. The treaty negotiated between King Stephen and Henry of Anjou in the summer of 1153 would carry ominous undertones for Gervase, but there is no evidence of any immediate change in his status when his father died a year later. Probably

74 Chaplais, 'The Original Charters of Herbert and Gervase', p. 104, no. 8; *Westminster Abbey Charters*, no. 266.

75 *Westminster Abbey Charters*, nos 264–5.

76 *Ibid.*, no. 268.

77 *Ibid.*, nos 254, 256–7, 259–60, 267.

78 *Ibid.*, nos 272–4.

79 Flete, *The History of Westminster Abbey*, p. 92.

80 Saltman, *Theobald, Archbishop of Canterbury*, pp. 507–8, no. 277; *Westminster Abbey Charters*, no. 195. On Alice de Condet's relationship to Earl Rannulf, see *Regesta III*, no. 178; Cronne, *The Reign of Stephen*, p. 287, n. 19.

81 *Gesta Stephani*, ed. and transl. K.R. Potter, introd. R.H.C. Davis (Oxford, 1976), p. 122.

Gervase performed the customary role of the abbot of Westminster at the coronation of Henry II, and he was at court shortly before the king embarked for the Continent in January 1156.[82] One royal charter, perhaps obtained on that occasion, ordered that Gervase was to have all his lands, tenants and liberties as any of his predecessors held them in the reign of King Edward, and to hold them as Edward and Henry I granted by their charters, with franchisal rights.[83] A charter of liberties, granted to Westminster in the name of Henry II, appears to date from the same time, but is of doubtful authenticity.[84] A writ of Henry II which does not name the abbot, but which appears to date from Gervase's abbacy, ordered the sheriff of Surrey to restore any part of the abbot's land in Claygate which had been misappropriated.[85] A further writ of Henry II, once again not naming the abbot, but apparently dating from this period, grants extensive legal exemptions in Paddington (Middlesex), Fanton (Essex) and Claygate, with rights in the wood and vill of Ditton (Surrey), but its tone and content suggest that it is one of a series of spurious writs on this subject.[86] The abbey's tenant at Hendon (Middx) took the opportunity of Henry II's accession to plead for a confirmation of his fee farm. Henry II issued a writ ordering the abbot and monks to comply,[87] and Abbot Gervase dutifully issued a confirmation to this effect.[88] These royal documents contain no overt indication that Gervase was under threat. His position was formally guaranteed by the writ concerning his jurisdiction over his lands,[89] although the very fact that he petitioned for it may indicate that he was feeling uncertain about his future prospects. On the other hand, entries on the Pipe Rolls for the early years of the reign indicate that Gervase was given some preferential treatment, with remission of routine exactions (murder fines levied on the tenants of specific hundreds, the *donum* of the shire, etc.) on his lands in several counties – in other words he was treated, for financial purposes, as a magnate in good standing with the king.[90]

The deposition of Gervase, when it came, was perhaps more sudden and less 'inevitable' than it appears with hindsight, and circumstances beyond his control perhaps contributed to the decision of Henry II to remove him from office. One such circumstance was most likely the flight into exile of Henry of Blois. This seems to have occurred late 1155, and he remained abroad, chiefly at Cluny, until some time in 1157, at any rate, and possibly until early

82 Richardson and Sayles, *The Governance of Medieval England*, p. 419.

83 *Westminster Abbey Charters*, no. 122.

84 *Ibid.*, no. 123.

85 *Ibid.*, no. 125.

86 *Ibid.*, no. 126.

87 *Ibid.*, no. 124.

88 *Ibid.*, no. 263. See also Harvey 'Fee Farms', pp. 135–6.

89 *Westminster Abbey Charters*, no. 122.

90 *The Great Rolls of the Pipe for the Second, Third and Fourth Years of the Reign of King Henry the Second A.D. 1155–1158*, ed. J. Hunter (London, 1844), pp. 124, 133, 135, 143, 156, 161–2, 169, 182.

1158.[91] His self-imposed absence evidently caused some inconvenience to the king, who enlisted Archbishop Theobald to write to him repeatedly, urging him to return. Theobald wrote in reassuring terms, but reading between the lines, it seems that the bishop feared actual physical harassment.[92] Theobald concluded one letter, dated by its editors to 'late 1157', with the following sentence:

> Our Lord the King has assured us of your safety, and except for two persons whom he excludes by name, you will be able to introduce to his favour anyone you please; and we shall rejoice at your return and gladly give you all the help or counsel that we can. Farewell.[93]

While these 'two persons' were perhaps confidential clerks of the bishop of Winchester, it is perhaps more likely that they were the two abbots dismissed within a short time of the date assigned to this letter. The precise date of Gervase's removal is uncertain, but it occurred late in 1157 or the early months of 1158.[94] Its mention in the Winchester Annals indicates the impact made there by the ousting of the bishop's nephew.[95]

Reginald, abbot of Reading, was ordered by the king to resign in 1158.[96] In 1154, but before he became king, Henry of Anjou had a disagreement with Reginald over the church of Berkeley. Reginald, formerly Keeper of the Seal to King Stephen, clearly owed his appointment early in 1154 to that king.[97] Reading, founded by Henry I,[98] housed his tomb, together with that of his infant great-grandson William.[99] In the late 1150s it was still the monastery which, above all others in England, was entrusted with interceding for the wellbeing of the descendants of Henry I. Moreover, it was entrusted with a powerful relic, the Hand of St James. This had been selected from the imperial treasures by the Empress Matilda, in her widowhood, given by her to her father Henry I, and donated by him to Reading in 1133. Following the burial of Henry I at Reading on 4 January 1136, it was appropriated by Henry of Blois, who retained it until he fled into exile. In 1155, the Hand was returned to Reading.[100] It is conjectural whether Henry II's demands for the return of the Hand prompted the bishop's flight. Given this sequence of

91 *English Episcopal Acta VIII. Winchester 1070–1204*, pp. xlvii, 219; cf. *Letters of John of Salisbury*, I, nos 36–8.

92 *Letters of John of Salisbury*, I, nos 37–8.

93 *Ibid*., no. 36, p. 66.

94 Knowles, Brooke and London, *Heads of Religious Houses*, p. 77.

95 Winchester Annals, *Annales Monastici*, II, ed. H.R. Luard, Rolls Series (1865), *sub an*. 1159. The date of these annals is slightly 'out' at this period.

96 *Reading Abbey Cartularies*, ed. B.R. Kemp, Camden Fourth Series, nos 31, 33 (1986–7), I, p. 26.

97 Richardson and Sayles, *The Governance of Medieval England*, pp. 256–7.

98 *Reading Abbey Cartularies*, I, pp. 13–19.

99 *Chronica Roberti de Torigneio*, in *Chronicles of the Reigns of Stephen, Henry II and Richard I*, IV, ed. R. Howlett (Rolls Series, 1889), p. 189.

100 K.J. Leyser, 'Frederick Barbarossa, Henry II and the Hand of St James', reprinted from

events, Abbot Reginald bore no responsibility for the alienation of the Hand from Reading, but was perhaps deemed to be less than wholehearted in his efforts to secure its return. Any dereliction of duty reflected not only on Reading abbey but also on the realm, since the Hand was perceived to guarantee the well-being of the *regnum* which sheltered it.[101]

The sequence of events which led up to the removal of Reginald and Gervase began with Henry II's return to England in April 1157, after successfully concluding his warfare against his brother Geoffrey. He embarked on a programme designed to underline his royal authority, having himself crowned at Lincoln about Christmas 1157, and at Worcester about Easter, 20 April 1158. The removal of the heads of the abbeys which were respectively the mausoleum of his dynasty and the coronation church date from around the period within which these ceremonies were held. Gervase, as a son of Henry's rival, and Reginald, as one of Stephen's confidential advisers, were evidently deemed unsuitable to remain in charge of these key churches. Other religious houses which had strong links with recent kings retained their existing heads, including those of Holy Trinity Aldgate, Battle, and Cirencester. Faversham, founded by Stephen, retained its existing abbot while, in Normandy, Stephen's nephew Henry de Sully remained abbot of the ducal monastery of Fécamp down to 1187. Henry II's concern was evidently to consolidate his royal authority in England itself. Throughout his reign, he intermittently took over the patronage of monasteries founded by one or another of his barons, a policy which carried both political and spiritual connotations.[102] Clearly his firm line on church-state relations in no way modified his belief that the monastic round of prayer helped to secure both his physical and his spiritual well-being.

Abbot Reginald, after spending some years as a monk of Grestain (Eure), in Normandy, was appointed prior of Luffield (priory) (Bucks. and Northants) in 1164, an office which he held for about ten years. In 1166, he was also installed as prior of Walden priory (Essex), holding this office to 1190, when he was promoted to be its first abbot.[103]

For Gervase, however, there was no happy ending, and he died on 25 August 1160.[104] There is no reason to believe that he was the bad abbot of later legend. The story that he dissipated the property of Westminster was probably spread by his successor, Abbot Lawrence, since it is found in sources emanating from Durham and St Albans, with both of which he had strong

English Historical Review, 90 (1975), pp. 481–506, in K. Leyser, *Medieval Germany and its Neighbours 950–1250* (London, 1982), pp. 215–40. See esp. pp. 225–6, 228, 230–1.

101 *Ibid.*, p. 225.

102 Elizabeth M. Hallam, 'Henry II as a founder of monasteries', *Journal of Ecclesiastical History*, 28 (1977), pp. 113–32; Emma Mason, 'The King, the Chamberlain and Southwick Priory', *Bulletin of the Institute of Historical Research*, 53 (1980), pp. 1–10.

103 Knowles, Brooke and London, *Heads of Religious Houses*, pp. 53, 75–6.

104 Flete, *The History of Westminster Abbey*, p. 90.

links.[105] The chronicle of John of Hexham was informed that Gervase wasted the property in a 'juvenile' manner[106] while at St Albans, Abbot Robert de Gorron was given to understand that Gervase's mismanagement resulted in there being nothing left for the food or clothing of the monks.[107] The ruinous condition of the estates in the West Midlands was caused by the men of Earl Robert of Gloucester (d.1147), and no doubt their recovery was under way before Gervase left office. Similarly, the ruinous state of many of the abbey buildings, which Robert de Gorron reported, was due to a devastating fire.[108] Abbot Lawrence, with his own reputation to consider, could be seen to achieve more if he could persuade others that his predecessor had allowed the condition of Westminster to run down. His main charges circulated in other monasteries, while Flete's story of the fee-farms was for the local readership. What gave support to Flete's allegations of economic mismanagement was that Westminster did suffer territorial losses, not through Gervase's activities, but in consequence of his deposition. In a lawsuit of 1201, it was alleged that, in the reign of Henry II, Aubrey de Vere held Feering of the abbey, but lost it unjustly:

> when Abbot Gervase of Westminster was disseized of his lands in England by the will of King Henry.[109]

No canonical proceedings were taken against Gervase, and he was dismissed simply on the royal *fiat*. Such an action was demeaning to Westminster, and also left a shadow over the careers of subsequent abbots. It was better to create an impression that he had deserved to be demoted.

Abbot Lawrence was described by Flete as a teacher (*professor*) of theology.[110] While studying in France, he attended the lectures of Hugh of St Victor (d.1141), on the advice of Maurice of Rievaulx, a former sub-prior of Durham who joined Rievaulx c.1138. During this period, Lawrence was evidently involved, at a distance, in the business of the bishopric of Durham. In 1143 he returned to England, bringing a letter from St Bernard on the subject of the current election dispute at Durham to Prior Roger and the convent there. Bernard commended Master Lawrence as someone who had worked faithfully and effectively on behalf of the prior and chapter.[111] Lawrence had a knack of enlisting the support of the right people at the right

105 Richardson and Sayles, *The Governance of Medieval England*, pp. 420–21.

106 *The Chronicle of John of Hexham*, in *Symeonis Monachi: Opera Omnia*, ed. T. Arnold, Rolls Series (1882–5), II, p. 330.

107 Thomas of Walsingham, *Gesta Abbatum Monasterii Sancti Albani*, ed. H.T. Riley, Rolls Series, I (1867), p. 133.

108 Richardson and Sayles, *The Governance of Medieval England*, pp. 20–21.

109 *Curia Regis Rolls*, I, pp. 464–5. I am grateful to the late Jennifer Bray for this reference and her comments on it.

110 Flete, *The History of Westminster Abbey*, p. 91.

111 F.E. Croydon, 'Abbot Lawrence of Westminster and Hugh of St Victor', *Medieval and Renaissance Studies*, II, ed. R. Hunt and R. Kliblansky (London, 1950), pp. 169–171.

time. Flete reported that he found favour with the Empress Matilda while she was Lady of the English.[112] Evidently Lawrence remained in the service of the church of Durham for a further ten years and was a participant in the proceedings leading up to the disputed election to the bishopric in 1153. When the archbishop of York quashed the election, Lawrence was excommunicated with the other electors. They were absolved by the papal legate, and the bishop-elect and the others set out for Rome, where the election was to be examined. Lawrence, however, turned aside from the party and joined the monastic community of St Albans.[113] Flete reported that Lawrence found favour with Henry II. This favour seems to have expressed itself in material terms, enabling Lawrence to achieve the repairs of those parts of the abbey which had suffered from fire damage, besides the recovery of those lands which were damaged by Earl Robert in the West Midlands.[114] But royal favour was gained at a price. Lawrence persuaded Abbot Robert de Gorron of St Albans that Westminster was destitute, and Robert accordingly gave him gifts to the value of nearly 200 marks, quite apart from initial donatives at the time of his entry.[115] It was not explained just how valuable horses, and silver cups and spoons, were going to help the allegedly undernourished, ill-clad monks, although these were perhaps intended as gifts to earn the royal *benevolencia*, either directly or through intermediaries. Lawrence achieved this only too well, enlisting the support of Henry II in a lawsuit against St Albans over the disputed estate of Aldenham.[116] A further grievance of the monks of St Albans was that their Prior Alquin, deposed on suspicion that he intended using a spurious abbey seal for his own ends, fled to Westminster, where he was well received by Abbot Lawrence.[117]

One big project which Lawrence successfully masterminded was the canonization of King Edward. When the subject was raised by several of the monks, Lawrence discussed the matter with some of the senior brethren, and it was then raised in the monastic chapter, where it was unanimously decided to go ahead, on the basis of the procedures outlined in the bull of Innocent II rejecting the petition of 1139. Well-prepared lobbying brought widespread written support from the English bishops, probably responding in the late summer of 1160. Lawrence then travelled to Normandy, where he gained the support of Henry II for the project, and on to Paris, where he had similar success with the legates of Pope Alexander III, Cardinals Henry and Otto, and a delegation was then sent to the pope. Alexander discussed the matter thoroughly, and examined the documentary evidence. Then, with the consent of the cardinals, he authorized the bulls of canonization, which were

112 Flete, *The History of Westminster Abbey*, p. 92.
113 *Ibid.*, p. 143; John of Hexham, pp. 329–30.
114 Flete, *The History of Westminster Abbey*, p. 92.
115 Thomas of Walsingham, *Gesta Abbatum*, p. 133.
116 *Ibid.*, p. 134.
117 *Ibid.*, pp. 107–110.

dated at Anagni, on 7 February 1161.[118] Lawrence then enlisted the support of his kinsman, the Cistercian abbot Ailred of Rievaulx, to re-write and update the earlier *Life* of the Confessor.[119] Henry II's incessant travel, and pressing business at times when he was in England, caused a delay before the solemn Translation could be held, and this gave the opportunity for Lawrence and a select few of the monks to inspect Edward's body and satisfy themselves that it remained incorrupt, as a saint's should be.[120]

Unfortunately, during the delay, the crisis began to build up over Henry II's 'ancestral customs' regarding the relationship between the monarch and the clerical hierarchy, the Constitutions of Clarendon. Despite the growing tension, the king was joined by almost all the bishops, as well as by other magnates, for the solemn ceremony of St Edward's Translation, which was held on 13 October 1163.[121] Happily all was concluded before the dispute between Henry II and Archbishop Thomas Becket reached its climax at Northampton a year later.

Lawrence is said to have visited Durham apparently some time after the Council of Woodstock (July 1163) but before that of Northampton (October 1164). A Westminster monk travelled the few miles out to the hermitage of Finchale, to pay his respects to the hermit Godric. Their talk turned to the newly-elected archbishop, and Godric asked the monk to convey to Becket his prophecy that, although he would suffer exile, he would eventually triumph. In fact, Lawrence himself took the message to the archbishop.[122] In the early stages of the dispute, such an action might seem advantageous from a professional point of view, since, on the surface, Godric's prophecy appeared to depict that Becket, in his lifetime, would become all-powerful. However, once the storm broke, Lawrence seems to have kept his head down.

Late in 1160, Gilbert Foliot, while still bishop of Hereford, wrote warmly in support of the canonization of King Edward.[123] After Gilbert became bishop of London, in 1163, he inherited the on-going dispute between his see and the abbey, but personal relations between him and Lawrence seem to have been unaffected. In 1169, Lawrence wrote to Pope Alexander III in support of the bishop who was then under attack by the exiled Becket.[124]

118 Richard of Cirencester, *Speculum Historiale de Gestis Regum Angliae*, ed. J.E.B. Mayor, Rolls Series, 2 vols (London, 1863–9), II, pp. 321–3; F. Barlow, *Edward the Confessor*, pp. 277–81.

119 *The Life of Ailred of Rievaulx by Walter Daniel*, transl. and introd. F.M. Powicke (Oxford, 1950, reprinted 1978), p. xxxvi.

120 Richard of Cirencester, *Speculum Historiale*, II, pp. 324–5; Barlow, *Edward the Confessor*, pp. 281–3.

121 Richard of Cirencester, *Speculum Historiale*, II, p. 326; Barlow, *Edward the Confessor*, p. 283.

122 Reginald of Durham, *Libellus de Vita et Miraculis S. Godrici, heremitae de Finchale*, ed. J. Stevenson, Surtees Soc., 20. (1847), pp. 236–8.

123 *Letters and Charters of Gilbert Foliot*, no. 133.

124 *Materials for the History of Thomas Becket*, VI, ed. J.C. Robertson, Rolls Series VI (1882), pp. 621–2, no. DXIX.

Apart from this one letter, there is little else surviving to indicate Lawrence's views during the course of the dispute. His attendance is not recorded, for instance, at the Great Councils of Clarendon and Northampton.

The delegation to the papal court which successfully petitioned for the canonization of King Edward acquired two further papal bulls. These, like those granting the canonization, were also issued at Anagni on 7 February 1161. The Westminster delegation evidently included both Roger the infirmarer and Walter the sacrist, who each obtained a bull confirming property pertaining to their respective offices.[125] Some senior member of their party perhaps remained in Anagni, or returned there, in order to secure for Westminster the bull which granted to Abbot Lawrence and his successors the right to wear mitre and ring, on Sundays and other solemn festivals, during Mass and in processions within the abbey, and during papal and episcopal synods. This privilege was dated 18 April, and while the most likely year for its issue would be 1161, when it is known that a Westminster delegation travelled to the *curia*, Alexander III is known to have visited Anagni in April in other years of his pontificate, including, perhaps, 1160 and certainly in 1173.[126] It is likely that Lawrence would seek to acquire the dignified status of mitred abbot as soon as Westminster acquired a *bona fide* royal saint of its own, and the grant was most likely obtained in 1161. In 1173 the delegation would have set out during the last months of Lawrence's life, since he died on 10 or 11 April in that year.[127] If 1173 was in fact the year in which this privilege was requested, it was in practice Lawrence's gift to his successors, for the grant would not have taken effect during his lifetime.

One of the other bulls granted by Pope Alexander III to Abbot Lawrence confirmed the abbey's privileges and possessions, and especially its cells of Great Malvern, Hurley and Sudbury. This effectively confirmed the bull relating to these cells which Adrian IV granted to Abbot Gervase in June 1157, although Alexander stated that he was following a precedent set by Eugenius III.[128] The need to seek a renewed confirmation in 1163 indicates that one or another of the dependent priories was again restive. It is testimony to the perceived urgency of the case that Lawrence sent a deputation to the pope at Sens just as the Translation of King Edward was about to take place. Alexander III granted the bull on 6 October, and it is highly unlikely that the delegation could have returned to Westminster within a week so as to join in the festivities.

One further bull of Alexander III was addressed to Abbot Lawrence, confirming the privileges and possessions of Westminster, and particularly its exemption from the jurisdiction of the bishop of London. This grant was

125 *Westminster Abbey Charters*, nos 169–70.
126 *Ibid.*, no. 173 and note.
127 Knowles, Brooke and London, *Heads of Religious Houses*, p. 77.
128 *Westminster Abbey Charters*, no. 166.

issued from Tusculum on 3 December 1171.[129] This confirmation reinforced the exemption from episcopal jurisdiction granted by Innocent II in 1133.[130] Although relations between Abbot Lawrence and Bishop Gilbert Foliot had been good in recent years, the issue may well have continued to be contested on the part of the archdeacons of the diocese of London. The timing of the petition for this confirmation is interesting in another way, coming as it did when King Henry II was still unreconciled to the pope in the wake of Becket's murder. Although Henry's Continental lands were under sentence of Interdict, England was not, but the pope had confirmed the sentences of excommunication pronounced by the late archbishop against those bishops who opposed him.[131] Late 1171 would be an opportune time to bolster the jurisdiction of the abbot of Westminster against that of the bishop of London. Papal legates, commissioned to negotiate with Henry, travelled in the opposite direction in the autumn of 1171, although formal talks did not begin until the following May. The king, meanwhile, was in Ireland, and bad weather in the Irish Sea disrupted communications.[132] With more pressing matters in hand, he would be unlikely to hear that the abbot of Westminster was in communication with the pope from whom he was estranged.

Formal contacts between Westminster and the bishop's bureaucrats were variable in the level of amicability they displayed. This was only to be expected, given the wide scope of the bishop's jurisdiction, and also the extensive interests of the abbot of Westminster. Direct confrontation between Lawrence and Gilbert occurred over dues which the bishop claimed from the church of St Margaret's Westminster.[133] On a personal note, abbot and bishop confronted one another over the abbot's tenant, Roger of Darnford, who was related to the bishop through a marriage connection. When a direct appeal failed, Gilbert enlisted the support of the archdeacon of Canterbury, Geoffrey Ridel, who was also an influential royal officer. The bishop pointed out that not only Abbot Gervase and the convent, but also the Empress Matilda, had confirmed the Darnford inheritance, and yet Lawrence was trying to withhold it.[134] Both Lawrence and Gilbert were to some extent constrained by the vested interests of the communities which they represented, but, despite these, a working relationship persisted between them, and Lawrence attested occasional *acta* of the bishop.[135]

While in many respects Lawrence seems to have operated effectively in the corridors of power, there is comparatively little evidence of his obtaining

129 *Papsturkunden in England*, I, no. 113.

130 *Westminster Abbey Charters*, no. 155.

131 W.L. Warren, *Henry II* (London, 1973), p. 520.

132 *Ibid.*, p. 530.

133 *Letters and Charters of Gilbert Foliot*, no. 229; A. Morey and C.N.L. Brooke, *Gilbert Foliot and his Letters* (Cambridge, 1965), p. 223.

134 *Letters and Charters of Gilbert Foliot*, no. 230; see *Westminster Abbey Charters*, nos 98, 136, 271, 341.

135 *Letters and Charters of Gilbert Foliot*, nos 391, 422.

concessions for his abbey from Henry II. One writ, probably dating from Lawrence's abbacy, ordered the clerk John of Bushey to render to the abbot the tithes due from Aldenham;[136] a second writ, in which the abbot is not named, and which, consequently, may date from the interregnum between Gervase and Lawrence, ordered that the abbey was to enjoy the liberties conceded in earlier royal writs.[137] The only other royal writ to name Abbot Lawrence peremptorily ordered him to restore to a plaintiff land in Sunbury and Teddington (Middx).[138] Lawrence, however, contrived to draw the ensuing litigation into his own court, and extracted from the plaintiff a quitclaim of the land in question, granting a compensatory three virgates in lieu of the three hides which were claimed.[139]

A further indicator of Lawrence's standing with the king is given by the nature of entries relating to him on the Pipe Roll. The financial outlay involved in fining for a charter confirming the liberties of the abbey could be recouped, over a period of time. At Michaelmas 1161, for instance, exemptions were granted to Westminster from murder-fines, imposed on hundreds in which their lands lay, in Essex, Hertfordshire, Surrey and Sussex, – these totalled £3 11s 2½d.[140] A year later, exemption from the murder-fine imposed on Corby hundred, Northamptonshire, saved the abbey 4s 2d,[141] while exemption from geld on the abbey's lands in Berkshire, Buckinghamshire and Bedfordshire, Essex and Hertfordshire, Gloucestershire, Lincolnshire, Northamptonshire, Staffordshire, Surrey, Sussex and Worcestershire, brought a total saving of £53 1s 4d.[142] Things did not always go so well for the abbot however. At Michaelmas 1165 it was noted that he had been amerced £100.[143] This entry, made under the London and Middlesex account, presumably related to some major offence committed by Lawrence himself, rather than by tenants on his lands. A year later, £50 was still owing on this amercement,[144] and £50 was still owing at Michaelmas 1169.[145] At Michaelmas 1173 the entry read that the abbot owed £25 on the amercement 'but he is dead'.[146] A similar entry is found for 1174.[147]

Members of the Scottish royal family occasionally had business which brought them to Westminster, and the abbot was quick to take advantage of this. King Malcolm IV, on his way to, or from, the Toulouse expedition of

136 *Westminster Abbey Charters*, no. 128.
137 *Ibid.*, no. 131.
138 *Ibid.*, no. 133.
139 *Ibid.*, no. 452.
140 *Pipe Roll 7 Henry II*, pp. 14, 44, 66, 69.
141 *Pipe Roll 8 Henry II*, p. 8.
142 *Ibid.*, pp. 8, 19, 29, 31, 41, 44, 47, 57, 61, 70, 72.
143 *Pipe Roll 11 Henry II*, p. 33.
144 *Pipe Roll 12 Henry II*, p. 132.
145 *Pipe Roll 15 Henry II*, p. 171.
146 *Pipe Roll 19 Henry II*, p. 184.
147 *Pipe Roll 20 Henry II*, p. 11.

1159, was persuaded to confirm a grant of land in Tottenham which his predecessors had made for the soul of Queen Matilda (Malcolm's great-aunt).[148] In June 1170, King William I 'the Lion' attended the coronation, at Westminster, of the Young King, and this was most likely the occasion on which he confirmed the same property.[149]

Given the arbitrary style of Angevin government, it was clearly advantageous to be able to do small favours for those who had influence at court. There is some evidence of Lawrence's activity in this field, although the question must remain open as to how far Lawrence actively went out of his way to be obliging, and how far he was under pressure. The latter is clearly demonstrated in evidence, given some time after his death, by Bartholomew de Vendôme, by this time archbishop of Tours, that Queen Eleanor 'requested' Lawrence to represent him to the church of Ockendon (Essex), which he did.[150] Notables at court could hint that certain perquisites in the abbot's gift would be acceptable. Mr Ralph de Beaumont, physician to Lawrence, but also to the king, was granted the church of Bloxham by Lawrence and the convent.[151] Richard of Ilchester, an even more powerful figure, received from Abbot Lawrence a grant of a house in the Fishmarket in London.[152] He was supposed to hold this house of the abbey, but instead granted it to John Burgundian. On the advice of the convent, Lawrence confirmed the house to John, contriving as he did so to increase its rent.[153] Lawrence and Richard acted together when, in their capacity as 'friends' of the bishop of Lincoln, Robert de Chesney, they 'requested' him to grant the perpetual vicarage of Datchworth to the clerk Elias.[154] In the mid 1160s, when this transaction took place, Richard was officially archdeacon of Poitou, but he was also rector of Datchworth,[155] a benefice which the abbot had evidently considered it prudent to grant him.

The wheels of government of church and state were kept turning by the constant flow of such patronage. Powerful figures no doubt angled for the most lucrative of Westminster's benefices, even though some of these were required for the abbot's clerks, such as Maurice, whom Lawrence appointed perpetual vicar of Sawbridgeworth (Herts.).[156] The enforced allocation of churches was a serious matter, since their cumulative income, annual pensions and the like, played an important part in maintaining the abbey's cash-flow. Once installed, and having agreed an annual fixed payment, an

148 *Westminster Abbey Charters*, no. 103.
149 *Ibid.*, no. 104.
150 *Ibid.*, no. 463.
151 *Ibid.*, no. 286.
152 *Ibid.*, no. 277.
153 *Ibid.*, no. 278. For Richard's charter, see N. Moore, *History of St Bartholomew's Hospital*, I (London, 1918), pp. 73–4.
154 *Westminster Abbey Charters*, no. 222.
155 *Ibid.*, no. 468.
156 *Ibid.*, no. 284.

incumbent might remain in office for several decades. Stephen, presented by Lawrence to succeed his father Ralph, held the church of Hendon (Middx) for some forty-three years,[157] while Nigel, presented by Lawrence to Kelvedon (Essex), remained its parson until shortly before 1218.[158]

Lawrence's charters depict him treating Westminster's churches as sources of income: with the assent of the convent he assigned the church of Sawbridgeworth (Herts.) to provide lights for the high altar, and wine and a pittance in the refectory in annual commemoration of his parents, previous monks and benefactors.[159] Similarly Lawrence granted the church of Easthampstead to Hurley Priory, to provide extra food on the feast of St Edward.[160] He confirmed to the nuns of Kilburn the grants made to them by Abbots Herbert and Gervase.[161]

Two disputes between Westminster and Lawrence's former abbey, St Albans, were settled by compromise. One of these, concerning Aldenham in Hertfordshire, was settled on 29 September 1165;[162] the other, concluded by exchanging lands near Sandridge and Wheathampstead (Herts.), was ended in 1167 or 1168.[163] The only other charters of Lawrence which relate to landed transactions are the confirmation, by abbot and convent, to Baldwin Crisp, of some tenements in London[164] and a slightly later document in which they modified the rents due during Baldwin's lifetime.[165] The latest of the surviving abbatial writs concerning the Westminster sanctuary was issued in Lawrence's name.[166]

At Westminster, Lawrence left a reputation as an eloquent preacher, who delivered numerous sermons appropriate to the various seasons of the church's year. On the feast of St Peter's Chains (1 August), one of the major festivals observed at the abbey, he preached on the text 'Herod the king sent a hand so that it might afflict those of the church.'[167] Flete clearly considered it one of Lawrence's more memorable efforts, but, if delivered during the Becket dispute, it might be thought to have subversive overtones. The text for Lawrence's sermon on the feast of St Mary Magdalene (22 July), was 'Mary entered the house of Simon, and there she prostrated herself at the feet of the Lord.'[168] Presumably the sermon which followed exemplified the doctrine of penance.

Lawrence's concerns for his spiritual welfare are shown in his assignment of income from the churches of Wandsworth and Battersea for the commemorating of the anniversary of his death. These churches were appropriated to the use of the monastic infirmary since, said Flete, Lawrence always gave attention to the cure of the sick, as prescribed in the Rule of St

157 *Ibid.*, no. 459.
158 *Ibid.*, no. 211, note.
159 *Ibid.*, no. 283.
160 *Ibid.*, no. 285. See also no. 302.
161 *Ibid.*, no. 280.
162 *Ibid.*, no. 281.
163 *Ibid.*, no. 282.
164 *Ibid.*, no. 275.
165 *Ibid.*, no. 276.
166 *Ibid.*, no. 279.
167 Flete, *The History of Westminster Abbey*, p. 91.
168 *Ibid.*, pp. 91–2.

Benedict.[169] For his anniversary, Lawrence also assigned rents from the villeins in Battersea to support the infirmary, together with money to be expended on the poor, on the anniversaries of the deceased (monks of the abbey).[170] His assignment of the churches to the infirmary was confirmed by Pope Lucius III in 1185.[171]

As abbot, Lawrence was primarily required to be an administrator, and perhaps an ecclesiastical politician, but he kept up his contacts with the abbey of St Victor. One letter of his, to his 'kinsman', Abbot Hervey (*Ervisius*) (1162–1172), commends its bearer, John, who was himself a kinsman of the current prior of Westminster and a member of the *familia* of the abbot. A second letter, dated 1166, commends another John, nephew of Lawrence himself. It was intended that these young men would study at St Victor, as Lawrence himself apparently did.[172] Abbot Hervey left a somewhat unsatisfactory reputation at St Victor. He was said to be an Englishman, and during the Becket dispute a number of English exiles found refuge at his abbey.[173] Interception by the agents of Henry II of correspondence between Lawrence and Hervey would be one possible explanation of the heavy amercement imposed on Lawrence in 1165.

Following the death of Lawrence, on 10 or 11 April 1173, there was a vacancy in the abbacy down to early July 1175.[174]

169 *Ibid*., p. 94. *The Rule of St Benedict*, ed. J. McCann (London, 1952), caps. 31, 36.
170 Flete, *The History of Westminster Abbey*, p. 95.
171 *Westminster Abbey Charters*, no. 177; Flete, *The History of Westminster Abbey*, p. 95.
172 Croydon, 'Abbot Lawrence of Westminster and Hugh of St Victor', pp. 170–71.
173 *Westminster Abbey Charters*, no. 400, note.
174 Knowles, Brook and London, *Heads of Religious Houses*, p. 77.

4

The Abbots 1175–1222

Abbot Walter was an outsider, but one with a well-established monastic background. He was a former monk of Winchester and was prior there from about 1173. The year in which he became abbot of Westminster is uncertain. Some evidence indicates that he was elected about July 1175, but the election may have occurred a year later, when he is said to have been blessed as abbot.[1] Compared to some of his predecessors, Walter has bequeathed a less conspicuous reputation, but apparently adopted an understated yet businesslike approach towards his responsibilities. The few royal charters obtained at this period reflect a quiet determination to stabilize Westminster's existing rights and properties. One charter of Henry II, perhaps dating from the abbatial interregnum rather than from Walter's subsequent abbacy, ordered the royal officers in Gloucestershire and Worcestershire that the (unnamed) abbot and monks were under the royal protection. Their possessions must be treated as though they were royal demesne, and tenants of the abbey were to be compelled to render the service they owed.[2] The other charter of Henry II which appears to date from this period is a confirmation of the manor of Denham (Bucks.). Its language, however, indicates that it is a spurious product of the scriptorium.[3]

Richard I's charter of liberties for the abbey, dated 6 October 1189, is also a dubious document, which follows the lines of similarly suspect documents issued in the names of earlier twelfth-century kings, although an argument may be made in favour of its authenticity.[4] Its date, 6 October 1189, is also that of a succinct writ in which the king ordered that the abbey was to hold its entire liberty, as conceded in his own charter and in those of his predecessors.[5] There are problems in assessing the relationship between this charter of

1 D. Knowles, C.N.L. Brooke and V.C.M. London, *The Heads of Religious Houses England and Wales 940–1216* (Cambridge, 1972), pp. 77, 80.

2 *Westminster Abbey Charters 1066–c.1214*, ed. Emma Mason, assisted by the late Jennifer Bray, continuing the work of the late D.J. Murphy, London Record Society, 25 (London, 1988), no. 137.

3 *Ibid.*, no. 138.

4 *Ibid.*, no. 140.

5 *Ibid.*, no. 141.

Richard's, the charter of liberties mentioned above and a further writ dated 7 October 1189, granting exemption from pleas, gelds, (communally-levied) murder fines, sheriff's aids and other exactions. There is evidence that the terms of this writ were rigorously observed in the first half of Richard's reign, and again in the early years of John's reign.[6] Considering the financial loss to the Crown, and the consequent gain to Westminster, a fine of one mark (13 shillings and four pence) was very low, especially in the light of the financial pressures which Richard was currently placing on his kingdom. On the other hand, he did quitclaim these revenues for the souls of his parents, and it was also possible for Westminster's petitioners to represent the concession as a simple confirmation of an earlier concession made by Henry II.[7] Richard's departure from England on 12 December 1189 evidently gave rise to a feeling of apprehension at Westminster. The kingdom was initially entrusted to co-justiciars: Hugh du Puiset and William Longchamp. On 16 December 1189, within a few days of Richard's crossing to Calais, Hugh was requested to issue a writ in the king's name, ordering that the monks and their possessions were to be protected as was the royal demesne. They were not to be disseized of any free tenement which they held on the day when the king last crossed from England into Normandy, and were not to be impleaded over any tenement except in the presence of the king, his chief justiciar or the chancellor. It was highly unusual for Hugh du Puiset, whilst acting jointly with William Longchamps, to issue writs on his sole authority, and this one for Westminster seems to be a unique survival.[8] It appears that the abbot and monks were quick to recognize that it would be inadequate to defend their interests. On 26 January 1190, a further writ was obtained, again in the king's name, but issued on the initiative of William Longchamp, who attested it as bishop of Ely and Chancellor. It notified royal officers in whose bailiwicks the abbey held lands or rents that Westminster, its lands, rents, men and possessions had been received into the king's possession, to be protected as though they were royal demesne. The abbey's charters, obtained from the king or his predecessors, were to be seen and heard in their bailiwicks, and the rights which they guaranteed were to be upheld.[9]

During Walter's abbacy, delegations were sent to the pope on two, or more probably three, distinct occasions. One bull of Alexander III, issued at Anagni on 13 September in some uncertain year between 1175 and 1180, addressed to Abbot Walter and the convent, granted to Walter and his successors that, since they already had papal permission to wear mitre and ring, they might also wear the dalmatic tunicle and sandals on solemn days

6 *Ibid.*, no. 142 and note.

7 King Henry's charter is printed in *Regesta Regum Anglo-Normannorum*, II, ed. C. Johnson and H.A. Cronne (Oxford, 1956), p. 389, no. CCCXXVII; calendared *ibid.*, no. 1987, where it is suggested that this is a writ of Henry II; *Westminster Abbey Charters*, no. 131.

8 *Westminster Abbey Charters*, no. 145.

9 *Ibid.*, no. 146.

within the monastery and its dependencies, in processions, in papal, legatine and episcopal synods.[10] It has been suggested that this bull was granted in 1176.[11] Arguably, Walter would have taken the earliest opportunity to enlarge the privileges regarding the wearing of high-status vestments which had already been obtained by Abbot Lawrence.

Two further bulls obtained on Walter's behalf from Pope Alexander III contain circumstantial evidence of the abbot's representatives pursuing the papal entourage across north-eastern Italy as Alexander tried to reach satisfactory peace terms, first with the Emperor, Frederick Barbarossa and then with the Lombard league. By the earlier of these bulls, dated at the Rialto, Venice, on 2 April 1177, the pope granted to Walter the right to wear gloves during solemn Mass on festivals.[12] Alexander III travelled on to Ferrara, to reassure the league and to agree the details of the peace conference.[13] The abbot's men were in hot pursuit. Petitioning the pope on 18 April, they secured a further bull, addressed to Walter and the convent, confirming the possessions of the abbey, its exemption from the jurisdiction of the bishop of London, and prohibiting the alienation of the churches of Oakham (Rutland), Ashwell (Herts.), Staines (Middx), Aldenham and Wheathampstead (Herts.), with their chapels.[14] This last clause was perhaps intended less as a restraint on the abbot than a curb on the covetousness of senior royal clerks who kept an eye open for lucrative benefices. In 1173, for instance, Ashwell had acquired a new incumbent in the person of Walter Map, presented by Henry II during the vacancy which preceded Walter's election to the abbacy.[15] There is no hint in the dating of any of the papal bulls for Westminster that the abbot was represented at the Third Lateran Council in 1179. On the other hand, the parson of Ashwell was there, maintaining a high profile with his refutation of Waldensian beliefs.[16] Arguably he was there to represent the interests of the king and, perhaps, those of the abbot of Westminster.

During Walter's abbacy, two further papal bulls were obtained. The first, issued by Pope Lucius III at Verona, on 17 March, probably in 1185, notified

10 W. Dugdale, *Monasticon Anglicanum*, revised H. Caley, H. Ellis and B. Bandinel (6 vols in 8, London, 1817–30), I, p. 311, no. LXX; calendared *Westminster Abbey Charters*, no. 174.

11 *Regesta Pontificum Romanorum ad annum 1198*, ed. P. Jaffé, 2nd edn, 2 vols (Leipzig, 1885–88), II, p. 299, no. 12734.

12 *Papsturkunden in England*, ed. W. Holtzmann, 3 vols, Abhandlungen der Gesellschaft der Wissenschaften in Göttingen, phil.-hist. Klasse, Berlin, Göttingen (I = neue Folge XXV, 1930–31; II = 3 Folge XIV–XV, 1935–36; III = 3 Folge XXXIII, 1952), I, no. 143; calendared *Westminster Abbey Charters*, no. 175.

13 I.S. Robinson, *The Papacy 1073–1198: Continuity and Innovation* (Cambridge, 1990), p. 495.

14 *Papsturkunden in England*, I, no. 144; calendared *Westminster Abbey Charters*, no. 176.

15 *Curia Regis Rolls*, VI, p. 93. See also Walter Map, *De Nugis Curialium: Courtier's Trifles*, ed. and transl. M.R. James; revised C.N.L. Brooke and R.A.B. Mynors (Oxford, 1983), pp. 496–7.

16 Walter Map, *De Nugis Curialium*, pp. 124–7.

the abbot and convent that he confirmed to the infirmary the churches of Battersea and Wandsworth, donated by the late Abbot Lawrence.[17] This bull confirmed, in effect, that granted by Alexander III to Roger the infirmarer in February 1161.[18] Some time after that earlier bull was issued, these churches came into the possession of Richard of Ilchester, most likely through assertion of his influence as bishop of Winchester (1174–88), but just possibly through an extension of his known transactions with Abbot Lawrence. An *actum* of Richard's, issued at some uncertain date between March 1178 and December 1188,[19] appropriating the churches to the abbey infirmary, perhaps resulted from his being made aware of this bull of Pope Lucius.

Concern over the abbey's rights in its churches prompted Walter to send to the pope one further delegation, which reached Pope Clement III at the Lateran in July 1189. His earlier bull issued for Westminster granted that, when the churches of which they were patrons fell vacant, the abbot and convent might appropriate the tithes, in order to support the brethren, their guests and the poor.[20] A second bull, addressed to Abbot Walter and the convent on 20 July, confirmed the abbey's possessions, especially the five churches of Oakham, Ashwell, Staines, Aldenham and Wheathampstead; excluding episcopal intrusion into St Margaret's Westminster, and confirming all pensions from churches held before the Third Lateran Council.[21] Given the expense, and the logistical difficulties involved in sending a delegation to the papal curia, it is clear that Abbot Walter regarded the safeguarding of the income and patronage of the parish churches controlled from Westminster as valuable long-term resources, well worth the outlay incurred in their defence.

Nearer home, however much Walter and his monks resisted the intrusion of the bishop of London, dealings with him were necessary from time to time over presentations to the abbey's churches. Conflicting claims to jurisdiction over the little nunnery of Kilburn, which perhaps arose during Walter's abbacy, were resolved in Westminster's favour.[22] Abbot Walter and the convent assented to Bishop Gilbert Foliot's confirmation, made c.1176–78, of a hospital established by Ralph Brito in Bordwadestone (in Brentford, Middx).[23] Conversely, when Abbot Walter and the convent presented a

17 *Papsturkunden in England*, I, no. 232; calendared *Westminster Abbey Charters*, no. 177.

18 *Papsturkunden in England*, I, no. 85; calendared *Westminster Abbey Charters*, no. 169.

19 *English Episcopal Acta VIII. Winchester 1070–1204*, ed. M. Franklin (Oxford, 1993), no. 188; calendared *Westminster Abbey Charters*, no. 231.

20 *Papsturkunden in England*, I, no. 261; calendared *Westminster Abbey Charters*, no. 178.

21 *Papsturkunden in England*, I, no. 262; calendared *Westminster Abbey Charters*, no. 179.

22 *The Letters and Charters of Gilbert Foliot*, ed. Z.N. Brooke, A. Morey and C.N.L. Brooke (Cambridge, 1967), no. 463. The editors comment: 'The nature of the case, and the formulas suggest an early date and it is not impossible that this is an act of Gilbert the Universal (1128–1134)'; calendared *Westminster Abbey Charters*, no. 205.

23 *The Letters and Charters of Gilbert Foliot*, no. 464. See also *Westminster Abbey Charters*, no. 206 and note.

parson to Greenford and Hanwell, the bishop issued a formal notification that he had instituted this new incumbent.[24]

Westminster's concern to safeguard its rights over its parish churches, manifest in the papal bulls acquired during Walter's abbacy, was also reflected nearer home, in a detailed confirmation obtained from Gilbert Foliot, between 1180 and 1187, of the abbey's churches throughout the London diocese, with the pension due from each carefully enumerated.[25] Probably the further confirmations of Westminster churches made by Gilbert's successor, Richard Fitz Nigel, were requested in the time of the next abbot.[26]

Abbot Walter enlisted the intervention of Gilbert Foliot, in his capacity as papal legate, to pronounce on legal disputes arising over some of the abbey's churches, including Feering (Essex),[27] and those of Doddington and Thorpe-on-the-Hill (Lincs.).[28] Gilbert Foliot was also enlisted by Walter and the convent in an unofficial capacity, to attempt to win the recognition of the bishop of Worcester to a prior whom Walter had clandestinely instituted to the dependent priory of Great Malvern.[29] Abbot Walter took every care to safeguard the abbey's churches, even applying to Bartholomew de Vendome, archbishop of Tours, when defending his right to the advowson of Ockendon Church.[30] When outright victory was impossible, Walter and the convent safeguarded their right to the advowson of Deene by presenting the candidate of Hugh, bishop of Lincoln (presumably the other party in a contest over the church).[31] Following a dispute over the church of St Magnus the Martyr, near London Bridge, Walter and the monks agreed to share its advowson equally with Prior Henry de Soilly and the convent of Bermondsey.[32] Another church near London Bridge, St Margaret's Bridge Street *alias* Fish Street, proved easier to retain, and Walter and the convent made a presentation, reserving an annual pension to the abbey Chamber.[33] During Walter's abbacy, the grant of a church was occasionally made, with the consent of the convent, to some small religious house. The church of Easthampstead (Berks.) was given to their dependent cell of Hurley,[34] while that of St Alban,

24 *The Letters and Charters of Gilbert Foliot*, no. 468. See also *Westminster Abbey Charters*, no. 210.

25 *The Letters and Charters of Gilbert Foliot*, no. 462. See also *Westminster Abbey Charters*, no. 211 and note.

26 *Westminster Abbey Charters*, nos 212 and 213.

27 *The Letters and Charters of Gilbert Foliot*, nos 465–6; *Westminster Abbey Charters*, nos 207–8.

28 *The Letters and Charters of Gilbert Foliot*, no. 467; *Westminster Abbey Charters*, no. 209.

29 *The Letters and Charters of Gilbert Foliot*, no. 239.

30 *Westminster Abbey Charters*, no. 463.

31 *English Episcopal Acta IV. Lincoln 1186–1206*, ed. D.M. Smith (London, 1986), no. 209; *Westminster Abbey Charters*, no. 223.

32 *Westminster Abbey Charters*, nos 287, 368.

33 *Ibid.*, no. 369.

34 *Ibid.*, no. 302.

Wood Street, in London, was granted to the suburban Hospital of St James.[35] Walter rationalized the management of outlying tithes, in Lincolnshire, by granting them to his clerk, Mr Nicholas.[36]

Property transactions dating from Abbot Walter's time include a number in which land was granted or confirmed to tenants in the city of London or its immediate vicinity.[37] In one, contrasting, instance, Walter and the convent, in full chapter, granted confraternity to the prominent City personality Brichtmar of Haverhill, and his family, in return for land outside Ludgate.[38] Following a lawsuit, land in Paddington (Middx) was obtained on 31 May 1185, in exchange for corrodies granted to the defendants and their wives.[39] In Surrey, Walter leased a mill and its appurtenant land in Sutton to one of the abbey's sergeants,[40] and on 29 September 1176 granted to another tenant land in Penge on a long lease.[41] The manor of Benfleet (Essex) with its church and the manors of Fanton and Paglesham, which had formerly been assigned to the abbey's pittancer, were granted by Walter to the convent.[42] However, during the last year of his life, he granted the vill of Paglesham, apart from its church, to Nicholas of Paglesham and his heirs.[43] Walter also excluded the church, and the tithes, from his grant of the manor of Denham (Bucks.) to Martin de Capella, who in return would owe the abbot an annual service of hospitality.[44]

Lands further afield, in the West Midlands, were the subject of several of Abbot Walter's charters. The manor of Perton, Staffs., restored by King Richard, was granted for life to the bishop of Coventry, Hugh de Nunant, on 2 February 1190.[45] In Worcestershire, Abbot Walter admitted Geoffrey de St Leger, son of the previous tenant, to two knights' fees in Strensham.[46] Another substantial tenancy, in which Abbot Walter admitted a son to succeed his father, comprised the vills of Upton Snodsbury and Bricklehampton, with three virgates in Wick.[47] Abbot Walter and the convent also granted land between Todenham and Wolford, Glos., to the king's Chamberlain, Ralph Fitz Stephen, in exchange for having the abbot's demesne corn ground.[48]

The outlying properties presented occasional difficulties in Walter's time. Notwithstanding the royal grants of liberties which were periodically obtained, at Michaelmas 1178 his tenants in Doddington and Thorp were deemed liable to render a murder-fine.[49] On the other side of England, the abbot of Pershore accounted at the Exchequer for £40 at Michaelmas 1185, because he had dispossessed both the abbot of Westminster and the prior of

35 *Ibid.*, no. 288.
36 *Ibid.*, no. 303.
37 *Ibid.*, nos 289–95.
38 *Ibid.*, no. 388.
39 *Ibid.*, no. 296.
40 *Ibid.*, no. 297.
41 *Ibid.*, no. 298.
42 *Ibid.*, no. 299.
43 *Ibid.*, no. 300.
44 *Ibid.*, no. 301.
45 *Ibid.*, no. 304.
46 *Ibid.*, no. 490.
47 *Ibid.*, no. 305.
48 *Ibid.*, no. 306.
49 *Pipe Roll 24 Henry II*, p. 7.

(Great) Malvern of property.[50] Charters surviving in Walter's name create an impression that he was a competent manager. That was the impression given by Flete, recording Walter's death on the feast of Saints Cosmas and Damian, 27 September 1190.[51] The later twelfth century witnessed a steady inflation, however, and Walter could not altogether avoid its consequences. For several years after his death, from Michaelmas 1192 to Michaelmas 1201, the Pipe Rolls record a debt of £16 13s 4d which Walter had owed to Aaron the Jew of Lincoln.[52] Even when the estates were managed profitably, there were other expenses, such as those incurred over lawsuits, or petitions to the papal court, which the regular cash-flow could not meet.

Yet Westminster's endowment still rendered its abbacy a substantial prize. In the absence of King Richard, a power-struggle between the justiciars whom he had appointed resulted, in the spring of 1190, in the supremacy of William Longchamp.[53] During the vacancy in the abbacy, following Walter's death, the abbey would be in royal hands, i.e. in the custody of the justiciar. Since the king's accession, Longchamp had been directly involved in Westminster's concerns on several occasions.[54] His position as justiciar both enabled him to be cognizant of the abbey's wealth and also gave him the opportunity to utilize it to the advantage of one of his brothers. Longchamp's efforts to intrude this man into the abbacy are recorded by two contemporary chroniclers, Ralph Diceto, writing from St Paul's London,[55] and Richard of Devizes, a monk of St Swithun's, Winchester.[56] Neither writer named this brother of Longchamp, although Richard of Devizes said that he was a monk of Caen (in Normandy).[57] Richard of Devizes related that Longchamp, through making amazing demands, and through persistency, first persuaded a party among the monks of Westminster, and subsequently the whole convent, to allow this man to profess residence at Westminster, so that, on the day on which he made his profession he might be elected abbot unanimously. This highly irregular agreement was recorded, and ratified with the seal of Westminster.[58] Of Longchamp's various brothers who were in England at this period, Robert is most likely to have been introduced into Westminster.[59] He

50 *Pipe Roll 31 Henry II*, p. 124.

51 John Flete, *The History of Westminster Abbey*, ed. J. Armitage Robinson (Cambridge 1909), p.96, although the year is given as '2 Richard I', i.e. 1191.

52 *Pipe Roll 3 and 4 Richard I*, p. 306; *Pipe Roll 5 Richard I*, p. 163; *Pipe Roll 6 Richard I*, p. 181; *Pipe Roll 7 Richard I*, p. 116; *Pipe Roll 8 Richard I*, p. 294; *Pipe Roll 9 Richard I*, p. 163; *Pipe Roll 2 John*, p. 151; *Pipe Roll 3 John*, p. 260.

53 J.T. Appleby, *England without Richard 1189–1199* (London, 1965) pp. 48–50.

54 *Westminster Abbey Charters*, nos 140, 146, 300, 304.

55 Radulfi de Diceto, *Opera Historica*, ed. W. Stubbs, 2 vols, Rolls Series (1876), II, pp. 100–101.

56 *The Chronicle of Richard of Devizes of the Time of King Richard the First*, ed. J.T. Appleby (London, 1963), pp. 39, 54–5.

57 *Ibid.*, p. 39.

58 *Ibid.*, pp. 38–9.

59 Knowles, Brooke and London, *Heads of Religious Houses*, pp. 46, 84. The justiciar's

is never listed among the abbots, though, and it appears that the agreement did not take effect. The length of Robert's subsequent monastic career indicates that he was still a very young man at this juncture, and formalities were perhaps delayed until he reached the canonical age for priesting. The delay, from whatever cause, proved fatal to his chances. In the course of 1191 a coup was staged against the unpopular William Longchamp, who left England at the end of October. Richard of Devizes related that the monks of Westminster took this opportunity to annul the agreement made concerning Longchamp's brother, and with the connivance of Count John (the future king) they elected their prior as their abbot. Without delay he received from Richard Fitz Nigel, the bishop of London, benediction as abbot and his abbatial crozier.[60] Longchamp's brother made a formal appeal, in the presence of reliable witnesses, against this second election, but was unable to obtain his hoped-for promotion. His self-esteem suffered a blow, and he left in confusion, taking with him however, the letter promising him the abbacy.[61] If, as seems likely, this disappointed candidate was Robert de Longchamps, he was not left out in the cold for long. By June 1194, at latest, he was prior of Ely, and in 1197 became abbot of St Mary's, York, an office which he held down to his death in 1239.[62]

William Postard, prior of Westminster, became abbot in 1191 on the removal of this intruder. As Devizes hinted, William owed his election, to some extent, to Count John.[63] Moreover he committed the abbey to a substantial fine of 1,500 marks (£1000), due to the Crown, but managed to pay off this whole sum within seven years. Flete, noting this achievement with satisfaction, stated that the fine was paid to secure his confirmation as abbot.[64] What was actually paid for, though, was permission for the monks to have an abbot of their own choice, rather than one imposed from above, whether by Longchamp,[65] or by his successor as justiciar, Walter of Coutances. Abbot William's election took place on 9 October 1191, and his blessing (by the bishop of London) on 13 October.[66] Both ceremonies therefore occurred while Longchamp was still in England, but in the unstable political situation, his downfall was already assured. The fine for free election was, presumably, imposed by Walter of Coutances.

The determined effort by Abbot William to pay off the fine placed a heavy burden on the abbey's finances, yet the wherewithal was promptly found to

brothers also included Henry (a layman) and Osbert. I am grateful to Stephen Church for clarification on the Longchamp family.

60 *The Chronicle of Richard of Devizes*, p. 54.

61 *Ibid.*, pp. 54–5.

62 Knowles, Brooke and London, *Heads of Religious Houses*, pp. 46, 84.

63 *The Chronicle of Richard of Devizes*, p. 54.

64 Flete, *The History of Westminster Abbey*, p. 98.

65 Barbara Harvey, *Westminster Abbey and its Estates in the Middle Ages* (Oxford, 1977), p. 64n.

66 Knowles, Brooke and London, *Heads of Religious Houses*, p. 77.

send a delegation to Pope Celestine III in Rome, in order to petition him for bulls variously designed to uphold the dignity of the abbot of Westminster and also to safeguard the abbey from further harassment of the kind which had evidently been experienced during the interregnum and the political unrest of recent months. This delegation was sent off within a few weeks of William's blessing as abbot, since all of the bulls which were obtained are dated at St Peter's, 13 January 1192. In one bull, Abbot William and his successors were granted the right to wear the mitre, annulets, gloves, dalmatic and sandals, together with sacerdotal vestments of benediction.[67] This bull largely confirmed the combined substance of the series of grants by Pope Alexander III, although that permitting Abbot Walter to wear gloves had omitted mention of his successors' rights in that respect.[68] The second of Pope Celestine's bulls exempted the abbey from any ecclesiastical jurisdiction other than his own; prohibited anyone from violently entering the church or despoiling its goods, and ordering the restitution of good wrongfully taken.[69] The terms of this bull certainly appear to reflect the abbey's insecure position during the recent abbatial interregnum. The third bull excommunicated those who had stolen the goods of the abbey, or had harmed it in any other way. Permission was granted to appeal against bishops, but the chapter was ordered to maintain good discipline, in order to avoid giving any pretext for intrusion.[70] The terms of this third bull again appear to reflect the conditions pertaining in the previous year, and also the grounds on which intruders justified their activities.

A further Westminster delegation was sent to the *curia* in the spring of 1199. Three of the bulls which were obtained on this occasion are dated at the Lateran, 23 April. In one of these, Pope Innocent III confirmed the liberties and immunities of Westminster, and its 'ancient and reasonable customs'.[71] A second bull, addressed to all English prelates, ordered that the privileges and indulgences granted to the abbey, by reason of its special relationship with the apostolic see, were to be observed.[72] In the third of these bulls dated 23 April, Innocent III observed that he had heard that certain benefices, intended for the use of the chapter, and for the poor (i.e. through the ministrations of the almonry), had occasionally been assigned, at the insistence of certain magnates, to their clerks. He ordered that the church of Sawbridgeworth (Herts.), assigned to the sacristy, and other churches assigned to hospitality or other pious uses, were not to be diverted

67 *Papsturkunden in England*, I, no. 301.

68 Cf. *ibid.*, I, no. 143.

69 *Ibid.*, I, no. 302; *Westminster Abbey Charters*, no. 181 and note.

70 *Papsturkunden in England*, I, no. 300; *Westminster Abbey Charters*, no. 182 and note.

71 *The Letters of Pope Innocent III (1198–1216), Concerning England and Wales: a Calendar, with an Appendix of Texts*, ed. C.R. Cheney and M. Cheney (London, 1967), p. 203, no. 104; *Westminster Abbey Charters*, no. 183 and note.

72 *Letters of Pope Innocent III (1198–1216)*, p. 203, no. 105; *Westminster Abbey Charters*, no. 184 and note.

to other ends.[73] Three further bulls, to the same effect as the three summarized here, were issued by Pope Innocent III on 8 April in an unspecified year of his pontificate.[74] Since they are now known only in the form of memoranda, it is not clear whether they were obtained by the delegation of 1199, but found to be lacking in some necessary details, or whether they represent the outcome of a later mission to Pope Innocent III, in the time of Abbot William de Humez. What is clear, however, is that the Westminster delegation of 1199 did not act solely, or even predominantly, in accordance with the wishes of Abbot William Postard. The pope's ruling concerning the revenues of Sawbridgeworth and other churches was probably issued in response to an appeal by the sacrist, the almoner and other *seniores*, against arbitrary managerial decisions taken by the abbot in his efforts to clear the obligations arising from the crisis of 1190–91. The pope issued a further bull on 30 April 1199, in which he prohibited the abbot from alienating the churches or other possessions pertaining to the whole community, without the consent of the chapter, or the greater and wiser part of it.[75] William Postard is not named in this writ, but it was clearly obtained as a check on his recent activities. His success in clearing the debt due to the Crown in return for the convent's right to a free election was perhaps achieved by an arbitrary rationalization of Westminster's assets, which would have antagonized the *seniores*. Innocent III upheld their complaint in line with the long standing papal view that monastic property was inalienable.[76]

The rising inflation of the later twelfth century, intensified by the pressures exerted on those owing debts to the Crown, combined to make William Postard's task a difficult one. Aspirations on the part of the obedientiaries to control the revenues of their respective offices sat uneasily with their wish to secure the right of free election. William Postard appears to have been the first of the post-Conquest abbots who was freely elected, and the Crown would not relax its oversight of such a wealthy and important abbey without substantial recompense.[77] Innocent III's bull of 30 April did take account of the abbot's dilemma, in contrast to the much stricter prohibition on alienation of monastic property set out in the *Decretum* of Gratian. Alienations were to be permitted, provided the chapter consented to them.[78]

Several of William Postard's charters depict him assigning income for the

73 Dugdale, *Monasticon Anglicanum*, I, p. 312a, no. LXXIII; *Westminster Abbey Charters*, no. 185 and note.

74 *Westminster Abbey Charters*, notes to nos 183–5.

75 *Letters of Pope Innocent III (1198–1216)*, p. 203, no. 113; *Westminster Abbey Charters*, no. 186 and note.

76 For the papal view on the inalienability of monastic property, see H.G. Richardson, 'The Coronation in Medieval England', *Traditio*, 16 (1960), pp. 151–3. See, however, Harvey, *Westminster Abbey and its Estates*, p. 84.

77 Harvey, *Westminster Abbey and its Estates*, p. 94 and n. 3. She comments on the 'astonishing' sum paid to secure Postard's election: *ibid.*, p. 89 and n. 1; cf. p. 64n.

78 *Ibid.*, p. 84.

use of the convent or of one or another of the monastic offices. The convent received his confirmation of the church of (South) Benfleet (Essex), with the manor, and the appurtenant lands and manors of Fanton and Paglesham.[79] A related *actum* of Richard Fitz Nigel, bishop of London, dating from c.1192, granted the church of South Benfleet to the convent, specifically allocating it to the use of the pittancer.[80] By a two-way exchange of charters between Abbot William and Juliana, abbess of Godstow, the sacrist was guaranteed an annual pension of five marks from the church of Bloxham (Oxon.) to maintain altar lights.[81] The abbey Chamber, and its chamberlain, also gained from transactions made in the name of William Postard. In granting the church of Sunbury to its new rector, Gilbert of Cranford, he exacted an annual pension of two marks, payable to the chamberlain.[82] In 1196 the bishop of London, Richard Fitz Nigel, confirmed this pension at the petition of the abbot.[83] Abbot William, acting with the convent, occasionally made an exceptional demand on the Chamber revenues, for instance, on 27 August 1198, assigning from it an annual payment of five marks to the son of a former seneschal, until they recompensed him with lands elsewhere.[84] On another occasion when a temporary demand was to be made on its funds, William assigned to the Chamber rents adequate to meet the commitment.[85]

The abbey infirmary gained an annual pension of 21 marks (£14) from the churches of Oakham and Hambleton by a grant made by Abbot William to the convent, to ensure the commemoration of his anniversary.[86] In 1197 or 1198, Hugh, bishop of Lincoln, confirmed a pension from these churches of thirty marks (£20) due annually to the monks, to maintain a hospital.[87] The abbey kitchener received an annual payment of £8 from the vill of Parham, which William granted to the convent, except for the advowson of its church. While the abbot would receive the homage of any incoming tenant, the convent would gain financially by receiving the relief which he paid.[88] On 4 November 1199, the abbot, represented by James the cellarer, received a quitclaim of the advowson from Baldwin of Parham.[89]

William's surviving charters show him active in the land market,

79 *Westminster Abbey Charters*, p. 317.

80 Dugdale, *Monasticon Anglicanuum*, I, p. 309, no. LIX; *Westminster Abbey Charters*, no. 214.

81 *Westminster Abbey Charters*, nos 323, 481; cf. no. 225.

82 *Ibid.*, no. 315.

83 *Ibid.*, no. 217.

84 *Ibid.*, no. 310.

85 *Ibid.*, no. 308.

86 *Ibid.*, no. 321.

87 *English Episcopal Acta IV. Lincoln 1186–1206*, no. 212.

88 *Westminster Abbey Charters*, no. 326.

89 *Ibid.*, no. 325.

arranging profitable transactions both in London and its suburbs;[90] and also further afield.[91]

The intermittent friction with St Alban's abbey revived in the early summer of 1194 in a dispute over franchisal rights at Aldenham, settled by compromise.[92] The abbot, represented by his chamberlain, Stephen, embarked on litigation in 1194–95 to defend Sulby (Northants) against a claimant, although the farm of this manor was assigned to the chamber.[93] Further litigation in that year, in which the abbot was represented by his seneschal, Theobald, failed to recover the advowson of Holwell (Herts.), although in the ensuing settlement an annual pension of one mark was secured for the almonry of the abbey.[94] In 1192, the abbot and convent, having failed in litigation to secure the advowson of Datchworth, obtained an annual pension of £1 from its incumbent.[95] Control over rights of advowson, and entitlement to pensions from churches, continued to be an administrative priority of William Postard.[96] The revenues of a parish church depended for their stability, however, on the expectation that all parishioners, including the more affluent and those who maintained large households, would have regular recourse to the parish church. If they did not, then the income from oblations would dwindle. The parish of St Margaret's, Westminster, was being infiltrated, in the late twelfth century, by men who were prominent in public life. They needed a residential base in the vill, but wanted this to contain the fashionable status-symbol of a private chapel. One such notable was a chamberlain of the Exchequer, Robert Mauduit, whom William Postard accepted as a tenant on abbey property, and to whom he conceded the right to have a private chapel. Careful provision was made, though, to ensure that St Margaret's, Westminster, would not suffer undue depletion of the oblations which might accrue from members of the chamberlain's household.[97] In a time of financial stress, there were advantages in having a neighbourly acquaintance with a high-ranking Exchequer official.

Another eminent resident of the vill in the later 1190s was Henry Marshall, bishop of Exeter. He, too, petitioned successfully for the right to have a private chapel, which was granted on conditions which safeguarded the

90 *Ibid.*, nos 307, 309, 395.

91 *Ibid.*, nos 314, 316, 319, 322, 324.

92 *Ibid.*, no. 318.

93 *Three Rolls of the King's Courts 1194–95*, ed. F.W. Maitland, Pipe Roll Society, XIV (1891), p. 128. See also *Pipe Roll 7 Richard I*, p. 33; *Pipe Roll 8 Richard I*, p. 190; Harvey, *Westminster Abbey and its Estates*, p. 356; *Westminster Abbey Charters*, nos 195, 339, 479.

94 *Three Rolls of the King's Court 1194–95*, p. 127. See also Harvey, *Westminster Abbey and its Estates*, p. 346.

95 *Westminster Abbey Charters*, no. 320.

96 *Ibid.*, nos 218, 322.

97 *Ibid.*, nos 311–12.

rights of St Margaret's.[98] A third notable whom Abbot William confirmed in property in Westminster was William of Ely, the king's treasurer.[99] Fortunately for St Margaret's, the treasurer did not maintain a chapel in this town-house.

The allegations, implied in the bulls of Pope Innocent III, that Abbot William acted high-handedly, are not readily sustained on the evidence of his surviving *acta*. In those cases where he is depicted as acting alone, he is invariably assigning revenues to the convent.[100] In all other instances, the convent is associated with the abbot in the transaction. It is arguable that some of his independent transactions were negotiated by means of the final concord which was increasingly used to conclude lawsuits in this period. Of those final concords in which William is named, two associate the convent with him.[101] In four other cases the abbot appears to act alone, although in the last case he is represented by the cellarer.[102] On this slight evidence, it is impossible to argue that he used the device of the collusive lawsuit to evade any restraints which the convent might impose on him. The only other case where he was not associated with the convent was in the franchisal dispute with St Albans, but this was not the sort of case which the pope had in mind. William Postard died on 4 May 1200,[103] seemingly under a cloud, according to the papal bulls, despite his having been elected on a popular vote.

The vacancy which followed lasted barely six months, ending in the election, on 30 November 1200, of Ralph Arundel. His blessing as abbot took place on the ensuing 17 December, coincidentally (and ominously, as events transpired) the same date on which Gervase had been blessed.[104] Ralph had previously been prior of Westminster's dependent cell of Hurley.[105] There is some evidence to suggest that in his youth he had been an outspoken member of the monastic community of Canterbury cathedral priory. Feelings there were sharply divided in the later 1160s over the exiled Archbishop Thomas Becket. There was some tentative, and perhaps indirect, communication between John of Salisbury, one of the most active propagandists on Becket's behalf, and the monk Ralph Arundel. This monk then apparently wrote to John, assuring him of his support for the archbishop, and John replied, to the effect that he was willing to keep in touch with him if Ralph agreed.[106] This line of communication was then used to forward a bull from Pope Alexander III, addressed to the English church, which Ralph read

98 *Ibid*., no. 230; cf. no. 445.
99 *Ibid*., no. 313.
100 *Ibid*., nos 308, 317, 321, 326.
101 *Ibid*., nos 310, 320.
102 *Ibid*., nos 314, 316, 324–5.
103 Knowles, Brooke and London, *Heads of Religious Houses*, p. 77.
104 *Ibid*., p. 77.
105 *Ibid*., p. 92.
106 *The Letters of John of Salisbury, II (1163–1180)*, ed. W.J. Millor and C.N.L. Brooke (Oxford, 1979), no. 246.

out in chapter early in 1168. He was denounced to Ranulf de Broc, who was the custodian of Canterbury on the king's behalf, and was banished from the monastic community.[107] This banishment perhaps took the form of a transfer to Westminster.[108] Although he arrived there in disgrace, his support for Becket's cause would earn him a greatly enhanced status after the archbishop's canonization, and would account for the eventual election of this outsider as prior of the daughter house of Hurley. By 1200, the prior of Hurley would be in line for higher things.

The chief point against this identification of the outspoken monk of Canterbury with the abbot of Westminster is that the latter died only in 1223,[109] some fifty-five years after the episode at Canterbury. If these two monks were identical, Ralph was very young when he was sent into exile, and well into his seventies at the time of his death. Detailed evaluation of patterns of age at monastic profession, and of subsequent life-expectancy, have been made by Barbara Harvey from the much fuller documentation of late-medieval Westminster.[110] On the data available from that period, the hypothesis proposed for Ralph Arundel's career is by no means impossible. There is, too, a resemblance of outlook between the young monk of Canterbury who was prepared to go it alone, against the wishes of his community, and the independent initiatives of an abbot who acted without consulting his monastic chapter.

In some respects, Abbot Ralph acted in a manner calculated to enhance his standing in the eyes of the monks, although objections could be raised to each of these actions. He assigned an annual sum of £4 in silver, from the manor of Islip, to the sacristy, to maintain lights around the feretory of King Edward.[111] Islip, birthplace of King Edward, was granted by that king to Westminster, but the abbey was unable to secure possession of it after the Norman Conquest, despite producing a number of spurious writs claiming this manor. In the twelfth century, the De Courcy family acquired Islip, but in 1203 Robert de Courcy gave his allegiance to King Philip Augustus of France. Westminster, bringing forward the spurious charters in evidence, petitioned King John for the restitution of the manor. This was granted, but Abbot Ralph was required to fine 200 marks (£133 6s 8d) and two palfreys.[112] Given this financial outlay, the chapter would have hoped to maximize subsequent returns from the land, whereas the assignment to the sacristy would make inroads into these. In the time of Ralph's successor, it was found

107 *Ibid.*, no. 247.
108 *Ibid.*, note to no. 246.
109 Knowles, Brooke and London, *Heads of Religious Houses*, p. 77.
110 Barbara Harvey, *Living and Dying in England 1100–1540: The Monastic Experience* (Oxford, 1993), pp. 112–45.
111 Westminster Abbey Domesday (Muniment Book 11), f. 370r.
112 *Rotuli Chartarum in Turri Londoniensi asservati, 1199–1216*, ed. T. Duffus Hardy (Record Comm., London, 1837), p. 139b; *Westminster Abbey Charters*, no. 149 and note.

preferable to substitute the proceeds of the abbey's fulling-mill at Wandsworth to maintain the feretory lights.[113]

Ralph negotiated with the Prior, Robert Moulsham, and the convent, who proposed the celebration of four additional feasts with copes and processions. After the liturgy, wine and pittances would be served at the ensuing meal. The abbot, on his part, in response to a petition from the monks, restored their manor of Benfleet, which he had been holding at farm from them.[114] Under the urbane prose of the prior's charter there lurked some hard bargaining. Prior Robert and his monks clearly objected to Abbot Ralph's decision to hold their manor. It had been confirmed to them by Abbot William in the 1190s, and Ralph had perhaps made a unilateral decision to take control of it again. Ralph's related charter is short and to the point. Addressing the tenants at Benfleet, he simply notes the restitution of this manor to the monks, 'which manor pertains to the pittancer's office to which it was anciently assigned', although he had been holding the manor by the will and concession of the monks.[115] The fact that they had to bargain for its return suggests that their concession had been made reluctantly. A second manor of the convent's which Ralph appears to have attempted to control was Parham in Sussex. This was 'conceded and confirmed' to the convent by Abbot William, with the exception of the advowson, on the understanding that the convent, in his place, would render the £8 due annually to the convent's kitchener.[116] Ralph apparently resumed control, over-riding the monks' warden in the vill. The convent fought back, however, and obtained from Ralph a grant of Parham, together with its advowson, and without prejudice to the existing grant of 8 shillings per day payable to the abbey kitchen from the abbot or his bailiff. Homage and relief were assigned respectively to abbot and convent, as in Abbot William's charter, but there are signs of a recent dispute in the additional provision that the convent might appoint any monk or layman as warden of Parham, and the abbot had no authority to dismiss him. The same would apply to any parson whom the convent appointed. Ralph states that he had made this concession of his 'spontaneous will in the chapter of Westminster; sealed it with his own seal, and placed it on the altar of St Peter, prince of the Apostles'. Anyone presuming to infringe its provisions would incur anathema. For good measure, the witnesses included the staff of the Exchequer; the abbey's seneschal and sergeants, and other leading residents of the vill. Somehow these proceedings lack the 'spontaneity' claimed by the abbot.

A third instance in which Ralph perhaps tried to withhold a concession made by his predecessor was in the case of the pension of 21 marks (£14) due annually from the churches of Oakham and Hambleton towards the monks' infirmary. This pension was granted by William Postard, in return for the

113 Westminster Abbey Domesday, f. 370r.

114 *Westminster Abbey Charters*, no. 345.

115 *Ibid.*, no. 332.

116 *Ibid.*, no. 326.

commemoration of the anniversary of his death.[117] Abbot Ralph perhaps tried to recover this pension, since he is recorded as having 'conceded' and 'confirmed' it to the convent for his soul and those of his parents and ancestors. Future abbots were exhorted, on pain of anathema, to uphold his concession.[118] Despite its high-flown language, this document probably represents a third instance in which the abbot was obliged to back-track, under pressure from a resentful prior and convent. Seven of those witnesses who had attested Abbot William's charter concerning the pension were assembled to witness Ralph's concession. It was perhaps after the infirmary pension was confirmed that Abbot Ralph and the convent jointly confirmed a grant by the parson of Oakham, Robert de Ardre, to William de Remis, of two virgates in Thorpe which were to be held of Oakham church.[119]

One fact which perhaps affected Ralph's land-management policies was the proximity of the abbey to the royal court and especially to the senior personnel of the Exchequer and the judiciary. Clearly there were occasions when such powerful neighbours could, and would, support the interests of the abbey, by drawing on their own expertise and professional contacts. There were advantages in accepting such men as tenants of the abbey, whether within the vill itself, or on lands further afield. One of the most powerful of all such contacts was Geoffrey Fitz Peter, Justiciar from 1198 to 1213. Abbot Ralph granted him the manor of Claygate, Surrey, to hold for life, on terms which seem reasonable on economic grounds, in that he owed an annual rent of £3, payable to the almonry, while he himself had to provide the livestock.[120] The rent was higher than the value of this manor in 1086,[121] and Westminster would receive the benefits of any improvements which he made. Geoffrey stated, in the charter in which he acknowledged these conditions, that he had received the manor from Abbot Ralph and the convent. Perhaps the grant was willingly made by the convent, but it was an almonry endowment which was being leased out, seemingly on Abbot Ralph's initiative. Geoffrey Fitz Peter's marriage to Beatrice de Say, the heiress of the Mandeville family, brought him the Mandeville barony of Pleshy in 1190.[122] With this, presumably, came the Mandevilles' patronal interest in Hurley priory. Ralph was probably acquainted with Geoffrey Fitz Peter well before either man received his highest office. Requests by the justiciar for tenurial favours would be difficult to refuse.

Almonry interests were again in question when Geoffrey, in his capacity as founder and patron of the small Gilbertine house of Shouldham, in Norfolk, petitioned the abbot and convent of Westminster for a grant of all

117 *Ibid.*, no. 321.
118 *Ibid.*, no. 336.
119 *Ibid.*, no. 337.
120 *Ibid.*, no. 484.
121 Harvey, *Westminster Abbey and its Estates*, p. 358 and note 3.
122 I.J. Sanders, *English Baronies. A Study of their Origin and Descent 1086–1327* (Oxford, 1960), p. 71.

tithes pertaining to them in Clakelose Hundred in return for an annual payment of £1 10s to the almoner of Westminster.[123] The deal was struck, and the nuns and brethren of Shouldham acknowledged that they had received these tithes, on these terms, from Abbot Ralph and the convent.[124] These tithes were probably a recent acquisition since they are not enumerated in the detailed confirmations granted by Pope Adrian IV and his successors. Westminster had no landed interests in Norfolk which could have served as a base from which to gather this income, so that its collection cannot have been very cost-effective. At the same time, Abbot Ralph was once again taking the lead in disposing of the convent's goods. It would not be prudent to oppose the Justiciar in matters such as these, while any link, patronal on Geoffrey's part, between him and Abbot Ralph, stretching back through the 1190s, would also make any refusal psychologically difficult.

Other grants made by Ralph to men prominent in public life did not overtly threaten the interests of the convent. The monks' consent was recorded in his grant of land in Longditch Street to Ralph Fitz Stephen;[125] in a grant to their clerk, Alexander of Swerford, of houses in London, between Ludgate and Fleet Bridge;[126] and in a confirmation made at the petition of the king's chamberlain, Robert Mauduit and his wife, of gifts made to provide lights for the Lady Altar.[127]

At Michaelmas 1201, in a dispute with Aubrey de Vere (seemingly not the earl of Oxford of that name), Ralph received from him a quitclaim of the manor of Feering (Essex), in return granting to Aubrey the manor of Little Coggeshall.[128] Litigation between the abbot and William de Ginnes and his wife Matilda resulted in the couple quitclaiming land in Battersea, at Easter 1204.[129] The seemingly interminable skirmishing with St Albans abbey resurfaced during Ralph's abbacy in a dispute over the view of frankpledge in Aldenham (Herts.), settled by compromise.[130] Ralph was active in the oversight and defence of Westminster's parish churches. In 1208, acting jointly with his own convent and the prior and convent of Bermondsey, he made a presentation to the church of St Magnus the Martyr in London.[131] In March of the same year, Ralph and the convent presented a cleric to the church of Todenham (Glos.).[132]

Ralph was active in defending the abbey's rights of advowson in its widely-scattered parish churches. In London, he secured a quitclaim from Anselm son of Hakon of the advowson of St Clement, Candlewick Street, Eastcheap;[133] he embarked on litigation to retrieve the advowson of Ashwell, Herts., after its long-serving rector, Walter Map, eventually died;[134] and he

123 *Westminster Abbey Charters*, no. 476.
124 *Ibid.*, no. 477.
125 *Ibid.*, no. 328.
126 *Ibid.*, no. 327.
127 *Ibid.*, no. 329.
128 *Ibid.*, no. 331.
129 *Ibid.*, no. 330.
130 *Ibid.*, no. 333.
131 *Ibid.*, no. 220.
132 *Ibid.*, no. 233.
133 *Ibid.*, no. 363.
134 *Curia Regis Rolls*, VI, p. 93.

secured the advowson of Parham, Sussex, granting to the defeated litigant participation in the spiritual benefits afforded by the abbey.[135] In Lincolnshire, he embarked on legal action to secure the advowsons of Doddington and Thorp.[136] When, in 1210, a defeated litigant quitclaimed the advowson of Uppingham in Rutland, he and his heirs were admitted to the spiritual benefits and prayers of the abbey.[137] Most of these actions were initiated and concluded in the secular courts, but when Ralph was defending his claim to lands pertaining to Launton church (Oxon.) against the prior of Bicester, he alleged that these were granted in free alms, so the case was taken to the church courts.[138] One of Ralph's last acts as abbot, which can be firmly dated, was his presentation, made with the convent, of a parson to Launton church, in October 1213.[139]

In the wider world, Abbot Ralph seems in general to have maintained amiable relations with those who mattered, although in 1205 he was amerced 20 marks to have the king's goodwill.[140] More often, Ralph could persuade these dignitaries to do something for his abbey. The papal legate, John of Salerno, in London during August 1201, granted two indulgences – one to enable Westminster to enhance its liturgy on certain feast days which normally fell in Lent, and the other to encourage worshippers at the abbey on the feast of St Peter in Chains.[141] The legate Nicholas de Romanis, in England in the autumn of 1213, in the wake of King John's surrender to the papacy, granted to Westminster, on 11 October 1213, a further indulgence designed to enlarge the congregations on several feast days. Increased offerings were for the use of the sacrist, who was to administer these faithfully.[142]

This legate meant to ensure that the monastic life at Westminster was properly conducted, and it was Abbot Ralph who came in for his closest scrutiny and censure. Complaints had been raised by the convent concerning Ralph's management of the endowments. Flete reports that the legate spent eighteen days at Westminster, having detailed discussions with the convent on the reform of the administration of their temporalities and spiritualities.[143] There followed a lull of about three months, during which time the legate presumably consulted the pope.[144] Soon after Christmas, Ralph Arundel was deposed on the authority of the papal legate, who sent the abbot of Waltham,

135 *Westminster Abbey Charters*, no. 334.

136 *Curia Regis Rolls*, IV, p. 48; *Pipe Roll 7 John*, p. 236; *Pipe Roll 9 John*, p. 52; *Rotuli de Oblatis et Finibus*, ed. T. Duffus Hardy (Record Comm., London, 1835), p. 336.

137 *Westminster Abbey Charters*, no. 338.

138 D.M. Stenton, *English Justice between the Conquest and the Great Charter 1066–1215* (London, 1965), pp. 46–7; *Curia Regis Rolls*, IV, p. 291.

139 *Westminster Abbey Charters*, no. 227.

140 *Rotuli de Oblatis et Finibus*, p. 325.

141 *Westminster Abbey Charters*, nos 191–2.

142 *Ibid.*, no. 193.

143 Flete, *The History of Westminster Abbey*, p. 100.

144 Harvey, *Westminster Abbey and its Estates*, p. 84.

to execute the sentence of deposition. On 23 January 1214, Ralph's seal was broken during the meeting of the Chapter. However, in view of his former dignity, the legate, and the abbot of Waltham as his representative, assigned to Ralph the manors of Teddington and Sunbury, but reserving the advowson of Sunbury to the incoming abbot. Ralph eventually died on 12 August 1223, outliving his successor by more than a year.[145]

William de Humez, a Norman by birth, began his monastic career at St Étienne, Caen and at some uncertain date he was transferred to its dependent priory of Frampton in Dorset. From there he was elected abbot of Westminster on 4 May 1214, and was blessed on 25 May.[146] Frampton, founded on a former royal manor within a few years of the Norman Conquest, accumulated a substantial endowment.[147] Even before the loss of Normandy culminated in the loss of Rouen in 1204, King John ordered a survey to be begun of the value of the English lands belonging to Norman monasteries. Their lands were seized by the Crown, but the prior of Frampton offered 100 marks for the custody of the abbot of Caen's manors. He paid half this sum on 5 October. The second instalment is not recorded, but in the following year he donated a palfrey, the value of which is unstated. The terms agreed were that, having completed his initial fine for custody, he would farm the lands for £80 per annum.[148] If this unnamed prior was William de Humez, he had demonstrated both the managerial skills and the correct political attitude required of an abbot of Westminster. Undoubtedly William de Humez was recognized as having useful talents, since soon after his election he was required to join more senior royal representatives on an embassy to King Philip Augustus of France.[149]

One of the most urgent tasks facing the new abbot was the recovery of properties alienated by Ralph Arundel without the consent of the convent. This project involved litigation, with the aim of recovering 40 acres of land in Pershore (Worcs.), another 40 acres in Feering (Essex), and a carucate of land in Wheathampstead.[150] According to Flete, there had been 'much controversy and conflict' in Abbot Ralph's lifetime over his unauthorized alienations,[151] but as the law stood, property alienated by a monastic head without the consent of his convent could be recovered only after the end of his

145 Flete, *The History of Westminster Abbey*, p. 100; Knowles, Brooke and London, *Heads of Religious Houses*, p. 77.

146 Knowles, Brooke and London, *Heads of Religious Houses*, p. 77.

147 D. Knowles and R.N. Hadcock, *Medieval Religious Houses England and Wales* (London, 1971), p. 88.

148 D. Matthew, *The Norman Monasteries and their English Possessions* (Oxford, 1962, reprinted Westport, CT, 1979), pp. 72–3.

149 *Rotuli Litterarum Patentium in Turri Londiniensi asservati*, ed. T. Duffus Hardy, Record Comm., I, i (London, 1835), f. 140b.

150 *Curia Regis Rolls*, VIII, pp. 212, 265; *ibid.*, X, p. 187. See also *Westminster Abbey Charters*, no. 331.

151 Flete, *The History of Westminster Abbey*, p. 100.

abbacy, and it was essential to resort to litigation.[152] Flete's account of the abbacy of William de Humez highlights his agreement with the monks whereby he assigned to their kitchen annual revenues totalling £150 11s 9d, drawn from the revenues of manors and rents of assize, and ratified by charter.[153] If, for any reason, such as debts, lawsuits or chance occurrences, the convent was not able to draw rents from these sources to that amount, then there would be a return to the former payment of 8 shillings a day. This agreement dates from within the first year of William's abbacy.[154] Subsequently the abbot, with the assent of the convent, set out in a further charter assignments of income to augment the revenues of several of the major monastic offices. A rent of 40 shillings, from the manor of Hampstead, was granted to augment the revenues for the kitchen in addition to the manors and rents listed in his previous charter. He granted the rent of 40 shillings won from Ivo of Deene in the Curia Regis, together with all the tithes of Pershore, which the abbot received from the monks of Great Malvern, in an agreement made between them by the authority of papal judges-delegate, to the infirmarer, in order to commemorate his anniversary; to alleviate (the sufferings) of the convent and also of one hundred poor people. Moreover, because he honoured and revered St Edward the king, he wanted the feast of the saint's Translation to be venerated solemnly, in copes, with due devotion, and therefore assigned for this purpose 20 shillings from the land of Robert Basset in Sutton (Glos.).[155] Abbot William's concern for the proper maintenance of St Edward's shrine is also reflected in his assignment of the revenues of the fulling-mill at Wandsworth to maintain lights around the feretory, in lieu of the assignment of £4 from the manor of Islip, previously allocated by Abbot Ralph.[156] The cult of St Edward also prompted Abbot William and the convent to make a confraternity agreement with Abbot Hugh II and the convent of Bury St Edmunds. It was noted in this agreement that the patrons of their respective houses were both sanctified kings and kinsmen.[157]

William de Humez faced problems on several fronts: Norman by birth, he had to adjust to living in an England which was now politically cut off from his Norman homeland; secondly, he was introduced, as an outsider, and an alien one at that, into a large monastic community which was keenly and vocally aware of its rights *vis-à-vis* the abbot; thirdly, as abbot, he had to try to retrieve the tenurial damage caused by his predecessor – lands, rents and

152 Harvey, *Westminster Abbey and its Estates*, p. 84.

153 Flete, *The History of Westminster Abbey*, p. 101.

154 *Documents Illustrating the Rule of Walter de Wenlok, Abbot of Westminster 1283–1307*, ed. Barbara F. Harvey, Camden Fourth Series, 2 (1965), pp. 215–16; Harvey, *Westminster Abbey and its Estates*, pp. 85–6.

155 Westminster Abbey Muniment 32354, which carries a fragment of the abbot's seal.

156 Westminster Abbey Domesday, f. 370r.

157 *Memorials of St Edmund's Abbey*, ed. T. Arnold, Rolls Series, 3 vols (1890–96), II, p. 251.

services were scattered over much of southern England, and had to be defended vigorously. In the early months of 1215, and in the presence of the judges of the Curia Regis, the abbot engaged in a plea against his tenant Ivo of Deene, over the rendering of a service of hospitality which Ivo owed annually for the manor of Deene (Northants) and which he had been withholding. Ivo now acknowledged his obligation to render this service. In return, he was to hold the manor in perpetuity, rendering £18 annually, whereas he had formerly rendered only £16.[158]

During the abbacy of William de Humez, continuing rapid inflation made it essential to maximize returns. In Worcestershire, he confirmed the manor of Longdon to Robert Foliot, rendering an annual service of hospitality, together with an annual farm of £28. This represented a sharp increase in his obligations.[159]

One further challenge facing the abbot was to safeguard Westminster and its properties from the ravages of civil war. There were already ominous political tensions at the time when William became abbot, and by the early months of 1215 England was in a state of civil war. From mid-May 1215, rebel forces were in London, and the abbey was at their mercy. Westminster's plight is apparent in a letter patent, issued by King John on 24 October 1215, when he was engaged in the siege of Rochester. He ordered his knights, sergeants and other soldiers of his army that they were not to enter the precincts of the abbey, the abbey church or its cemetery. They were not to permit others to enter, nor were they to cause, or permit others to cause, injuries to the monks, or to the king's men dwelling there, since the abbey, its men, all residents and its property were under the royal protection.[160] It is conjectural how far such a charter would deter even royalist troops. In 1216 it did not inhibit a party of rebels who, when denied admission to the abbey, seized the royal regalia.[161]

By 1218, the country was sufficiently recovered for the abbot to resume the work of trying to recover the lands and other properties lost by earlier alienations, and perhaps augmented by the recent disturbances. On 17 July 1218 he received from John of Besford a renunciation of claims to Besford chapel.[162] Shortly afterwards, the abbot, represented by Brother Richard of Barking, was successful in a lawsuit against Bartholomew of Benfleet, gaining half a hide of land in Benfleet, held by Basil the chaplain. He gave some land in exchange, with seventeen and a half marks of silver.[163]

158 F.M. Stenton, *The First Century of English Feudalism 1066–1166*, 2nd edn (Oxford, 1961), pp. 267–9.

159 Westminster Abbey Domesday, f. 304.

160 *Westminster Abbey Charters*, no. 151.

161 Carpenter, *House of Kings*, p. 24.

162 Westminster Abbey Muniment, 22443. See also Westminster Abbey Muniment 22486; Westminster Abbey Domesday, f. 577.

163 *Feet of Fines for Essex (1182–1326)*, ed. R.E.G. Kirk and E.F. Kirk, Essex Archaeological Society, 2 vols (Colchester, 1899–1928), I, p. 50, no. 12.

In mid-November 1220, he secured from Robert King land in Pensham (Worcs.).[164] Shortly after this, in 1220–21, and represented by his attorney Robert of Croxley, he was involved in litigation with Robert de Vere, earl of Oxford, over land in Feering and Kensington.[165] Robert of Croxley again represented the abbot in the early months of 1222, successfully re-establishing Westminster's long-held title to the church of Wennington against Gilbert of the Marsh. In return for renouncing his claim, Gilbert and his heirs were admitted into confraternity with Westminster.[166]

William de Humez was careful to learn the lessons of his predecessor's mistakes, while upholding the dignity of the office of abbot. As one instance of this, in his charter concerning the maintenance of lights at King Edward's feretory, he talks of the convent 'unanimously and voluntarily' agreeing to the new sources of finance, but also of 'Abbot Ralph, our predecessor of good memory'.[167] During William's time, too, work was begun on building the Lady Chapel.[168] The initiative, however, came from the prior and convent, rather than from the abbot, as their charters indicate.

One matter in which the abbot was certainly required to take the lead was in facing up to a renewed attempt by the bishop of London to assert his jurisdiction over Westminster. The new bishop, Eustace de Fauconberg, was in office from the spring of 1221, but had been royal treasurer since November 1217.[169] In that capacity he would have been in close proximity to the abbot and monks through his work at the Exchequer. Flete is clear that the canons of St Paul's were with him in this dispute, probably reminding him of the claims of his see. Arbitrators, acceptable to both parties, were called in: Stephen Langton, archbishop of Canterbury; Peter des Roches, bishop of Winchester; Richard Poore, bishop of Salisbury; together with Thomas, prior of Merton and Richard de Mores, prior of Dunstable. They declared that Westminster was totally exempt from the jurisdiction of the bishop of London; the church of Staines should be converted to the use of the abbey, but that the manor of Sunbury and its church were to go to the bishop of London. The church of St Margaret's, Westminster, with its whole parish, chapels and tithes, and the clergy and laity living there, was to be entirely exempt from the jurisdiction of the bishop of London and that of his Official, and Westminster was answerable solely to the pope.[170] Sunbury was

164 Westminster Abbey Muniment, 22453.

165 *A Calendar of the Feet of Fines for London and Middlesex I: Richard I to Richard III*, ed. W.J. Hardy and W. Page (London, 1892), no. 34. See also *Westminster Abbey Charters*, nos 331, 456.

166 *Feet of Fines for Essex*, p. 61, no. 93.

167 Westminster Abbey Domesday, f. 370r.

168 R.A. Brown, H.M. Colvin and A.J. Taylor, *The History of the King's Works*, I (London, 1963), p. 131.

169 J. Le Neve, *Fasti Ecclesiae Anglicanae 1066–1300. I. St Paul's, London*, compiled Diana E. Greenway (London, 1968), pp. 2, 54.

170 Flete, *The History of Westminster Abbey*, pp. 101–2.

a demesne manor, valued at £6 in 1086, which had been held by the abbey since King Edward's time.[171] The arbitrators would perceive the need to make some concession to the bishop and his chapter, but in other respects Westminster was fully vindicated. The rule of William de Humez ended on a note of triumph. He died on 20 April 1222.[172]

The abbots discussed in this chapter differed from one another in various ways – background, nationality, age at appointment, and ambitions – but some common threads run through their careers. In the first place, several of them clearly liked to have their kinsmen among their close advisors. Commentators on the abbacy of Gervase have occasionally remarked on the attestations to his charters by his brothers Amalric and Ralph. The underlying implication is that such transactions were dubious ones.[173] However, the successors of Gervase were equally liable to call on their kinsmen to witness their deeds. John, nephew of Abbot Lawrence, witnessed one of his charters, and the abbot's brother Ralph witnessed another, as well as a grant made to the abbey by Leofwine Kepe.[174] His position in the witness lists indicates that he was in clerical orders. Charters of Abbot Walter are attested by his brother Alexander,and by his nephew Walter de Doniton (Donnington), who was a clerk,[175] while a charter of Abbot William Postard is witnessed both by his brother Arnulf and also by his nephew Nicholas. Mr Arnulf, Ernald or Ernulf Postard evidently served as a clerk both to Abbot William and to his successor Ralph Arundel.[176] In the social climate of the day, kinsmen generally supported one another's interests, and the more successful members of a family would bring the others forward into public life. It was quite usual, therefore, for the charters of even the most reputable clerics to include mention of their kinsmen, in one capacity or another. For instance, the editors of Bishop Gilbert Foliot's letters and charters indexed some twenty-four other individuals with the surname Foliot.[177] It would have been more remarkable if the charters of twelfth-century abbots of Westminster had contained no attestations by their kinsmen.

The *Rule of St Benedict* set out plainly the duties of an abbot,[178] and all members of the community would know what was required of the man who currently held office. The abbot, in addition to meeting the requirements of

171 Harvey, *Westminster Abbey and its Estates*, pp. 24n., 113n., 124, 354.

172 Knowles, Brooke and London, *Heads of Religious Houses*, p. 77.

173 Amalric and Ralph attest Westminster Abbey Charters, nos 258, 263, 269. See Harvey, 'Abbot Gervase de Blois and the Fee Farms of Westminster Abbey', *Bulletin of the Institute of Historical Research*, 40 (1967), p. 134.

174 For John, see *Westminster Abbey Charters*, no. 284; for Robert, *ibid.*, nos 280, 404.

175 *Ibid.*, nos 291, 297, 300, 303, 490.

176 For the joint attestations of Arnulf and Nicholas, *ibid.*, no. 321. For Arnulf, Ernald, Ernulf Postard see also *ibid.*, nos 307, 312–13, 323, 336, 353, 441 and 481.

177 *Letters and Charters of Gilbert Foliot*, pp. 560–61.

178 *The Rule of St Benedict*, ed. and transl. J. McCann (London, 1952), cap. 2. See also cap. 64.

the Rule, needed also the managerial skills required of the head of a large enterprise. He commanded a considerable work-force, if one may so term the monks, clerks, lay servants and also the employees on far-flung estates. He needed the business-sense to manage those lands, combined with the personal skills to enable him to administer these in co-operation with, rather than in opposition to, an increasingly articulate monastic chapter. Royal government was becoming increasingly pervasive, so that the abbot had to defend the revenues and franchisal rights of his house by all legitimate means, while at the same time he must adhere to the requirements of the growing body of canon law, and the rulings of the pope as expressed through a steady flow of letters and the agenda of visiting legates. These pressures were enough for any individual, so that the intellectual achievements of Abbot Gilbert Crispin and, perhaps, those of Abbot Lawrence, were all the more remarkable.[179] It was enough for the majority of abbots in the period covered by this study to fulfil their basic obligations, and much to their credit that they performed as well as they did. The range of pressures on them rendered the abbacy something of a hot seat. Gervase, as has been demonstrated, was dismissed on political grounds, rather than for any failure to live up to the role of abbot. Conversely Ralph Arundel was removed for being an over-zealous administrator, unwilling to work with, rather than in isolation from, his chapter. The one abbot who may have been an outright failure was Geoffrey, but his shortcomings are swathed in a blanket of silence. Successful abbots needed to walk warily in the corridors of power, and needed to maintain a network of useful connections. This know-how was probably always essential – even in the period between the Tenth-Century Reform and King Edward's assumption of the role of patron. Religious communities in general had most esteem for those of their heads who could best defend their interests. Even when little is known of the earlier abbots the manner in which this knowledge is presented, on Edwin or Vitalis for instance, reflects the presuppositions of the monastic community.

With all the demands on their time and energies the wonder of it is that the abbot was able to continue to observe the monastic routine as fully as he did. The Customary of the abbey, dating from the mid 1270s, indicates that throughout the thirteenth century, the abbot of Westminster was still expected to attend almost all of the daily offices (except prime), and the daily chapter, and to dine in the refectory.[180] On the other hand, there was a gap between expectations and actuality. The abbots began to live in quarters of their own, within the precincts, in the twelfth century. Barbara Harvey, in her study of Walter de Wenlock, abbot from 1283 to 1307, demonstrated that he lived off-precinct, in his own residence, La Neyte, even when in the neighbourhood of Westminster, and that on occasion he travelled with the

179 See Harvey, *Westminster Abbey and its Estates*, p. 95.

180 *Documents Illustrating the Rule of Walter de Wenlok, Abbot of Westminster, 1283–1307*, pp. 9–10.

retinue appropriate to a great magnate.[181] This isolation developed from the division of goods between abbot and monks in 1225, and La Neyte was bought for the abbot's use.[182]

Before that period the abbots were probably more in evidence at Westminster, when their attendance was not required at the royal court, and they were not inspecting their far-flung estates. The latter occupation increasingly predominated, as is demonstrated by a steady diminution in the numbers of attestations of abbots to royal charters. This falling-off occurred steadily between c.1050 and c.1100, while in the course of the twelfth century the political role of abbots dwindled still further.

Evidence for the abbots' regular travels around his estates is found in a charter of Abbot Herbert, who wrote of a projected, and seemingly routine, visit to Great Malvern.[183] Abbot Walter, confirming the manor of Denham (Bucks.) to Martin de Capella, c.1182, required in return, in addition to the rent, an annual service of hospitality at fifteen days' notice.[184] Another charter of Abbot Walter's, granted to the royal chamberlain Ralph Fitz Stephen, included the provision that Ralph would arrange for the grinding of corn pertaining to the abbot's manor house (*dominica curia*) before Walter's arrival at Todenham (Glos.).[185] This obligation to render hospitality could prove onerous. Following a lawsuit in January 1192, Abbot William Postard quitclaimed to his tenant William of Darnford an annual service of hospitality in the vill of Deerhurst (Glos.), and would receive in lieu an annual payment of 40 shillings.[186] Payment of this substantial sum was evidently preferable to the upheaval caused by a visit from the abbot, and transactions between Abbot William de Humez and two of his tenants indicate the extent of the arrangements required. A final concord was made in the Curia Regis at Westminster, on 2 February 1215, between the abbot and Ivo of Deene (Northants), after Ivo had been withholding a service of hospitality. It was now agreed that, when the abbot needed to exercise his right to this service at Deene, he would notify Ivo by writ, two weeks in advance of his visit. On the day of the abbot's arrival, seven of his officials would travel ahead of him, and take over the various household offices. These men comprised the seneschal, who would assume custody of the abbot's hall; the chamberlain, who was in charge of the *camera* (in this context a room for private use, rather than the normal Westminster usage of a finance office); the pantler, in charge of the stores and the bread; the butler, with oversight of the buttery and the drink; the usher, controlling the door; the cook, in charge of the kitchen; and the marshal, in control of the stabling. Ivo and his men were to receive the

181 *Ibid.*, p. 10.

182 Harvey, *Westminster Abbey and its Estates*, pp. 87, 414.

183 *Westminster Abbey Charters*, no. 248A.

184 *Ibid.*, no. 301. See also British Library Harleian Charter 85 A 11.

185 *Westminster Abbey Charters*, no. 306.

186 *Ibid.*, no. 324. A charter in the name of Abbot Gervase, which also refers to this tenancy, is a forgery (*ibid.*, no. 271).

abbot and his retinue in an honourable manner. Ivo would also make adequate provision, from his own goods, for food and drink and other essentials appropriate to the honourable reception due on the first day of the abbot's arrival. On the next day, the abbot and his retinue were to be served dinner (a midday meal at this period) in an honourable manner, but after dinner on that day neither the abbot nor his men might demand drink more than once, by way of custom. They were not to have anything else from Ivo's own goods unless they wanted to buy it. However if the abbot chose to delay the whole of that (second) night at Ivo's house, he should buy everything he needed, at a just price. A reckoning must be kept, and accounts drawn up, between the servants of the abbot and Ivo and his servants. What the abbot and his men had of Ivo's goods was to be reckoned up and allowed to Ivo in his farm which he was to render at the next term. On the first night of the abbot's arrival, Ivo was to provide two candles to burn in the abbot's presence. These were to be of wax, both one pound in weight. The abbot's chamberlain was to have any remnant of them which remained unburnt. Ivo must also give 12 pence to each of the named officials of the abbot. On account of the damage and expense which Westminster abbey had incurred through the withholding of this hospitality, which Ivo denied having to render, Ivo increased his farm by forty shillings. Ivo and his heirs would hold the manor of Deene in perpetuity, with all its appurtenances (except the advowson and presentation of the church, retained by the abbot and his successors), from the abbot and his successors, rendering the hospitality as described. Ivo would also render £18 sterling annually to Westminster for the manor, for which he previously rendered £16, payable in quarterly instalments.[187]

Abbot William's agreement with Robert Foliot over the manor of Longdon (Worcs.) is undated, but set out similar terms to those contained in the agreement made with Ivo of Deene. In this case, too, the making of the agreement on hospitality was the occasion for increasing the farm of the manor, here raised from £24 to £28. Robert was required to swear on the Gospels, in Chapter, that no use would ever be made of his old charter which set the farm at £24. If it ever came into his hands, he would restore it without creating any difficulties. His son Reginald was made to swear a similar oath. The wording of the agreement hints that Robert, trying to evade the burden of large-scale entertaining, had conveniently 'lost' the old charter. The surviving charters which relate to the abbots' right of hospitality indicate that they travelled on a regular circuit through their lands in the West Midlands, and also visited those further east.

During the period under discussion, most of the abbots were imposed on the abbey by the king. Herbert, although a former monk of the house, was

[187] F.M. Stenton, *The First Century of English Feudalism*, pp. 267–9. See also *ibid.*, pp. 71–3; *Westminster Abbey Charters*, no. 480; G. Edwards, 'The Royal Household and the Welsh Lawbooks', *Transactions of the Royal Historical Society*, fifth series, 13 (1963), pp. 163–76, esp. pp. 168–9.

probably chosen by King Henry I, rather than elected by the chapter, while the manner of Lawrence's election is uncertain. William Postard was the elected choice of the monks, but only on payment of a heavy fine to the Crown.[188] Ralph Arundel is said by Flete to have been *electus in abbatem*, which ought to signify that his elevation resulted from free election, but his subsequent activities indicated that this was not necessarily a recommendation. The last of the abbots encompassed in this study, William de Humez, was another outside appointment. However, from 1222 until 1533 the monks chose their own abbot, normally without any difficulties being raised. The king would simply grant licence to elect, and would give his formal assent to the man who emerged as abbot.[189]

Abbots were buried in the cloister at Westminster. The exceptions were Ralph Arundel, who was buried in the nave, and Geoffrey, dismissed to Normandy. Flete carefully locates each tomb and records its epitaph. Those who now try to locate the tomb of any given abbot have an uphill task, because these monuments have been re-arranged over the centuries. The stones are now very much worn away, although an attempt has been made to identify some of the tombs on the basis of their materials and on stylistic grounds, insofar as surviving fragments of the figure sculpture and the epitaphs permit.[190] Most epitaphs, like that surviving for Gervase, are succinct, but Flete records rather longer ones for Gilbert Crispin and Lawrence.[191]

It has been argued, on technical grounds, that whereas the tomb which can be identified as that of Gervase does date from the 1160s, those tombs carrying the longer epitaphs were constructed together, but not before the 1180s.[192] For some reason, new stones, with florid epitaphs, were then designed for Gilbert and Lawrence.[193]

188 Harvey, *Westminster Abbey and its Estates*, p. 64, n. 2.
189 *Ibid.*, p. 94.
190 Freda Anderson, 'The Westminster Abbots: A Problem of Identity', *Church Monuments*, IV (1989), pp. 3–15.
191 Flete, *The History of Westminster Abbey*, pp. 85, 87, 88, 91, 94, 96, 98, 102.
192 Anderson, 'The Westminster Abbots', p. 13.
193 Flete, *The History of Westminster Abbey*, pp. 87, 94.

5

The Visible Monks

Most of the monks of Westminster necessarily remain invisible, immersed in the rounds of the liturgy. Their movements at all times of the day were prescribed by the Rule and by customs derived from Lanfranc's *Monastic Constitutions* which in turn was embedded into the mid-thirteenth-century *Customary*.[1] A minority of the monks, though, attained one or another of the senior offices within the community or else some lesser position of responsibility. These men have left their mark in the archives, chiefly because of the part they played in instigating, or in responding to, property transactions.

The priors, naturally, are the best-documented of the obedientiaries. The *Customary* indicated that the abbot still played a regular part in the life of the community.[2] In practice, though, he began to withdraw from the common life of the abbey early in the Anglo-Norman period. There is circumstantial evidence for this distancing before the end of Gilbert Crispin's abbacy, and conversely the priors emerged into prominence as the officials with practical responsibility for supervising the daily life of the community.[3] The priors, with rare exceptions, came up through the ranks, in contrast to the abbots, who were usually imposed from outside, during the period covered by this study. Consequently the priors could take the moral high ground, representing the economic interests of the community as a whole, in the face of those abbots who had an arbitrary managerial style. Given the extent of the monastic endowment which the convent regarded as its own, it was, of course essential that the priors themselves, and the obedientiaries as a whole, should be good administrators.[4] Smooth administration leaves few surface traces, but from time to time the wording of the Westminster charters hints

1 J. Armitage Robinson, *Gilbert Crispin, Abbot of Westminster* (Cambridge, 1911), p. 28. See also *Customary of the Benedictine Monasteries of St Augustine, Canterbury, and St Peter, Westminster*, ed. E. Maunde Thompson, Henry Bradshaw Society, XXIII and XXVIII (1902, 1904).

2 *Documents Illustrating the Rule of Walter de Wenlok, Abbot of Westminster, 1283–1307*, ed. Barbara F. Harvey, Camden Fourth Series, 2 (1965), pp. 9–10.

3 Barbara F. Harvey, *Westminster Abbey and its Estates in the Middle Ages* (Oxford, 1977), pp. 132–3.

4 On the importance of good managerial skills, see John Van Engen, 'The "Crisis of

at tough bargaining between the prior, representing the monastic interest, and a high-handed abbot.[5] Some able administrators rose to the top of the hierarchy: Abbot Edwin was a former monk of the house; Abbot Herbert was a former almoner of Westminster; and Abbot William Postard was a former prior of the house.[6] By being an active prior, a monk could also gain a public reputation which might cause him to be promoted to higher things elsewhere. Abbot Walter had formerly been prior of Winchester; Abbot Ralph had been prior of the dependent cell of Hurley; and William de Humez had been prior of the alien priory of Frampton.[7] For day-to-day purposes, of course, all three had been effectively in charge of their respective priories, although in important matters Ralph and William were subject to their respective mother-houses, just as Abbot Vitalis had been, in his earlier days at Bernay.[8]

The first prior of Westminster to leave any real trace in the records was Robert, active in the late eleventh century, and presumably of Norman origin, as his name indicates. He witnessed two surviving charters of Abbot Gilbert Crispin.[9] One of these may perhaps date from 1086,[10] which would indicate that Robert was a very experienced administrator by the time he was elected abbot of Bury St Edmunds in 1102. His appointment perhaps owed something to the fact that his predecessor there, another Robert, was deposed at the Council of Westminster at Michaelmas 1102. Prior Robert, 'a man of great religion', was conveniently at hand to commend himself to the assembled prelates. Before his consecration could take place, however, Archbishop Anselm went into exile for the second time, in April 1103. Nevertheless, Robert proved a diligent abbot-elect, supervising the building of Bury's cloister, chapter-house, refectory, dormitory and *camera*. Since his years at Westminster coincided with the later phase of construction there, most of his adult life would have been spent in the middle of a building site. Following the archbishop's return to England in 1107, Robert was consecrated on 15 August, but died on 16 September in the same year. He was remembered at Bury as an excellent administrator, distinguished among its abbots for his achievements in acquiring and safeguarding its lands.[11]

Cenobitism" Reconsidered: Benedictine Monasticism in the Years 1050–1150', *Speculum*, 61 (1986), p. 20.

5 *Westminster Abbey Charters 1066–c.1214*, ed. Emma Mason, assisted by the late Jennifer Bray, continuing the work of the late D.J. Murphy, London Record Society, 25 (London, 1988), nos 317, 326, 335–6.

6 D. Knowles, C.N.L. Brooke and Vera C.M. London, *The Heads of Religious Houses England and Wales 940–1216* (Cambridge, 1972), pp. 76–7.

7 *Ibid.*, pp. 77, 80, 92.

8 *Ibid.*, p. 77.

9 *Westminster Abbey Charters*, nos 236, 241.

10 *Ibid.*, no. 236.

11 Armitage Robinson, *Gilbert Crispin*, p. 29; Knowles, Brooke and London, *Heads of Religious Houses*, p. 32.

At Westminster, Edwy was the next prior to leave any trace in the surviving charters. His name indicates that he was of English parentage, and his promotion to high office under a Norman abbot probably indicates both his own abilities and also the ongoing presence of a substantial body of ethnic Englishmen in the chapter in the early twelfth century. Edwy is now known from an unusual letter, which he sent jointly with Abbot Herbert, to Prior Warin of Worcester and to Dom Uhtred, its precentor, concerning the runaway monk of Malvern who had fled to Westminster, leaving unfinished the missal he was writing for Worcester cathedral priory.[12] At this distance in time, it is impossible to say whether the underlying notes of compassion and practical good sense owe more to Edwy or to Herbert: although in a case such as this, the initiative would be more likely to come from the prior.

The order of succession of the next three priors is slightly conjectural, due in large part to the troubled career of Osbert de Clare, undoubtedly the best-known of the priors of Westminster. His manner was evidently very confrontational. He was exiled from Westminster in the time of Abbot Herbert, and demoted, and possibly exiled again, while Gervase was abbot. Osbert has left a highly articulate series of letters which chart the wrongs which he perceived to have been done to him.[13] His chief claim to fame, though, is his initiative in producing a considerable volume of forged charters, most of them very elaborate, and designed to uphold Westminster's title to its lands, and its claims to extensive franchisal privileges. Osbert's initiatives, both in this respect, and in his energetic promotion of the cult of St Edward, are discussed in later chapters.

Prior Osbert made a sedate appearance in one charter of Abbot Herbert's, in which they are depicted acting jointly in establishing the small nunnery of Kilburn, probably in the earlier part of 1134. Osbert had been exiled for some time during Herbert's abbacy, but he was prior of Westminster between 1134 and the early part of Gervase's abbacy.[14] In a charter issued for the nuns of Kilburn, Abbot Gervase and the convent granted them land in Gore, in the manor of Knightsbridge, as they were seized of it by 'our brother Osbert de Clare'.[15] During his mission to the papal court in December 1139, Osbert used the style of prior. Pope Innocent II's letter of 9 December addressed to Abbot Gervase and the monks, in which he told them that he rejected their petition for the canonization of King Edward, makes it plain that Osbert had created a favourable reputation for himself at the *Curia*. This had enabled

12 *Westminster Abbey Charters*, no. 248A.

13 *The Letters of Osbert de Clare, Prior of Westminster*, ed. E.W. Williamson, introd. J. Armitage Robinson (London, 1929).

14 For the foundation of Kilburn, see *Westminster Abbey Charters*, no. 249. The dates of Prior Osbert's periods of exile and demotion are uncertain: *Letters of Osbert de Clare*, pp. 19, 86; Frank Barlow, *Edward the Confessor* (London, 1970), pp. 272–7.

15 *Ibid.*, no. 265.

him to prompt the pope to write to the legate in England, Henry of Blois, ordering the recovery of those goods of Westminster's which had been wrongfully alienated.[16] 'Our dear son Osbert, prior of the royal monastery of Westminster', also persuaded the pope to write to King David of Scotland, urging him to confirm Westminster's title to the land from which the income supported the commemoration of Edith Matilda's anniversary.[17] The last of the series of bulls obtained on this occasion, in which Abbot Gervase is ordered to reform his administration, is highly suspect in its present form.[18] Any genuine, but simpler, original on which it is based, may perhaps have mentioned Osbert, but if so, he is tactfully edited out of the document as it now survives, and of which he was most likely the author. It is uncertain at what stage this censorious document was composed and publicly cited at Westminster. A likely occasion would be in 1141 when the empress appeared triumphant and the time perhaps seemed ripe to press for the demotion of Abbot Gervase, the son of the imprisoned king. Political expediency was perhaps reinforced by alleged papal censure. Gervase and Osbert had been able to co-operate in the early years of Gervase's abbacy, and Osbert, as prior, attested Gervase's grant to William de Wenden and his wife Adelaide of her late father's lands.[19] Osbert's demotion, and possibly a renewed exile, during Gervase's reign, was most likely caused by the production of the censorious forged bull.

At intervals during Gervase's abbacy, two further men are recorded with the title of prior of Westminster. One of these priors, Hugh, was elected and consecrated abbot of Bury St Edmunds in 1157 (around the time that Gervase was deposed), and remained in office down to his death in 1180.[20] Hugh gradually lost his grip on the administration there, however, with the result that there was much mismanagement and growing indebtedness. The financial and managerial crisis at his death formed the opening section of Jocelin of Brakelond's *Chronicle*.[21]

The other prior of Westminster recorded during Gervase's abbacy was

16 W. Dugdale, *Monasticon Anglicanum*, revised H. Caley, H. Ellis and B. Bandinel, 6 vols in 8 (London, 1817–30), I, p. 308, no. LIV; *Letters of Osbert de Clare*, pp. 87–8, no. 19; calendared *Westminster Abbey Charters*, no. 158. See also *Letters of Osbert de Clare*, no. 20; calendared *Westminster Abbey Charters*, no. 159.

17 *Papsturkunden in England*, ed. W. Holtzmann, 3 vols, Abhandlungen der Gesellschaft der Wissenschaften in Göttingen, phil.-hist. Klasse, Berlin, Göttingen (I = neue Folge XXV, 1930–31; II = 3 Folge XIV–XV, 1935–6; III = 3 Folge XXXIII, 1952), I, no. 25; calendared *Westminster Abbey Charters*, no. 160.

18 Barbara F. Harvey, 'Abbot Gervase de Blois and the Fee-Farms of Westminster Abbey', *Bulletin of the Institute of Historical Research*, 40 (1967), pp. 128–9.

19 *Westminster Abbey Charters*, no. 254.

20 Knowles, Brooke and London, *Heads of Religious Houses*, p. 32.

21 *The Chronicle of Jocelin of Brakelond*, transl. and ed. H.E. Butler (London, 1949), pp. 1–15.

Elias, who witnessed the abbot's grant to Gerin, the king's minister.[22] He is also the first witness to Abbot Gervase's confirmation of the manor of Deerhurst to William of Darnford.[23] That document, as it now survives, is in a highly suspicious form, since there are indications that several clauses have been added by a thirteenth-century scribe.[24] Gervase did issue a confirmation to William early in his abbacy, though, and this was confirmed by the Empress Matilda at sometime between 1141 and 1147.[25] If the thirteenth-century scribe retained the framework of Gervase's grant to William, this indicates that Elias was in office at any rate from the mid-1140s for the remainder of Gervase's abbacy. Certainly he was still prior after Gervase was deposed. A further confirmation to William of Darnford, this time issued in the name of the convent of Westminster, and referring to Gervase as 'former abbot', was issued in 1158. Prior Elias was the chief witness, followed by Osbert de Clare.[26] The elderly Osbert seemingly lived out his days as an untitled but elder statesman among the monks of Westminster.

Abbot Lawrence brought in as prior an outsider, an old acquaintance with a reputation for sharp practice. This was Alquin, who was deposed from his position as prior of St Albans following the discovery of an illicit seal which, it was implied, he intended to use to ratify unauthorized transactions. He fled to Westminster, where Lawrence, himself a former monk of St Albans, admitted him to the community, to the indignation of the chapter of St Albans. When the office of prior became vacant, Alquin was promoted.[27] At Durham, where Lawrence had once been employed as a secular clerk, the community subsequently commemorated 'Alcuin', monk of Westminster.[28] Alquin's term of office at Westminster is uncertain. It is conjectural whether he was the prior on whose behalf Abbot Lawrence wrote to the abbot of St Victor, requesting that his kinsman John be allowed to study in the schools.[29]

Prior Richard held office at some time during the abbacy of Walter (1175x1190), and witnessed his grant to the king's chamberlain, Ralph Fitz Stephen.[30] Richard was perhaps the unnamed prior who was designated, in Abbot Walter's charter for the Hospital of St James, to receive the solemn

22 *Westminster Abbey Charters*, no. 261.

23 *Ibid.*, no. 271.

24 Barbara F. Harvey, 'Fee-Farms', pp. 131–2.

25 *Regesta Regum Anglo-Normannorum 1066–1154*, 4 vols, ed. H.W.C. Davis, C. Johnson, H.A. Cronne and R.H.C. Davis (Oxford, 1913, 1956, 1968, 1969), III, no. 259; calendared *Westminster Abbey Charters*, no. 98.

26 *Westminster Abbey Charters*, no. 341.

27 *Gesta Abbatum Monasterii Sancti Albani*, ed. H.T. Riley, 3 vols, Rolls Series (London, 1867–9), I, pp. 107–110; E.H. Pearce, *The Monks of Westminster*, Notes and Documents Relating to Westminster Abbey, no. 5 (Cambridge, 1916), p. 44.

28 Pearce, *The Monks of Westminster*, p. 44.

29 *Patrologiae cursus completus, series Latina*, ed. J.P. Migne, 221 vols (Paris, 1844–64) 196, col. 1385, no. VII.

30 *Westminster Abbey Charters*, no. 306.

oath of the sisters of the hospital to observe the conditions under which they were to hold the church of St Alban, Wood Street.[31]

Robert Moulsham held the office of precentor c.1200, and in that capacity he began to attract a regular income for the Lady Altar of the abbey.[32] His activities on behalf of this altar are well-documented, and most likely led to his subsequently being elected prior. Promotion of the cult of the Blessed Virgin was as much his preserve as the project to ensure the canonization of King Edward had been that of Osbert de Clare. When Robert became prior, he retained direct responsibility for the welfare of the Lady Altar, and for the securing of its revenues.[33] As prior, though, he had also a wider remit, including responsibility for securing the estates of the convent. He recovered the manor of Benfleet for the convent from Abbot Ralph, granting in return on the monks' behalf the celebration of four feast-days with copes and processions, wine and pittances, as the abbot had requested.[34] This concession provides a rare glimpse of the outlook of early thirteenth-century monks, indicating that they regarded processions, with their additional chanting, as a chore, even though they would be regaled afterwards by wine and appetite-tempting dishes. After all, it was their revenues, not those of the abbot, which were to pay for these treats. Prior Robert's establishment of separate funding for the Lady Altar, and its successor, the distinctive Lady Chapel, established his posthumous reputation at Westminster, and the anniversary of his death was commemorated, a rare honour for priors in this period.[35]

Richard of Barking, who succeeded Abbot William de Humez in 1222, had previously been prior.[36] He was simply styled 'monk' when he acted on behalf of Abbot William in a lawsuit in 1218–19.[37] His subsequent appointment as prior was presumably due to his natural abilities. The office of prior called for determination and energy, and carried with it considerable responsibility. At the same time, as the careers of several priors demonstrate, it could serve as a step on the ladder to higher things.

The other obedientiaries were rarely documented by name in the period covered by this study. When they were named, this was for some unusual reason. For instance, it is deduced that Roger the infirmarer and Walter the sacrist headed the delegation to the papal *Curia* early in 1161, to secure the canonization of King Edward. On the same day as the bulls proclaiming the canonization were issued, Alexander III granted each a bull confirming a church, or churches, the revenues of which pertained to his office.[38] Walter

31 *Ibid.*, no. 288.

32 *Ibid.*, nos 441, 442.

33 *Ibid.*, nos 346–8, and, probably, no. 408. See also no. 387.

34 *Ibid.*, no. 345.

35 Harvey, *Westminster Abbey and its Estates*, pp. 39, 388–9.

36 John Flete, *The History of Westminster Abbey*, ed. J. Armitage Robinson (Cambridge, 1909), p. 103.

37 *Feet of Fines for Essex I: 1182–1272*, ed. R.E.G. Kirk (Colchester, 1899), p. 50, no. 12.

38 *Papsturkunden in England*, I, nos 85–6.

was probably the Walter de Rokesbure, sacrist of Westminster, who was later commemorated at Durham.[39] James the Cellarer was named when he represented Abbot William Postard in a lawsuit of 4 November 1199.[40] Ralph, the almoner in the latter part of Henry II's reign, was named as a witness to a miracle ascribed to the hermit Godric of Finchale, while Peter, the almoner in King John's reign, was named as conveying money to a donor in exchange for his donation.[41] Two of the successors to Robert Moulsham, in his capacity as warden, or proctor, of the Lady Altar, are known from the 1220s or thereabouts. These are Walter, recorded as leasing a messuage to a tenant in Westminster,[42] and Henry of Colchester, who is recorded leasing land in Knightsbridge (Middx) to a tenant.[43] Stephen was chamberlain during the abbacy of Walter and of William Postard.[44] In witness-lists he takes precedence over laymen, and was presumably in charge of the Chamber, rather than a domestic chamberlain. Other officers, such as the precentor,[45] are usually not identified by name in Westminster's documents of this period although Thomas the cellarer was listed among the debtors of the financier William Cade, who was active in the earlier part of Henry II's reign.[46]

While most offices called simply for orderly and business-like habits, both the sacrist and the archdeacon might find life becoming rather too exciting at times. These officers shared between them the oversight of those who fled to sanctuary in the abbey – absconding criminals who might try to use their refuge as a base for further dubious deeds, or at any rate be likely to behave in an antisocial way within the precincts. Among their other duties, the monastic archdeacon had to disarm anyone who arrived carrying weapons, while the sacrist had to enforce good order, making sure there was always adequate lighting.[47]

The monastic community at Westminster probably never comprised more than eighty monks, the number for which Abbot Gilbert Crispin made

39 Pearce, *The Monks of Westminster*, p. 45.

40 *Westminster Abbey Charters*, no. 325.

41 Reginald of Durham, *Libellus de Vita et Miraculis S. Godrici, heremitae de Finchale*, ed. J. Stevenson, Surtees Soc., 20 (1847), p. 362; *Westminster Abbey Charters*, no. 485.

42 For Walter, see Westminster Abbey Muniment, no. 23638(d).

43 For Henry, see Westminster Abbey Muniment, no. 16218.

44 *Westminster Abbey Charters*, nos 319, 369; *Three Rolls of the King's Court . . . 1194–95*, ed. F.W. Maitland, Pipe Roll Soc., XIV (1891), p. 128.

45 *Westminster Abbey Charters*, no. 251.

46 H. Jenkinson, 'William Cade, a financier of the twelfth century', *English Historical Review*, 28 (1913), p. 227.

47 *Westminster Abbey Charters*, no. 349 and note; *Customary of the Benedictine Monasteries of Saint Augustine, Canterbury, and Saint Peter, Westminster*, II, 42ff, 47–8, 61, 268. See also Jane Sayers, 'Monastic Archdeacons', in C.N.L. Brooke, D.E. Luscombe, G.H. Martin and Dorothy Owen, eds, *Church and Government in the Middle Ages: Essays Presented to C.R. Cheney on his 70th Birthday* (Cambridge, 1976), pp. 177–203, esp. pp. 185–8.

financial provision.[48] Most of those living in the period covered by this study have remained anonymous, although a minority can be identified from references in charters or other documents.[49]

Occasional casual references indicate that in the eleventh century, Westminster, like some of the other larger religious houses, afforded some form of oversight of, and protection for, individual women wishing to live the religious life.[50] Women who can be identified include Brihtgyva the wife of Ælnoth, 'who took the nun's veil because she had no children'.[51] At some time in or before King Edward's reign, Ælfwynn the nun held Datchworth and Watton of Westminster.[52] These women, like some of their male counterparts, are known because property which they held or conveyed came into the possession of the abbey. The names of such individual religious sometimes occur in charters which are spurious in their present form, but which contain a substratum of hard facts. There is no reason to doubt the existence of these individuals or that they donated specific lands to Westminster. Even the legendary anchorite Wlsy or Wlsin, whose vision of St Peter is said to have motivated the re-building of the ancient abbey on Thorn Island, perhaps actually existed.[53]

Sources recording, or purporting to record, mid-eleventh-century transactions, also help in identifying monks of that period. An entry in Domesday Book concerns lands given to Westminster by King Edward, together with his godson Baldwin. This young man, whose name indicates that he was of Flemish, or perhaps of Lotharingian ancestry, evidently became a monk of the house.[54] Native English monks of Westminster, known from donations granted by themselves, or on their behalf, when they entered Westminster, include Ælfnoth; Alfwold of St Botulph's Gate; the son of Living; the son of Ælfwine Faremann; and Ægelwin son of Brihtmaer, a late entrant.[55] An even more hesitant donor was Wlsy Lickescoppe, who gave land in return for the spiritual benefits of confraternity 'whether or not he became a monk'.[56]

Sulcard, the eleventh-century chronicler, is of uncertain ethnic origin. His statement that he had seen the old church of Westminster implies that he had been a monk of the house in King Edward's reign, although due to the comparatively slow supercession of the old church by the new, this

48 Harvey, *Westminster Abbey and its Estates*, p. 28.

49 Pearce, *The Monks of Westminster*, is the pioneering study in this area.

50 Sally Thompson, *Women Religious: The Founding of English Nunneries after the Norman Conquest* (Oxford, 1991), p. 3.

51 The 'First Charter' of King William I for Westminster, printed in *Calendar of Charter Rolls*, IV, p. 334.

52 *Anglo-Saxon Writs*, ed. Florence E. Harmer, 2nd edn (Stamford, 1989), no. 79.

53 Flete, *The History of Westminster Abbey*, p. 45.

54 Barlow, *Edward the Confessor*, p. 191.

55 'First Charter' of King William I, *Cal. Charter Rolls* IV, pp. 333–4. For Alfwold, see also *Regesta*, I, XXXI. For Aelfnoth, citizen of London, see also Westminster Abbey Muniment, XXVI; calendared in *Regesta*, I, no. 251.

56 *Cal. Charter Rolls*, IV, p. 334.

conjecture is unproven. He was buried in the cloister, but moved by Henry III to a marble tomb in the new chapter house. The epitaph on this, *Sulcard major est* (Sulcard is the greater), ranked him above Abbot Edwin.[57]

Following the Norman Conquest, the names of new recruits quickly came to include those who were 'French', that is French in language and culture, including Normans, but perhaps also men from further south. Among these men was Reinald, a chaplain of William I;[58] and, probably, the monks Herbert, Nicholas and William, who witnessed a charter dating from c.1086.[59] William the chaplain, perhaps identical with this third witness, is known from one charter of Abbot Gilbert's.[60] One anonymous monastic recruit of this period was a Jew of London who converted to Christianity as a result of the arguments used by Abbot Gilbert in debate against the learned Jew from Mainz. This anonymous convert accepted baptism and became a monk at Westminster.[61] A second anonymous monk was detailed, early in 1093, to carry to the Norman abbey of Bec a message for Prior Baldric from his abbot, Anselm, who was on a visit to Westminster. Anselm commended to Prior Baldric the bearer of the letter, 'a monk of the lord Abbot Gilbert, whom I want you to receive with special kindness'. Anselm was probably in England in an effort to gain from King William II a confirmation of Bec's English lands. Anselm reported that the king still delayed to respond to the request, but the monk would tell them much more than could be entrusted to writing.[62]

The abbey was not averse to admitting to its own chapter individual monks who had compelling reasons to leave the monasteries to which they had been professed. The *Rule of St Benedict* prescribed stability, and ordered that monks were not to wander around from house to house looking for a more congenial community.[63] Westminster, however, occasionally admitted men who had been professed elsewhere, but had some strong reason for moving on. In the cases discussed in this chapter, it will be seen that all such recruits had some particular expertise or experience which would render them valuable members of their adopted community.

One such recruit was Maurice, clerk in the *familia* of Bishop Wulfstan of Worcester.[64] When the bishop died (in January 1095) Maurice, his

57 B.W. Scholz, 'Sulcard of Westminster: "Prologus de Construccione Westmonasterii" ', *Traditio*, 20 (1964), pp. 59–61. See, however, Harvey, *Westminster Abbey and its Estates*, pp. 372–3, note 9.

58 Westminster Abbey Muniment, XXVI (The *Telligraphus*); calendered *Regesta*, I, no. 251.

59 *Westminster Abbey Charters*, no. 236.

60 *Ibid*., no. 242.

61 Armitage Robinson, *Gilbert Crispin*, p. 82.

62 *Ibid*., p. 20.

63 *The Rule of St Benedict*, ed. and transl. J. McCann (London, 1952), caps. 1, 79.

64 *Hemingi Chartularium ecclesiae Wigorniensis*, ed. T. Hearne, 2 vols (Oxford, 1723), II, p. 424; *The Vita Wulfstani of William of Malmesbury*, ed. R.R. Darlington, Camden Third Series, XL (1928), p. xxxvi, note 2.

subdeacon, became a monk of Westminster, where he survived 'for full twenty years, a pattern of devotion'. In his new capacity he related having seen at Worcester a document recording a vision of the Christ Child experienced by King Edward.[65] Members of an episcopal *familia* were usually earmarked for higher things, but the death of the English Bishop Wulfstan and the arrival of the 'French' Samson put an end to such expectations on the part of the late bishop's English clerks. The name Maurice probably disguises an Englishman. Another of Wulfstan's secular clerks, Frewin, subsequently became a monk at Worcester itself.[66] While Westminster and Worcester were far apart, under prevailing conditions of travel, the existence of Westminster's substantial estates in Worcestershire would lead to frequent contact between monks of the cathedral priory and the abbey's representatives. Maurice is named, together with several other deceased monks of Westminster, in the abbey's entry on the Mortuary Roll of Abbot Vitalis of Savigny. The other monks listed with Maurice were Riculf, Turstin and William, probably all of 'French' ancestry, and the English Aegeluuard. Abbot Vitalis of Savigny died on 16 October 1122 so that all these Westminster monks were dead by that date, or at least by the time his Mortuary Roll reached England.[67]

When Abbot Gilbert and the convent gave to Great Malvern priory land adjoining Powick, two monks of Westminster, Hugh and Warner, were sent to perambulate its boundaries.[68] Warner was also present at the translation of St Etheldreda and other early saints, which took place at Ely in 1107.[69]

Monks sent on missions such as those to Bec or to Powick were probably men who had had some experience of the wider world before they entered religion. One such was Wulfric, an Englishman by his name, and a moneyer by profession. He is known to have struck coins both of William II and of Henry I. His occupation was a lucrative one, and he was enabled to give the church of St Bartholomew, Sudbury, to the abbey when he became a monk at Westminster, a donation which King Henry conceded.[70]

Not all East Anglian benefactors were equally sure that the monastic life was for them. When Henry son of Wilfrid received a life tenancy of the manor of Ockendon, Essex, terms were agreed to cover the eventuality that he, and subsequently his unnamed heir, might become monks of the abbey, but evidently they had their doubts. Many people, at this period, entered

65 Armitage Robinson, *Gilbert Crispin*, p. 31.

66 *Vita Wulfstani*, p. 36.

67 Armitage Robinson, *Gilbert Crispin*, p. 27. See also Rouleau du Bienheureux Vital, Abbé de Savigny, in *Rouleaux des Morts du IXe au XVe siècle*, ed. L. Delisle, Libraire de la Société de l'Histoire de France (Paris, 1866; reprinted Johnson Reprint Corporation, New York, 1968), item XXXVIII.

68 *Westminster Abbey Charters*, no. 243, note.

69 Pearce, *The Monks of Westminster*, p. 41, where it is suggested that Warner was a former monk of Bec.

70 *Westminster Abbey Charters*, no. 72.

religious houses when age and infirmity set in, and Henry's negotiations probably represented a form of insurance for his declining years.[71]

The more active monks continued to travel far afield on authorized business. A letter of Prior Osbert de Clare mentions a visit which he made to Prior Hugh of St Pancras, Lewes, in the company of Brothers Gregory and Godefrid.[72] Since Lewes lay at the far side of the Sussex Weald, their journey would be an arduous one, over difficult trackways. Brother Godefrid can probably be identified with the monk Godfrey, who, in 1133, reported to Pope Innocent II the intrusion into the abbey of Gilbert 'the Universal', bishop of London, eager to assert his jurisdiction. This episode occurred on the Feast of SS Peter and Paul, 29 June, and the pope's bull, issued in response to Westminster's plea for protection, was dated 30 September.[73] At least Godfrey did not have to brave the Alpine passes in winter, although trekking through Italy in the heat of summer would have its own discomforts, before he caught up with the pope in Pisa.

In Abbot Herbert's time, too, a monk from Worcestershire was received at Westminster. He was a monk of Great Malvern, a dependent cell of Westminster's, which perhaps encouraged the abbey to accept him. They then learned that he had been engaged in writing a missal for the chapter of Worcester, and sent him on there, with a supportive letter, which hints that he had good reason for leaving his own community.[74] Despite the intriguing information contained in this letter, this monk was not named.

Monks who were active during the abbacy of Gervase were named in several of his charters. Godric Lobbe may have flourished rather earlier, but he is known from a transaction between the abbot and the chapter of St Martin le Grand, in which it is stated that Godric had granted the church of St Agnes in London to Westminster, on the day on which he was made a monk of their church.[75] One charter of Abbot Gervase is attested by the monks Ansgod, Richard *de Bissea* (?Bushey, Herts.), and Hugh a novice monk.[76] It has been suggested that this trio represent some of the alien monks whose advice Gervase was accused of taking.[77] Both Ansgod and Richard, however, attested another charter of Gervase which, although spurious in its present form, is based on a genuine charter, from which it appears to take its witness-list.[78] Richard also witnessed a third charter of the abbot.[79] Probably he was a confidential advisor of Gervase, although there is no evidence to indicate that he was from another monastic community. This

71 *Ibid*., no. 247.
72 *Letters of Osbert de Clare*, no. 1.
73 *Papsturkunden in England*, I, no. 17; Flete, *The History of Westminster Abbey*, pp. 48–9.
74 *Westminster Abbey Charters*, no. 248A.
75 *Ibid*., no. 257.
76 *Ibid*., no. 258.
77 Harvey, 'Fee-Farms', p. 134.
78 *Westminster Abbey Charters*, no. 271; see also Harvey, 'Fee-Farms', pp. 131–3.
79 *Westminster Abbey Charters*, no. 270.

third charter is also witnessed by the monk John,[80] while three monks – Richard de Hair, Roger Branc, and W. Capes – witness yet another of Gervase's charters.[81] The latter can possibly be identified with the William Capes listed with Thomas the cellarer as a debtor of William Cade.[82]

Each abbot probably selected his own advisors from among the monastic community. Those who attested charters of Abbot Lawrence include Geoffrey,[83] and Peter of Windsor, who witnessed two charters.[84] One unnamed monk, who was evidently entrusted with confidential business involving other religious houses, is known to have visited the hermit, Godric of Finchale, on two occasions, while on business which involved the cathedral priory of Durham, a few miles from Godfric's hermitage. This monk is also recorded on a mission to Canterbury cathedral priory.[85]

Abbot Walter's advisors from within the monastic community appear to have included Alexander and Martin, who witnessed the same two charters.[86] These documents probably have a third monastic witness in common, Ralph 'the monk', [87] who can most likely be identified with Ralph de Arundel.[88] This last attestation is not followed by any style. At the time the charter was issued, the future abbot of that name may already have been a monk of Westminster's dependent cell of Hurley, but of course he may equally have become a *senior* of Westminster before being promoted to the position of prior of its daughter house. One charter of Abbot William Postard's is witnessed by three of his monk-chaplains, Adam, Gilbert and Philip.[89] By this abbacy, though, attestations of monks were giving way to those of the secular clerks employed by the abbot, and the actual status of other possible members of the monastic community is open to conjecture. Witnesses to charters of the late twelfth and early thirteenth century who are styled 'chaplain' were probably chaplains of the current abbot, but there is a slight possibility that some of these chaplains were employed in the household of one or other of the notables who were establishing residences in the vill of Westminster, and who maintained private chapels.[90] Frequent attestations by any individual indicate that he was an inmate of Westminster. A charter granted to the abbey by Rose *la custerere* is witnessed by Alexander,

80 *Ibid.*, no. 270.
81 *Ibid.*, no. 254.
82 Jenkinson, 'William Cade, a Financier of the Twelfth Century', p. 227.
83 *Westminster Abbey Charters*, no. 281.
84 *Ibid.*, nos 277–8.
85 Reginald of Durham, *Libellus de vita et miraculis S. Godrici, heremitae de Finchale*, pp. 236–9.
86 *Westminster Abbey Charters*, nos 306, 490.
87 *Ibid.*, p. 490.
88 *Ibid.*, no. 306.
89 *Ibid.*, no. 308.
90 *Ibid.*, nos 230, 312.

Richard and Simon, all styled chaplain.[91] Alexander 'the chaplain' witnessed two further charters,[92] while Alexander 'the priest' witnessed two more.[93] Richard 'the priest' witnessed one of those attested by Alexander 'the priest'.[94] Simon 'the chaplain' witnessed two of those attested by Alexander 'the chaplain', [95] including one witnessed by Alexander 'the clerk',[96] and one without either of these associates. This last document is, however, attested by Salomon the chaplain,[97] who also attests two further charters.[98] As Salomon 'the priest', he attests one charter witnessed by Alexander 'the priest'.[99] Roger 'the chaplain' witnesses one of those attested by Salomon 'the chaplain',[100] and one without any obvious colleague.[101] Robert 'the chaplain' witnesses one charter, seemingly without associates.[102] William 'the chaplain', however, witnesses one charter in conjunction with Salomon 'the chaplain'.[103] Clearly the monastic chaplains of this period were not uniformly accorded this style by Westminster's scribes. Fully-professed monks usually took priest's orders, and the style of priest, which evidently carried a status of its own, was used interchangeably with that of chaplain.

Westminster's dependent cell of St Bartholomew's, Sudbury, probably contained only two inmates at any given time. Ivo gave two parts of his demesne tithe of *Torp* when he became a monk there, in the reign of Henry I.[104] Towards the end of the twelfth century, two Sudbury monks, Robert de Clara and Martin, witnessed a donation to the cell.[105] In the reign of Richard I, Mr Robert son of Godric, of Sudbury, joined the priory, donating land to it, with the consent of his heir, and confirming an earlier grant.[106] This charter reinforces the likelihood that recruitment was largely local, but it is conjectural whether Westminster monks were sent, at times, to reinforce the community in numbers and in standards of observance.

91 *Ibid.*, no. 387.
92 *Ibid.*, nos 392, 451.
93 *Ibid.*, nos 444, 460.
94 *Ibid.*, no. 460.
95 *Ibid.*, no. 392, 480.
96 *Ibid.*, no. 480.
97 *Ibid.*, no. 445.
98 *Ibid.*, nos 416, 440.
99 *Ibid.*, no. 444.
100 *Ibid.*, no. 416.
101 *Ibid.*, no. 406.
102 *Ibid.*, no. 390.
103 *Ibid.*, no. 440.
104 Dugdale, *Monasticon Anglicanum*, III, p. 459, no. II.
105 Westminster Abbey Muniment, no. 20759.
106 Westminster Abbey Muniment, no. 20766.

6

Scribes and Clerks of Westminster Abbey

Scribes or clerks working between the abbacy of Edwin and that of Herbert can rarely be identified by name. Sometimes, though, the work of one man can be singled out and on rare occasions his preoccupations, and the influences upon him, can be glimpsed. Sulcard, the historian of the abbey, at work c.1080, certainly drew on the early archives of the house, but he cannot be firmly identified as one of its scribes, let alone as one of its numerous forgers.[1]

A second Westminster writer who possibly worked on the abbey's charters was the monk Warner, most likely to be identified with the man of that name who energetically examined the remains of St Etheldreda of Ely, when she was translated in 1106. Warner was reputedly the author of a book of homilies and of a collection of extracts from early Patristic writers.[2] One contemporary of Warner's was William, a clerk of Abbot Gilbert in the later 1090s.[3] He can perhaps be identified with the William the chaplain who witnessed a charter of Gilbert's towards the end of his abbacy.[4] These men tentatively identified as among the scribes of the abbey were apparently all in monastic orders. Just when secular clerks first began to be employed is conjectural. Apparently Abbot Gervase's clerks were seculars, but since Herbert's clerks cannot be positively identified, the approximate date of the changing pattern of employment cannot now be determined.

The very anonymity of the scribes of the late eleventh and earlier twelfth centuries adds a further dimension of uncertainty to any examination of their work, since it was over these very decades that the bulk of Westminster's

1 *The Crawford Collection of Early Charters and Documents now in the Bodleian Library*, ed. A.S. Napier and W.H. Stevenson (Oxford, 1895), p. 92; B.W. Scholz, 'Two Forged Charters from the Abbey of Westminster and their Relationship with St Denis', *English Historical Review*, 76 (1961), pp. 471–2.

2 On Warner's participation in the examination of St Etheldreda's remains, see *Liber Eliensis*, ed. E.O. Blake, Camden Third Series, XCII (1962), p. 232; and for his writings, Richard Widmore, *A History of the Church of St Peter of Westminster* (London, 1751, p. 22.

3 *Westminster Abbey Charters, 1066–c.1214*, ed. Emma Mason, assisted by the late Jennifer Bray, continuing the work of the late Desmond J. Murphy, London Record Society, 25 (1988), no. 488.

4 *Ibid.*, no. 242.

output of forged charters was produced. There were various reasons why the monks should be put to work composing such documents – including the staking of a claim in properties wrongfully alienated, or about to become so; the assertion of franchisal rights and privileges in the abbey's various estates; and, very important, the assertion of exemption from the jurisdiction of the bishop of London. But little can be deduced about the men behind this output. The terminology of the forged Great Charter of King Edgar owes something to Frankish formularies, and more especially to documents in the archives of the French royal abbey of St Denis. While French-speaking monks arrived after the Norman Conquest, the direct link with St Denis is not easily proven.[5] Further major charters, the Second Charter of King Edward, and the Great Charter of Dunstan, also display features in common with charters of the abbey of St Denis which had intermittently maintained links with England since the earlier seventh century.[6] A former monk of St Denis perhaps took up residence in Westminster, but the inspiration for the charters may equally have come through an intermediary. Baldwin, abbot of Bury St Edmunds (1065–1097/8), was a former monk of St Denis, and it has been suggested that he played a key role in instigating the output of forged charters both at Westminster and at other houses.[7]

A charter in the name of King Offa was almost certainly concocted in the late eleventh century.[8] Further charters in the names, respectively, of Edgar, Ethelred and Dunstan, and over thirty in the name of King Edward, have all given rise to suspicion, to a greater or lesser degree. That is not to say that all are equally dubious, but rather that they may have undergone some 'improvement'.[9] English scribes were certainly employed in the *scriptorium* well into Gilbert Crispin's term of office, as is shown by the English-language sanctuary writs.[10] By Abbot Gilbert's time, the royal court was no longer issuing writs in the English language, so that it is likely that an English-language writ addressed by King William I to Abbot Gilbert was actually drawn up by an English scribe at Westminster and then presented at the royal court for sealing.[11] As the races merged linguistically in mid-twelfth-century

5 *The Crawford Collection*, pp. 91–2.

6 Scholz, 'Two Forged Charters from the Abbey of Westminster', pp. 469–70, 472.

7 Antonia Gransden, 'Baldwin, Abbot of Bury St Edmunds, 1065–1097', in R. Allen Brown, ed., *Anglo-Norman Studies, IV, Proceedings of the Battle Conference 1981* (Woodbridge, 1982), pp. 65–76.

8 The 'originals' of this grant are: Westminster Abbey Muniment II (twelfth-century) and Westminster Abbey Muniment III (eleventh- or twelfth-century). Printed: *Cartularium Saxonicum*, ed. W. de Gray Birch, 3 vols and index (London, 1885–93), I, 245. For further discussion, see P.H. Sawyer, *Anglo-Saxon Charters, an Annotated List and Bibliography* (London, 1968), no. 124; *Anglo-Saxon Writs*, ed. Florence E. Harmer, 2nd edn (Stamford, 1989), p. 501; Barbara Harvey, *Westminster Abbey and its Estates in the Middle Ages* (Oxford, 1977), p. 345.

9 *Westminster Abbey Charters*, table on pp. 321–2.

10 *Ibid.*, nos 238–9.

11 *Ibid.*, no. 42.

England,[12] practices in the *scriptorium* would merge, too, so that it is exceptional to find in a charter of Abbot William Postard that the scribe was using French numerals and measurements.[13]

The suspect Anglo-Saxon charters indicate that forgery was probably well under way at Westminster long before Prior Osbert de Clare assumed control of the *scriptorium*'s operations. Osbert's zealous promotion of the cult of King Edward, and of the privileged status of his great church, indicate that the prior saw himself as a man with a mission. By promoting his objectives he also drew attention to his own claims to high office – anticipating the *dictum* current in Westminster circles some seven hundred years later, that to succeed in life a man must persevere in promoting his own subject, one which he uniquely understands.[14]

Osbert's leading role in the production of forged charters has long been recognized, but he worked with a team of highly professional scribes.[15] Although these men are not known by name, Pierre Chaplais demonstrated that certain men were responsible for writing particular groups of forgeries. He showed that one of Abbot Herbert's scribes wrote the three great charters in the name of Edward the Confessor.[16] Another scribe, whose hand occurs in charters of Abbot Gervase, wrote writs attributed to King Edward, and to William I, not only for Westminster but also for other religious houses. He even wrote a forged charter in the name of Gervase's father, King Stephen.[17] Chaplais also showed clearly that Prior Osbert was the mastermind in this ongoing enterprise, drafting texts even if he did not write out the formal versions.[18] The production team did not confine its activities to the more impressively-worded charters, such as the solemn diplomas and papal bulls for which they are now best known. The texts of genuine grants of land were sometimes embellished by the addition of clauses which accorded to the property certain fiscal or jurisdictional exemptions and privileges. Late eleventh-century writs were sometimes enhanced by the addition of a place of issue, or by a set of attestations.[19] The attestations of certain eminent late eleventh-century personalities – Walkelin, bishop of Winchester; William of

12 *Dialogus de Scaccario*, ed. and transl. C. Johnson with corrections by F.E.L. Carter and D.E. Greenway (Oxford, 1983), p. 53.

13 *Westminster Abbey Charters*, no. 309.

14 The importance to a man in public life of 'having a subject' recurs in several of the novels of Anthony Trollope. See, for instance, *Phineas Finn* (reprinted Harmondsworth, 1972), p. 553.

15 P. Chaplais, 'The Original Charters of Herbert and Gervase, Abbots of Westminster (1121–1157)', in P.M. Barnes and C.F. Slade, eds, *A Mediaeval Miscellany for Doris Mary Stenton*, Pipe Roll Soc., new series, XXXVI (1960), pp. 89–110; reprinted in P. Chaplais, *Essay in Mediaeval Government and Administration* (London, 1981), pp. XVIII 89–110, *passim*, and esp. pp. 96–7.

16 *Ibid.*, pp. 91–2.

17 *Ibid.*, p. 97

18 *Ibid.*, pp. 91–6.

19 *Westminster Abbey Charters*, pp. 10–11.

St Calais, bishop of Durham; Robert, count of Meulan; Robert d'Oilly; Roger Bigod and Ivo Taillebois – occur on one genuine charter for Westminster but were perhaps added later.[20] This particular combination of 'the great and the good' evidently appealed to the staff of the Westminster *scriptorium* and their attestations were added *en bloc* to at least ten charters of doubtful authenticity.[21]

While the scribe's hand can be used as a test of the authenticity of an original charter, cartulary copies cannot be examined in this way. On the other hand, it is still possible to detect cases where a scribe, concocting a supposed royal grant, inadvertently juxtaposed individuals who did not simultaneously bear the titles with which they are credited.[22] The individual scribes, or at any rate their supervisors, were not complacent about the quality of their output, as is shown by the survival of two or more texts relating to the same property, each embellished fractionally more than its predecessor.[23] Most such addenda would be intended to maximize the financial returns from any given property. One additional reason for adding a place of issue and a particular set of witnesses to some eleventh-century charters was, apparently, to imply that William I habitually kept the Christmas feast at Westminster, marking the occasion by the gift of a manor or two to the abbey.[24] In the gusto with which these charters were expanded, and attestations (chiefly 'the usual ones') were added, the scribes overlooked the fact that, by providing virtually identical witness-lists for two distinct grants, in two separate instances they effectively assigned a second donation to the abbey at the same Christmas.[25] No doubt the abbot would have welcomed such generosity, and doubtless King William preferred the company of some of his magnates to that of others, yet the coincidences reveal a forger with more enthusiasm than finesse.

Most of the expanded charters dated, or purported to date, from the reign of William I. The scribes amended the wording of these so as to strengthen Westminster's title to the lands in question by 'demonstrating' that certain

20 *Regesta Regum Anglo-Normannorum*, I, ed. H.W.C. Davis (Oxford, 1913), p. 129, no. XXXVIII; calendared *Westminster Abbey Charters*, no. 37.

21 The relevant texts are printed respectively in *Anglo-Saxon Writs*, pp. 493–4; J. Armitage Robinson, *Gilbert Crispin, Abbot of Westminster* (Cambridge, 1911), pp. 129–31, nos 4–5; *Regesta*, I, nos XII, XXXI, XXXVII and XLIV. One occurs in Westminster Abbey Domesday (Muniment Book 11), f. 278v, and another in British Library, MS Cotton Faustina A III, f. 64v. They are calendared in *Westminster Abbey Charters*, nos 11–12, 25, 28, 30, 35–6, 38, 40, 46. I am grateful to David Bates for discussion on this point.

22 See, for instance, *Westminster Abbey Charters*, notes to nos 11, 13.

23 For instance *ibid.*, nos 62–4, 70, 106.

24 *Ibid.*, nos 11, 28, 34, 38.

25 Identical attestations occur in *Regesta*, I, no. 234 and no. XXXVII; calendared *Westminster Abbey Charters*, nos 28 and 38. Witness lists which are almost identical have been added to *Regesta*, I, no. XII and *ibid.*, no. 143; calendared *Westminster Abbey Charters*, nos 11, 34.

lands were held before the Norman Conquest,[26] or at latest by the time of the Domesday Survey.[27] Charters of Henry I were occasionally 'improved' in order to incorporate grants of franchisal rights[28] and a few charters of Stephen were imaginatively and extensively enlarged so as to increase the returns from the land in question.[29]

To add authenticity to the end product, the handwriting of genuine royal writs for Westminster was carefully followed by the scribes, some of whom proved more adept at this work than others. The imitator would most often be required to produce another text in the name of the king who granted the original, but on one occasion, the hand of one of King Stephen's scribes was imitated to produce a purported writ of Henry I.[30] While Prior Osbert, and those who worked under his directions, were probably responsible for the large output of dubious documents which survive for the period down to 1154, it is clear that they were followed by well-trained successors capable of adjusting texts issued in the name of King Henry II.[31] A charter of Abbot Gervase was amplified as late as the thirteenth century.[32] The lavish terms of charters allegedly issued for Westminster by successive twelfth-century kings at, or soon after, their coronation seem unnaturally generous. Those surviving in the names of Henry I, King Stephen and Henry II are clearly not authentic.[33] That issued in the name of Richard I closely follows the earlier texts. It bears the king's Great Seal, which was probably removed from one of his genuine grants for the abbey.[34] By 1189, it is unlikely that the royal seal would be affixed to a document drafted in a monastic *scriptorium* although the two 'originals' of Henry II's charter may indicate that a text of this was drafted, and then fair-copied, at the abbey, with a view to presenting it for authentication.[35] Richard's charter is dated 6 October 1189, only three days

26 *Westminster Abbey Charters*, nos 17, 20.

27 *Ibid*., no. 44.

28 *Ibid*., nos 62–4, 74.

29 *Regesta Regum Anglo-Normannorum, III, 1135–1154*, ed. H.A. Cronne and R.H.C. Davis (Oxford, 1968), nos 928–9, 939–41.

30 T.A.M. Bishop, *Scriptores Regis* (Oxford, 1961), pp. 8–9 and Plates VI–VII. For further discussion on questions of authenticity, see Chaplais, 'The Original Charters of Herbert and Gervase', *passim*.

31 *Westminster Abbey Charters*, nos 123, 126, 129, 138.

32 *Ibid*., no. 217. For discussion of the reasons for making this late forgery, see Barbara Harvey, 'Abbot Gervase de Blois and the Fee Farms of Westminster Abbey', *Bulletin of the Institute of Historical Research*, 40 (1967), pp. 139–41.

33 *Regesta Regum Anglo-Normannorum*, II, ed. C. Johnson and H.A. Cronne (Oxford, 1956), no. I; *Regesta III*, no. 929. Stephen's charter closely follows the text of that in the name of Henry I. Henry II's charter exists as two 'originals': Westminster Abbey Muniment, XLIII and BL Cotton Charter VI.5; calendared *Westminster Abbey Charters*, no. 123. It closely follows the grants in the names of Henry I and Stephen, and is clearly a late-twelfth-century forgery; Chaplais, 'Original Charters', p. 96, note 6.

34 *Westminster Abbey Charters*, no. 140.

35 On the question of the royal authentication, in the twelfth century, of documents drawn up in a monastic *scriptorium*, see R. Mortimer, 'The Charters of Henry II: What

after his coronation. It is arguable that on that occasion he was shown the reputed grants of his predecessors, gave his verbal assent to their terms, and an undertaking to ratify a similar charter in his own name, which was prepared in the abbey's *scriptorium*. Certainly there is little change in the wording from one to another in the series, apart from adjustments to the attestations and the dating clauses.

The scribes of the abbey would not always be employed on such prestigious projects. There would always be a certain volume of routine documents to be drafted, many of them leaving little trace in the archives. Once documents had outlived their useful life, the parchment, an expensive commodity, was likely to be recycled, as with a number of charters dating from the decades around 1200, which were later trimmed to matching dimensions and stitched together so that the reverse sides provided material for an account roll.[36] Another of the scribes' routine activities would be the provision of liturgical manuscripts, likely to be worn out with constant use, hence Abbot Gervase's provision of revenues for the repair of books.[37]

From the time of Abbot Gervase, the clerks and scribes of the abbey can be named with growing confidence. This is due in part to the larger numbers of charters surviving from each abbacy. The texts of many of the older charters survive only in the form of cartulary copies. In the case of genuine charters, other than the forged showpiece documents, it was generally the case that, the older they were, the more likely the copyist would abridge the witness list to a mere *Hiis testibus* ('with these witnessing'). Gervase's charters, however, were rarely abridged.[38]

By the mid-twelfth century, the professional style is usually 'clerk' rather than 'scribe'. Probably many such clerks were recompensed for their services by being presented to benefices in the gift of Westminster. One possible case of this kind is that of Alger the clerk, who was granted land in Ham (Essex), formerly held by his grandfather Puncelin.[39] On the other hand, this charter may be an early instance of the well-documented practice of later abbots of recompensing clerks with lands in the Home Counties. Two further clerks who were perhaps also parochial clergy were Master Leofwin, formerly a tenant of Westminster at Wheathampstead (Herts.),[40] and Alured the clerk of Wheathampstead who, with his son William, attested a charter of Abbot Gervase.[41]

are the Criteria for Authenticity?' in Marjorie Chibnall, ed., *Anglo-Norman Studies, XII, Proceedings of the Battle Conference 1989* (Woodbridge, 1990), pp. 119–34; see esp. p. 21.

36 *Westminster Abbey Charters*, p. 6 and no. 347.

37 *Ibid*., no. 251.

38 *Ibid*., no. 256, is exceptional in being a charter of Gervase surviving, in abridged form, only in the cartularies of Reading abbey.

39 *Westminster Abbey Charters*, no. 267.

40 *Ibid*., no. 269.

41 *Ibid*., no. 267.

When named clerks recur in successive charters, however, it is likely that they represent some of those currently employed at the abbey. These would, by this period, be men in secular orders, rather than monastic scribes. Elias the clerk witnessed two charters of Abbot Gervase,[42] and, as Elias son of Goldwin, was granted land in London, from which the annual rent was to contribute towards the cost of the monks' clothing.[43] Master Hervey, ranked among the abbot's clerks, witnessed two charters of Gervase.[44] Ralph the clerk witnessed three charters of this abbot,[45] and in two of them took precedence over the clerk Maurice.[46] Probably several clerks were employed at any given period, but their identification is not always a straightforward matter. In one charter of Abbot Gervase, confirming to a tenant land in London, the witnesses include Robert, clerk of the Tower, together with other local clergy and residents. These included a woman, Philomena, whose attestation is immediately followed by that of Amand the clerk, and then by Master Hervey and Elias the clerk.[47] Since Amand does not recur elsewhere in the abbey's charters, it may be deduced that he, like Robert, was a Londoner who witnessed on behalf of the recipient.

There was some continuity of clerical personnel after the succession of Abbot Lawrence. While Elias 'the chaplain'[48] can more likely be identified as a monk than as the clearly secular clerk employed by Gervase, Elias the clerk is not to be confused with a namesake in the service of the bishop of Lincoln, presented to the church of Datchworth at the request of Abbot Lawrence.[49] Mr Ralph, who witnessed one of Lawrence's charters, can probably be identified with Ralph the clerk of Gervase's time,[50] while Gervase's clerk Maurice was probably the Master Maurice who witnessed two of Lawrence's charters.[51] In his capacity as perpetual vicar of Sawbridgeworth, he was also assigned an income from that church, on payment of an annual pension of £15 to the abbey.[52] Since Abbot Lawrence himself had studied in the schools, it is not surprising that he chose to employ a number of fellow-graduates. Even so, it is uncertain that these were increasingly recruited during his abbacy, since *magistri* were clearly not accorded their academic title in every witness-list, as already demonstrated in the cases of Maurice and Ralph. Roger the clerk, who witnessed both one grant of Abbot Lawrence[53] and also a confirmation made to the abbey,[54] can probably be identified with the Mr Roger of Lulworth who witnessed another of Lawrence's charters.[55]

Simon the clerk (never *magister*) witnessed four of Lawrence's surviving charters.[56] He also witnessed a confirmation made to the abbey of the church

42 *Ibid.*, nos 255, 270.
43 *Ibid.*, no. 258.
44 *Ibid.*, no. 255; see also 258.
45 *Ibid.*, nos 263, 265, 269.
46 *Ibid.*, nos 263, 265.
47 *Ibid.*, no. 255.
48 *Ibid.*, no. 277.
49 *Ibid.*, nos, 222, 468.
50 *Ibid.*, no. 275
51 *Ibid.*, nos 275, 280.
52 *Ibid.*, no. 284.
53 *Ibid.*, no. 275.
54 *Ibid.*, no. 470.
55 *Ibid.*, no. 285.
56 *Ibid.*, nos 275, 280, 284–5.

of Sawbridgeworth,[57] and can probably be identified with the abbatial clerk Simon of Denham.[58] On one occasion he is specifically designated 'clerk of Abbot Lawrence'.[59] This raises the possibility that other clerks were employed by the monastic chapter, although that is unproven. Further clerks who each attested one charter of Abbot Lawrence included Robert,[60] Mr Gregory,[61] and Mr Walter de Constant. It is tempting to identify this last attestation with that of the Cornish cleric who eventually became in turn bishop of Lincoln and archbishop of Rouen.[62] Whether or not that is the case, he was still quite junior when attesting Lawrence's charter, in fifth place among the witnesses, and with both Roger of Lulworth and Simon the clerk taking precedence over him.

Mr Maurice, clerk of Abbot Walter, was probably identical with the clerk Maurice who served Gervase and Lawrence, and was seemingly junior to the clerk Ralph. The latter can perhaps be identified with Ranulf the clerk of Feering, who retained Feering church when he joined the Arrouaisian community of Missenden. It was recovered for Westminster c.1176–80, when Maurice was presented.[63] One man who undoubtedly owed his advancement to Abbot Walter was his nephew Walter, who attested one charter of his with the style of clerk and another without it.[64] In 1184 Abbot Walter and the convent presented Geoffrey 'de Turre' (of the Tower), clerk, as perpetual vicar of the church of St Margaret Eastcheap.[65] The clerks Jordan,[66] Michael,[67] and Richard[68] each attested one charter of Abbot Walter. Mr Geoffrey of Norwich,[69] and Thomas[70] witnessed two. The confirmation by the archdeacon of the church of Datchworth to Elias was witnessed by Mr Hugh, Mr Jordan and Thomas, clerk and *tornatus*.[71] Mr Nicholas witnessed two charters of Abbot Walter and also the grant which Geoffrey de St Leger made to him. Nicholas was instituted to two churches in Lincolnshire, Doddington and Thorpe-on-the-Hill, from which he received annual pensions.[72] Two further clerks, who probably witnessed on behalf of recipients of grants, rather than as members of the abbot's entourage, were Robert the clerk de *Becham* (?Beckenham),[73] and Mr William de Actun.[74] Alexander, a clerk in the time of Abbot Walter, or of Lawrence, was perhaps employed by William de Mandeville, earl of Essex.[75] Vivian the clerk identified himself as the

57 *Ibid.*, no. 470.
58 *Ibid.*, no. 404.
59 *Ibid.*, no. 285.
60 *Ibid.*, no. 275.
61 *Ibid.*, no. 277.
62 *Ibid.*, no. 285; John Le Neve, *Fasti Ecclesiae Anglicanae 1066–1300. III. Lincoln*, compiled Diana E. Greenway (London, 1977), pp. 2, 35.
63 *Westminster Abbey Charters*, no. 207.
64 *Ibid.*, nos 297, 300.
65 *Ibid.*, no. 194.
66 *Ibid.*, no. 298.
67 *Ibid.*, no. 290.
68 *Ibid.*, no. 303.
69 *Ibid.*, nos 297, 304.
70 *Ibid.*, nos 297, 304.
71 *Ibid.*, no. 468.
72 *Ibid.*, nos 298, 306, 490; for the Lincolnshire churches *ibid.*, nos 209, 224.
73 *Ibid.*, no. 298.
74 *Ibid.*, no. 301.
75 *Ibid.*, no. 464.

scribe of a charter granted to the convent by Leofwine Kepe in the reign of Henry II.[76]

From the later twelfth century onwards, there are growing uncertainties involved in identifying the abbot's clerks. In part this was due to the growing numbers of charters relating to properties in London, and naturally attested by London clergy; secondly, with the increasing use of Westminster, in place of Winchester, as the focus of the royal government, frequent contacts developed between the administrators of Westminster abbey and the personnel of the Exchequer. While this is discussed in detail in a later chapter, it should be born in mind at this juncture that not all clerks witnessing charters of the abbot of Westminster in the later twelfth century were necessarily men in his employment. In the late twelfth century, another obstacle to the satisfactory identification of the abbey's scribes is that occupational surnames were emerging. In a late twelfth-century charter, for instance, attention was drawn to the fact that Clerk was the cognomen of Ralph, and not his professional designation.[77] Abbot William Postard's clerks included his brother, Mr Ernulph, *alias* Ernald.[78] This man witnessed several grants by the abbot and was involved in the negotiations between Westminster and Godstow nunnery over the church of Bloxham.[79] As Mr Ern[ulph] he witnessed a charter granted to the abbey[80] and was himself a tenant of the house, holding land in the vill of Westminster.[81] Albin the clerk is named in four charters in this period,[82] and Mr Simon de Baresworth attested three.[83] Mr Adam of Cranford and Gilbert of Cranford, clerk, had an interest in Westminster's church of Sunbury (Middx), and were possibly employed by Abbot William.[84]

Mr John of Winchester, the last witness (customarily the scribe's place) to a grant of Abbot William, was possibly one of his clerks.[85] Mr Elias,[86] probably not the mid-twelfth-century clerk of that name, Richard the clerk,[87] and William the clerk[88] were possibly employed by Abbot William Postard. On the other hand Sawal the clerk, a resident of Westminster in the later twelfth century,[89] and Thomas of Newgate, scribe,[90] were perhaps employed at the Exchequer rather than by the abbot. Clerks and scribes of Abbot Ralph Arundel are even more difficult to identify with any certainty. One charter of his was witnessed by Ernulf Postard, but without any professional designation.[91] Hereward the scribe witnessed three grants made to the abbey in this period.[92] Four clerks – Ralph,[93] Richard de Stapelek,[94] Stephen of Barking[95]

76 *Ibid*., no. 404.
77 *Ibid*., no. 406; see also no. 407.
78 *Ibid*., no. 312.
79 *Ibid*., nos 307, 313, 323, 481.
80 *Ibid*., no. 353.
81 *Ibid*., no. 441.
82 *Ibid*., nos 406, 415, 416, 457.
83 *Ibid*., nos 307, 323, 481.
84 *Ibid*., no. 315.
85 *Ibid*., no. 322.
86 *Ibid*., no. 456.
87 *Ibid*., no. 352.
88 *Ibid*., no. 456.
89 *Ibid*., no. 406.
90 *Ibid*., no. 313.
91 *Ibid*., no. 336.
92 *Ibid*., nos 417, 444, 480.
93 *Ibid*., nos 466, 467.
94 *Ibid*., no. 484.
95 *Ibid*., no. 461.

and Walter[96] – were perhaps employed by the abbot. Nicholas Fitz Geoffrey, scribe of one grant made by John Testard to Isabel Mauduit,[97] was perhaps employed on the staff of the Exchequer, since Isabel and her husband, the chamberlain Robert Mauduit, drew on the expertise of his official clerks, a point which is to be considered in more detail in a later chapter. Similarly, given the frequency with which financial officers were surnamed 'of Ely', it is likely that Henry the clerk 'of Ely', resident of St Clement's parish and father of Walter,[98] was employed at the Exchequer. The clerks Elias and Thomas, jointly attesting one charter of c.1200, were perhaps employed in the administration of the archdiocese of Canterbury, as were other witnesses to the charter in which they occur.[99]

One abbey clerk, at an early stage of his career, was Alexander of Swerford. He was employed by Abbot Ralph, and was granted some of Westminster's houses between Ludgate and Fleet Bridge.[100] He may be identical with the clerk Alexander who attested other charters issued about the same time.[101] Louis the clerk of the Exchequer,[102] *alias* clerk of Rockingham,[103] probably owed his start in life to the Mauduit family, castellans of Rockingham in the twelfth century, and he evidently worked as a subordinate of Robert Mauduit in the Exchequer.[104] His professional expertise was also available in a private capacity. He wrote the charter by which Abbot William granted property in Longditch to Robert Mauduit, and that whereby he granted to Robert Mauduit a private chapel in his town house,[105] one by which Isabel Mauduit granted properties to the Lady Altar,[106] and that whereby Nicholas Fitz Geoffrey son of Fredesent granted to the abbey a rent to provide lights for the Lady Altar.[107] In addition he witnessed charters granted by Abbot William,[108] Abbot Ralph,[109] and Prior Robert Moulsham,[110] as well as numerous charters of benefactors.[111] The recorded

96 *Ibid.*, no. 390.
97 *Ibid.*, no. 421.
98 *Ibid.*, no. 393.
99 *Ibid.*, no. 482.
100 *Ibid.*, no. 327.
101 *Ibid.*, nos 335, 346, 423, 439, 480. All are attested by known members of the Exchequer staff.
102 *Ibid.*, nos 414, 424, 426, 432.
103 *Ibid.*, nos 311, 443–4.
104 *The Beauchamp Cartulary Charters 1100–1268*, ed. Emma Mason, Pipe Roll Society, new series, 43 (London, 1980), p. xxxij, nos 185, 188, 190–2, 194–8, 213, 218, 226–7, 229–30.
105 *Westminster Abbey Charters*, nos 311–312.
106 *Ibid.*, no. 422.
107 *Ibid.*, no. 443.
108 *Ibid.*, no. 321.
109 *Ibid.*, no. 335.
110 *Ibid.*, no. 346.
111 *Ibid.*, nos 407, 412, 414, 420, 423, 424, 426–7, 429, 432, 441–2, 444, 458, 461.

activities of Louis of Rockingham and Alexander of Swerford, in relation to the abbey, suggest that while Louis initially became involved with Westminster because the Exchequer chamberlain and his wife wanted their dealings with the abbey to be precisely recorded, he developed an interest of his own, hence his willingness to act as a witness in so many transactions on the abbey's behalf. Alexander, on the other hand, evidently started out as a clerk of the abbot, but was offered the opportunity of joining the Exchequer staff. Later he was to become one of its most distinguished officials.[112]

Such interaction of the abbey's clerks and those of the Exchequer might be thought to work to Westminster's advantage, leading to the adoption of the latest techniques of drafting documents. The weight of the evidence does not, however, support this theory. Charters were dated in relation to the most notable events to have come to the notice of the scribe responsible for drafting the document. A charter of Abbot Walter's is dated 'Michaelmas six years after the coronation of Henry the Young King and the martyrdom of Blessed Thomas' [Becket], i.e. 29 September 1176.[113] A charter of Abbot William's specified that the term of a lease would begin at 'Easter next after the death of the abbot of Caen who came to England with Master Philip, bishop-elect of Durham'. Abbot Robert of Caen died on 11 April 1196, and Easter that year was on 21 April.[114] When the summoner of the abbey leased out his office for twelve years, he specified that the term would begin at 'The Feast of St John the Baptist next after the election of Hugh of Wells as bishop-elect of Lincoln, in the eleventh year of King John and in the ninth year of the blessing of Ralph as abbot of Westminster' (i.e. 24 June 1209).[115] Hugh of Wells, as a recent royal chancellor, would probably be a familiar figure to the abbey's clerks, but they did not emulate his practice of having documents dated by day and month. Similarly, while royal *acta* were now enrolled, and Hugh, once installed in Lincoln, was to pioneer the keeping of episcopal registers, Westminster had not as yet devised any satisfactory means of registering the *acta* of the abbot and monks. The great cartularies of the abbey date only from the late thirteenth century onwards. Meanwhile, given the fragile nature of charters, some of those who had dealings with the abbey, and notably men who were involved in the royal administration, wanted to ensure the safe-keeping of their recorded transactions with Westminster. Before royal *acta* began to be enrolled in the 1190s, the officials in royal government, or those who had dealings with them, occasionally fined to have their private charters copied on to the Pipe Rolls.[116] By analogy, royal

112 Matthew Paris, *Chronica Majora*, ed. H.R. Luard, IV, Rolls Series (1877), pp. 587–8; F.M. Powicke, *King Henry III and the Lord Edward* (Oxford, 1947), pp. 90–91; R.C. Stacey, *Politics, Policy and Finance under Henry III, 1216–1245* (Oxford, 1987), pp. 41–2, 257.

113 *Westminster Abbey Charters*, no. 298.

114 *Ibid.*, no. 307 and note.

115 *Ibid.*, no. 402.

116 *Beauchamp Cartulary*, pp. xv, xxix, xlj, no. 312 note.

officials having business with the abbey wanted their transactions recorded in some comparably sacrosanct document. Ralph Fitz Stephen, a prominent member of the royal court, acquired a lease of abbey property in Westminster, c.1200x1203. He ensured that the resulting charter stated that the terms had been agreed in full chapter, that these terms were to be transcribed into the abbey's martyrology, and that a chirograph, or authenticated duplicate, of the charter, was deposited in the abbey's Treasury.[117] The chamberlain Robert Mauduit and his wife Isabel, with other benefactors of the Lady Altar, likewise successfully petitioned Ralph to have their names recorded in the martyrology.[118]

The scribes varied their prose style according to the people directly involved in the transaction in question. The grandly-resounding phrases of the big set-piece forgeries in the names of King Edward[119] and King William[120] were in a special category of their own. In the case of genuine charters relating to current transactions, the practice varied between a brisk and business-like style in charters directed towards rank-and-file tenants, and a markedly more florid style, usually, although not invariably, adopted when the recipient was in clerical or religious orders, or else was a person of considerable consequence. An early example of this florid style appears in a charter of Abbot Vitalis to an unidentified Gerald.[121] This same florid style was adopted in charters granted in the name of the abbot to the monks, probably to underline the inviolable nature of their property rights. For instance, 'florid' charters in the name of Abbot Herbert were addressed to Great Malvern Priory, Worcester cathedral priory, and the nuns of Kilburn.[122] Similar elaborate prose is found in Abbot Gervase's assignment of the manor of Kelvedon to provide lights for the high altar; in his two charters for the nunnery of Kilburn; and in a letter addressed to Earl Geoffrey de Mandeville (patron of Hurley), asking him to ensure that the monks of that house enjoy

117 *Westminster Abbey Charters*, no. 328.

118 *Ibid.*, no. 329.

119 Great Charter: (BL Cotton Faustina A.III, ff. 114v–120). First Charter, W. Dugdale, *Monasticon Anglicanum*, revised H. Caley, H. Ellis and B. Bandinel, 6 vols in 8 (London, 1817–30), I, p. 293, no. iv. Second Charter (Westminster Abbey Domesday ff. 40v– 41r; BL Cotton Faustina A.III, ff. 30r–31v). Third Charter (Westminster Abbey Domesday, ff. 41r–43v; BL Cotton Faustina A.III, ff. 31v–37v); see also *Anglo-Saxon Writs*, pp. 289–94; Sawyer, *Anglo-Saxon Charters*, nos 1011, 1039, 1041, 1043.

120 First Charter (printed in full: *Calendar of Charter Rolls*, *IV*, pp. 330–336). Second Charter (Westminster Abbey Muniment, XXVII (b)). Third Charter (BL Cotton Faustina A III, ff. 44v–49r; see also Westminster Abbey Domesday, ff. 51r–52v). Fourth Charter (BL Cotton Charter Aug. II, part 54; see also BL Cotton Faustina A III, ff. 51r–53v; Westminster Abbey Domesday ff. 96r–97v). Telligraphus (Westminster Abbey Muniment, XXVI; Westminster Abbey Domesday, ff. 46v–49r; BL Cotton Faustina A III, ff. 120r–128v).

121 *Westminster Abbey Charters*, no. 234.

122 *Ibid.*, nos 243, 248A, 249, 250.

their rights of pannage.[123] Scribes writing charters in the name of Abbot Lawrence adopted florid prose for his writ to the sheriff of Middlesex, concerning the abbey's right to offer sanctuary; in his confirmation of his predecessors' charters to the nuns of Kilburn; in his grant of the church of Sawbridgeworth to the use of the sacristy; in his grant of the church of Easthampstead to Hurley Priory, to encourage its inmates to celebrate the feast of St Edward; and, to some extent, in his grant of the church of Bloxham to Mr Ralph de Beaumont, a royal clerk.[124] Charters in the name of Abbot Walter employed florid prose to confirm to the convent the manors of Benfleet, Fanton and Paglesham; and to 'concede' the church of Easthampstead to Hurley Priory. A mildly florid style was also adopted in making a grant of tithes to Walter's clerk Mr Nicholas.[125] Abbot William Postard's charter 'conceding and confirming' to the royal chamberlain Robert Mauduit the right to have a private chapel in his house in Longditch is rather more floridly worded than his actual grant to Robert of property in Longditch.[126] The fully-florid style was used in the charters in William's name which granted to the convent the church of Benfleet with the manor, and the appurtenant Fanton and Paglesham; in the charter which granted them a pension from churches in Rutland; in that which conceded the church of Bloxham to the nuns of Godstow; and in that which 'conceded and confirmed' the vill of Parham to the convent.[127] A florid style was also used when confirming to the royal treasurer, William of Ely, property in Westminster, and a more moderately florid style when granting the church of Sunbury to Gilbert of Cranford.[128] The sanction of the anathema was invoked in two charters granted to the convent by Abbot William Postard, one confirming to them the church and manor of Benfleet, with appurtenant lands, and the other confirming an income to the infirmary from churches in Rutland.[129] Similarly, two elaborately-worded grants by Abbot Ralph to the convent, one confirming the vill of Parham, and the other confirming the pension from the churches in Rutland, were reinforced by threatening the use of the anathema against anyone infringing its terms.[130] Conversely, a low-key introduction of the anathema clause occurs in a charter addressed to Abbot Ralph and 'conceded' by Prior Robert Moulsham and the convent, granting the celebration of four additional feasts annually with copes and processions, in return for their manor of Benfleet, which he had been holding at farm.[131]

The inclusion of the ancient anathema clause in the documents discussed here indicates the solemnity with which the convent treated any arrangements for the management of their property, particularly when dealing with such high-handed administrators as Abbots William and Ralph. Most

123 *Ibid.*, nos 252, 264–6.
124 *Ibid.*, nos 279–80, 283, 285–6.
125 *Ibid.*, nos 299, 302–3.
126 *Ibid.*, nos 311–12.
127 *Ibid.*, nos 317, 321, 323, 326.
128 *Ibid.*, nos 313, 315.
129 *Ibid.*, nos 317, 321.
130 *Ibid.*, nos 335–6.
131 *Ibid.*, no. 345.

charters in Ralph's name are in simple prose, although a florid style was again used in one addressed to the chamberlain Robert Mauduit, confirming that the gifts which he, his wife Isabel and other benefactors had made to the Lady Altar would be entered into the abbey's martyrology.[132] Clearly, for such solemn reasons as this, solemn prose was deemed essential.

There were certain situations in which the Westminster scribes disregarded their usual convention of employing elaborate prose in documents addressed to fellow clerics and religious. The monastic community at St Albans, in particular, was addressed in prosaically-worded charters dating from the abbacies of Lawrence, William Postard and Ralph Arundel.[133] All three charters were designed to record agreements terminating territorial or franchisal disputes, which had perhaps prompted ill-feeling between the communities. Additionally, it was perhaps deemed advisable to use the plainest possible language in order to obviate the recurrence of misunderstandings, actual or alleged. Charters of Abbot Walter granting properties to the Hospitals of St Bartholomew's and St James's were plainly worded, and, after a briefly florid opening, so was one to the nuns of Clerkenwell.[134] One further bluntly-worded charter issued by Abbot Walter was addressed to Hugh de Nunant, bishop of Coventry, on 2 February 1190. Shortly after his accession, King Richard I had confirmed to Westminster its manor of Perton, Staffs., but now, in presence of the justiciars, William de Longchamp and Hugh du Puiset, and other notables, the abbot granted the manor to Nunant to hold for life.[135] Westminster might well object to the indefinite loss of control over this manor, but in February 1190 Nunant was too strong to be resisted. He had bought the shrievalty of Staffordshire in 1189 and then entered into a violent conflict with the monks of Coventry, with a view to supplanting them with secular canons. On 22 October 1189, before the bishops assembled at Westminster for an episcopal consecration, he made an emotional appeal, complaining of being attacked by his monks. A number of the bishops sided with him since, as secular clerics they too had difficulty in dealing with their respective monastic chapters. Archbishop Baldwin (himself a Cistercian monk) thwarted a widespread move against monastic chapters, but Hugh du Nonant was able to displace his monks for the time being, and feelings ran high between regular and secular clerics.[136] In this climate of opinion, it would be difficult for Abbot Walter to refuse Hugh's 'request' for a life grant of Perton, but the plain language of the charter no doubt expressed the feelings of the community at Westminster.

Most charters granted to Westminster were in plain prose, although bishops, heads of religious houses and other senior clerics generally employed

132 *Ibid.*, no. 329.
133 *Ibid.*, nos 282, 318, 333.
134 *Ibid.*, nos 288, 292–3.
135 *Ibid.*, no. 304.
136 J.T. Appleby, *England without Richard 1189–1199* (London, 1965), pp. 27–9.

language comparable with Westminster's own florid style.[137] The parson of Hendon, the nuns of Shouldham and the abbess of Godstow also employed florid prose, although in each case the circumstances surrounding the grant may indicate that the charter was written by Westminster scribes.[138] Two clerics who employed a plain style were Turold, Master of St James's Hospital, whose financial resources perhaps did not run to employing an eloquent scribe,[139] and Osbert, abbot of Bec, acknowledging a rent due to Westminster from property in London.[140] This charter was sealed in the Husting Court, where unequivocal language would be appreciated. On the other hand, two prominent City personalities made grants in very florid language. The nature of these transactions suggests that a Westminster scribe may have been employed in each case. Andrew Bucherel, when about to join the Third Crusade, made a grant in return for the annual commemoration of his *obit*,[141] while Brichtmar of Haverhill made a grant in return for confraternity for himself and his family.[142] In such cases, high flown language would denote Westminster's commitment to its reciprocal spiritual obligations. Other secular donors who employed elaborate language in their charters for the abbey, Isabel Mauduit; Geoffrey de Mandeville (I) and the *curialis* Peter Fitz Herbert, were well placed to employ expert clerks on their own behalf.[143]

Overall, the information gained from the surviving charters of the activities of Westminster's scribes is rather uneven in quality. The illuminated manuscripts produced at Westminster were almost all seized at the Dissolution. The Liber Regalis and the Litlyngton Missal were spared, when it was pointed out that these both contained a text of the coronation liturgy, together with that of the royal burial service (and illustrations of royal burials).[144] The loss of the other luxury manuscripts makes it impossible to evaluate the overall activities of the scribes working in this area. In the case of charters, many are now known only from cartulary copies, and some of these are clearly abridged. This, combined with the fading out of the practice of naming the scribe who wrote any given document, generates uncertainties not only about the identities of the scribes, but also about their methods of working. Since many charters produced in the period under discussion would have been destroyed in later centuries, having outlasted their usefulness, there can be no complete record of the scribes who worked at Westminster. The question of which named scribe trained which of his identifiable successors is purely conjectural, as is any calculation of the usual length of a scribe's employment at the abbey. The *Magistri*, in particular, would have completed their formal education, probably including some training in the *ars dictamini* (the technical skills required when drafting charters) before being recruited

137 *Westminster Abbey Charters*, nos 365, 400, 401, 463, 468, 482–3.
138 *Ibid.*, nos 459, 477, 481.
139 *Ibid.*, no. 392.
140 *Ibid.*, no. 361.
141 *Ibid.*, no. 352.
142 *Ibid.*, no. 388.
143 *Ibid.*, nos 422, 450, 462, 487.
144 *Ibid.*, p. 7.

to the abbey *scriptorium*. At this distance in time, it can only be deduced that, while some came to Westminster as complete outsiders, others were themselves the sons of scribes of the abbey, and had perhaps spent their early years in a parsonage-house attached to one or another of its churches. This conjecture is likely one, given that recruitment to all professions and trades operated largely on a father-to-son basis. But even when a young scribe had grown up imbued, through family table-talk, with the requirements of his profession, there were inevitable constraints upon the manner in which his skills were deployed, arising from the pressures of the moment as these affected the abbot and his monks.

7

The Abbey and the Hierarchy of the Church

In the Anglo-Norman period, members of the clerical hierarchy are frequently addressed, in royal charters issued for Westminster, in their capacity as administrators in the secular sphere. This aspect of their responsibilities gradually dwindled in the course of Henry I's reign, as the numbers of secular administrators increased, and tailed away in the reign of Stephen and the early years of Henry II. Conversely the earlier decades of the twelfth century were marked by a steady increase in the volume and range of the activities of the higher clergy in their capacity as ecclesiastical administrators. The present chapter is concerned with these varying roles of the clerical hierarchy as they impinged upon the life of the abbey.

The more notable of the surviving Anglo-Saxon clerics continued to exercise the secular responsibilities which had been theirs in late Anglo-Saxon times. Very soon after the Norman Conquest, Archbishop Ealdred of York (d.1069), a former bishop of Worcester, was jointly notified, together with his successor, Bishop Wulfstan, and the new Marcher lord, Earl William Fitz Osbern, that William I confirmed Westminster in its lands of Pershore and Deerhurst.[1] Not long afterwards Bishop Wulfstan and an unnamed abbot of Evesham, probably the formidable Æthelwig (d.1077), acted with Regenbald the royal chancellor in presiding over a lawsuit which secured for the abbot of Westminster his demesne in Worcestershire. The subsequent confirmatory writ of William I named Vitalis (1076–85) as abbot of Westminster, but there are strong grounds for arguing that the lawsuit was heard in an earlier year.[2] In an English-language writ of William I concerning Westminster's

1 W. Dugdale, *Monasticon Anglicanum*, revised H. Caley, H. Ellis and B. Bandinel (6 vols in 8, London, 1817–30), I, p. 301, no. XL; calendared *Regesta Regum Anglo-Normannorum 1066–1154*, 4 vols, ed. H.W.C. Davis, C. Johnson, H.A. Cronne and R.H.C. Davis (Oxford, 1913, 1956, 1968, 1969), I, no. 32; *Westminster Abbey Charters 1066–c.1214*, ed. Emma Mason, assisted by the late Jennifer Bray, continuing the work of the late D.J. Murphy, London Record Society, 25 (London, 1988), no. 4.

2 *Regesta Regum Anglo-Normannorum*, I, no. XXVII; calendared *ibid.*, no. 213, and *Westminster Abbey Charters*, no. 22. On the date of the lawsuit, see Simon Keynes, 'Regenbald the Chancellor (*sic*)', in R. Allen Brown, ed., *Anglo-Norman Studies*, X, *Proceedings of the Battle Conference 1987* (Woodbridge, 1988), pp. 185–222, esp. pp. 210–11.

land in Perton, Bishop Leofwine of Lichfield (deposed 1070) was addressed in his capacity as an administrator of Staffordshire,[3] while Archbishop Stigand (deposed 1070), in his capacity as an administrator in Surrey, was notified by William I of his grant to Westminster of land in Battersea and Pyrford.[4]

The incoming Continental clerics exercised a similar function. Bishop Walkelin of Winchester (1070–98) was addressed in several writs which survive in the name of King William I, relating to Westminster's estates in Surrey and Hampshire, but the real extent of his dealings with Westminster is uncertain, since none of the writs in genuine in its present form.[5] In one of the writs, Wulfwold, the English abbot of Chertsey (c.1058–84) is also addressed.[6] In the least-suspect of the group, one of Walkelin's fellow-administrators is named as Hugh (de Aurea Valle), bishop of London (d.1084).[7] Hugh was also addressed in the so-called Fourth Charter of William I, an outright forgery.[8] Hugh's predecessor, William, although a Continental cleric, had been appointed by King Edward in 1051, and remained in office until his death in 1075. In his capacity as an administrator in Essex and Middlesex, he is addressed in four writs issued for Westminster's benefit by William I. Two of these are undoubtedly genuine[9] while two have an authentic base combined with later attestations.[10] A fifth writ addressed to the bishop, concerning Westminster's Essex manor of Wennington, is perhaps based on a genuine grant, but shows more signs of re-working.[11] Bishop Maurice (1085–1107), in his capacity as an administrator of London, is addressed only in one royal writ of doubtful authenticity, confirming to the abbey St Mary Newchurch, which Westminster fought a long and losing battle to retain.[12]

Westminster acquired a considerable amount of property in the widespread diocese of Lincoln. Several surviving writs concerning this are addressed to Bishop Rémy of Lincoln. Two which are undoubtedly genuine

3 Dugdale, *Monasticon Anglicanum*, I, p. 301, no. XXXIX; calendared *Regesta Regum Anglo-Normannorum*, I, no. 25; *Westminster Abbey Charters*, no. 5.

4 Dugdale, *Monasticon Anglicanum*, I, p. 301, no. XXXV; calendared *Regesta Regum Anglo-Normannorum*, I, no. 45; *Westminster Abbey Charters*, no. 6.

5 *Westminster Abbey Charters*, nos 13, 17, 21, 24, 34.

6 *Ibid.*, no. 13.

7 *Ibid.*, no. 24, probably based on a genuine grant.

8 *Ibid.*, no. 33; also calendared in *Regesta Regum Anglo-Normannorum*, I, no. 144.

9 Dugdale, *Monasticon Anglicanum*, I, p. 301, no. XXXVII; *Regesta Regum Anglo-Normannorum*, I, no. XI; calendared *ibid.*, nos 86 and 87; and also *Westminster Abbey Charters*, nos 9–10.

10 *Regesta Regum Anglo-Normannorum*, I, no. XII; *Anglo-Saxon Writs*, ed. Florence E. Harmer, 2nd edn (Stamford, 1989), p. 494; calendared *Westminster Abbey Charters*, nos 11–12.

11 *Anglo-Saxon Writs*, p. 493; calendared *Westminster Abbey Charters*, no. 35.

12 Dugdale, *Monasticon Anglicanum*, I, p. 302, no. XLV; calendared *Regesta Regum Anglo-Normannorum*, I, no. 278, and *Westminster Abbey Charters*, no. 40.

order, respectively, that Westminster is to have possession of the manor of Doddington with its appurtenant soke of Thorpe (Lincs.), and that the monks were to have their manor of Ayot St Lawrence (Herts.).[13] Since Rémy held office for many years, his name was inevitably one which appealed to the twelfth-century forgers of Westminster. In a second series of writs, Rémy is notified that the king has confirmed to the abbey its manor of Aldenham (Herts.); he is ordered that the monks are to have their manor of Islip (Oxon.), and informed that the king has confirmed them in certain churches, with appurtenant lands, in Rutland.[14] Even charters such as these, which are essentially fabrications, demonstrate the major role played by eleventh-century bishops in local government, and the consequent need for a monastic community such as Westminster to maintain good relations with those diocesan bishops in whose sees they held land. By the late eleventh-century, Westminster held lands in most counties in southern England.

Osmund, bishop of Salisbury (1078–99), was notified of the king's confirmation to the abbey of land in Wiltshire.[15] The responsibilities of Lanfranc, archbishop of Canterbury, and Odo, bishop of Bayeux, included participation in national government and it was probably for this reason that they were jointly notified by William I of his grants to the abbey of various rights and properties in Surrey, Sussex, London and Worcestershire.[16] Additionally, the archbishop and the bishop, who was also earl of Kent, had specific interests in that shire. A highly suspect charter in the name of William I, addressed to them jointly, notified them of his confirmation to Abbot Vitalis and the monks of the manor and church of Lessness.[17]

In the reign of William Rufus, the monks were still struggling to secure control of St Mary Newchurch in London, and they obtained from the king a writ notifying Maurice, bishop of London, and his fellow-recipients that the king confirmed the church as his father had done.[18] Even though powerful laymen were addressed jointly with the bishop in this and in comparable writs, and even though the diocesan bishop was customarily the first of any such batch of recipients to be named, yet the regular practice of addressing

13 Dugdale, *Monasticon Anglicanum*, I, p. 301, no. XLI; *Regesta Regum Anglo-Normannorum*, I, no. XXXVIII; calendared *ibid.*, nos 212, 235; *Westminster Abbey Charters*, nos 31, 37.

14 *Regesta Regum Anglo-Normannorum*, I, nos IX–X, XLIV; calendared *ibid.*, nos 52–3, 275; *Westminster Abbey Charters*, nos 2–3, 46.

15 *Regesta Regum Anglo-Normannorum*, I, no. LXX; calendared *ibid.*, no. 417; *Westminster Abbey Charters*, no. 32.

16 *Regesta Regum Anglo-Normannorum*, I, no. XX; calendared *ibid.*, no. 166; *Westminster Abbey Charters*, no. 19.

17 Dugdale, *Monasticon Anglicanum*, I, p. 302, no. XLVI; calendared *Regesta Regum Anglo-Normannorum*, I, no. 54; *Westminster Abbey Charters*, no. 20.

18 J. Armitage Robinson, *Gilbert Crispin, Abbot of Westminster*, Notes and Documents Relating to Westminster Abbey, No. 3 (Cambridge, 1911), p. 137, no. 10; calendared *Regesta Regum Anglo-Normannorum*, I, no. 306; *Westminster Abbey Charters*, no. 49.

him on matters of property underlines his continuing role in secular government in the last years of the eleventh century.

Bishops still bore such responsibilities in the reign of Henry I. Texts survive of two writs in his name, addressed to Richard de Belmeis I, bishop of London (1108–27), concerning the interests of Westminster, although both relate to its parish churches. Richard was ordered to render justice to the abbot following an incident when armed men broke into his church of Wennington overnight.[19] Richard was also addressed in a fabricated writ, which in reality was composed some years after the end of his episcopate. In this document he was ordered to see that the abbey received possession of several churches in London: St Margaret, Eastcheap; St Lawrence, Candlewick Street; St James Garlickhithe; and also St Magnus the Martyr.[20] Probably there had been obstacles which prevented Westminster from exercizing control of all of these, but the difficulties were most apparent in the case of St Magnus's, which was also claimed by the priory of Bermondsey. A long-running dispute triggered further forgeries, and was settled by compromise only in 1182.[21] Richard was also addressed in a writ issued by Edith Matilda, the king's first wife, who notified the bishop and other officials in London that she had granted to Abbot Gilbert a tenement on the abbot's wharf.[22]

Administrative oversight of the kind indicated in these writs would be deemed well within the competence of any diocesan. Richard de Belmeis, for instance, had recognized talents as an administrator. In the early years of the century the king had appointed him as justiciar-sheriff of Shropshire, when it became a fully-integrated English county, after the fall of the house of Montgomery.[23] In the latter part of Henry I's reign, the bishop of London (unnamed) was among the officials notified by Henry I that he had conceded to Richard de Balta land in Hampstead which he was to hold of the abbey.[24] A charter of dubious authenticity, addressed to Bishop Gilbert 'the Universal', notified him that the abbey was to hold peacefully the church of St Magnus the Martyr.[25]

Robert Bloet, bishop of Lincoln, was among the dignitaries of Lincolnshire whom Henry I, early in his reign, notified of a series of exchanges of

19 Armitage Robinson, *Gilbert Crispin*, p. 149, no. 31; calendared *Regesta Regum Anglo-Normannorum*, II, no. 1538; *Westminster Abbey Charters*, no. 84.

20 Armitage Robinson, *Gilbert Crispin*, p. 148, no. 30; calendared *Regesta Regum Anglo-Normannorum*, II, no. 1177; *Westminster Abbey Charters*, no. 70.

21 The church of St Magnus was listed among properties confirmed to Bermondsey priory in a charter of Henry I, of doubtful authenticity; *Regesta Regum Anglo-Normannorum*, II, no. 1990. See also *Westminster Abbey Charters*, nos 70 note, 287.

22 Armitage Robinson, *Gilbert Crispin*, p. 155, no. 38; calendared *Regesta Regum Anglo-Normannorum*, II, no. 1180; *Westminster Abbey Charters*, no. 97.

23 R.R. Davies, *The Age of Conquest: Wales 1063–1415* (Oxford, 1991), pp. 40–41.

24 *Regesta Regum Anglo-Normannorum*, II, no. CCLXIX; calendared *ibid.*, no. 1758; *Westminster Abbey Charters*, no. 88.

25 *Regesta Regum Anglo-Normannorum*, II, no. CCCIV; calendared *ibid.*, no. 1883; *Westminster Abbey Charters*, no. 93.

land, in consequence of which Abbot Gilbert recovered his manor of Doddington.[26] The abbey had leased its manor of Lessness, Kent, to Robert Bloet at some time in the reign of William Rufus. Bloet, however, became negligent about rendering his dues, and Henry I ordered him to honour them.[27] The writ on this subject, issued at Woodstock, clearly dates from the last years of Bloet's life, and its sharp tone suggests that it was composed about the time of his disgrace, which in turn led to his death. As a major public figure, Robert Bloet could probably evade his obligations with impunity, but once his downfall appeared imminent, those with grievances against him would press their case. Other diocesan bishops named in writs of Henry I concerning Westminster's property include William Giffard, bishop of Winchester, notified about the king's confirmation of four hides in Tooting (Surrey) to Abbot Gilbert and the monks;[28] and Herbert Losinga, bishop of Norwich, who was informed that the king had conceded to Westminster the church of St Bartholomew, Sudbury (Suffolk), donated by Wulfric the moneyer when he became a monk at the abbey.[29] One further writ of Henry I, of questionable authenticity, addressed the leading minister Roger, bishop of Salisbury, and officials in Oxfordshire, Surrey and Middlesex, notifying them of the king's restoration, to Abbot Herbert and the convent, of Battersea, Islip, Pyrford and Shepperton.[30]

Some residual role in secular government was evidently still exercised by bishops in Stephen's reign, and not solely because of the comparatively weak state of the royal administration. In a writ dating from no later than 1137, the unnamed bishop of London (probably Anselm of Bury, whose occupation of the see was brief), was notified, together with leading officials of Middlesex, that the king had conceded to Richard de Balta the tenancy in Hampstead which he held of the abbot and convent.[31] Another charter addressed to the unnamed bishop, together with officials in Essex, and probably dating from early in the reign, informed them of the king's grant to the abbey of assarts in Kelvedon.[32]

Occasional writs of similar purport were issued by King Henry II. One, probably dating from early in his reign, informed the bishop of Norwich,

[26] Armitage Robinson, *Gilbert Crispin*, p. 145, no. 26; calendared *Regesta Regum Anglo-Normannorum*, II, no. 818; *Westminster Abbey Charters*, no. 61.

[27] Armitage Robinson, *Gilbert Crispin*, p. 157, no. 42; calendared *Regesta Regum Anglo-Normannorum*, II, no. 1383; *Westminster Abbey Charters*, no. 81.

[28] Armitage Robinson, *Gilbert Crispin*, pp. 142–3, no. 21; calendared *Regesta Regum Anglo-Normannorum*, II, no.1173; *Westminster Abbey Charters*, no. 60.

[29] Dugdale, *Monasticon Anglicanum*, III, p. 459, no. I; calendared *Regesta Regum Anglo-Normannorum*, II, no. 1178; *Westminster Abbey Charters*, no. 72.

[30] *Regesta Regum Anglo-Normannorum*, II, no. CCCIII; calendared *ibid.*, no. 1881; *Westminster Abbey Charters*, no. 83.

[31] *Regesta Regum Anglo-Normannorum*, III, no. 925; calendared *Westminster Abbey Charters*, no. 108.

[32] *Regesta Regum Anglo-Normannorum*, III, no. 932; calendared *Westminster Abbey Charters*, no. 114.

William de Turba, that he confirmed to the monks of Sudbury (which by this time was a little cell of Westminster), two thirds of the tithe of *Torp*.[33] In a further writ, purportedly dating from the earlier part of the reign, but in fact a forgery, Henry II is depicted as ordering Hilary, bishop of Chichester, that the monks are to have their vill of Parham.[34]

The decline of the role of the bishops in secular administration was matched by the steady rise of papal jurisdiction, a process which can be noted in Westminster's muniments. The earliest papal bulls for Westminster are all forgeries. One, in the name of Pope John XIII (965–72), confirming estates in Essex, Hertfordshire, Middlesex, Surrey and Sussex, is embedded in a spurious charter of King Edgar, which is actually a product of Osbert de Clare.[35] Recited in full, in the spurious Great Charter of King Edward, and also in abridged form in the spurious First Charter of Edward, is the well-known letter purportedly issued by Pope Leo IX in 1049, granting to King Edward that, in order to obviate political dangers, he may commute his vows of making a pilgrimage to Rome. Instead, he must found a monastery dedicated to St Peter.[36] A letter in the name of Pope Nicholas II, allegedly sent in response to a petition from King Edward, confirms and extends the privileges of the abbey, styles it the repository of the royal regalia, and exempts it from episcopal jurisdiction. This text is in fact recited within the spurious Third Charter of Edward.[37] A further essay in comparable vein is a purported bull of Pope Paschal II, supposedly dating from 1101x1114, informs King Henry I that the abbey is under the special protection of St Peter; that it is exempt from the jurisdiction of the bishop of London, and that he, Paschal, confirms its status as the coronation church, and its possession of all its lands and churches.[38] These texts convey more of the preoccupations of Prior Osbert and his associates than they do of the papal attitude towards the abbey. No genuine bull for Westminster survives from any pontificate earlier than that of Innocent II (1130–1143), but from his time onwards the bulls preserved by the abbey are normally authentic. The expense, the dangers and the

33 Dugdale, *Monasticon Anglicanum*, III, p. 459, no. II; calendared *Westminster Abbey Charters*, no. 130.

34 T.A.M. Bishop, *Scriptores Regis: Facsimiles to Identify and Illustrate the Hands of Royal Scribes in Original Charters of Henry I, Stephen and Henry II* (Oxford, 1961), Plate VI (b), facsimile; calendared *ibid*., no. 553; *Acta of Henry II and Richard I*, ed. J.C. Holt and R. Mortimer, List and Index Society Special Series, 21 (1986), no. H 290; *Westminster Abbey Charters*, no. 129.

35 *Monasticon Anglicanum*, I, pp. 291–3; calendared P.H. Sawyer, *Anglo-Saxon Charters: an Annotated List and Bibliography* (London, 1968), no. 774.

36 *Papsturkunden in England*, ed. W. Holtzmann, 3 vols, Abhandlungen der Gesellschaft der Wissenschaften in Göttingen, phil.-hist. Klasse, Berlin, Göttingen (I = neue Folge XXV, 1930–1931; II = 3 Folge XIV–XV, 1935–6; III = 3 Folge XXXIII, 1952), I, no. 2; calendared *Westminster Abbey Charters*, no. 152.

37 *Codex Diplomaticus Aevi Saxonici*, ed. J.M. Kemble, 6 vols (London, 1839–48), IV, pp. 183–5, no. DCCCXXV; calendared *Westminster Abbey Charters*, no. 153.

38 *Papsturkunden in England*, I, no. 9; calendared *Westminster Abbey Charters*, no. 154.

difficulties involved in a journey to the papal *curia* (traditionally but by no means invariably located in Rome), ensured that the abbot and his *seniores* would send a deputation only in order to secure objectives which were of crucial concern to them, whether this affected their property, their revenues, their jurisdictional rights or their status compared to that of the other great Benedictine houses in England.

The pope's political difficulties, whether caused by an anti-pope, by the Emperor or by the Romans, frequently caused him to travel extensively, so that it would be up to any delegation to locate him as best they could. It was at Pisa that Pope Innocent II issued, in 1133, a bull authorizing Henry I to take the abbey under his protection. Additionally this bull excluded the abbey from the jurisdiction of the bishop of London.[39] By this date, the monks of Westminster had developed a strong sense that their house should be exempt from the control of the bishop. The legendary dedication of the abbey by St Peter was cited in support of its view, although, when initially introduced by Sulcard, in the late eleventh century, this apocryphal story was perhaps simply intended to indicate that Westminster enjoyed special divine favour, on a par with certain famous Continental abbeys which made similar claims.[40] The Westminster delegation which attended the Second Lateran Council, and was probably led by Abbot Gervase, received from Pope Innocent a solemn privilege, dated 22 April 1139. The pope stated in this that he took Westminster under his protection as (he was given to understand that) his predecessors, Leo IX (1049–54) and Nicholas II (1058–61) had done. He also confirmed the abbey in its privileges and possessions.[41]

Another bull issued on the same day was requested by Henry (of Blois), the bishop of Winchester, in order to protect the lands of the abbey's tenant, Gilbert of Hendon.[42] In 1138, the pope had quashed the election of Anselm of Bury as bishop of London.[43] Bishop Henry was put in charge of the vacant see.[44] In this capacity, he would have the same administrative responsibilities in the diocese as has been demonstrated in the case of its bishops. Both Gervase, and his predecessor Herbert, had granted land to Gilbert of Hendon but differences arose between the parties.[45] The bull would ease the situation for both Gilbert and Henry. Indirectly it would also serve to record the

39 *Papsturkunden in England*, I, no. 17; calendared *Westminster Abbey Charters*, no. 155.

40 B.W. Scholz, 'Sulcard of Westminster: "*Prologus de Construccione Westmonasterii*" ', *Traditio*, 20 (1964), pp. 72–3.

41 *Papsturkunden in England*, I, no. 21; calendared *Westminster Abbey Charters*, no. 156.

42 *Papsturkunden in England*, I, no. 20; calendared *Westminster Abbey Charters*, no. 157.

43 John Le Neve, *Fasti Ecclesiae Anglicanae 1066–1300. I. St Paul's London*, compiled Diana E. Greenway (London, 1968), p. 1.

44 Ralph de Diceto, *Abbreviationes Chronicorum*, *Opera Historica*, ed. W. Stubbs, Rolls Series, 2 vols (1876), I, p. 252.

45 *Westminster Abbey Charters*, no. 107; see also nos 104, 124, 263.

abbey's proprietorial interest in the land but would be of direct use to Westminster only when Hendon became a demesne manor at a much later date.[46]

The Westminster mission of December 1139 failed to secure the canonization of King Edward,[47] but obtained a papal bull requiring Henry of Blois, both legate and administrator of the London diocese, to secure the restitution to the abbey of misappropriated lands.[48] This bull predates the losses which were undoubtedly caused to the abbey's estates by the unrest in Stephen's reign, and most likely reflects difficulties still facing the abbey in its efforts to recover estates lost as far back as the interregnum before Abbot Herbert's election. One separate, and minor, territorial concern was to secure the land which supported Edith Matilda's anniversary. To this end, a further bull was obtained from the Pope, and addressed to the late Queen's brother, King David of Scotland. Since this bull in effect confirmed Westminster's interest in the land, a copy was kept at Westminster, and appears in several of its cartularies.[49] The series of bulls issued by Innocent II for Westminster in 1139 inspired the production, presumably by Prior Osbert, of a forgery designed to underline the role of the convent in the management of its lands, and to enhance the status of the abbey as depository of King Edward's regalia.[50]

The two bulls granted by Pope Eugenius III for Westminster, in 1146 and 1151 respectively, are generally-worded confirmations of pre-existing privileges.[51] As indicated in Chapter Three, it is likely that they were obtained on Westminster's behalf by visitors to the *curia* who had an agenda of their own, rather than by a deputation from the abbey. Given the expense and uncertainties involved in the sending of any deputation to Rome, the abbot and monks would have used the occasion to obtain a more positively-worded bull in each case if they had sent a direct representative. At the same time, it is interesting to see that the Cistercian Eugenius III evidently had no grievance against Abbot Gervase in person, no matter what his opinion of the abbot's father and paternal uncle. The Westminster delegation which reached the *curia* in the latter part of May 1157, on the other hand, had a definite

46 On Hendon, see Barbara F. Harvey, *Westminster Abbey and its Estates in the Middle Ages* (Oxford, 1977), p. 352.

47 *Monasticon Anglicanum*, I, p. 308, no. LIV; calendared *Westminster Abbey Charters*, no. 158.

48 *The Letters of Osbert de Clare, Prior of Westminster*, ed. E.W. Williamson, introd. J. Armitage Robinson (London, 1929); calendared *Westminster Abbey Charters*, no. 159.

49 *Papsturkunden in England*, I, no. 25; *The Acts of Malcolm IV, King of Scots 1153–1165*, ed. G.W.S. Barrow (Edinburgh, 1960), pp. 290–91, no. 319; calendared *Westminster Abbey Charters*, no. 160.

50 John Flete, *The History of Westminster Abbey*, ed. J. Armitage Robinson, Notes and Documents Relating to Westminster Abbey, no. 2 (Cambridge, 1909), pp. 90–91; calendared *Westminster Abbey Charters*, no. 161.

51 *Foedera, conventiones, literae et cujuscunque generis acta publica*, ed. T. Rymer, 20 vols (London, 1704–35), I, i, f. 14; *Papsturkunden in England*, I, pp. 286–8, no. 47; calendared *Westminster Abbey Charters*, nos 162–3.

commission to obtain a bull which would reinforce the abbey's control over its cell of Great Malvern.[52] A week later, the deputation received a second bull which reinforced the first and also confirmed the abbey's control over its other cells of Hurley and of Sudbury.[53] For good measure, a general confirmation of the abbey's privileges, exemptions and lands was also obtained.[54]

The revival of the project to obtain the canonization of King Edward led to the dispatch to the *curia* of a delegation which would have had to traverse the Alpine passes in the bleak midwinter. They would travel in hope of success, though, following the demonstration of support for the beleaguered Alexander III which was given by King Henry II in 1160.[55] Their mission was amply rewarded: one bull addressed to Abbot Lawrence and the convent announced that King Edward was to be canonized as a Confessor,[56] while a second bull to the same effect was generally addressed to the English clergy, and hence suitable for circulation among them.[57] Abbot Lawrence also requested an appropriate recompense for two obedientiaries who, presumably, led the delegation. Roger the infirmarer received a confirmation of the churches of Battersea and Wandsworth, revenues from which would support the infirmary; while Walter the sacrist received a confirmation of the church of Sawbridgeworth, so that its revenues would provide lights for the sacristy altar.[58] All four bulls were issued at Anagni on 7 February 1161. Ongoing concern to ensure control over the abbey's daughter-houses prompted a new deputation to the pope, by now at Sens, early in October 1163.[59] Dependent cells might aspire to become independent, but equally, energetic diocesan bishops might attempt to monopolise oversight of these daughter-houses. Certainly determination to evade the claim by the bishop of London to exercise jurisdiction over the abbey itself prompted the sending of a new delegation to the pope, by then at Tusculum, early in December 1171.[60] The exempt status secured by the abbey on this occasion was symbolically reinforced by another bull, obtained at some uncertain date, but perhaps as late as the spring of 1173, whereby Abbot Lawrence was permitted to wear mitre

52 *Papsturkunden in England*, I, no. 68; calendared *Westminster Abbey Charters*, no. 164.

53 *Papsturkunden in England*, I, no. 70; calendared *Westminster Abbey Charters*, no. 166.

54 *Papsturkunden in England*, I, no. 69; calendared *Westminster Abbey Charters*, no. 165.

55 Frank Barlow, 'The English, Norman and French Councils Called to Deal with the Papal Schism of 1159', reprinted from *English Historical Review*, 51 (1936), pp. 264–8, in F. Barlow, *The Norman Conquest and Beyond* (London, 1983), pp. 297–301.

56 Flete, *The History of Westminster Abbey*, p. 93; calendared *Westminster Abbey Charters*, no. 167.

57 Dugdale, *Monasticon Anglicanum*, I, pp. 308b–309, no. LV; calendared *Westminster Abbey Charters*, no. 168. For correspondence leading up to the canonization, see Frank Barlow, *Edward the Confessor* (London, 1970), pp. 309–24.

58 *Papsturkunden in England*, I, nos 85–6; calendared *Westminster Abbey Charters*, nos 169–70.

59 *Papsturkunden in England*, I, no. 101; calendared *Westminster Abbey Charters*, no. 171.

60 *Papsturkunden in England*, I, no. 113; calendared *Westminster Abbey Charters*, no. 172.

and ring on solemn occasions.[61] Abbot Walter followed up this privilege by obtaining from Alexander III two further bulls which authorized him to wear dalmatic tunicle, sandals and gloves.[62] The superior standing of the abbot was now plain for all to see.

The status claimed by the abbot, on behalf of his house, was necessarily demonstrated in this visible way, to counteract the assertion, not only of the power of diocesan bishops, but also that of the secular authorities. Several of the abbey's most profitable churches were liable to fall prey to predatory outsiders, usually men who had obtained the king's support. A bull granted by Alexander III at Ferrara in 1177 was designed to deal with both of these threats to the abbey.[63] The lucrative churches singled out for special mention in this bull were not the only ones which the abbey was in danger of losing. Those of Battersea and Wandsworth were equally at risk, but from their diocesan bishop, the powerful Richard of Ilchester. A bull obtained from Pope Lucius III, c. March 1185, was intended to help retrieve them.[64]

By the 1180s, the great inflation of the twelfth century was making a real impact, and the abbot and convent needed to augment their income as best they could. A bull was obtained from Pope Clement III in July 1189, permitting the abbot and convent to appropriate the tithes of the churches of which they were patrons, when vacancies occurred, for the support of the brethren, their guests and the poor. At the same time, they were required to establish vicarages for the priests of these churches (guaranteeing them an income, mainly from the lesser tithes), and to pay their synodal dues.[65] The delegation which secured that bull at the Lateran had to wait for two weeks before gaining a second, surprisingly eclectic bull which again confirmed the group of five churches which were at risk of alienation. Simultaneously it prohibited any bishop or archbishop from saying Mass in St Margaret's, Westminster, or from holding a synod there, exempted the abbey from the control of the bishop of London, and confirmed all pensions from churches which the abbey held before the Third Lateran Council. Conventionally the two widely-differing issues, of parish churches and their pensions, on the one hand, and exemption from episcopal control on the other, would have been the subjects of two distinct bulls. Their odd juxtaposition in this one, combined with the delay before this bull was obtained, may hint at a cash-flow problem faced by the delegation, and a consequent search for some economical means of achieving their objectives.

The bishop of London attempted to assert his authority at this period, on

61 *Papsturkunden in England*, I, no. 118; calendared *Westminster Abbey Charters*, no. 173.

62 Dugdale, *Monasticon Anglicanum*, I, p. 311, no. LXX; *Papsturkunden in England*, I, no. 143; calendared *Westminster Abbey Charters*, nos 174–5.

63 *Papsturkunden in England*, I, no. 144; calendared *Westminster Abbey Charters*, no. 176.

64 *Papsturkunden in England*, I, no. 232; calendared *Westminster Abbey Charters*, no. 177.

65 *Papsturkunden in England*, I, no. 261; calendared *Westminster Abbey Charters*, no. 178.

the grounds that Westminster's internal discipline was less than satisfactory.[66] This issue continued to be among the abbey's major priorities over the next few years, and in January 1192 a bull was obtained from Pope Celestine III exempting the abbey from any episcopal authority other than his own, and simultaneously ordering the restoration of any of its property which had been misappropriated.[67] Losses had presumably occurred during the interregnum between the death of Abbot Walter and the election of William Postard. The recent threats to the dignity of Westminster, whether prompted by attempted episcopal intrusion or by the activities of Robert de Longchamp and his supporters, were countered by a reassertion of the dignity of the house, and a second bull obtained on 13 January confirmed William Postard's right to wear the accoutrements of a mitred abbot.[68] On the other hand, representations on the bishop's behalf had clearly reached Celestine III. In a third bull issued on the same date as the others, while on the one hand he ordered the excommunication of those who had stolen the goods of the abbey and also granted leave to appeal against the activities of bishops, he also ordered the chapter to maintain good discipline, in order to avoid giving any pretext for intrusion.[69] Most likely, the restiveness in the chapter against Robert de Longchamp, and the monks' subsequent rejection of him, had been represented to the pope as a state of indiscipline which it was the bishop's duty to investigate and subdue. An outsider's understanding or, more precisely, his tendentious representation of the recent state of affairs in Westminster, is suggested in a passage by Richard of Devizes. As an inmate of St Swithun's, Winchester, he wrote scathingly of Westminster's rejection of Robert de Longchamp, depicting the monks as turncoats, rather than as victims of Robert's powerful brother, William.[70]

The next Westminster delegation to the *curia* obtained from Pope Innocent III a series of bulls dated 23 April 1199. Two of these essentially confirmed the status which the abbey had acquired in recent years. One of them confirmed the liberties and immunities of the abbey, together with its 'ancient and reasonable customs'.[71] The second bull was a companion to this, generally addressed to all English prelates, and ordering that the privileges and indulgences granted to the abbey, by reason of its special relationship

66 *Papsturkunden in England*, I, no. 262; calendared *Westminster Abbey Charters*, no. 170. See also the ensuing note.

67 *Papsturkunden in England*, I, no. 302; calendared *Westminster Abbey Charters*, no. 181.

68 *Papsturkunden in England*, I, no. 301; calendared *Westminster Abbey Charters*, no. 180.

69 *Papsturkunden in England*, I, no. 300; calendared *Westminster Abbey Charters*, no. 182.

70 *The Chronicle of Richard of Devizes of the Time of King Richard the First*, ed. J.T. Appleby (London, 1963), pp. 54–5.

71 *The Letters of Pope Innocent III (1198–1216), Concerning England and Wales: a Calendar, with an Appendix of Texts*, ed. C.R. Cheney and Mary Cheney (Oxford, 1967), p. 203, no. 104; calendared *ibid.*, p. 19, no. 104; *Westminster Abbey Charters*, no. 183.

with the apostolic see, were to be observed.[72] But the struggle to recover a financial equilibrium, and the need to acknowledge obligations to recent benefactors, constrained Abbot William Postard to take decisions which were unpopular with the chapter. The monastic delegation took this opportunity to make representations to the pope, and in a third bull issued on 23 April, Innocent III ordered that the financial assets of the abbey were to be used in a fitting way.[73] There is evidence that two separate delegations set out to achieve the objectives secured in these three bulls, since brief memoranda survive of three bulls, dated 8 January, in some unspecified year, and encompassing the provisions of the three issued on 23 April 1199.[74] The delegation of April 1199 evidently decided that the bull concerning improper alienations was not worded strongly enough. Fortified by the long-maintained papal view that monastic property was inalienable, they petitioned for a further bull. This was issued on 30 April, and specifically prohibited the abbot from making any alienations without the consent of the chapter, or at any rate, that of the greater and wiser part.[75] Abbot William Postard had in fact proved a most efficient manager, although his recovery of financial solvency was evidently achieved by arbitrary methods. Indignant monks, no doubt prompted by *seniores* who had been on a nearly-equal footing with him in his pre-abbatial days, could vent their feelings in the knowledge that the papacy firmly upheld the view that monastic property was inalienable.[76] Innocent, like his predecessors and successors, was largely reliant on the statement of facts as represented by each petitioning delegation. If William Postard did not suspect that the delegation would press for this fourth bull, then his side of the case would remain unrepresented.

Westminster was occasionally able to obtain a privilege or an indulgence from a papal legate who was in England on official business. A legate was usually dispatched by the pope to resolve some major problem which had arisen within the *ecclesia anglicana*. As the machinery of papal government expanded, it was seen to impinge on that of the secular authorities. The Norman kings of England, and indeed their immediate successors, were wary of the possible consequences of admitting a legate, whose pronouncements might put a strain on the loyalties of previously-reliable clerics. Consequently not all legates who were dispatched were permitted to enter the realm, and of those who were admitted, not all were free to move around the country and conduct business as they pleased. On the other hand, when they

72 *The Letters of Pope Innocent III (1198–1216)*, p. 203, no. 105; calendared *ibid*., p. 19, no. 105; *Westminster Abbey Charters*, no. 184.

73 Dugdale, *Monasticon Anglicanum*, I, p. 312a, no. LXXIII; calendared, *The Letters of Pope Innocent III (1198–1216)*, p. 19, no. 106; *Westminster Abbey Charters*, no. 185.

74 Notes to *Westminster Abbey Charters*, nos 183–5.

75 *The Letters of Pope Innocent III (1198–1216)*, p. 203, no. 113; calendared *ibid*., p. 20, no. 113; *Westminster Abbey Charters*, no. 186.

76 On the papal view on the inalienability of monastic property, see H.G. Richardson, 'The Coronation in Medieval England', *Traditio*, 16 (1960), pp. 151–3.

were in England, they were likely to pass through London – and perhaps to use Westminster as a base for their activities.[77] Since legatine privileges and indulgences carried considerable prestige, the abbot and monks tried to make the most of their opportunities. Given the time that it would take to draft, and then to fair-copy any letter of privilege, ready for formal approval, it would be necessary to alert the scriptorium, and to have a petition ready for their eminent visitor. He himself had pressing business to attend to, and the monks would need to make the most of a fleeting opportunity. The most usual request was for the grant of an indulgence of a specific number of days of remission (from purgatory) for those visiting the abbey on certain feast days. A survey of those named indicates the rise and fall in the popularity of particular cults, a subject covered in a later chapter.

The first legate who undoubtedly granted a privilege for Westminster was the cardinal priest John of Crema. He arrived in England by 25 March 1125, travelled throughout England and into Scotland, and then, on 8 September, held a legatine council at Westminster shortly before he left for home.[78] The abbot and monks would have their best opportunity to petition him for a privilege on this latter date. At the request of Abbot Herbert and the convent, and on the grounds that King Edward 'of blessed memory' and Edith Matilda were buried in the abbey, he granted to all the faithful visiting the abbey on the feast of SS Peter and Paul, 29 June, or within its octave, an indulgence of forty days.[79] King Henry I had put some difficulties in the way of the legate's arrival, and even when he did enter the country, his one real achievement was to hold his council.[80] The monks made the most of his presence at Westminster, both by obtaining this indulgence and then by using it as a model for others. Some years earlier, in the summer of 1121, another legate, the cardinal priest Peter Pierleoni, had visited England. Henry I made it plain that he was unwelcome, and he soon left. It is unlikely that Westminster obtained any privilege from him during his brief stay.[81] Peter was a member of a leading Roman family and he was highly influential in Rome. He was a candidate in the papal election of December 1124, and again in that of February 1130. On this occasion he had the support of a majority of the cardinal priests and deacons, but that of only two of the cardinal-bishops, even though at his election the proper formalities were observed better than at that of his rival, who took the name of Innocent II. Peter assumed the name of Anacletus II, and initially his position was the

77 *Councils and Synods, with Other Documents Relating to the English Church, I, 871–1204*, ed. D. Whitelock, M. Brett and C.N.L. Brooke, 2 parts (Oxford, 1981), ii, no. 130, p. 733; no. 139, p. 768; no. 146, p. 810; no. 184, p. 1075; *II, 1205–1313*, ed. F.M. Powicke and C.R. Cheney, 2 parts (Oxford, 1964), i, no. 25.

78 *Councils and Synods*, I, part ii, no. 129, pp. 730–41.

79 Westminster Abbey Domesday (Muniment Book 11), f. 389v; calendared *Westminster Abbey Charters*, no. 189.

80 M. Brett, *The English Church under Henry I* (Oxford, 1975), pp. 42–3.

81 *Ibid.*, p. 41.

stronger.[82] It is conjectural just when the monks of Westminster decided that they wanted some legatine grants in his name. One of two such documents seems to be a slightly extended version of the indulgence granted by John of Crema in 1125.[83] The privilege, in the name of Peter Pierleone, was probably drawn up about the same time as the indulgence ascribed to him.[84] The outer limits for the fabrications would seem to be between September 1125, when John of Crema left England, and late 1130 or early 1131, by which time it was plain that Anacletus's rival, Innocent II, was gaining widespread recognition, thanks to the support of the reforming leaders, even though the schism continued until the death of Anacletus in 1138.[85] Since Westminster obtained a privilege from Innocent II in September 1133,[86] it is unlikely that forged privileges in the name of his rival, even when still styled a cardinal, would have any perceived appeal at Westminster by that date. One of the two documents in Peter Pierleone's name grants an indulgence of forty days to those visiting the abbey on the feast of SS Peter and Paul, and also on that of St Peter in Chains (1 August).[87] The other document confirms the abbey in its possessions, present and to come; grants an indulgence to those visiting on the feast of SS Peter and Paul; permits five or three deacons and five or three subdeacons to participate in the Mass on seven especially solemn festivals, and pronounces anathema on anyone disturbing the abbey in its possessions.[88] Its wording suggests that this and the companion document are the work of Prior Osbert and his associates, composed while Peter Pierleone's star was in the ascendant.

There was an interval of almost thirty years between the grant of John of Crema and the date of the next legatine document. During the intervening years, legates did occasionally visit England. Alberic, bishop of Ostia, came in 1138, and on 13 December presided over a synod held in Westminster abbey, in the course of which Abbot Gervase was consecrated.[89] However there is no evidence that his abbey obtained any legatine grant on this occasion.

Similarly no grant survives in the name of Imar of Tusculum, who was in England in the early months of 1145.[90] He was sent to England just when

82 I.S. Robinson, *The Papacy 1073–1198. Continuity and Innovation* (Cambridge, 1990), pp. 63, 69–70, 72–3, 75–6, 382, 444–6.

83 The indulgence in the name of Peter Pierleone (*Papsturkunden in England*, I, no. 13; calendared *Westminster Abbey Charters*, no. 187) may be compared to that granted by John of Crema in 1125 (*Westminster Abbey Charters*, no. 189).

84 *Papsturkunden in England*, I, no. 12; calendared *Westminster Abbey Charters*, no. 188.

85 Robinson, *The Papacy 1073–1198*, pp. 445–6; Colin Morris, *The Papal Monarchy. The Western Church from 1050 to 1250* (paperback edn, Oxford, 1991), pp. 183–4.

86 *Papsturkunden in England*, I, no. 17; calendared *Westminster Abbey Charters*, no. 155.

87 *Papsturkunden in England*, I, no. 13; calendared *Westminster Abbey Charters*, no. 187.

88 *Papsturkunden in England*, I, no. 12; calendared *Westminster Abbey Charters*, no. 188.

89 Frank Barlow, *The English Church 1066–1154* (London, 1979), pp. 93, 130.

90 A. Morey and C.N.L. Brooke, 'The Cerne Letters of Gilbert Foliot and the Legation of Imar of Tusculum', *English Historical Review*, 63 (1948), pp. 526–7; Barlow, *The English Church 1066–1154*, p. 111.

both Archbishop Theobald and Henry, bishop of Winchester, were trying to persuade the *curia* of their respective claims to be appointed permanent legate in England.[91] Under the circumstances, Westminster could not tactfully petition for a legatine privilege.

The next legatine document issued for Westminster was in fact granted in France, by the cardinal-priest Henry of Pisa, a letter addressed to Hilary, bishop of Chichester, Robert de Chesney, bishop of Lincoln, and Nigel, bishop of Ely. Writing at the request of Abbot Lawrence, he urged them to attend the forthcoming translation of King Edward, following his canonization.[92] The canonization took place in February 1161, and Abbot Lawrence took measures in good time to try to ensure that the subsequent translation would be well-attended. Henry of Pisa was legate in France, 1160–1162, and Abbot Lawrence visited him in Paris with evidence in support of the canonization which Henry and his colleague urged the pope to accept.[93] While the cardinal was in Normandy, in the spring of 1162, the bishops of Chichester and Lincoln visited the duchy.[94] At that period, Becket was barely elected to Canterbury, and there could be no anticipation of the clash between king and archbishop, which in turn might curtail attendance at the translation. Lawrence was leaving nothing to chance, hence his willingness to cross the Channel to enlist the support of the legate, even when the king himself preferred to keep such officials at arm's length.

There then follows another long interval before the date of the next known legatine document granted to Westminster. It was issued in London, in August 1201, by the cardinal priest, John of Salerno.[95] In consideration of the abbey's special relationship with the Holy See, he permitted the solemn chanting of the angelic hymn *Gloria in Excelsis Deo* on the feast of the Purification of the Blessed Virgin (2 February) if it fell after Septuagesima Sunday, on the Feast of the Annunciation (25 March) and on the feast of St Benedict (21 March).[96]

Customarily the *Gloria* was not sung between Septuagesima Sunday and the night of Holy Saturday.[97] The feast of the Purification might fall within the pre-Lenten period following Septuagesima and the other two would almost invariably fall within Lent. All three were, however, major feasts.

91 Robinson, *The Papacy 1073–1198*, p. 160.

92 Westminster Abbey Domesday, f. 388r–v; calendared *Westminster Abbey Charters*, no. 190.

93 Barlow, *Edward the Confessor*, pp. 311 and n. 1; 312.

94 R.W. Eyton, *Court, Household and Itinerary of King Henry II* (Dorchester and London, 1878), p. 56.

95 On the cardinal's visit to England, see *Councils and Synods*, I, ii, no. 184, pp. 1074–5.

96 Westminster Abbey Muniment, 12733; calendared *Westminster Abbey Charters*, no. 191.

97 *The Monastic Constitutions of Lanfranc*, ed. and transl. D. Knowles (London, 1951), p. 17, but see also p. 30.

Abbot Ralph Arundel apparently had a taste for elaborate ceremonial,[98] and it was perhaps on his initiative that this legatine concession was obtained. Monks, in contrast, whether at Westminster or at its daughter-house of Hurley, evidently required some special inducement before they agreed to undertake any additional chanting.[99]

Probably on the same occasion, Cardinal John of Salerno granted an indulgence of forty days to those visiting the abbey on the feast of St Peter in Chains (1 August).[100]

King John's prolonged dispute with Pope Innocent III put a curb on any immediate prospects of obtaining further indulgences, but a few months after his surrender to the papacy in 1213, Nicholas de Romanis, the cardinal bishop of Tusculum, arrived in England. On 11 October, he granted an indulgence of twenty days to those visiting the abbey on the feast of St Peter, on that of St Edward and on that of the Holy Relics. No abbot of Westminster, nor any other individual, might presume to claim a customary right in the offerings made on the feast of SS Peter and Paul, or on that of St Peter in Chains, nor divert those offerings to the use of anyone other than the sacrist, who must administer such revenues faithfully. Anyone infringing this ordinance would incur excommunication.[101]

Nicholas had come briefed to achieve a variety of objectives, ranging from the political to the financial.[102] Among other business, though, was the hearing of the grievances of the monks of Westminster against the high-handed rule of Abbot Ralph Arundel. From the wording of his indulgence it appears that he quickly came to agree with the monks that the abbot had been diverting to other uses funds which the convent deemed to be customarily restricted to specific purposes. Ralph was eventually deposed in January 1214.[103] Not long afterwards the legate's nephew, Mr Robert, son of Robert, was presented to Westminster's church of Launton (Oxon.) by the new abbot

98 *Westminster Abbey Charters*, no. 345.

99 *Ibid.*, nos 302, 345.

100 *Ibid.*, no. 192. While the text simply mentions a 'feast of St Peter' that of St Peter in Chains is probably intended, as in an earlier and probably spurious indulgence in the name of the legate Peter Pierleone (*ibid.*, no. 187).

101 *Ibid.*, no. 193. Nicholas de Romanis, cardinal-bishop of Tusculum, was in England from c. Michaelmas (29 September) 1213, and visited both London and Westminster (*Chronica Rogeri de Wendover liber qui dicitur Flores Historiarium*, ed. H.G. Hewlett, Rolls Series, 3 vols (1886–89), II, pp. 93–4). He was in London 30 September – 2 October, and at Wallingford about the beginning of November 1213 (*Councils and Synods*, II, i, 20–21). See also Angelo Mercati, 'La prima Relazione del Cardinale Nicolo de Romanis sulla Legazione in Inghilterra (1213)', in *Essays presented to R.L. Poole*, ed. H.W.C. Davis (Oxford, 1927), pp. 274–89.

102 *Selected Letters of Pope Innocent III Concerning England (1198–1216)*, ed. C.R. Cheney and W.H. Semple (London, 1953), nos 60–62, 64–5, 70–71.

103 Harvey, *Westminster Abbey and its Estates*, pp. 83–4.

and the monks.[104] A connection between the two events may be deduced, even though unproven.

While legates would often find Westminster a convenient stopping-off place, whether or not they planned to hold a council there, other dignitaries would also pass through on occasion, leaving memories of their visits, as with Philip of Poitou, the bishop-elect of Durham.[105] Legates, of course, intermittently played a prominent role in the politics of Henry III's reign. While the present study does not extend into that period, one legatine ruling may be mentioned here. Cardinal Guala, who played a major part in restoring peace after the civil war of 1215–17, wrote after leaving England for the benefit of Westminster, on 5 November 1219, stating that, although the coronation of Henry III had necessarily been held in Gloucester, this in no way compromised Westminster's status as the coronation church.[106]

Following the Concordat of Avranches of 1172, canon law jurisdiction played an increasingly important role in disputes over clerical property. These judges, usually men with some reputation for knowledge of the canon law, might well be near neighbours of the litigants. In March 1184, for instance, the prior of St Saviour, Bermondsey, and Nicholas the archdeacon of London, resolved a dispute between rival claimants to the church of St Margaret Eastcheap. Westminster's candidate, Geoffrey de Turre, was presented by Abbot Walter and the monks, and instituted by the judges as perpetual vicar. The other candidate evidently had a good case too, since he was assigned an annual pension from this church, together with adequate food and clothing until another church was found for him.[107]

More often, the panels of papal judges delegate who heard pleas about the abbey's property were led by bishops, who also had dealings with Westminster in their episcopal capacity. Even though these individuals were able to keep their two roles distinct, yet their knowledge of, and attitude towards, Westminster acquired in one capacity would inevitably influence their response in the other. For this reason it is as well to consider in turn each of the eminent clerics who has left in the archives of Westminster documentary evidence of his dealings with the abbey.

The slight evidence of contact between Archbishop Anselm and Westminster abbey dates from his earlier years as abbot of Bec, and is therefore

104 *Rotuli Hugonis de Welles, episcopi Lincolniensis*, ed. W.P.W. Phillimore, Canterbury and York Soc., 3 vols (1907–9), I, p. 70.

105 *Westminster Abbey Charters*, no. 307. See also John Le Neve, *Fasti Ecclesiae Anglicanae 1066–1300. II. Monastic Cathedrals*, compiled Diana E. Greenway (London, 1971), p. 30. See also p. 14.

106 Richard of Cirencester, *Speculum Historiale de Gestis Regum Angliae*, ed. J.E.B. Mayor, 2 vols, Rolls Series (1863–9), II, p. 37. Richard cited a tract written for King Richard II by William of Sudbury, another monk of Westminster, who wrote that the legate's letter had been preserved by the monks 'to this day'. A copy of Guala's letter survives in BL Cotton Faustina A. III, f. 263r–v.

107 *Westminster Abbey Charters*, no. 194.

discussed in a later chapter.[108] The earlier part of Theobald's archiepiscopate coincided with the unrest of Stephen's reign, which in turn is reflected in the content of those documents which he issued for the benefit of Westminster. The earliest is a mandate dating from between December 1148 and the early months of 1150, and addressed to Robert de Chesney, bishop of Lincoln. The monks of Westminster had complained of the seizure of property by three landholders in the East Midlands: Alice de Condet (a sister of Ranulf, earl of Chester); John de Stuteville; and Robert Foliot. Theobald himself had already written to each of the three of them, and now ordered Robert de Chesney (as their diocesan bishop) to deploy ecclesiastical censure.[109] At some time in the last years of Stephen's reign – perhaps when it was becoming apparent that he would not found a dynasty – the monks of Westminster requested Theobald to confirm a series of grants which they had purportedly received from the king. By this time Theobald was papal legate and, given the recent extension of canon law jurisdiction, it would be hoped that his authority, at any rate, would be acknowledged by any new dynasty. Theobald's confirmation encompassed the contents of a series of charters for Westminster granted in Stephen's name.[110] Only one of these was genuine[111] although Theobald's attestation appears on all.[112]

In his capacity as resident papal legate, Theobald gave verdicts in two lawsuits involving Westminster. He pronounced in favour of Abbot Gervase in his dispute with William of Ockendon over the advowson of Ockendon church.[113] On another occasion, following a complaint by Gervase, he wrote to Geoffrey Bataille and Richard de Fracheville, ordering them, under pain of anathema, to quit within fifteen days the manor of Kelvedon (Essex), into which they had violently intruded.[114] No doubt the endemic unrest of Stephen's reign had facilitated this intrusion. Like visiting legates, Theobald was also petitioned to grant an indulgence to those visiting the abbey on certain feast days.[115] The question of Westminster's preferred feast days and cults is discussed in more detail in a later chapter, but it should be noted here that the festivals listed by Theobald were by no means identical with those promoted in the indulgence granted about thirty years previously by John of

108 *Ibid.*, nos 26, 50n.

109 *Ibid.*, 195 and note. For Alice de Condet's kinship to Earl Ranulf, see *Regesta Regum Anglo-Normannorum*, III, no. 178; H.A. Cronne, *The Reign of Stephen 1135–54* (London, 1970), p. 287, note 19.

110 A. Saltman, *Theobald, Archbishop of Canterbury* (London, 1956; reprinted 1969), pp. 505–6, no. 275; calendared *Westminster Abbey Charters*, no. 197.

111 *Regesta Regum Anglo-Normannorum*, III, no. 938; calendared *Westminster Abbey Charters*, no. 118.

112 *Regesta Regum Anglo-Normannorum*, III, nos 938–41; calendared *Westminster Abbey Charters*, nos 118–21. One of the forgeries appears to date from the thirteenth century (*Regesta* III, no. 940; calendared *Westminster Abbey Charters*, no. 120).

113 *Westminster Abbey Charters*, no. 198.

114 *Ibid.*, no. 199.

115 *Ibid.*, no. 200.

Crema.[116] Later archbishops, over the period covered by this study, have not left traces of their activities in Westminster's archives. There is no direct mention of Thomas Becket, although, after his death, the monks did present his nephew John to the church of St James Garlickhithe.[117]

In their dealings with the bishop of London, the monks had to walk warily. They needed their diocesan bishop to support their title to lands and income, and to authorize the institution of their nominees to churches of which they held the advowson. At the same time, the monks' long-standing claim to enjoy exemption from the control of their diocesan brought them into friction with him. The earliest surviving charter of a bishop of London for Westminster is one dating from between late November 1120 and January 1127. In this, Richard de Belmeis I grants that the convent may hold the church of Sawbridgeworth (Herts.) with its tithes and other appurtenances, since Henry I gave it to them with his advice and consent and as he, Richard, gave them seisin at the hands of Archdeacon Roger (Fitz Robert, archdeacon of Middlesex).[118] Richard's successor, Gilbert the Universal, is not represented in the abbey's archives, although it has been suggested that a charter surviving among those ascribed to Bishop Gilbert Foliot may in fact have been issued by the earlier Gilbert.[119] That charter confirms Westminster's jurisdiction over Kilburn nunnery, founded during Herbert's abbacy, when it would be natural to enlist the support of the diocesan bishop. Gilbert the Universal is better remembered for the story of his intrusion into the abbey during Mass on the feast of SS Peter and Paul, when he is said to have appropriated the offerings of the altar.[120] Gilbert's claims to assert jurisdiction over Westminster prompted the abbey's successful petition to Pope Innocent II for exemption from diocesan control.[121] Bishop Gilbert's immediate successor, Anselm of Bury (1136–8), has left no trace in Westminster's archives. No document directly granted to Westminster by Bishop Robert de Sigillo is recorded at the abbey, although his formal assent is recorded to an agreement between two clerks concerning a pension due from Westminster's church of St Matthew, Friday Street, in the City of London. This document, drawn up in the chapter of St Paul's, was witnessed by Archdeacon Richard, several of

116 *Ibid.*, no. 189.

117 *Ibid.*, no. 365.

118 *Ibid.*, no. 203; see also no. 86.

119 *Ibid.*, no. 205. The identity of the grantor is raised in *Letters and Charters of Gilbert Foliot*, ed. Z.N. Brooke, A. Morey and C.N.L. Brooke (Cambridge, 1967), no. 463, note.

120 Everett U. Crosby, *Bishop and Chapter in Twelfth-Century England* (Cambridge, 1994), p. 323. On this episode and its consequences, see M. Brett, *The English Church under Henry I* (Oxford, 1975), p. 55. See also Beryl Smalley, 'Gilbert the Universal', *Recherches de théologie ancienne et médiévale*, VII (1935), pp. 245–7.

121 *Papsturkunden in England*, I, no. 17. The forged bulls of Pope Nicholas II and Pope Paschal II, discussed above (calendared, *Westminster Abbey Charters*, nos 153–4), were probably composed about the time that resistance to the bishop became a major issue.

the bishop's clerks and some canons.[122] Soon after King Edward's canonization, Bishop Richard de Belmeis II (the archdeacon of the previous document), granted an indulgence of forty days to all those visiting Westminster on the feast of his Deposition, and on that of his Translation (a ceremony which the bishop did not live to witness).[123]

Bishop Gilbert Foliot, in his role as papal judge-delegate, presided at the hearing of a suit between Abbot Walter and Ranulf the clerk of Feering. This man was alleged to have retained the church of Feering (Essex) after he became a monk (*sic*) at Missenden (Bucks.). Gilbert restored this church to the abbot, and at his request, bestowed it on his clerk, Mr Maurice.[124] Ranulf as an inmate of Missenden was actually an Arrouaisian canon, and his effrontery in retaining Feering church was probably due to his being a brother of the late Pope Adrian IV, a kinship which had perhaps brought him influential contacts. In a second, more detailed record of his verdict in this case, Gilbert Foliot stated that Ranulf's son N. guaranteed his father's undertaking to make restitution, and as security, pledged the whole fee which he held of the abbot of St Albans.[125] These two records were perhaps drawn up on the same occasion, since their attestations are identical. The second document may reflect precautions considered advisable in the light of second thoughts. One further verdict by Gilbert Foliot concerned Westminster's claim to the advowson to two churches in Lincolnshire, Doddington and Thorpe on the Hill. Once Westminster's title was assured, and Abbot Walter and the monks had presented their clerk, Mr Nicholas, several of the other claimants, clergy of the diocese of Lincoln, headed by the vice-archdeacon of Stow, Mr Alexander, were granted the churches in return for pensions payable to Nicholas.[126]

Gilbert Foliot was also involved with Westminster in a variety of transactions over which he presided in his capacity as diocesan bishop. His possible role in confirming Westminster's jurisdiction over Kilburn nunnery has been discussed above.[127]

When the *curialis* Ralph Brito founded and endowed a hospital in Bordwadestone, later represented by Boston House, in Brentford (Middx), the bishop obtained the consent, both of William of Northolt, the parson of Hanwell – since the hospital lay within the bounds of that parish, and also

122 *Westminster Abbey Charters*, no. 380. On St Matthew's, Friday Street, see also *ibid.*, nos 211, 255.

123 *Ibid.*, no. 204.

124 *Letters and Charters of Gilbert Foliot*, no. 465; calendared *Westminster Abbey Charters*, no. 207.

125 *Letters and Charters of Gilbert Foliot*, no. 466; calendared *Westminster Abbey Charters*, no. 208.

126 *Letters and Charters of Gilbert Foliot*, no. 467; calendared *Westminster Abbey Charters*, no. 209.

127 *Letters and Charters of Gilbert Foliot*, no. 463; calendared *Westminster Abbey Charters*, no. 205.

the consent of Abbot Walter and the convent.[128] This church had been included in Archbishop Theobald's confirmation for Westminster.[129] Some years after the hospital was founded, the bishop is recorded instituting Henry of Bayeux as parson of both Greenford and Hanwell, on the presentation of Abbot Walter and the convent.[130] Since the bishop clearly recognized the abbey's title to this church, it is surprising to find it omitted from a list of those, both in the City of London and also in Essex, Hertfordshire and Middlesex, which he confirmed to the abbey.[131]

Because so many individuals might bring forward a claim to one or other of Westminster's churches, the support of the respective diocesan bishops was invaluable. This was particularly so in the London diocese, where influential clerics, and others in high places, concentrated many of their interests. But the need for the bishop's goodwill was not allowed to compromise the abbey's claim to be exempt from his jurisdiction, a privilege claimed in several papal bulls which the abbey obtained in the course of the twelfth century.[132] The uneasy relationship between bishop and abbot is clearly visible in documents surviving from the time of Abbot Lawrence. On the one hand, he supported Gilbert Foliot during the Becket dispute.[133] Lawrence also witnessed Gilbert's verdict in a dispute between two rival religious houses.[134] On the other hand rights of jurisdiction could give rise to conflicts between the parties. According to Abbot Lawrence, the church of St Margaret, Westminster, was exempt from rendering synodal dues to the bishop, a claim which the bishop strongly contested.[135] Similarly disputes could arise over property, and these were intensified when family interests were concerned. Roger of Darnford claimed to hold, of Westminster, in inheritance, land in which his territorial predecessor had been confirmed by Abbot Gervase; by the convent separately; and by the Empress Matilda.[136] Notwithstanding these confirmations, Abbot Lawrence tried to deny Roger's right to succeed to the tenancy. Roger, though, was a kinsman by marriage of Gilbert Foliot, who wrote to the

128 *Letters and Charters of Gilbert Foliot*, no. 464; calendared *Westminster Abbey Charters*, no. 206.

129 Saltman, *Theobld*, pp. 505–6, no. 275; calendared *Westminster Abbey Charters*, no. 197.

130 *Letters and Charters of Gilbert Foliot*, no. 468; calendared *Westminster Abbey Charters*, no. 210.

131 *Letters and Charters of Gilbert Foliot*, no. 462; calendared *Westminster Abbey Charters*, no. 211.

132 For instance, *Papsturkunden in England*, I, nos 17, 113; calendared *Westminster Abbey Charters*, nos 155, 172.

133 *Materials for the History of Thomas Becket, Archbishop of Canterbury*, ed. J.C. Robertson and J.B. Sheppard, 7 vols, Rolls Series (1875–85), VI, pp. 621–2, no. DXIX, dating from 1169.

134 *Letters and Charters of Gilbert Foliot*, no. 391.

135 *Ibid.*, no. 229 and notes.

136 *Regesta Regum Anglo-Normannorum*, III, no. 259; *Westminster Abbey Charters*, nos 98, 271, 341.

powerful Geoffrey Ridel, at that time archdeacon of Canterbury, asking him to use his influence with the king on Roger's behalf.[137]

Gilbert's successor, Richard Fitz Nigel, was enlisted repeatedly on Westminster's behalf. He issued two charters confirming the churches held by the abbey throughout his diocese, the first of these generally worded[138] and the second listing each church with its pension and any other appurtenances.[139] Evidently he was receptive to representations that the abbey needed to augment the official income of various obedientiaries. He granted the church of South Benfleet so that its revenues would augment the pittancer's office. A vicarage was established to support the chaplain who would serve the church, and consent for this was obtained from the parson, Ivo of Cornwall, archdeacon of Derby.[140] A second office to benefit from the bishop's attention was the sacristy. Richard confirmed a pension of £2 annually, payable from the church of Staines (Middx) to pay for the improved lighting of the abbey church.[141] Thirdly, at the petition of Abbot William Postard and the convent, the bishop established an annual pension of 2 marks (£1 6d 8d) payable annually by the rector of Sunbury (Middx), to the abbey chamber.[142] The bishop is also recorded, on occasion, instituting clergy to one or another of Westminster's parish churches. When Ivo of Cornwall, in his capacity as parson of South Benfleet, presented the chaplain John of Thrapston to its perpetual vicarage, the arrangements for financing this were again clearly specified.[143] On the other hand, when he instituted Joseph the chaplain, on the representation of Abbot William Postard and the convent, to St Martin's, Ludgate, it was stated that Joseph would render to the monks the pension formerly due from it. Richard's eye for financial detail no doubt owed something to his long former service as royal treasurer. In that capacity he had occupied, as a tenant of the abbey, a substantial group of houses and other buildings, but confirmed these to his kinsman William of Ely, a canon of St Paul's,[144] who succeeded him in his office of royal treasurer.[145] Abbot William Postard confirmed this transfer,[146] which King John further confirmed to William, after the bishop's death.[147] Following a political miscalculation during the civil war towards the end of King John's reign, William lost

137 *Letters and Charters of Gilbert Foliot*, no. 230.

138 *Westminster Abbey Charters*, no. 212.

139 *Ibid.*, no. 213.

140 *Ibid.*, no. 214.

141 *Ibid.*, no. 216.

142 *Ibid.*, no. 217.

143 *Ibid.*, no. 215.

144 John Le Neve, *Fasti Ecclesiae Anglicanae 1066–1300. I. St Paul's London*, compiled Diana E. Greenway (London, 1968), p. 35.

145 H.G. Richardson, 'William of Ely, the King's Treasurer', *Transactions of the Royal Historical Society*, 4th series, 15 (1932), pp. 45–90, esp. pp. 79–80; calendared *Westminster Abbey Charters*, no. 219.

146 *Westminster Abbey Charters*, no. 313.

147 *Rotuli Chartarum in Turri Londoniensi asservati 1199–1216*, ed. T. Duffus Hardy, Record

his office of treasurer.[148] Early in the next reign, he 'gave and confirmed' the houses, their courtyard and an unattached stable to the monks, who, however, allowed him to continue to occupy the premises, in return for an annual payment of one pound of incense on the feast of the Ascension, in addition to the candle of 2 pounds weight which he customarily rendered on the feast of the Translation of St Edward.[149] These costly items reflect both the desirability of the property and the assumption that a (former) royal treasurer was unlikely to have cash-flow problems.

Richard of Ely's successor as bishop of London, William de Sainte Merè Eglise, had, as diocesan, oversight of several of Westminster's parish churches. On 14 April 1208, on the presentation of Abbot Ralph Arundel and the convent, and the prior and convent of Bermondsey, the bishop instituted Mr Simon de Valenciis, clerk, to the church of St Magnus the Martyr, London Bridge, reserving the pensions due respectively to the two religious houses.[150] Mr Simon was probably an older kinsman of the Mr Simon of London, *alias* de Valenciis, who was an episcopal clerk, and prebendary of Thame, in the bishopric of Lincoln, 1241–c.1259.[151] The Simon de Valenciis of King John's reign is unlikely to be identical with this prebendary who was active fifty years later, but may well be identical with the Mr Simon of London who witnessed two charters of Abbot Ralph;[152] witnessed two grants made to Westminster in the early thirteenth century;[153] made two grants to the abbey, respectively of land in London and in Westminster; in both of which he identified himself as son of Walter Black (*Niger*).[154] On 5 October 1213 he was instituted by Hugh of Wells, bishop of Lincoln, to Westminster's church of Launton.[155] Some years later, William de Sainte Merè Eglise himself made a presentation to Westminster's church of Wennington (Essex), in order to terminate a vacancy of several years while the advowson was contested between Abbot William de Humez and the monks on the one hand, and the knight Gilbert de Tany on the other. Not wishing to leave the church any longer without an incumbent, the bishop cited the authority of the Fourth Lateran Council (of 1215) for his decision to institute his clerk Thomas Fitz Henry, who would hold the church for life, rendering the annual pension, said to have been due from ancient times, to whichever litigant was able to

Comm. (London, 1837), p. 49a, membrane 10; calendared *Westminster Abbey Charters*, no. 147.

148 Richardson, 'William of Ely', pp. 55–8.

149 *Westminster Abbey Charters*, no. 439; Richardson, 'William of Ely', p. 89.

150 *Westminster Abbey Charters*, no. 220; see also nos 287, 368.

151 John Le Neve, *Fasti Ecclesiae Anglicanae 1066–1300. III. Lincoln*, compiled Diana E. Greenway (London, 1977), p. 102.

152 *Westminster Abbey Charters*, nos 328, 335.

153 *Ibid.*, nos 420, 424.

154 *Ibid.*, nos 356, 431.

155 *Ibid.*, no. 227.

prove his case.[156] Abbot William eventually established Westminster's claim to the advowson of Wennington in the early months of 1222, in a lawsuit against Gilbert de Marisco, who received a grant of confraternity in return for relinquishing his claims.[157] This latter litigant was perhaps a kinsman (but was not an heir) of Gilbert de Tany, lord of Aveley (Essex) who died in 1221.[158] The bishop, like his predecessor, was responsive to Westminster's requests for permission to increase the income of its major offices. After consulting Cardinal Guala and others, he permitted the abbey to appropriate the church of Staines (Middx), so that its income was assigned to the almonry. Certain tithes were reserved for the vicar, who would be presented to the bishop by the abbot and convent, reserving the rights of the current vicar in the church of Teddington.[159]

Westminster possessed several churches in the large diocese of Lincoln, and hence had intermittent dealings with its bishops. Bishop Robert de Chesney was one of those prelates whose help was solicited in fostering the cult of King Edward, in the wake of his canonization. Probably around the celebrations which marked his translation, the bishop granted an indulgence of twenty days, and participation in all the spiritual benefits of the church of Lincoln, to everyone who visited the tomb of St Edward on the feasts of his Deposition and his Translation, and within their quindenes.[160] Some years later, Robert de Chesney notified Nicholas de Sigillo, the archdeacon of Huntingdon, and the clergy and laity of Huntingdonshire and Hertfordshire, that, at the request of 'his friends' Abbot Lawrence and Richard of Ilchester, the archdeacon of Poitiers, he had confirmed the perpetual vicarage of Datchworth to Elias the clerk.[161] Richard of Ilchester was already an influential figure in the mid 1160s, when that presentation was made. Both Abbot Lawrence and Robert de Chesney would find it advantageous to be able to call on his goodwill.

Hugh of Avallon, better remembered as St Hugh of Lincoln, had various dealings with Westminster. Some time between September 1186 and October 1188, he instituted his own clerk, Mr Edmund, as parson of Deene (Northants) on the presentation of Abbot Walter and the convent, reserving

156 BL Cotton Faustina A. III, f. 247r–v. For Gilbert de Tany, see I.J. Sanders, *English Baronies. A Study of their Origin and Descent 1086–1327* (Oxford, 1960), p. 4. The bishop's justification for intervening perhaps derived from his interpretation of statutes 45 and 65 of the Fourth Lateran Council: *Sacrorum Conciliorum Nova et Amplissima Collectio*, ed. J.D. Mansi, *et al.*, 54 vols in 59, (Graz, 1960–61), XXII, pp. 1030, 1054.

157 *Feet of Fines for Essex*, ed. R.E.G. Kirk, 2 vols, A.D. 1182–1326 (Colchester, 1899–1928), I, no. 93.

158 Sanders, *English Baronies*, p. 4.

159 BL Cotton Faustina A. III, ff. 255r–256r; see also f. 256r–v.

160 *English Episcopal Acta. IV. Lincoln, 1186–1206*, ed. D.M. Smith (London, 1986), Appendix I, no. XIX; calendared *Westminster Abbey Charters*, no. 221.

161 *English Episcopal Acta. IV. Lincoln 1186–1206*, Appendix I, no. XX; calendared *Westminster Abbey Charters*, no. 222.

the perpetual vicarage held for life by Simon the clerk, together with all episcopal customary rights and the dignity of the church of Lincoln.[162] In the early 1190s, the bishop confirmed to Mr Nicholas of Westminster (a clerk of the abbot),[163] the churches of Thorpe-on-the-Hill and Doddington (Lincs.) as he held them by grant of the abbot of Westminster, in return for an annual pension of two besants (4 shillings), excepting the perpetual vicarage held by Mr Alexander, the archdeacon of Stow, who held the churches for life, and rendered a pension of £5 annually to Mr Nicholas, and also reserving the episcopal customs and the dignity of the church of Lincoln.[164] Since Nicholas had been instituted to these churches by the then papal judge-delegate, Bishop Gilbert Foliot, Mr Alexander had acquired the reversion of the subsidiary rights in them which had earlier been assigned to Robert Code and the clerk Haket.[165] The discreet wording of the bishop's charter may indicate that Alexander, one of his own diocesan dignitaries,[166] had been resisting the payment due annually to one of the abbot's confidential clerks.

About five or six years later again, the bishop confirmed to the abbot and convent the churches of Oakham and Hambleton, in Rutland, which Westminster had received from King William I, so that the monks received annually from the incumbent a pension of thirty marks (£20) towards the maintenance of a hospital, reserving the customs and dignity of the church of Lincoln.[167] There is a clear discrepancy between this pension of thirty marks, which the bishop believed would accrue jointly to the abbot and convent, and the allocation of only twenty-one marks (£14) which Abbot William Postard granted to the monks for the infirmary, in return for the celebration of his anniversary.[168] His apparent reservation of the balance for his own purposes illustrates the belief of his monks that his managerial style was altogether too high-handed.[169] Moreover, to obtain even this diminished allocation, the abbot required them to undertake the additional commemoration of his anniversary. As demonstrated above, such increased obligations were regarded without enthusiasm unless accompanied by some inducement, but William Postard's top-slicing of the pension scarcely came into that

162 *English Episcopal Acta. IV. Lincoln 1186–1206*, no. 209; calendared *Westminster Abbey Charters*, no. 223. See also no. 338, in which the Simon of Deene may be identical with this vicar.

163 On Mr Nicholas, see *Westminster Abbey Charters*, no. 209.

164 *English Episcopal Acta. IV. Lincoln 1186–1206*, no. 210; calendared *Westminster Abbey Charters*, no. 224.

165 *Letters and Charters of Gilbert Foliot*, no. 467; calendared *Westminster Abbey Charters*, no. 209.

166 Le Neve, *Fasti Ecclesiae Anglicanae 1066–1300. III. Lincoln*, pp. 45, 110.

167 *English Episcopal Acta. Lincoln 1186–1206*, no. 212; calendared *Westminster Abbey Charters*, no. 226 and note.

168 *Westminster Abbey Charters*, no. 321.

169 This belief on the part of the convent led to the monks' successful petition for a papal bull upholding their rights. *The Letters of Pope Innocent II (1198–1216)*, p. 203, no. 113; calendared *Westminster Abbey Charters*, no. 186.

category. Disagreements between the abbot and his monks, however, were outside the bishop's remit. On the other hand, in his capacity as a papal judge-delegate, acting with the abbot of St Albans, John de Cella, and Benedict, the abbot of Stratford Langthorne, he resolved, to Westminster's disadvantage, a dispute between the abbot and monks, on the one hand, and the abbess and nuns of Godstow on the other, over the church of Bloxham (Oxon.).[170] This had certainly been held by Westminster during the time of Abbot Gervase, when the incumbent was Robert de Chesney, in his pre-episcopal days.[171] In the time of Abbot Lawrence, the incumbent was the royal physician, Mr Ralph de Beaumont,[172] but Henry II subsequently conveyed the church to Godstow, where his mistress Rosamund Clifford (d.c.1176) was buried. A series of confirmations by dignitaries of church and state, including one from Pope Celestine III in 1191, strengthened the nuns' title. Under the circumstances, Westminster could scarcely hope to recover its property, and settled for an agreed pension of 5 marks (£3 6s 8d) annually.[173]

Hugh's immediate successor, William of Blois, bishop of Lincoln 1203–1206,[174] did not, apparently, have any significant dealings with Westminster. The next bishop of Lincoln, Hugh of Wells (1209–1235), would probably have been an old acquaintance of the *seniores* of the abbey, in his former capacity as keeper of the royal seal.[175] However, within the period under discussion, his one known direct transaction with Westminster was his institution of Mr Simon of London to the church of Launton (Oxon.), on the presentation of its patrons, Abbot Ralph and the convent, but reserving to Henry de Colwell his perpetual vicarage there. The bishop's formal notification was dated at London, on 5 October 1213.[176] This was about the time that the legate Nicholas de Romanis began to investigate the monks' allegations against Abbot Ralph. Despite the agreement negotiated by Hugh of Wells, Simon challenged Henry's occupancy of the vicarage. On 14 October 1214, papal judges-delegate resolved this dispute, leaving Henry in peaceful possession of his vicarage in return for certain payments to Simon.[177] In the event, the persecuted vicar outlasted the parson, and was still perpetual vicar when Mr Robert, son of Robert, nephew of Nicholas de Romanis, was presented to that church.[178]

170 *English Episcopal Acta. IV. Lincoln 1186–1206*, no. 211; Jane Sayers, *Papal Judges-Delegate in the Province of Canterbury 1198– 1254: a Study in Ecclesiastical Administration* (1971), Appendix B, pp. 354–5, no. 5.

171 *Westminster Abbey Charters*, no. 253.

172 *Ibid.*, no. 286.

173 *Ibid.*, no. 225 and note; see also nos 323, 481.

174 Le Neve, *Fasti Ecclesiae Anglicanae 1066–1300. III. Lincoln*, p. 3.

175 *Ibid.*, p. 3.

176 *Westminster Abbey Charters*, no. 227.

177 Westminster Abbey Muniment 15684; Westminster Abbey Domesday f. 276r–v. See also *The Letters of Pope Innocent III*, p. 149, no. 901; p. 264, no. 901; Sayers, *Papal Judges-Delegate*, p. 291, no. 76; p. 297, no. 5.

178 *Rotuli Hugonis de Welles*, I, p. 70.

While Westminster's main parochial interests lay in the dioceses of London and Lincoln, they also held parochial churches elsewhere. In addition they had dealings with various other prelates who came into contact with them over a variety of business. In the Chichester diocese their main possession was Parham with its church.[179] Their title to the church was effectively secured when the advowson was quitclaimed to Abbot William Postard by Baldwin of Parham in November 1199.[180] Probably as a result of this, the abbey came into the possession of a writ of Hilary, bishop of Chichester (1147–69), ordering William son of Gervase and Mr Serlo that they were not to exact any secular service from the virgate of land given by William son of Odo to St Peter's church, Parham, and to the bishop's clerk, Alberic.[181] Church lands were vulnerable, especially in time of unrest, and in circumstances where predators had powerful patrons. Mr Serlo was a clerk of Queen Alice, who, with her second husband, William d'Aubigny, earl of Arundel, eventually promised restitution of exactions they had taken from churches in the diocese of Chichester.[182]

Westminster's interests did not extend as far north as the diocese of Durham, but Bishop Hugh du Puiset (1153–1195) was a cousin of Abbot Gervase, and most probably it was on the grounds of their kinship that he granted an indulgence of ten days and the prayers of the church of Durham to all those visiting the abbey on the Petrine feasts.[183] Similarly, Westminster had no landed or parochial interests in the Exeter diocese, but in the latter part of the twelfth century, as the palace of Westminster increasingly became the main focus of royal government, so those with interests to protect found it convenient to have a residence in the vill. Among these incomers was Henry Marshal, bishop of Exeter (1194–1206), who obtained the permission of Abbot William Postard and the convent to build a chapel in Longditch Street, for the use of himself and his episcopal successors, and his *familia*, on the understanding that the rights of the abbey, and of its parish church of St Margaret's, would not be injured.[184]

The Surrey properties of Westminster abbey, right up to the south bank of the Thames opposite London and Westminster, lay in the diocese of Winchester, and hence its bishop had oversight of the abbey's parish churches in that neighbourhood. The churches of Battersea and Wandsworth were granted by Abbot Lawrence for the use of the abbey's infirmary, a concession

179 *Westminster Abbey Charters*, nos 325–6, 334–5.

180 *Ibid.*, no. 325.

181 *The Acta of the Bishops of Chichester 1075–1207*, ed. H. Mayr-Harting, Canterbury and York Soc. (1964), pp. 114–15, no. 55; calendared *Westminster Abbey Charters*, no. 228.

182 *The Chartulary of the High Church of Chichester*, ed. W.D. Peckham, Sussex Record Soc., XLVI (1961), no. 297. See also *Papsturkunden in England*, II, no. 57, dated 1148.

183 *Westminster Abbey Charters*, no. 229.

184 *Ibid.*, no. 230.

which was confirmed by Pope Alexander III in February 1161,[185] and reconfirmed by Pope Lucius III between 1182 and 1185.[186] The need to gain this second confirmation was perhaps prompted by difficulties experienced in retaining the churches, since the bishop of Winchester apparently asserted control over them at some time. Most likely it was in response to this mandate of Pope Lucius that Richard of Ilchester, bishop of Winchester (1173–88), 'granted' these churches, in honour of St Katherine, to support the infirmary chapel. A vicarage was to be established, with perpetual vicars, presented by the abbot and convent, and instituted by, and answerable to, the bishop of Winchester.[187] This episcopal charter was later produced before the bishop's successor, Godfrey de Lucy, who inspected and confirmed it, specifying the annual pensions to be rendered by the perpetual vicars from these churches.[188] Richard of Ilchester was a powerful figure. At times he acted in association with Abbot Lawrence,[189] and to some extent also with Abbot Walter,[190] but his prominent position in political life enabled him to take liberties which were not available to others. Some years after his death Herbert le Poer, archdeacon of Canterbury, who was probably his son,[191] quitclaimed to Abbot William Postard and the convent the land called New Court at Staines (Middx), which his father took from the abbey and treated as his own demesne, although Herbert himself, while continuing to hold it, rendered 10 shillings (annually).[192]

Westminster's extensive lands in the West Midlands would have held a number of parish churches. However the lands themselves have left little trace in the twelfth-century muniments of the abbey, when most were farmed on long leases. Rights of advowson over some of the churches on these estates were perhaps exercised in practice by the respective farmers, but this was not always the case. Mauger, bishop of Worcester (1200–1212), instituted Mr Simon as parson of Todenham (Glos.) at the presentation of Abbot Ralph Arundel and the convent, reserving parochial and episcopal dues.[193]

On rare occasions, the bishops of Continental dioceses had occasion to become involved with the abbey. The archbishop of Rouen, Walter de Coutances, granted an indulgence to those visiting Westminster on a series of

185 *Papsturkunden in England*, I, no. 85; calendared *Westminster Abbey Charters*, no. 169.
186 *Papsturkunden in England*, I, no. 232; calendared *Westminster Abbey Charters*, no. 177.
187 *English Episcopal Acta. VIII. Winchester 1070–1204*, ed. M.J. Franklin (Oxford, 1993), no. 188; calendared *Westminster Abbey Charters*, no. 231.
188 *English Episcopal Acta. VIII. Winchester 1070–1204*, no. 249; calendared *Westminster Abbey Charters*, no. 232.
189 See for instance, *Westminster Abbey Charters*, nos 222, 277–8, 281, 468.
190 *Ibid.*, nos 287, 361.
191 On the kinship of Herbert le Poer to Richard of Ilchester, see C. Duggan, 'Richard of Ilchester, Royal Servant and Bishop', *Transactions of the Royal Historical Society* 5th series, 16 (1966), p. 3 and n. 3; John Le Neve, *Fasti Ecclesiae Anglicanae 1066–1300. IV. Salisbury*, compiled Diana E. Greenway (London, 1991), p. 3 and n. 3.
192 *Westminster Abbey Charters*, no. 457.
193 *Ibid.*, no. 233.

major festivals, on the Petrine feasts, and those of King Edward.[194] Walter was said to be a Cornishman by birth, and his earlier career had been spent in England, where he was successively archdeacon of Oxford and bishop of Lincoln.[195] He was subsequently archbishop for upwards of twenty-two years,[196] but the most likely period when he would have issued this indulgence would be during his brief spell as Justiciar of England, from about October 1191 to late 1193.[197]

The bishop of Séez, Froger, similarly had cross-Channel interests, if not on so conspicuous a level. At some stage he acquired the London church of St James, Garlickhithe, perhaps in recompense for diplomatic services. In 1167 and again in 1170, he acted on behalf of Henry II in negotiations with Thomas Becket. Subsequent to the archbishop's murder and canonization, he perhaps felt the need to expiate any offence he might be deemed to have incurred by such activities. In any event, he granted his London church to John, a nephew of Thomas Becket. This new incumbent would render an annual pension to Westminster. Froger's need to make restitution to the kindred of Becket is indicated by the appearance of several of its members among the witnesses to this transaction. These include Mary Becket, abbess of Barking (whose own promotion represented one element in the restitution made by the king himself); Theobald, another nephew of Becket; and Stephen, a kinsman of his.[198]

One further Continental cleric whose interests overlapped with those of Westminster was Bartholomew de Vendôme, archbishop of Tours. In a formal statement made to Archbishop Richard, Ranulf Glanville the Justiciar and the other judges, he declared that he had formerly held Ockendon church, to which he had been presented by the late Abbot Lawrence at the request of Queen Eleanor. Bartholomew's evidence was given in response to a request by Abbot Walter when he was contesting the advowson of Ockendon against 'a certain knight'.[199]

While several of the episcopal charters discussed above indicate that diocesan bishops themselves habitually instituted clergy newly-presented to parochial churches, a few of the Westminster charters record the involvement of archdeacons. The earliest, dating from c.1164x1166, is a confirmation by Nicholas de Sigillo, archdeacon of Huntingdon, to Elias the clerk, of the perpetual vicarage of Datchworth (Herts.). Elias was the joint candidate of Abbot Lawrence and Richard of Ilchester, archdeacon of Poitou, the parson of this church. Elias would render two *aurei* annually to Richard so

194 *Ibid.*, no. 401.

195 Le Neve, *Fasti Ecclesiae Anglicanae 1066–1300. III. Lincoln*, p. 2 and n. 3.

196 Walter's career is discussed by L. Delisle, in his *Introduction to Recueil des Actes de Henri II* (Paris, 1909), pp. 106–13.

197 F. West, *The Justiciarship in England 1066–1232* (Cambridge, 1966), pp. 74–8.

198 *Westminster Abbey Charters*, no. 365 and note.

199 *Ibid.*, no. 463.

long as he remained parson, and would subsequently render this to the abbey.[200]

Records also survive of two institutions made by another Nicholas, the archdeacon of London (1162–89).[201] On the presentation of Abbot Walter and the convent he instituted Geoffrey of Bedford to St Margaret's, Bridge Street (or Fish Street), from which Geoffrey would pay an annual pension of 10 shillings to the abbey chamber.[202] That transaction occurred at some uncertain date between 1175 and 1189. A shorter span encompasses the period within which Nicholas, on the joint presentation of Abbot Walter and the convent, and of Prior Henry de Soilli and the convent of Bermondsey, who shared between them the advowson of St Magnus the Martyr, acting through his Official, received his nephew, Mr Nicholas, as parson of this church and inducted him into possession of it.[203] No doubt all concerned considered this a prudent appointment, in view of unforeseen difficulties which might occasionally call for the archdeacon's intervention. Westminster kept a vigilant eye on its existing advowsons. These were both a source of income, in the form of annual pensions rendered by the incumbents, and were also a means of providing for the abbey's expert clerks. Lawrence son of William 'conceded and resigned' the right which he claimed in the advowson of St Martin, Ludgate, and was recompensed with a grant of confraternity.[204] He had acquired this 'chapel' together with the land to which it pertained, from his uncle, Lawrence of Stanstead, who stated that this chapel was 'founded on my fee'.[205] Arguably, of course, this 'fee' may have been land held of the abbey, hence the expression 'conceded and resigned'. Another London resident, Anselm son of Hakon, quitclaimed to Abbot Ralph and the convent the church of St Clement, Candlewick Street, off Eastcheap, renouncing any future claim to the advowson.[206]

Property rights apparently interested the monks of Westminster more than did the niceties of the canon law regarding clerical celibacy. Abbot Lawrence and the convent presented Ralph to the church of Hendon (Middx), and subsequently Ralph's son Stephen was presented in turn. Following his institution by Bishop Gilbert Foliot, he held the church for forty-three years. In view of Stephen's long incumbency the monks probably felt the need to document the circumstances in which he acquired his benefice, to prevent any kinsman of his from claiming the right to the advowson in succession to him. Stephen, in this document (probably drafted in the *scriptorium*), is made to describe the monks as 'true patrons' of the church of

200 *Ibid.*, no. 468.
201 On Archdeacon Nicholas, see Le Neve, *Fasti Ecclesiae Anglicanae 1066–1300. I. St Paul's London*, p. 9.
202 *Westminster Abbey Charters*, no. 369.
203 *Ibid.*, no. 368.
204 *Ibid.*, no. 359.
205 *Ibid.*, no. 358.
206 *Ibid.*, no. 363.

Hendon.[207] The annual pension of 2 marks (£1 6s 8d) rendered by Stephen to the sacristy had apparently remained unchanged for the duration of his tenure, which, for him at any rate, was gratifying in a period of high inflation.

It is possible that Westminster did increase the pensions due from its Rutland churches of Oakham and Hambleton, about the end of the twelfth century, when James le Salvage was their incumbent. His charters recording his solemn undertaking to render these sums evidently anticipated some difficulty being raised by the pope and the diocesan bishop (of Lincoln), presumably on the grounds that the customary dues were being dramatically increased. He undertook to pay either the thirty marks (£20) from Oakham church itself, or else from his Kentish churches of Swanscombe and Stockbury.[208] Similarly, he would render twenty marks (£13 5s 8d) from the church of Hambledon.[209] The elaborate prose of his charters (perhaps products of the Westminster *scriptorium*) indicates the seriousness of his undertakings. James was a member of the *familia* of Archbishop Hubert Walter,[210] and then in 1206 he served as clerk to King John.[211] His total income would render him able to make the annual payments, while his undertaking about Oakham was attested by the hard-headed Archbishop Hubert, together with other dignitaries.

The possible difficulties arising from a parson's longevity, already witnessed in Hendon, were echoed at Kelvedon in Essex. There Nigel of Kelvedon, the parson, presented by Abbot Lawrence, died around the beginning of Henry III's reign, having occupied the living for over forty years. The circumstances of his presentation would have faded from memory, and a claim to the advowson was brought forward by Baldwin Fillol, a member of a prominent local family. Abbot William de Humez, however, stated the case in a way which Baldwin could not refute, and the advowson was secured for Westminster.[212] An interesting feature of this case is that Westminster apparently preferred to conduct cases of darrein presentment in the secular courts, rather than contest rights of advowson in church courts. In this, as in other aspects of ecclesiastical law and politics, the Westminster ethos was evidently pragmatic, rather than doctrinaire.

207 *Ibid.*, no. 459.

208 *Ibid.*, no. 482. I am grateful to the late Nicholas MacMichael for his help in identifying these churches.

209 *Ibid.*, no. 483.

210 *English Episcopal Acta. III. Canterbury 1193–1205*, ed. C.R. Cheney and E. John (Oxford, 1986), p. 307 nn. 11–12.

211 *Rotuli Chartarum 1199–1216*, f. 165b; calendared *Westminster Abbey Charters*, no. 150.

212 Westminster Abbey Muniment 1007.

8

The Abbey and the Royal Court

Links between the abbey and the courts of the early regional kingdoms may be deduced from the gifts of Offa of Mercia and earlier shadowy, if not legendary, royal benefactors.[1] More firmly, there is evidence of benefactions by King Edgar of lands in south-east England, while his former thegn, Aelfhelm Polga, bequeathed land in Brickendon (Herts.).[2] In the mid eleventh century, the construction of a new royal palace on Thorn Island ensured that king and monks would be close neighbours, whenever his itinerary brought him to the London area. Down to the middle decades of the twelfth century, it appears likely that when the king was in residence in the palace he normally heard Mass in the abbey. This is implied in an episode which occurred in 1155, during the long-running dispute between the abbot of Battle and the bishop of Chichester. The abbot tried to petition Henry II by waylaying him at early Mass in the abbey, but was interrupted when the bishop came hurrying up, and their rival claims distracted the king's attention throughout almost the whole of the liturgy. Before the end of this reign, however, a chapel was constructed within the royal palace.[3] Because of the juxtaposition of the palace and the monastic precincts, abbots claimed to exercise certain ecclesiastical rights over the palace. The abbot claimed the prerogative of granting licence for the celebration of the divine office in its oratories, and, together with the monks, he claimed the customary right of holding within the palace certain 'stations' and processions.[4] Westminster has not been identified as a venue for the Christmas court before December 1065, when the court assembled there in preparation for the reconsecration

1 Barbara Harvey, *Westminster Abbey and its Estates in the Middle Ages* (Oxford, 1977), pp. 20–22, 345–6.

2 *Ibid.*, 341–2, 346, 353–4, 359. For the grant by Aelfhelm Polga, *ibid.*, p. 23.

3 For the Battle-Chichester episode, see *The Chronicle of Battle Abbey*, ed. and transl. Eleanor Searle (Oxford, 1980), pp. 156, 200. On the construction of the palace chapel, see Barbara Harvey, *Living and Dying in England 1100–1540: the Monastic Experience* (Oxford, 1993), p. 3; H.M. Colvin, ed., *The History of the King's Works*, 6 vols (H.M.S.O., 1963–82), I, p. 493.

4 College of Arms, London, MS Young 72, f. cxlvi.

of the abbey.[5] Late evidence indicates, however, that at least one Easter court was held there in Edward's reign.[6] Several identified lay benefactors of this period are not known to have been members of Edward's court,[7] but others clearly had official responsibilities: Denham (Bucks.) was donated by the thegn Ulstan,[8] although the Tostig who, with his wife Leofrun, gave Claygate, is unlikely to have been Tostig Godwineson.[9] The manor of Deene (Northants.) was recorded as a donation of King Edward, although his chamberlain Hugh, *alias* Hugolin, was perhaps associated with it.[10] Hugolin was buried in the cloister of the abbey, although when rebuilding of Westminster took place in the reign of Henry III, his remains, with those of others buried in the cloister, were removed to the entrance to the chapter house. The fifteenth-century monastic historian John Flete described 'the noble Hugolin, chief chamberlain of the holy King Edward, always devoted to God and to that king, and the most faithful knight of all the nobles of the realm'. He added that the original inscription on his tomb read:

> O Hugolin, whom this place holds, you fell unjustly; You are celebrated in praise, because you are equal to the martyrs in your death.[11]

It may be that he lost his life in defence of King Edward's reputation, or of his endowments to the abbey.[12] During Edward's reign, Hugolin possibly had charge of the royal treasure. That is certainly the implication of a story told in detail by Ailred of Rievaulx in his version of the *Life of the Holy King Edward*.[13] Hugolin's importance in Edward's administration is indicated by the extent of his recorded landholdings, and his style and prominence in surviving charters.[14]

Links between the abbey and officials of the royal court continued in subsequent reigns. In the short reign of Harold II, the thegn Ingulf gave

5 *The Life of King Edward who Rests at Westminster*, attributed to a monk of Saint-Bertin, ed. and transl. Frank Barlow, 2nd edn (Oxford, 1992), p. 111; Martin Biddle, 'Seasonal Festivals and Residence: Winchester, Westminster and Gloucester in the Tenth to Twelfth Centuries', in R. Allen Brown, ed., *Anglo-Norman Studies, VIII, Proceedings of the Battle Conference 1985* (Woodbridge, 1986), p. 69.

6 *The Life of King Edward*, p. 103, and notes.

7 Harvey, *Westminster Abbey and its Estates*, pp. 342, 343, 344, 348, 351.

8 *Ibid.*, p. 338.

9 *Ibid.*, p. 358.

10 *Ibid.*, p. 355 and n. 4.

11 John Flete, *The History of Westminster Abbey*, ed. J. Armitage Robinson (Cambridge, 1909), p. 83.

12 Frank Barlow, *Edward the Confessor* (London, 1970), pp. 165–6. On Hugolin see also *ibid.*, pp. 150, 335.

13 *Vita Sancti Edwardi Regis*, *Patrologia Latina*, ed. J.P. Migne, CXCV, col. 746; Frank Barlow, *The English Church 1000–1066*, 2nd edn (London, 1979), pp. 123–4.

14 Simon Keynes, 'Regenbald the Chancellor (*sic*)', in R. Allen Brown, ed., *Anglo-Norman Studies, X, Proceedings of the Battle Conference 1987* (Woodbridge, 1988), pp. 190 n. 36, 207.

Paglesham (Essex) to Westminster.[15] Albert the Lotharingian, a royal clerk after the Norman Conquest, held churches and their appurtenant lands in Rutland, which were subsequently granted to Abbot Gilbert Crispin by William II.[16] King Edward had intended that extensive estates in Rutland should accrue to Westminster on the death of Queen Edith, but that delayed bequest was not fulfilled.[17] Albert was among the beneficiaries substituted by William I, and the subsequent reversion to Westminster was presumably due to diligent petitioning on the part of the abbot. Albert's tenure no doubt resulted from his position at court, and while his son Hugh succeeded to his prebend in St Paul's[18] he was evidently not in a position to match whatever offer Gilbert Crispin made to secure the churches, the value of which had increased in recent decades.[19]

In the later eleventh century, Westminster claimed the land called Chalkhill, in Kingsbury (Middx), on the grounds that it had been donated by Thurstan, a housecarl of King Edward, and confirmed by that king. A confirmation was eventually obtained from William I, but the date of this transaction is uncertain since, while the charter has an authentic base, its attestations, and probably also its franchisal clauses, have been added at a later date. Between Thurstan's occupancy of the land and William I's grant of it to the abbey, this estate was held by William, the king's chamberlain, the tenant *sub abbate* in 1086.[20] Probably the land was disputed between chamberlain and monks for some time before William conceded the rights of the monks, in order that his friend Hubert might receive the monastic habit at Westminster. William himself was recompensed with a grant of confraternity. This settlement was recorded in the forged *Telligraphus* but the circumstances surrounding Westminster's acquisition of this property are probably correct.[21] This donor has been identified with the known 'William, the king's chamberlain of London',[22] but it is arguable that he was in fact William Mauduit I, a

15 Harvey, *Westminster Abbey and its Estates*, p. 343. Alnod of London, who also made a donation in this reign, was probably not a courtier (*ibid.*, p. 359).

16 W. Dugdale, *Monasticon Anglicanum*, revised H. Caley, H. Ellis and B. Bandinel, 6 vols in 8 (London, 1817–30), I, p. 301, no. XLIII; J. Armitage Robinson, *Gilbert Crispin, Abbot of Westminster* (Cambridge, 1911), p. 139 no. 14.; see also *Westminster Abbey Charters 1066–c.1214*, ed. Emma Mason, assisted by the late Jennifer Bray, continuing the work of the late Desmond J. Murphy, London Record Society, 25 (1988), nos 55–6. On Albert, see also John Le Neve, *Fasti Ecclesiae Anglicanae 1066–1300, I, St Paul's London*, compiled Diana E. Greenway (London, 1968), p. 59.

17 Harvey, *Westminster Abbey and its Estates*, pp. 27, 47, 356–7.

18 Le Neve, *Fasti Ecclesiae Anglicanae 1066–1300, I, St Pauls*, p. 59.

19 *Domesday Book sive Liber Censualis*, ed. A. Farley, 2 vols (Record Comm., 1783), I, f. 294.

20 Harvey, *Westminster Abbey and its Estates*, p. 349 and n. 6; *Regesta Regum Anglo-Normannorum, I, 1066–1100*, ed. H.W.C. Davis with R.J. Whitwell (Oxford, 1913), pp. 120–21, no. XII; *Westminster Abbey Charters*, no. 11.

21 Westminster Abbey Muniment XXVI; Armitage Robinson, *Gilbert Crispin*, p. 130; Harvey, *Westminster Abbey and its Estates*, pp. 39, 386.

22 Armitage Robinson, *Gilbert Crispin*, p. 130.

chamberlain of the Treasury, whose descendants were chamberlains of the Exchequer.[23] In 1086 'William the chamberlain' was a tenant of the abbey in Ockendon, Essex, as well as in Middlesex.[24]

In the earlier twelfth century few royal officers are recorded as tenants or benefactors of the abbey. Abbot Gervase conceded to the king's *minister*, Gerin, who was also the man of the abbot, the land of Endiff (near Charing, in Westminster). Gerin had bought this from Walkelin, and would now render the abbot one pound of pepper annually for the tenancy. Unusually in a charter of this date, the witnesses were said to be *astantes et audientes* (standing around and listening) when Walkelin, with his son Robert, and William, Walkelin's brother, granted seisin to Gerin.[25] The beneficiary of this grant can probably be identified with the knight Gerin, who witnessed another charter of Abbot Gervase.[26] Prior Osbert de Clare, when compiling a dossier of miracles ascribed to King Edward's mediation, for use with the first attempt at obtaining the king's canonization, reported that the knight Gerin, keeper of the royal palace of Westminster, fell ill with a quartan fever. However, at Osbert's prompting, he kept vigil at the king's tomb on the night of 5 January. 'And Edward heard Gerin and Christ [heard] Edward.'[27] It is possible that Gerin was the ancestor of the Robert Fitz Gerin who was a resident of Westminster in the reigns of Richard I and John,[28] although an alternative conjectural ancestor for this man would be Gerin the engineer (*ingeniator*), another resident of Westminster during the abbacy of Gervase.[29]

If courtiers, other than the keeper of the palace, were not often in evidence at Westminster during the Anglo-Norman period, this was because the Norman kings governed a wider realm than did Edward, and would usually come to Westminster only for solemnities.

One event guaranteed to bring any king to Westminster was, of course, his consecration and coronation. The death of King Edward at Westminster, in a time of political instability, prompted the immediate coronation there of Harold II on 6 January 1066.[30] The subsequent claim of William I to be Edward's lawful successor ensured that on Christmas Day 1066, he too was consecrated in the great church which Edward had rebuilt.[31] The traumatic events of 1066 ensured that precedents were established for the abbey's claim to be the sole coronation church. When political circumstances necessitated

23 Emma Mason, 'The Mauduits and their Chamberlainship of the Exchequer', *Bulletin of the Institute of Historical Research*, 49 (1976), pp. 1–23.

24 Harvey, *Westminster Abbey and its Estates*, pp. 71n; 343n.

25 *Westminster Abbey Charters*, no. 261.

26 *Ibid.*, no. 269.

27 *The Life of King Edward*, pp. 158–9.

28 *Westminster Abbey Charters*, nos 313, 440.

29 *Ibid.*, no. 255.

30 *The Anglo-Saxon Chronicle*, ed. Dorothy Whitelock, with D.C. Douglas and Susie I. Tucker (London, 1961), C(D), *sub an.* 1065; E *sub an.* 1066.

31 *Ibid.*, (D).

the coronation of Henry III being held at Gloucester on 28 October 1216, the abbey subsequently succeeded in having its own rights confirmed by virtue of a letter issued by Cardinal Guala, on 5 November 1219.[32] Coronations were usually infrequent events, occurring at irregular intervals. While the consecration itself was normally performed by the archbishop of Canterbury, or on rare occasions the archbishop of York, as in both ceremonies in 1066, the abbot also had a part to play in the ceremonial, prompting the king or queen in the various stages of the ritual, while the monks would provide the choral element in the liturgy.[33] The solemnities, attended by famous and infamous notables, would provide a break from the monastic routine. The unpredictable turn of political events surrounding all the royal accessions before that of Henry II no doubt provided much food for thought and speculation during the monks' allotted evening recreation period. On the other hand, the fear caused by the firing of the surrounding houses, which marred the ceremonial of William I's coronation,[34] and the pogrom which followed that of Richard I,[35] while providing grounds for concern, did not directly threaten the monastic chapter.

In the later eleventh century, the monks would most frequently see the king and his court at his crown-wearing, held on the three greatest feasts of the Church's year: Christmas, Easter and Pentecost. The venues for these ceremonies varied. The precedents which established Westminster as one of the locations for these gatherings were Edward's Christmas court of 1065 and Harold II's Easter court of 1066.[36] William I is known to have held four of his Christmas courts at the abbey. These included his first, coinciding with his coronation. He also held three courts there at Pentecost, including that of 1068, when his wife Matilda was solemnly consecrated as queen.[37] William Rufus held his first and fourth Christmas courts at Westminster, besides his

32 Richard of Cirencester, *Speculum Historiale de Gestis Regum Angliae*, ed. J.E.B. Mayor, 2 vols, Rolls Series (1863–9), II, p. 37.

33 For Harold II's coronation by Archbishop Ealdred, see *The Chronicle of John of Worcester, II, 450–1066*, ed. R.R. Darlington and P.M. McGurk, Oxford Medieval Texts (Oxford, 1995), pp. 600–601; *Chronicle of the Archbishops of York* in *Historians of the Church of York and its Archbishops*, ed. J. Raine, 3 vols, Rolls Series (London, 1879, 1886, 1894), II, p. 348; and for that of William I, see *Anglo-Saxon Chronicle, sub an.* 1066 (D). Detailed references to the role of the abbots (and latterly of the dean, as his replacement) are found in *Three Coronation Orders*, ed. J. Wickham Legg, Henry Bradshaw Society, XIX (London, 1900), p. 190. On the role of the abbot, and the (monastic) choir, see also J. Wickham Legg, *English Coronation Records* (Westminster, 1901), pp. xxvi–xxvii.

34 Guillaume de Poitiers, *Histoire de Guillaume le Conquérant*, ed. and transl. R. Foreville (Paris, 1952), pp. 220–21; *The Ecclesiastical History of Orderic Vitalis*, ed. Marjorie Chibnall, 6 vols (Oxford, 1969–80), II, pp. 184–5.

35 *The Chronicle of Richard of Devizes of the Time of King Richard the First*, ed. J.T. Appleby (London, 1963), p. 3.

36 *The Life of King Edward who Rests at Westminster*, pp. 112–13; *Anglo-Saxon Chronicle, sub an.* 1066 (C, D); Biddle, 'Seasonal Festivals and Residence', p. 69.

37 Biddle, 'Seasonal Festivals and Residence', p. 64.

last two Pentecost courts.[38] Henry I held seven of his Christmas courts at Westminster between 1100 and 1109, five Pentecost courts between 1102 and 1109, and another in 1121.[39] None of the Norman kings is recorded as holding an Easter court there. At the great courts, the magnates of church and state assembled to give advice, if required, on matters of state, while the festivities would also serve as a form of social bonding, intended to contribute towards the political stability of the realm. The ritual element in the proceedings was the king's solemn crown-wearing, when he appeared before his magnates in all the glory of his regalia. This ceremonial underlined his position as the anointed ruler.[40] William of Malmesbury, translating the *Life of St Wulfstan* in the latter part of Henry I's reign, ascribed the introduction of this ceremonial to William I.[41] According to William of Malmesbury, the ceremony was regularly observed in the reigns of William I and William II, but Henry I allowed it to decline.[42] John of Worcester antedates the ceremonial to the reign of King Edward. Setting the scene for an anecdote, he related how, one Easter Day, when Edward 'as usual' held his royal court at Westminster, after the liturgy, but still wearing his crown, he returned in state to the court and sat down to dine.[43] John, writing in the middle of Henry I's reign, perhaps assumed that the Anglo-Norman ceremonial had an earlier history.[44] Westminster's involvement in the ritual was well rewarded. A mandate of Henry I, dating from no later than 1107, informed Eudo the dapifer and Herbert the chamberlain that on all feasts when he wore his crown in the churches of Westminster, Winchester and Gloucester these were to have an allowance, and their cantors an ounce of gold, since Bishop Maurice of London had testified that this was customary in the reigns of the king's predecessors.[45] Unfortunately the confirmation of this privilege was soon

38 *Ibid.*, p. 65.

39 *Ibid.*, p. 67.

40 *Ibid.*, pp. 51–63, esp. p. 57. For a romanticized description of William II's Pentecost court of 1099, see *L'estoire des Engleis by Geffrei Gaimar*, ed. A. Bell, Anglo-Norman Text Society, 14–16 (Oxford, 1960), 5969–6104.

41 *The Vita Wulfstani of William of Malmesbury*, ed. R.R. Darlington, Camden Society, 3rd Series, XL (1928), pp. 34, 84. See also B. Golding, *Conquest and Colonization: The Normans in Britain, 1066–1100* (Basingstoke, 1994), p. 92.

42 William of Malmesbury, *De Gestis Regum Anglorum*, ed. W. Stubbs, 2 vols, Rolls Series (1887–9), II, p. 335.

43 *The Life of King Edward who Rests at Westminster*, p. 103; *The Chronicle of John of Worcester, II, 450–1066*, p. 648.

44 For arguments refuting the suggestion that crown-wearings can be traced back to King Edward's time, see H.E.J. Cowdrey, 'The Anglo- Norman *Laudes Regiae*', reprinted from *Viator*, 12 (1981), pp. VIII, 37–78 in Cowdrey's *Popes, Monks and Crusaders* (London, 1984), pp. 37–78, at p. 50, n. 46. See also Janet L. Nelson, 'The Rites of the Conqueror', reprinted from R. Allen Brown, ed., *Anglo-Norman Studies, IV, Proceedings of the Battle Conference 1981* (Woodbridge, 1982), pp. 117–32, 210–21, in Nelson's *Politics and Ritual in Early Medieval Europe* (London, 1986), pp. 375–401, at p. 397.

45 Armitage Robinson, *Gilbert Crispin*, p. 141, no. 18; calendared *Westminster Abbey Charters*, no. 58.

followed by the lapse of this ceremonial. By providing the liturgical setting for the visual glorification of the monarchy, the abbey was contributing to the political success of the realm. Virtually everyone of political consequence would assemble for the great courts. It was essential that the participants in the festivities should include all loyal subjects, all visiting allies, actual or potential, and all those who might defect if they believed themselves to be slighted. The royal hall built in the earlier eleventh century was too small for the steadily growing throng of those who were politically useful. Its rebuilding was commissioned by William Rufus, determined to create a hall spacious enough to fulfil its political function.[46] Some similarities have been identified between the surface decoration of the new hall and that of the contemporary claustral buildings at the abbey.[47] Architectural inspiration, however, was one of the lesser of the benefits to be derived from close, if intermittent, proximity to the king.

The Anglo-Norman kings, like their predecessors and successors, travelled incessantly around their lands. The abbot, accompanied by his entourage, might be required to attend the royal court in various locations. The English Edwin clearly attended court in order to obtain those benefits which were granted to himself and his monks, but rarely attested grants made to others and his movements beyond Westminster are uncertain.[48] Geoffrey, who apparently did not obtain anything for the abbey, is known to have attested only one royal charter, issued at Windsor in 1072, and recording the suit between Archbishops Lanfranc and Thomas.[49] Vitalis travelled widely in southern England, sometimes obtaining grants for his abbey and on other occasions witnessing grants to other beneficiaries. Besides attending the court locally, he is recorded at Berkeley, *Wiht* and Winchester.[50] In 1080, he attested a charter issued in Normandy.[51] While Abbot Gilbert did not, apparently, have to travel overseas, he attended the royal court on occasion at Bushey, Cornbury, Dover, Gloucester, Lincoln, Nottingham, Winchester and Windsor, besides more frequent attendances in London and Westminster. Sometimes he took the opportunity to petition for privileges for his abbey, but on other occasions he is recorded merely attesting grants for others.[52] Probably Gilbert was the last of the abbots of Westminster to be summoned

46 On the architecture and dimensions of the hall, see Frank Barlow, *William Rufus* (London, 1983), pp. 132, 372 and n. 146, plate 10. Henry of Huntingdon, a late source for this reign, reported that the king said the hall was not big enough by half for his purposes: *Henrici Huntendunensis Historia Anglorum*, ed. T. Arnold, Rolls Series (1879), p. 231.

47 R.D.H. Gem, 'The Romanesque Rebuilding of Westminster Abbey', in R. Allen Brown, ed., *Anglo-Norman Studies, III, Proceedings of the Battle Conference 1980* (Woodbridge, 1981), p. 60.

48 *Regesta Regum Anglo-Normannorum, I, 1066–1100*, nos 11, 22, 52, 53, 237.

49 *Ibid.*, no. 64.

50 *Ibid.*, nos 95, 126, 128, 137, 148, 174, 205, 212–14, 216–17.

51 *Ibid.*, no. 127.

52 *Ibid.*, nos 236, 278–9, 315, 328, 338, 370, 381, 402, 429, 436–7, 455; *Regesta Regum*

to court with any great frequency. Since the middle decades of the eleventh century, secular clerks had been gaining in stature and influence at the expense of monks, whose active role in court circles correspondingly declined. Abbot Herbert attended the council at Northampton on 8 September 1131, attesting a charter issued for Salisbury, but this was only the second known occasion when he was named as a witness to a royal grant.[53] His presence at court can be deduced on other occasions when grants were issued for the benefit of his abbey, but even here, it is possible that he obtained more than one grant on each occasion that he enlisted the king's support. Herbert's attendance may be deduced at Waltham, at Windsor and at Woodstock.[54]

Abbot Gervase occasionally travelled with his father, King Stephen. For instance, they were probably together at Godstow nunnery, and certainly at Shrewsbury early in 1139.[55] Gervase, styled the king's son, witnessed a royal charter for the Knights Templar, issued at London c.1147–53. He also acted in a judicial capacity at a gathering in the king's chapel within the Tower of London. Here King Stephen, together with the bishops of Winchester and Ely, the abbot of Westminster and several barons, considered the charters and written narratives of Battle Abbey, which were brought to them by the abbot of Battle in defence of the liberties of his house, and which were read out to the assembly by the bishop of Winchester.[56] Charters issued by King Stephen for Westminster were usually issued either at London or at Westminster, but one was granted at Clare early in the reign,[57] and another at St Albans, between 1149 and 1152.[58] The presence of Gervase on both occasions is likely, but unproven.

Contacts of other kinds had long been maintained between Westminster and the royal court. There is some evidence to indicate that on occasion the abbey housed prisoners of state. The twelfth-century writer Geoffrey Gaimar stated that King Cnut temporarily committed the infant sons of Edmund Ironside to the care of the abbot of Westminster.[59] While Geoffrey wrote a romance *History of the English*, he made extensive use of early sources,

Anglo-Normannorum, II, 1100–1135, ed. C. Johnson and H.A. Cronne (Oxford, 1956), nos 488, 544, 547–9, 677, 702, 769, 818, 828, 851, 918, 1173, 1180.

53 *Regesta Regum Anglo-Normannorum, II, 1100–1135*, no. 1715. Herbert's earlier attestation is to *ibid.*, no. 1301.

54 *Ibid.*, nos 1247–8, 1251–2, 1383, 1416, 1879, 1881.

55 *Regesta Regum Anglo-Normannorum, III, 1135–1154*, ed. H.A. Cronne and R.H.C. Davis (Oxford, 1968), nos 366, 819.

56 For the Templars' charter, *ibid.*, no. 859. The judicial gathering in the Tower is recorded in *The Chronicle of Battle Abbey*, p. 200.

57 *Regesta Regum Anglo-Normannorum III, 1135–1154*, no. 927.

58 *Ibid.*, no. 938. Three forgeries, based in part on this grant, all purport to have been issued at St Albans (*ibid.*, nos 939–41).

59 *L'estoire des Engleis by Geffrei Gaimar*, 4491–2, 4507.

including texts of the *Anglo-Saxon Chronicle* which are now lost.[60] It is arguable, therefore, that his statement is correct. On the other hand, Geoffrey was writing after the publicization of the abbey's claims to offer sanctuary,[61] so that he may reflect twelfth-century assumptions. Moreover, Westminster, like other abbeys, did hold an occasional political prisoner later in the eleventh century. Æthelric, bishop of Durham, resigned in 1056, when he was replaced by his brother Æthelwine. During the northern rebellion early in the reign of William I, Æthelwine was implicated with the rebels in 1069 and fled. He was outlawed, and joined the English rebels at Ely. Here he was captured, subsequently deposed, and imprisoned at Abingdon abbey. Æthelric, meanwhile, was taken to Westminster to face unspecified charges. He was held in custody there down to his death in 1072.[62]

An occasional royal visit might owe something to personal, rather than to political interests. When Bernard, a former chaplain of Queen Edith-Matilda, was appointed bishop of St David's, Archbishop Ralph planned to consecrate him in the chapel of Lambeth Palace, but the queen particularly wanted to attend the ceremony, which was accordingly held at Westminster abbey on 19 September 1115.[63]

In 1118 Queen Edith was buried in the abbey, near her kinsman, King Edward.[64] Following the death of Abbot Vitalis of Savigny on 16 October 1122, his mortuary roll duly reached Westminster. Here, the monks' entry requested prayers for King Edward and the abbots Vitalis (of Westminster) and Gilbert Crispin. Requests were inserted for prayers on behalf of kings Offa and Edgar, besides Queen Edith-Matilda and six named monks.[65] These petitions on behalf of Edward and Edith-Matilda slightly predate evidence that the abbey was fostering their cults.[66]

The proximity of Westminster Hall, offering as it did the scope for

60 Ian Short, 'Gaimar's Epilogue and Geoffrey of Monmouth's *Liber vetustissimus*,' *Speculum*, 69 (1994), pp. 323–43.

61 *Westminster Abbey Charters*, nos 238–40, 248.

62 Golding, *Conquest and Colonization*, pp. 42–3, 156. Godric, abbot of Winchcombe from 1054, was deposed in 1066 and was subsequently in the custody of Abbot Æthelwig of Evesham: Emma Mason, *St Wulfstan of Worcester c.1008–1095* (Oxford, 1990), p. 198. See also pp. 128, 147.

63 Eadmer, *Historia Novorum in Anglia*, ed. M. Rule, Rolls Series (London, 1884), pp. 235–6; Armitage Robinson, *Gilbert Crispin*, pp. 25–6.

64 *Anglo-Saxon Chronicle*, *sub an.* 1118 (E); Harvey, *Westminster Abbey and its Estates*, p. 373 and n. 6; *Customary of the Benedictine Monasteries of St Augustine, Canterbury and St Peter, Westminster*, ed. E. Maunde Thomson, Henry Bradshaw Society, XXIII, XXVIII (London, 1902–4), II, p. 45.

65 Rouleau du bienheureux Vital, abbé de Savigny, *Rouleaux des morts du IXe au XVe siècle*, ed. L. Delisle (1866, reprinted New York 1968), XXXVIII, pp. 315–16, no. 100; Armitage Robinson, *Gilbert Crispin*, p. 27.

66 The earliest clear evidence on the fostering of these two cults dates from 1125: *Westminster Abbey Charters*, no. 189, although two related charters, probably spurious, purport to date from 1121: *ibid.*, nos 187–8. Three writs issued by Abbot Gilbert concerning the abbey's right to offer sanctuary, and perhaps also that surviving in the

semi-formal contacts with the royal court, must surely have brought all manner of political gossip to the cloister. But, as Martin Brett has observed, the monks surprisingly made no effort to draw on such material in order to write a chronicle.[67] The abbey certainly did not lack intelligent and fluent scribes, but their interests were seemingly channelled into charter production, whilst the most conspicuously erudite of the abbots, notably Gilbert and Lawrence, directed their energies towards more obviously scholarly pursuits. It may be that royal foundations preferred to abstain from publicizing any work which might be perceived to contain injudicious, or even disloyal, political comment. As Brett observed, Queen Edith-Matilda's Augustinian foundation of Holy Trinity Aldgate also produced singularly little in the way of historical works.[68]

Just as leaders of the clerical hierarchy occasionally convened councils at Westminster, so too were secular Councils held at the neighbouring palace.[69] These gatherings provided the occasion for intermittent close contact with the king during the twelfth century, when direct royal interest in the abbey appeared to be minimal. It has been suggested that King Stephen appears to have held a council at Westminster in 1136 or 1137.[70] King Henry II's Councils held at Westminster included those of March and October 1163, the Council, or Synod, of 1175, and a gathering in 1184 which has also been described as a Council.[71] The abbey itself was the venue for the translation of the newly-canonized St Edward, on 13 October 1163, attended by Henry II,[72] who also attended the coronation at Westminster of his son, the Young King, on 24 May 1170.[73]

While direct royal contact with the abbey was largely confined to formal occasions such as these, there was, during the twelfth century, simultaneously occasional contact in the form of pleas on the part of the abbot and monks which resulted in legal decisions taken by the king in person.

name of Abbot Gilbert, indicate that King Edward's cult was already being fostered: *ibid.*, nos 238–40, 248.

67 Martin Brett, 'The annals of Bermondsey, Southwark and Merton', in D. Abulafia, M. Franklin and M. Rubin, eds, *Church and City 1000–1500: Essays in Honour of Christopher Brooke* (Cambridge, 1992), p. 279.

68 Brett, *ibid.*, p. 279.

69 *Councils and Synods, with Other Documents Relating to the English Church, I, A.D. 871–1204*, ed. D. Whitelock, M. Brett and C.N.L. Brooke, 2 vols (Oxford, 1981), part ii, nos 113, 115, 121, 130, 132, 139, 143, 156, 158, 168, 169, 174, 175, 182, 183.

70 Graeme White, 'Continuity in Government', in E. King, ed., *The Anarchy of Stephen's Reign* (Oxford, 1994), p. 119. A conciliar setting is here proposed for the plea brought by the prior and canons of Holy Trinity Aldgate against the castellan of the Tower of London, for which, see *Regesta Regum Anglo-Normannorum, III, 1135–1154*, no. 506.

71 R.W. Eyton, *Court, Household and Itinerary of King Henry II* (London, 1878), pp. 60, 64, 190, 259; W.L. Warren, *Henry II* (London, 1973), pp. 97, 465–6, 470, 477, 597.

72 Richard of Cirencester, *Speculum Historiale*, II, pp. 325–6; Barlow, *Edward the Confessor*, p. 283.

73 *Gesta Regis Henrici Secundi Benedicti Abbatis*, ed. W. Stubbs, 2 vols, Rolls Series (London, 1867), I, p. 5.

Obviously all royal charters issued for Westminster were in one sense a response to an appeal made to the king himself, but discussion is focused here on those which contain some internal indication of the deliberations which took place. From the reign of William I, the earliest such document is a writ addressed to the sheriff and officers of Essex, notifying them that the king, on the advice of his barons, has granted to the abbey the manor of Feering in Essex, with three houses in Colchester, held by Earl Harold (Godwineson) when King Edward died (5 January 1066) and which were subsequently held by William himself. These properties were now granted to Westminster by agreement and in exchange for Windsor, granted to them previously by King Edward.[74] A mandate to the sheriffs of Essex and Surrey, concerning the protection of Westminster's lands, probably resulted from some deliberations at court, since the rival claimant was Anselm, abbot of Bec, who might have expected support from the king.[75] A writ of William II ordered the restoration of Broomfield (Essex) to the abbey, which had been misappropriated by Thurold, the dapifer of the king's uncle, Odo, bishop of Bayeux.[76] Most probably this restoration was made after the collapse, in 1088, of the rebellion in which Bishop Odo had played so large a part.[77] The prevailing opinion in the royal court would be equally hostile to the bishop's subordinates. A specific record of litigation before judges nominated for the purpose is contained in another writ of William II dating from 1091–5. On his orders, and in the presence of the bishop of Durham (William of St Calais), (Wakelin) the bishop of Winchester, Eudo dapifer, Ivo Taillebois, and Robert Dispenser, Abbot Gilbert Crispin had proved his title to the land of Cippenham and Burnham (Bucks.), granted by the king's father. William accordingly instructed Hugh de Beauchamp and the men of Buckinghamshire that the abbot was to hold the land peaceably, with all customary rights.[78] Another mandate of William II, addressed to Hugh of Buckland and the sheriff and men of Middlesex, ordered that the abbey was to hold peacefully the land of Yeoveney, which was pasture pertaining to the manor of Staines. In the time of the king's father, Abbot Vitalis had proved his title to this against Walter Fitz Oter. No one was to be permitted to cause any damage or disturbance, nor need Abbot Gilbert answer for that land except in presence of those bishops and barons acting as judges who were present when the title to that land was defended. The king strongly forbad anyone from misappropriating anything or depleting the property in any way. The land was to be

74 *Regesta Regum Anglo-Normannorum, I, 1066–1100*, no. XVII; calendared *Westminster Abbey Charters*, no. 16.

75 *Regesta Regum Anglo-Normannorum, I, 1066–1100*, no. XXIX; calendared *Westminster Abbey Charters*, no. 26.

76 Florence E. Harmer, *Anglo-Saxon Writs*, 2nd edn (Stamford, 1989) p. 507; calendared *Westminster Abbey Charters*, no. 48.

77 *Anglo-Saxon Chronicle*, (E), *sub an*. 1088.

78 Armitage Robinson, *Gilbert Crispin*, p. 136, no. 9; calendared *Westminster Abbey Charters*, no. 51.

held just as it was when it was granted by King Edward, without any deterioration.[79] Not all petitions to the royal court had such a satisfactory outcome. The clerk Alward of London had given the City church of St Mary Newchurch to Westminster and, in two confirmatory writs issued by William II, the king stated that his father had confirmed it to the abbey.[80] Such a writ was perhaps issued by William I, but the document to this effect which survives in his name is, in its present form, clearly the work of the twelfth century forgery team,[81] as is the First Charter of William I, in which Newchurch is also confirmed.[82] A further confirmatory writ in the name of Henry I names the donor as Goslan. In other respects it appears genuine, although the possibility remains that it was drafted by the team to add strength to their case.[83] In fact, Newchurch had been misappropriated in the latter part of William II's reign by Eudo *dapifer*, a seneschal of William II. Eudo conveyed it to his own foundation, the abbey of St John at Colchester.[84] The Colchester claim to Newchurch was later supported by the production of blatant forgeries, but it was this abbey, and not Westminster, which retained Newchurch.[85] The royal writs which Westminster obtained represent the outcome of successive pleas before the king, but evidently Gilbert Crispin was outmanœuvred by Eudo.

The abbot was more successful in the case of Westminster's land in Tooting (Surrey), held since the reign of Harold II.[86] The monks' title was evidently challenged early in the reign of Henry I, who notified William Giffard, bishop of Winchester (the diocese in question) and his French and English barons in Surrey, that he granted the land to Abbot Gilbert and the monks, to be held as peacefully as in previous reigns, and forbidding anyone to cause them injury. The abbot was not to be required to answer for the land before anyone but the king himself.[87] The rival claimant was not identified, but perhaps here, as in Feering (Essex), discussed above, Westminster was coming under pressure from the abbey of Bec, which held the manor of

79 Armitage Robinson, *Gilbert Crispin*, p. 138, no. 12; calendared *Westminster Abbey Charters*, no. 53.

80 Armitage Robinson, *Gilbert Crispin*, p. 137, nos 10–11; calendared *Westminster Abbey Charters*, nos 49, 54.

81 Armitage Robinson, *Gilbert Crispin*, p. 131, no. 5; calendared *Westminster Abbey Charters*, no. 40.

82 *Calendar of Charter Rolls*, IV, pp. 330–36 (full text printed); calendared *Westminster Abbey Charters*, no. 1.

83 Armitage Robinson, *Gilbert Crispin*, p. 159; calendared *Westminster Abbey Charters*, no. 90.

84 The foundation of this abbey is dated to 1096. Building work began in 1097: D. Knowles and R.N. Hadcock, *Medieval Religious Houses England and Wales*, 2nd edn (London, 1971), pp. 62–3.

85 Armitage Robinson, *Gilbert Crispin*, pp. 158–66.

86 Harvey, *Westminster Abbey and its Estates*, p. 359.

87 Armitage Robinson, *Gilbert Crispin*, p. 142, no. 21; calendared *Westminster Abbey Charters*, no. 60.

Upper Tooting, or Tooting Bec, from before 1086.[88] Henry I personally presided over the negotiations concerning a complex series of land transfers, and then notified the outcome to Robert Bloet, bishop of Lincoln, Ranulf Fitz Ranulf, and the 'French and English' barons of Lincolnshire. Hugh de *Euremou* restored the manor of Doddington to Westminster and to Abbot Gilbert.[89] William I had confirmed Abbot Vitalis (1076–85) in possession of Doddington, which the abbey received from Ailric son of Meriet.[90] Subsequently Hugh received Doddington from Abbot Gilbert in the presence of King William II, in exchange for the manor of Duxford (Cambs.) which Hugh had given to Abbot Gilbert. But Henry I restored the manor of Duxford to Count Eustace; he gave an exchange to it to Hugh; and therefore Hugh restored the manor (of Doddington) to Westminster abbey.[91] For good measure, Westminster obtained a copy of Hugh's companion notification to 'his lord' Robert Bloet, and the barons of Lincolnshire, of his restoration of Doddington to the abbey.[92]

A somewhat different case which came before the king's court between the spring of 1114 and the early months of 1116, concerned Wulfric, a moneyer at Sudbury in the reign of William II and the early years of Henry I. He became a monk at Westminster abbey, to which he donated the church of St Bartholomew at Sudbury. The validity of this grant was challenged and the case came before the king's court, where it was pleaded in presence of his barons perhaps during the council held in September 1115. The verdict was favourable to Westminster, and Henry I 'conceded' the church to the abbey. Accordingly a writ was issued, notifying the outcome to Herbert Losinga, bishop of Norwich, Haimo the dapifer, the burgesses of Sudbury and the royal officers in Suffolk.[93] The most likely opponent of Wulfric's donation would have been Herbert Losinga, as diocesan bishop, although the king's officers had perhaps queried the validity of the donation made by Wulfric from property which he had held in his capacity as a royal servant.

While Westminster acquired properties in several dioceses, individuals from other regions who had designs on abbey properties were sometimes too powerful to resist without royal intervention. In the time of William II, Robert Bloet, bishop of Lincoln, reached an agreement with Abbot Gilbert

88 Marjorie Morgan, *The English Lands of the Abbey of Bec* (Oxford, 1946), pp. 12, 149; J.E.B. Gover, A. Mower and F.M. Stenton, with A. Bonner, *The Place-Names of Surrey*, English Place-Name Society, XI (reprinted 1982), p. 35.

89 Armitage Robinson, *Gilbert Crispin*, p. 145, no. 26; calendared *Westminster Abbey Charters*, no. 61.

90 Dugdale, *Monasticon Anglicanum*, I, p. 301, no. XLI; calendared *Westminster Abbey Charters*, no. 31.

91 Armitage Robinson, *Gilbert Crispin*, p. 145, no. 26; calendared *Westminster Abbey Charters*, no. 61.

92 Armitage Robinson, *Gilbert Crispin*, p. 144, no. 25; calendared *Westminster Abbey Charters*, no. 475.

93 Dugdale, *Monasticon Anglicanum*, III, p. 459, no. I; calendared *Westminster Abbey Charters*, no. 72.

and the monks, whereby he was admitted as tenant of their manor of Lessness, in Kent. At some later date, possibly during the long vacancy after Gilbert's death, he over-rode the terms of this agreement. It was only after the accession of Abbot Herbert that a successful petition was made to King Henry I, ordering the bishop to abide by their agreed terms.[94] The very proximity of the abbey to the palace of Westminster perhaps caused the abbot and monks to find themselves in difficulties with magnates of church or state who were often in the king's company. A dignitary might signify his wish to become the tenant of a Westminster estate on favourable terms, in return for enlisting the king's help in some matter. Subsequently, though, any obligations due to Westminster from the property might be conveniently overlooked. Some such train of events evidently led to the grievance about Lessness, and a comparable one arose over Westminster's land in Battersea. It appears that a tenancy here was granted to Ranulf the chancellor, who died in January 1123. However the sheriff of Surrey, Gilbert, apparently took control of the estate and gave seisin of part of it to Hugh Fitz Hedric. A plea by Abbot Herbert to the king resulted in his issuing a writ ordering restitution to the abbey.[95] A further complaint to Henry I secured a writ ordering Hugh Mascherell to restore to the abbey the tithe of Roding, which his brother (Roger Mascherell) gave, together with arrears.[96] Presumably Hugh, as Roger's feudal superior, had declined to ratify his donation. Hugh Mascherell was a substantial tenant of the Mandevilles,[97] and could not be called to account without royal assistance.

Already in Henry I's reign, comparable disputes were being heard by accredited judges in his name, and direct evidence of any king presiding over legal arguments is less readily identifiable in the Westminster charters from the 1120s onwards. It is possible, however, but by no means certain, that King John directly presided over the deliberations which at long last secured Westminster's control over its manor of Islip (Oxon.), the birthplace of King Edward. In his resulting charter, John states that Islip was granted on the evidence of royal charters and the testimony of law worthy men of the manor. Abbot Ralph and the monks lodged their petition for this manor after the previous holder, Robert de Courcy, joined Philip Augustus in 1203. All known earlier Westminster charters relating to Islip are in fact spurious, and, whether or not this was apparent to the chancery staff, Westminster had to fine heavily for the restoration.[98] Proximity to the monarchy in the

94 Armitage Robinson, *Gilbert Crispin*, p. 157, no 42; calendared *Westminster Abbey Charters*, no. 81.

95 *Regesta Regum Anglo-Normannorum, II, 1100–1135*, no. CLXXI; calendared *Westminster Abbey Charters*, no. 82.

96 *Regesta Regum Anglo-Normannorum, II, 1100–1135*, no. CCCII; calendared *Westminster Abbey Charters*, no. 92.

97 *Westminster Abbey Charters*, no. 92, note.

98 *Rotuli Chartarum in Turri Londoniensi asservati 1199–1216*, ed. T. Duffus Hardy, Record Comm. (London, 1837), f. 139b; calendared *Westminster Abbey Charters*, no. 149.

Anglo-Norman period resulted in occasional windfalls, such as an annual grant of 10 shillings ordered by Henry I to be paid from the royal alms, as mentioned in the king's rolls.[99] While the writ ordering the payment was addressed to Richard de Monte, sheriff of Oxfordshire, the rolls in question cannot be identified with any certainty. Other *ad hoc* royal benefactions included Edith Matilda's grant of a tenement on the abbot's wharf,[100] and the daily grant which Henry I later established to meet the costs of a light burning before Matilda's tomb.[101] The original grant of land in Tottenham made by Matilda's brother David, while earl of Huntingdon, to finance the yearly celebrations of her anniversary[102] was confirmed when he became King of Scots and subsequently by his son and grandsons.[103]

99 Armitage Robinson, *Gilbert Crispin*, p. 149, no. 32; calendared *Westminster Abbey Charters*, no. 71.

100 Armitage Robinson, *Gilbert Crispin*, p. 155, no. 38; calendared *Westminster Abbey Charters*, no. 97.

101 Armitage Robinson, *Gilbert Crispin*, p. 156, no. 39; calendared *Westminster Abbey Charters*, no. 79.

102 *The Acts of Malcolm IV, King of Scots, 1153–65, together with Scottish Royal Acts prior to 1153*, ed. G.W.S. Barrow, *Regesta Regum Scottorum*, I (Edinburgh, 1960), no. 6; calendared *Westminster Abbey Charters*, no. 99.

103 *The Acts of Malcolm IV*, nos 13–14, 36, 154; *The Acts of William I, King of Scots 1165–1214*, ed. G.W.S. Barrow with W.W. Scott, *Regesta Regum Scottorum*, II (Edinburgh, 1971), no. 52; calendared *Westminster Abbey Charters*, nos 100–104.

9

The Abbey and the Courts

Certain charters of the abbots and monks of Westminster which reflect their use of the legal system during the twelfth century and the early thirteenth illustrate its expansion in this period. The progression can be charted from legal decisions taken by the king himself, as discussed in the previous chapter, through the orders given by the king to small groups of magnates to hear individual cases, then to the pleading of cases before the Exchequer, sitting in its legal capacity. By the late twelfth century, additional courts included that of the justices of the Bench at Westminster, and those of the small teams of itinerant justices, active when an eyre was in progress, besides the *coram rege* court, held in presence of the king himself. These three courts were all known as the *Curia Regis*, the king's court, even though he actually sat only in the last of these.[1] Westminster abbey brought pleas before all these courts in the twelfth century, while resorting most frequently to the Exchequer court, as a matter of practical convenience.

The gradual diminution of direct royal involvement in the abbey's legal difficulties was parallelled by a gradual rise in recourse to courts of various kinds. Matters of local interest were heard before lesser courts. The abbey defended its franchisal rights and exemptions as adjuncts to effective control over its estates. In London, recourse was had to the court of Husting, while in Westminster the abbot and monks, assembled in chapter, constituted a court of another kind, distinct both from the abbot's personal court and also from the halimote, or manorial court. Assemblies of this sort were held both in the vill of Westminster and also on other substantial manors of the abbey. All these courts played their part in securing the property rights of the abbot and monks.

Over the Anglo-Norman period, cases were increasingly heard by a group of judges appointed *ad hoc* by the king. A writ of William II, dating from 1091x1095, informed Hugh de Beauchamp and his loyal French and English men of Buckinghamshire that, on his orders, Abbot Gilbert Crispin defended his title to the land of Burnham and Cippenham, granted to him

1 R.V. Turner, *The King and his Courts: The Role of John and Henry III in the Administration of Justice 1199–1240* (Ithaca, N.Y., 1968), pp. 1–2. See also pp. 9–25.

by William I. The judges deputed to hear this case (and who gave a verdict in the abbot's favour) were (William de St Calais), bishop of Durham; (Walkelin), bishop of Winchester; Eudo dapifer; Ivo Taillebois; and Robert Dispenser. Accordingly the king ordered Hugh that the abbot was to hold these lands peaceably, with all customary rights. His writ was attested by the two episcopal judges.[2] A writ of Henry I, issued for Westminster at some uncertain date between May 1108 and January 1127, ordered the bishop of London, Richard de Belmeis I, to render justice to the abbot of Westminster in a case concerning those men who, armed and by night, broke into his church at Wennington (Essex). If the bishop failed to act, then the king's barons of the Exchequer would cause justice to be done.[3]

In another writ issued c.1130x1133, King Henry I informed his barons and loyal men of Sussex and Middlesex that Abbot Herbert, by the judgement of the king's (unnamed) barons, defended his title to the land of Parham and that of *Mapeleford* in their presence, at the Exchequer. Consequently Herbert Fitz Herbert could no longer claim any right in that land. The abbot might hold it in demesne, if he chose, and could do as he pleased with it. The king ordered that the abbot was to hold this land well and peacefully, and without any counter-claim, as he had defended his title to it. This writ was attested by (Roger), bishop of Salisbury,[4] who had perhaps headed the bench of judges who heard this case. However, the writ which he issued in 1130, jointly with Geoffrey Rufus, pardoning the abbot 800 silver marks, appears not to relate to these disputed lands, but rather represents a large instalment of the fine which Herbert owed Henry I for the recovery of lands unjustly dispersed after the death of Gilbert Crispin.[5]

Westminster appears to be the only religious house which has preserved writs recording litigation at the Exchequer in Henry I's reign. These documents comprise the only evidence to indicate that the Exchequer acted as a court of law in this period, and there are no wider indications that it performed this function on a regular basis. It has been suggested that the proximity of the monks to the Exchequer officers was the sole reason why the abbey was able to enlist their involvement in its legal concerns during the Anglo-Norman period.[6]

By the reign of Henry I, the community at Westminster was evidently

2 J. Armitage Robinson, *Gilbert Crispin, Abbot of Westminster* (Cambridge, 1911), p. 136, no. 9; calendared *Westminster Abbey Charters 1066–c.1214*, ed. Emma Mason, assisted by the late Jennifer Bray, continuing the work of the late Desmond J. Murphy, London Record Society, 25 (1988), no. 51.

3 Armitage Robinson, *Gilbert Crispin*, p. 149, no. 31; *Westminster Abbey Charters*, no. 84.

4 *Curia Regis Rolls*, VI, pp. 176–7, where it is cited in a lawsuit of 1211; calendared *Westminster Abbey Charters*, no. 96.

5 *Westminster Abbey Charters*, no. 73 and note.

6 Paul Brand, ' "*Multis Vigiliis Excogitatem et Inventam*": Henry II and the Creation of the English Common Law', *The Haskins Society Journal*, II, ed. R.B. Patterson (1990), pp. 206–7.

encountering a growing volume of litigation in one court and another, since it was defending its interests either by fining for writs prohibiting impleading, or in some instances by requiring the staff of the *scriptorium* to fabricate writs granting the abbey quittance from pleas.[7] King Stephen confirmed the abbey's title to Parham and *Mapeleford*. Evidently the dispute had reopened since Henry I issued his writ on this matter, but it is not clear whether there was a renewal of litigation in the courts, or an appeal was made directly to King Stephen, since the resulting writ appears to date from the abbacy of his son Gervase.[8] During much of Stephen's reign, royal government was at its most effective in the south-east of England. Consequently, it has been suggested that in the course of this reign, Westminster came to replace Winchester as the centre of the financial administration, at any rate after 1141. Possibly the change occurred before the downfall of Roger of Salisbury in June 1139, since, in his capacity as justiciar, he appears to have issued writs at Westminster.[9] Exchequer sessions were very brief in this period, but could prove profitable for the abbey. By the latter part of the reign of Henry II, the sacristan of Westminster was claiming the 'ancient right' of a payment of 2 shillings in the Michaelmas term, in return for providing ink for both the Upper and the Lower Exchequer.[10] This payment, while contributing only minutely to the abbey's substantial income, is indicative of the regular close contact between its personnel and some of the most influential men in the realm. The Exchequer sessions were not always held at Westminster in Henry II's reign: Northampton was the venue in 1169, for instance, while in 1175 the Exchequer met at Oxford,[11] it met often enough at Westminster, however, to ensure regular contact with the abbey, and the gradual establishment of a relationship which could be mutually profitable to the monks and to some of the most senior Exchequer officers. The evidence for this is at its strongest in the latter part of King Richard's reign, and that of John, although the process was under way in the time of Henry II.

At Michaelmas 1165, litigation at the Exchequer between Abbot Lawrence of Westminster, on the one hand, and Abbot Robert de Gorron of St Albans, together with Robert Taileboys and his brothers Roger and Simon on the other, ended in a quitclaim by Abbot Robert and the Taileboys brothers of various charges which they had brought against Westminster abbey and its abbot, 'both in woodland and in field'. In return for this concession, Abbot Lawrence gave the brothers 23 marks (£15 6s 8d) with the

7 *Westminster Abbey Charters*, nos 73, 74, 93, 105, 106.

8 *Regesta Regum Anglo-Normannorum*, III, ed. H.A. Cronne and R.H.C. Davis (Oxford, 1968), no. 935; *Westminster Abbey Charters*, no. 117 and note.

9 Graeme White, 'Continuity in Government', in E. King, ed., *The Anarchy of Stephen's Reign* (Oxford, 1994), p. 132. See also E.J. Kealey, *Roger of Salisbury, Viceroy of England* (Berkeley, Los Angeles, London, 1972), pp. 259–60, no. 23.

10 *Dialogus de Scaccario*, ed. and transl. C. Johnson with corrections by F.E.L. Carter and D.E. Greenway (Oxford, 1983), p. 12.

11 *Pipe Roll 15 Henry II*, p. 73; *Pipe Roll 21 Henry II*, p. 11.

consent of Abbot Robert. Lawrence and his monks also quitclaimed to the Taileboys brothers quittance of pannage for twenty pigs in Aldenham wood annually. This seemingly mundane dispute was heard before a panel of eminent administrators acting as royal justices: Nigel, bishop of Ely; Geoffrey Ridel, archdeacon of Canterbury; Richard of Ilchester, archdeacon of Poitiers; Richard Fitz Nigel, the royal treasurer; Guy Rufus, dean of Waltham; Robert de Beaumont, earl of Leicester; Richard de Lucy; the royal chamberlains Henry Fitz Gerold and William Mauduit; Simon Fitz Peter; Alan de Neville; Geoffrey 'the monk'; William Fitz Andelin, the king's marshal; and Philip of Daventry.[12] No doubt Abbot Lawrence was fortunate to have the opportunity to focus the attention of this distinguished panel upon his territorial dispute with an abbey which also had personal grievances against him.[13] The precedents set by Westminster were soon followed by others, and from the latter part of Henry II's reign there is wider evidence of litigation being heard at sessions of the Exchequer.[14] Down to 1179, final concords concluding suits heard in this royal court normally call it 'the king's court at Westminster', adding that the concords were made 'at the Exchequer'. Most such references are to occasions, the brief half-yearly sessions at Easter and Michaelmas, rather than to an institution, although the Exchequer court was indeed turning into an institution in the course of Henry II's reign. Surviving final concords indicate that there was no essential difference between the personnel of 'the king's court at Westminster' and that of 'the king's court at Westminster at the Exchequer', suggesting that at this period these two institutions were one.[15] In the thirteenth century, the collusive final concord was used to give added validity to an amicable transfer of land. The concords of earlier generations, though, are more likely to represent the conclusion of genuine lawsuits, especially when the nature of the preceding assize is identified.

The gradual stabilization of the Treasury and the Exchequer at Westminster in the course of Henry II's reign, and the establishment of the Chancery there during the reign of John, did much to enhance the profitability of the abbey's vill, increasing the demand for suburban residences and augmenting the profits of the retail trade.[16] While such economic developments would be welcome to the monks, greater importance perhaps continued to be attached to the proximity of the royal justices, since the maintenance of good relations with regular members of the bench would help secure the abbey's wider

12 *Westminster Abbey Charters*, no. 281 and note.

13 For the views of St Albans abbey on Abbot Lawrence, see Thomas of Walsingham, *Gesta Abbatum Monasterii Sancti Albani*, ed. H.T. Riley, I, Rolls Series (1867), pp. 107–10, 112, 133–4.

14 Brand, '*Multis Vigiliis Excogitatam et Inventam*', pp. 207–8.

15 *Ibid*., p. 208. On the evolution of this court in the later twelfth century, *ibid*., pp. 211–15.

16 Richard Mortimer, *Angevin England 1154–1258* (Oxford, 1994), pp. 63, 65, 183. See also Gervase Rosser, *Medieval Westminster 1200–1540* (Oxford, 1989), pp. 18–21.

territorial interests. Litigation between Abbot Walter and his monks, on the one hand, and Prior Bertram and his monks of St Saviour's, Bermondsey, in 'the king's court at Westminster' at the Easter session of the Exchequer was concluded by a final concord, dated 23 April 1182, when the two religious houses agreed to share equally the rights of advowson in the church of St Magnus the Martyr near London Bridge. On this occasion, the judges were headed by Richard of Ilchester, bishop of Winchester; and Ranulf de Glanville, the justiciar; acting with Richard Fitz Nigel, the royal treasurer and nine others.[17]

Three years later, on 31 May 1185, a final concord terminated a suit 'in the king's court at Westminster' between Abbot Walter, and the brothers Richard and William of Paddington. These men surrendered the whole tenement which they held of the abbey in Paddington, 'and whatever right they had in it', in return for 40 marks (£26 13s 4d) and four corrodies in Westminster abbey. Those allocated to Richard and William would run for twelve years, while those for their wives would be held for life, and were augmented by pittances. The judges who heard this case comprised John of Oxford, bishop of Norwich; Ranulf de Glanville, justiciar; Richard Fitz Nigel; Godfrey de Lucy; Hubert Walter; William Basset; and Nigel Fitz Alexander.[18] It is clear that the judges were sitting in a purely legal capacity, since the Easter session of the Exchequer was long past, and their eminence may reflect the legal complexity of the case, as well as being indicative of the calibre of judges which the wealthy Westminster could interest in its pleas.[19]

While the very proximity of senior administrators could be turned to advantage, the protection of Westminster's interests was further enhanced when a writ was obtained on 16 December 1189, ordering that the monks and their possessions were to be treated as was the royal demesne. They were not to be disseized of any free tenement which they held on the day when the king last crossed from England into Normandy, nor were they to be impleaded over any tenement, except in the presence of the king, his chief justiciar or the chancellor. Richard I had crossed to Calais four days before this writ was issued on the sole authority of Hugh du Puiset, bishop of Durham and co-justiciar.[20] But even though Westminster's interests were safeguarded at the highest level in the secular courts, this protection was of little use when they came under pressure from leading ecclesiastics. Only a few weeks after the protective writ was obtained, Abbot Walter was constrained to make a life-grant of the abbey's recently re-acquired manor of Perton, Staffs., to Hugh de Nunant, bishop of Coventry.[21] The pressure

17 *Westminster Abbey Charters*, no. 287.

18 *Ibid.*, no. 296. See also Barbara Harvey, *Living and Dying in England 1100–1540: The Monastic Experience* (Oxford, 1993), pp. 196, 240.

19 Harvey, *Living and Dying in England*, p. 196.

20 *Westminster Abbey Charters*, no. 145 and note. See also no. 146 and notes.

21 *Ibid.*, no. 304.

which Hugh was able to bring to bear resulted from the support which a recent ecclesiastical gathering had given to him in his dispute against his own monastic chapter.[22] On the other hand, Hugh de Nunant was listed among the 'barons of the king's Exchequer' who were present in the *Curia Regis* at Westminster when an agreement was reached between Abbot Walter and the monks, on the one hand, and Nicholas of Paglesham on the other, in which the conditions were defined under which Nicholas would hold the vill of Paglesham. An agreement had already been ratified between the parties in the chapter of Westminster, but the attestations of the judges of the *Curia Regis* were evidently seen as enhancing the stability of the arrangements. William Longchamp, bishop of Ely, presided in his capacity as royal chancellor, together with Hugh du Puiset, bishop of Durham, and Hugh de Nunant, 'and other barons of the king's Exchequer'. The latter are not named, while the remaining identified witnesses appear to have been tenants of the abbey and residents of the vill.[23]

While canon lawyers claimed jurisdiction over suits of advowson, the abbot and monks of Westminster usually pleaded such cases in the secular courts, as required by Clause 1 of the Constitutions of Clarendon. On 4 December 1192, a final concord ended a suit heard in the *Curia Regis* at Westminster between Abbot William Postard and the monks, on the one hand, and Hugh of Buckland on the other, over the advowson of Datchworth (Herts.). This lawsuit had been initiated 'by writ of recognition' (of *darrein presentment*). The abbot and convent quitclaimed the advowson to Hugh and his heirs, on the understanding that, before any clerk whom they presented was instituted to the church, or gained admission to it, he would first swear in the chapter at Westminster that he would render 20 shillings annually to the abbot and convent at Michaelmas, once he was instituted. Assent to this agreement was obtained from William of Buckland, who was the tenant of the abbot of Westminster in the vill of Datchworth. William was the lord there of Hugh of Buckland (the abbey's under-tenant).[24] The bench of judges comprised Walter de Coutances, archbishop of Rouen (the justiciar); Roger Fitz Reinfrid; Robert of Whitefield; Osbert Fitz Hervey; Simon of Pattishall; and Hugh of Chacombe. Whatever their disposition towards the abbey, the Buckland family was well-entrenched. Some eighty years previously, an earlier William of Buckland had been admitted as a tenant of Abbot Gilbert in estates in Buckinghamshire, Hertfordshire and Middlesex,[25] while an earlier Hugh of Buckland had administrative responsibilities in various shires in the reigns of William II and Henry I.[26]

22 J.T. Appleby, *England without Richard 1189–1199* (London, 1965), pp. 27–9.

23 *Westminster Abbey Charters*, no. 300.

24 *Ibid.*, no. 320. For the Constitutions of Clarendon on advowsons (Clause 1), see *English Historical Documents II, 1042–1189*, ed. D.C. Douglas and G.W. Greenaway, 2nd edn (London, 1981), pp. 766–70, no. 126, at p. 767.

25 *Ibid.*, no. 242.

26 *Ibid.*, nos 53, 59, 68, 85, 97, 320, 488.

The *Curia Regis* at Westminster was again the venue, on 26 November 1197, for a suit between Ailward of Charing and his wife Hawise, plaintiff, and Abbot William Postard, defendant, over three virgates of land in Teddington, about which a recognition of *Mort d'Ancestor* was summoned between them in that court. In the resulting final concord, the abbot acknowledged that the land belonged by right and inheritance to the plaintiffs, to be held of him and his successors in perpetuity, by free service of one mark (13s 4d) annually, and also the forinsec service. In return for this agreement, the plaintiffs gave the abbot 20 shillings sterling.[27] On this occasion it was not the abbot who had chosen to bring a suit in the *Curia Regis* but the tenants, who evidently considered that their claim to hereditary right would be best defended there. Litigants might prefer the expense of a suit in the *Curia Regis* if they thought that any lesser court would pronounce automatically in favour of the abbot. Teddington, for instance, had been granted to the abbey by King Edward.[28]

Comparable reasoning perhaps prompted another plaintiff, Walter son of Thurstan of Colham, to bring a suit against Abbot William Postard and his monks in the course of 1198. In this case the suit was over the seneschalcy of the abbey.[29] By the resulting final concord, dated 27 August 1198, Walter quitclaimed this office to the abbot and his successors. In return, the abbot and monks granted him an annual payment of 5 marks (£3 6s 8d), from the abbot's chamber, until they eventually rendered him £10 worth of rents in the course of his life, or a lesser sum, if that would satisfy him.[30] While the natural forum for such a dispute might be the Chapter of Westminster, or else the abbot's court, Walter could conclude that his only chance of an objective hearing would be before the *Curia Regis* and that an action brought there was worth the expenditure, given the rewards of the office. Other laity in dispute with the abbey evidently reached a comparable conclusion. Stephen of Turnham and his wife Edelina were plaintiffs in a suit of *Mort d'Ancestor* which they brought against Abbot William Postard, over one and a half virgates of land and two hides of land (perhaps two separate tenements) in Battersea. By the ensuing final concord, drawn up in the *Curia Regis* on 11 November 1198, they quitclaimed this land to the abbot and his successors, but in return he gave them a plot of land in the vill of Westminster, opposite the Church of the Holy Innocents (St Mary le Strand), which they and their heirs would hold in perpetuity at an annual rent of one pound of pepper or 6 pence. Not unnaturally, the couple required that the abbot and his successors would warrant them in their occupancy against all comers.[31] A suit of advowson was

27 *Ibid.*, no. 316.

28 Barbara Harvey, *Westminster Abbey and its Estates in the Middle Ages* (Oxford, 1977), p. 354.

29 *Curia Regis Rolls*, I, p. 138.

30 *Westminster Abbey Charters*, no. 310. My thanks are offered to Barbara Harvey for her comments on the unusual wording of this document.

31 *Westminster Abbey Charters*, no. 314.

again contested in the *Curia Regis* at Westminster when the plaintiff Baldwin of Parham brought a suit against Abbot William Postard, represented on this occasion by James the Cellarer, over the advowson of Parham (Sussex). There was a recognition (of *darrein presentment*), following which Baldwin quitclaimed all his right in the advowson, in return for one mark of silver.[32] The surviving final concords from the abbacies of Lawrence, Walter and William Postard, appear, therefore, to have terminated genuinely adversarial litigation.

The final concord concluding the earliest lawsuit in the *Curia Regis* which involved Abbot Ralph Arundel has, however, a collusive appearance. Westminster had acquired the manors of Little Coggeshall and Feering from William I, with other lands, in exchange for Windsor.[33] In the course of litigation in the *Curia Regis* at Westminster, in Michaelmas term 1201, Aubrey de Vere claimed to hold Feering for an annual farm of £40, by virtue of a grant dating from the time of Abbot Gervase.[34] However, at the conclusion of the lawsuit, he quitclaimed this manor to the abbot and his successors, in return for its appurtenant manor of Little Coggeshall, which he and his successors would hold in perpetuity, at an annual rent of 2 shillings, due at Michaelmas, besides answering for the forinsec service.[35]

Abbot Ralph's next recorded litigation in the *Curia Regis* concluded in a very detailed final concord. At its outset, it appears collusive in nature, although its further details may represent the outcome of some hard bargaining over pasture rights. This lawsuit was heard in Easter term, 1204, when Abbot Ralph was the plaintiff against William de Ginnes and his wife Matilda, over a carucate of land in Battersea. They acknowledged that this land belonged by right to the abbot and his abbey, and in return he granted it to them, to hold for 20 shillings annually. The couple then quitclaimed, for themselves and Matilda's heirs, all their land and woodland in Penge, which the abbot and his successors might do with as they pleased, on the understanding that the couple and Matilda's heirs might have common of herbage in their woodland in Penge, and exclusive pannage for thirty pigs. In the event that the abbot or his successors wanted to make an assart in the wood, then a sufficient area would be excluded from the assart to sustain the thirty pigs; up to forty *animalia* (presumably cattle, since goats were excluded) and up to a hundred sheep. The abbot then received William's homage for that land in the *Curia Regis*.[36] Matilda was presumably the heiress of this land, but recognition of her rights, and of those of her husband, in their Battersea property was secured only by a curtailment of their use of their woodland in Penge. Suits in the *Curia Regis* over such modest landholdings may scarcely

32 *Ibid*., no. 325.
33 Harvey, *Westminster Abbey and its Estates*, p. 341.
34 *Curia Regis Rolls*, I, pp. 464–5.
35 *Westminster Abbey Charters*, no. 331.
36 *Ibid*., no. 330.

have been cost-effective, although the verdict of its august judges would be a good guarantee against further contests.

The *Curia Regis* was an obvious forum in which to debate control over the abbey's substantial outlying estates. Abbot William Postard had made an inheritable grant of the vill of Doddington, Lincs., to his knight William Picot, in return for an annual payment of £12.[37] Abbot Ralph, however, experienced difficulties in keeping this tenant to the terms of his agreement and in 1205 he produced a charter, in the form of a chirograph, identifying its appendant seal as that of his predecessor. Picot, though, challenged the authenticity of this document. The only significant difference in its terms from those of Abbot William's known charter is the inclusion, with Doddington, of Thorpe [on-the-Hill].[38] John de Grey, bishop of Norwich, took an interest in the suit, which had evidently begun locally, and he fined one palfrey so that the case could be transferred to the *Coram Rege* court.[39]

Parham, in Sussex, was another such isolated property. Here the advowson was claimed by Thomas de Preston, who brought an assize of *darrein presentment* against Abbot Ralph in Easter term 1208. This concluded with the plaintiff acknowledging that the abbot and convent were rightful possessors of the advowson, and in return he was granted confraternity.[40] The outlying vill of Parham was more vulnerable than most of Westminster's properties. The abbey's title to it was challenged by the prominent *curialis* Peter Fitz Herbert, who was embroiled in a long-running lawsuit with the abbot and monks, waged between 1211 and 1214.[41] The abbey's title to Parham dated from the late tenth century.[42] Peter's claim to the vill revived one made earlier in the twelfth century by Herbert Fitz Herbert, even though both Henry I and King Stephen had upheld Westminster's title.[43] But, however good the abbey's title, it was vulnerable to pressure from those with influence. The abbey needed the goodwill of prominent courtiers in order to obtain favourable verdicts in other cases. In 1214, Peter Fitz Herbert obtained a series of concessions from the abbey, culminating in a payment to him of £100. He acknowledged receipt of this in a letter addressed to the barons of the Exchequer and the justices of the Bench [Court], informing them that the suit had ended in a concord agreed in the *Curia Regis*. Since he was called away on urgent royal business, he requested the barons of the Exchequer to

37 *Ibid*., no. 322.

38 *Curia Regis Rolls*, IV, pp. 13, 45–6, 48; *Westminster Abbey Charters*, no. 322n. Abbot William had not described his charter as being in the form of a chirograph, whereas Ralph's clearly was.

39 *Rotuli de Oblatis et Finibus in Turri Londiniensi asservati, tempore Regis Johannis*, ed. T. Duffus Hardy (Record Comm., London, 1835), p. 336. See also *Pipe Roll 7 John*, p. 236; *Pipe Roll 9 John*, p. 52.

40 *Westminster Abbey Charters*, no. 334.

41 *Curia Regis Rolls*, VI, pp. 119, 133, 176–7, 215, 287, 296, 393; VII, p. 239. See also Turner, *The King and his Courts*, p. 256.

42 Harvey, *Westminster Abbey and its Estates*, p. 359.

43 *Westminster Abbey Charters*, nos 96, 117.

carry out the terms of the concord, and to make a chirograph in the *Curia Regis*. He assigned Mr Jocelin the king's Marshal to take delivery of this chirograph on his behalf. He would also ratify anything which Jocelin negotiated with the abbot and monks, and Jocelin was also to ensure the exchange of their respective charters recording the agreement.[44]

The *Curia Regis* was again the venue, early in 1215, for a suit between Abbot William de Humez, plaintiff, and his tenant Ivo of Deene, defendant, which established the full extent of the service of hospitality due to the abbot when his annual travels brought him to Simon's manor of Deene.[45] As a matter of convenience, it would generally suit the abbots to have cases against their more distant tenants heard in the *Curia Regis* at Westminster. Additionally the status of this court would add weight to any verdict delivered there; while they could generally expect a favourable verdict, given the apparently smooth working relationship between the abbey and the personnel of this court, in the late twelfth century and the early thirteenth.

The texts of the charters of the abbots and monks in this period indicates that men who served as judges often had responsibilities in the Exchequer, while those engaged in either capacity might also be tenants of the abbey. At the same time, a growing specialization was taking place within official circles, leading to a gradual differentiation between the bench of justices at the court of Common Pleas and the barons of the Exchequer.[46] This process was under way, but by no means completed, at Michaelmas 1189, when William Postard, at that time still prior, made a payment to the Exchequer in order to have enrolled on the Pipe Roll a memorandum of the quitclaim which William of Eynsford (III) made to the monks of his life-tenancy in Benfleet (Essex), and his restoration, of the charter recording his tenancy, which he made in the *Curia Regis*, in presence of the Barons of the Exchequer.[47] The prior's use of the Pipe Roll in order to record a tenurial transaction is an early instance of a practice which was also followed by staff of the Exchequer, including the chamberlain William Mauduit (III) in 1193, and Mr Roger of Charlecote who did likewise in 1202.[48] Doubtless some Exchequer officer advised Prior Postard on the use of the Pipe Roll for this purpose. William Mauduit's son and heir, Robert Mauduit (II), maintained a close relationship with the abbey. He had a residence on abbey property, and was permitted to

44 *Ibid.*, no. 487.

45 F.M. Stenton, *The First Century of English Feudalism 1066–1166*, 2nd edn (Oxford, 1961), pp. 267–9, no. 17. See also *ibid.*, pp. 71–3.

46 Richard Heiser, 'The Households of the Justiciars of Richard I: An Inquiry into the Second Level of Medieval English Government', *The Haskins Society Journal*, II (1990), pp. 230–31.

47 *Westminster Abbey Charters*, no. 344.

48 *The Beauchamp Cartulary Charters 1100–1268*, ed. Emma Mason, Pipe Roll Society, new series, 43 (1980), p. xxix, no. 312n. Mr Roger's enrolment was of a grant he had recently received from Mr Jocelin the Marshal (of the Exchequer: cf. *ibid.*, nos 312 and 314), who perhaps advised Roger on the advisability of recording it in this way.

maintain a private chapel in this '*curia*'.[49] He and his wife, Isabel Bassett, were benefactors of Westminster,[50] and Robert attested charters for the abbey.[51] Mr Jocelin Marshal similarly attested charters on behalf of the abbot and monks,[52] and he was also rector of Westminster's church of St Matthew, Friday Street.[53] Robert and his wife were granted confraternity,[54] and Robert's *obit* was ceremoniously commemorated there.[55]

A third eminent Exchequer officer associated with Westminster was Alexander Swerford. He was described as 'our clerk' when Abbot Ralph and the convent granted him some houses in London, between Ludgate and Fleet Bridge, between 1206 and 1214. Even at this time, however, it may be that he was chiefly employed in the Exchequer, since the abbot's grant was witnessed by leading Exchequer personalities, headed by William of Ely, the royal treasurer; William of Cornhill; the chamberlain Robert Mauduit and Mr Jocelin Marshal.[56] The tenancy granted to Alexander perhaps represented the equivalent of a retaining fee, so that the abbot and monks could call on his expertise from time to time. Over the ensuing decades, Alexander became one of the most eminent of the Exchequer staff. Matthew Paris, recording his death in 1246, commented on his exceptional knowledge of the Exchequer's archives and of its practices.[57] The full extent of his dealings with the abbey is uncertain, since it is not clear whether he is to be identified in every, or even in any, case, with the man, or men, variously described as Alexander the clerk[58] and Alexander, clerk of the Exchequer.[59] The latter was closely associated with Edith, daughter of Geoffrey de Barra. They had children, but were not recorded as being married.[60] Ambitious clerks, hoping for ecclesiastical preferment, would exercise discretion when recording personal matters. A similarly reticent couple were Rose *la custerere* and Ralph Mauduit, who

49 *Westminster Abbey Charters*, nos 311–12.

50 *Ibid.*, nos 329, 422, 450.

51 *Ibid.*, nos 321, 327, 335, 409, 427, 449, 450.

52 *Ibid.*, nos 327, 335, 409, 434, 446.

53 David Crouch, *William Marshal: Court, Career and Chivalry in the Angevin Empire 1147–1219* (Harlow, 1990), p. 146. Jocelin's career and his connection with William Marshal are discussed *ibid.*, pp. 145–6, 206–7. Jocelin had some connection with William Turpin, an officer of the King's Chamber: *Beauchamp Cartulary*, nos 310–14.

54 *Westminster Abbey Charters*, no. 329.

55 Westminster Abbey Muniments, nos 3455, 3456.

56 *Westminster Abbey Charters*, no. 327.

57 Matthew Paris, *Chronica Majora*, ed. H.R. Luard, IV, Rolls Series (1877), pp. 587–8. See also F.M. Powicke, *King Henry III and the Lord Edward* (Oxford, reprinted 1966), pp. 90–91; R.C. Stacey, *Politics, Policy and Finance under Henry III 1216–1246* (Oxford, 1987), pp. 41–2, 257.

58 *Westminster Abbey Charters*, nos 335, 346, 423, 439, 464, 480.

59 *Ibid.*, nos 414, 424, 426. On the probability that there were simultaneously two, or more, Exchequer employees named Alexander, see H.G. Richardson, 'William of Ely, the King's Treasurer', *Transactions of the Royal Historical Society*, fourth series, 15 (1932), p. 88.

60 *Westminster Abbey Charters*, nos 413–14.

made the abbey a joint grant, to take effect after their deaths. This donation, of a messuage in the vill of Westminster, for their souls and that of King Henry II, was made in King John's reign.[61] Ralph had been in the royal service towards the end of Henry II's reign.[62] Rose was more affluent, and carried more social cachet, than her cognomen indicated. She was the widow of William Turpin, an officer of the Chamber (personal finance office) of Henry II. William had granted to Rose, c.1177, land outside Ludgate, of which Osmund the carter and his wife Ermengard had made him heir in the *Curia Regis*. Rose was invited to donate this land to any church she chose, for the good of her soul and those of William and King Henry II. William's stature in the royal court is indicated by the eminence of the witnesses to his charter, headed by William Fitz Ralph, seneschal of Normandy; Stephen de Marzai, seneschal of Anjou, and Manser Biset.[63] William Turpin probably died shortly before Michaelmas 1194.[64] Rose evidently retained this land near Ludgate for some years before granting it to the abbey in King John's reign.[65] It was this same Ludgate property which was then granted by Abbot Ralph and the monks to Alexander Swerford.[66] Its renewed occupation by a senior financial officer may be more than fortuitous, and is perhaps indicative of its desirability in other respects.

Successive royal treasurers were among the most notable of the abbey's tenants in the vill of Westminster. Richard Fitz Nigel, royal treasurer in Henry II's reign, bishop of London in his last years, held a messuage with houses and outbuildings, which he conveyed in 1196 to his successor as treasurer, William of Ely, a near kinsman, who would now become the abbey's tenant.[67] Abbot William Postard confirmed this transfer.[68] William remained in office down to the civil war at the end of John's reign. Then, together with his fellow-canons of St Paul's, he supported Prince Louis of France when he was invited into England by the rebels. William lost his position as treasurer (having apparently delivered the records of the Exchequer to the prince).[69] He remained a tenant of the abbey, however. At some date between September 1218 and February 1221 he restored the property to the monks, who would, however, allow him to remain in occupation for the time being. Evidently he had been reconciled to the regency government, since his grant was made for the soul's of Kings Henry, Richard and John, while his witnesses included the papal legate, Pandulph Masca, bishop of Norwich; Hubert de

61 *Ibid.*, no. 435.
62 *Pipe Roll 34 Henry II*, p. 17.
63 *Westminster Abbey Charters*, no. 386.
64 *Beauchamp Cartulary*, no. 312 and note.
65 *Westminster Abbey Charters*, no. 387.
66 *Ibid.*, no. 327.
67 Richardson, 'William of Ely', pp. 79–80, no. 1; calendared *Westminster Abbey Charters*, no. 219.
68 *Westminster Abbey Charters*, no. 313.
69 Richardson, 'William of Ely', pp. 55–8.

Burgh, the justiciar; and Eustace de Fauconberg, the royal treasurer.[70] Before April 1224 William had been replaced as tenant of this property by Hubert de Burgh.[71]

Whatever the pressure of their other commitments, the senior personnel could make time to ratify dealings of their members with the abbey; it was 'at the petition and instance of the king's barons' that Abbot William Postard granted licence to the royal chamberlain Robert Mauduit to have a private chapel in his house in the vill of Westminster.[72] William of Ely witnessed this grant, together with a slightly earlier one by which the abbot granted the tenancy of the property to Robert. The justice Simon of Pattishall also witnessed both of these, as did a series of lesser officials.[73] Attestations of senior Exchequer staff were obtained when Robert's wife Isabel acquired property from a resident of the vill of Westminster;[74] when Robert's clerk, William 'of the Temple', acquired a tenancy in the vill;[75] and when the Exchequer employee William English was granted a messuage by Prior Robert Moulsham.[76] Such prominent officials occasionally witnessed transactions between comparatively modest residents of the vill,[77] but the most impressive witness-list of all occurs on Abbot Ralph's solemn grant and confirmation to the convent of the vill of Parham.[78] Some of those who occasionally attested Westminster charters, men employed at the Exchequer in a lesser capacity, were in effect witnessing in their capacity as residents of the vill, and neighbours of the people involved in the various transactions.[79]

Many disputes between the abbey and rival litigants were resolved in local courts. In the years after the Norman Conquest, royal writs were often addressed to groups of notables, both ecclesiastical and lay, either ordering them to resolve a dispute or else to see that justice was done in accordance with the king's decision. Those named were the leading officials responsible for exercising justice in the king's name, and writs were addressed to recipients in

70 *Westminster Abbey Charters*, no. 439. On the extension of this property while in William's occupancy, see *ibid.*, nos 437–8. The premises lay in the Endiff district: see Rosser, *Medieval Westminster*, pp. 18–21.

71 Richardson, 'William of Ely', pp. 90–91, no. IX. See also Rosser, *Medieval Westminster*, p. 20.

72 *Westminster Abbey Charters*, no. 312.

73 *Ibid.*, nos 311–12.

74 *Ibid.*, no. 421. The land, with its charter, was donated by Isabel to the abbey: *ibid.*, no. 422.

75 *Ibid.*, no. 446.

76 *Ibid.*, no. 346.

77 *Ibid.*, nos 409, 486.

78 *Ibid.*, no. 335.

79 *Ibid.*, no. 336. For instance, in nos 311–12, the attestations of senior Exchequer personnel are followed by those of the more prominent residents of the vill, and only then by those of the lesser members of the Exchequer staff (although the rising clerk, Louis of Rockingham, takes the traditional concluding place, as scribe of these charters).

most parts of southern England and the Midlands.[80] While the principal recipients were personally addressed, it would be intended that the writs would be read out in the shire court, in order to publicize the abbey's title to the lands in question. The device of including the thegns of the shire or shires in which the land lay would ensure that the message reached most of those capable of unlawfully occupying the estate in question. In the reigns of William I and his sons, there was a long chronological overlap between writs addressed to a small group of eminent men and those specifically addressed to one particular sheriff or another. One of the earliest surviving Westminster writs in the latter category, from an uncertain date in the reign of William I, notified Sweyn, the sheriff of Essex, of the king's confirmation of land in Tilbury, donated to the abbey by Geoffrey de Mandeville.[81] The wide spread of the abbey's lands, including its large estates in the West Midlands, helps account for the long survival of writs with multiple addressees. The regional notables were not merely administrators, nor yet simply those concerned with upholding the king's rights in a region, although that was one of their duties.[82] Sometimes they constituted a panel of judges, as when Bishop Wulfstan and [Æthelwig] the abbot of Evesham, gave a verdict in a suit concerning Westminster's lands in Worcestershire.[83] In other cases, as with a writ of William I, addressed to notables in Essex and Surrey, ordering them to render justice to Abbot Vitalis, it appears that the king had already delivered his verdict.[84] In view of the endemic violence resulting from tenurial disputes in the decades after the conquest, the abbey's hold over its lands would often be uncertain.[85] The intervention of the regional magnates would greatly enhance the abbey's chances of securing its possessions.

Increasingly, however, the individual sheriff and his shire jurors may be glimpsed in the charters acting in a similar capacity. It seems clear that, after an initial appeal to the king on the part of the abbey, matters were being delegated to the sheriff. For instance, in a writ issued by Henry I in 1129, the sheriff of Essex, Aubrey de Vere, was ordered to convene the shire court in order to hear the dispute between the archbishop of Canterbury and the abbot of Westminster, over the land of Alestan [in West Ham]; to cause a verdict to be delivered on which party had the better title, and to deliver lawful seisin accordingly.[86] While sheriffs therefore had their uses for the abbey, the monastery aspired to render only minimal reciprocal obligations.

80 *Ibid.*, nos 2–7, for instance.

81 *Ibid.*, no. 23.

82 *Ibid.*, no. 8, for instance.

83 *Ibid.*, no. 22. See also no. 51.

84 *Ibid.*, no. 26.

85 Prior occurrence of violent dispossession is implied in writs of William I for Westminster: for instance, W. Dugdale, *Monasticon Anglicanum*, revised H. Caley, H. Ellis and B. Bandinel, 6 vols in 8 (London, 1817–30), I, p. 301, nos XXXIV, XXXVII; calendared *Westminster Abbey Charters*, nos 7, 9.

86 *Westminster Abbey Charters*, no. 91.

A writ of Henry I dating from c.1121 notified the sheriffs of those shires where St Peter and the abbot held land that Abbot Herbert was to hold his lands, men and property quit of pleas and suits, shire and hundred courts, as Westminster held them TRE and as confirmed by a charter of King Edward.[87] A writ of King Stephen notified his officers in Essex that he quitclaimed to the abbey and the monks the sheriff's aid, *alias* justice-aid at the rate of 1 shilling annually on each hide in Essex.[88] A seemingly-spurious writ produced in the abbey's *scriptorium* extended the exemptions enjoyed by the abbey[89] although general exemption from sheriff's aids and other exactions was in fact granted by Richard I on 7 October 1189.[90] Extensive franchisal rights within the abbey's lands had long been claimed in the abbey's more dubious charters, but were actually confirmed by Henry II c.1156.[91] Another writ of Henry II, perhaps issued a year or two after the previous one, ordered his sheriffs throughout England to ensure that the abbey enjoyed its liberty.[92] It was perhaps in consequence of this that the abbey's lands in several shires were exempted from the murder fine when this was levied in ensuing years.[93]

The abbey was not altogether exempt from the intrusion of sheriffs into its lands. A writ issued in the name of Henry II, c.1158, ordered the abbot (Lawrence) to render right to Hugh Fitz Warner over lands in Teddington and Sunbury, otherwise the sheriff of Middlesex would do so.[94] The abbot pursued the matter 'in the court of Westminster' but it is uncertain whether this phrase indicates the *Curia Regis*, or the court of the abbot himself. In the event, Hugh surrendered his claim, together with his royal writ, but was compensated by the grant of an equivalent holding.[95] The sheriff of Surrey, on the other hand, was ordered by the king, c.1158, to investigate possible disseisin of the abbot from his land in Claygate, and to restore him, if he had been wrongfully dispossessed, to any land he held there at the death of Henry I.[96] The exemptions from routine shire justice claimed by,[97] and especially those granted to, Westminster, combined to ensure that its archives contain comparatively few records from this period relating to shrieval administration of justice. Many of the abbey's more remote estates were in any case farmed on long leases in this period, and documents relating to them are

87 *Ibid.*, no. 80.

88 *Ibid.*, no. 113.

89 *Ibid.*, no. 126.

90 *Ibid.*, no. 142.

91 *Ibid.*, no. 122.

92 *Regesta Regum Anglo-Normannorum, II, 1100–1135*, ed. C. Johnson and H.A. Cronne (Oxford, 1956), p. 389, no. CCCXXVII; calendared *Westminster Abbey Charters*, no. 131.

93 *Pipe Rolls 2–4 Henry II*, p. 135; *Pipe Roll 7 Henry II*, pp. 66, 69; *Pipe Roll 8 Henry II*, p. 8.

94 *Westminster Abbey Charters*, no. 133.

95 *Ibid.*, no. 452.

96 T.A.M. Bishop, *Scriptores Regis* (Oxford, 1961), plate xxv(b); calendared *Westminster Abbey Charters*, no. 125.

97 Bishop, *Scriptores Regis*, plate vi(b); calendared *Westminster Abbey Charters*, no. 129.

consequently rare. On the other hand, suits were occasionally pleaded by the abbot in presence of the itinerant justices. Since the abbot was still entitled at this time to exercise a brief annual right of hospitality at Deene, Northants,[98] it was perhaps convenient for him to time his visit to Northampton to coincide with the visit of the justices in January 1192 (the timing of which he would know from contacts at Westminster itself). Abbot William Postard quitclaimed a right of hospitality which he had been claiming against William of Darnford, in the vill of Deerhurst (Glos.) and in return, it was agreed that his tenant would render him 40 shillings annually.[99] Rationalization of the abbatial itinerary perhaps prompted the abbot to initiate a collusive suit in this instance.

When an eyre was conducted in Bedfordshire and Buckinghamshire, in the autumn of 1195,[100] two of the abbot's subordinates were deputed to plead cases on his behalf. At Bedford, Theobald, his seneschal, acted in a suit against Simon Malory (*Malhore*), representing his wife Alice, over the church of Holwell (Herts., *Helewell*), which was at that time in Bedfordshire.[101] The suit concluded in a concord by which the abbot (through Theobald) acknowledged Simon's right to the advowson, reserving 1 mark (13s 4d) annually which the almoner of Westminster was accustomed to receive from that church for the abbey's almonry.[102] Subsequently Stephen, the chamberlain (*camerarius*), was deputed by the abbot to contest a suit against Geoffrey de Insula, concerning land in Sulby (Northants).[103] In Michaelmas term 1210, Abbot Ralph, represented by Odo the goldsmith, was plaintiff in a suit against Simon of Deene, defendant, represented by his son Ivo, concerning the advowson of Uppingham church (Rutland). King John presided at the hearing of the suit of *darrein presentment*, together with five other judges. The case concluded with the defendant acknowledging the abbot's right to the advowson, and in return Simon and his heirs were accepted into confraternity with the abbey.[104]

The intermittent disputes between Westminster and St Alban's Abbey, were waged in various courts. In the later 1160s, their argument was simply territorial, and was resolved in presence of Nicholas, the sheriff of Hertfordshire, in a meeting of the shire court. Abbot Lawrence, with the assent of his monks and of the tenants of the disputed land in Sandridge granted it to Abbot Simon and his monks, together with a further plot acknowledged to

98 Stenton, *The First Century of English Feudalism*, pp. 267–9.

99 *Westminster Abbey Charters*, no. 324.

100 *Three Rolls of the King's Court in the Reign of King Richard the First A.D. 1194–1195*, ed. F.W. Maitland (Pipe Roll Society XVI, 1891, reprinted Vaduz, 1966), pp. XXVII–VIII.

101 On Holwell, see *Westminster Abbey Charters*, no. 166. Following a later alteration in county boundaries, it was subsequently in Hertfordshire.

102 *Three Rolls of the King's Court . . . 1194–1195*, p. 127.

103 *Ibid.*, p. 128.

104 *Westminster Abbey Charters*, no. 338.

belong to Westminster. In return, Abbot Simon, with the assent of his monks and the advice of his men, granted in exchange to Abbot Lawrence and his monks an equivalent amount of land in Sandridge adjacent to his land in Wheathampstead, with the assent of Gregory, the priest of Sandridge, to whom right (of tenancy) pertained.[105]

A dispute between Abbot William Postard of Westminster, and Abbot Warin of St Albans concerned the view of frankpledge in Aldenham (Herts.), and suit of the hundred-court. This case was evidently heard in the *Curia Regis* in the summer of 1194, but the parties quickly requested permission to make a (final) concord.[106] The resulting agreement is not the standard form of a final concord, but in that of a chirograph. It was agreed that the abbot of St Albans was entitled to send any one of his bailiffs to the view of frankpledge in Aldenham and would hear the oath being taken. The abbot of Westminster's bailiff would receive any pledges which resulted from the view of frankpledge and these would belong to the abbot of Westminster, transmitted through his bailiff. It was further agreed that every year, on the day of the view of frankpledge, the bailiff of the abbot of St Albans would receive by the hand of the bailiff of the abbot of Westminster two besants or 4 shillings sterling, whether there were any forfeitures or not. But it was not permitted to exact anything else from the abbot of Westminster or from his bailiff, or from the men of Aldenham for the view of frankpledge, except for suit of the hundred-court as it was anciently accustomed to be rendered and also excepting pleas of the Crown. This agreement was sealed by both parties, but the abbot of Westminster's copy has lost the seal (of the abbot of St Albans). This was perhaps removed, to signify cancellation, when a new agreement was made a few years later. This second agreement, between Abbot John of St Albans and Abbot Ralph of Westminster, set out exactly the same terms.[107] The few minor alterations in the wording do not convey any change of substance and it is not clear why a new charter was drawn up. Perhaps the initial agreement had not worked well in practice, but if so, no new safeguards were devised. In both documents, the abbot of Westminster was deemed to have the right to hold the view of frankpledge, while the compensatory payment to the abbot of St Albans went some way towards acknowledging his rival claims to the franchise. On both sides, principles and privileges were upheld, but without much monetary profit.

Nearer home, the abbot and convent had recourse to a number of local courts. Within the City of London, they were substantial property-holders. As their possessions increased, they would inevitably be drawn into litigation, but in the earlier twelfth century a determined effort was made to minimize its impact by securing legal exemptions and immunities. The first clear indication that this process was under way occurs in a writ of Edith

105 *Ibid.*, no. 282.

106 *Three Rolls of the King's Courts*, pp. xvi–xix (for the date), 7, 28.

107 *Westminster Abbey Charters*, no. 333.

Matilda, dating from 1113x1118. In this, she notified the bishop, sheriff and barons of London that she had conceded to Abbot Gilbert a tenement, formerly held of her by Hugh of Buckland, with sake and soke and customary rights.[108] During the vacancy which followed the death of Abbot Gilbert, the abbey suffered extensive losses of lands in various parts of England. Abbot Herbert, on his appointment, immediately set out to repair the damage and obtained a series of writs from Henry I in 1121–22 which were so worded as to ameliorate the abbey's financial predicament,[109] to assist in the recovery of lands wrongfully alienated,[110] and to confirm certain legal exemptions said to have been granted by King Edward and applicable to all the estates of the abbey.[111] Two further writs in this series specifically confirmed the abbey's liberties and privileges in the City of London, said to have been granted by King Edward.[112]

Two English-language writs in Edward's name concede to Westminster extensive judicial and financial rights within the City, although it is unlikely that either of them is genuine.[113] Similar privileges were also incorporated in the spurious Third Charter of King Edward, which has been identified as a product of the abbey's *scriptorium* in the earlier twelfth century.[114] The spurious Fourth Charter of King William I, allegedly dating from 2 January 1081, was designed to uphold Westminster's property and commercial rights within the City, besides conferring on the abbey a wide range of judicial exemptions.[115] Comparable immunities were bestowed on the abbey in four spurious writs surviving in the name of William I.[116] All are probably the

108 Armitage Robinson, *Gilbert Crispin*, p. 155, no. 38; calendared *Westminster Abbey Charters*, no. 97.

109 *Regesta Regum Anglo-Normannorum*, II, no. CXXV. See also *ibid.*, no. CXXVI; calendared *Westminster Abbey Charters*, nos 73–4.

110 *Regesta Regum Anglo-Normannorum*, II, no. CXXX; calendared *Westminster Abbey Charters*, no. 75.

111 Armitage Robinson, *Gilbert Crispin*, pp. 163–4; calendared *Westminster Abbey Charters*, no. 76.

112 *Formulare Anglicanum* compiled T. Madox (London, 1702), nos LXV, CCCCXCVI; calendared, respectively, *Westminster Abbey Charters*, nos 78 and 77.

113 *Anglo-Saxon Writs*, ed. and transl. F.E. Harmer, 2nd edn (Stamford, 1989), nos 105–6; discussed *ibid.*, pp. 296–7.

114 *Concilia Magnae Britanniae et Hiberniae* ed. D. Wilkins, 4 vols (London, 1737), I, pp. 319–20. On the authenticity of this writ, see *Anglo-Saxon Writs*, p. 290; P. Chaplais, 'The Original Charters of Herbert and Gervase, Abbots of Westminster (1121–1157)', reprinted from *A Medieval Miscellany for Doris Mary Stenton*, ed. P. Barnes and C.F. Slade, Pipe Roll Soc., new series, XXXVI (London, 1962), pp. 89–110, at p. 91, in P. Chaplais, *Essays in Medieval Diplomacy and Administration* (London, 1981), p. XVIII, 91.

115 *Westminster Abbey Charters*, no. 33. Chaplais, 'Original Charters', p. XVIII, p. 92.

116 Armitage Robinson, *Gilbert Crispin*, pp. 129–30, no. 4; p. 131, no. 5; *Regesta Regum Anglo-Normannorum 1066–1154*, I, ed. H.W.C. Davis with the assistance of R.J. Whitwell (Oxford, 1913), XXX, XLV and no. 251; calendared *Westminster Abbey Charters*, nos 36, 39, 40, 43.

handiwork of the *scriptorium* in the 1120s or the 1130s. This conjecture is supported by the fact that in one case such exemptions are particularly associated with (the lost) St Mary Newchurch.[117] In genuine royal writs obtained from William II, in an effort to recover control over this church, no mention is made of such exemptions and privileges,[118] nor are they mentioned in a further charter, issued for the same purpose, by Henry I.[119] On the other hand, the spurious Charter of Liberties, allegedly issued for Westminster by Henry I at his coronation, does confirm such privileges, said to have been granted by King Edward and King William I.[120]

The commercial potential of London was borne in mind by King Edward when he decided to rebuild the abbey.[121] The monks would be well aware of the advantages to be gained from expanding their properties in the City, and of being able to control them as they pleased. The approximate timespan within which the genuine writs were obtained, first from Edith Matilda and then from King Henry, suggests that the monks were increasingly concerned to establish their legal privileges in the City between c.1115 and c.1122. It is conjectural whether the *scriptorium* designed the English writs in King Edward's name for use when petitioning King Henry, or whether these, together with the Latin writs and charters which 'confirmed' the abbey's legal status in London, were produced retrospectively. The energy devoted to this project suggests an awareness of a growing assertiveness on the part of the City's rulers.[122] The privileges confirmed by the royal grants, whether the genuine or the spurious ones, were exemptions of a traditional and generally-worded kind. No document conferred exemption from the court of Husting or from the Folkmoot. Although its records survive only from the thirteenth century, the Husting court existed in the eleventh century, or even earlier.[123] The Folkmoot, a general gathering of the Londoners, was probably the older court of the two, but it met infrequently, whereas the smaller Husting court

117 Armitage Robinson, *Gilbert Crispin*, p. 131, no. 5; calendared *Westminster Abbey Charters*, no. 40.

118 Armitage Robinson, *Gilbert Crispin*, p. 137, nos 10–11; calendared *Westminster Abbey Charters*, nos 49, 54.

119 Armitage Robinson, *Gilbert Crispin*, p. 159; calendared *Westminster Abbey Charters*, no. 90.

120 *Regesta Regum Anglo-Normannorum*, II, no. 1; calendared *Westminster Abbey Charters*, no. 57.

121 *The Life of King Edward who Rests at Westminster*, ed. F. Barlow, 2nd edn (Oxford, 1992), pp. 68–9.

122 Susan Reynolds, 'The Rulers of London in the Twelfth Century', *History*, 57 (1972), pp. 34–41.

123 D. Keene and V. Harding, *A Survey of Documentary Sources for Property Holding in London before the Great Fire*, London Record Society, 22 (1985), p. 2. See also Pamela Nightingale, 'The Origin of the Court of the Husting and Danish Influence on London's Development into a Capital City', *English Historical Review*, 102 (1987), pp. 559–78.

met regularly on Mondays, in Henry I's reign, transacting a wide range of business.[124]

Early in the reign of King Stephen, a writ was obtained from him, addressed to Andrew Buccuinte (justiciar of London) and the citizens, ordering that the men in the soke of St Peter were to be quit of the Hustings and the Folkmoot, as fully as their charter attested. If anyone made a claim against them, let justice be done.[125] The earlier charter referred to here is perhaps a genuine writ of Henry I, from 1121–1122, which conferred legal exemptions on merchants residing on the abbey's land in London.[126] However, this contains no specific exemption from the Folkmoot nor from the Court of Husting. Neither does a later writ of Henry I, protecting from harassment the merchants in the soke of St Peter and of the abbot of Westminster and prohibiting intrusion into the soke, as conceded by King Edward and by William I.[127] Perhaps the scope of the Husting Court had been expanding over the fifteen or so years since Henry I's writ had been issued. The profitability of the abbey's lands in London depended in large part upon the freedom of its tenants to engage in their commercial transactions without undue restraint, whether in the form of actions against them in the City's courts, or else in the shape of a requirement to render suit of court.

The abbot and monks would not want to compromise their formal exemption from the jurisdiction of the courts of the City by having any avoidable recourse to them. On the other hand, there were advantages to be had in publicizing certain of their agreements reached with their tenants. A grant of a tenancy in London which Abbot Gervase made to his clerk Elias son of Goldwin was notified 'to all barons and citizens of London'.[128] The grant by which Gervase and the convent 'conceded' to Godwin Loffa of Bishopsgate land in Langbourn Ward was notified 'to the sheriff and all barons of London',[129] as was their confirmation of the grant of land in London which John son of Ralph made to the church of St Pancras, Lewes.[130] In effect, the Husting court was notified of the arrangement made in each case, but there is no further evidence that either Gervase or Lawrence made use of this procedural device. Abbot Walter, however, openly utilized the Husting Court, which was effectively the county court of the City. Common pleas, pleas about land or about the probate of testaments were heard there, and it was the appropriate forum in which to enrol private deeds. In the later twelfth

124 C.N.L. Brooke, assisted by G. Keir, *London 800–1216: The Shaping of a City* (London, 1975), pp. 249–50.

125 *Regesta Regum Anglo-Normannorum, III*, no. 927.

126 *Formulare Anglicanum*, no. CCCCXCVI; calendared *Westminster Abbey Charters*, no. 77.

127 *Regesta Regum Anglo-Normannorum*, II, no. CXXVIII; calendared *Westminster Abbey Charters*, no. 89.

128 *Westminster Abbey Charters*, no. 258.

129 *Ibid.*, no. 259.

130 *Ibid.*, no. 260.

century it was particularly useful when citizens were publicizing transactions concerning land.[131] It was apparently this aspect of its work which appealed to Abbot Walter and his monks. In 1184, the abbot and monks 'conceded' to the nuns of Clerkenwell the house, belonging to their fee, which Alulf Fitz Fromund gave them in Bread Street, situated between the house of Ralph de Quatremars and that of Warin the turner. The nuns would hold it in perpetuity, rendering 30 pence annually to the chamberlain of the abbey. Walter and the monks also 'conceded' them another plot of land pertaining to their fee in Eastcheap, adjoining the land of Simon of Paris which Osbert Becche gave them, for which the nuns would render two shillings annually to the chamberlain of the abbey. This grant, witnessed by the sheriff of London and several prominent citizens, 'was made in the full Husting of London'.[132]

In another charter, of uncertain date, Abbot Walter and the convent confirmed to Nicholas, son of Randulf Duchet, their land bordering the Thames, lying between that of the nuns of Haliwell and that of Ralph, brother of Joyce the vintner, 'which was adjudged to us in the full Husting', and which Nicholas would now hold in fee and inheritance, at an annual rent of sixteen pence. The abbot and monks acknowledged their obligation to warrant Nicholas against all counter-claimants, and also acknowledged that they were not entitled to raise the rent. Nicholas, in return, gave them a gersum of 40 shillings.[133]

In 1183–84, an agreement was reached between Osbert, abbot of Bec, and his convent, and the chamberlain of Westminster, acknowledging the obligation of Bec to render to Westminster 15 shillings annually, for land and a house, namely *Musterlingebur*, pertaining to Westminster's fee, which Richard, prior of Ruislip, obtained from the wife of Stephen the healer. The annual payment to Westminster would be made by the Prior of Ruislip (a cell of Bec). 'This mutual agreement was . . . more fully recorded in the Husting of London'.[134] Clearly the Husting court afforded useful publicity for property-holders when their tenants changed, enabling the landlord to ensure the ongoing payment of his rent.

According to a document of c.1118x1120, which defined the monks' share of the abbey's property, they had been assigned 'all rents in London'.[135] Consequently they also made independant use of the court of Husting to secure their rights in the property assigned to them. A pair of final concords was drawn up in this court at some date between 1179 and 1181. In one case the other party to the agreement comprised Peter of Sutton and his wife

131 Keene and Harding, *Survey of Documentary Sources for Property Holding in London*, p. 2.

132 *Westminster Abbey Charters*, no. 292; *Cartulary of St Mary, Clerkenwell*, ed. W.O. Hassall, Camden Soc., Third Series, LXXI (1949), no. 235.

133 *Westminster Abbey Charters*, no. 289.

134 *Ibid.*, no. 361.

135 *Ibid.*, no. 339.

Margaret; and in the other case the second party comprised John Tresgod and his wife Amy. The women were co-heiresses with a reversionary interest in land in Dowgate, from which the monks received 8 shillings annually. The land was occupied by an under-tenant, although the mesne tenant was Mirabel, daughter of Oger, who curently held the land for life, without owing rent for it. However after her death, or her entry into a nunnery, or her vacating the land for any other reason, the property would be divided between the two couples, each of whom would owe 4 shillings annually to the Chamber of the abbey. This pair of agreements was witnessed by a number of leading citizens 'and the whole Husting'.[136] The description of the charters as final concords indicates that there had been some preceding litigation, perhaps focused on the conditions of Mirabel's tenure, and in particular on her rent-free occupancy.

On other occasions, grants made by Abbot Walter and the convent, although not said to have been made in the Husting court, were attested by some of the most eminent citizens of the day, and the likelihood is that these transactions took place there. One such grant dates from 1184,[137] but the others were made on various unspecified occasions during Walter's abbacy.[138] In the time of Walter's successors, William Postard and Ralph Arundel, further properties in London were acquired by the abbey. Several such grants, attested by prominent citizens, were presumably made in the Husting court,[139] as were others made by one Londoner to another, of properties which were subsequently acquired by Westminster.[140] One such grant was made to the rector of St Matthew's Friday Street (one of Westminster's parish churches) in A.D. 1200, 'in presence of all the parishioners'. The first witness was Henry Fitz Ailwin, 'at that time mayor of London', and among the others were John Fitz Herlicun, 'at that time alderman of our ward', and several other prominent citizens.[141]

It was convenient to uphold in the Husting court the title to newly-acquired lands, as to those where the conditions of tenancy were changing, although the abbey also maintained franchisal rights. The 'soke of St Peter and of the abbot of Westminster', confirmed by Henry I,[142] was one of several controlled by privileged individuals or corporations within the City of London, These included the soke of Saint Martin le Grand, popularly known as

136 *Ibid.*, nos 342–3.
137 *Ibid.*, no. 293.
138 *Ibid.*, nos 290, 294–5. My thanks are due to Vanessa Harding for discussion on this point.
139 *Ibid.*, nos 353, 355, 363, 364, 371, 377, 378.
140 *Ibid.*, nos 366, 367, 372, 381.
141 *Ibid.*, no. 381.
142 *Regesta Regum Anglo-Normannorum*, *II*, no. CXXVIII; calendared *Westminster Abbey Charters*, no. 89.

'the soke of William de Sainte Merè Eglise' during his time as Dean of St Martins;[143] and the soke of the bishop of London.[144]

At Westminster itself, there were several terms used to describe the assembly (or assemblies) in which business was ratified. Property transactions should, as a matter of routine, be approved jointly by abbot and monks, so that any abbatial charter omitting the formula denoting their consent carries a suspicious air.[145] The phraseology by which such consent was conveyed varied, both from one abbot, and his various scribes, to another and also from one sort of transaction to another. In a particularly solemn charter, Abbot Herbert states that he has made a grant 'at the petition, and with the consent, of this chapter, . . . And I have confirmed this concession before the high altar, in presence of the convent, and placed the grant upon the altar.'[146] Solemn ritual, rather than the formalities of court procedure, are denoted in this instance. More usually Herbert's charters included phrases such as 'with the common assent of the chapter';[147] 'with the common assent of the whole chapter';[148] or 'with the common assent and advice of the whole chapter'.[149] While different shades of meaning may be conveyed by each variation, the changes may be due to nothing more than the preferences of particular scribes. In all cases, it is clear that the proposed transaction had been discussed by the abbot and monks presumably, even if not explicitly in the chapter-house.

Traditional allegations that Gervase acted high-handedly have been largely dispelled.[150] Sometimes his charters include phrases such as 'at the petition and with the common consent of our chapter';[151] 'with the common advice of all our chapter'; [152] or 'with the common assent and advice of the whole chapter'.[153] A thirteenth-century forgery which may be based on a genuine grant of his employs the phrase 'with the unanimous consent of our whole convent'.[154] More often the simple phrase 'and the whole convent' was

143 *Westminster Abbey Charters*, no. 382. See also M.B. Honeybourne, 'The Sanctuary Boundaries and Environs of Westminster Abbey and the College of St Martin-le-Grand', *Journal of the British Archaeological Association*, new series, 38 (1932), pp. 316–32.

144 *Westminster Abbey Charters*, no. 375. See also H.W.C. Davis, 'London Lands and Liberties of St Paul's 1066–1135', in A.G. Little and F.M. Powicke, eds, *Essays in Medieval History Presented to Thomas Frederick Tout* (Manchester, 1925), pp. 45–59.

145 Barbara Harvey, 'Abbot Gervase de Blois and the Fee Farms of Westminster Abbey', *Bulletin of the Institute of Historical Research*, 40 (1967), p. 134.

146 *Westminster Abbey Charters*, no. 244.

147 *Ibid.*, no. 246.

148 *Ibid.*, no. 247.

149 *Ibid.*, no. 250.

150 Harvey, 'Fee Farms', pp. 127–41.

151 *Westminster Abbey Charters*, no. 253.

152 *Ibid.*, no. 252.

153 *Ibid.*, no. 265.

154 *Ibid.*, no. 271.

used.[155] An agreement between Abbot Gervase and Prior Robert of Merton was made 'with the assent of each chapter'.[156]

The phraseology changes in the time of Abbot Lawrence. His charters usually employed terms such as 'and the convent of that place';[157] 'with the assent of his convent';[158] 'with the common assent and will of the whole of our chapter';[159] 'having been provided with the advice of our brothers in their common deliberations'[160] or 'with the common advice of our brothers'.[161] The elaborate phraseology of the erudite Lawrence gave way to plainer language in Abbot Walter's time. His charters used terms such as 'and the convent of that place',[162] or else 'and the whole convent of that place'.[163] On the other hand, it is from Walter's abbacy that clearer evidence survives of the emergence of the chapter as, in some sense, a legal forum. When an agreement was made with the hospital of St James, its brethren were required to take a solemn oath to observe its terms 'in the presence of the chapter of Westminster'.[164] Similarly, a donation by Brichtmar of Haverhill was reciprocated by a grant of confraternity to himself and all his family, made by Abbot Walter 'and the whole convent in full chapter'.[165] An agreement between Walter and the convent and Nicholas of Paglesham was rendered doubly secure, since Nicholas first swore in the chapter that he would observe its terms, and then the resulting chirograph was ratified in the *Curia Regis*.[166]

The use of the chapter virtually as a legal forum is also explicit in the charters of Abbot William Postard. For instance, when he and the convent quitclaimed the advowson of Datchworth to Hugh of Buckland, it was specified that any clerk to be presented to that church, should before he was instituted, first swear in the chapter of Westminster that he would render the annual pension due.[167] Abbot William Postard made his solemn grant of Parham to the monks in the chaper 'with the whole convent present'.[168] Similarly, a grant by Abbot Ralph and the convent to Ralph Fitz Stephen of Boulogne was said to have been made 'by the convent in full chapter',[169] while a grant made to Abbot Ralph by Prior Robert Moulsham and the monks was confirmed 'in full chapter'. Anyone subsequently infringing its terms would incur the sentence of anathema 'in full chapter'.[170] The abbots Walter, William and Ralph associated the convent with their acts as a matter of routine, and the additional citation of the chapter in an institutional sense was, in these cases, evidently designed to add solemnity to particular transactions. While the monks assembled in the chapter-house for their daily

155 *Ibid.*, nos 255, 256, 259, 260, 262, 263, 266, 267, 269.
156 *Ibid.*, no. 268.
157 *Ibid.*, nos 275, 276, 284.
158 *Ibid.*, no. 282.
159 *Ibid.*, no. 283.
160 *Ibid.*, no. 277.
161 *Ibid.*, no. 278.
162 *Ibid.*, nos 288, 289, 292, 293, 300.
163 *Ibid.*, nos 290, 291.
164 *Ibid.*, no. 288.
165 *Ibid.*, no. 388.
166 *Ibid.*, no. 300.
167 *Ibid.*, no. 320.
168 *Ibid.*, no. 326
169 *Ibid.*, no. 328.
170 *Ibid.*, no. 345.

chapter (meeting) when routine business was discussed, this gathering could also become a solemn assembly in order to impress visiting dignitaries or to overawe potentially troublesome tenants.

Another assembly, quite distinct from the first, was the court which the abbot was entitled to hold in his capacity as a major territorial lord. King Henry I, when ordering the restoration to Abbot Herbert of lands wrongfully alienated (during the recent abbatial vacancy), ordered that if anyone tried to establish a claim to these, then Herbert was empowered to judge the dispute in his own court.[171] In another writ of about the same date, i.e. 1121 (x1122), the king confirmed extensive judicial exemptions and franchisal rights to Herbert throughout his estates, citing a charter of privileges granted by King Edward. All pleas, including those of murder and robbery, were to be heard on respective abbatial estates where, by implication, Herbert held courts.[172]

In the time of Abbot Lawrence, Hugh Fitz Warner quitclaimed land in Sunbury and Teddington before being compensated with another property. This quitclaim was made 'in the court of Westminster', which appears, from the identity of the witnesses, to be the abbot's own court (and not the *curia regis*). Hugh surrendered into the hand of the abbot the royal writ which he had obtained in pursuance of his suit, and swore in the hand of Alan the dapifer that he would observe the agreement.[173] The writ in question ordered the abbot to render justice without delay to Hugh, otherwise the sheriff of Middlesex would do so.[174] Obviously the abbot would not want to risk having his jurisdictional rights over-ridden by the sheriff. Once the case was in his own court, Lawrence could secure a verdict which met his managerial requirements while fending off the intrusion of royal officials.

A comparable case occurred during the reign of King John, when Richard Testard produced a royal writ in order to make a claim in the abbot's court against Robert of Bagnor and his wife Derewenn, over a rent of 12 pence in the vill of Westminster. Richard proved his title, but then quitclaimed the rent to the Lady Altar, in order to provide lights for it. The resulting charter was witnessed by several leading residents of Westminster, including Odo the reeve; the Exchequer clerks Louis and Alexander; and lay officials of the abbey.[175] The court of the abbot of Westminster also heard cases from further afield. When Celestria, widow of Daniel de Aqua of Aldenham (Herts.), and her son Thomas quitclaimed to Thomas de Camera a messuage and land in Aldenham, they renounced their claim to the property 'in presence of the whole court of Westminster'. The preponderance of Westminster residents

171 *Regesta Regum Anglo-Normannorum, II*, no. CXXX; calendared *Westminster Abbey Charters*, no. 75.

172 *Regesta Regum Anglo-Normannorum, II*, no. CXXIX; calendared *Westminster Abbey Charters*, no. 80.

173 *Westminster Abbey Charters*, no. 452.

174 *Ibid.*, no. 133.

175 *Ibid.*, no. 423.

attesting the resulting charters indicates that the court met there, and not in Aldenham, although a few men from there naturally acted as witnesses.[176]

The halimote (hall-moot) of Westminster was a further court which dealt with grants and sales of land within the vill. A series of transactions conducted under its auspices date from the abbacies of William Postard and Ralph Arundel. The only one of these which can be dated fairly closely, to the year from September 1197 to September 1198, is a 'concession and confirmation' by Walter son of Cecily to the unnamed abbot of Westminster (in fact William Postard) of 13 shillings' worth of rents from tenements behind the church of St Clement-beyond-the-Bar (i.e. St Clement Danes), due in all from five named tenants. The abbot and convent would render 3 shillings annually to the farm of Westminster for the rents, but retain the surplus. Walter undertook to warrant the rents, or else to make an exchange of equal value, by view of the neighbours. He received a gersum in return for his grant 'which was made publicly, in the full halimote of the aforesaid abbot of Westminster'. The abbot's seneschal and the reeve of Westminster headed a substantial list of prominent Westminster residents.[177]

Several further transactions which took place in the halimote are known from the reign of King John. When the clerk Henry of Ely confirmed to the abbot and convent a messuage in St Clement's parish, he and his son and heir Walter swore 'in the full halimote of Westminster' that they would firmly keep to the agreement which they had made with the monks.[178] Similarly 'the whole halimote of Westminster' witnessed a grant of rent made by Odo the goldsmith to the Lady Altar.[179]

The halimote was the forum not only for transactions between the abbey and its tenants, but also those between residents of Westminster. All were effectively tenants of the abbey, so that a watching brief was kept on all changes of occupancy which led to changes in those liable to render rent or other dues. One such grant was made by William Little to Alexander son of Henry, and Edith, daughter of Geoffrey de Barra, and their sons, who would hold a certain plot of land of William at an annual rent in inheritance. The couple were empowered to designate as heirs whichever of their sons they chose. The witnesses included the reeve of Westminster, Odo the goldsmith.[180] A further transaction which occurred in the halimote was the sale, by Marwanna daughter of William, to the king's treasurer, William of Ely, of her messuage at Endiff (in Westminster). She held this messuage by right and inheritance, and sold it at the petition, and with the assent, of her son William. He never had seisin of this property, even though he and his wife

176 *Ibid.*, nos 466–7.

177 *Ibid.*, no. 395. On the composition of the halimote, see also Rosser, *Medieval Westminster*, p. 231.

178 *Ibid.*, no. 393.

179 *Ibid.*, no. 425.

180 *Ibid.*, no. 413.

Alice lodged there at Marwanna's pleasure. Therefore neither he nor any heir of his could claim any right in the messuage. In addition to the price paid to Marwanna, William of Ely paid £1 to her son William, and 1 shilling to Alice, who witnessed the transaction and confirmed that she had no dower rights in the transaction, since her dower comprised only one third of William's acquired property and a gold ring.[181] A companion charter was ratified by Marwanna's son William 'son of Absalon', together with his wife Alice. This covered the same ground as his mother's charter, with the added information that William had no children by Alice, nor any hope of any. His grant, like his mother's was witnessed by the reeves of Westminster, Henry Sumer and Richard Testard.[182] When these witness without title, but in company with other leading Westminster residents, it is likely that the transaction took place in the halimote.[183]

A halimote, or some equivalent court, probably existed on at least the more substantial Westminster manors, although evidence for their existence at this period is fragmentary. Abbot Herbert, 'with the common consent of the chapter', granted to Leofgar and his heirs the land of Coggeshall (Essex) in fee-farm, for 40 shillings annually, together with the land called Half-Hide for a further 3 shillings annually, so that he might hold it freely on condition that he rendered suit of court 'at the halimote of our vill', unless the abbot specifically enjoined (otherwise).[184] Similarly, when Abbot Walter granted the vill of Paglesham, a member of Benfleet (Essex) to Nicholas of Paglesham, to hold at an annual rent of £9, due to the abbey's pittancer, he ordered that Nicholas 'or his heirs' must attend the abbey's pleas of Benfleet 'as the head of the manor', when summoned.[185] Courts of a manor, or of a vill, could function effectively only when the more affluent and influential tenants were present, hence the imposition of such duties upon Leofgar and Nicholas.

181 *Ibid.*, no. 437.
182 *Ibid.*, no. 438.
183 *Ibid.*, nos 428–9, for instance.
184 *Ibid.*, no. 246.
185 *Ibid.*, no. 300.

10

Tenants and their Lands: the Outer Estates

The magisterial work of Barbara Harvey on the estates of the abbey, their accumulation, consolidation and management over the centuries from the foundation of the West Minster down to the Dissolution, is the definitive book on this subject.[1] The present chapter is not intended to emulate such comprehensive coverage of Westminster's lands but rather to focus on some aspects of their management between the abbacy of Edwin and that of Ralph Arundel, as revealed both in the charters granted by the abbots and monks and also in those which were granted to them.

While some of the abbey's estates had been held since the time of King Offa of Mercia,[2] and others were given or confirmed by King Edgar,[3] the great increase in Westminster's lands occurred as a result of King Edward's extensive endowment, augmented to some extent by those of other benefactors.[4] King Edward was commemorated for his generosity, even though his endowments largely followed the prevailing royal practice of re-distributing lands which had been lost by other religious houses owing to political circumstances beyond their control. Many of the benefactions made to favoured religious houses by kings and nobles in the late Anglo-Saxon period previously belonged to communities which had succumbed to Viking attacks.[5]

The recent history of the Mercian estates granted by King Edward to Westminster had a comparable but somewhat different history, having belonged to establishments which succumbed to the attacks of Ealdorman Ælfhere and his associates during the reaction which followed the death of King Edgar. The most substantial of King Edward's donations in south-west Mercia comprised the two-hundred hide estate of Pershore (Worcs.) and the

1 Barbara Harvey, *Westminster Abbey and its Estates in the Middle Ages* (Oxford, 1977).

2 Notably Aldenham and Titeburst, Herts.; *ibid.*, pp. 345–6.

3 For instance, one of the Fanton manors, and Ham, both in Essex; Datchworth with Watton, and Holwell, Herts.; Paddington and possibly Westminster itself, in Middlesex; Morden, Surrey; *ibid.*, pp. 341–2, 346, 353–4, 358.

4 *Ibid.*, pp. 24–7.

5 Robin Fleming, 'Monastic Lands and England's Defence in the Viking Age', *English Historical Review*, 100 (1985), 247–65.

estate in Deerhurst (Glos.) of fifty-nine hides, with its appurtenant manors.[6] It was perhaps no coincidence that this latter grant rendered Westminster a neighbour of the French royal abbey of St Denis.[7] Westminster's other more remote manors included Doddington and Thorpe in Lincolnshire,[8] Deene and Sudborough in Northamptonshire,[9] Launton (Oxon.)[10] and Perton (Staffs.).[11] Although the largest number of the abbey's estates were concentrated within a fairly compact radius of London, there were further outlying properties in the remoter parts of Hertfordshire and Essex, besides isolated properties in Easthampstead (Berks.), Eversley (Hampshire) and Parham (Sussex).[12] Westminster consequently had to administer properties which were more widely distributed than those of most other English Benedictine houses. Since much of the land had been acquired comparatively recently, consolidation barely began before the Norman Conquest and settlement gave rise to new problems.[13]

In Worcestershire the two-hundred hide estate based on Pershore had been donated by King Edward 'exempt and free from every claim, as he held it in his own lordship. The whole shire bears witness to this.'[14] This exemption therefore placed the estate beyond the scope of the sheriff's jurisdiction, as were a total of five further hundreds, held by other ecclesiastical proprietors, 'therefore, as the sheriff states, he loses much in revenue'.[15] It has long been maintained that these monastic immunities, and notably Worcester's triple-hundred of Oswaldslow, were granted by King Edgar in order to safeguard the endowments of the reformed monastic houses against territorial claims raised by the secular magnates. The king for his part, gained the loyalty of his newly-created religious magnates, whose franchisal and tenurial powers now acted as a political counterbalance to those of the lay aristocracy.[16] Patrick Wormald, however, when investigating the antiquity of Worcester's liberty of Oswaldslow, argued that there is no convincing evidence for its existence before the Norman Conquest.[17] On the other hand, 'the whole shire' confirmed the existence of the liberties of Oswaldslow in

6 Harvey, *Westminster Abbey and its Estates*, pp. 344–5, 360–64.
7 *Anglo-Saxon Writs*, introd. and ed. F.E. Harmer, 2nd edn (Stamford, 1989), p. 293.
8 Harvey, *Westminster Abbey and its Estates*, p. 348.
9 *Ibid.*, pp. 355–6.
10 *Ibid.*, p. 356.
11 *Ibid.*, p. 357.
12 *Ibid.*, pp. 337, 345, 359–60. For the overall distribution of Westminster's estates, *ibid.*, maps and tables on pp. 471–4.
13 P.E. Clarke, *The English Nobility under Edward the Confessor* (Oxford, 1994), p. 55.
14 *Domesday Book*, ed. A. Farley, 2 vols (London, 1783), I, 174b.
15 *Ibid.*, I, 172.
16 E. John, *Orbis Britanniae and other Studies* (Leicester, 1966), pp. 56–60, 172–9.
17 P. Wormald, 'Oswaldslow: an "immunity"?', in N. Brooks and C. Cubitt, eds, *St Oswald of Worcester. Life and influence* (London, 1996), pp. 117–28. See also Julia Barrow, 'How the Twelfth-Century Monks of Worcester Perceived their Past', in P. Magdalino, ed., *The Perception of the Past in Twelfth-Century Europe* (London, 1992), pp. 69–74.

1086, just as they did those of Westminster's double hundred.[18] The acceptance of Wormald's theory may indicate a conspiracy on the part of the leading men of the shire to vouch for the antiquity of Oswaldslow. By implication (and in the interests of demonstrating a convincing consistency and, perhaps, reciprocity) such claims were perhaps extended by the shire jurors to encompass liberties enjoyed by the other leading monastic proprietors. A conspiracy on this scale would not be unprecedented, given that a few years before the Domesday Survey was held the leading men of the shire, French as well as English, combined to uphold Bishop Wulfstan's jurisdictional claims against those of the 'French' Abbot Walter of Evesham.[19] But any plan to claim the long history of the existence of Oswaldslow and, perhaps, of the other great monastic franchises in Worcestershire, would necessarily have been made within a year or two of the Norman Conquest. Urse d'Abetot, sheriff in 1086, when he accepted the authenticity of these franchises, so detrimental to his own official position, was already constructing Worcester castle, evidently in his capacity as sheriff, before the death of Archbishop Ealdred in 1069.[20] Any conspiracy would pre-date this earlier development, and perhaps received an impetus when it became obvious that the great earldom of Mercia was about to be dismantled.[21]

On the other hand, Wormald's view about the newness of the liberties in 1086 may be accepted without necessarily hypothesizing any deliberate plot. Westminster justified the existence of its own liberty of Pershore on the grounds that the abbey succeeded to the rights enjoyed by King Edward.[22] The position in Worcestershire was complicated in that, while a Norman sheriff was appointed by the early months of 1069, his authority was counterbalanced by that of Abbot Æthelwig of Evesham, authorized by King William to exercise wide legal powers throughout the West Midlands and to pronounce on the law in contentious cases.[23] Æthelwig in turn acted jointly with Bishop Wulfstan in a legal capacity,[24] while the bishop was

18 *Domesday Book*, I, 172c, 174.

19 Emma Mason, *St Wulfstan of Worcester* (Oxford, 1990), pp. 135–9.

20 *The Beauchamp Cartulary Charters: 1100–1268*, ed. Emma Mason, Pipe Roll Soc., new series, xliii (1980), pp. xlviij–lij.

21 *The Ecclesiastical History of Orderic Vitalis*, ed. Marjorie Chibnall, II (Oxford, reprinted 1990), pp. 214–19, 256–9; Mason, *St Wulfstan of Worcester*, p. 148.

22 *Domesday Book*, I, 174. The classic discussion of the association of franchisal privileges with a former royal manor is that by Helen Cam, '*Manerium cum hundredo*: The Hundred and the Hundredal Manor', *English Historical Review*, 47 (1932), pp. 353–76, see esp. pp. 359, 371–2. However, the ecclesiastical liberties in Worcestershire are singled out as exceptions to the rule.

23 R.R. Darlington, 'Aethelwig, Abbot of Evesham', *English Historical Review*, 48 (1933), pp. 1–22, 177–98.

24 *Regesta Regum Anglo-Normannorum, I, 1066–1100*, ed. H.W.C. Davis, assisted by R.J. Whitwell (Oxford, 1913), no. XXVIII; calendared *Westminster Abbey Charters*, ed. Emma Mason, assisted by the late Jennifer Bray, continuing the work of the late D.J. Murphy, London Record Society, 25 (1988), no. 22.

among the leading administrators of secular jurisdiction within the shire.[25] In such circumstances franchisal immunities might easily have 'emerged' on their respective estates, while, in the interests of Benedictine solidarity, the bishop and abbot acknowledged Westminster's privileges which were perhaps claimed by virtue of holding land 'of ancient royal demesne'.

But recognition of Westminster's franchise did not automatically ensure the safety of its territorial endowment in the aftermath of the Norman Conquest and the break-up of the earldom of Mercia. Urse the sheriff quickly built up a very powerful territorial position in Worcestershire, controlling, in addition to his own modest tenancy-in-chief, land held in farm from the king, together with numerous estates held of others. In particular, he held more than sixty-one hides of the bishop and cathedral priory, and a further fifty hides as a tenant of Westminster abbey.[26] The monks of the cathedral priory certainly represented him as having seized several of their estates without justification, even though at times they exaggerated their case against him.[27]

Sheriffs, by the nature of their powers, were well placed to augment their lands by improper means. In a writ which has been dated to 1077, King William I ordered a select group of magnates to summon the sheriffs and convey his orders that they must return to 'his' bishoprics and abbacies all the demesne, and demesne land, which 'his' bishops and abbots, whether through carelessness, fear or greed, had given them out of the demesne of 'his' bishoprics and abbacies, and which the sheriffs had consented to hold, or which they had seized by violence.[28] As this writ shows, sheriffs not only seized control of ecclesiastical lands, but also accepted them as 'gifts' from churchmen. There might be occasions when an ecclesiastic wanted such a powerful person as an ally, or else was too frightened to deny him control of lands which he coveted. The king's repeated reference to the ecclesiastical proprietors and their offices as 'his' indicates his perception of his control over the church hierarchy and its possessions. Endowments were intended to support the cathedrals and abbeys in their liturgical round, which in turn upheld the safety of the realm, a concept which can be traced back to the Old Testament.[29] Any serious depletion of their revenues might hinder this essential activity whilst aggrandizing sheriffs so that they evolved into territorial

25 W. Dugdale, *Monasticon Anglicanum*, revised H. Caley, H. Ellis and B. Bandinel, 6 vols in 8 (London, 1817–30), I, 301, no. XL; calendared *Westminster Abbey Charters*, no. 4.

26 *Beauchamp Cartulary*, pp. xviij–xx.

27 Mason, *St Wulfstan of Worcester*, p. 153.

28 *Placita Anglo-Normannica*, ed. M.M. Bigelow (London, 1879), pp. 4–5; for translation and comment, see *English Historical Documents, II, 1042–1189*, ed. D.C. Douglas and G.W. Greenaway, 2nd edn (London, 1981), p. 463, no. 38.

29 Emma Mason, '*Pro Statu et Incolumnitate Regni Mei*: Royal Monastic Patronage 1066–1154', in S. Mews, ed., *Religion and National Identity*, Studies in Church History, 18 (Oxford, 1982), pp. 99–117. For the Old Testament precedents for this belief, see, for instance, Ezra, 6: 10.

magnates and threatened the very stability which they were appointed to uphold. But in the case of Urse's well-publicized acquisition of ecclesiastical lands in Worcestershire, Judith Green has suggested that part, at least, of this activity perhaps had royal sanction, on the grounds that the sheriff's territorial position must be enhanced vis a vis those of the entrenched tenants-in-chief.[30]

Urse was a tenant of Westminster abbey in the Worcestershire vills of Besford, Birlingham, Broughton Hacket, Comberton, Eckington, Grafton, Longdon, Naunton Beauchamp, North Piddle, Peopleton, Powick, Upton Snodsbury and Wick. These tenancies totalled over fifty hides, even allowing for the fact that the Domesday Survey does not record the precise hideage on his land in Powick.[31] While these holdings combined to render him one of the most substantial tenants of the abbey, he has left little trace in its charters. The sheriff is not addressed in either of two writs issued by King William I, concerning Westminster's lands in Gloucestershire and Worcestershire. The earlier of these, written in English, was issued in the first years of the reign. Archbishop Ealdred (d.1069), Bishop Wulfstan and Earl William Fitz Osbern, with the thegns of Gloucestershire, Worcestershire and Oxfordshire, were notified that he confirmed to Westminster the lands in Pershore and Deerhurst which were granted by King Edward.[32] Later in the reign, a further writ was obtained, notifying the king's officials and French and English men throughout Worcestershire and Gloucestershire that William had 'conceded' to Westminster and its monks the manors of Pershore and Deerhurst, towards their diet. While the text is almost certainly based on a genuine writ, as it now survives in cartulary copies, it has been heavily embellished by the addition of franchisal rights. The attestations, which also appear to have been added, indicate a date of 1081x1084.[33] Westminster may well have sought such a second writ, in Latin, in view of the difficulties which were being experienced in securing the properties in south-west Mercia.

There were particular problems in Worcestershire. Early in the reign a lawsuit in defence of the Worcestershire lands was heard before Bishop Wulfstan, (Æthelwig) the abbot of Evesham, and Regenbald the chancellor, who upheld Westminster's claims. Further difficulties apparently ensued, because some years later Abbot Vitalis found it necessary to apply for a royal writ ordering the restitution of his Worcestershire demesne land, insofar as that lawsuit established his title to it.[34]

30 Judith Green, 'The Sheriffs of William the Conqueror', in R. Allen Brown, ed., *Anglo-Norman Studies, V, Proceedings of the Battle Conference, 1982* (Woodbridge, 1983), p. 144.

31 *Domesday Book*, I, 174–5; *Beauchamp Cartulary*, xix.

32 Dugdale, *Monasticon Anglicanum*, I, p. 301, no. XL; calendared *Westminster Abbey Charters*, no. 4.

33 *Westminster Abbey Charters*, no. 28.

34 *Regesta Regum Anglo-Normannorum*, I, no. XXVIII; calendared *Westminster Abbey*

Despite this series of writs, Westminster continued to experience difficulties in Worcestershire. A nine-hide estate in Comberton, pertaining to its Pershore estate, was held in 1086 by Gilbert Fitz Turold, together with a berewick of a further ten hides.[35] Urse d'Abetot's brother, Robert Dispenser, a royal steward, was a tenant of Worcester cathedral priory at that time,[36] but was not a tenant of Westminster's estate in Worcestershire. Some time after the Survey was completed, though, he bought from Gilbert Fitz Turold his 'land and manor' of Comberton. He also acquired the abbey's manor of Wick, in Pershore, which he held at farm from Abbot Gilbert Crispin. In the reign of William II, and probably in 1095–96, Robert made a restoration 'for his soul', of both tenancies. Wick, as an estate held in farm, would be due to revert to the abbey on Robert's death. His purchase of Comberton had perhaps not been sanctioned by the abbot, and in any event he appears to have been dissuaded from conveying his tenancy to any successor. The restoration of these lands was made by proxy, in a symbolic ritual by which Robert's brother Urse, and Robert's unnamed wife, placed on St Peter's altar in the abbey two silver candelabra; a thurible, an altar cloth and a tapestry. The ceremony was witnessed by several prominent *curiales*, by Robert's own men, by other barons of the king, and by several of the abbot's men, indicating the great importance which Abbot Gilbert placed upon the recovery of these lands.[37] The nature of the transaction suggests that Robert was gravely ill, and he certainly died in the late 1090s.[38] Early in the reign of Henry I, Westminster reinforced its title by obtaining from Henry I a writ informing Urse and his barons of Worcestershire that he had 'conceded' to the abbey the land of Comberton which Robert Dispenser 'gave'.[39] A document which may date from c.1118–1120, during the vacancy which followed Abbot Gilbert's death, lists the weekly farm of the monks. In this Comberton was named among five manors which collectively rendered £32 for allowances and pittances.[40]

The other Worcestershire manors have left little trace in this period. Abbot Herbert granted the manor of Powick to the monks of Westminster's cell of Great Malvern, to hold at an annual farm of £24 per annum, so long as they were obedient to their mother church. The abbot would have all

Charters, no. 22. On Regenbald, see S. Keynes, 'Regenbald the Chancellor (*sic*)', in R. Allen Brown, ed., *Anglo-Norman Studies, X, Proceedings of the Battle Conference, 1987* (Woodbridge, 1988), pp. 185–222, esp. pp. 210–11.

35 *Domesday Book*, I, 175.

36 *Ibid.*, I, ff. 172, 173, 173, 174; *Beauchamp Cartulary*, p. xx.

37 *Westminster Abbey Charters*, no. 488.

38 *Beauchamp Cartulary*, p. xx.

39 J. Armitage Robinson, *Gilbert Crispin, Abbot of Westminster* (Cambridge, 1911), p. 147, no. 28; calendared *Westminster Abbey Charters*, no. 66.

40 *Westminster Abbey Charters*, no. 339.

customary rights in that manor which he had in all other manors which were similarly held at farm.[41]

For much of the twelfth century though, the Worcestershire manors gave rise to little in the way of formal transactions. Tenants on the west-Mercian estates were not always scrupulous in rendering the service due. When, in 1166, Abbot Lawrence returned his *carta*, enumerating the knight-service due to him, he listed nine tenants (including the king, who owed service on one fee) who answered for a total of eighteen knights' fees, and some fractions of fees, in Worcestershire and Gloucestershire. All these men acknowledged the service due from them, and rendered it, but the earl of Gloucester (Robert's son, William) was withholding the service due from two fees in Gloucestershire, and other men were withholding the service due from one and a half out of two further fees in Worcestershire. The large holdings of Urse d'Abetot were now represented by the seven knights' fees for which his grandson William de Beauchamp answered, and a further half fee held by Walter de Beauchamp.[42]

Some years later, Geoffrey de St Leger rendered homage to Abbot Walter and was permitted to succeed to the two knights' fees in Strensham (Worcs.) which his father Reginald held of previous abbots. Geoffrey's mother was granted the use of the tenement for her lifetime, but if she died, or became a nun or gave up the land for any reason, Geoffrey would pay to Walter the full feudal relief, and the abbot or his successors would then give him a charter.[43] Reginald de St Leger had not been listed by Abbot Lawrence, but he did include a Reginald de *Stainlinge*, who answered for two knights' fees in Worcestershire and Gloucestershire.[44]

Not all of the west-Mercian tenants held their land by knight-service. In another agreement made with a tenant in this region, Abbot Walter and the monks 'conceded and confirmed' in fee and inheritance, to Robert of Wick and his heirs their vill of Upton Snodsbury, which Abbot Lawrence and the monks 'conceded' by charter to his father, Peter of Wick. In return, Robert would render £6 annually to the farm of Pershore. Moreover, they 'conceded' to him their vill of Bricklehampton, to hold in fee and inheritance, which his father held by charter, 'conceded' by Abbot Lawrence and the convent. Robert would render £4 annually in return to the farm of Pershore. Abbot Walter and the convent further 'conceded' three virgates of land in their vill of Wick, to be held freely, by hereditary right, as Abbot Lawrence and the convent granted by charter to Peter of Wick. Robert would render for these 8s 4d annually to the farm of Pershore.[45] King William I had granted

41 *Ibid.*, no. 243.
42 *Liber Niger Scaccarii*, ed. T. Hearne (London, 1774), pp. 51–2.
43 *Westminster Abbey Charters*, no. 490.
44 *Liber Niger Scaccarii*, p. 51.
45 *Westminster Abbey Charters*, no. 305.

Wick-by-Pershore to Abbot Vitalis, together with the royal rights in Droitwich, an important centre of salt-production.[46]

In Gloucestershire, the big estate in Deerhurst was the subject of a series of grants made at intervals in the twelfth century. The whole manor, with its outliers, was valued at £41 in King Edward's reign, and £40 in 1086, 'of which £26 related to the lord's manor and £14 to the lands of the lesser men'.[47] Abbot Gervase and the monks 'gave and conceded and confirmed' the manor of Deerhurst with all its appurtenances to William of Darnford in fee-farm, and he would render them £30 annually. This grant was made not later than c.1141.[48] During the hostilities between King Stephen and the Empress Matilda, whose forces dominated the west country, William obtained from her a charter 'conceding' this manor to him as it had been granted by Gervase and the monks.[49] Since the chief witness was the earl of Gloucester, it may be deduced that William held his estate peacefully. After the deposition of Abbot Gervase, but apparently before the election of Lawrence, William of Darnford obtained from the monks of Westminster a confirmation of the manor, still at the £30 farm.[50] He obtained a further confirmation of the manor from King Henry II, at some date between 1172 and 1184.[51] He perhaps petitioned for this, following the death of Abbot Lawrence in 1173, since the abbatial lands would then fall into royal custody. The monks, on the other hand, evidently feared a more generalized destabilization of their lands in West Mercia. At some stage, perhaps coincidental both with this vacancy and with the Great Revolt of the king's sons, a writ was obtained from Henry II, ordering his officers in Gloucestershire and Worcestershire that the (unnamed) abbot and monks and their possessions were under his protection, and their property was to be treated as royal demesne. All tenants of the abbey were to be compelled to render the service they owed, without delay.[52] If William of Darnford was among those defaulting tenants, the ensuing brusque chivvying by royal officers might prompt him to seek royal confirmation of his tenancy. Neither the charter of Gervase nor that of the monks had imposed any duty of rendering a service of hospitality, yet on 22 January 1192, Abbot William Postard brought a suit before the itinerant justices at Northampton, in which he claimed this service from the William

46 *Regesta Regum Anglo-Normannorum*, I, no. XX; *Domesday Book*, I, 174.

47 *Domesday Book*, I, 166.

48 *Westminster Abbey Charters*, no. 271. While Gervase probably did make a grant of Deerhurst, this text, as it now survives, represents a later re-working; Barbara Harvey, 'Abbot Gervase de Blois and the Fee-Farms of Westminster Abbey', *Bulletin of the Institute of Historical Research*, 40 (1967), pp. 139–41.

49 *Regesta Regum Anglo-Normannorum, III, 1135–1154*, ed. H.A. Cronne and R.H.C. Davis (Oxford, 1968), no. 259.

50 *Westminster Abbey Charters*, no. 341.

51 Westminster Abbey Muniment 32669; calendared *Westminster Abbey Charters*, no. 136.

52 *Westminster Abbey Charters*, no. 137.

of Darnford of his own day. The suit ended with the abbot quitclaiming the service to William, in return for 40 shillings annually.[53] The abbot's aim, from the start, had perhaps been to obtain this monetary payment, since the customary annual farm, well below that prescribed in 1086, took no account of the inflationary pressures of the later twelfth century.

Abbot Walter had, however, been in the habit of making a regular visit to his west-Mercian manors. Together with the convent, he 'conceded and confirmed' to the king's chamberlain, Ralph Fitz Stephen, land between their vill of Todenham (Glos.) and Ralph's vill of Wolford, so that Ralph could strengthen his mill-pond. In return he would have the abbot's demesne corn ground in readiness for his arrival and during his stay.[54]

The outlying manor of Perton, Staffs., had a chequered tenurial history. It had been granted by King Edward but the abbey's control over it wavered in the aftermath of the Norman Conquest. A writ (in English) was obtained from King William I, probably no later than 1068, in which he notified Bishop Leofwine of Lichfield, Edwin, earl of Mercia, and the thegns in Staffordshire that Perton belonged to Westminster, and that it was to be protected for the abbey by Abbot Ethelwig (of Evesham) and Thurkill the sheriff.[55] Thurkill, however, had been replaced by the mid 1070s,[56] and Ethelwig died in 1077.[57] Perton was evidently soon lost, but was temporarily recovered (probably after some undocumented negotiations) when William I, constable of Cheshire, granted it in alms for his wife's soul, quit of scutage and secular services. The abbey then held Perton during the time of Hugh, earl of Chester (d.1101), and presumably during the lifetime of the constable. On his death, c.1130, he was succeeded as constable by his son, William II. Westminster lost control of the manor, but obtained from King Henry I a writ ordering the constable to restore it, together with anything taken from it unjustly.[58] Whether or not that writ proved effective, Westminster did not control Perton later in the twelfth century, until it was restored by Richard I, 'after inspecting the charters of his predecessors'. Obviously such a remote manor would have to be farmed, and there were those only too ready to take control of it. On 2 February 1190, Abbot Walter and the convent granted it for life to Hugh de Nunant, bishop of Coventry, to hold for £2 annually.[59] This was identical with its value in 1086, and no account was taken of the

53 *Ibid.*, no. 324.

54 *Ibid.*, no. 306.

55 Dugdale, *Monasticon Anglicanum*, I, p. 301, no. XXXIX; calendared *Westminster Abbey Charters*, no. 5.

56 Green, 'The Sheriffs of William the Conqueror', p. 130.

57 D. Knowles, C.N.L. Brooke and V.C.M. London, *The Heads of Religious Houses England and Wales 940–1216* (Cambridge, 1972), p. 47.

58 T.A.M. Bishop, *Scriptores Regis* (Oxford, 1961), plate XVIII (a); calendared *Westminster Abbey Charters*, no. 98.

59 *Westminster Abbey Charters*, no. 304.

inflation of recent decades. Nunant's position in north-west Mercia no doubt ensured his tenure on favourable terms.[60] He died on 27 March 1198.[61]

Across country, the Lincolnshire manor of Doddington was equally remote from Westminster, and presented occasional managerial problems. A writ of William I notified Rémy, bishop of Lincoln, Hugh the sheriff and the other barons of Lincolnshire that Westminster and Abbot Vitalis were to have the manor of Doddington and its appurtenant soke of Thorpe, which were granted by Ailric son of Meriet.[62] In the Domesday Survey, the abbot of Westminster is recorded as holding part of Ailric's former estate. Among the *clamores* for the Kesteven district of Lincolnshire, the abbot claimed the land and soke of Ailric son of Meriet against a certain Baldwin, asserting that he was entitled to all the component parts, since the chief manor had been granted to the abbey. The whole shire court supported the abbot's title and the king's writ perhaps confirmed this verdict.[63]

Doddington was too remote to be managed directly. Abbot Gilbert Crispin granted it to Hugh de *Evremou*, in presence of King William II, in exchange for the manor of Duxford (Cambs.). Early in the next reign, however, Henry I restored Duxford to Count Eustace of Boulogne, and gave Hugh a grant in exchange. Hugh, in turn, restored the manor of Doddington to Abbot Gilbert in the king's presence. Westminster's title was reinforced by a royal writ which informed the bishop of Lincoln and the notables of Lincolnshire of this series of transactions.[64] To be doubly sure, Hugh de *Evremou* was prompted to address a writ to 'his lord', Bishop Robert Bloet, and the barons of Lincolnshire, notifying them of his restoration of the manor of Doddington to Westminster and the background to this.[65] The weekly farm of the monks, dating from c.1118–1120, assigned to them all rents from Doddington.[66] Tenure of Doddington became difficult in Stephen's reign, perhaps during the vacancy following the death of Abbot Herbert, but perhaps in the course of hostilities between the king's supporters and those of the Empress. A writ of King Stephen ordered Gerbod de Scalt that the monks were to be allowed to hold their manor of Doddington peacefully. Gerbod must not seize anything; nor exact any forfeiture, nor intrude into any part of it, because the king would not warrant the manor to anyone except the abbey and its monks.[67]

60 Harvey, *Westminster Abbey and its Estates*, p. 357.

61 E.B. Fryde, D.E. Greenway, S. Porter and I. Roy, eds, *Handbook of British Chronology*, 3rd edn (London, 1986), p. 253.

62 Dugdale, *Monasticon Anglicanum*, I, 301, no. XLI.

63 *Westminster Abbey Charters*, no. 31 note.

64 Armitage Robinson, *Gilbert Crispin*, p. 145, no. 26; calendared *Westminster Abbey Charters*, no. 61.

65 *Westminster Abbey Charters*, no. 475.

66 *Ibid.*, no. 339.

67 *Regesta Regum Anglo-Normannorum*, III, no. 933; calendared *Westminster Abbey Charters*, no. 115.

Abbot William Postard and the monks granted the manor, except for the advowson of the church, to 'our knight' William Picot, to hold in fee and inheritance, rendering £12 annually to the abbey's chamberlain. If at any time William or his heirs should have need of the advice and help of the abbot and monks, in order to defend (their tenure of) this manor, this would be supplied through the abbey's charters and muniments, through the intervention of any one of the community, to defend the manor when and where necessary, with their expenses.[68] It appeared from the foregoing that William Picot anticipated trouble from his neighbours, but in the event it was he who caused trouble to Westminster. Abbot William's charter had clearly reserved the advowson of the church for the abbot and monks, but in 1205 the advowson of Doddington and Thorp-on-the-Hill was claimed by William Picot. Abbot Ralph Arundel produced a charter of Abbot William and the convent, in form of a chirograph, reciting the terms outlined above, and he identified the appendant seal as that of his predecessor, although Picot challenged the authenticity of the document.[69]

The Sussex manor of Parham had been a possession of Westminster from the late tenth century.[70] The income from a mill there pertained to the monks' weekly farm early in the twelfth century, as did rents from Chollington in Sussex.[71] Towards the end of Henry I's reign, Herbert Fitz Herbert (son of Herbert the chamberlain) claimed Parham. However Abbot Herbert proved his title both to Parham itself and to *Mapeleford*, by judgement of the barons of the Exchequer, and an ensuing writ of Henry I notified his barons in Sussex and in Middlesex that the abbot might hold these lands in demesne.[72] Some years later, during the abbacy of Gervase, Westminster experienced difficulties from an unnamed litigant who was evidently trying to establish tenancy rights. On the evidence of the earlier verdict, King Stephen accordingly notified his officials in Sussex and Middlesex that the abbot might hold the lands of Parham and *Mapeleford* in demesne if he wished, and do as he pleased with it. He was to hold these peacefully, in accordance with King Henry's charter.[73] In the 1190s, Abbot William Postard granted the vill to the convent, apart from the advowson of the church, and the monks would pay £8 annually to the convent kitchener. If any homage fell due (i.e. from a newly-admitted tenant), the abbot would receive it in person, although any relief (due from a new tenant) would be

68 *Westminster Abbey Charters*, no. 322.

69 *Curia Regis Rolls*, IV, pp. 13, 45–6, 48.

70 Harvey, *Westminster Abbey and its Estates*, p. 359.

71 *Westminster Abbey Charters*, no. 339. William I confirmed land in Challington in 1076x82; *Regesta Regum Anglo-Normannorum*, I, no. XX; calendared *Westminster Abbey Charters*, no. 19.

72 *Curia Regis Rolls*, VI, pp. 176–7; calendared *Westminster Abbey Charters*, no. 96.

73 *Regesta Regum Anglo-Normannorum*, III, no. 935; calendared *Westminster Abbey Charters*, no. 117.

rendered to the monks.[74] A more elaborate agreement was drawn up in or after 1206, between Abbot Ralph Arundel and the convent, which succeeded in driving a hard bargain with him. The monks would now hold the advowson as well as the vill, but the new arrangements would not prejudice the existing grant to the abbey's kitchen, which was now said to be 8 shillings daily. Homage and relief were again allocated respectively to abbot and convent. The monks were entitled to appoint as warden of the vill anyone they chose, whether monk or layman. The abbot had no right to dismiss either this warden or any parson whom the convent appointed to the church.[75]

The assignment of income from Parham to the church was a short-lived arrangement. Abbot William Humez, very soon after his election on 4 May 1214, drew up new arrangements for financing the monks' kitchen, which would give it a total annual income of £150 11s 9d annually from several designated manors, but rents from Parham played no part in making up this total.[76] One reason for its omission was, perhaps, the litigation over Parham instigated in the *curia regis* by the *curialis*, Peter Fitz Herbert in 1214. Evidently he relinquished his claim to the manor only on payment of £100 and in return for other, unspecified, favours.[77] The case was perhaps still *sub judice* when the new abbot was negotiating with the monks over the financing of their diet.

Some smaller outlying estates which gave rise to dispute were in Rutland. King Edward's reversionary grant of Martinsley wapentake in Rutland failed to take effect after the death of Queen Edith in 1075,[78] but Westminster did secure an interest in some lands appurtenant to churches held there by a former royal clerk. The earliest surviving genuine texts concerning these are two writs of William II. In one, he notified his grant to Westminster, and to Abbot Gilbert, of those churches in Rutland, with their lands, which Albert the Lotharingian held of the king.[79] A second writ ordered W. the sheriff to act justly towards the abbot of Westminster over the churches in Rutland, together with their customary rights, which Osbern the clerk held of him.[80] The churches were not named in either writ. In 1086 Albert the clerk held the churches of Oakham, Hambleton and St Peter's, Stamford, which belonged to Hambleton. These, together with their appurtenant lands, had

74 *Westminster Abbey Charters*, no. 326.

75 *Ibid.*, no. 335.

76 *Documents Illustrating the Rule of Walter de Wenlok, Abbot of Westminster, 1283–1307*, Camden Fourth Series, 2 (1965), pp. 215–16.

77 *Westminster Abbey Charters*, no. 487.

78 Harvey, *Westminster Abbey and its Estates*, p. 27.

79 Dugdale, *Monasticon Anglicanum*, I, p. 301, no. XLIII. On Albert the Lotharingian, see John Le Neve, *Fasti Ecclesiae Anglicanae 1066–1300, I, St Paul's London*, compiled Diana E. Greenway (London, 1968), p. 59.

80 Armitage Robinson, *Gilbert Crispin*, p. 139, no. 14; calendared *Westminster Abbey Charters*, no. 56.

been worth £8 in King Edward's reign, but were now worth £10.[81] A writ of William I, which is certainly spurious in its present form, notified his confirmation to the abbey and monks of the churches of Uppingham and Wardley in Rutland, and that of Belton (Lincs.), together with their appurtenant lands, tithes and chapels.[82] All three writs survive only as cartulary copies, and there is a possibility that Osbern (Herbert in one variant text) is a scribal error for Albert.[83] On the other hand, there may have been two clerks, holding two distinct groups of churches. The writ in the name of William I, in its original form, perhaps identified those held by Osbern. Later the abbey had interests in churches in both groups.[84] Land in Uppingham was seized by Robert de Stuteville during the unrest in Stephen's reign, when Westminster enlisted the assistance of Archbishop Theobald in ordering its restoration.[85] The churches of Oakham and Hambleton rendered substantial pensions to Westminster in the reign of King John,[86] probably on account of the substantial tithes accruing from the tenants on the appurtenant lands. In 1206 the rector of Oakham, the royal clerk James Salvage, obtained, in return for the considerable fine of three palfreys, a grant from King John exempting the tenants of these churches from owing suit of shire or hundred courts, and of the obligation to render sheriffs' aids.[87]

Westminster held some small estates in Northamptonshire,[88] but these seemingly gave rise to few recorded administrative difficulties in the period under discussion. Rents from Sulby contributed to the monks' weekly farm, c.1120.[89] It appears that Westminster held the manor as a tenant of Robert Foliot. During Stephen's reign the monks informed Archbishop Theobald that he had seized their land in Sulby, an act for which he incurred the archbishop's censure. The archbishop's mandate was conveyed to him via the bishop of Lincoln, who was ordered to threaten spiritual penalties in case of recalcitrance.[90] Robert and his wife Margaret quickly granted the manor of

81 *Domesday Book*, I, f. 294.

82 Dugdale, *Monasticon Anglicanum*, I, p. 301, no. XLII; calendared *Westminster Abbey Charters*, no. 46.

83 *Westminster Abbey Charters*, no. 56 note.

84 Emma Mason, 'Westminster Abbey's Rutland Churches', *Rutland Record* 5 (1985), pp. 163–6.

85 A. Saltman, *Theobald, Archbishop of Canterbury* (London, 1956; reprinted New York, 1969), pp. 507–8, no. 277.

86 *Westminster Abbey Charters*, nos 482–3.

87 *Rotuli Chartarum in Turri Londoniensi asservati 1199–1216*, ed. T. Duffus Hardy, Record Comm. (London, 1837), f. 165b; *Rotuli de Oblatis et Finibus in Turri Londiniensi asservati, tempore regis Johannis*, ed. T. Duffus Hardy, Record Comm. (London, 1835), p. 365; *Pipe Roll 8 John*, p. 53.

88 Harvey, *Westminster Abbey and its Estates*, pp. 355–6.

89 *Westminster Abbey Charters*, no. 339.

90 Saltman, *Theobald, Archbishop of Canterbury*, pp. 507–8, no. 277. On Sulby, see *Westminster Abbey Charters*, no. 195 note.

Sulby to the monks, to hold for the service of one knight, as they had rendered to the grantors' predecessors in the reign of Henry I. Margaret was a daughter of Richard de Reinbuedcurt, from whom the abbey evidently acquired this tenancy. Robert Foliot's *carta*, returned in 1166, listed the abbot of Westminster as holding one fee of old enfeoffment of his barony.[91]

Elsewhere in Northamptonshire, the abbey had some interests in Islip. In the early twelfth century Westminster was recorded as having one hide of land there, on which four of the king's sokemen were tenants.[92] The abbey's rights in the land of these sokemen were specifically reserved when the church there was granted by Abbot Gervase to Elias 'the dean' at an annual pension of half a mark (a sum which implies only a limited return from tithes). This grant was witnessed by clergy from Sudborough and Deene, in both of which places Westminster also held land.[93] The manor of Deene was variously recorded as the gift of King Edward, or that of his chamberlain Hugelin.[94] It was held of the abbot by a service of hospitality, and early in 1215 Abbot William d'Humez brought a lawsuit against his tenant Simon of Deene in order to reaffirm his rights in this service.[95] The importance laid on these rights indicates that the abbots were in the habit of travelling to inspect their Northamptonshire estates. In a separate transaction, about the same time or slightly earlier, Simon and his son Ivo granted, by charters, two half-virgates of land in Deene to Henry Sumer, to be held in hereditary right at an annual rent of one pound of pepper. Henry then granted this land to the monks, to provide lights for the Lady Altar.[96] Henry Sumer was a prominent resident of the vill of Westminster, as shown by his frequent attestations to charters usually without any title, although he was, for a time, reeve of Westminster,[97] and was also a sergeant of Westminster abbey.[98] Probably he acquired his tenancy in Deene through favour of the abbot.

A few outlying manors lay in other shires. In Oxford, another Islip, the birthplace of King Edward, together with a half-hide at Marston, was said to have been donated by him at the time the abbey was rededicated. This is probably correct, even though there is some doubt about the authenticity of surviving texts relating to his grant.[99] The land in Marston was confirmed to

91 *Westminster Abbey Charters*, no. 479 and note.

92 The Northamptonshire Survey, *VCH Northamptonshire*, I, pp. 357–8 (on its date), 365.

93 *Westminster Abbey Charters*, no. 270. See also Harvey, *Westminster Abbey and its Estates*, pp. 355–6.

94 Harvey, *Westminster Abbey and its Estates*, p. 355 and note 4.

95 F.M. Stenton, *The First Century of English Feudalism 1066–1166*, 2nd edn (Oxford, 1961), pp. 71–3, 267–9.

96 *Westminster Abbey Charters*, no. 480.

97 *Ibid.*, nos 437–8.

98 *Ibid.*, no. 297.

99 *Anglo-Saxon Writs*, nos 103–4. See also P.H. Sawyer, *Anglo-Saxon Charters: an Annotated List and Bibliography* (London, 1968), nos 1147–8.

the abbey within two years of the Norman Conquest.[100] Islip itself was among lands restored to Westminster in a writ of Henry I, seemingly dating from c.1121 to 1123, but the authenticity of this document has been challenged.[101] In the twelfth century Islip was held by the De Courcy family. However Robert de Courcy joined Philip Augustus of France in 1203, and so incurred the forfeiture of his English lands. Westminster seized this opportunity to petition for Islip, and presented in support of its claim the earlier writs which it possessed concerning this manor. Whether or not it was apparent to the Chancery staff that these texts are spurious, the abbey was required to pay heavily for King John's restoration of Islip.[102]

From the period under discussion, only sporadic documentation now survives on Westminster's estates in other shires. The Hampshire manor of Eversley, donated by King Edward, was probably confirmed by King William I, although his writ now survives only in a spurious form.[103] Early in the twelfth century, Richard Fitz William confirmed to the almonry of the abbey two thirds of the tithes of his fee of *Buchetuna* (probably Buckton, Herefordshire) both from the demesne land and from that of the villeins, as his father William granted it.[104] Since this place lies in the far north-west of the shire, collection of this income cannot have been very cost-effective. Finally, among the outer ring of properties, was some land in Cricklade, Wilts., granted to the abbey by Robert Fitz Wimarc. This was confirmed by King William I in 1078 or later. In 1086 the abbot held in chief the church of Cricklade, together with 'many' burgesses and the third penny of the vill (i.e. one-third of the profits of local justice).[105] This Cricklade estate was one of only five where the abbey is recorded as holding burgess-tenants (the others were Ashwell, Droitwich, Pershore and Staines). The Cricklade property was perhaps not very lucrative, more especially since the Domesday Survey also records that the king himself held the third penny there. Evidence of later Westminster involvement is lacking.[106] No other estate was held in Wiltshire before 1399.[107]

In Berkshire, Easthampstead was granted to Westminster by King Edward,

100 Dugdale, *Monasticon Anglicanum*, I, p. 301, no. XXXIV; calendared *Westminster Abbey Charters*, no. 7.

101 *Regesta Regum Anglo-Normannorum, II, 1100–1135*, ed. C. Johnson and H.A. Cronne (Oxford, 1956), no. CCCIII; *Westminster Abbey Charters*, no. 83 and note.

102 *Rotuli Chartarum*, f. 139b; *Westminster Abbey Charters*, 149 and note; *Rotuli Litterarum Clausarum in Turri Londiniensi asservati (1204–27)*, ed. T. Duffus Hardy, 2 vols, Record Comm. (London, 1833–44), 15a; 32b; *Pipe Roll 6 John*, p. 112; *Rot. de Oblati et Fin.*, 222.

103 Westminster Abbey Muniments XXIII (2); calendared *Westminster Abbey Charters*, no. 34, and note; Harvey, *Westminster Abbey and its Estates*, p. 345.

104 *Westminster Abbey Charters*, no. 478.

105 *Regesta Regum Anglo-Normannorum*, I, no. LXX; *Westminster Abbey Charters*, no. 32 and note.

106 Harvey, *Westminster Abbey and its Estates*, p. 101 and note.

107 *Ibid.*, p. 360.

and was held by the abbey in 1086. Probably this manor was granted to Hurley priory early in its history, long before it is recorded in 1225 as being held by Hurley for £5 per annum.[108] This may be deduced from the fact that the church of Easthampstead was 'conceded' to the priory by Abbot Lawrence,[109] and subsequently 'given and conceded' to it by Abbot Walter.[110] The vill of Hurley itself, together with the surrounding woodland, with some exceptions, was granted to Westminster by Geoffrey de Mandeville I, c.1085–86, with the specific intention that it should form the initial endowment of Hurley Priory, of which he was founder.[111]

Windsor had been donated to Westminster abbey by King Edward, but when William I was creating Windsor Forest he took the manor but gave in exchange others in Essex[112] and Surrey,[113] which are discussed below. However, eight hides of land pertaining to Westminster's manor of Pyrford lay within the newly-formed Windsor Park and Forest and were acquitted of geld and scot by William I and his sons.[114]

In Buckinghamshire Westminster held in Denham an estate assessed at ten hides, which was granted to the abbey by the thegn Wulfstan in the reign of King Edward. At that time it was worth £10, but only £7 in 1086.[115] An annual income of £1 10s from Denham church was included in the revenues which Abbot Herbert assigned to the High Altar of the abbey.[116] In 1172 Martin de Capella held land in Denham of Westminster.[117] The terms on which he originally obtained his tenancy are unknown, but were perhaps considered at Westminster to be too favourable to him and a potential threat to the abbey's title. The staff of the scriptorium composed a charter which purported to be a confirmation by King Henry II to Westminster of the manor of Denham, which Martin de Capella held, to hold in demesne. This text was probably drafted in 1181x1182,[118] and intended to safeguard the abbey's title to Denham before a new tenancy agreement was made between Abbot Walter and Martin. The abbot and convent 'conceded and confirmed' the manor of Denham to Martin, to be held in inheritance, except for the church with its tithes and oblations, which would be retained by Westminster. In return for the manor, Martin would render £15 annually. Moreover he

108 *Westminster Abbey Charters*, no. 462; Harvey, *Westminster Abbey and its Estates*, p. 337.

109 *Westminster Abbey Charters*, no. 285.

110 *Ibid*., no. 302.

111 *Ibid*., no. 462.

112 Dugdale, *Monasticon Anglicanum*, I. no. XXXVII; *Regesta Regum Anglo-Normannorum*, I, no. XVII; calendared *Westminster Abbey Charters*, nos 9, 16.

113 Harvey, *Westminster Abbey and its Estates*, pp. 27–8, 338.

114 Armitage Robinson, *Gilbert Crispin*, p. 29n, p. 141 no. 19; calendared *Westminster Abbey Charters*, nos 44, 65.

115 *Domesday Book*, I, f. 145.

116 *Westminster Abbey Charters*, no. 244.

117 *Pipe Roll 18 Henry II*, p. 47.

118 *Westminster Abbey Charters*, no. 138.

would render the abbot an annual service of hospitality, of which he would receive fifteen days' notice in order to make preparations. Martin would hold the manor freely with everything pertaining to his fee-farm, holding his land in the same manner as did the other fee-farmers of the land of St Peter (of Westminster).[119] The service of hospitality was quitclaimed to Henry de Capella, in the reign of King Henry III, in return for a further £3 per annum,[120] a sum indicative of the substantial scale on which this service was required to be performed.

Westminster's other estate in Buckinghamshire comprised eight hides at East Burnham, which included Cippenham. The estate was held before 1066 by three thegns, who paid an annual customary due of 5 *ora* to the monastery of Staines. At that time the total estate was worth £6 annually. Westminster was granted the land by King William, before 1086, when it was worth £5 2s 4d.[121] In the early 1090s, Abbot Gilbert proved his title to these lands on the king's orders. William II accordingly instructed the men of Buckinghamshire that the abbot was to hold the estate peacefully.[122] In the last years of his abbacy Gilbert drew up an agreement with William of Buckland. It was stated that William and his heirs would hold (East) Burnham and Cippenham in fee and inheritance, rendering £2 10s annually for all service apart from the king's common geld. They would also hold Tetworth and Tonge (in Huntingdonshire) for £3 annually, except for the king's geld, and he would hold in fee the courtyard in front of his house for 4 pence annually. Moreover he would hold Chelsea (Middx) for £4 annually, except for the king's geld, for his lifetime, but Chelsea would revert to Westminster on his death. Whenever the king levied a scutage of £1 on each knight's fee, William would acquit the abbey of this sum (i.e. he himself would render the king the scutage due from his fee). He would render £2 at Christmas and £2 at the Feast of the Ascension for Chelsea and would render 55s 2d for his fee at the Feast of the Annunciation and the same amount eight days before Michaelmas.[123] The 'weekly farm of the monks' assigned to them all rents from Cippenham.[124] William of Buckland was building up a strong position for himself in this region, as his father Hugh had done earlier. In 1119, William was sheriff of Berkshire and may also have been sheriff of Buckinghamshire.[125] The goodwill of such a rising official would be an asset to Westminster in the administration of its lands in the shires to the north of London.

119 *Ibid*., no. 301. On Martin, see also *ibid*., no. 315 and compare the attestations to these two charters.

120 British Library Harleian Charter 85 A 11.

121 *Domesday Book*, I, f. 145.

122 Armitage Robinson, *Gilbert Crispin*, p. 136, no. 9; calendared *Westminster Abbey Charters*, no. 51.

123 *Westminster Abbey Charters*, no. 242.

124 *Ibid*., no. 339.

125 Judith A. Green, *The Government of England under Henry I* (Cambridge, 1986), pp. 166, 201, 202n, 206n, 237–8, 283, 285, 286.

The land which he held of the abbey in Tetworth and Tonge appears not to have given rise to any further negotiations in the period under discussion, throughout which it comprised the only Huntingdonshire property of Westminster.

In contrast several of the Hertfordshire estates gave rise to successive administrative arrangements. The manor of Aldenham was reputedly given to the abbey by King Offa of Mercia and was confirmed by King Edgar.[126] A writ in the name of William I, confirming the estate to Abbot Edwin, appears to be a complete fabrication.[127] The estate was held in demesne, and although its value dropped considerably in the wake of the Norman Conquest, the income from tithes accrued to the abbey. In the earlier twelfth century there was no problem in collecting these, but the disturbances of Stephen's reign evidently led to the tithes being withheld. In the early years of Henry II's reign the abbot appealed to the king, who issued a writ *praecipe* ordering the clerk John of Bushey to render to the abbot, justly and without delay, the tithes pertaining to his parish of Aldenham.[128] The vill of Bushey lay a short distance to the south of Aldenham, and although Westminster held no land there, it did acquire some tithes, by the reign of Henry I if not earlier. As with those due from John of Bushey in Aldenham, these too were apparently withheld in Stephen's reign. The abbey obtained a writ of right from Henry II, ordering Geoffrey de Jarpunville to restore the tithes without delay, or else be constrained to do so by the bishop of Lincoln (i.e. under threat of incurring spiritual penalties).[129] One difficulty in administering Aldenham was that it lay within the sphere of influence of the abbey of St Albans. Moreover, Abbot Lawrence was a former monk of that house and received material support from it when he was elected to Westminster. His subsequent ingratitude triggered recriminations and led to a tenurial dispute which was resolved only by the eminent officials who comprised the Exchequer court at Michaelmas 1165. The outcome was that Abbot Robert, on behalf of his monks, together with Robert Tailleboys, with his brothers Roger and Simon, for themselves and their heirs, quitclaimed to Abbot Lawrence the claim which Abbot Robert made against him and his abbey on behalf of Robert Tailleboys and his brothers in Aldenham. Abbot Lawrence, in return, gave the brothers 23 marks (£15 6s 8d), with the consent of Abbot Robert; and also granted them right of pannage for 20 pigs annually in Aldenham wood.[130] While this wood was a valuable asset in itself, the demographic and consequent economic pressures of the later twelfth century, which led to so much assarting across the country, prompted the abbey to take advantage of

126 Harvey, *Westminster Abbey and its Estates*, p. 345.

127 *Regesta Regum Anglo-Normannorum*, I, no. IX; calendared *Westminster Abbey Charters*, no. 2.

128 Westminster Abbey Domesday (Muniment Book 11), f. 203v; calendared *Westminster Abbey Charters*, no. 128.

129 *Westminster Abbey Charters*, no. 127.

130 *Ibid.*, no. 281.

the demand for more cleared land. Abbot William Postard accordingly granted two virgates of assart to Geoffrey Picot and his heirs, land lying between the recipient's houses and the abbot's wood, which would render half-yearly payments of 6s 8d.[131]

The rising population of the period led to growing numbers of men being answerable to franchisal courts, and thereby generating increasing profits of justice for the holders of these franchises. Both St Albans and Westminster claimed to control the inhabitants of Aldenham for this purpose, but the ensuing dispute between the parties was settled in the early summer of 1194.[132] In the reign of King John the dispute was renewed between Abbot John of St Albans and Abbot Ralph Arundel of Westminster, but was resolved on terms similar to the earlier settlement.[133] When land in Aldenham changed hands, transactions took place in the abbot's court, presumably a manorial court held there, and in presence of the seneschal of Westminster.[134] The manor of *Titeburst* had been acquired with Aldenham, and rents totalling 20 shillings contributed to the weekly farm of the monks.[135]

Some distance to the north of Aldenham lay Wheathampstead, donated to the abbey by King Edward.[136] In c.1167x1169 a dispute broke out between Westminster and St Albans over a plot of land in the neighbouring Sandridge. Abbot Lawrence, with the assent of his monks and the advice and assent of his men 'to whom the right in that land pertained', in the presence of Nicholas the sheriff and that of many men of the shire court of Hertfordshire, granted the disputed land to Abbot Simon and the monks of St Albans, together with another plot of land 'which was known to belong by right to St Peter (of Westminster)'. In return, Abbot Simon, with the assent of his monks and on the advice of his men, granted to Westminster an equivalent amount of land in Sandridge bordering on his land in Wheathampstead. This was done with the assent of Gregory, the priest of Sandridge 'to whom the right in that land pertained'.[137]

Something of Wheathampstead's management earlier in the twelfth century is known from a charter of Abbot Gervase, by which he granted land there to Robert, his marshal, and his heirs. Previous occupants of its component parts, who had held short tenancies, subsequently quitclaimed, included William of Cowley; Gerold, the chamberlain of Abbot Herbert; Master Leofwine; and Richard Osumull, besides Godwine the swineherd. Seemingly all these lands suffered in the troubles of Stephen's reign, because they were said to be wasted and rendered no taxation. Robert, though, would now hold them as a tenancy assessed at three virgates, an arrangement approved by the

131 *Ibid.*, no. 319.
132 *Ibid.*, no. 318.
133 *Ibid.*, no. 333.
134 *Ibid.*, nos 466–7.
135 *Ibid.*, no. 339. See also Harvey, *Westminster Abbey and its Estates*, p. 346.
136 Harvey, *Westminster Abbey and its Estates*, p. 347.
137 *Westminster Abbey Charters*, no. 282.

chapter of Westminster and by the judgement of worthy men of the vill of Wheathampstead. Accordingly he was granted his charter, and his homage was received in the chapter.[138]

Slightly to the north-east of Wheathampstead lay the vill of Ayot St Lawrence. In the middle decades of the eleventh century Westminster claimed to hold an estate of two and a half hides there, granted by the thegn Ælfwine Gottone in King Edward's reign, but perhaps subsequently held by him as a sub-tenant of the abbey. The confirmatory writ now surviving in King Edward's name appears to be a later fabrication, but he did perhaps issue a simpler version of such a writ. This was seemingly produced in evidence when the successful request was made to William I for a further confirmation in the 1080s.[139] In 1086 the estate was held of Westminster by Geoffrey de Mandeville, but was subsequently lost.[140]

An estate in Datchworth with Watton was granted to the abbey by King Edgar, and confirmed by King Edward.[141] In the first years of William I's reign, a further confirmatory writ was obtained, addressed to Edmund the sheriff, Ælfwine Gottune (presumably identical with the donor of Ayot St Lawrence) and Leofwine Scune, ordering them that the abbey was to have full possession of its land in Watton and Datchworth, and an enquiry was also to be made into royal rights there.[142] In the middle decades of the twelfth century, William of Buckland obtained a tenancy there, and in 1192 the tenant was Hugh of Buckland.[143] These men were members of that family which had been dominant in Berkshire and Buckinghamshire early in the century. Datchworth church was a valuable living in the possession of Westminster. In the mid-twelfth century the abbot and monks appointed the powerful royal official Richard of Ilchester as rector, and with his agreement they then, c.1164x1166, appointed their clerk Elias to the perpetual vicarage there.[144] In the mid-twelfth century, Robert Fitz Ralph was tenant of the Valognes fee, from which he held the manor of Woodhall in Watton. At the time of his marriage he granted half of his 'vill of Watton' to his wife Katherine, as her dower. Since his charter was acquired by Westminster, the abbey presumably acquired this land in due course.[145] Also near Datchworth lay Mardley (now Mardleybury), from which rents totalling 15 shillings contributed to the weekly farm of the monks.[146]

Land in Wormley, in south-east Hertfordshire, was donated by the master-

138 *Ibid.*, no. 269.

139 *Anglo-Saxon Writs*, pp. 310–11; no. 91, pp. 356–7; *Regesta Regum Anglo-Normannorum*, I, no. XXXVIII.

140 Harvey, *Westminster Abbey and its Estates*, pp. 72, 74.

141 *Ibid.*, p. 346.

142 Dugdale, *Monasticon Anglicanum*, I, 301, no. XXXVI.

143 Harvey, *Westminster Abbey and its Estates*, p. 346.

144 *Westminster Abbey Charters*, no. 468.

145 *Ibid.*, no. 474 and note.

146 *Ibid.*, no. 339.

mason Leofsin Dodesone, and confirmed to Westminster by King Edward. There was some trouble in securing possession, and a further confirmatory writ was obtained from William I. However this, too, failed to take effect and the abbey held nothing there in later years.[147]

The manor of Stevenage had been granted by King Edward and was held in demesne.[148] Consequently little documentation relating to it survives from the period under discussion. As in the case of Aldenham, any property transfers directly affecting Westminster were conducted in the presence of the seneschal of Westminster abbey.[149]

At Sawbridgeworth, in the extreme east of Hertfordshire, Westminster acquired the church, with its appurtenant lands, tithes and rights, by a grant made by Henry I, following the death, in November 1120, of Otwel Fitz Count, who was drowned in the wreck of the White Ship.[150] Accordingly Richard de Belmeis I, bishop of London, formally granted this church to the abbey with its tithes and other appurtenances, adding that the king's grant was made on his advice and with his consent. On his instructions Roger Fitz Robert, the archdeacon of Middlesex, conveyed seisin.[151] Westminster initially staffed this church with some of its monks, but they evidently suffered harassment from the local inhabitants, as well as from over-zealous officials of William d'Aubigny 'the Breton', who had custody of the lands of Otwel Fitz Count. Following an appeal to him, he issued a writ designed to protect the monks, and ordered that in the event of any allegations or pleas arising from their occupancy, these were to be reserved until they could be heard in his presence. His officers were to act justly towards the monks, their tenants, their tithes and their other rights.[152] The harassment had probably been financial in its origins and prompted by the fact that William himself was answerable to the king for the Fitz Count estate. Evidently the property pertaining to the church was quite substantial, because Westminster went to the expense of applying to the king for a writ ordering that the entire supplies and goods which the abbey's officers at Sawbridgeworth could swear to be their demesne possessions were to be quit of toll, passage dues and all customary exactions.[153] In 1161 Abbot Lawrence granted the church to the Sacristy of the abbey, so that its revenues could provide lights for the altar besides wine and a pittance on the Second Feast of St Agnes (28 January), to commemorate the anniversary of the deaths of his father and mother, and of

147 *Ibid.*, no. 27 and note.

148 Harvey, *Westminster Abbey and its Estates*, p. 346.

149 *Westminster Abbey Charters*, no. 473. However, transfers between tenants did not require the seneschal's presence; *ibid.*, nos 471–2.

150 Armitage Robinson, *Gilbert Crispin*, p. 156, no. 40; calendared *Westminster Abbey Charters*, no. 86.

151 *Westminster Abbey Charters*, no. 203.

152 *Ibid.*, no. 469.

153 Armitage Robinson, *Gilbert Crispin*, pp. 156–7, no. 41; calendared *Westminster Abbey Charters*, no. 87.

the predecessors and benefactors of the monks.[154] At the same time, Pope Alexander III was requested to confirm this church to the use of the Sacristy, which he did on 7 February 1161.[155] The other person with a strong interest in the matter was the current feudal lord. The wife of the late Otwel Fitz Count had been Margaret de Ria, whose first husband had been William de Mandeville I. The fortunes of this family were somewhat chequered.[156] From 1166, its head was William's grandson, William earl of Essex, who agreed to confirm the church to Westminster.[157] It was worth the trouble and expense of obtaining these confirmations since its incumbent rendered the substantial annual pension of £15,[158] the bulk of which doubtless accrued from the rents and tithes rendered by the tenants of the appurtenant lands.

Westminster had estates scattered throughout the large shire of Essex. Nearest to London were lands in West and East Ham. In the reign of King Edward, Alestan held a manor of eight hides and thirty acres in West Ham. After the Norman Conquest this was given by William I to Rannulf Peverel and Robert Gernon, but by the latter part of Henry I's reign, possession was disputed between the archbishop of Canterbury and the abbot of Westminster. A writ of Henry I, dating from 1129, ordered Aubrey de Vere, sheriff of Essex, to convene the shire court in order to determine which litigant had the better case, and to put him in lawful seisin.[159] Westminster's claim to this estate was perhaps an extension of its earlier interests in East Ham, where it had been confirmed in an estate by King Edgar.[160] In the period 1144x1156, Abbot Gervase and the monks granted to Alger the clerk the land in Ham which his grandfather Puncelin earlier held, to be held of the abbey at an annual rent of £3.[161]

Some distance to the east lay Ockendon, an estate in North Ockendon, which was sometimes documented jointly with Feering, another estate in the north-east of the county. This association stemmed from the fact that they had been given jointly by King William, as part of the exchange by which he obtained Windsor.[162] The grant of these two estates was notified by William I in two writs dating from no later than 1075. One of these, written in English, notified William bishop of London; Sweyn the sheriff and the thegns of Essex

154 *Westminster Abbey Charters*, no. 283.

155 *Papsturkunden in England*, ed. W. Holtzmann, 3 vols, Abhandlungen der Gesellschaft der Wissenschaften in Gottingen, phil.hist. Klasse, Berlin, Gottingen (I = neue Folge XXV, 1930–31; II = 3 Folge XIV–XV, 1935–6; III = 3 Folge XXXIII, 1952), I, no. 86.

156 C. Warren Hollister, 'The Misfortunes of the Mandevilles', *History*, 58 (1973), pp. 18–28.

157 *Westminster Abbey Charters*, no. 470.

158 *The Letters and Charters of Gilbert Foliot*, ed. A. Morey and C.N.L. Brooke (Cambridge, 1967), no. 462; calendared *Westminster Abbey Charters*, no. 211.

159 *Regesta Regum Anglo-Normannorum*, II, no. CCIV; calendared *Westminster Abbey Charters*, no. 91.

160 Harvey, *Westminster Abbey and its Estates*, p. 342.

161 *Westminster Abbey Charters*, no. 267.

162 Harvey, *Westminster Abbey and its Estates*, p. 343. See also p. 341.

that the abbey was to have Feering and Ockendon in exchange for Windsor 'as he first granted them'. Sweyn was to convey them to the abbey from whoever currently held them, and all alienated goods and possessions were to be restored within eleven nights from the reading out of this writ (in the shire court).[163] The second writ, in Latin, was addressed to the same recipients. It was worded more succinctly, but stated that Earl Harold Godwineson held the lands in King Edward's reign.[164] A further Latin writ, addressed to Sweyn the sheriff and his officers, between 1070 and 1082, notified them of the king's grant of Feering, with three appurtenant houses in Colchester, as it was held by Earl Harold at the death of King Edward, and as William himself held it. The grant was made on the advice of his barons, in exchange for Windsor.[165] But Feering was still not secure. Yet another writ was obtained between September 1092 and March 1093. William Rufus informed Peter de Valognes, sheriff of Essex, and his officers, that he had 'conceded' the manor of Feering to Abbot Gilbert, with its customary rights, which Abbot Vitalis held, and his other predecessors 'in the reign of King Edward'.[166] Evidently the abbey's determination to secure this manor had led the monks to cite anachronistic rights when petitioning for this writ. Whether or not the claim to have held Feering in Edward's reign was challenged by other interested parties, Westminster continued to experience hindrance in its administration of both Feering and Ockendon. Early in Henry I's reign a writ was obtained in which he ordered his barons and officers of Essex that the abbey was to hold these estates freely, with all customary rights, as granted by William I.[167] The ongoing problem which made it necessary for Westminster to obtain this series of writs was perhaps that successive sheriffs and their officers had continued to regard these estates, and particularly Feering, as royal demesne.

Rents of 5 shillings from Ockendon contributed towards the weekly farm of the monks.[168] In 1125 Abbot Herbert and the convent granted to Henry, son of Wilfred, for his lifetime the manor of Ockendon, at an annual rent of £10. He would give a further £1 annually from his church of St Alphege. If Henry wished to become a monk, he would be received at Westminster without further formalities and one heir of his would succeed to this tenancy, paying an annual rent of £11 for the manor. If this heir wished to become a monk, he too would be admitted, and then Ockendon, with all improvements made to it, would revert to Westminster.[169] Subsequent tenants are

163 Dugdale, *Monasticon Anglicanum*, I, p. 301, no. XXXVII; calendared *Westminster Abbey Charters*, no. 9.
164 *Regesta Regum Anglo-Normannorum*, I, no. XI.
165 *Ibid.*, no. XVII.
166 Armitage Robinson, *Gilbert Crispin*, p. 140, no. 17; calendared *Westminster Abbey Charters*, no. 50.
167 Armitage Robinson, *Gilbert Crispin*, p. 143, no. 22.
168 *Westminster Abbey Charters*, no. 339.
169 *Ibid.*, no. 247.

not recorded in the period under discussion, but the annual farm remained at £10 per annum.[170]

By the beginning of King John's reign, Aubrey de Vere was claiming the manor of Feering but following his plea in the *Curia Regis* at Westminster, at Michaelmas 1201, he quitclaimed this manor to Abbot Ralph, in return for the appurtenant manor of Little Coggeshall, which he would hold at an annual rent of 2 shillings, and render the forinsec service.[171] The manor of Coggeshall was also appurtenant to Feering and was granted by Abbot Herbert and the convent to Leofgar, and his heirs, to hold in fee-farm, together with the land of Half-hide, currently held by Norman. Leofgar would render £2 annually for Coggeshall, and 3 shillings annually for Half-hide.[172]

Slightly to the south-west of Feering lay the manor of Kelvedon, which was granted to the abbey by Guthmund and confirmed by King Edward.[173] This estate was enlarged by a grant made by King Stephen, probably at the beginning of his reign, by which he donated forty acres of assarts there.[174] The political unrest during Stephen's reign probably facilitated the intrusion into Kelvedon by Geoffrey Bataille and Richard de Fracheville. Abbot Gervase and the convent complained to Archbishop Theobald, who directed a mandate to the offenders, ordering them to restore the land to Westminster within fifteen days, under pain of anathema.[175]

The associated, but geographically-distinct manor of Kelvedon Hatch was held by Ailric in the reign of King Edward.[176] In 1066, during the reign of Harold II, Ailric fell ill after returning from a naval battle against William of Normandy. He gave the manor to Westminster, but according to the jurors giving evidence to the Domesday commissioners in 1086, the abbey held this land without any confirmatory royal writ.[177] Subsequently Abbot Gervase, with the assent of the convent, assigned this manor of Kelvedon Hatch to provide for lights and other things necessary for the high altar.[178]

The Essex manor of Benfleet was donated by King William I, possibly in part-exchange for Windsor (Berks.).[179] In the early twelfth century, it was listed with other manors assigned to provide allowances and pittances to the monks.[180] Some managerial disagreement evidently arose between the abbot

170 *Documents Illustrating the Rule of Walter de Wenlok*, p. 215.
171 *Westminster Abbey Charters*, no. 331.
172 *Ibid.*, no. 246.
173 Harvey, *Westminster Abbey and its Estates*, p. 342.
174 *Regesta Regum Anglo-Normannorum*, III, no. 932; calendared *Westminster Abbey Charters*, no. 114.
175 Saltman, *Theobald, Archbishop of Canterbury*, pp. 508–9, no. 278.
176 Harvey, *Westminster Abbey and its Estates*, p. 343.
177 *Westminster Abbey Charters*, no. 12 and note.
178 *Ibid.*, no. 252.
179 Harvey, *Westminster Abbey and its Estates*, p. 340.
180 *Westminster Abbey Charters*, no. 339.

and convent in the time of Abbot Walter, who issued a confirmation of the manor to the convent, together with Fanton and Claygate, 'because these manors were known to have belonged since ancient times to the office of the pittancer'.[181] At some uncertain date, William of Eynsford III acquired from the prior and convent a life grant of Benfleet, at an annual farm of £24, but surrendered the charter relating to this to Prior William Postard in the *Curia Regis*, in the presence of the Barons of the Exchequer. For added security, the prior paid to have a memorandum of this surrender enrolled on the Pipe Roll of Michaelmas 1189.[182] In his later capacity as abbot, William Postard earned a reputation for high-handedness, and one instance of this seems to have been an attempt to control Benfleet, with the appurtenant Fanton and Paglesham. Pressure from the convent presumably lay behind his solemn 'concession and confirmation' of these properties to the monks, who claimed that these manors were known to have pertained to the pittancer's office since ancient times.[183] Abbot Ralph Arundel contrived to obtain the manors to hold at farm from the monks, although he too eventually restored and quitclaimed them again to the prior and convent, as pertaining to the pittancer's office.[184] A reciprocal charter was issued on this occasion by Prior Robert Moulsham, granting in return the celebration of four named feasts, with copes and processions, after which wine and pittances would be served.[185]

Fanton, frequently associated with Benfleet in charters of this period, contained two manors held by Westminster, one confirmed by King Edgar and the other allegedly confirmed by King Edward but later disputed with William I.[186] Fanton was among several scattered manors listed in three spurious charters surviving in the name of Henry I, as being exempt from a range of franchisal and fiscal obligations.[187] All three purport to date from the earlier part of this reign. More firmly, the weekly farm of the monks lists Fanton with other manors assigned to finance allowances and pittances.[188] A genuine writ of King Stephen, dating from the early years of his reign, granted exemptions to Fanton and the other estates listed in the spurious charters in the name of Henry I, although a second text to the same effect appears to be spurious.[189] One further spurious charter, this time purporting

181 *Ibid.*, no. 299.
182 *Ibid.*, no. 344.
183 *Ibid.*, no. 317.
184 *Ibid.*, no. 332.
185 *Ibid.*, no. 345.
186 Harvey, *Westminster Abbey and its Estates*, p. 341. See also *Anglo-Saxon Writs*, pp. 105, 295.
187 Armitage Robinson, *Gilbert Crispin*, pp. 143–4, nos 23–4; calendared *Westminster Abbey Charters*, nos 62–4.
188 *Westminster Abbey Charters*, no. 339.
189 *Regesta Regum Anglo-Normannorum*, III, nos 936–7; calendared *Westminster Abbey Charters*, nos 105–6.

to date from the early years of Henry II, was also designed to secure franchisal and fiscal exemptions for Fanton and the other estates.[190]

Paglesham was donated to Westminster by the thegn Ingulf, in the reign of Harold II.[191] It was listed among those manors contributing to the monks' pittances and allowances,[192] but in 1190, Abbot Walter and the convent granted the vill, except the church, to Nicholas of Paglesham and his heirs, at an annual rent of £9 to the pittancer.[193]

Wennington was donated to the abbey by Aetsere Swearte and Aelfgyth in 1042–44.[194] William I, in a writ which is suspect in its present form, but perhaps containing a genuine core, ordered, c.1080–85, that Abbot Vitalis and the monks were to have the manor of Wennington with its church and the appurtenant soke of Alveley, as 'Eadser and Ealvida' granted and King Edward conceded.[195] Henry I ordered Richard de Belmeis I, bishop of London (1108x1127) to render justice to the abbot, since armed men had broken into Wennington church by night.[196] Wennington, like the Essex manors mentioned above, contributed to the regular provision of allowances and pittances.[197]

Land in Wheatley was donated to Westminster by Sweyn of Essex, and confirmed by his widow at his burial. Abbot Gilbert Crispin, however, granted this land to Sweyn's son Robert, at an annual rent of £3.[198] The weekly farm of the monks included a payment of £3 from Wheatley 'for the service of the Lord's Supper'.[199] The annual rent of £3 originally donated by Sweyn of Essex, was confirmed to Westminster in 1191x1202 by Geoffrey, count of Perche, with the consent of his wife Matilda. Geoffrey's interest in this rent was somewhat convoluted: the lands of Sweyn's grandson, Henry of Essex, had escheated to Henry II in 1163. The king's daughter, Matilda, wife of Henry the Lion, duke of Saxony, had a daughter, also named Matilda, who married Geoffrey in 1189 before he became count of Perche. As her marriage portion the younger Matilda conveyed part, at least, of the lands formerly held by Henry of Essex.[200] The efforts made to secure this estate, like those concerning Islip (Oxon.) mentioned above, illustrate the long corporate

190 *Westminster Abbey Charters*, no. 126.
191 Harvey, *Westminster Abbey and its Estates*, p. 343.
192 *Westminster Abbey Charters*, no. 339.
193 *Ibid.*, p. 300.
194 Harvey, *Westminster Abbey and its Estates*, p. 344.
195 *Formulare Anglicanum* ed. T. Madox (London, 1702), no. LXI; calendared *Westminster Abbey Charters*, no. 35.
196 Armitage Robinson, *Gilbert Crispin*, p. 149, no. 31; calendared *Westminster Abbey Charters*, no. 84.
197 *Westminster Abbey Charters*, no. 339.
198 *Ibid.*, no. 237.
199 *Ibid.*, no. 339.
200 *Ibid.*, no. 465 and note.

memories of the monks of Westminster which were brought into play when defending their tenurial interests.

Roding, in Essex, rendered tithes to Westminster, which appear to have been granted by Roger Mascherel, but his brother Hugh, as his feudal lord, evidently declined to ratify this grant. A writ of Henry I, dating from the latter part of his reign, ordered Hugh to restore the tithe to Westminster, together with any arrears.[201] In 1180x87 Gilbert Foliot, bishop of London, confirmed to Westminster the tithes of White Roding which pertained to the precentor's office.[202] A charter of William de Mandeville, earl of Essex (1166x89) confirming the whole of Roding to Geoffrey Fitz Walter, perhaps found its way into Westminster's muniments as a result of some further tithe dispute.[203]

A mill in Stratford, bequeathed by Ailnoth, was confirmed to Westminster by William I, c.1076x85.[204] The revenue from this mill contributed to the monks' weekly farm, towards which Ilteney also rendered 24 shillings.[205]

The manor of Moulsham, in Chelmsford, with the land of Broomfield, which Wlmar held of the abbey, were confirmed to Abbot Gilbert by William I, c.1085x87, with all customary rights, as King Edward conceded.[206] However the land in Broomfield was wrongfully taken by Thurold, the dapifer of Odo, bishop of Bayeux. Evidently Abbot Gilbert appealed to William II, since he ordered his officers in Essex to restore this land to Westminster. He also confirmed the abbey's possessions in Moulsham, as granted by King Edward and confirmed by William I.[207]

One grant which did not take effect at all was that by Geoffrey de Mandeville I, of land and marshland in Tilbury. William I notified Sweyn of Essex, at that time sheriff, that he confirmed the grant, but Westminster did not hold this land in Tilbury at a later date. Its misappropriation was possibly the work of Sweyn himself.[208] His benefaction in Wheatley, discussed above, was perhaps made in reparation. Westminster's Essex properties seem also to have suffered some harassment from officials of Anselm, abbot of Bec. Abbot Vitalis (1076–85) evidently petitioned William I, who ordered his officials that Vitalis was to have justice against Anselm.[209]

201 *Regesta Regum Anglo-Normannorum*, II, no. CCCII; calendared *Westminster Abbey Charters*, no. 92.
202 *Letters and Charters of Gilbert Foliot*, no. 462.
203 *Westminster Abbey Charters*, no. 464.
204 Armitage Robinson, *Gilbert Crispin*, p. 128, no. 2.
205 *Westminster Abbey Charters*, no. 339.
206 *Anglo-Saxon Writs*, p. 507.
207 *Ibid.*, p. 507; calendared *Westminster Abbey Charters*, no. 48.
208 Armitage Robinson, *Gilbert Crispin*, p. 127, no. 1; calendared *Westminster Abbey Charters*, no. 23.
209 *Regesta Regum Anglo-Normannorum*, I, no. XXIX; calendared *Westminster Abbey Charters*, no. 26.

11

Tenants and their Lands: the Inner Circle

At the same time that officials of the abbey of Bec were harassing Westminster's lands in Essex, they were also impeding its control over some of its lands in Surrey, most likely in the Tooting area, and consequently the same writ was applicable to these.[1]

The Surrey manor of Battersea (and Wandsworth) together with that of Pyrford, was granted to Westminster by William I, in part-exchange for Windsor (Berks.).[2] This grant was notified to the relevant officials in the shire by William I, in an English-language writ, dating from 1066xApril 1070. In the Anglo-Saxon period, Battersea was held by the nuns of Barking until their house was destroyed by Viking raiders in 870. Battersea had a strategic value in that it commanded an important ford on the Thames. In the years leading up to the Norman Conquest, it was held by Harold Godwinson.[3] Those initially notified of the king's grant to Westminster comprised Archbishop Stigand (deposed c. 11 April 1070), Count Eustace and the king's thegns in Surrey. The successive upheavals of the late 1060s rendered the addressees inadequate as guarantors of the abbey's title and the *scriptorium* concocted two subsequent versions, taking the opportunity to assume increasing franchisal privileges. One such writ, purportedly dating from 1070x1082, was addressed to Bishop Walkelin of Winchester and bore the attestations of Archbishop Lanfranc and Odo, bishop of Bayeux. A second such writ, while generally addressed to the officials in Surrey, was extended to include an even wider range of judicial privileges.[4] One further, but genuine, writ of 1076x1082 notified Archbishop Lanfranc and Bishop

1 *Regesta Regum Anglo-Normannorum, I, 1066–1100*, ed. H.W.C. Davis, assisted by R.J. Whitwell (Oxford, 1913), no. XXIX; calendared *Westminster Abbey Charters*, no. 26.

2 Barbara Harvey, *Westminster Abbey and its Estates in the Middle Ages* (Oxford, 1977), p. 357.

3 *Westminster Abbey Charters*, ed. Emma Mason, assisted by the late Jennifer Bray, continuing the work of the late D.J. Murphy, London Record Society, 25 (1988), no. 6 and note. See also Robin Fleming, 'Monastic Lands and England's Defence in the Viking Age', *English Historical Review*, 100 (1985), pp. 256, 262.

4 *Regesta Regum Anglo-Normannorum*, I, nos XVIII–XIX; calendared *Westminster Abbey Charters*, nos 17–18.

Odo that the king granted to Abbot Vitalis and the monks hunting rights in Battersea woods, with the tithe of two hundred houses near the church. This royal grant incorporated lesser ones for which the monks had evidently petitioned: land in Chollington (Sussex), one house there and two in London, with Wick-by-Pershore (Worcs.) and the tithes of all the king's property in Droitwich (Worcs.).[5] In the reign of Henry I Battersea was held of the abbey by Ranulf the chancellor, an official with a particularly unfavourable reputation, who died in January 1123. Henry I subsequently ordered Gilbert the sheriff to restore it to Abbot Herbert, and specifically that part of the land of which Gilbert unjustly delivered seisin to Hugh Fitz Hedric.[6] The text and contents of this writ were used by the staff of the Westminster *scriptorium* to draft a more detailed version, ordering the restoration of further lands, held by 'the chancellor', including both Battersea and Pyrford in Surrey, together with Shepperton (Middx) and Islip (Oxon.).[7] Two spurious charters in the name of King Stephen granted quittance of gelds, Danegeld and certain other exemptions on twenty-eight hides in Battersea, with quittance of geld on forty-four hides.[8] Both grants purportedly date from early 1150 x *ante* 3 May 1152. Battersea evidently caused no further problems until 1198, when an assize of *Mort d'Ancestor* was held between Stephen of Turnham and his wife Edelina, and Abbot William Postard, over one and a half virgates and two hides of land in Battersea. The couple quitclaimed their right in these in return for land in the manor of Westminster, by the Thames, next to the church of the Holy Innocents.[9] One further agreement with tenants survives from this period, between Abbot Ralph and William of Ginnes and his wife Matilda. The abbot granted the couple, and Matilda's heirs, a carefully-identified carucate of land in Battersea, while they in turn quitclaimed all their right in the wood and land of Penge, although the abbot granted them some limited grazing rights there, i.e. specific rights of herbage and pannage.[10]

Morden, in Surrey, was confirmed to the abbey by King Edgar and was held in demesne at all times.[11] Consequently it has left little trace in the archives of this period. Indications that it was augmented are found in one spurious writ, supposedly dating from 1076xApril 1084, whereby William I is

5 *Regesta Regum Anglo-Normannorum*, I, no. XX.

6 *Regesta Regum Anglo-Normannorum, II, 1100–1135*, ed. C. Johnson and H.A. Cronne (Oxford, 1956), no. CLXXI. On Ranulf the chancellor, see notes to *Westminster Abbey Charters*, nos 82–3; Judith A. Green, *The Government of England under Henry I* (Cambridge, 1986), p. 28.

7 *Regesta Regum Anglo-Normannorum*, II, no. CCCIII; calendared *Westminster Abbey Charters*, no. 83.

8 *Regesta Regum Anglo-Normannorum, III, 1135–1154*, ed. H.A. Cronne and R.H.C. Davis (Oxford, 1968), nos 940–41.

9 *Westminster Abbey Charters*, no. 314.

10 *Ibid.*, no. 330.

11 Harvey, *Westminster Abbey and its Estates*, p. 358.

depicted as notifying his officials in Surrey that he confirmed to Westminster three hides: one in Balham and the other two in Walton near Morden, donated by Geoffrey (*sic*), son of Count Eustace of Boulogne, on behalf of his wife Beatrice, and with the consent of Geoffrey de Mandeville. However there is no record of Westminster's holding this land in 1086, while the wording of the charter is reminiscent of the efforts of the Westminster forgers. The donor of this land is better known as Godfrey of Bouillon, advocate of the Holy Sepulchre.[12]

Wandsworth, as mentioned above, was granted by William I together with Battersea,[13] and little further is recorded of it over the period under discussion, except that Abbot Gervase, and Robert, prior of Merton, exchanged land there in order to facilitate Westminster's construction of mills. Later evidence suggests that these were possibly fulling-mills.[14]

Claygate, in Surrey, was granted to Westminster by Tostig and his wife Leofrun, and confirmed to the abbey by King Edward in or after 1058. A writ in the name of William I, spurious in its present form, but perhaps based on a genuine grant, notified dignitaries and officials in Surrey that he confirmed to Westminster, Abbot Edwin and the brethren the 'little manor' of Claygate, with appurtenant rights in Long Ditton and its woods, and with legal and fiscal exemptions.[15] Three spurious writs in the name of Henry I, all purportedly dating from the earlier part of his reign, quitclaimed Claygate and its appurtenant land, held since King Edward's reign in the wood of Long Ditton, from a range of legal and financial exactions.[16] By the time these writs were fabricated, these lands were evidently assigned to the almonry, and the exemptions, if acknowledged by the appropriate officials, would have increased the revenues from this property considerably. A genuine writ of King Stephen, dating from the early years of his reign, quitclaimed similar legal and financial exemptions, so that the forged writs in his uncle's name perhaps represented successive drafts of a document which was intended to be presented for confirmation.[17] However, a second charter in Stephen's name, relating to these same properties, appears to be spurious. The main distinctive point in it (but shared with one of the spurious writs in Henry I's name)[18] is the statement that William I confirmed by charter the privileges claimed.[19]

12 *Regesta Regum Anglo-Normannorum*, I, no. XXV. See also *Westminster Abbey Charters*, note to no. 21.

13 *Regesta Regum Anglo-Normannorum*, I, nos XVIII–XIX.

14 *Westminster Abbey Charters*, no. 268 and note.

15 Harvey, *Westminster Abbey and its Estates in the Middle Ages*, p. 358; J. Flete, *The History of Westminster Abbey*, ed. J. Armitage Robinson (Cambridge, 1909), p. 141; *Westminster Abbey Charters*, no. 13 note.

16 J. Armitage Robinson, *Gilbert Crispin, Abbot of Westminster* (Cambridge, 1911), pp. 143–4, nos 23–4; calendared *Westminster Abbey Charters*, nos 62–4.

17 *Regesta Regum Anglo-Normannorum*, III, no. 936.

18 *Westminster Abbey Charters*, no. 64.

19 *Regesta Regum Anglo-Normannorum*, III, no. 937.

Both charters in Stephen's name indicate that the lands were administered by a monk-custodian. Part, at least, of the Claygate estate was evidently misappropriated during the unrest of Stephen's reign, since in a writ dating from no later than c. August 1158, Henry II ordered the sheriff of Surrey to reseize the abbot of any land which he held at the death of Henry I, and which had later been wrongfully taken.[20] The forgers of this period were as concerned as their predecessors to uphold the claims of the almonry to the revenues of Claygate and Ditton wood, and a further writ to this effect was concocted purportedly dating from before Michaelmas 1158.[21] Further land and customary rights in the vill of Claygate and Kingscroft were granted to the abbey in the later twelfth century by Gilbert of Claygate, who placed his grant on the high altar of the abbey church. In return he received one monk's corrody and one sergeant's corrody, with specified additions, and two houses on the land formerly held by Alice Picot, those nearest the abbey. Gilbert was appointed a sergeant in the house of the almonry, and was granted this office in perpetuity.[22] In the time of Abbot Ralph Arundel, Geoffrey Fitz Peter, earl of Essex (d.1213) received a grant for life of Claygate, for which he would render £3 to the almonry. He was required to stock the manor himself, and undertook to conserve the woodland. After his death, when the land reverted to Westminster, the abbot and convent would receive it with all improvements, except for any corn currently in the barn.[23] The earl's rent of £3 was favourable to him, considering that the value in 1086 had been £2 10s, while Claygate had been augmented fairly recently by the grant received from Gilbert of Claygate. A further six acres of land in Claygate was granted to Westminster, for the use of the almonry, by Roger son of Edward, to the west of the almoner's land, which he held of the fee which was formerly Gilbert's. In return, Roger received a *gersum* of 25s 8d sterling from Peter the almoner and would receive an annual rent of 18 pence.[24]

The more remote Surrey manor of Pyrford, granted by King William I together with Battersea,[25] was augmented, towards the end of his reign, by a grant of eight of its appurtenant hides which were in Windsor Forest in the royal demesne, to be held quit of scot and geld.[26] These financial exemptions were confirmed by William II and also by Henry I, c.1104x1107, who further exempted the land from 'the new geld'.[27] Pyrford was normally held in

20 T.A.M. Bishop, *Scriptores Regis* (Oxford, 1961), plate XXV (b); calendared *Westminster Abbey Charters*, no. 125.

21 Westminster Abbey Domesday (Muniment Book 11), f. 458v; calendared *Westminster Abbey Charters*, no. 126.

22 Westminster Abbey Domesday, f. 465v.

23 *Westminster Abbey Charters*, no. 484.

24 *Ibid.*, no. 485.

25 W. Dugdale, *Monasticon Anglicanum*, revised H. Caley, H. Ellis and B. Bandinel, 6 vols in 8 (London, 1817–30), I, p. 301, no. XXXV.

26 Armitage Robinson, *Gilbert Crispin*, p. 29 note 1.

27 *Ibid.*, p. 141, no. 19.

demesne, although like Battersea, it had been held for a time by Ranulf the chancellor in Henry I's reign.[28] Towards the end of the twelfth century, a tenancy of forty acres was granted to William Southall and his wife Denise. William was dispossessed by Walter de Reda, and appealed to King John, early in his reign, perhaps in April 1200 for his help in making the abbot reinstate him.[29]

Other Surrey properties gave rise to little in the way of litigation or of recorded administrative adjustments over this period. The manor of Tooting was given by Sweyn and confirmed by his kinsman, King Edward.[30] A writ of William I, confirming this estate of four hides to Westminster, stated that they were initially given by Sweyn, and were currently held by his nephew, Ailnoth of London.[31] A variant history of this land, found in Domesday Book, was that Ailnoth bought the land from Waltheof, who in turn acquired it from Sweyn, a kinsman of King Edward.[32] Henry I, early in his reign, confirmed the land to Westminster with the concession that the abbot was answerable only in the king's presence for any claim on it.[33] After this time, Tooting was largely unrecorded, and was perhaps included with the manor of Battersea and Wandsworth.[34]

Over the years the abbey acquired other small properties in Surrey. A mill was obtained from Gilbert of Wandsworth, together with thirty acres of land in Sutton. Both were granted by Abbot Walter to Westminster's sergeant Henry Sumer, who would render annually one pound of incense to the High Altar on the feast of the Translation of St Edward, and half a mark (6s 8d) annually to the almoner. If Henry was able to get possession of 6 shillingsworth of land which Gilbert unjustly detained, but which pertained to the mill, his cash rent would increase to 10 shillings annually.[35]

Another transaction of Abbot Walter's, firmly dated to 29 September 1176, was his grant of land outside their wood at Penge, to be held at an annual rent of 20 shillings for a term of thirty years, after which it would revert to the abbey in the same condition in which he received it, unless his heir was able to obtain a renewal of the lease from the abbot and convent. If William died within the agreed term, then his heir would hold the land for the length of time remaining.[36]

28 Harvey, *Westminster Abbey and its Estates*, p. 359; *Westminster Abbey Charters*, no. 83.
29 *Westminster Abbey Charters*, no. 148.
30 *Anglo-Saxon Writs*, introd. and ed. F.E. Harmer, 2nd edn (Stamford, 1989), p. 357, no. 92.
31 Armitage Robinson, *Gilbert Crispin*, p. 128, no. 2.
32 *Domesday Book*, ed. A. Farley, 2 vols (London, 1783), I, f. 32; Harvey, *Westminster Abbey and its Estates*, p. 359; *Anglo-Saxon Writs*, pp. 311–13, 357, no. 92.
33 Armitage Robinson, *Gilbert Crispin*, pp. 142–3, no. 21; *Westminster Abbey Charters*, no. 60 and note.
34 Harvey, *Westminster Abbey and its Estates*, p. 359.
35 *Westminster Abbey Charters*, no. 297.
36 *Ibid.*, no. 298.

One further transaction relating to Surrey was the grant obtained from Hugh son of Ingulf of half an acre in South Lambeth, next to the land of Walter the brewer, in the land known as Hide, in order to link up the water-course of the Winterburn with the Thames.[37]

Most of the lands in Kent which Westminster held in the later Middle Ages were acquired later than the period covered by this study. The one exception was Lessness. A writ of King Edward stated that the estate of Lessness which Ætsere bequeathed to the abbey was to be held by it, to provide food for the monks.[38] The Domesday Survey recorded Azor, probably identical with Ætsere, as the holder of Lessness in King Edward's reign, but it does not record his grant to the abbey.[39] A writ of William I notified dignitaries and officials in Kent that he confirmed the manor of Lessness, with its church, to the abbey, as King Edward conceded it, but this document is a forgery.[40] By 1086, Robert Latimer held Lessness of Odo of Bayeux.[41] The bishop had perhaps seized this land illegally, and it is arguable that the writ of King Edward, like that of William I, is a forgery, designed to help recover the land after Odo's downfall.[42] Westminster did, however, hold Lessness during the reign of William II, when Abbot Gilbert agreed that Robert Bloet, bishop of Lincoln (1093–1123), would hold it of him. Bloet, however, later failed to observe the agreed terms, and Abbot Herbert obtained from Henry I a writ, 1121x1123, ordering him to do so.[43] Nothing more is known of Westminster's interests in Lessness. The probable date, deduced on palaeographical grounds, when the forged writ of William I was written,[44] would suggest that the manor was lost again soon after Henry I's intervention.

In Middlesex the abbey held the substantial manor of Westminster (calculated at thirteen and a half hides) given, or confirmed, by King Edgar.[45] Various other estates in Middlesex were given or confirmed by Archbishop Dunstan, Ethelred II and King Edward, or granted by private individuals in the period down to c.1100.[46] Close to the abbey, a little to the west, lay the manor of Eye, approximating to part of the district later known as Ebury. The two are not identical since the abbatial residence of La Neyte was distinct. The name of Ebury was used only from the thirteenth century.[47] The 'little manor' of Eye was donated by Geoffrey de Mandville I for the soul of his first

37 *Ibid.*, no. 486.
38 *Anglo-Saxon Writs*, pp. 342–3, no. 76.
39 *Ibid.*, pp. 299–300.
40 *Formulare Anglicanum*, ed. T. Madox (London, 1702), no. LXII; *Facsimiles of English Royal Writs to A.D. 1100 presented to Vivian Hunter Galbraith*, ed. T.A.M. Bishop and P. Chaplais (Oxford, 1957), xxii, note 1.
41 *Domesday Book*, I, f. 6v.
42 *Anglo-Saxon Writs*, p. 300.
43 Armitage Robinson, *Gilbert Crispin*, p. 157, no. 42.
44 *Facsimiles of English Royal Writs*, xxii, note 1.
45 Harvey, *Westminster Abbey and its Estates*, pp. 354–5.
46 *Ibid.*, pp. 349–55.
47 *Ibid.*, p. 350.

wife, Alice, who was buried in the abbey cloister, and for the souls of himself and his children.[48] This grant was confirmed by William II,[49] and again by Henry I in the early years of his reign.[50] Nearby Chelsea seems to have evolved out of part of the manor of Westminster. It is first distinctly recorded c.1115x1117, as one of several estates granted in fee by Abbot Gilbert Crispin to William of Buckland, who undertook to render for it an annual rent of £4, together with scutage.[51] This manor was later granted by Abbot Gervase to his mother Damette in fee farm. She undertook to render an identical annual rent of £4, and, when the grant was made, she gave 40 shillings to the convent, and a pall worth 100 shillings.[52] The manor of Knightsbridge was confirmed to the abbey by King Edward.[53] A rent of 7 shillings from Knightsbridge contributed towards the weekly farm of the monks.[54] Land pertaining to Knightsbridge in Kensington Gore was granted by Abbot Herbert, c.1130x38, to the nuns of Kilburn, to make an assart,[55] and a renewed grant of this was made by Abbot Gervase.[56] Tithes in Kensington, granted to the almonry of Westminster by the ancestors of Aubrey de Vere III, earl of Oxford, were confirmed by him c.1191x1194.[57]

Paddington was confirmed to the abbey by King Edgar and also by Aethelred II.[58] Three spurious charters in the name of Henry I, purportedly issued in the earlier part of his reign, granted legal and financial exemptions to Paddington, with Fanton in Essex and Claygate (Surrey) for the benefit of the almonry.[59] A genuine grant to the same effect was issued by King Stephen early in his reign. He confirmed the exemptions as the almoner held them in the time of King Henry, and as King Edward's charter testified.[60] The spurious charters in the name of Henry II probably represent successive drafts of a version presented to Stephen as evidence for the earlier concession of these liberties. The text of another charter in Stephen's reign, conceding them in more detail, is probably spurious, although it may represent an instance of the beneficiary's scribe having written a text subsequently presented for ratification. It has been suggested that the third of those surviving in the name of Henry I was modelled on it.[61] This second writ of Stephen's also supplements

48 *Westminster Abbey Charters*, no. 436.

49 *Regesta Regum Anglo-Normannorum*, I, no. LXV; calendared *Westminster Abbey Charters*, no. 52.

50 Armitage Robinson, *Gilbert Crispin*, p. 142, no. 20.

51 *Westminster Abbey Charters*, no. 242.

52 *Ibid.*, no. 262.

53 Harvey, *Westminster Abbey and its Estates*, p. 353.

54 *Westminster Abbey Charters*, no. 339.

55 *Ibid.*, no. 250.

56 *Ibid.*, no. 265.

57 *Ibid.*, no. 456.

58 Harvey, *Westminster Abbey and its Estates*, p. 353.

59 Armitage Robinson, *Gilbert Crispin*, pp. 143–4, nos 23–4.

60 *Regesta Regum Anglo-Normannorum*, III, no. 936.

61 *Ibid.*, III, no. 937; Bishop, *Scriptores Regis*, p. 8 and note 4.

the three in the Henry I series, by stating that these privileges were confirmed by William I. However there is no such grant among his genuine charters for Westminster. As for the supposed grant of liberties made by King Edward, none in his name singles out Paddington, together with Fanton and Claygate, although several generalized grants of exemptions survive in his name.[62] One further spurious writ in the series relating to the liberties purportedly pertaining to Paddington and these other manors survives in the name of Henry II.[63] While the liberties claimed for Paddington were non-existent, the manor undoubtedly belonged to the abbey, and its tenancies were subject to scrutiny. On 31 May 1185, the brothers Richard and William of Paddington quitclaimed to Abbot Walter the tenement there which they held of the abbey in return for corrodies for themselves and their respective wives.[64]

Hampstead was granted to Westminster by Æthelred II.[65] A tenancy was granted by charter to Richard de Balta, to hold at an annual rent of £2. This was confirmed by Henry I in the 1120s,[66] and again by King Stephen, no later than 1137.[67] The manor does not feature again in charters of the period under discussion, but was redeemed from the fee-farmer during the abbacy of Richard de Crokesley (1248–58).[68]

Hendon, donated by Archbishop Dunstan,[69] was granted by Abbot Gilbert Crispin no later than 1102, to his man Gunter, in fee farm, for one week's farm every year.[70] Abbot Herbert confirmed the land to Gunter 'of Hendon' and his heir as it was held in Abbot Gilbert's day.[71] Subsequently though, and probably in the interval following Herbert's death, this heir, Gilbert of Hendon, experienced difficulty in establishing his title, but successfully appealed to King Stephen early in his reign, who ordered that he was to hold his land peacefully.[72] Possibly the inheritance of this tenancy by an heir had been considered unacceptable to the monks of Westminster. Gilbert of Hendon also appealed to Henry of Blois, bishop of Winchester, who was authorized by the pope to take charge of the vacant bishopric of

62 *Anglo-Saxon Writs*, nos 81–3, 105–6.

63 Westminster Abbey Domesday, f. 458v; calendared *Westminster Abbey Charters*, no. 126.

64 *Westminster Abbey Charters*, no. 296.

65 Harvey, *Westminster Abbey and its Estates*, p. 352.

66 *Regesta Regum Anglo-Normannorum*, II, no. CCLXIX; calendared *Westminster Abbey Charters*, no. 88.

67 *Regesta Regum Anglo-Normannorum*, III, no. 925.

68 Harvey, *Westminster Abbey and its Estates*, p. 352.

69 *Ibid*., p. 352.

70 *Westminster Abbey Charters*, no. 241. The latest limit of this grant is fixed by the attestation of Prior Robert, who was elected abbot of Bury St Edmunds late in 1102; D. Knowles, C.N.L. Brooke and V.C.M. London, *The Heads of Religious Houses England and Wales 940–1216* (Cambridge, 1972), p. 32.

71 *Westminster Abbey Charters*, no. 245.

72 *Regesta Regum Anglo-Normannorum*, III, no. 926.

London in 1138. The see was filled only in July 1141. Pope Innocent II notified Abbot Gervase, in April 1139, that, at the request of the bishop, he confirmed, and took under his protection, the lands which Gilbert of Hendon and his predecessors held of the abbey.[73] Notwithstanding this mandate, the monks continued to resist Gilbert's right to this hereditary fee-farm. Early in Henry II's reign he evidently appealed to the king, who ordered the abbot and monks to allow Gilbert to hold the manor of Hendon in fee-farm as peacefully as Abbots Gilbert and Herbert and the chapter granted it to his father, and to Gilbert himself, and as Gilbert or his father held it in the reign of Henry I, as the charter of that king bears witness.[74] King Stephen's writ did not mention any charter of Henry I,[75] and, if it ever existed, it has disappeared. The citation of such a writ was perhaps a politically-correct ploy, since this was scarcely the occasion on which to cite a writ of Stephen's. In any event, the monks of Westminster were well aware of the long previous history of Gilbert's claims, while Abbot Gervase was in no position to evade the mandate of Henry II. Accordingly, together with the convent, he 'conceded' the manor in fee-farm, for an annual rent of £20.[76] Although they were required to acknowledge the right of Gilbert to succeed to his father's fee-farm, something which they were evidently reluctant to accept, yet they now established, in explicit terms, their entitlement to a substantial rent. In view of the pressure of inflation which was beginning to be felt at this time, the outcome was by no means to their disadvantage, especially given the likelihood that the estate held by Gilbert comprised only three hides out of the twenty at which Hendon was assessed in 1086, when it was valued at £8.[77]

Westminster acquired some land in Tottenham, valued at £1 10s when it was granted by David, earl of Huntingdon, to provide lights, love-feasts and pittances on the anniversary of the death of his sister, Queen Edith-Matilda, and on those of his parents, Malcolm III, King of Scots, and Queen Margaret.[78] A mandate of Pope Innocent II was obtained by Prior Osbert's delegation to the papal *curia* in December 1139, requesting David, as King of Scots, to confirm Westminster's title to this land.[79] David accordingly 'conceded' his earlier grant, and notified those directly concerned. His son, Earl

73 *Papsturkunden in England*, ed. W. Holtzmann, 3 vols, Abhandlungen der Gesellschaft der Wissenschaften in Gottingen, phil.-hist. Klasse, Berlin, Gottingen (I = neue Folge XXV, 1930–31; II = 3 Folge XIV–XV, 1935–6; III = 3 Folge XXXIII, 1952), I, no. 20. See also Barbara Harvey, 'Abbot Gervase de Blois and the Fee-Farms of Westminster Abbey', *Bulletin of the Institute of Historical Research*, 40 (1967), p. 136.

74 *Westminster Abbey Charters*, no. 124.

75 *Regesta Regum Anglo-Normannorum*, III, no. 926.

76 *Westminster Abbey Charters*, no. 263.

77 Harvey, 'Fee-Farms', p. 135.

78 *The Acts of Malcolm IV, King of Scots 1153–1165, together with Scottish Royal Acts prior to 1153*, ed. G.W.S. Barrow (Edinburgh, 1960), no. 6.

79 *Ibid.*, pp. 290–1, no. 319; *Papsturkunden in England*, I, no. 25; *Westminster Abbey Charters*, no. 160.

Henry, and the latter's sons, Malcolm IV and William the Lion, also made confirmations.[80] David's charters concerning this land were all issued on occasions when he was either at Westminster or in London, and while it is not specified where the relevant charters of his descendants were granted, their presence in the vicinity of Westminster can be deduced on circumstantial grounds in each instance.

One small property in Middlesex, largely undocumented in this period, was Hanworth, which contributed £1 10s annually towards the monks' farm.[81] Another small estate in Middlesex, but one which is not readily identifiable, was that of *Mapeleford* or *Mapelefort*. Herbert Fitz Herbert claimed this, together with Parham in Sussex, against Westminster but Abbot Herbert was able to prove his title to these lands in presence of the barons of the Exchequer. A confirmatory writ was issued by Henry I, c.1130x1133.[82] Evidently the dispute was reopened, since a further confirmatory writ was obtained from King Stephen.[83] The land was not recorded again in the period under discussion, and its administration was presumably merged with that of one of the substantial manors in Middlesex.

Another under-documented estate was that of Chalkhill in Kingsbury, donated to Westminster, with royal assent, by Thurstan, a housecarl of King Edward.[84] This land was confirmed to the abbey by William I, to augment the diet of the monks.[85] This estate, which lay to the west of Watling Street, between Hendon and Harrow,[86] was perhaps never held by the abbey in demesne.[87]

The manor of Harrow pertained to the archbishopric of Canterbury, but one of its tenants granted land there to Westminster. Charters relating to this tenancy consequently became the property of the abbey, and the history of the land can be traced from c.1150 onwards. An estate of one and a half hides, held by Osmar at a rather earlier date, was confirmed to his son Edmund, a physician, at an annual rent of 5 shillings.[88] Edmund apparently died without heirs, since Richard of Dover, while archbishop and papal legate (May 1177 x September 1181) confirmed this land to Simon son of Osmar to

80 *Acts of Malcolm IV*, nos 13–14, 36, 154; *The Acts of William I, King of Scots 1165–1214*, ed. G.W.S. Barrow, with W.W. Scott (Edinburgh, 1971), no. 52.
81 *Westminster Abbey Charters*, no. 339.
82 *Curia Regis Rolls*,, VI, pp. 176–7. See also *Westminster Abbey Charters*, no. 96.
83 *Regesta Regum Anglo-Normannorum*, III, no. 935.
84 *Anglo-Saxon Writs*, p. 308, p. 344 no. 77.
85 *Regesta Regum Anglo-Normannorum*, I, no. XII. The place-name Cealchithe is wrongly identified there as Chelsea. See Harvey, *Westminster Abbey and its Estates*, p. 349 and note 6.
86 D. Sullivan, *The Westminster Corridor* (London, 1994), map A, facing p. 96.
87 Harvey, *Westminster Abbey and its Estates*, p. 349 and note 6.
88 A. Saltman, *Theobald, Archbishop of Canterbury* (London, 1956; reprinted New York, 1969), pp. 345–6, no. 124.

hold as Osmar proved his title to it.[89] A few years later, in 1182 or early 1183, the archbishop confirmed the land to Matilda, the daughter of Simon.[90] More than twenty years later again, in the period 1206x1213, Matilda 'de Paris' granted the estate to Westminster, which would now owe the 5 shillings rent to the archbishop. The income from the land would contribute towards the costs of the monks' clothing. In return for this grant, the monks would provide her with all necessities in food and clothing. To ensure that their title would not be challenged, they required her to hand over all relevant charters.[91]

Several of the manors lay in the west and south-west of Middlesex, including Sunbury, granted by Archbishop Dunstan, and Teddington, granted by King Edward. Both of these were demesne manors at this time.[92] Within Teddington, however, there was a three-virgate holding which is documented at times in the later twelfth century. Hugh Fitz Warner obtained from Henry II a writ of right ordering Abbot Lawrence to render justice to Hugh in respect of a three-virgate holding in Sunbury and Teddington.[93] However following litigation in the abbot's *curia*, he quitclaimed it and surrendered the royal writ of right. In return he was compensated by a tenancy of equivalent size in Teddington alone.[94] A holding of three virgates in Teddington, perhaps identical with this, was granted by Abbot William Postard to Ailward of Charing and his wife Hawise, in the *Curia Regis* at Westminster on 26 November 1197.[95] Shepperton, given to Westminster by Archbishop Dunstan and confirmed by King Edward, was held for some time in the early twelfth century by Ranulf the chancellor. Following his death in January 1123, Shepperton was restored to the abbey, together with other lands of Westminster's which he had held.[96] Not long after this, it was granted in farm to Robert Crevequer.[97]

Cowley Peachey was donated by Archbishop Dunstan. An estate there was held of the abbey in the early twelfth century by Hugh of Colham,[98] probably the man of that name who was appointed dapifer and proctor of the abbey in the last years of the eleventh century.[99] The annual rent at that time was presumably the £1 10s from Cowley included in the early twelfth century

89 *English Episcopal Acta, II, Canterbury 1162–1190*, ed. C.R. Cheney and B.E.A. Jones (Oxford, 1986), no. 69.
90 *Ibid.*, no. 70.
91 *Westminster Abbey Charters*, nos 460–61.
92 Harvey, *Westminster Abbey and its Estates*, p. 354.
93 Westminster Abbey Domesday, ff. 155v–156; calendared *Westminster Abbey Charters*, no. 133.
94 *Ibid.*, no. 452.
95 *Ibid.*, no. 316.
96 *Regesta Regum Anglo-Normannorum*, II, no. CCCIII. See also *Westminster Abbey Charters*, no. 83.
97 Harvey, *Westminster Abbey and its Estates*, p. 354.
98 *Westminster Abbey Charters*, no. 453.
99 *Ibid.*, nos 47, 488.

'monks' farm'.[100] Cowley descended to Hugh's son Richard and then to Richard's nephew, William of Northolt, archdeacon of Gloucester (and subsequently bishop of Worcester). William, c.1177x86, granted two hides of his inheritance to his sergeant Robert Simple, who would render the service due to the abbot and convent of Westminster, and also one besant (2 shillings) annually to William and his heirs, in recognition of his right in that land.[101] Walter of Greenford, nephew of William of Northolt, confirmed Robert Simple in this tenancy, in William's lifetime, together with an assart in Northolt, which Derewyn of Roxeth formerly held of William of Northolt. The agreement reached was that Robert Simple would undertake sole responsibility for the service due to the abbot and convent of Westminster, while the plaintiffs would warrant the land against Walter of Greenford.[102] On the same occasion, Roger of Missenden, nephew of William of Northolt, confirmed to Robert Simple and his heirs these same lands, to be held of William and his heirs.[103] In 1204, a dispute over the service due from this land concluded when Robert Simple undertook sole responsibility for rendering it to the abbot and convent of Westminster, while Roger de la Dune and Godfrey son of Ralph would warrant the land against Walter of Greenford.[104]

Staines was a demesne manor, donated by King Edward.[105] William I apparently issued a confirmatory writ, although the text, in its surviving form, appears inflated. At this period, 1081x86, the manor was a said to augment the diet of the monks,[106] although it was later assigned to the abbot's portion.[107] In the later twelfth century, land in Staines known as New Court was appropriated by Richard of Ilchester, the powerful royal official who became bishop of Winchester (1173–88). He treated it as his own demesne, although when his son, Herbert le Poer, succeeded to it, he rendered 10 shillings annually to the abbot, until he eventually quitclaimed it in 1191x94.[108] A much smaller tenement in Staines, held by Ralph Swift of Matthew of Staines, rendered 1s 6d annually, 6 pence of which Matthew granted annually to St Edward on the feast of his Translation (13 October).[109] The only other evidence of any sub-tenancy in Staines over the period under discussion concerns the appurtenant pasture land of Yeoveney, which Walter Fitz Oter acquired by some unauthorized means in the late eleventh century. Abbot Vitalis recovered his title to it in a lawsuit heard by unnamed 'bishops

100 *Ibid.*, no. 339.
101 *Ibid.*, no. 453.
102 *Ibid.*, no. 454 and note.
103 *Ibid.*, no. 455.
104 *Ibid.*, no. 454 and note.
105 Harvey, *Westminster Abbey and its Estates*, p. 354.
106 *Regesta Regum Anglo-Normannorum*, I, no. XXXVII. See also *Westminster Abbey Charters*, no. 38.
107 Harvey, *Westminster Abbey and its Estates*, p. 354.
108 *Westminster Abbey Charters*, no. 457.
109 *Ibid.*, no. 458.

and barons', and the land was subsequently confirmed to Abbot Gilbert by William II.[110] Some interests in Yeoveney were acquired late in the twelfth century by Richard de Barentin, and subsequently by his brother Thomas. These men were sons of Alexander de Barentin, a *pincerna* (butler) of King Henry II, and nephews of Richard of Ilchester.[111] At Michaelmas 1192, their wardship was granted to their cousin, Herbert le Poer, archdeacon of Canterbury, but was acquired at Michaelmas 1194 by William de Sainte Merè Eglise.[112] Richard came of age c.1195x96, when he made a grant in inheritance of certain Norman lands to William de *Ripuaria*, who would render Richard annually 40 shillings sterling at Yeoveney in England.[113] By Michaelmas 1212 Richard had been succeeded by his brother Thomas, who quitclaimed land in Yeoveney to Osbert, son of Alfred *de Lilleseye*, at a rent of 7 shillings annually, apart from the service due to the king, insofar as it pertained to the free land in that tenement.[114] The Barentin brothers perhaps acquired their initial interest in Yeoveney through the unauthorized presence of their influential uncle, Richard of Ilchester, in the adjacent Staines.

Hanwell, another demesne manor which was donated by Archbishop Dunstan,[115] gave rise to very little documentation in the period under discussion, apart from a claim to quittance on all secular service on one virgate there. This appeared in a complex forgery purporting to be a charter of King Stephen, dating from 1150x1152.[116] This claim to quittance was reiterated in a confirmation, by Archbishop Theobald, in his capacity as papal legate, of several grants by King Stephen.[117]

Westminster's interests in the city of London were well-developed by the period under discussion. King Edward's awareness of the commercial potential of the city was said to be one of the reasons for his decision to develop Westminster as his *Eigenkloster*.[118] Three of his writs for the abbey deal specifically with its rights in London. One, dating from the early years of his reign, ordered that the monks were to have the land and the wharf which Ulf the portreeve and his wife Cynegyth gave, as fully as they possessed it, together with full freedom in everything which arose there on land and on

110 Armitage Robinson, *Gilbert Crispin*, p. 138, no. 12.

111 *Westminster Abbey Charters*, nos 135, 139, 143–4.

112 *Pipe Rolls 3 and 4 Richard I*, p. 305; cf. *Pipe Roll 5 Richard I*, p.161; *Pipe Roll 6 Richard I*, pp. 20, 182. On Herbert le Poer, see John Le Neve, *Fasti Ecclesiae Anglicanae, 1066–1300, II, Monastic Cathedrals*, compiled Diana E. Greenway (London, 1971), p. 14 and note 1.

113 Westminster Abbey Domesday, f. 140v.

114 *Ibid.*, f. 140v. On Thomas's succession to Richard, see *Pipe Roll 14 John*, p. 85. Cf. *Pipe Roll 16 John*, p. 164; *Pipe Roll 2 Henry III*, p. 46; *Pipe Roll 3 Henry III*, p. 76; *Pipe Roll 14 Henry III*, p. 99.

115 Harvey, *Westminster Abbey and its Estates*, p. 352.

116 *Regesta Regum Anglo-Normannorum*, III, no. 941.

117 Saltman, *Theobald, Archbishop of Canterbury*, pp. 505–6, no. 275.

118 *The Life of King Edward who Rests at Westminster*, ed. and transl. Frank Barlow, 2nd edn (Oxford, 1992), pp. 68–9.

strand. While this writ substantially represents a donation of Edward's, its terms may have been enhanced by the monks.[119] Two further writs concerning London date from the later years of his reign. One, addressed to Bishop William, the portreeves Leofstan and Ælfsige and the burh thegns of London, notified them that he had granted to the abbey full freedom upon all its lands, with judicial and financial rights as fully and completely as he himself possessed them. He invoked a blessing on the man who increased the freedom of the abbey, and the honour of St Peter, and a curse on him who diminished them.[120] A second writ apparently dating from the last week of the king's life, and addressed to the same men, informed them that he had granted to Westminster, at its dedication, full freedom on all its lands, with a series of judicial privileges.[121] These writs, too, appear to represent King Edward's intentions for the abbey, including the emphasis on the commercial liberty known as 'showing'. On the other hand, they have almost certainly been elaborated.[122] Two writs in the name of William I which appear to date from the last years of his reign, and to confirm the privileges granted by the two later writs of King Edward, are themselves of doubtful authenticity. The second of William's writs elaborated on the abbey's rights in its marketplaces, with their stalls and shops, rents and meat-market, rights and tolls. All merchants who, in the time of King Edward, landed or put in at the soke or stalls or wharves of St Peter to stay there might now return under the king's peace.[123]

The abbey's active commercial presence in London during the later eleventh century readily accounts for the effort put into obtaining, or else producing in-house, documentation of its privileged status in the city. A third, and even more elaborate version of the privileges claimed in the spurious writs of William I is found in the so-called Fourth Charter of King William, supposedly dating from 2 January 1081. This too confirms the property and privileges of the abbey in London, and grants protection to the merchants residing on the soke of St Peter.[124] Houses and land were acquired there at this time.[125] Interest focused on the accumulation of sites with a mercantile potential, including the *curia*, with its houses and its wharf lying at the head of London Bridge, which were acquired from Alwold of St Botolph's gate, and were said to have been held since the time of King Edward.[126] The value of residential rents was already considerable, as indicated by the £3 required annually by Abbot Vitalis in return for the land called *Vuerc*, in the city,

119 *Anglo-Saxon Writs*, no. 75 and p. 308.
120 *Ibid.*, no. 105.
121 *Ibid.*, no. 106.
122 *Ibid.*, pp. 332–4.
123 *Regesta Regum Anglo-Normannorum*, I, nos 215 (=XXX), 216.
124 *Westminster Abbey Charters*, no. 33.
125 *Regesta Regum Anglo-Normannorum*, I, no. XX; Armitage Robinson, *Gilbert Crispin*, p. 128, no. 2.
126 *Regesta Regum Anglo-Normannorum*, I, no. XXXI.

which he granted to Gerald and his heirs.[127] One long-running grievance of the monks was their failure to secure St Mary Newchurch with its appurtenant lands and houses, granted to them by Alward of London and confirmed by William I.[128] This church, also known as 'St Mary Woolchurch' or 'St Mary of Westcheap', was confirmed by William II on two occasions[129] and subsequently by both Henry I and King Stephen,[130] but entirely without success. The powerful official Eudo dapifer had taken possession of Newchurch and conveyed it to the abbey of St John's, Colchester, which upheld its title by a series of blatant forgeries.[131]

King Henry I confirmed the lands in London given by the three daughters of Deorman, in return for rights of confraternity and burial. The fact that his confirmation was necessary indicates that the women's father was the Deorman the moneyer named on coins of King Edward and of William I.[132] This confirmation dates from the earlier part of the reign, as does another confirming several City churches with their appurtenant lands, houses and parishes.[133] A further confirmation of the abbey's lands and customary rights in the City extended over future acquisitions.[134] Particular care was taken to obtain writs protecting the financial immunities of the merchants living on the abbey's land[135] or, more specifically, residing in the soke of St Peter, as Kings Edward and William I were said to have conceded.[136] All rents from London properties at this time contributed towards the monks' farm.[137] The king ordered that the chamberlains and sheriffs were to render to the sacrist of Westminster in perpetuity a halfpenny daily from the farm of London, to maintain a light at the tomb of his first wife, Queen Edith-Matilda.[138] She herself had conceded to Abbot Gilbert a tenement on the abbot's wharf in London, together with sake and soke and customary rights.[139] A charter of King Stephen, dating from the early years of his reign, ordered that the men of the soke of St Peter were to be quit of the Hustings and Folkmoot, as their charter attested.[140]

Probably during the vacancy between Abbots Herbert and Gervase, the monks notified the citizens of London that they had conceded to Eorlwin,

127 *Westminster Abbey Charters*, no. 234.
128 Armitage Robinson, *Gilbert Crispin*, p. 131, no. 5.
129 *Ibid.*, p. 137, nos 10–11.
130 *Ibid.*, p. 159. King Stephen's writ named the donor of this church as Gislan.
131 *Ibid.*, pp. 158–66.
132 *Ibid.*, pp. 147–8, no. 29; *Westminster Abbey Charters*, no. 68 and note.
133 Armitage Robinson, *Gilbert Crispin*, p. 148, no. 30; see also *Regesta Regum Anglo-Normannorum*, II, no. CCCIV.
134 *Formulare Anglicanum*, no. LXV.
135 *Ibid.*, no. CCCCXCVI.
136 *Regesta Regum Anglo-Normannorum*, II, no. CXXVIII.
137 *Westminster Abbey Charters*, no. 339.
138 Armitage Robinson, *Gilbert Crispin*, p. 156, no. 39.
139 *Ibid.*, p. 155, no. 38.
140 *Regesta Regum Anglo-Normannorum*, III, no. 927.

brother of Wlfwin, in fee and inheritance, the land with the building on it which Godric Catepol held of their chamberlain in Eastcheap. Eorlwin would render 7 shillings annually, whether or not there was any outbreak of fire (which would destroy the building).[141] Geoffrey de Mandeville II, earl of Essex, was granted control of the Tower of London by the Empress, in the summer of 1141. It was probably about this time that he granted to the abbey land in London with an annual rental of 20 shillings, due on the anniversary of his mother, for the use of the monks in the refectory.[142] This grant is an early instance of similar ones of later date whereby the monks were induced to chant heartily during the commemoration of a particular *obit*, heartened by the thought of a particularly good meal afterwards.

Several charters of Abbot Gervase record him granting out property in London, including a church, in return for rents.[143] In one case this would contribute towards the clothing of the monks.[144]

The spurious charter of liberties surviving in the name of Henry II included a confirmation of the lands granted by citizens of London,[145] an indication of the steady build-up of Westminster's property portfolio in the City. Abbot Lawrence is recorded on several occasions negotiating with tenants their rents on City properties, including some in Cheap and in the Fishmarket.[146] Similar charters in the name of Abbot Walter variously relate to land bordering the Thames, in the parish of St Mary Staining Lane, several in Friday Street, Bread Street, Cheap and Aldersgate.[147] While most of these properties were residential, one grant included a third-share in a seld (a stall in a covered market-hall).[148] On occasion the monks are recorded, acting without the abbot, in the administration of their City properties, for instance, in transactions with co-heiresses, dating from c.1179x1181 over land in Dowgate.[149]

Abbot William Postard is also recorded, although with less frequency than his recent predecessors, both negotiating rents within the City[150] and also obtaining, by means of an exchange, land in the Strand (described as being near 'the White Monastery of the Holy Innocents', i.e. St Mary le Strand.[151] Over this period, Westminster's focus of interest was apparently shifting from the City towards its western suburbs and the immediate neighbourhood of the abbey itself, although one charter of Abbot Ralph records a rental agreement concerning houses between Ludgate and Fleet Bridge.[152]

The charters granted to Westminster by citizens of London conveyed properties in many of its parishes. The standardized format does not usually indicate whether the monks had deliberately tried to build up their holdings

141 *Westminster Abbey Charters*, no. 340.
142 *Ibid.*, no. 350.
143 *Ibid.*, nos 256–60.
144 *Ibid.*, no. 258.
145 *Ibid.*, no. 123.
146 *Ibid.*, nos 275–8.
147 *Ibid.*, nos 289–95.
148 *Ibid.*, no. 295.
149 *Ibid.*, nos 342–3.
150 *Ibid.*, nos 307–8.
151 *Ibid.*, no. 309.
152 *Ibid.*, no. 327.

in particular areas. Some of the properties acquired in this way had an obvious commercial potential. William *de Camera* and his wife Eluva Lombard granted land with buildings and a wharf, c.1191x11196.[153] Land, with an appurtenant wharf, in the parish of St Mary at Hill, was also acquired from William Fitz Alulf in 1201x1202.[154] The location of this parish, which bordered on the Thames, was perhaps a consideration when other interests were acquired there at a slightly earlier date.[155] Possibly too, there was a commercial potential in the property in the parish of St Margaret 'towards London Bridge' i.e. Bridge Street, or New Bridge Street, acquired from Matilda de Paris in the reign of King John.[156] Richard Blund granted one of his stalls in the parish of St Nicholas Shambles in the mid-twelfth century.[157] Rather later, rent from land was acquired in West Cheap, located between two identified shops and presumably therefore itself commercial premises.[158] Rent was also acquired, in King John's reign, from a shop in the Fishmarket.[159] Some grants of land or rent did not specify the parish in which they lay, even though the premises were clearly identified in relation to those of their immediate neighbours. This applies, perhaps surprisingly, to a grant by Henry Fitz Ailwin, soon to become London's first mayor.[160] Similarly, Andrew Bucherel, about to set out for Jerusalem, perhaps on the Third Crusade, identified the rent which he granted simply as that from land in London pertaining to the monks' fee. He also bequeathed money to enable the monks to buy a further property which would bring in a rent income. In return, the monks would commemorate the anniversary of his death and those of his ancestors. If he did return from the Holy Land, he undertook not to retract any part of his donation.[161] Other property transactions in the late twelfth and early thirteenth centuries related variously to lands in Ludgate,[162] *Musterlingebur*,[163] the parish of St Alphege, Cripplegate, and also land in the direction of the Tower of London,[164] and in the parish of St Faith 'in the crypt of St Paul's'.[165]

Suburban properties, lying outside Ludgate, were acquired from several individuals between the last years of Henry II's reign and that of King John.[166] Interests were also acquired, about the same time, in Fleet Street,[167] and in the parish of St Clement Danes.[168]

Fuller documentation, however, survives from transactions relating to properties in the immediate vicinity of the abbey. The earliest, dating from 1083x1086, is a grant by Abbot Gilbert Crispin to William Baynard of the berewick of Tothill in Westminster, to be held for the service of one knight,

153 *Ibid.*, no. 353.
154 *Ibid.*, no. 377.
155 *Ibid.*, nos 378–9.
156 *Ibid.*, no. 371. See also nos 370, 372–3.
157 *Ibid.*, no. 385.
158 *Ibid.*, no. 355.
159 *Ibid.*, no. 356.
160 *Ibid.*, no. 351.
161 *Ibid.*, no. 352.
162 *Ibid.*, nos 358–60.
163 *Ibid.*, no. 361.
164 *Ibid.*, no. 362.
165 *Ibid.*, no. 364.
166 *Ibid.*, nos 386–91.
167 *Ibid.*, no. 392.
168 *Ibid.*, nos 393–6.

as it had earlier been held by the thegn Wulfric Bordewate.[169] The area soon had a commercial potential, indicated by a writ of King Henry I, dating from c.1129x1133, in which he instructed Richard Basset and Aubrey de Vere that the abbot was to have his stalls in the 'new work' as in the old, as he had ordered. This 'new work' was possibly some building project ordered by the king, outside the abbey precincts, while the abbot's stalls were perhaps for a fair or for a market.[170]

Residential property in Westminster begins to be documented from the time of Abbot Gervase, who 'conceded' to Gerin, the king's minister, the land of Endiff which he had bought from Walkelin and his heirs.[171] This land lay slightly down-river, between the abbey and Charing.[172] A valuable boost to the profitability of the manor of Westminster came c.1150 x *ante* May 1152, with a grant from King Stephen of quittance of geld on six and a half hides.[173] The monastic *scriptorium* then used this grant as a basis for a forgery in which the king was represented as quitclaiming not only gelds, but also other customary financial exactions.[174] Residential development increased markedly in the later twelfth century, when the royal government was increasingly concentrated at Westminster, so that dignitaries and officials found it advisable to maintain a residence there. In 1194x98, Henry Marshall, bishop of Exeter, bought land in Longditch Street, Westminster, from Geoffrey Picot and built on it a chapel (presumably adjoining his residence) for the use of visiting staff of the Exeter diocese. It was agreed that, while the divine office might be celebrated there, the chapel was not to function to the prejudice of the abbey church, nor to that of St Margaret's Westminster, in which parish the land was situated.[175] At much the same time as this was agreed, Abbot William Postard and the convent confirmed to the king's chamberlain, Robert Mauduit (II), their houses in Longditch, together with the lands and meadows which William, the usher of Abbot Walter 'gave and conceded' to the abbey.[176] The abbot also granted Robert licence to have a chapel in his residence in Longditch, under restrictions designed to ensure that St Margaret's Westminster did not suffer financial loss, and provided that the chapel functioned only when Robert and his wife were in residence.[177] Longditch Street continued to be an area preferred by dignitaries; Abbot Ralph and the chapter granted land there to Ralph Fitz Stephen of

169 *Ibid.*, no. 236.

170 Armitage Robinson, *Gilbert Crispin*, p. 157, no. 43. See also *Westminster Abbey Charters*, no. 94, note.

171 *Westminster Abbey Charters*, no. 261.

172 J.E.B. Gover, A. Mawer, and F.M. Stenton, with S.J. Madge, *The Place-Names of Middlesex*, English Place Name Society, XVIII (Cambridge, 1942), p. 168.

173 *Regesta Regum Anglo-Normannorum*, III, no. 938.

174 *Ibid.*, nos 939, 941.

175 *Westminster Abbey Charters*, no. 230.

176 *Ibid.*, no. 311.

177 *Ibid.*, no. 312.

Boulogne, who would render a rent due to the high altar, besides the forinsec service.[178] Another eminent resident of this period was the king's treasurer, William of Ely, admitted by Abbot William Postard c.1196, as tenant of certain houses and lands formerly held by Richard Fitz Nigel (*alias* 'of Ely'), bishop of London, and granted by the bishop to William.[179] Property continued to be acquired in the district around the church of St Mary le Strand. Abbot William and the convent quitclaimed to Henry Fitz Reygner a rent of 3 shillings 'at the gate of his house' in exchange for land between St Mary le Strand and the Thames. Its width varied from 31 ells to 37, in the middle, then narrowing to 34 ells. In length it was 102 ells.[180] On 11 November 1198 this irregularly-shaped plot was granted to Stephen of Turnham and his wife Edelina, in exchange for one and a half virgates and two hides of land in Battersea.[181]

The promotion of the Lady Altar of the abbey generated many property transactions. Three charters of Prior Robert Moulsham record transactions by which he granted out various tenements in Westminster in return for rents due to the Lady Altar: to William English of Westminster (an Exchequer officer);[182] to Geoffrey Picot;[183] and to Adam, a sergeant of the church of Westminster.[184]

The extent of urbanization and the management of this urban property in Westminster, between approximately 1190 and 1216, are well documented.[185] There are grants (which were sometimes clearly sales) of property to the Lady Altar;[186] transactions between individuals concerning land which was subsequently acquired by the monks, who then used the income to support it,[187] besides the tenancy agreements made by the prior in his capacity as warden or proctor of the Altar.[188] This proliferation of transactions relating to small, usually residential, properties, reflects the fact that, following the death of King Edward in January 1066, there was no sustained royal patronage of the abbey until the time of Henry III. Meanwhile, if the monks wanted to extend their endowment, or to finance a new project such as the Lady Altar, they had to look elsewhere for support. The vast majority of those who donated lands to the abbey over the period under discussion were,

178 *Ibid.*, no. 328.

179 *Ibid.*, no. 313. The bishop's grant to William is printed by H.G. Richardson, 'William of Ely, the King's Treasurer', *Transactions of the Royal Historical Society*, fourth series, 15 (1932), pp. 79–80, no. I.

180 *Westminster Abbey Charters*, no. 309.

181 *Ibid.*, no. 314.

182 *Ibid.*, no. 346.

183 *Ibid.*, no. 347.

184 *Ibid.*, no. 348.

185 *Ibid.*, nos 405–51.

186 *Ibid.*, nos 407–8, 410–12, 414–15, 417–18, 420, 422–7.

187 *Ibid.*, nos 405–6, 409, 413, 416, 419, 421, 428.

188 *Ibid.*, nos 346–8.

therefore either citizens of London or else residents of the suburb of Westminster. Sometimes, reciprocal concessions such as grants of confraternity[189] or of burial in the abbey,[190] or of the recording of the benefactor's name in the abbey's martyrology[191] were granted in those cases where the transaction was indeed one of gift rather than a lightly disguised sale.

By one means and another the abbot and monks were able to consolidate their holdings in certain parts of London and Westminster, mainly with the intention of generating a good rent income. Even in London rents were occasionally acquired for the Lady Altar.[192] Perhaps the majority of City tenements in areas such as Ludgate[193] for instance, were residential. On the other hand, there was a pronounced interest both in wharves, and in plots fronting the Thames,[194] and also in commercial areas, where individual shops were acquired.[195] Occasionally a building was specifically said to be of stone,[196] which indicates that often others were not. The move towards the increased use of building-stone is traditionally said to have occurred during the mayoralty of Henry Fitz Ailwin, during the reigns of Richard and John, when stone walls were encouraged in order to lessen the spread of fires.[197]

In the vill of Westminster, property transactions focused on Charing,[198] on Longditch[199] and on Tothill Street,[200] together with some concentration on St James's, which takes its name from a leper-house of that dedication.[201] The gradual urbanization of the whole vill from the late twelfth century onwards has been documented in further detail by Gervase Rosser.[202]

189 *Ibid.*, nos 235, 329, 334, 338, 359, 388, 400.
190 *Ibid.*, nos 237, 388, 436.
191 *Ibid.*, nos 328–9, 385.
192 *Ibid.*, no. 356.
193 *Ibid.*, no. 358.
194 For example, *ibid.*, 353.
195 *Ibid.*, nos 356–7.
196 For example, *ibid.*, no. 370.
197 *London Assize of Nuisance 1301–1431: a Calendar*, ed. Helena M. Chew and W. Kellaway, London Record Soc., 10 (1973), ix; T. Baker, *Medieval London* (London, 1970), p. 202.
198 *Westminster Abbey Charters*, 390.
199 *Ibid.*, nos 230, 311–12, 328, 442, 444–5.
200 *Ibid.*, nos 236, 407, 427, 447–51.
201 *Ibid.*, 390, 427, 441.
202 G. Rosser, *Medieval Westminster 1200–1540* (Oxford, 1989).

12

Westminster Abbey in the Monastic World

Westminster, like most of the larger monasteries, controlled a number of small houses, or cells, and from time to time took action to ensure that these neither tried to become too independent, nor fell under the control of some rival religious house. The abbots of Westminster also took action, from time to time, to ensure the safety of the endowments of these cells.

Hurley (Berks.) was founded in 1085x86, when Geoffrey de Mandeville I made a grant to Westminster of the church of St Mary of Hurley, with the whole vill and the surrounding wood, except for the land of Edric the reeve, and that of the rustics of Waltham St Laurence, Berks., which he retained. Osmund, bishop of Salisbury, was present at the dedication of the church of Hurley, and confirmed further specified endowments. Geoffrey obtained from William I confirmation of these endowments, and Abbot Gilbert declared anathema on everyone who infringed this gift. Geoffrey made the grant for his soul; for that of his wife Lesceline, who counselled this benefaction; and for that of his deceased wife Alice, the mother of his sons. The stability of this grant was ensured by the attestations of Lesceline and of Geoffrey's sons, together with the presence of the diocesan bishop.[1] At a later date, probably c.1144x1166, a scribe working at Hurley wrote a much more elaborate version of this charter, together with supposed confirmations of the priory's endowments by King Henry I and Geoffrey de Mandeville (II). While the lands claimed in the forgeries did not differ from those listed in Hurley's genuine charters of the period, the fabrications were much more explicit about the rights said to have been given with them.[2] Westminster's concern

1 *Westminster Abbey Charters 1066–c.1214*, ed. Emma Mason, assisted by the late Jennifer Bray, continuing the work of the late Desmond J. Murphy, London Record Society, 25 (1988), no. 462. See also J. Armitage Robinson, *Gilbert Crispin, Abbot of Westminster* (Cambridge, 1911), pp. 32–3.

2 P. Chaplais, 'The Original Charters of Herbert and Gervase, Abbots of Westminster (1121–1157)', reprinted from *A Medieval Miscellany for Doris Mary Stenton*, ed. Patricia M. Barnes and C.F. Slade, Pipe Roll Society, new series, XXXVI (London, 1962), in Chaplais, *Essays in Medieval Diplomacy and Administration* (London, 1981), pp. XVIII, 89–110 and Addendum (unnumbered), at pp. 97–8. See also Barbara Harvey, *Westminster Abbey and its Estates in the Middle Ages* (Oxford, 1977), pp. 337–8.

for the economic viability of Hurley is reflected in a charter of Abbot Gervase, addressed to Earl Geoffrey de Mandeville, and notifying him that he has granted to Prior William of Hurley part of the pannage which Westminster held in Edmonton (Middx) from the time of the first Geoffrey de Mandeville. The earl was urged to confirm this grant and to notify his officers of it.[3] The uncertainty about the dates of the term of office of Prior William[4] renders it unclear whether the Geoffrey to whom Gervase wrote was Geoffrey the first earl (1140–44) or his son, who was earl from c. January 1156. Prior William was still in office when Abbot Lawrence granted to the priory the church of Easthampstead (Berks.), to provide extra food for the brothers on the feast of St Edward.[5] The abbot did not mention the consent of the monks of Westminster to this grant, although the omission may be inadvertent, and the result of the unusually grandiose prose. Yet some disquiet seems to have arisen, either at Westminster or at Hurley, since Abbot Walter subsequently issued a further charter, more plainly worded, and clearly associating the convent of Westminster with his 'grant and concession' of the church to Hurley.[6]

Great Malvern (Worcs.) was a second of Westminster's cells. It originated as a hermitage established in the later eleventh century by Aldwin, a monk of Worcester. Discouraged by initial hardships, he planned to make the pilgrimage to Jerusalem, but Bishop Wulfstan (1062–95) predicted the future success of a monastery on the site. When William of Malmesbury re-wrote Wulfstan's *Life*, c.1124–42, he noted that Great Malvern held some thirty inmates.[7] But while Aldwin was a former monk of Worcester, his hermitage lay on land donated by Earl Æthelwine (or Odda), whose estates were later given by King Edward to Westminster.[8] Great Malvern is not mentioned in the Domesday Survey, so that the development from hermitage to priory presumably took place during the abbacy of Gilbert Crispin. Abbot Gilbert and the convent are said to have given to Great Malvern lands adjoining Powick, when the boundaries of these were perambulated by the Westminster monks Hugh and Warner.[9] In c.1126–27, King Henry I confirmed Abbot Gilbert's donation of land in Baldenhall, together with other lands and churches which he granted, besides the gifts of other benefactors, chiefly members of

3 *Westminster Abbey Charters*, no. 266.

4 D. Knowles, C.N.L. Brooke and Vera C.M. London, *The Heads of Religious Houses England and Wales 940–1216* (Cambridge, 1972), p. 92.

5 *Westminster Abbey Charters*, no. 285.

6 *Ibid.*, no. 302.

7 *The Vita Wulfstani of William of Malmesbury*, ed. R.R. Darlington, Camden Third Series, XL (London, 1928), p. 26; William of Malmesbury *De Gestis Pontificum Anglorum*, ed. N.E.S.A. Hamilton, Rolls Series (London, 1870), pp. 285–6.

8 *Vita Wulfstani*, pp. xli–xlii; Harvey, *Westminster Abbey and its Estates*, p. 30.

9 W. Dugdale, *Monasticon Anglicanum*, revised H. Caley, H. Ellis and B. Bandinel, 6 vols in 8 (London, 1817–30), III, pp. 447–8; *Calendar of Patent Rolls 1374–77*, p. 282. See also *Westminster Abbey Charters*, no. 243 note.

the FitzPons family. The monks of Great Malvern were to be quit of the rent of 4 shillings paid by their predecessors for Baldenhall, and the sum was to be allocated to their credit at the Tallies (the forerunner of the Exchequer) as ordered by King William I.[10] The manor of Powick was granted at farm to Great Malvern by Abbot Herbert and the convent of Westminster for £24 annually. They were to hold the manor so long as they remained obedient to Westminster, and the abbot would exercise those customary rights which he held in other manors similarly at farm.[11] Some time before August 1134, a monk of Great Malvern absconded and made his way to Westminster. Abbot Herbert and Prior Edwy listened to the monk's excuse for his defection and considered it a reasonable one. They were prepared to admit him to Westminster, with the status of a professed monk of the house, until they discovered that he had begun work on a missal for Worcester cathedral priory. They accordingly sent him back to Worcester, with a letter addressed to Prior Warin, Uhtred the precentor and the monks, asking them to show mercy to him and treat him well until Herbert's next visit to the region when he hoped to learn more of the reasons for the monk's absconding.[12]

Another, but much smaller cell, was also founded in the time of Abbot Gilbert. This was Sudbury in Suffolk, which owed its origins to the donation of St Bartholomew's church there by the moneyer Wulfric, when he became a monk of Westminster. There followed some dispute, which was adjudged to the abbey in the royal court, in presence of the king's barons. Subsequently, c.1114x1116, Henry I notified the bishop of Norwich, Herbert Losinga, and officials in Suffolk that he upheld the abbey's title.[13] The cell was always a small one, with perhaps two inmates at any time, neither of them dignified with the title of prior.[14] Recruitment, however, was perhaps largely local, rather than achieved by the secondment of monks from Westminster. A writ of King Henry II notified William de Turba, bishop of Norwich, and the barons of Suffolk, that he confirmed to the monks of St Bartholomew's, Sudbury, two parts of the tithe of *Torp*, which Ivo gave from his demesne when he became a monk there, to hold as Henry I had confirmed by charter.[15]

Hurley, Great Malvern and Sudbury were the only recognized cells of Westminster, and the monks were determined to ensure that the inmates of all three acknowledged the abbey's rights over them. Great Malvern, however, attempted to secure its independence, apparently by trying to play off the abbey against the bishop of Worcester. Malvern obtained a papal

10 *Regesta Regum Anglo-Normannorum, II, 1100–1135*, ed. C. Johnson and H.A. Cronne (Oxford, 1956), no. 1490.

11 *Westminster Abbey Charters*, no. 243.

12 *Ibid.*, no. 248A.

13 Dugdale, *Monasticon III*, p. 459, no. I; *Westminster Abbey Charters*, no. 72.

14 D. Knowles and R.N. Hadcock, *Medieval Religious Houses England and Wales* (London, 1971), p. 77.

15 Dugdale, *Monasticon*, III, p. 459, no. II; *Westminster Abbey Charters*, no. 130.

privilege, but Abbot Gervase refused to recognize it. Adrian IV deputed Archbishop Theobald to hear the case, and Gervase was then supported by Gilbert Foliot, at this time bishop of Hereford, and by Abbot Hamelin of Gloucester and Abbot Reginald of Pershore. Theobald accordingly put pressure on the monks of Malvern, who eventually prostrated themselves at the feet of Gervase, asked pardon and abandoned their papal privilege. Walter, bishop of Rochester, and Silvester, abbot of St Augustine's, mediated peace between the parties. Archbishop Theobald concluded his report to the pope by reiterating that Great Malvern had always been subject to Westminster, adding that any weakening of its rights would be detrimental to the customs of all monasteries. Finally he asked the pope to give a sympathetic hearing to the 'just petitions' of Gervase.[16] This request was met when a Westminster delegation reached the Lateran in the Spring of 1157. On 25 May, Pope Adrian IV addressed a bull to Gervase and the convent, confirming the abbey's jurisdiction over Great Malvern.[17] A week later, on 1 June, a further bull was obtained, confirming Westminster's rights over all three cells, in addition to its various churches and chapels.[18] This was reinforced by a bull of Pope Alexander III, dated at Sens on 6 October 1163, and addressed to Abbot Lawrence, confirming Westminster's control over Great Malvern, Hurley and Sudbury.[19] Having secured control over Great Malvern, however, Westminster was not always equally observant of the rights of the diocesan bishop. In the later twelfth century, there were two known occasions on which the abbot attempted to institute a new prior into Great Malvern without the consent of the bishop of Worcester. The first such episode was certainly instigated by Abbot Walter, and it was probably on his initiative that the second occurred, although the situation was resolved only after his death.[20]

The church of Sawbridgeworth was served by monks in the 1120s, but most likely they acted only in a pastoral capacity.[21] No attempt seems to have been made to develop this site as a cell.

One further small religious house associated with Westminster, although not confirmed as a dependency as the official cells were, was the female community which became in time the nunnery of Kilburn (Middx). In the

16 A. Saltman, *Theobald, Archbishop of Canterbury* (reprinted New York, 1969), pp. 88–9; *The Letters of John of Salisbury, I (1153–1161)*, ed. W.J. Millor and H.E. Butler, revised C.N.L. Brooke (London, 1955), pp. 80–81, no. 45.

17 *Papsturkunden in England*, ed. W. Holtzmann, 3 vols, Abhandlungen der Gesellschaft der Wissenschaften in Göttingen, phil.-hist. Klasse, Berlin, Göttingen (I = neue Folge XXV, 1930–31; II = 3 Folge XIV–XV, 1935–6; III = 3 Folge XXXIII, 1952), I, no. 68.

18 *Ibid.*, no. 70.

19 *Ibid.*, I, no. 101.

20 Mary G. Cheney, *Roger, Bishop of Worcester 1164–1179* (Oxford, 1980), pp. 374–6. See also *The Cartulary of Worcester Cathedral Priory (Register I)*, Pipe Roll Society, new series, XXXVIII (London, 1968), nos 301, 303.

21 *Westminster Abbey Charters*, no. 469 and note.

later eleventh century and the early twelfth, a number of Benedictine monasteries afforded protection to small groups of women leading a religious life. In the course of the twelfth century, many of these female commmunities were transformed into small nunneries. John Flete, the fifteenth-century historian of Westminster, wrote that the founding members of the Kilburn community were former maids-in-waiting to Queen Edith-Matilda, the first wife of King Henry I.[22] If that was the case, then they presumably comprised a rather informal religious community in the interval between her death in May 1118 and the first recorded documentation, in the form of two charters issued for them by Abbot Herbert. In that which appears to be the earlier of the two, dating from c.1134, the abbot, together with Prior Osbert de Clare and the monks, and with the assent of Gilbert the Universal, bishop of London, granted the hermitage of Kilburn, which Godwin built, and its lands, to three maidens: Emma, Gunhild and Christine. At the request and petition of this same Godwin the hermit, they would hold this property in alms, for the redemption of the souls of the monks, on the same conditions and with the same liberty which King Ethelred granted Hampstead to the church of Westminster and King Edward confirmed it. Godwin would be master of the community for his lifetime. After his death the community of women was, with the advice of the abbot, to elect as his replacement a suitable man of mature years. No one, not even the abbot or the prior, might intrude except with the express permission of the inmates, who would hold their possessions in the same way that the monks held theirs. The initial benefactions comprised 30 shillings' worth of the 60 shillings' worth of alms which Sweyn, father of Robert of Essex, gave to the abbey. Ailmar the priest also gave some land in Southwark, which rendered 2 shillings per annum.[23] In a slightly later charter Abbot Herbert, with the assent and advice of the convent, granted to the 'handmaids of God' (*ancillae Dei*) of the church of St John the Baptist, Kilburn, land to assart in Gore, which pertained to the abbey's manor of Knightsbridge.[24] Abbot Gervase granted to the *ancillae Christi* of Kilburn a full monastic corrody formerly belonging to Ailmar the hermit, and which he now confirmed with the advice and consent of the whole chapter. The abbot and monks also granted the corrody of Abbot Gilbert and were confirmed in possession of a third corrody which they were formerly granted by charter.[25] From now on the community, provided it remained small, would not go short of food or drink, including claret on feast days, or of tasty pittances. Abbot Lawrence confirmed the grants which his predecessors Herbert and Gervase had earlier granted to the *ancillae Christi* of Kilburn.[26] For a time, jurisdiction

22 John Flete, *The History of Westminster Abbey*, ed. J. Armitage Robinson (Cambridge, 1909), p. 88.

23 *Westminster Abbey Charters*, no. 249.

24 *Ibid.*, no. 250.

25 *Ibid.*, no. 264.

26 *Ibid.*, no. 280. See also Barbara Harvey, *Living and Dying in England 1100–1540: The Monastic Experience* (Oxford, 1993), pp. 239–40.

over this community was contested between the abbot and convent, on the one hand, and the bishop of London on the other. It was resolved when Bishop Gilbert confirmed to the (unnamed) abbot and his successors jurisdiction over the cell, rendering it permanently exempt from the jurisdiction of the bishop of London. The abbot and convent were empowered to administer the cell personally and through proctors. The identity of the bishop, and therefore also the date of his concession, are uncertain. Although the charter has been published with those of Bishop Gilbert Foliot (1163–87), its editors accept the possibility that the document is an act of Gilbert the Universal (1128–34).[27] A renewed agreement was made in 1231 between Bishop Roger Niger and Abbot Richard of Barking.[28] The question of jurisdiction which would naturally be raised by the diocesan bishop was perhaps compounded by the question of the women's status. In the abbots' charters they are termed *ancillae Dei* (or *Christi*) which is not the usual term for a nun. John Flete described Kilburn as 'a cell of canonesses'.[29] Sally Thompson, observing that later *magistri* of Kilburn seem not to have had any particular links with Westminster, remarks that one, Master Alexander of St Paul's, can possibly be identified with a known canon of the cathedral. She suggests that the women of the Kilburn community did not follow the Benedictine rule, and perhaps had a link with St Paul's.[30]

Confraternity agreements linked Westminster into an association of another kind. The earliest was with Durham cathedral priory, recorded in a *conventio* negotiated between Bishop William of St Calais and Abbot Vitalis, some time between 1080 and 1085. It was agreed that if either bishop or abbot died, then commemoration would be made for him in the other house as in his own. If any monk of Durham died, then seven full offices would be said for him by the convent, one priest would chant a mass for him, and the other brethren would chant the Psalter. Laymen who did not know the Psalter would recite the Paternoster (the Lord's Prayer) 150 times. The monks of Durham would do the same for the monks of Westminster.[31] An additional link with Durham was that these two monastic communities, together with those of Christ Church and St Augustine's Canterbury, shared their observance of the customary drawn up by Archbishop Lanfranc. William of St Calais made a total of fourteen confraternity agreements, including two with the Norman houses of Fécamp and Caen.[32] Westminster itself had an agreement with Fécamp, mentioned in Abbot Herbert's first charter for Kilburn, where it was stated that one of his benefactions was made

27 *The Letters and Charters of Gilbert Foliot*, ed. A. Morey and C.N.L. Brooke (Cambridge, 1967), p. 491, no. 463 and note; see also *Westminster Abbey Charters*, no. 205.

28 Dugdale, *Monasticon*, III, p. 428, no. IX.

29 Flete, *The History of Westminster Abbey*, p. 87.

30 Sally Thompson, *Women Religious: the Founding of English Nunneries after the Norman Conquest* (Oxford, 1991), p. 63.

31 *Westminster Abbey Charters*, no. 235.

32 Frank Barlow, *The English Church 1066–1154* (London, 1979), pp. 187–8.

for the repose of the souls of all monks of Westminster and for all the brethren of Fécamp, both living and dead.[33] This association with Fécamp probably dated from the time of Abbot Vitalis, who had once been a monk of that house.[34] In the early twelfth century (c.1115x24) Westminster was among twenty-eight Benedictine houses which had confraternity links with Rochester.[35]

While confraternity agreements would be made primarily with other Benedictine houses, personal links with communities attached to different traditions would occasionally lead to others. This was evident in the agreement between Abbot Guerin and the convent of St Victor, Paris, and the unnamed prior and monks of Westminster, probably drawn up either during the abbatial vacancy at Westminster between 1173 and 1175 or that in 1190–91. Guerin obtained the unanimous consent of his brethren that they would annually commemorate the deceased brethren of Westminster on 1 May, with vespers of nine *lections*, vigils and solemn Mass, and in return requested the prayers of the monks of Westminster.[36] The link with St Victor was made by Abbot Lawrence in his pre-monastic days, when he probably studied there, since he has been suggested as the author of a report of lectures given by Hugh of St Victor. Lawrence's style of *Magister* may imply that he subsequently taught in the Schools. Later, as abbot of Westminster, Lawrence wrote to his kinsman, Abbot *Ervisius* (?Hervey) of St Victor, commending to him a certain John, kinsman of the prior of Westminster, who wanted to study in the Schools. A similar letter, written c.1166, commended Lawrence's own nephew, another John. Abbot *Ervisius*, reputedly an Englishman, left an unsatisfactory reputation. During the Becket dispute, numerous English exiles were at his abbey.[37] Evidence for the full extent of Westminster's confraternity agreements is patchy, since the original document would be vulnerable to decay, and registration in an appropriate volume was not always ensured. For instance, while the agreement with St Victor was copied into Westminster's most prestigious cartulary, it was not suitably registered at the abbey of St Victor.[38] Westminster's confraternity agreements would probably be recorded in its martyrology, but this is now lost. Such agreements continued to be made beyond the period covered by this study. One between Westminster and Bury St Edmunds dates from the time of Abbot William de Humez[39] although practical links with such another prestigious Benedictine

33 *Westminster Abbey Charters*, no. 249.

34 *Regesta Regum Anglo-Normannorum, I, 1066–1100*, ed. H.W.C. Davis with R.J. Whitwell (Oxford, 1913), no. 91.

35 Barlow, *The English Church 1066–1154*, p. 188.

36 *Westminster Abbey Charters*, no. 400 and note.

37 *Ibid.*, note; F.E. Croydon, 'Abbot Lawrence of Westminster and Hugh of St Victor', *Medieval and Renaissance Studies*, II, ed. R. Hunt and R. Klibansky (1950), pp. 169–71.

38 *Westminster Abbey Charters*, no. 400 and note.

39 *Memorials of St Edmund's Abbey*, ed. T. Arnold, 3 vols, Rolls Series (1890–96), II, p. 251.

house would have existed much earlier, if only through contact at councils convened at Westminster. The energetic involvement of Abbot Samson of Bury (1182–1211) in the secular concerns of his abbey would also have brought him to the vicinity of Westminster,[40] where he held land from Wimund the baker. Samson 'conceded and confirmed' this tenement to William de Castellis, c.1206x1211, at an annual rent of 1 mark, comprising 11 shillings due to Wimund and 28 pence to Walter of London. In addition William would provide stabling for fifteen horses for the abbot and his successors, at their expense, whenever they came to court in person.[41]

Dealings with other religious houses were usually over property rights. For the most part these were rights in land and rents, or perhaps franchisal rights, but on occasion ecclesiastical dues were involved. This was the case in Pershore (Worcs.) notwithstanding King Edward's generous grant of lands to Westminster.[42] While Abbot Gilbert Crispin acknowledged Pershore's rights, his charter has not survived, and the earliest one to do so is in the name of Abbot Herbert. He notified his French and English men of his lands of Pershore, and of the (double) hundred, that, on peril of their souls, they should render all rights and customary dues which they owed to the church of St Mary and St Eadburga of Pershore, the mother-church of the hundred, which it had in the time of Herbert's predecessors, in tithes and alms and all other services which they owed that church, justly, without tumult and without any denial. He further ordered them that they were not to disrupt or deny the rights of that mother church at any time, because of any official whom they had over them.[43] Later there was a renewal of the problem, perhaps in part because of the disruption to Westminster's estates by the troops of Robert earl of Gloucester during the unrest of Stephen's reign.[44] Pershore enlisted the support both of the diocesan and also of the archbishop. John of Pagham, bishop of Worcester (1151–57) confirmed to Pershore two parts of all tithes in the hundred of Pershore and other benefits which had been conceded by Abbot Gilbert Crispin.[45] Some time between 1150 and 1161, Archbishop Theobald issued a confirmation in similar terms,[46] and a further one was obtained from Richard of Dover, c.1174x81.[47]

40 *The Chronicle of Jocelin of Brakelond*, transl. and ed. H.E. Butler (London, 1949), *passim*. For his dealings with London merchants, *ibid*., pp. 75–7.

41 Rodney Thomson, 'Twelfth-century Documents from Bury St Edmunds Abbey', *English Historical Review*, 92 (1977), p. 813, no. 18.

42 Harvey, *Westminster Abbey and its Estates*, pp. 360–64.

43 B.R. Kemp, 'The Mother Church of Thatcham', *Berkshire Archaeological Journal*, LXIII (1967–68), p. 21, note 32; P. Chaplais, 'The Original Charters of Herbert and Gervase', Addendum. On the dedication of Pershore abbey, see Alison Binns, *Dedications of Monastic Houses in England and Wales 1066–1216* (Woodbridge, 1989), p. 81.

44 Flete, *The History of Westminster Abbey*, p. 92.

45 PRO, E315/61 (The Pershore Cartulary), f. 104v.

46 Saltman, *Theobald, Archbishop of Canterbury*, pp. 420–21, no. 199.

47 *English Episcopal Acta, II, Canterbury 1162–1190*, ed. C.R. Cheney and B.E.A. Jones (Oxford, 1986), no. 181.

Certain tithes, though, remained due to Westminster. William of Northolt, bishop of Worcester (1186–90), confirming the presentation by Prior Walter and the convent of Great Malvern of the clerk Andrew to the church of St Andrew's, Pershore, noted that, as perpetual vicar, he would render a yearly pension of 10 marks to the monks of Great Malvern, of which 8 marks represented tithes due to the abbot of Westminster from his court in Pershore and its appendages, comprising Wick, Pinvin, Pensham and Birlingham.[48] This pension was of comparatively recent origin. The church was dedicated by Bishop Simon only in 1147.[49] Some time after Andrew's institution, however, a dispute over tithes broke out. He sided with Prior Walter (c.1177–c.1216) and the convent of Great Malvern against the abbot and convent of Pershore, and agreement between the parties was reached only on 24 June 1204.[50] Later again, Prior Thomas de Wick of Great Malvern granted the advowson of St Andrews to Abbot William de Humez of Westminster, no earlier than c.1216x1218.[51] The prolonged multi-party disagreement was exacerbated by differences over the manor of electing a prior of Great Malvern. Concessions on the procedures conceded by Abbot William de Humez, and arrangements for his annual visit to his Worcestershire properties, were published by Prior Thomas Wick of Great Malvern, c.1216x1227.[52]

Most of Westminster's transactions with other houses were relatively simple and resolved within a much shorter time-span. In the period under discussion, there were relatively few recorded transactions with religious communities of any kind in London or its vicinity. The Cluniac priory of St Saviour, Bermondsey, on the south bank of the Thames, disputed with Westminster the control of the advowson of St Magnus Martyr, near London Bridge. The case was resolved in the *Curia Regis* on 23 April 1182,[53] and a joint presentation was made a few years later.[54] A further joint presentation was made in April 1208.[55]

Several hospitals of one kind and another feature in the abbey's twelfth-century charters. In 1184, Abbot Walter granted to St Bartholomew's hospital in London three tenements, variously in Friday Street and in Bread Street, to be held in return for rents due to the monks' Chamber.[56] A grant to Westminster by King Stephen, of quittance of geld and customary exactions on six and a half hides of the manor of Westminster, was made 'because his

48 Westminster Abbey Muniment 22497. For Prior Walter's presentation of Andrew, see Westminster Abbey Domesday (Muniment Book 11) f. 648v.

49 Westminster Abbey Muniment, no. 22495.

50 Westminster Abbey Muniment, no. 22492.

51 Dugdale, *Monasticon Anglicanum*, III, p. 449, no. VII.

52 BL, MS Cotton Faustina A III, ff. 276v–277v.

53 *Westminster Abbey Charters*, no. 287.

54 *Ibid.*, no. 368.

55 *Ibid.*, no. 220.

56 *Ibid.*, no. 293.

court and palace, and the infirmary of St Giles are established there'.[57] The leper-house of St Giles-in-the-Fields was founded by Queen Edith-Matilda.[58] Another leper hospital, lying closer to the abbey, was that of St James, from which St James's park and its environs take their name. Abbot Walter granted to the sick women, and the brethren of this hospital, the church of St Alban, Wood Street, in the City of London, for an annual pension of 1 mark (13s 4d) payable to the abbey's chamber. Provided the pension was paid regularly, the inmates of St James's were entitled to retain all other offerings made to that church. The brethren of the hospital, in presence of the chapter of Westminster, and the women in presence of the prior of Westminster, who was sent to them, swore on the Sacrament to uphold this agreement faithfully.[59] St Alban's, Wood Street, was said to be the chapel of a palace of King Offa of Mercia, and a writer of St Albans abbey later recorded that an abbot of Westminster (Vitalis or Crispin – the writer was uncertain) had granted St Albans abbey the right of alternating presentation to this church. However Bishop Gilbert Foliot confirmed the (whole) church to Westminster, with a pension of 1 mark.[60]

In the reign of King John, Turold, at that time Master of St James's, together with the brethren and sisters, 'conceded and confirmed' to Westminster the grant made to the abbey by Reginald, baker of Richard (Fitz Nigel), bishop of London, of land in Fleet Street belonging to the fee of the hospital, which Reginald held of St James's. Westminster would render to St James's the same annual rent of 3 shillings which Reginald did formerly.[61]

One further ecclesiastical community in London which had dealings with the abbey was the college of St Martin le Grand, whose chapter comprised high-flying secular clerics who were usually royal clerks.[62] Abbot Gervase and the convent granted to the college the church of St Agnes in London with its lands and other appurtenances as Godric Lobbe held them, and which he donated to Westminster when he became a monk there. St Martin's would render 7 shillings annually.[63] During the latter part of Stephen's reign, the Dean of St Martin's was Henry of Blois, the uncle of Abbot Gervase,[64] and Barbara Harvey has suggested that this relationship perhaps influenced the

57 *Regesta Regum Anglo-Normannorum, III, 1135–1154*, ed. H.A. Cronne and R.H.C. Davis (Oxford, 1968), no. 938; see also no. 939.

58 C.N.L. Brooke with Gillian Keir, *London 800–1216: the Shaping of a City* (London, 1975), p. 319.

59 *Westminster Abbey Charters*, no. 288.

60 *Ibid.*, no. 288 note; *Letters and Charters of Gilbert Foliot*, no. 462.

61 *Westminster Abbey Charters*, no. 392.

62 R.H.C. Davis, 'The College of St Martin-le-Grand and the Anarchy 1135–54', reprinted from *London Topographical Record*, 23 (1974), pp. 9–26, in Davis, *From Alfred the Great to Stephen* (London, 1991), pp. 237–54, see esp. pp. 248–52.

63 *Westminster Abbey Charters*, no. 257.

64 Davis, 'The College of St Martin-le-Grand', pp. 241–2, 248, 250–51.

terms of this grant.[65] At some time between 1180 and 1187, St Agnes (within Aldersgate) was among the churches confirmed to Westminster by Gilbert Foliot, bishop of London.[66] Given its location, though, it was administratively convenient for both Westminster and St Martins to permit its being leased to the canons.[67]

Most of Westminster's dealings with religious houses further afield have already been discussed in earlier chapters, notably in those on the abbots and on tenants and their lands, and therefore they are now simply summarized in their monastic context. The most long-running and hard-fought disputes were with other Benedictine houses, including the long-running battle to recover St Mary Newchurch from St John's, Colchester, a contest waged in the last years of the eleventh century and the early years of the twelfth.[68] There was the on-going dispute with St Albans in that part of Hertfordshire where their territorial and franchisal interests adjoined.[69] Reading Abbey acquired an interest in some of Westminster's land in London, when its tenant became a monk of Reading, and ensuing differences between the two houses came before Queen Eleanor in her capacity as regent, 1156x1157.[70] The Cluniac house of St Pancras, Lewes (Sussex) also became Westminster's tenant in respect of tenements in London.[71] The Norman abbey of Bec also became a tenant of Westminster in London, after earlier disagreement in an area where the latter's English lands bordered on those of Westminster.[72] Conversely, an amicable exchange was made between the abbey and the Augustinian Merton Priory over lands in Surrey.[73]

In addition to the cell of Kilburn, discussed above, a few further transactions involved nunneries. The most hotly contested was that with the Benedictine house of Godstow, over Westminster's parish church of Bloxham (Oxon.), which the nuns acquired following the burial at Godstow of Rosamund Clifford, a mistress of King Henry II.[74] The nuns of Clerkenwell, in London, became tenants of the abbey in respect of tenements in Bread Street and Eastcheap, for which they would render rent to the abbey Chamber.[75]

65 Barbara Harvey, 'Abbot Gervase de Blois and the Fee-Farms of Westminster Abbey', *Bulletin of the Institute of Historical Research*, 40 (1967), p. 134.

66 *Letters and Charters of Gilbert Foliot*, no. 211.

67 Davis, 'The College of St Martin-le-Grand', p. 239; D. Keene and Vanessa Harding, A *Survey of Documentary Sources for Property-holding in London before the Great Fire*, London Record Society, 22 (1985), map facing p. 248.

68 *Westminster Abbey Charters*, nos 40, 49, 54, 90, 109, 244; Armitage Robinson, *Gilbert Crispin*, pp. 158–66.

69 *Westminster Abbey Charters*, nos 281–2, 318, 333.

70 *Ibid.*, no. 256 note; *Reading Abbey Cartularies*, I, ed. B. Kemp, Camden Fourth Series, 31 (1986), nos 462 and note, 466.

71 *Westminster Abbey Charters*, no. 260.

72 *Ibid.*, nos 26, 361.

73 *Ibid.*, no. 268.

74 *Ibid.*, nos 225, 323, 481.

75 *Ibid.*, no. 292.

The Gilbertine nuns of Shouldham were granted the abbey's tithes in Clakelos Hundred, Norfolk, in return for an annual rent of £1 10s. In terms of cost-effectiveness, this was a rational managerial decision, but it was also an offer which Abbot Ralph and the monks could scarcely refuse, given that it was 'requested' by the patron of Shouldham, Geoffrey Fitz Peter, earl of Essex and Justiciar.[76]

76 *Ibid.*, nos 476–7; F. West, *The Justiciarship in England 1066–1232* (Cambridge, 1966), pp. 96–177; see also R.V. Turner, *The English Judiciary in the Age of Glanvill and Bracton c.1176–1239* (Cambridge, 1985), p. 124.

13

The Abbey and the Laity

Westminster, like other Benedictine abbeys, employed a considerable number of laity on its staff. At the top of this hierarchy was the officer known as the dapifer, in the Anglo-Norman period, and later termed the seneschal. Both terms may be translated as 'steward', and the office-holder witnessed many, but not all, property transactions directly relating to the abbey. A writ of William II notified his confirmation of the grant by Abbot Gilbert and the convent to Hugh of Colham and his heirs of being dapifer of the abbey, and proctor under the abbot of Westminster.[1] Hugh witnessed, without title, the restoration by Robert Dispenser of Comberton and Wick, c.1095/6 x ante 1098.[2] The grant by Robert's brother Urse de Abetot, sheriff of Worcester, to the 'brethren' of Great Malvern of tithes in Bransford and Powick, 1096x1108, is witnessed by Hugardo dapifer, an attestation which may be that of Hugh of Colham, representing Westminster's interests in its cell.[3] Hugh held an estate of two hides in Cowley (Middx) of the abbot and convent of Westminster.[4]

Gregory the dapifer witnessed the second of Abbot Herbert's charters for the nuns of Kilburn, c.1130x1136.[5] He also witnessed a charter of the convent of Westminster, 'conceding' land in Eastcheap, London, to Eorlwin brother of Wlfwin, c.1136–38.[6] Gregory's attestation occurs on two charters of Abbot Gervase: one granting to William de Wenden and his wife Adelaide the lands and offices of Walter Stantus,[7] and another granting to the female community of Kilburn land at Gore in the manor of Knightsbridge.[8] When

1 *Westminster Abbey Charters 1066–c.1214*, ed. Emma Mason, assisted by the late Jennifer Bray, continuing the work of the late Desmond J. Murphy, London Record Society, 25 (1988), no. 47.

2 *Ibid.*, no. 488.

3 T. Habington, A *Survey of Worcestershire*, Worcestershire Historical Society, V, 2 vols (Oxford, 1893–99), II, variant texts on pp. 178, 283.

4 *Westminster Abbey Charters*, no. 453.

5 *Ibid.*, no. 250. The attestations to the first of the two have been omitted from the surviving cartulary copy of this text.

6 *Ibid.*, no. 340.

7 *Ibid.*, no. 254.

8 *Ibid.*, no. 265.

Geoffrey de Mandeville, earl of Essex, granted land in London to the convent of Westminster, c.1140x1144, Gregory was virtually the only representative of the abbey who attested with members of the earl's entourage.[9] His attestations overall varied between that of 'dapifer', and 'dapifer of Westminster'.

Alan the dapifer was in office c.1161x1173, when Hugh Fitz Warner quitclaimed land in Middlesex to Abbot Lawrence, and swore with his hands placed between those of Alan (in token of fidelity) to observe the agreement.[10] Alan witnessed one charter of Abbot Lawrence confirming to a tenant land in London, and another by which the abbot granted the church of Easthampstead (Berks.) to Hurley priory.[11] Since neither Alan nor his predecessor Gregory is known to have used any form of surname, it is unclear whether either was a descendant of Hugh of Colham.

From the time of Abbot Walter onwards, however, it seems that Hugh's descendants did not hold this office, which now changed its title to that of seneschal. Geoffrey Picot occupied this post from some uncertain date, and was in office January x September 1190.[12] His few surviving official attestations are those of 'seneschal' and 'seneschal of the abbot'.[13] However it is likely that some of his attestations which do not carry an official title also date from his time as seneschal, notably to grants made by, or to, Abbot Walter.[14] In one instance, he witnessed a charter of Walter's in company with his nephew William Picot and his son Richard.[15] Geoffrey Picot also occurs in charters dating from the time of Abbot William,[16] including one attested by Theobald of Feering as seneschal[17] and others attested by Theobald's successor, Richard de Dol.[18] In the mid 1190s, Geoffrey held land in Longditch, Westminster,[19] and was granted land in Aldenham (Herts.) by Abbot William Postard.[20]

Theobald of Feering (Essex) is known to have held the office of seneschal from 1191x1194 to some time after September 1197, over which period his attestations occur variously as 'seneschal', 'seneschal of Westminster', 'seneschal of the abbot' and 'our (i.e. the abbot's) seneschal'.[21] Like his predecessor, he occasionally attested without a title, apparently during his time in office.[22]

The hereditary claims of the descendants of Hugh of Colham had been overlooked in the recent appointments to his office, until one of them

9 *Ibid.*, no. 350.
10 *Ibid.*, no. 452.
11 *Ibid.*, nos 275, 285.
12 *Ibid.*, no. 300.
13 *Ibid.*, nos 297, 300, 302.
14 *Ibid.*, nos 289, 303, 490.
15 *Ibid.*, no. 304.
16 *Ibid.*, nos 319, 352, 409.
17 *Ibid.*, no. 322.
18 *Ibid.*, nos 466–7.
19 *Ibid.*, nos 230, 445.
20 *Ibid.*, no. 319.
21 *Ibid.*, nos 319, 321–3, 395, 409, 457, 481.
22 *Ibid.*, nos 360, 456. 23. *Rotuli Curiae Regis. Rolls and Records of the Court Held before the King's Justiciars or Justices, I. From the Sixth Year of King Richard I to the Accession of King John*, ed. F. Palgrave, Record Comm. (London, 1835), p. 138.

brought a lawsuit over it in the *Curia Regis*.[23] This was concluded on 27 August 1198, by a final concord made between Walter, son of Thurstan of Colham, plaintiff, and Abbot William Postard and the convent. Walter quitclaimed, for himself and for his heirs, his right in the seneschalcy of the abbey. In return, he would receive an annual payment of 5 marks (£3 6s 8d) from the abbey's Chamber, until he was recompensed with £10 worth of rents for his lifetime, or less if it should be acceptable. The annual payment indicates acceptance of Walter's claims, and of the expectation of any seneschal that he could derive profit from his official activities. At the same time, the monks' hopes that they could placate him with less than the requisite £10 in annual rents may indicate their assertion that the claims of the Colham family had lapsed through disuse. Conversely, the odd wording of this phrase perhaps indicates an obligation only to render £10 worth of rents 'in the course of his life'.[24]

The next known seneschal, Richard de Dol, was perhaps in office during the last years of William Postard's abbacy,[25] and was certainly active in this post throughout the abbacy of Ralph Arundel. His attestations vary between 'seneschal of Westminster', 'seneschal of the abbot', and 'seneschal of the abbot of Westminster'.[26] Further attestations of Richard de Dol, without any title, probably also date from his term of office, since in most cases he is the leading witness who appears to represent the interests of the abbey.[27] Richard held land in the vill of Westminster and leased a plot to Ralph Testard at an annual rent of 3 shillings, but subsequently granted 2 shillings of this annually to the abbey, to provide lights for the high altar.[28]

Julian Chenduit, who attested charters while Richard was seneschal,[29] was perhaps envisaged as a potential successor, and certainly took precedence immediately after him on several occasions.[30] Julian appears to have been appointed seneschal when William de Humez became abbot, but in one curious instance, while Julian attested as seneschal of Westminster, the attestation of Richard de Dol took precedence.[31] Julian was certainly seneschal

23 *Rotuli Curiae Regis. Rolls and Records of the Court held before the King's Justiciars or justices, I. From the sixth year of King Richard I to the accession of King John*, ed. F. Palgrave (Record Comm., London, 1835), p. 138.

24 *Westminster Abbey Charters*, no. 310 and note.

25 *Ibid.*, no. 411.

26 *Ibid.*, nos 328, 333, 335, 356, 422, 433, 442, 447–9, 461, 466–7, 473, 482, 484–5; *The Beauchamp Cartulary Charters: 1100–1268*, ed. Emma Mason, Pipe Roll Society, new series xliii (1980), nos 192, 197–8.

27 *Westminster Abbey Charters*, nos 327, 337, 402–3, 423, 425–6, 428, 441, 476–7.

28 *Ibid.*, nos 419–20.

29 *Ibid.*, nos 328, 333, 424, 426, 484, 486.

30 *Ibid.*, nos 328, 426, 461.

31 Westminster Abbey Domesday (Muniment Book 11), f. 304r. See also Westminster Abbey Muniment 17317. The Richard who attests as seneschal c.1225 may be of a younger generation: Westminster Abbey Domesday ff. 101r–102r.

towards the end of William's abbacy,[32] and attested at various times throughout it.[33] While the majority of his attestations appear on charters relating to properties in the locality of Westminster, he, like his predecessors, was occasionally involved in transactions relating to Westminster's interests further afield, such as dues liable to be rendered to the abbot's court in Pershore (Worcs.).[34]

The abbot of Westminster, in common with the heads of other old Benedictine houses, owed knight-service to the king. The *carta* returned by Abbot Lawrence in 1166 showed that the bulk of the land which rendered knight service lay in Worcestershire and Gloucestershire. The king himself answered for the service of one knight in *Stokes*; William de Beauchamp (III) owed the service of seven knights; Walter de Beauchamp, half a knight; Walter de Clifford, one-fifth of a knight; William Folet, one knight; Hugh Poher, three knights; Henry de Newmarket, two knights; Reginald de Stainlinge, two knights; Peter of Studley, two separate knight's fees. All these tenants acknowledged the knight-service due, and rendered the amount required of their respective lands. Further knight-service was owed by the following men, most of whom were making difficulties about rendering it. The earl of Gloucester owed the service of two knights for land in Gloucestershire, which he rendered down to the most recent campaign in Wales (1165) but later withheld; Ralph of Monmouth owed the service of one knight in Worcestershire and Gloucestershire, but withheld it; Walter de Meine owed the service of one knight in Worcestershire, but his undertenant in the fee, William de Stanton, withheld half; An(s)got Duredent owed the service of half a knight in Buckinghamshire; Walkelin owed the service of a third part of a knight in Surrey; Richard de Keimes owed the service of half a knight in Essex, and all three men apparently acknowledged their obligations. However, in Middlesex Walter Fitz Robert owed the service of one knight, which he withheld. All these men, or their predecessors, were enfeoffed in the time of Henry I (d.1135) and none was enfeoffed more recently.[35] These dues, if rendered, would have rendered the service of a further six and three quarters knights. Most of the abbot's knights do not feature to any extent in the Westminster charters of the period, but the Buckinghamshire tenant An(s)got Duredent witnessed a series of charters dating from c.1177 x May 1186, seemingly at the instigation of William of Northolt and his nephew, and relating to land in Cowley (Middx).[36] The identification of the abbot's knights is occasionally possible: for instance William Baynard, who owed Abbot Gilbert Crispin the service of one knight

32 *Westminster Abbey Charters*, no. 439.

33 Westminster Abbey Muniments, 17319, 17439; Westminster Abbey Domesday, f. 166v.

34 Westminster Abbey Domesday, f. 292v–293r.

35 *Liber Niger Scaccarii*, ed. T. Hearne, I (London, 1774), pp. 51–3.

36 *Westminster Abbey Charters*, nos 453–4.

for land in the berwick of Tothill, Westminster,[37] or William Picot who owed Abbot William Postard a knight's service for land in Lincolnshire.[38]

The agreements made by Abbot Walter and his successors with certain tenants over hospitality due to the abbot on his visits to outlying estates indicate that he travelled with a substantial retinue.[39] A whole bevy of officials, including seneschal, chamberlain, pantler, butler, usher, cook and marshal, habitually accompanied the abbot on his seasonal tours around his more remote estates. Geoffrey the chamberlain held office in the early years of the thirteenth century.[40] Together with his colleagues, he would take charge of any household whose owner owed a service of hospitality to ensure that everything ran smoothly for the abbot during his brief stay. The mobilizing of this entourage was probably the responsibility of the marshal. Robert the marshal is known from the time of Abbot Gervase, while a later Robert filled the same office during the abbacy of William Postard.[41] Walter the marshal was in office in 1209.[42] The entourage would also include esquires of the abbot such as John, active in the time of Abbot Gervase.[43]

Various officials of the abbot's household are readily identifiable, including his usher (*hostiarius*), a man of some status. In the time of Abbot Walter, his usher was William of Hurley.[44] His successor in the time of Abbot William Postard was James.[45] Bartholomew the usher was in office in June 1209, during the abbacy of Ralph Arundel.[46] William of Hurley's widow, Pavia of Westminster (*alias* of Longditch in Westminster), identified him as a former butler (*pincerna*).[47] In the time of Abbot William Postard, there was a butler named Thomas, who was perhaps identical with Thomas the son of William of Hurley.[48] However, another butler, named John, was also in office 1191x1198.[49] Gerold, chamberlain (*camberarius*) of Abbot Herbert, held land of the abbey in Wheathampstead (Herts.).[50]

Abbot Gervase granted to William of Wenden and his wife Adelaide, daughter of Walter Stantus, all Walter's tenements, together with his offices within and without the church, 'since Adelaide was Walter's most lawful

37 *Ibid.*, no. 236.
38 *Ibid.*, no. 322.
39 *Ibid.*, no. 301; F.M. Stenton, *The First Century of English Feudalism 1066–1166*, second edn (Oxford, 1961), pp. 71–2, 267–9.
40 *Westminster Abbey Charters*, nos 402–3, 447–8, 466–7, 482, 484.
41 *Ibid.*, nos 269, 307, 318, 353.
42 *Ibid.*, no. 402.
43 *Ibid.*, no. 254.
44 *Ibid.*, nos 311, 405. *Beauchamp Cartulary*, nos 183, 189, 190.
45 *Westminster Abbey Charters*, nos 307, 309.
46 *Ibid.*, no. 402.
47 *Beauchamp Cartulary*, no. 191, and for her *alias*, *ibid.*, no. 193.
48 *Westminster Abbey Charters*, nos 315, 319; cf. *Beauchamp Cartulary*, nos 192–3. As Thomas, son of Pavia, he attests *Westminster Abbey Charters*, no. 419.
49 *Westminster Abbey Charters*, no. 309.
50 *Ibid.*, no. 269.

heir'. The couple would hold these things as Walter Stantus did, and as Geoffrey, Adelaide's brother, quitclaimed these to them from the day of their marriage.[51] The offices in question were the sergeanties of the vestibule and the buttery, identified in the account of how a later William de Wenden surrendered them to Abbot Walter de Wenlock (1283–1307) with all corrodies, stipends and other perquisites.[52] The formal nature of the transfer of office indicates both the stature which it bestowed on its incumbent in the local community and also its presumed profitability. This is explicit in the case of the office of summoner, which was held by Nicholas son of Geoffrey in the earlier part of Ralph Arundel's abbacy.[53] However, c.24 June 1209, he 'demised and conceded' to Robert of Croxley and his heirs or assigns, his ministry of being summoner in Westminster Abbey, together with a monks's corrody and other appurtenances, besides the land pertaining to that office. These were to be held for twelve years, in return for 50 shillings which Robert gave him. The office would revert to Nicholas and his heirs at the end of the term.[54] Subsequently, though, Nicholas made an open-ended 'concession and confirmation' of this office to Robert of Croxley, to hold for an annual payment of 4 pence. Robert in return gave a gersum of 100 shillings sterling.[55]

Already by c.1118x1120 there were sergeanties of the bakery, brewery, kitchen, infirmary, vineyard and yard.[56] William 'of the infirmary' was perhaps sergeant there in the late twelfth century.[57] Walkelin 'of the almonry' may similarly have held a sergeanty there, in the late twelfth and early thirteenth century,[58] and, in the first years of the thirteenth century, Thomas brother of Pancras was sergeant of the sacristy.[59] William, servant of the church,[60] was probably answerable to the sacrist. Frequently a charter dating from the time of Abbot William Postard or Abbot Ralph Arundel was witnessed by several of the sergeants acting together, although their attestations do not indicate their respective spheres of activity. In order of frequency of attestation, Geoffrey was the most prominent,[61] then Adam,[62] followed

51 *Ibid*., no. 254 and note.
52 John Flete, *The History of Westminster Abbey*, ed. J. Armitage Robinson (Cambridge, 1909), p. 117.
53 *Westminster Abbey Charters*, nos 393, 437–8, 440.
54 *Ibid*., no. 402.
55 *Ibid*., no. 403.
56 *Ibid*., no. 339.
57 *Ibid*., nos 360, 444.
58 *Ibid*., nos 328, 417–19, 445.
59 *Ibid*., no. 328.
60 *Ibid*., no. 419.
61 *Ibid*., nos 297, 302, 348, 360, 378, 387, 407, 412, 423, 430, 433, 443–4, 451, 458.
62 *Ibid*., nos 360, 378, 387, 407, 412, 423, 430, 433, 443–4, 451, 458, 461.

closely by John;[63] others included William[64] and William Stutel,[65] Ralph,[66] Randulf,[67] and Alan.[68] Ralph the baker[69] and Gerard the cook[70] were possibly abbey employees, as, more certainly, were Ivo of the Kitchen and, probably, Roger the cook.[71] Nicholas[72] and Richard[73] 'of the cellar' were active c.1199–1216. Richard the doorkeeper is recorded in the time of Abbot Walter.[74] Gerin the engineer (*ingeniator*) is known from the time of Abbot Gervase.[75] Servants or sergeants in the various household offices were entitled to a daily corrody, as was Gilbert of Claygate when he was appointed to work in the almonry, and the janitor was also entitled to one.[76] As Barbara Harvey has pointed out, the extensive provision of corrodies of varying kinds, not simply to abbey servants, but also to those who purchased a long-term interest in them, or who were allocated one in return for a grant of their tenements, had a major impact on the capacity of the almonry to provide for the genuine poor of the neighbourhood.[77]

Bailiffs, not usually identified by name, were employed on the abbey's estates,[78] as were officials of other kinds.[79] Edric of the Garden presumably managed the abbey's crops of fruit and vegetables on the site later known as Covent ('the convent's') Garden.[80]

Craftsmen employed at the abbey are sometimes identified, including stone-masons employed on King Edward's rebuilding programme. These include Leofsi Duddesunu, *alias* Leofsi of London, later reputed to have granted land to Westminster, as did Godwine Greatsyd; and Teinfrith the churchwright, to whom King Edward granted land at Shepperton (Middx). The first two were clearly English, but it has been argued that the name Teinfrith is Continental Germanic.[81] As men of substance, they were likely to have been among the leaders of the work in progress, if not the actual design-team. A

63 *Ibid.*, nos 378, 387, 407, 412, 430, 433, 443–4, 451, 461.
64 *Ibid.*, nos 360, 378, 412, 419, 423, 458.
65 *Ibid.*, nos 387, 433.
66 *Ibid.*, nos 360, 407, 443–4, 451.
67 *Ibid.*, no. 490.
68 *Ibid.*, no. 302.
69 *Ibid.*, no. 404.
70 *Ibid.*, no. 423.
71 *Ibid.*, no. 419.
72 *Ibid.*, nos 348, 356, 378, 387, 402, 408, 411–12, 414, 419, 421–4, 429–30, 432–3, 441–5, 447–8, 451.
73 *Ibid.*, nos 410, 412, 414, 419, 432–3.
74 *Ibid.*, no. 297.
75 *Ibid.*, no. 255.
76 Westminster Abbey Domesday, f. 465v; Barbara Harvey, *Living and Dying in England 1100–1540: the Monastic Experience* (Oxford, 1993), p. 240.
77 Harvey, *Living and Dying*, pp. 189, 191–2, 194, 204, 207.
78 *Westminster Abbey Charters*, nos 271, 318, 333, 335, 339.
79 *Ibid.*, nos 87, 107.
80 *Ibid.*, nos 408, 417–18, 449–50.
81 R.D.H. Gem, 'The Romanesque Rebuilding of Westminster Abbey', with a reconstruction

century or so later, several of the painters attested charters, and it is possible to trace to some extent the sequence of their employment. Richard was probably one of the earliest, active in Henry II's reign.[82] About the same time, William and his sons Simon and Burchard were working at Westminster.[83] Simon and Burchard were there in c.1182x86, while Simon was apparently still working in John's reign.[84] Finally Eustace emerged in this reign and was certainly employed at Westminster in June 1209.[85] The careers of Simon and Eustace, if not also that of Burchard, cover the period when Westminster's earliest surviving psalter was decorated by two artists of widely differing abilities, but their part, if any, in this, is not documented.[86]

The focus of the present study upon the abbey itself precludes any detailed examination of the inhabitants of the neighbouring vill. The work of Gervase Rosser, based on the extensive muniments of the abbey, has charted the intensifying urbanization of the vill, and the consequent activities of its inhabitants.[87] It need only be observed here that the proliferation of documentation from c.1200, generated by the wish to build up an endowment in rents for the Lady Altar, makes it possible to know the identities of the occupants of whole groups of tenements. Property transactions between tenants of the abbey would be witnessed by the reeves. Richard the reeve attested one charter of Abbot Herbert, and several of those of Abbot Gervase.[88] Edward was in office in the later twelfth century and down to 1194 and perhaps a year or two longer.[89] Roger Enganet was subsequently reeve in 1197x1198.[90] Henry Sumer was a sergeant of the abbey who was granted land and a mill in Surrey by Abbot Walter. He also acquired land in Deene (Northants), which he granted to the Lady Altar.[91] He is also recorded as reeve c.1198x1212.[92] His term of office coincided with that of Richard Testard,[93] but they seem to have been in office only briefly. Odo the goldsmith was reeve in the reign of King John. Later, from 1218, he was

by W.T. Ball, *Proceedings of the Battle Conference on Anglo-Norman Studies, III, 1980*, ed. R. Allen Brown (Woodbridge, 1981), pp. 39, 204–5.

82 *Westminster Abbey Charters*, no. 405.

83 *Ibid.*, no. 404.

84 *Beauchamp Cartulary*, no. 183; *Westminster Abbey Charters*, nos 447–8.

85 *Beauchamp Cartulary*, no. 197. *Westminster Abbey Charters*, nos 402, 443–4.

86 F. Wormald, 'Paintings in Westminster Abbey and Contemporary Paintings', *Proceedings of the British Academy*, XXXV (1949), pp. 161–76, see esp. pp. 162–3.

87 G. Rosser, *Medieval Westminster 1200–1540* (Oxford, 1989), see especially chapter 1.

88 *Westminster Abbey Charters*, nos 250, 258, 261, 263, 265, 269.

89 *Ibid.*, nos 289, 303, 318, 406. *Beauchamp Cartulary*, nos 187, 189, 194–6. It has been suggested that his immediate successor was Richard de Dol (Rosser, *Medieval Westminster*, pp. 328, 330) but the charter cited, Westminster Abbey Muniment 17323, in fact names him as seneschal (*Westminster Abbey Charters*, no. 411).

90 *Westminster Abbey Charters*, nos 395, 416.

91 For Henry's land in Surrey, *ibid.*, no. 297; on his Northamptonshire benefaction, *ibid.*, no. 480.

92 *Ibid.*, nos 437–8.

93 *Ibid.*, nos 437–8. On the Testard family in the later twelfth century and the earlier

'keeper of the works of the king's houses of Westminster'. He continued in the royal service until 1239, an administrator directing the rebuilding and refurbishing of the Palace and St Stephen's Chapel.[94] While these officials and their neighbours are chiefly known from their frequent attestations to charters which directly concerned the interests of Westminster abbey, they were also involved in transactions between inhabitants of the vill, including the Exchequer chamberlains William Mauduit (III) and his son Robert (II).[95]

Among the more casual inhabitants of the vill were those men who evaded the course of justice by fleeing to Westminster's celebrated sanctuary. The abbey cherished its privileged status in possessing this immunity which was 'documented' in some of its forged charters.[96] A series of abbatial writs, notifying sheriffs of the flight of fugitives, was also preserved, evidently as successive models of the genre. From these we may glimpse some of the individuals who rushed to Westminster. The earliest such writs to survive date from the time of Abbot Gilbert Crispin, who sent letters in English to notify the sheriff of Surrey of the flight of Deorman *de Cleareton*, and to N. sheriff of Essex of the flight of an unidentified R.[97] Before the end of Gilbert's abbacy, such writs were written in Latin, the language in which he issued a generally-addressed notification of the flight of Jordan.[98] Another generally-addressed writ was issued by Abbot Herbert, following the flight of Jordan of Worcester.[99] Abbot Gervase wrote to Aylwin the sheriff of Sussex about the flight of Tubern of the Weald, and to R. the sheriff of Sussex about another fugitive whose name has not survived.[100] The last in the series was a notification by Abbot Lawrence to Brithstan (? Brihmer de Haverhill), sheriff of Middlesex, that Siward of Dunstable had sought sanctuary because of a

thirteenth, see *Curia Regis Rolls* XIV, p. 217, p. 339 no. 1584. In that lawsuit, Richard Testard's mother is named as Juliana. His father, who was not named in the account relating to the descent of the contested land, was in fact Robert Testard: *Beauchamp Cartulary*, no. 199.

94 For Odo as reeve, see *Westminster Abbey Charters*, nos 328, 347, 390, 410, 413–14, 418–19, 423–4, 434, 447–8, 450. On his role as Keeper of the Works, see R. Kent Lancaster, 'Artists, Suppliers and Clerks: the Human Factors in the Art Patronage of King Henry III', *Journal of the Warburg and Courtauld Institutes*, 35 (1972) pp. 97–8.

95 *Beauchamp Cartulary*, nos 183–200.

96 The right to offer sanctuary to fugitives is included both in a purported bull of Pope John (XIX) and also in the so-called Third Charter of King Edward: Flete, *The History of Westminster Abbey*, pp. 51, 53. For the latter text, see also P. Chaplais, 'The Original Charters of Herbert and Gervase, Abbots of Westminster (1121–1157)', reprinted from *A Medieval Miscellany for Doris Mary Stenton*, ed. Patricia M. Barnes and C.F. Slade, Pipe Roll Society, new series, XXXVI (London, 1962), pp. 89–110, in Chaplais, *Essays in Medieval Diplomacy and Administration* (London, 1981), XVIII, pp. 89–110 at pp. 93–5.

97 *Westminster Abbey Charters*, nos 238–9.

98 *Ibid.*, no. 240.

99 *Ibid.*, no. 248.

100 *Ibid.*, nos 272–3.

charge of theft.[101] But the privileged status of a sanctuary had to be balanced against the inconvenience caused by such restive inmates. There survives from the early thirteenth century the text of the form of an oath which fugitives were required to swear on the Gospels in the hope that this would curb their more anti-social tendencies. First: they were required to say truthfully why they had fled, and whom they had injured. Secondly: that while the fugitive remained, he would uphold the rights, privileges and customs of the abbey. Thirdly: that he would obey all judgements and verdicts imposed there, and would not appeal against them except to the apostolic see. He would faithfully uphold peace there. If he had fled on account of debt, he would state how he hoped to satisfy his creditors, and would undertake any litigation in a sedate manner, without becoming garrulous or contentious. He swore that he would not offer for sale (to pilgrims or other visitors to the abbey) any surplus from his daily allocation of food, without the special permission of the archdeacon or of his deputy. Similarly, except with the express permission of these officials, he would not admit into his house or provide food for any fugitive or fugitives, or other suspect persons. He would not wear defensive arms within the sanctuary without permission, and any he had on his arrival would be handed over to the archdeacon or his deputy. Except with their special permission, he would not leave the sanctuary by day or night, except to reach a legal agreement with his adversaries. He would not defame or defraud any other fugitive. He would not voluntarily commit any violence within the sanctuary, and would do his best to stop any which occurred. These undertakings applied to the whole sanctuary precinct. Within the abbey church itself, the sacrist had the duty of maintaining good order, and was particularly required to maintain adequate lighting.[102] The oath was presumably designed to put a stop to practices which were actually occurring. Reading between its lines, we can envisage the archdeacon and his deputy waging an uphill struggle against quarrelsome and violent criminals on the run, sometimes using the sanctuary as a base for operations, or running a sideline in the take-away food trade. Whatever the inconvenience, though, Westminster cherished its special status, one shared in this region only with the canons of St Martin-le-Grand.[103] The widespread recognition of Westminster's privileged sanctuary is reflected in an anecdote by the twelfth-

101 *Ibid*., no. 279.

102 *Ibid*., no. 349 and note. On the archdeacons of Westminster, see also Jane Sayers, 'Monastic Archdeacons', in C.N.L. Brooke, D. Luscombe, G. Martin and D. Owen, eds, *Church and Government in the Middle Ages* (Cambridge, 1976), pp. 177–203, esp. pp. 185–8.

103 M.B. Honeybourne, 'The Sanctuary Boundaries and Environs of Westminster Abbey and the College of St Martin-le-Grand', *Journal of the British Archaeological Association*, new series, 38 (1932), pp. 316–32; R.H.C. Davis, 'The College of St Martin-le-Grand and the Anarchy 1135–54', reprinted from *London Topographical Record*, 23 (1974), pp. 9–26, in Davis, *From Alfred the Great to Stephen* (London, 1991), pp. 237–54. See esp. pp. 238–40.

century writer Geoffrey Gaimar of how the infant sons of Edmund Ironside were briefly housed at the abbey after the triumph of King Cnut, before the victor took them away again.[104]

Anecdotal evidence highlights the fact that violence was never far away from the abbey. William the Conqueror was said to have used the royal hall at Westminster as a base for operations against English resistance in 1066,[105] while his coronation was marred by the firing of houses in the vill, when his troops panicked at the unexpected shouts of acclamation.[106] There was further violence in 1141 when the Londoners attacked the empress there.[107] At the close of the period under discussion the abbey was again under threat. Rebel troops controlled London in 1215, but the monks apparently suffered as much inconvenience from incursions by the forces of King John.[108]

The unique position of Westminster as the coronation church, its convenience as a venue for councils to which the great and the good were convened, and the wide geographical spread of its lands, which impinged on those of so many others, ensured that a wide range of well-known personalities of the period would be brought into contact with the monks, and not always in a context which would seem likely from the more publicized aspects of their careers. To mention only a few: Anselm, the future saintly archbishop, was something of a predator from Westminster's viewpoint;[109] Hugh de Evremou, the son-in-law of the English freedom-fighter, Hereward the Wake, temporarily occupied a Westminster manor;[110] while the kinsfolk of the recently-martyred Thomas Becket basked in his reflected glory.[111] The A. de Condet whom Archbishop Theobald reprimanded for withholding a rent from the

104 *L'estoire des Engleis by Geffrei Gaimar*, ed. A. Bell, Anglo-Norman Text Society, 14–16 (Oxford, 1960), 4491–2, 4507. See also *The Chronicle of John of Worcester, II, 450–1066*, ed. R.R. Darlington and P.M. McGurk, Oxford Medieval Texts (Oxford, 1995), pp. 502–3, for Cnut's treatment of the children, but without mention of Westminster.

105 *The Carmen de Hastingae Proelio of Guy, Bishop of Amiens*, ed. Catherine Morton and Hope Muntz, Oxford Medieval Texts (Oxford, 1972), pp. 42–3.

106 *The Ecclesiastical History of Orderic Vitalis*, ed. Marjorie Chibnall, Oxford Medieval Texts, II (new edn 1990), pp. 184–5.

107 R.H.C. Davis, *King Stephen 1135–1154*, 3rd edn (Harlow, 1990), p. 57.

108 *Rotuli Litterarum Patentium in Turri Londiniensi asservati*, ed. T. Duffus Hardy, I, part i (1201–1216), Record Comm. (London, 1835), f. 165b; *Westminster Abbey Charters*, no. 151.

109 *Westminster Abbey Charters*, no. 26.

110 J. Armitage Robinson, *Gilbert Crispin* (Cambridge, 1911), p. 145, no. 26. On the relationship between Hugh de Evremou and Hereward the Wake, see J.H. Round, *Feudal England*, 2nd edn (New York, 1964), pp. 132–4, 137.

111 *Westminster Abbey Charters*, nos 294–5, 365, 382, 384. On the role of Mary Becket, abbess of Barking, in promoting his cult, see Jocelin Wogan-Browne, ' "Clerc u lai muine u dame": Women and Anglo-Norman Hagiography in the Twelfth and Thirteenth Centuries', in Carol M. Meale, ed., *Women and Literature in Britain 1150–1500* (Cambridge, 1993), pp. 62, 67, 83.

abbey, during the unrest of Stephen's reign,[112] was in fact Alice, the twice-widowed sister of Ranulf earl of Chester. She has some status as a patron of literature, having commissioned a vernacular translation of the Book of Proverbs into rhyming couplets.[113]

112 A. Saltman, *Theobald, Archbishop of Canterbury* (reprinted New York, 1969), pp. 507–8, no. 277; *Westminster Abbey Charters*, no. 195 and note.

113 A charter of King Stephen for Ranulf earl of Chester included, 'for love of the said earl', a restoration to Alice de Condet of all her land of Horncastle and her other lands: *Regesta Regum Anglo-Normannorum, III, 1135–1154*, ed. H.A. Cronne and R.H.C. Davis (Oxford, 1968), no. 178. On Alice, see *Les Proverbes de Salemon by Sanson de Nantuil*, ed. C. Claire Isoz, III, Anglo-Norman Text Society (London, 1994), pp. 11–18; I. Short, 'Patrons and Polyglots: French Literature in Twelfth-Century England', in Marjorie Chibnall, ed., *Anglo-Norman Studies, XIV, Proceedings of the Battle Conference 1991* (Woodbridge, 1992), p. 243.

14

The Cults Observed at Westminster

The Petrine dedication of the West Minster is hinted to have been one of the features which prompted King Edward to choose it as his burial church.[1] This dedication is recorded in a charter of King Edgar,[2] and was probably that of any church on Thorn Island at an earlier date. In fact it is indirectly supportive of Westminster's claims to have enjoyed a (more-or-less) continuous existence from the seventh century, and to have enjoyed subsequently the patronage of King Offa the Great of Mercia.[3] The legendary story of the West Minster's dedication by St Peter during the episcopate of Mellitus, bishop of London (604–c.617) could provide inspiration to later generations of monks, eager to evade the jurisdiction of the bishop of London. Bernhard Scholz has argued, however, that this was not a consideration with Sulcard. In his view, the story should rather be seen as belonging to a group of narratives of supernatural dedications, relating to some of the more prestigious churches of western Europe. The cult of St Peter was evidently predominant at Westminster when Sulcard wrote, and Abbot Vitalis clearly prompted him to give the considerable amount of attention which he did to miracles ascribed to St Peter.[4]

Both Abbot Herbert and Abbot Gervase referred, on occasion, to St Peter as advocate of Westminster.[5] Writs issued by Abbots Gilbert, Herbert and Gervase following the arrival of fugitives to the abbey all refer to them as seeking the altar of St Peter.[6] A grant was made by Abbot Lawrence, dating from 1161, to 'God and the altar of St Peter', to provide lights before the

1 *The Life of King Edward who Rests at Westminster*, ed. and transl. Frank Barlow, 2nd edn (Oxford, 1992), pp. 66–7.

2 W. Dugdale, *Monasticon Anglicanum*, ed. B. Bandinel, J. Caley and H. Ellis, 6 vols in 8 (London, 1817–30), I, p. 291, no. 2.

3 Alison Binns, *Dedications of Monastic Houses in England and Wales 1066–1216* (Woodbridge, 1989), pp. 19–20.

4 B.H. Scholz, 'Sulcard of Westminster: "*Prologus de Construccione Westmonasterii*" ', *Traditio*, 20 (1964), pp. 72–3.

5 *Westminster Abbey Charters 1066–c.1214*, ed. Emma Mason, assisted by the late Jennifer Bray, continuing the work of the late D.J. Murphy, London Record Society, 25 (London, 1988), nos 244, 252.

6 *Ibid.*, nos 240, 248, 272–3.

Blessed Sacrament and the relics of the saints contained in the altar.[7] A charter of Abbot Walter specified that a rent of a pound of incense was due annually to the altar of St Peter on the feast of the Translation of St Edward.[8] Abbot William Postard, 'conceding and confirming' to the convent the church and manor of Benfleet, with Fanton and Paglesham (Essex), placed the charter on 'the altar of St Peter, prince of the Apostles',[9] and did likewise when granting the monks the vill of Parham.[10] A similar ritual gesture was made by Abbot Ralph Arundel when he 'granted, conceded and confirmed' Parham to the convent.[11] In two instances, later eleventh-century donations, one made by Robert son of Sweyn of Essex, together with his mother, and the other by Geoffrey de Mandeville, were placed on the altar of St Peter by their grantors.[12] The altar of St Peter was not invariably so named, and in other charters reference is simply made to the 'great altar'[13] or simply 'the altar'.[14] Throughout the period under discussion St Peter was abundantly documented as dedicatee of the abbey[15] and, similarly, influential clerics were enlisted to promote his cult.[16] Abbot William Postard twice cited St Peter as guarantor of an anathema to be incurred by anyone infringing the abbey's rights in its properties,[17] as did Prior Robert of Moulsham.[18] St Peter was also described as the 'special protector' of the abbey in a forged bull of Pope Paschal II.[19] Abbot Herbert, assigning revenues for the service of the High Altar, included 15 shillings due to the abbot from the High Altar on the two feasts of St Peter, and all the '*gylds* (?*recte* gelds) of St Peter', 'our lord'.[20] The abbey's soke in the City of London was similarly known as the 'soke of St Peter'.[21] The feast of St Peter's Chains, first promoted in a spurious indulgence

7 *Ibid*., no. 283.
8 *Ibid*., no. 297.
9 *Ibid*., no. 317.
10 *Ibid*., no. 326.
11 *Ibid*., no. 335.
12 *Ibid*., nos 237, 436.
13 *Ibid*., nos 225, 244, 312, 328, 404, 420.
14 *Ibid*., no. 253.
15 *Ibid*., p. 350 and references listed there.
16 *Ibid*., nos 187–8, 192–3, 200, 209.
17 *Ibid*., nos 317, 326.
18 *Ibid*., no. 345.
19 *Papsturkunden in England*, ed. W. Holtzmann, 3 vols, Abhandlungen der Gesellschaft der Wissenschaften in Göttingen, phil.-hist. Klasse, Berlin, Göttingen (I = neue Folge XXV, 1930–31; II = 3 Folge XIV–XV, 1935–6; III = 3 Folge XXXIII, 1952), I, no. 9. See P. Chaplais, 'The Original Charters of Herbert and Gervase, Abbots of Westminster (1121–1157)', reprinted from A *Medieval Miscellany for Doris Mary Stenton*, ed. Patricia M. Barnes and C.F. Slade, Pipe Roll Society, new series, XXXVI (London, 1962), pp. 89–110, in Chaplais, *Essays in Medieval Diplomacy and Administration* (London, 1981), pp. XVIII, 89–110 and Addendum at p. 92.
20 *Westminster Abbey Charters*, no. 244.
21 *Ibid*., no. 112.

ascribed to Peter Pierleoni,[22] was encouraged by Hugh du Puiset, bishop of Durham,[23] and was also fostered by Nicholas de Romanis, the legate visiting in October 1213.[24] In England, this feast marked Lammas-Day, the festival of the wheat harvest. Sulcard reported that it drew crowds of worshippers. Throughout the Middle Ages it continued to be highly regarded.[25]

While there is evidence throughout the period under discussion that the cult of St Peter remained pre-eminent among those observed at Westminster, it should be noted that sporadic attempts were also made to promote that of St Paul – perhaps in a conscious bid to dilute the claims of the diocesan bishop. The feast of St Peter and St Paul (29 June) was first promoted in two forged legatine charters in the name of Peter Pierleoni. Their purported date was 1121, and they were probably written a few years later,[26] following receipt of a genuine indulgence granted in 1125 by the legate John of Crema which encouraged this joint feast. In the later twelfth century, a further attempt was made to promote this feast, by means of an indulgence granted by Hugh du Puiset.[27] A grant to the abbey by Leofwine Kepe, in the latter part of the reign of Henry II, was made on the feast of Saint Peter and Saint Paul.[28] These two saints were jointly cited by Abbot Ralph Arundel as sanctioning the anathema which would fall on those infringing his donation of the vill of Parham.[29] In King John's reign, the tenant of land in London, acknowledging a rent due to the Chamber, identified the abbey as 'the church of the blessed apostles Peter and Paul of Westminster'.[30] Similarly the legate Nicholas de Romanis, granting an indulgence on 11 October 1213, reserved for the sacrist the offerings made on the feast of St Peter and St Paul.[31]

Lesser cults mentioned in charters of the period include that of St Agnes, whose Second Feast (28 January) was to be observed with enhanced solemnity at the instance of Abbot Lawrence, since it coincided with the anniversary (of the deaths) of his parents.[32] Another female saint venerated in the later twelfth century was St Katherine, to whom the infirmary chapel was dedicated. In her honour, Richard of Ilchester, bishop of Winchester, granted the tithes and offerings of the churches of Battersea and Wandsworth, so that these would support the monks in the infirmary.[33] The cult of St Margaret of Antioch grew in popularity in England in the later Anglo-Saxon period, and St Margaret was the dedicatee of the parish church of the vill of Westminster, which is clearly documented from the time of Abbot Herbert and perhaps dated from the reign of King Edward.[34] The cult of the Blessed Virgin

22 *Ibid.*, no. 187.
23 *Ibid.*, no. 229.
24 *Ibid.*, no. 193.
25 Scholz, 'Sulcard of Westminster', p. 73.
26 *Papsturkunden in England*, I, nos 12–13; *Westminster Abbey Charters*, nos 187–8.
27 *Westminster Abbey Charters*, no. 229.
28 *Ibid.*, no. 404.
29 *Ibid.*, no. 335.
30 *Ibid.*, no. 373.
31 *Ibid.*, no. 193.
32 *Ibid.*, no. 283.
33 *Ibid.*, no. 231.
34 *Ibid.*, no. 244. See also G. Rosser, *Medieval Westminster 1200–1540* (Oxford, 1989), pp. 251–2.

displayed a great upsurge of popularity at Westminster around the end of the twelfth century, when a sustained programme developed of accumulating lands and rents for the maintenance of the Lady Altar. Its proctor, Robert of Moulsham, successively precentor and prior, was in charge of this activity.[35] This promotion of the cult of the Blessed Virgin continued beyond the chronological scope of the present study, when subsequent proctors active on her behalf included Henry of Colchester[36] and Walter.[37] The building of a proper Lady Chapel dates from the abbacy of William de Humez.[38] The altar of the Holy Trinity, which was beginning to be singled out for donations during the abbacy of Ralph Arundel,[39] also continued to attract grants of land and rent in the time of William de Humez.[40]

A further focus for veneration, and one which proved more popular than most, was the feast of the Holy Relics. In a charter of Abbot Herbert, it was said that a grant was made 'for the honour of all relics reposing in this Church'.[41] A charter of Abbot Gervase contains the phrase 'on account of the honour and reverence of all the saints whose relics repose in our church'.[42] Archbishop Theobald, when papal legate (1150x1161), granted an indulgence applicable to those visiting the abbey on the feast of the Holy Relics.[43] A charter of Abbot Lawrence, however, conveyed his benefaction to St Peter's altar, to provide lights 'before the Body of Christ, and the relics of the saints which are contained therein'.[44] Walter of Coutances, archbishop of Rouen, and justiciar 1191x93, granted an indulgence to those visiting the abbey on certain feasts, including that 'of the holy relics which are gloriously contained in that church'.[45] It received further sanction in an indulgence granted by the legate in 1213.[46] The feast of the Holy Relics was celebrated on 16 July. In the period under discussion, the most prized item in this collection was the girdle of the Blessed Virgin, donated by King Edward.[47] Relics were categorized by John Flete as those of the Saviour, of the

35 *Westminster Abbey Charters*, nos 346–8, 408, 411, 425, 429–30, 441–2. However, the late twelfth-century reference to 'St Mary of Westminster' (*sic*) appears to be a scribal error for 'St Peter', *ibid.*, no. 396.

36 Westminster Abbey Muniment 16218.

37 Westminster Abbey Muniment 23638 (d).

38 Barbara Harvey, *Westminster Abbey and its Estates in the Middle Ages* (Oxford, 1977), p. 64.

39 *Westminster Abbey Charters*, no. 431.

40 Westminster Abbey Muniments 17319, 17439. Both are attested by Julian Chenduit as seneschal, and Odo the goldsmith as reeve.

41 *Westminster Abbey Charters*, no. 244.

42 *Ibid.*, no. 252.

43 A. Saltman, *Theobald, Archbishop of Canterbury* (London, 1956, reprinted New York, 1969), p. 509, no. 279.

44 *Westminster Abbey Charters*, no. 283.

45 *Ibid.*, no. 401.

46 *Ibid.*, no. 193.

47 Harvey, *Westminster Abbey and its Estates*, p. 44.

Blessed Virgin, of the Apostles, Martyrs, Confessors, and Virgins.[48] The earliest donations were reputed to be by Kings Sebert and Offa, and the collection continued to accumulate from the tenth century onwards.[49] In 1247, King Henry III donated a phial of the Precious Blood of Christ. In due course, the festival of the Holy Relics became one of the most popular along with that of St Peter's Chains.[50]

The cult of St Edward was never popular in comparison with these two. As Frank Barlow has shown, the cult originated among surviving members of Edward's court.[51] It was not a cult venerated at the abbey when Sulcard was at work.[52] According to Osbert de Clare, writing in 1138, Edward's tomb was opened in 1102, in the presence of Gundulf, bishop of Rochester, and other notables. The body was found to be incorrupt.[53] This circumstance perhaps inspired the wording of the earliest surviving abbatial writs concerning the Westminster sanctuary. The English-language writs in Gilbert's name depict the fugitives as having fled to 'Christ and St Peter and King Edward's rest'.[54] A Latin writ in Gilbert's name depicts the fugitive fleeing to the 'body' of King Edward.[55] This phrase is echoed in a writ of Abbot Herbert.[56] By the time of Abbot Gilbert, fugitives are said to have fled to the tomb of King Edward,[57] and this is repeated in the one sanctuary writ surviving in the name of Abbot Lawrence.[58] On this evidence, then, it may be suggested that the cult was first tentatively considered in the time of Abbot Gilbert and that a hesitant wish to promote it continued into the abbacy of Herbert. There were evidently doubts, however, about its viability to stand alone. While the papal legate John of Crema was in England, between March and September 1125, the grant of an indulgence was obtained from him, made on the grounds that King Edward and Edith Matilda were buried in the abbey.[59] This was echoed in one of the forgeries ascribed to an earlier legate, Peter Pierleoni, and supposedly dating from 1121.[60] The association of Queen Edith-Matilda with her kinsman indicates that the monks, while trying to maximize the potential of possessing these two royal tombs, were uncertain which person, if either, was capable of inspiring a viable cult. The queen had been a

48 John Flete, *The History of Westminster Abbey*, ed. J. Armitage Robinson (Cambridge, 1909), pp. 68–73.

49 *Ibid.*, p. 18.

50 Harvey, *Westminster Abbey and its Estates*, p. 44.

51 *The Life of King Edward who Rests at Westminster*, p. xxxii; F. Barlow, *Edward the Confessor* (London, 1970), pp. 256–62.

52 Scholz, 'Sulcard of Westminster', pp. 71–2.

53 Barlow, *Edward the Confessor*, pp. 267–9.

54 *Westminster Abbey Charters*, nos 238–9.

55 *Ibid.*, no. 240.

56 *Ibid.*, no. 248.

57 *Ibid.*, no. 272–4.

58 *Ibid.*, no. 279.

59 *Ibid.*, no. 189.

60 *Papsturkunden in England*, I, no. 13; *Westminster Abbey Charters*, no. 187.

benefactor of the abbey.[61] A few years after her death, and possibly in January 1121, Henry I ordered a daily payment of a half-penny from the farm of London to maintain a light before her tomb.[62] The queen's brother, David earl of Huntingdon, granted land in Tottenham to provide lights, love-feasts and pittances on her anniversary and on those of his parents.[63] He reaffirmed this grant in 1141, and further confirmations were obtained from his son and grandsons.[64] Westminster would naturally want to retain any such endowments, but even allowing for the initial legatine and comital grants, there is no indication that Edith Matilda's cult enjoyed any popularity.

Attempts to promote the queen's cult had a certain urgency, in that the canons of Holy Trinity Aldgate also aspired to house her tomb.[65] In this era of Augustinian expansion, it would be doubly essential to retain Matilda's tomb, and any potential cult, for the Benedictine Westminster.

There was little long-term potential for the queen's cult at Westminster, and further efforts focused on Edward alone. While the first petition for his canonization, in 1139, was a failure,[66] the second, in 1161, was a success,[67] and eminent churchmen were enlisted to help promote his cult more widely.[68] Abbatial charters reflected this change. Abbot Herbert wrote of 'our good patron King Edward, founder of this church',[69] or 'our King Edward, founder of our church',[70] a phrase also used by Abbot Gervase.[71] Promotion of the cult was encouraged by successive abbots, who sometimes specified renders of candles, incense, or even of pepper (possibly with the garnishing of pittances in mind) on Edward's feast-day.[72] Abbot Lawrence encouraged the popularity of the cult at Westminster's daughter-house of Hurley by providing extra food on his feast day,[73] a gesture followed by Abbot Walter, who expressed the hope that its inmates would celebrate the occasion with greater

61 J. Armitage Robinson, *Gilbert Crispin, Abbot of Westminster* (Cambridge, 1911), p. 155, no. 38; *Westminster Abbey Charters*, no. 97.

62 Armitage Robinson, *Gilbert Crispin*, p. 156, no. 39; *Westminster Abbey Charters*, no. 79.

63 *The Acts of Malcolm IV, King of Scots 1153–1165, together with Scottish Royal Acts prior to 1153*, ed. G.W.S. Barrow, Regesta Regum Scottorum, I (Edinburgh, 1960), no. 6.

64 *Ibid.*, nos 13–14, 36, 154; *The Acts of William I, King of Scots 1165–1214*, ed. G.W.S. Barrow, with W.W. Scott, Regesta Regum Scottorum, II (Edinburgh, 1971), no. 52.

65 *The Cartulary of Holy Trinity Aldgate*, ed. G.A.J. Hodgett, London Record Society, 7 (London, 1971), p. 230.

66 Dugdale, *Monasticon Anglicanum*, I, p. 308, no. LIV; *Westminster Abbey Charters*, no. 158.

67 Barlow, *Edward the Confessor*, pp. 323–4, no. 14; Dugdale, *Monasticon Anglicanum*, I, pp. 308b–309, no. LV; *Westminster Abbey Charters*, nos 167–8. For the development of the cult down to this juncture, see *The Life of King Edward who Rests at Westminster*, pp. 150–63.

68 *Westminster Abbey Charters*, nos 190, 204, 221, 401.

69 *Ibid.*, no. 244.

70 *Ibid.*, no. 250.

71 *Ibid.*, no. 265.

72 *Ibid.*, nos 297, 313, 360.

73 *Ibid.*, no. 285.

devotion and honour.[74] A Westminster forgery in the name of King Henry II ascribed his confirmation of the manor of Denham (Bucks.) to his devotion to St Edward;[75] a very considerable fine was rendered to King John for the 'restoration' of King Edward's birthplace of Islip (Oxon.)[76] and Abbot Ralph Arundel invoked Edward's authority in enforcing an anathema to be incurred by anyone impeding the convent's enjoyment of the vill of Parham.[77] Yet the promotion of the cult beyond the abbey walls met with little recorded success in this period. One rare reference to it occurs in a confirmation of a rent of 6 pence, made 'to St Edward, patron of the church of Westminster' by Matthew of Staines, a charter dating from the reign of King John.[78] There was still a need for Westminster to enlist the help of eminent clerics to promote the cult of their saint,[79] while the arrangements made by Abbot Ralph to maintain appropriate lights around his feretory were amended by William de Humez.[80] Only in the reign of Henry III, when religious corporations vied to express their recognition of Edward's merits, would there be much public recognition of St Edward.[81]

74 *Ibid.*, no. 302.

75 *Ibid.*, no. 138.

76 *Rotuli Chartarum in Turri Londoniensi asservati 1199–1216*, ed. T. Duffus Hardy, Record Comm. (London, 1837), f. 139b.; *Westminster Abbey Charters*, no. 149.

77 *Westminster Abbey Charters*, no. 335.

78 *Ibid.*, no. 458.

79 *Ibid.*, nos 193, 401.

80 Westminster Abbey Domesday (Muniment Book 11), f. 370r.

81 British Library MS Cotton Faustina A III, ff. 261v–262v.

15

Conclusion

The great abundance of the muniments of Westminster abbey ensures that any treatment of its history must be selective, first in chronological span and then in the approach taken to the materials available from the chosen period. This study has focused on the abbey from the perspective of its people, as depicted in the charters of the period, its monastic inhabitants, their lay employees, benefactors, tenants and others with whom the monks came into contact.

While the abbots, from the time of Vitalis onwards, can be viewed as clearly defined individuals, this is rarely the case with the monks, apart, of course, from Prior Osbert de Clare. More often there is a pen-portrait of one or another of the donors, including those compelled by force of circumstances to become donors, or in fact vendors, such as Matilda de Parys,[1] or Marwenna and her daughter-in-law Alice, 'who had no children, and no hope of any'.[2]

Looming over the community was the royal court and in particular the Exchequer and its officers: William of Ely, a royal treasurer and the 'most dear and special friend' of the abbey;[3] Gerin 'the king's minister', probably the Gerin, keeper of the royal palace, who was healed by the posthumous mediation of King Edward;[4] and the Exchequer chamberlain Robert Mauduit and his wife Isabel Basset, devotees of the cult of the Blessed Virgin and promoters of the Lady Altar.[5] Conversely the name of the powerful Richard of Ilchester recurs in the charters, for good and for ill.[6] His kinsfolk were themselves tenants of the monks, and his nephew Adam was a frequent testator of charters relating to the vill.[7] Charters, primarily concerned with

1 *Westminster Abbey Charters, 1066–c.1214*, ed. Emma Mason, assisted by the late Jennifer Bray, continuing the work of the late Desmond J. Murphy, London Record Society, 25 (London, 1988), nos 371–3, 460–61.

2 *Ibid.*, nos 437–8.

3 *Ibid.*, no. 313.

4 *Ibid.*, no. 261 and note.

5 *Ibid.*, nos 329, 446–7, 449–50.

6 *Ibid.*, nos 135, 139, 144, 222, 227–8, 231–2, 281, 287, 361, 437–8, 457, 468.

7 *Ibid.*, nos 288, 387, 413–14, 416, 422, 437–8, 440, 443–4, 446–8, 451; *The Beauchamp*

property of one kind and another, give little indication of the spiritual impact made by the liturgy. In this splendid setting, the prayers of the monks would seem to potential benefactors to be exeptionally efficacious. A hint of the spiritual attraction of Westminster is gained from the request of Robert Mauduit (II), made slightly beyond the period covered by this study, that his *obit* should be celebrated in the same manner as those of Abbots Lawrence and William Postard, and with ringing of bells by the gild.[8]

The perspectives of historians, even when working on the same period and drawing on much the same categories of material, will vary as much as will those who edit film, or sound-bites. Consequently one person will not view the life of medieval Westminster as another would, given that each historian will have a personal bias arising from many factors – hence the scope of 'possible history', as Eleanor Searle has termed it.[9] Moreover the focus, in the present study, on the evidence of the charters, with their inbuilt emphasis on property and privileges, draws attention away from other aspects of the monastery's life in this period, including the fact that the abbots both planned projects and also fell under penalizing constraints, which led them into the debt of Jewish moneylenders.[10] The imbalance in the nature of surviving sources hinders the capacity of the reader to grasp the total impact of this great community as it went about its daily business. Yet the urge of individuals to be commemorated there – whether by having their names entered in the martyrology,[11] by securing burial rights,[12] or those of confraternity,[13] all testify to a belief, current throughout the period covered by this study, that the individual could best achieve spiritual salvation through the mediation of St Peter of Westminster.

Cartulary Charters: 1100–1268, ed. Emma Mason, Pipe Roll Society, new series, xliii (London, 1980), nos 183–6, 191–2, 199–200.

8 Emma Mason, 'The Mauduits and their Chamberlainship of the Exchequer', *Bulletin of the Institute of Historical Research*, 49 (1976), pp. 22–3.

9 Eleanor Searle, 'Possible History', *Speculum*, 61 (1986), pp. 779–86.

10 C. Roth, *The History of the Jews in England*, 3rd edn (1964, reprinted Oxford, 1979), pp. 5, 7, 16, 41.

11 *Westminster Abbey Charters*, nos 328–9, 385.

12 *Ibid.*, nos 237, 388, 436.

13 *Ibid.*, nos 329, 334, 338, 359, 388.

Appendix 1

Westminster Abbey and the Monarchy between the Reigns of William I and John 1066–1216

The lavish patronage bestowed on Westminster Abbey by Edward the Confessor, and later by Henry III, ensured its status as the church which preeminently enjoyed royal favour and was designated by each as his mausoleum.[1] During the intervening reigns, the prestige of the abbey was less assured. The present paper seeks to examine the extent to which the genuine charters issued from, or for, Westminster between 1066 and 1216 testify to any special relationship with the monarchy. Omitted from the discussion is any detailed examination of the voluminous output of forgeries, largely produced in the third and fourth decades of the twelfth century by Prior Osbert de Clare, his associates and their immediate successors. These documents represent an imaginative campaign at Westminster to revive the dwindling prestige of the abbey by reasserting its rights and claims but do not reflect the status of the house as it was perceived by detached observers.[2]

JMH = *Journal of Medieval History*; WAD = Westminster Abbey Domesday; WAM = Westminster Abbey Muniment; *BIHR* = *Bulletin of the Institute of Historical Research.*

The Leverhulme Trust, the Nuffield Foundation and the British Academy have generously funded successive phases of my work on the Westminster Abbey charters dating from between 1066 and 1214. A volume of these charters has recently been published by the London Record Society. I am grateful to the late Dr Jennifer Bray for her assistance throughout this project; to Miss Barbara Harvey, Dr Diana Greenway, Dr Jane Sayers and Dr David Bates for their views on the documents discussed here; and to the staff of Westminster Abbey Library for much patient help. Professor Frank Barlow kindly read and commented on an earlier version of this paper, which was delivered in abridged form on 9 May 1987, during the Twenty-second International Congress on Medieval Studies, held at the Western Michigan University, Kalamazoo, Michigan. Comments made there by Dr Susan Ridyard and Dr Brian Golding have been incorporated in the revision of this paper, with subsequent ones by Professor Martin Biddle.

1 On King Edward's decision, see the *Vita Ædwardi regis*, ed. and trans. Frank Barlow, London 1962, 44–6. On King Henry, see *Charter Rolls 1226–57*, 306; Barbara Harvey, *Westminster Abbey and its Estates in the Middle Ages*, Oxford 1977, 28–9; Steven H. Wander, 'The Westminster Abbey sanctuary pavement', *Traditio* xxxiv (1978), 137–56, esp. p. 153.

2 Many of the major forgeries are discussed by Pierre Chaplais, 'The original charters of

First published in *The Journal of Ecclesiastical History*, 41 (1990)

The genuine documents are examined for evidence of the extent to which Westminster was recognised as a royal burial church; the frequency with which grants were made for the spiritual welfare of the royal family, whether by the king or by others; the intensity of interest in the abbey displayed by successive kings; the popularity of the cult of Edward the Confessor and the extent to which the current dynasty was perceived to share kinship with him.

King Edward rebuilt and generously endowed the abbey of St Peter of Westminster, intending that it should be his mausoleum. He was buried there in 1066, as was his widow, Queen Edith, in 1075.[3] The tomb of Queen Matilda, first wife of Henry I, joined theirs in 1118.[4] Her burial at Westminster was probably fortuitous, the result of her death at the adjacent palace, since the canons of her foundation of Holy Trinity, Aldgate, in London, had hoped to secure her burial in their own church.[5] Yet the late queen had been profoundly conscious of her descent from the house of Wessex,[6] and she perhaps ultimately chose to be buried beside its last consecrated ruler.

In 1066 both Harold II Godwinson and William I urgently needed to establish themselves as legitimate successors of King Edward. The obvious

Herbert and Gervase, abbots of Westminster (1121–1157)', in *A Medieval Miscellany for Doris Mary Stenton*, ed. Patricia M. Barnes and C. F. Slade (Pipe Roll Society, NS xxxvi, 1962), 89–99. See also B. W. Scholz, 'Two forged charters from the Abbey of Westminster and their relationship with St-Denis', *EHR* lxxvi (1961), 466–78. Surviving charters for Westminster issued in the name of King Edward, or of those of his predecessors, are listed in chronological sequence, with comments on their authenticity, by P. H. Sawyer, *Anglo-Saxon Charters: an annotated list and bibliography*, London 1968. The charters of William I are being re-edited by Dr David Bates, and I concur with his views regarding the authenticity, or otherwise, of those documents issued for Westminster by both William I and William II. The *Regesta Regum Anglo-Normannorum I: 1066–1100*, ed. H. W. C. Davis with R. J. Whitewell, Oxford 1913, omits several charters issued for Westminster by William I, and its comments on others are erroneous. Editorial comment on the authenticity of Henry I's charters for Westminster in the *Regesta Regum Anglo-Normannorum II: 1100–1135*, ed. C. Johnson and H. A. Cronne, Oxford 1956, cannot invariably be sustained. Full texts of all King Stephen's charters for Westminster are printed in the *Regesta Regum Anglo-Normannorum III: 1135–1154*, ed. H. A Cronne and R. H. C. Davis, Oxford 1968, where nos 928–9, 939–41 are designated as forgeries. The editors appear undecided about no. 937, but this can also be shown to be a forgery on textual grounds.

3 *Vita Ædwardi*, 44–6. On Queen Edith's funeral, see *The Anglo-Saxon Chronicle*, trans. and ed. Dorothy Whitelock, with D. C. Douglas and Susie I. Tucker, London 1961, D, E, 158. King Edward's rebuilding of Westminster was paralleled by Queen Edith's rebuilding of the nunnery of Wilton, where her namesake, the royal St Edith, was buried, *Vita Ædwardi*, 46–7. The queen retained an association with this house in her widowhood, ibid. 100, and perhaps intended that its church should be her mausoleum. By according her a ceremonious funeral at Westminster, King William ensured that Wilton would not become the focus of yet another tomb-cult of a member of the former royal house.

4 ASC, E, 186; Harvey, *Westminster Abbey*, 373 and n. 6.

5 *The Cartulary of Holy Trinity Aldgate*, ed. G. A. Hodgett (London Record Soc. vii, 1971), nos 13, 997.

6 Judith A. Green, *The Government of England under Henry I*, Cambridge 1986, 10–11.

means of symbolising this continuity was to inaugurate their rule in the church which housed his tomb. These precedents were followed by their successors, thus ensuring recognition of Westminster as the coronation church.[7] Both Harold and William were buried in churches which they had earlier patronised, and their successors, down to 1216, similarly selected their mausolea on the basis of personal preference.[8] This separation of royal burial from inauguration rituals parallels earlier developments in France. The Capetian kings retained Rheims as the coronation church, thus symbolising their continuity with their Carolingian predecessors, while the abbey of St-Denis was the mausoleum of the earlier Capetians, who gained important advantages from association with this powerful cult.[9] There was also, perhaps, a wish to disassociate the ritual of king-making from the site of a predecessor's obsequies.[10]

As the twelfth century progressed, ecclesiastical foundations attached increasing value to their possession of royal remains which became, in effect, status symbols. In both realms, successive kings founded or endowed churches as their mausolea. Each founder intended to be buried alone or, at most, with the immediate members of his family, perhaps in order to ensure an exclusive concentration of monastic intercessions.[11] Henry I's foundation of Reading, and Stephen's of Faversham, illustrate this point.[12]

Meanwhile, at Westminster, King Edward's tomb gradually became a focus of veneration. The progressive stages in the development of his cult are recorded in the *Vita Ædwardi regis*, completed by an anonymous writer c. 1067; the *Vita beati Eadwardi regis Anglorum*, by Prior Osbert de Clare, completed in 1138, to accompany the first petition for canonisation; and the *Vita sancti Edwardi regis*, which the Cistercian abbot, Ailred of Rievaulx, was

7 Harvey, op. cit. 25.

8 In some instances, choice was influenced by political considerations, Emma Mason, 'Pro statu et incolumnitate regni mei: royal monastic patronage 1066–1154', *Studies in Church History* xviii (1982), 99–117; Elizabeth M. Hallam, 'Royal burial and the cult of kingship in France and England, 1066–1330', *JMH* viii (1982), 359–80; Emma Mason, 'St Wulfstan's staff: a legend and its uses', *Medium Ævum* liii (1984), 157, 170–1.

9 Gabrielle M. Spiegel, 'The cult of St Denis and Capetian kingship', *JMH* i (1975), 43–69.

10 Parallel considerations to those which prompted Harold II and William I in their choice of coronation church influenced German rulers. Aachen Cathedral, where Charlemagne was buried, Einhard and Notker the Stammerer, *Two Lives of Charlemagne*, trans. L. Thorpe, Harmondsworth 1969, 84–5, was the coronation church of rulers descended from a series of dynasties, Boyd D. Hill Jr, *Medieval Monarchy in Action*, London 1972, 25, 61, 85, 101; Otto of Freising, *The Deeds of Frederick Barbarossa*, trans. and intro. C. C. Mierow, New York 1953, new edn 1966, 53, 116–17.

11 Hallam, 'Royal burial', 363–4, 367.

12 On Reading, see *Reading Abbey Cartularies* i, ed. B. R. Kemp (Camden Society, 4th ser. xxxi, 1986), 13–19 and nos 1–2. On Faversham, see W. Dugdale, *Monasticon Anglicanum*, 6 vols, rev. H. Caley et al., London 1817–30, iv. 573 no. 3. See also Hallam, op. cit. 369.

commissioned to write after King Edward's canonisation in 1161, in readiness for the translation of his remains in 1163.[13]

In the years following King Edward's death, there is no positive evidence of the encouragement of his cult by anyone. It may be conjectured that a few Westminster monks, perhaps an 'English faction', lent it some support. Queen Matilda, conscious of her English ancestry, would have had a vested interest in encouraging the cult in the early years of the twelfth century but this is only a hypothesis.[14] Miracle stories indicate that Edward's cult had its devotees among Londoners in the reign of Henry I,[15] and there is evidence in the Westminster archives that the cult was actively promoted by the Norman abbot, Gilbert Crispin (1085–1117/8).[16] Native cults were rapidly adopted by various Norman prelates,[17] and Gilbert was by no means the first Norman abbot to see the potential for his monastery in promoting an unofficial English cult.[18] King Edward's tomb was employed at Westminster as a powerful reinforcement of the abbey's claim to afford sanctuary to fugitives from all over England. Indeed, the earliest sustained, genuine evidence for the existence of Edward's cult at Westminster is contained in a series of eight abbatial writs, concerning the flight to the abbey of named individuals and usually addressed to the named sheriff of a particular shire.

The earliest such writs to survive are three issued in the name of Abbot Gilbert Crispin. In two of these, the sheriff was informed that the fugitive had fled to 'Christ, St Peter and King Edward',[19] while a third depicts the fugitive as seeking 'the altar of St Peter and the body of King Edward'. This identical phrase occurs in the one writ on this subject surviving in the name of Abbot Herbert (1121–*c*. 1136).[20] Of Herbert's other surviving charters one, granting to the abbey the rents from certain churches, was made 'to the honour of God and of St Peter, our advocate . . . and for the repose of our good patron, King Edward, devoted founder of this church'. Another was

13 *Vita Ædwardi*, pp. xiv–xli; Frank Barlow, *Edward the Confessor*, London 1970, 256–85, where ancillary evidence on the development of the cult is also considered. See also B. W. Scholz, 'The canonization of Edward the Confessor', *Speculum* xxvi (1961), 38–60. He suggests that the 'book of miracles' presented to Pope Alexander III with the second petition for canonisation was actually the *Vita* as revised by Osbert de Clare, ibid. 49–50; cf. Barlow, op. cit. 278.

14 See, however, Derek Baker, ' "A nursery of saints": St Margaret of Scotland reconsidered', in *Medieval Women*, ed. D. Baker, Oxford 1978, 122–5.

15 *Vita Ædwardi*, 124–8.

16 J. Armitage Robinson, *Gilbert Crispin, Abbot of Westminster*, Cambridge 1911, 13–18.

17 Susan J. Ridyard, '*Condigna Veneratio*: post-Conquest attitudes to the saints of the Anglo-Saxons', *Anglo-Norman Studies IX. Proceedings of the Battle Conference 1986*, ed. R. Allen Brown, Woodbridge, 1987, 179–206.

18 In *c*. 1077 the Norman abbot of Evesham, Walter de Cérisy, produced in support of his claim to certain lands the relics of the English St Ecgwine, *Placita Anglo Normannica*, ed. M. M. Bigelow, London 1879, 18.

19 Armitage Robinson, *Gilbert Crispin*, 37; *Monasticon* i, 310 no. 64. Only seven writs and charters survive in the name of Abbot Gilbert.

20 Armitage Robinson, op. cit. 37; *Monasticon* i, 310 no. 62.

made 'for the soul of our King Edward, founder of our church'.[21] Both charters are of uncertain date and show that the late King Edward, while acknowledged as patron and founder, was regarded as being in need of prayers himself, rather than as an intercessor. None of the other charters surviving in Abbot Herbert's name has any bearing on the development of King Edward's cult, although three legatine indulgences, discussed below, date from the early years of this abbacy.

Abbot Gervase (1138–c. 1157) is known to have issued three writs concerning fugitives who had fled to Westminster. In two of these the fugitive is said to have fled to 'the mercy of God, the altar of St Peter and the tomb of King Edward',[22] while the equivalent phrase in the third writ is 'the mercy of God and St Peter, and the tomb of King Edward'. This identical phrase is found in the one writ concerning fugitives which survives in the name of Abbot Laurence (*c.* 1158–73).[23] The third writ of Abbot Gervase further cites 'the dignity of our church and of King Edward' as grounds for sparing the fugitive in life and limb.

In his other charters, Gervase depicted King Edward as someone to be prayed for. His grants to the nuns of the abbey's dependent cell of Kilburn were variously made 'for the soul of King Edward' and 'for the soul of our King Edward, the founder of our church'.[24] This abbot continued to acknowledge the abbey's traditional patron, and his grant of the manor to provide lights before the sacrament was made out to reverence to 'St Peter, prince of the apostles, our advocate'.[25] Recognition of St Peter as advocate recurs in documents issued by later abbots.

It was at the outset of Gervase's abbacy that the first attempt was made to secure the canonisation of King Edward, but this project had already been planned by Prior Osbert de Clare as part of his wider programme to reassert Westminster's rights and claims.[26] The petition was rejected by Pope Innocent II, because of the scanty evidence produced to demonstrate King Edward's sanctity and the lack of widespread support for the petition through the realm.[27]

The second, successful, petition for Edward's canonisation was organised by Abbot Laurence,[28] and recognition of Edward's enhanced status might therefore be anticipated in this abbot's charters. Yet, apart from Laurence's one sanctuary writ, which itself follows a model provided by Abbot Gervase,

21 Chaplais, 'Original charters', 100–1; *Monasticon* i. 307 no. 50; ibid. iii. 426 no. 2. Ten charters survive in Abbot Herbert's name.

22 Ibid. i. 310 no. 61. WAD (Muniment Book 11), for. 79v.

23 WAD, fo. 79v; *Monasticon* i, 310 no. 63.

24 Ibid. iii. 427 nos 4 and 5. The texts of twenty-four writs and charters survive in the name of Abbot Gervase.

25 WAD, fo. 377v.

26 Barlow, *Edward the Confessor*, 272–6.

27 *Monasticon* i, 308 no. 54.

28 Barlow, op. cit. 278–80.

there is only one other document surviving in the name of Abbot Laurence which relates to Edward's cult. This charter grants a church to the dependent cell of Hurley, so that its revenues would enable the brethren to enjoy a more lavish menu on the feast of St Edward and thus demonstrate a greater devotion towards him.[29] This aspiration was reiterated in a subsequent charter issued for Hurley by Abbot Walter (1175–90).[30] Only one other of Walter's charters reflects the existence of Edward's cult – a grant of a mill in return for a pound of incense due annually to the altar of St Peter on the feast of the Translation of St Edward.[31]

Similarly, from the abbacy of Walter's successor, William Postard (1191–1200), there survives only one charter which hints at the existence of the cult. This is a confirmation of property in Westminster, which was made to the King's treasurer, William of Ely, in return for a candle weighing two pounds, which was due annually on the feast of the Translation of King Edward.[32] This rent is also cited in the prior grant of the land to William of Ely by his kinsman Richard Fitz Nigel, bishop of London, and in a related confirmation by King John.[33] Finally, Edward's cult is mentioned in only one charter of those surviving from the abbacy of Ralph Arundel (1200–14). Granting the vill of Parham to the convent of Westminster, he declared that anyone impeding their control over it would incur anathema 'by the authority of the blessed apostles Peter and Paul, and of King Edward and all the saints of God'.[34] This is the sum total of evidence for the observance of Edward's cult in more than 120 abbatial writs and charters. It might be argued that if more such documents had survived these would contain further evidence, although abbatial charters, concerned with the management of endowments, were not designed to reflect the existence of the royal cult to any marked extent.

Nor do the charters of rank-and-file donors[35] display any widespread evidence of veneration for St Edward. More than 130 charters relating to Westminster's interests in this period survive in the names of non-royal laity and of lesser clerics. Half of these cannot be expected to reflect the royal cult, since they comprise a few administrative writs, together with a much larger number of grants of land by donor A to donor B, the eventual grantor of the property to Westminster. Yet of the direct grants, only seven, scarcely more

29 WAM 2280. Abbot Laurence's surviving charters total twelve.

30 WAM 2270.

31 WAM 1767. Walter's surviving charters total twenty.

32 H. G. Richardson, 'William of Ely, the king's treasurer (? 1195–1215)', *Transactions of the Royal Historical Society*, 4th ser. xv (1932), 80–1 no. 2. William Postard's surviving charters total twenty.

33 Ibid. 79–80 no. 1; *Rotuli chartarum in Turri Londoniensi asservati 1199–1216*, ed. T. Duffus Hardy, London 1837, 49a, m.10.

34 WAD fos 572r–3r. Abbot Ralph's surviving charters total twelve.

35 For an analysis of these, see Emma Mason, 'The donors of Westminster Abbey charters: c. 1066–1240', *Medieval Prosopography* viii/2 (1987), 1–17.

than 10 per cent, reflect any awareness either of the cult of St Edward or of any special relationship between the abbey and the monarchy.

Two charters of lay donors reflect an awareness of the cult of St Edward. Late in the twelfth century, Laurence *cognomen diabolus* granted a fee in Ludgate, London, which he and his successors would hold of the monks at an annual rent of a pound of pepper due on the feast of the Translation of St Edward.[36] In King John's reign, Matthew of Staines granted 'to God and Blessed Edward, patron of the Church of Westminster', an annual rent of 6*d.* in the vill of Staines (Middlesex), which was to be paid annually to 'Blessed Edward . . . on the day of his translation'.[37] Matthew's reference to St Edward as patron of Westminster is unique among ordinary lay donors in this period. It might be suggested that the expression was dictated by the monks who were to receive this benefaction, but it that case, the phrase would be expected to be found recurring in the charters of other donors. As demonstrated in the charters of Abbot Walter and Abbot William, cited above, specification of the feast of St Edward's Translation for the payment of rent was the initiative of Westminster, rather than of the layman involved in the transaction. A rent of a large quantity of incense, or of a large candle, had an obvious use on such a major feast day (major at least in the eyes of the Westminster monks, though perhaps not in those of the surrounding laity). Similarly the rent of pepper due from Laurence *diabolus* would have a culinary use in the generous pittances which the monks enjoyed on festivals.[38]

Concern for the spiritual welfare of one or more of the Angevin kings was expressed in five further charters, granted by, or on behalf of, men who enjoyed some measure of official status. William de Mandeville, earl of Essex (1166–89), confirmed to Westminster a church which it had held in the time of his ancestors 'for the soul of my lord, King Henry'.[39] William Turpin, an officer of the royal Chamber, granted land outside Ludgate, London, to his wife Rose, c. 1177. She was empowered to donate this land to any church she pleased, 'for our souls, and for the soul of my lord King Henry . . . to the honour of God and of the Blessed Virgin Mary'. It pleased Rose, in her widowhood, to grant the land to the Lady Altar at Westminster, but she did not name King Henry among the resulting spiritual beneficiaries.[40] Rose made a further grant to the abbey in association with Ralph Mauduit. Their messuage in Westminster was donated 'for the soul of King Henry and for the

36 WAD, fo. 474v.

37 WAD, fo. 136r.

38 Miss Barbara Harvey's recent work on the monastic diet at Westminster confirms both the generous quantity of the pittances enjoyed on feast days and also the remarkable extent to which the dishes were highly seasoned.

39 BL, MS Cotton Charter x. 1.

40 WAM 13844, 13845.

health of our souls'.[41] Since Ralph was a minor royal official,[42] it was perhaps he who was concerned for the king's spiritual welfare. More surprisingly, perhaps, London's first mayor, Henry Fitz Ailwin (d. 1212), granted rent in London 'for the safety of the soul of King Henry . . .'[43] a king who had not favoured the aspirations of the Londoners towards greater self-government.[44] Slightly later than these grants is another, made *c.* 1218 x 1221. William of Ely, formerly royal treasurer, granted to the abbey certain property in Westminster 'for the souls of Henry, Richard and John, kings of the English, and for the soul of Richard, bishop of London . . .'.[45] In 1216, William had joined the invading forces of Prince Louis, probably taking with him his official records. Understandably, the resurgent regency government would not reinstate him in office.[46] Yet in his declining years William atoned for his defection by enlisting the spiritual support of the monks for his former patrons.

In charters of the laity, therefore, there is no evidence of widespread recognition either of St Edward as a potent intercessor or of Westminster as a major source of spiritual support for the monarchy. After the royal government became centred at Westminster in the later twelfth century, it was only natural that a proportion of the *curiales* would make donations to their nearest big church. The royal officials cited above simply manifested in their charters the gratitude towards their former patrons which was traditionally expected in government circles, and the wording of their grants does not suggest that they regarded the intercessions of the monks of Westminster as being exceptionally efficacious on behalf of the kings of England. In addition to the above-mentioned grants, a somewhat larger number was made by contemporary exchequer officials, such as the chamberlain Robert Mauduit, Alexander of Swerford, later famed as the compiler of the *Red Book of the Exchequer*, or the marshall Jocelin Fitz Hugh. Their donations were made for their own spiritual welfare and that for their families, and their charters contain no evidence that they considered Westminster to have any particular association with the monarchy. Indeed, the most high-ranking of these curial donors, Richard of Ilchester, bishop of Winchester, who made a grant in honour of St Katherine, dedicatee of the Infirmary chapel,[47] even contrived on another occasion to appropriate some of Westminster's land, to which his son, Herbert le Poore, succeeded in due course.[48] St Edward was scarcely even mentioned in the charters of rank-and-file donors. Most lay grants were made in honour of St Peter who, according to the late eleventh-century writer

41 Emma Mason, 'The Mauduits and their chamberlainship of the Exchequer', *BIHR* xlix (1976), 23.

42 *Pipe Roll 34 Henry II*, 17.

43 WAD, fos 485 v–6r.

44 C. N. L Brooke and Gillian Keir, *London: the shaping of a city*, London 1975, 40–1.

45 Richardson, 'William of Ely', 89–90 no. 8.

46 Ibid. 58.

47 WAD, fos 570v–1r.

48 WAM 16737.

Sulcard of Westminster, had himself dedicated the original church on Thorn Island.[49] In the reigns of Richard I and John, however, the laity of London and Westminster made an increasing number of grants to the altar of the Blessed Virgin Mary.[50] Donations to altars dedicated to Mary became common elsewhere in England at this period. The cult of the Virgin had been steadily gaining in popularity throughout the twelfth century, and Lady Chapels were proliferating.

English bishops and archbishops issued some thirty-nine charters for Westminster which survive from this period, but only three of these refer to the cult of the Confessor. Shortly after the canonisation of King Edward, Robert de Chesney, bishop of Lincoln, granted an indulgence of twenty days' remission, to those worshipping at the abbey during the *Depositio* and the Translation of the Confessor, and for fifteen days from the vigil of these ceremonies.[51] A similar indulgence, granting forty days' remission, was issued in the name of Richard de Belmeis (II), bishop of London.[52] Since he died in May 1162,[53] it seems that Westminster began soliciting such indulgences soon after the canonisation in 1161 and well before plans were completed for the translation.[54] Any major church would solicit such indulgences in anticipation of the translation of its new saint, and therefore these bishops were not necessarily devotees of the newly acclaimed St Edward. The dying Richard de Belmeis[55] was, however, remarkably magnanimous, given the sustained and successful resistance offered by the monks of Westminster to visitation by their diocesan.[56] Abbot Laurence also persuaded the cardinal legate, Henry of Pisa, to write to Bishops Hilary of Chichester, Robert de Chesney of Lincoln and Nigel of Ely, urging them to convene at Westminster for the Translation of St Edward.[57] Clearly a spontaneous outburst of devotion was not anticipated.

Only a generation after his canonisation, St Edward's feasts by no means topped the league of those popularly observed at Westminster. Walter de Coutances, archbishop of Rouen (1184–1207), probably during his brief period in control of the government of England, granted an indulgence of twenty days' remission to those visiting the abbey on the feasts of Christmas,

49 B. W. Scholz, 'Sulcard of Westminster: "Prologus de construccione Westmonasterii" ', *Traditio* xx (1964), 83–5.

50 A. G. Rosser, *Medieval Westminster: the vill and the urban community 1200–1540*, PhD diss., London University 1984, 86–92.

51 *English Episcopal Acta IV: Lincoln 1186–1206*, ed. David M. Smith, Oxford 1986, appendix I, no. 19.

52 WAD, fo. 393r.

53 John Le Neve, *Fasti Ecclesiae Anglicanae 1066–1300: I St Paul's, London*, compiled by Diana E. Greenway, London 1968, 2.

54 On the planning of the translation, see Barlow, *Edward the Confessor*, 282.

55 A. Morey and C. N. L. Brooke, *Gilbert Foliot and his Letters*, Cambridge 1965, 98.

56 *Papsturkunden in England*, 3 vols, ed. W. Holtzmann. Berlin-Göttingen, 1930/1–51, i. nos 17, 113, 144, 262, 302.

57 WAD, fo. 388.

Easter, Ascension and Pentecost; the Feast of the Holy Relics; all feasts of the Blessed Virgin and of St Peter, 'and of all the apostles', and on the two feasts of St Edward, king and confessor.[58] During the later decades of the twelfth century, Westminster's anxiety to attract pilgrims evidently led the abbot and monks to promote a variety of cults. That this was a comparatively recent development is shown by an indulgence of Hugh de Puiset, bishop of Durham (1153–95), presumably granted before King Edward's canonisation, since it promoted only the feasts of St Peter and St Paul.[59] A legatine indulgence granted in 1201 by John, cardinal priest of St Stephen in Celio Monte, omitted any mention either of St Edward's feasts or of that of the Holy Relics.[60] This last feast, and one (only) of St Edward were, however, listed with those of St Peter in an indulgence, granted on 11 October 1213, by the legate Nicholas, bishop of Tusculum.[61]

Papal bulls issued for Westminster before the second, successful petition for the canonisation of King Edward rarely reflected any special relationship between the abbey and the monarchy. The one exception is a bull of Innocent II, issued at the prompting of Prior Osbert de Clare, which describes Westminster as a royal monastery.[62] Bulls ranging in date from the pontificate of Innocent II to the early years of that of Alexander III include occasional confirmation of charters issued by King Edgar and by his grandson King Edward. Both are referred to as patrons of the abbey – and Edward as its *renovator*.[63] The bull of Alexander III notifying the abbot and monks of King Edward's canonisation refers to the antecedent petition of King Henry,[64] but nothing in the later bulls of this pope, nor in those of his successors, down to and including Innocent III, refers even obliquely to any continuing special relationship between the monarchy and the abbey.[65] There is no surviving evidence that Alexander, or his successors in this period, issued indulgences designed to foster the cult of St Edward. In the aftermath of the Becket dispute, there would be no enthusiasm in the papal curia for a royal tomb cult in England.

The royal writs and charters issued for Westminster present evidence of a fluctuating relationship between Crown and abbey. Later generations of

58 WAD, fo. 390v.

59 WAD, fo. 390r.

60 WAD, fo. 390r.

61 WAD, fo. 390.

62 *Papsturkunden* i. no. 25; *The Acts of Malcolm IV King of Scots 1153 – 1165*, ed. G. W. S. Barrow, Edinburgh 1960, appendix, no. 319.

63 *Papsturkunden* i, nos 21, 47, 69; WAD, fo.2.

64 Barlow, *Edward the Confessor*, 323–4 no. 14; John Flete, *The History of Westminster Abbey*, ed. J. Armitage Robinson, Cambridge 1909, 193.

65 Pope Alexander III's confirmation of the abbey's possessions, 6 Oct. 1163, *Papsturkunden* i. no. 101, is the only subsequent bull issued before the end of Innocent III's pontificate which even lists earlier named kings as benefactors.

monks esteemed William I as a benefactor,[66] but his posthumous reputation derived in part from the considerable numbers of writs and charters for Westminster which survive in his name. In fact, probably twenty of those ascribed to him are outright forgeries, and this figure does not include several otherwise genuine grants to which attestations were added at a later date. For purposes of the present argument, these are included among the twenty-five texts which represent authentic grants.[67] These documents largely reflect an attitude of perfunctory response towards requests for judicial support, of a kind he would have extended to any of his major abbeys, rather than one of spontaneous generosity towards, or personal interest in, Westminster itself. In a few instances, lands were confirmed 'as King Edward gave them',[68] but in no genuine writ is the late king referred to as William's kinsman. Ten writs and charters for Westminster survive in the name of William Rufus. All appear genuine, although in one case the attestations were perhaps added at a later date.[69] His writs, like those of his father, simply reflect an attitude of routine response towards petitions from the abbey.

Henry I was the other king of the Norman dynasty who was later recalled as a benefactor of Westminster.[70] His genuine writs and charters for the abbey total thirty-four, with a further six forged texts surviving in his name.[71] This gives a ratio of one mandate for almost each regnal year, approximately equal to those for his two immediate predecessors. However, it cannot be assumed that the documents were issued at such regular intervals. In any reign intermittent crises in Westminster's affairs no doubt prompted an occasional flurry of requests for writs. One well known writ of Henry I, dating from 1100 x 1107, ordered that Gloucester, Westminster and Winchester were to have an ounce of gold on each festival when the king wore his crown in one of these churches, as Bishop Maurice (of London) testified was the case in the time of the king's *antecessores*.[72] In the pre-Conquest era, Westminster is known to have been favoured with a royal visit on the occasion of major religious festivals only at the very end of Edward's reign. William I and William II were occasionally at Westminster either at Christmas or at Pentecost. Henry I usually celebrated Christmas there, and occasionally Pentecost, too, down

66 Flete, op. cit. 34, 71; WAD, fo. 2; *Papsturkunden* i. nos 47, 69, 101; Harvey, *Westminster Abbey*, 27–8.

67 These figures derive from my own recent work on the abbey's charters and coincide with the findings of Dr David Bates. See also above n. 2.

68 E.g. BL, MS Cotton Faustina A iii, fo. 60; see also Armitage Robinson, *Gilbert Crispin*, 140.

69 These figures are again derived from my own work and coincide with those reached by Dr Bates. See also above n. 2.

70 Flete, *Westminster Abbey*, 87; *Papsturkunden* i, nos 47, 69, 101.

71 These figures are derived from my own work. The spurious texts are those which are calendared in the *Regesta II*, as nos 489, 668 (which is, in fact, a conflation of two texts), 1177, 1240, 1883. See also above n. 2.

72 Armitage Robinson, *Gilbert Crispin*, 141 no. 18; J. H. Round, *The King's Sergeants*, London 1911, 322.

to 1109, but after that year the only major festival which he is known to have celebrated at Westminster was Pentecost 1121.[73] From the early years of the reign, when he was regularly making ceremonial visits to the abbey, there survives a writ for Westminster in which he appears to underline its role in upholding the spiritual welfare of the ruling dynasty. This grant was made for the souls of his father and brother, and for his own, and for those of his wife Queen Matilda and of their children.[74]

Only three later charters make any specific association between the spiritual welfare of Henry, or other members of his family, and benefactions to the abbey. These grants all date from the aftermath of the White Ship disaster, when the future of Henry's dynasty appeared uncertain. Early in 1121 he appointed Herbert as abbot of Westminster and granted a series of charters designed to ensure the recovery of rights and possessions which had been eroded during the vacancy following the death of Abbot Gilbert Crispin in 1117 or 1118. The language of these three charters is to some extent reminiscent of that of the Westminster forgeries, yet there are solid reasons for accepting the group as genuine. Two of the grants were made for the king's soul, and for that of his kinsman King Edward, together with those of Henry's ancestors and successors,[75] while the third more explicitly associates the fortunes of the Norman royal house with Westminster Abbey. This grant is additionally made for the souls of William I, William II and William Ætheling, those of the king's mother and of his late wife Queen Matilda.[76] It was perhaps hoped that confirmation by the bereaved King Henry of grants earlier made to the abbey by his 'kinsman' King Edward would be reciprocated by a satisfactory resolution to the succession crisis. Yet King Henry had no intention of allowing Westminster to assume a wider responsibility for the spiritual welfare of himself or his line. He founded Reading Abbey in the earlier part of 1121, probably intending from the outset that it should be his mausoleum.[77]

Westminster's most ambitious hopes might be dashed, but it was perhaps

73 Martin Biddle, 'Seasonal festivals and residence: Winchester, Westminster and Gloucester in the tenth to twelfth centuries', in *Anglo-Norman Studies VIII: Proceedings of the Battle Conference 1985*, ed. R. Allen Brown, Woodbridge, 1986, 51–72.

74 Armitage Robinson, op. cit. 144 no. 24; T. A. M. Bishop, *Scriptores regis*, Oxford 1961, no. 521, plate x (a).

75 Armitage Robinson, op. cit. 163–4; T. Madox, *Formulare Anglicanum*, London 1702, lxv.

76 Ibid. ccccxcvi.

77 *Reading Abbey Cartularies* i. 13–19 and nos 1–2. Before Henry's body was taken to Reading, his entrails were buried in the priory church of Notre-Dame-du-Pré, outside Rouen. William of Malmesbury, reporting this, added that Henry's mother had founded the church and that he himself had been a benefactor, *Historia Novella*, trans. and intro. K. R. Potter, London 1955, 14. The parish church had been founded by Henry's parents, but the monastic cell, which was a dependency of Bec, was regarded by the monks of Bec as being Henry's foundation. Orderic Vitalis, writing in Saint Evroul, reported that Notre-Dame-du-Pré had been begun by Henry's mother, and

in this very year that an attempt was made to realise the potential of the abbey's most recent royal burial, that of Queen Matilda, kinswoman of King Edward. She had anticipated spiritual benefits accruing to herself, her husband and children in return for a grant of land which she had made to the abbey in her later years.[78] Following her burial at Westminster in 1118, Henry I ordered a daily payment, in perpetuity, of one obol to provide a light before her sepulchre.[79] Moreover, the late queen's brother, Earl David, donated rent from land in Middlesex to provide another light, together with pittances on her anniversary, and also on the anniversary of the deaths of his father and mother (i.e. Malcolm III Canmore, king of Scots, and his wife Queen Margaret).[80]

The legate Peter Pierleoni was in England during the summer of 1121,[81] and texts of two indulgences for Westminster survive in his name, although the authenticity of both has been questioned. One indulgence grants, *inter alia*, forty days' remission to those of the faithful worshipping at the abbey on the feasts of Saints Peter and Paul.[82] The second indulgence appears to be an abridged variant of the first and purported to have been granted 'because King Edward, and Queen Matilda, of good memory, lie buried in that monastery'.[83] This latter document was perhaps shown to the legate John de Crema, when he was in England in 1125, and accepted by him, since a similarly worded indulgence survives in his name.[84] Further evidence from independent sources suggest that in the years after Queen Matilda's death she was popularly regarded as a saint,[85] but in the absence of official encouragement, whether from pope or king, her cult soon lapsed. Yet the fact that it was encouraged at Westminster, even if only for a few years after her death, indicates that in the 1120s the cult of Edward the Confessor was attracting little widespread popularity on its own.

completed by him. *The Ecclesiastical History of Orderic Vitalis* vi, ed. and trans. Majorie Chibnall, Oxford 1978, 450.

78 Armitage Robinson, *Gilbert Crispin*, 155 no. 38.

79 Ibid. 156 no. 39.

80 *The Acts of Malcolm IV*, no. 6.

81 Eadmer, *Historia Novorum*, ed. M. Rule (Rolls Series, 1884), 294–7.

82 *Papsturkunden* i. no. 12. See M. Brett, *The English Church under Henry I*, Oxford 1975, 41 n. 4; *Councils and Synods, with other documents relating to the English Church, I: 871–1204*, ed. D. Whitelock, M. Brett and C. N. L. Brooke, Oxford 1981, ii. 724; *Papsturkunden* i. 234–5.

83 Ibid. i. no. 13. See Brett, op. cit. 41 n. 4; *Councils and Synods I* ii. 724; *Papsturkunden* i. 237.

84 WAD, fo. 389v. The possibility remains that this text is a further fabrication, based on the earlier ones. On John of Crema's legatine visit and his convening of a council at Westminster, see *Councils and Synods I* ii. 731–41; *Chronicle of John of Worcester*, ed. J. R. H. Weaver (Anecdota Oxoniensia, 1908), 20–2.

85 Barlow, *Edward the Confessor*, 270 and n. 1, 272; Green, *Government of England*, 11 and n. 53. Queen Matilda had been actively engaged in religious patronage and good works in London, Brooke and Keir, *London 800–1216*, 315–23, hence, perhaps, a degree of spontaneous popular enthusiasm for her cult.

Even though Matilda's cult soon waned, Westminster vigorously upheld its title to the land which financed her second tomb-light. Her brother David, like Matilda and their mother Queen Margaret, was strongly conscious of his descent from the old English royal line,[86] and it perhaps seemed fitting to him that members of his family were commemorated in King Edward's church. In 1124, David succeeded to the Scottish throne, and thereafter Westminster's control over his endowment became more precarious, particularly after the outbreak of hostilities between the realms in the early years of King Stephen's reign. Reinforcement was sought at the highest level, and, in 1141, Prior Osbert de Clare successfully petitioned Pope Innocent II to urge David to confirm his earlier grant.[87] David's confirmation of this year was made for the soul of Matilda, and those of his father and mother, his ancestors and his successors.[88] In the preceding years, David's son, Earl Henry, had evidently exercised mesne lordship over the land from which the rent derived,[89] and he also issued a confirmation for Westminster.[90] Malcolm IV, king of Scots, Henry's son, confirmed the rent *c.* 1159, for the soul of Queen Matilda, that of King David, those of his own parents, and of all his ancestors and successors.[91] Malcolm's brother and successor, King William I, issued a similar confirmation *c.* 1170.[92] In granting these confirmations, members of the Scottish royal house were responding to petitions from Westminster when they happened to be in its neighbourhood, and it may be questioned whether David's successors were particularly concerned to associate themselves with King Edward's church.

During most of King Stephen's reign, the abbot of Westminster was his illegitimate son Gervase.[93] It is therefore surprising that only eleven genuine charters for Westminster survive in Stephen's name, representing a lower ratio to regnal years than for any of his three predecessors. One writ, stating his relationship to Gervase, ordered that the abbot's lands were to be protected as though they were royal demesne,[94] and it was possibly for the sake of Gervase that the king was willing to support the project to secure the canonisation of King Edward.[95]

86 Walter Daniel, *The Life of Ailred of Rievaulx*, trans. and intro. F. M. Powicke, Oxford 1950, repr. 1978, pp. xlii, xlvi and n. 2; Baker, 'A nursery of saints', 125; A. Squire, 'Aelred and King David', *Collectanea Sacri Ordinis Cisterciensium Reformatorum* xxii (1960), 356–77.

87 *Papsturkunden* i. no. 25; *Acts of Malcolm IV*, appendix no. 319.

88 Ibid. no. 13.

89 Ibid. no. 12; cf. no. 14.

90 Ibid. no. 36.

91 Ibid. no. 154.

92 *The Acts of William I, King of Scots 1165–1214*, ed. G. W. S. Barrow with W. W. Scott, Edinburgh 1971, no. 52. King David is not named individually.

93 D. Knowles, C. N. L. Brook and Vera C. M. London, *The Heads of Religious Houses: England and Wales 940–1216*, Cambridge 1972, 77.

94 *Regesta III*, no. 930.

95 Barlow, *Edward the Confessor*, 275.

Any wider intention of drawing on the hoped-for canonisation to enhance the status of England and its kings[96] is scarcely reflected in Stephen's charters for Westminster. Three charters, of varying dates, explicitly associate donations to the abbey with the well-being of Stephen's line and link it firmly to the preceding Norman dynasty. The earliest grant of *c.* 1135 x 1139, was made for the souls of Stephen, his wife and sons, for the repose and redemption of his dear father and for the well-being of his mother (i.e. the crusading Count Stephen of Blois and the Conqueror's daughter Adela), and for the soul of his uncle King Henry.[97] A second grant, of indeterminate date, was made for the souls of King Henry, Stephen himself and his wife Matilda, Stephen's son Eustace and his other sons (unnamed).[98] A third charter dates from *c.* 1150 x 1152, when Stephen's hopes of establishing a dynasty were fading. Its wording seeks to integrate the king firmly into the preceding royal line, and the grant is said to be made to the church of St Peter of Westminster for the souls of Stephen, his wife and sons, for that of King Henry, and for those of Stephen's other predecessors, kings of England.[99] Yet some years before Westminster received this third charter, any expectations that Stephen might assume a patronal role towards the abbey were finally dashed when, in 1148, the king founded the abbey of Faversham. This church was to become the mausoleum of his own immediate family for whom, and for Stephen's antecessors, kings of England, its monks were to intercede.[100]

The accession of Henry II boded ill for Stephen's son, Abbot Gervase. At the outset of the reign, he obtained from Henry II confirmation in the abbatial lands[101] but was then arbitrarily dismissed. The king did not wish to see a son of the house of Blois presiding over the coronation church. Simultaneously with his dismissal of Gervase, Henry took the opportunity to seize certain of Westminster's lands.[102]

96 Ibid.

97 *Regesta III*, no. 936.

98 Ibid. no. 932.

99 Ibid. no. 938.

100 *Monasticon* iv. 573 no. 3. A confirmation issued for Faversham by Henry II, at the request of Stephen's surviving son William, earl of Warenne, refer to the church 'ubi requiescant cognati mei, vicelicet Rex Stephanus, et Matilda regina, uxor eius, et Eustacius filius eorum'. Henry's charter was issued for his own soul, and those of all his kindred and *antecessores*, kings of England, ibid. iv. 573 no. 2.

101 *New Palaeographical Society: Facsimilies*, 1st ser. ii (1904), plate 98 (a).

102 *Curia Regis Rolls* i 464–5. Gervase's reputation was perhaps damaged by this territorial loss. He was subsequently depicted at Westminster as an unworthy abbot, Flete, *Westminster Abbey*, 88–91, but recent writers have demonstrated the falsity of most of the allegations agaist him, H. G. Richardson and G. O. Sayles, *The Governance of Medieval England*, Edinburgh 1963, 413–21; Barbara Harvey, 'Abbot Gervase de Blois and the fee-farms of Westminster Abbey', BIHR xl (1967), 127–41. Evidence of his concern for the abbey is reflected in his surviving charters, considerably more numerous than those of any other abbot in the period down to 1214.

There survive ten writs and charters of Henry II for Westminster, a ratio of one for every three-and-a-half years of his reign. None is indicative of any special relationship with the abbey, although one writ, directed to royal officers in Gloucestershire and Worcestershire, proclaimed that the king had taken Westminster and its goods under his protection.[103] This writ was probably issued in the vacancy which followed the death of Abbot Laurence in 1173.

Henry II lent his support to the second, successful petition to secure the canonisation of King Edward, although this was essentially a Westminster project.[104] Its success was due both to its careful preparation[105] and also to the political constraints which inclined Pope Alexander to favour any petition which was supported by Henry II, a much needed ally.[106] The canonisation of King Edward provided Henry with a saint among his royal predecessors, thus reinforcing his claims to assert his jurisdiction over the clergy in England. The subsequent translation occurred opportunely for Henry, just as the dispute over the Constitutions of Clarendon escalated.[107] Yet, there is no evidence in any of Henry's subsequent charters for Westminster to suggest that he used the cult of St Edward in furtherance of his political objectives.

Four writs for Westminster survive in the name of Richard I, all issued in the first months of his reign. Two date successively from 6 and 7 October 1189, the latter granting quittance of financial exactions on all land and tenants of the abbey, for the soul of Henry II and (the well being) of Queen Eleanor.[108] On 16 December 1189, the abbey was granted a general writ of protection, the equivalent of that applicable to the royal demesne. The monks were not to be dispossessed of any free tenement which they had held on the day the king last crossed from England to Normandy (11 December 1189), and pleas concerning the abbey's tenements were to be heard only before the king himself, the chief justiciar or the chancellor.[109] The fourth writ, dated 26 January 1190, was a general notification that the abbot, his lands, rents and tenements, were under the king's protection, and were to be defended as though they were royal demesne.[110] It seems as though the abbot and monks were apprehensive about the maintenance of law and order during Richard's imminent crusade, and that they accumulated these writs of protection in order to forestall any assaults on their property.

103 WAD, fo. 58r.

104 Barlow, *Edward the Confessor*, 279–80. Henry's letter supporting canonisation describes Edward as his kinsman but does not mention Westminster, ibid. 310. See also Scholz, 'The canonisation', 49–57.

105 Barlow, op. cit. 278–80.

106 Scholz, op. cit. 50.

107 Ibid. 55–60.

108 WAM xlvi; WAD, fo. 59. Richard's charter for liberties for the abbey (WAM xlv), like those ascribed to Henry I, Stephen and Henry II, is almost certainly spurious.

109 WAD, fo. 59r.

110 WAM xlvii.

From King John's seventeen-year reign, there survive only five writs and charters for Westminster, of which three relate to purely routine business. A fourth, dated 1 November 1204, restored to St Peter, St Edward, Abbot Ralph and the monks the manor of Islip (Oxon.), birthplace of King Edward, originally granted by him to Westminster at its dedication, and to which the abbey had proved its right by charters produced in the royal court.[111] This grant makes no mention of any return, but the royal records show that Abbot Ralph fined 200 marks and two palfreys for the restoration of Islip.[112] Earlier royal records contain less circumstantial detail, although an entry on the 1130 Pipe Roll shows that the benevolence of Henry I was also obtained at a price.[113]

The last of King John's writs, dated 24 October 1215, at the siege of Rochester, forbade the royal troops to intrude into the church of Westminster or its cemetery, or to cause any injury to the monks, since the king had taken this church into his protection, together with its goods, inmates and contents.[114] In time of civil war it was the least that could be done to protect the coronation church.

Westminster's efforts to establish a special relationship with the post-Edwardian monarchy can therefore be shown to have met with little success. Given the prior commitment of William I to his foundation of St Étienne, Caen, there was no possibility that he would consider designating Westminster as his mausoleum.[115] The patronage extended to St Peter's, Gloucester, by William Rufus, implies some special relationship between the king and his abbey, which he perhaps envisaged as a potential mausoleum.[116] His burial at Winchester was primarily due to his sudden death in the New Forest,

111 *Rotuli chartarum in Turri Londoniensi asservati 1199–1216*, ed. T. Duffus Hardy, London 1837, 139b.

112 *Pipe Roll 6 John*, 112, *Rotuli litterarum clausarum in Turri Londiniensi asservati (1204–27)*, 2 vols, ed. T. Duffus Hardy, London 1833–44, i. 15a, 32b; *Rotuli de oblatis et finibus in Turri Londiniensi asservati*, ed. T. Duffus Hardy, London 1835, 222.

113 Restoration of the goods of Westminster which had been unjustly dispersed cost Abbot Herbert a fine of 1,000 marks, *The Great Roll of Pipe for the thirty-first year of the reign of Henry I (Michaelmas 1130)*, ed. J. Hunter, London 1833, 150.

114 *Rotuli chartarum*, 165b.

115 William I bequeathed to St-Étienne his crown and regalia, which were bought back by William II in 1096–7, *Regesta I*, no. 397. Caen lay at a focal point in William I's *regnum*, Mason 'Pro statu', 104.

116 Frank Barlow, *William Rufus*, London 1983, 114–15, 428. Gloucester was one of the churches where Christmas crown-wearings were sometimes held in the reigns of William I and II, Biddle, 'Seasonal festivals', 64–5. On the benefactions of William II and his barons, see David Bates, 'The building of a great church: the abbey of St Peter's, Gloucester, and its early Norman benefactors', *Transactions of the Bristol and Gloucestershire Archaeological Society* cii (1984), 129–32. On the scale of building operations in this reign, see Christopher Wilson, 'Abbot Serlo's church at Gloucester (1089–1100): its place in Romanesque architecture', in *Medieval Art and Architecture at Gloucester and Tewkesbury* (The British Archaeological Association Conference Transactions for the year 1981, 1985), 52–83.

although this cathedral was an appropriate choice, since it housed the tombs of earlier kings, including those of Cnut, and of his son Harthacnut, King Edward's half-brother.[117]

The favour accorded to Westminster by Henry I, in the earlier part of his reign, perhaps raised the expectations of its inmates. Following the foundation of Reading Abbey, no further preferential treatment could be expected from him, and the new tomb-cult of Queen Matilda withered for lack of encouragement from Court. It was perhaps this dashing of recently raised hopes which motivated Prior Osbert and his associates to embark on their own imaginative documentation of Westminster's rights and privileges. While intermittent charters of King Stephen were worded so as to imply a special link between him and the abbey, he, too, preferred to establish a new mausoleum for his line. The greatly extended frontiers of the Angevin kings prompted the designation of a new cult church. Henry II was eventually buried at Fontevraud, where Richard I followed him in due course, with other members of their family.[118] King John decided early in his reign to be buried in England, and in his will he insisted on being buried beside the newly canonised St Wulfstan in Worcester Cathedral.[119]

In the period between the Norman Conquest and the death of King John, rejection as a royal mausoleum was perhaps the least of Westminster's grievances against the monarchy. William I's manipulation of its landholdings proved a mixed blessing;[120] possessions were successively alienated to meet the temporal needs of Stephen's mistress Damette[121] and the spiritual needs

117 On the burials of Cnut and Harthacnut in the Old Minster, Winchester, see *ASC*, 102, 106. Winchester was the usual venue for Easter crown-wearings when William I and II were in England, Biddle, op. cit. 64–5. In conversation with the present writer, Professor Biddle, suggested that William II had a particular regard for Winchester, as evidenced by his donations, including his grant to Bishop Walkelin of the right to hold an annual three day fair; cf. *Regesta I*, no. 377, *Regesta II*, no. 377a.

118 Elizabeth M. Hallam, 'Henry II, Richard I and the order of Grandmont', *JMH* i (1975), 165–8. The tombs of Henry II, Richard I, Henry's wife Eleanor and John's second wife Isabel can still be seen at Fontevraud. Those of John's sister Johanna and her son Raymond VII, count of Toulouse, were destroyed during the French Revolution.

119 Mason, 'St Wulfstan's staff', 157. John was attended in his last illness by the abbot of the Premonstratensian house of Croxton (Leics.), Roger of Wendover, *Flores Historiarum* ii, ed. H. G. Hewlett (Rolls Series, 1887), 196, and this abbey obtained his *intestina*, Barnwell Annals, in *Memoriale Fratris Walteri de Coventria*, 2 vols, ed. W. Stubbs (Rolls Series, 1872–3), ii. 232. In 1257, Croxton claimed to have John's heart, *Charter Rolls* i. 463; although Fontevraud also claimed to have his heart-burial, together with those of his son Henry III and other members of the English royal house. The crypt which housed these heart-burials was filled in during the French Revolution.

120 Harvey, *Westminster Abbey*, 27.

121 Flete, *Westminster Abbey*, 89. See also Harvey, 'Abbot Gervase de Blois', 131, 138. The manor of Chelsea was alienated to Damette by Gervase himself, but the extent of his father's prompting is unknown.

of Henry II's deceased mistress Rosamund Clifford;[122] an abbatial vacancy enabled Henry II to present Walter Map as parson of one parish church pertaining to Westminster,[123] and senior royal clerks occur suspiciously often as incumbents of others.[124] Indeed, the Norman and Angevin kings appear almost to have had a grudge against the abbey, perhaps because it was too close to the palace or because its claims were unacceptable.[125] Successive abbots of Westminster trod precariously in the corridors of power. In addition to the special case of Abbot Gervase, other abbots are known to have incurred heavy amercements for a variety of offences, and sometimes for no explicit reason.[126]

The tide turned only with the accession of Henry III. He was reared in an awareness of English traditions, actively supported Westminster and the cult of St Edward and even revived his saintly predecessor's exercise of thaumaturgical powers.[127] Until he assumed active patronage of the abbey, Westminster did not enjoy any special relationship with the post-Conquest monarchy. On the contrary, the abbey's genuine charters, read in conjunction with contemporary royal records, demonstrate that this church was by no means first among equals.

122 WAD, fos 378v–9r; PRO E. 164/20, fo. xiii; see also *Monasticon* iv. 364 no. 7, 365 no. 8, 366 no. 15.

123 *Curia Regis Rolls* vi. 93.

124 E.g. Froger, formerly royal almoner, WAD, fo. 476r; cf. R. W. Eyton, *Court Household and Itinerary of King Henry II*, London 1878, 336; Ralph de Beaumont, royal physician, WAD, fo. 378. Cf. J. E. Lally, 'Secular patronage at the court of King Henry II', *BIHR* xlix (1976), 173.

125 Lukewarmness towards Edward's foundation perhaps originated in his vacillating dispositions for the succession to the throne. On these, see Ann Williams, 'Some notes and considerations on problems connected with the English royal succession, 860–1066', *Proceedings of the Battle Conference on Anglo-Norman Studies, I: 1978*, ed. R. Allen Brown, Ipswich 1979, 164–6. An alternative interpretation of Edward's intentions, which depicts them as more constant, is that of Eric John, 'Edward the Confessor and the Norman succession', *EHR* xciv (1979), 241–67.

126 *Pipe Roll 2 Henry II*, 33; *Rotuli de oblatis et finibus*, 325.

127 Frank Barlow, 'The king's evil', *EHR* xcv (1980), 3–27, repr. in idem, *The Norman Conquest and Beyond*, London 1983, 23–47. See also Mason, 'St Wulfstan's staff', 171.

Appendix 2

'The Site of King-Making and Consecration': Westminster Abbey and the Crown in the Eleventh and Twelfth Centuries*

'From the era of its first foundation, this has been the venue for the royal consecration, the burial place of kings, and the repository of the royal insignia, and deservedly named from ancient times as the (spiritual) head of England and the diadem of the realm.'[1] This claim, made on behalf of Westminster Abbey by the fifteenth-century monk John Flete, is examined here with reference to its history between the reign of Edward the Confessor and that of John.

At Edward's accession the site of Westminster afforded a potential new base for the monarchy, since the economic expansion of the eleventh century, and growing mercantile traffic across the North Sea, rendered a royal presence in the London area increasingly desirable. The other major attraction of Westminster was its potential for upholding royal sovereignty. In England, as in France, certain cults were promoted in order to enhance the status and prestige of the king, and to reinforce his claims to rule by reference to the authority and power of particular saints.[2] St Peter (sometimes in association with St Paul) was the most popular dedication in seventh- and eighth-century England, but he was overtaken by the Blessed Virgin, and remained in second place to her down to the end of King John's reign. Early Petrine dedications sometimes resulted directly from a visit to Rome by the subsequent founder of a church, and the saint's popularity was enhanced by

* The Leverhulme Trust, the Nuffield Foundation, and the British Academy have generously funded successive phases of my work on the Westminster Abbey charters. I am grateful to the late Dr Jennifer Bray for her assistance throughout this project; to Miss Barbara Harvey, Dr Diana Greenway, Dr Jane Sayers, and Dr David Bates for their views on the documents discussed here, and to the staff of Westminster Abbey Library for much patient help.

1 John Flete, *The History of Westminster Abbey*, ed. J. Armitage Robinson (Cambridge, 1909), p. 63.

2 D. Rollason, *Saints and Relics in Anglo-Saxon England* (Oxford, 1989), p. 137.

First published in *The Church and Sovereignty c.590–1918. Essays in Honour of Michael Wilks*, Studies in Church History, Subsidia, 9 (Oxford, 1991) the comparative frequency with which English pilgrims travelled there.[3] Westminster's dedication to St Peter was one of its major attractions for King Edward, who is said to have venerated the saint with exceptional and special love. This comment occurs in his first *Life*, a work commissioned by his widow before the Westminster hagiographers began their work. The King would naturally select as his burial church one which was dedicated to St Peter, keeper of the keys of Heaven, although the biographer hints that the strategic and economic importance of London also determined Edward's choice.[4]

After the disruption of the line of succession which had caused his long exile, Edward evidently conceived the idea that his rule could be sustained if he maintained a similar relationship with Westminster as the French king did with the Abbey of St Denis, outside Paris, which afforded spiritual and political support to the French monarchy. King Edward was a benefactor of the Abbey of St Denis, to which he granted land in Taynton (Oxon.), c.1053–7, and the church of Deerhurst (Glos.).[5] Probably he had come to appreciate the potential of the cult of St Denis while he was living on the Continent. On the evidence of his writs concerning his enhancement of the endowments of Westminster, he had initiated plans for this own burial church by c.1050 at latest, and building work had perhaps also begun by this time.[6] Westminster was already moderately prosperous by the time King Edward became patron. His own effective donations comprises almost twice as much as it already possessed, and he intended that further estates should accrue to the abbey in due course. Even without these, Westminster was among the richest religious houses in England by 1066.[7]

Edward planned to build a new and much grander church dedicated to St Peter. This was located to the east of the old one, so that the monks would not be disturbed in their liturgical round. Prayers for the monarchy would continue without interruption, and a tithe of the royal revenues was assigned to meet the expenses of this intentionally spectacular building. In its size, Edward's church was equalled only by the great imperial churches of the Rhineland, at Mainz and Speyer. Contemporary continental building practice was echoed by the decision to create a completely new church rater than

3 Alison Binns, *Dedications of Monastic Houses in England and Wales 1066–1216* (Woodbridge, 1989), pp. 20–1.

4 *Vita Aedwardi Regis: The Life of King Edward who rests at Westminster, attributed to a monk of St. Bertin*, ed. and tr. F. Barlow (London, 1962), p. 44.

5 Florence E. Harmer, *Anglo-Saxon Writs*, 2nd edn (Stamford, 1989), no. 55, and pp. 243–4, 292–3, 538–9.

6 Ibid., pp. 294–5; R. D. H. Gem, 'The Romanesque rebuilding of Westminster Abbey', *Proceedings of the Battle Conference on Anglo-Norman Studies III. 1980*, ed. R. Allen Brown (Woodbridge, 1981), p. 34.

7 Barbara Harvey, *Westminster Abbey and its Estates in the Middle Ages* (Oxford, 1977), p. 27.

incorporate the structure of that which already existed on the site.[8] Edward's intention in commissioning a church on this scale was both to draw comparisons between his own rule and that of the most prestigious West European ruler of the day, and also to underline the fact that *his* West Minster signalled the revived prestige of the monarchy after the inglorious end to the rule of the interloping Danish dynasty. Whereas Cnut and Harthacnut had been buried with the kings of the legitimate line, in the old 'capital city' – Edward was deliberately choosing to focus his revived rule in the 'new capital'.

Concepts of sovereignty underlying Edward's rebuilding of Westminster are echoed in some of the coin types produced in his reign. In particular, a series issued from *c.*1053 onwards draws on the designs of coins issued both by recent German imperial rulers, notably Henry II, Conrad II (1027–39), and Henry III (1046–56), and, in one issue, the reverse echoes the gold *solidus* of the Byzantine Emperor Justin II (565–78). This issue was perhaps intended to depict the King in majesty, as he appeared at the solemn crown-wearings held on the major festivals of the Church. Later coin types depict Edward wearing a closed imperial crown.[9] Edward maintained contact with the imperial court, and his chief ambassador, Archbishop Ealdred, drew on his experiences there when he devised a new coronation *ordo*, used in the consecrations of Harold II and later of William I.[10] Ealdred's experiences during his travels to Rome (through imperial lands) and to the imperial court itself probably supplied the ideology underlying King Edward's later coin types and most likely added the 'imperial' dimension to the impetus to rebuild Westminster Abbey, although Edward also recruited able Continentals to his court, including Lotharingians, who were imperial subjects.

Imperial contacts inspired the majestic size of the new abbey, and contact with St Denis inspired its function, by the King's own years of exile in Normandy determined its architectural style. Edward's church is described in his near-contemporary *Life*; and a view of the church also appears on the Bayeax Tapestry.[11] Archaeological evidence is necessarily fragmentary, given that Henry III's church was constructed over the foundations of Edward's building, but it is clear that Westminster's architectural sources are not English. It was built on a much greater scale than any previous English church, and in overall length even outclassed near-contemporary monastic churches in Normandy. Specific features both of the east end and of the nave have parallels in Norman buildings. Analogies have been drawn between Westminster and Jumièges, but a case has recently been argued for Westminster's

8 *Vita Aedwardi Regis*, pp. 44–6; Gem, 'The Romanesque rebuilding of Westminster Abbey', pp. 36, 38, 44, 46.

9 Marion M. Archibald, 'Anglo-Saxon Coinage, Alfred to the Conquest', in Janet Backhouse, D. H. Turner, and Leslie Webster, eds, *The Golden Age of Anglo-Saxon Art* (London, 1984), nos 229–33.

10 Janet L. Nelson, *Politics and Ritual in early Medieval Europe* (London, 1986), pp. 390–9.

11 *Vita Aedwardi Regis*, pp. 45–6; Gem, 'The Romanesque rebuilding of Westminster Abbey', pp. 36–7.

influence upon the latter, rather than vice versa, as was formerly believed. Yet the architecture of Edward's Westminster was Norman, not English, even though two, and possibly three, of the masons associated with Westminster in his reign bore English names.[12] The Romanesque architecture of the abbey church was perceived in England as a novelty. William of Malmesbury, writing in the middle of Henry I's reign, observed, correctly, that it was King Edward who first commissioned a building in that style.[13] Purists in English monastic circles argued that full-blown Romanesque architecture was a distracting style, inappropriate in a building which was dedicated to spiritual purposes.[14] But for King Edward, the underlying purpose of this new church was to symbolize the majesty which was his by virtue of his consecration.

It is questionable how far he was effectively sovereign during his lifetime, given the tensions between his over-mighty subjects and the importunate claims of continental kinsmen. In the biography which Queen Edith commissioned after Edward's death, it was said that he was at leisure to spend most of his time in hunting and hawking, while his brothers-in-law, Earl Harold and Earl Tostig, defended the realm.[15] A king preoccupied in this way effectively abrogated his sovereignty, if indeed Edward had ever been in a position to assert it. As he aged, he enjoyed the further luxury of tapping the resources of the realm in order to finance his burial church, which embodied the image of monarchy which he wanted to project, but could not assert.

Queen Edith, meanwhile, 'was drawn to emulate that project of his',[16] a phrase which implies that she built a burial church of her own. The nunnery of Wilton, where she was educated, traces its royal connections from the time of King Edgar: Abbess Wulfthryth was the mother of his bastard daughter Edith. The latter, Edward's aunt, was designated a saint, albeit on remarkably slight grounds.[17] Queen Edith is said to have conferred her patronage on Wilton because of its cult of her royal namesake, and caused its wooden church to be rebuilt in stone, with all appropriate embellishments.[18] King Edward is said to have ordered the relics of other religious houses to be brought before her, so that she could choose those she wanted – presumably for Wilton.[19] The story, if factual, indicates the serious intent behind the Queen's rebuilding of Wilton. There are other instances of separate burial churches being commissioned for rulers and their wives, notably the

12 Gem, 'The Romanesque rebuilding of Westminster Abbey', pp. 39, 46–55.

13 William of Malmesbury, *De Gestis Regum Anglorum*, ed. W. Stubbs, 2 vols, *RS* (1887–9), I, p. 280.

14 R. Gem, 'England and the resistance to Romanesque architecture', in C. Harper-Bill, C. J. Holdsworth, and Janet L. Nelson, eds, *Studies in Medieval History presented to R. Allen Brown* (Woodbridge, 1989), pp. 129–39.

15 *Vita Aedwardi Regis*, p. 40.

16 Ibid., p. 46.

17 Ibid., pp. 94, 96.

18 Ibid., pp. 46–8.

19 *Chronica Abbatiae de Evesham ad annum 1418*, ed. W. D. Macray, *RS* (1863), p. 317.

foundations of Duke William and Duchess Matilda in Caen, so that the individual rebuilding of churches by Edward and Edith does not necessarily reflect either on the relationship between them of on the lack of heirs of the marriage. Both churches were consecrated in the course of 1065 – that of Westminster only on 28 December, following a ceremony which the King was too ill to attend.[20] Although he was buried in Westminster, political considerations prompted future kings to choose other churches for their burial,[21] until Henry III assumed the patronage of Westminster, although two queens-consort were buried in the abbey. Queen Edith, in her widowhood, retained her interest in Wilton, but William I caused her to be buried at Westminster, a fitting honour for the widow of the King whose lawful successor he claimed to be.[22] But it was one which had to be accorded, since Edith was also the sister of his rival, and her burial at Wilton, with its royal dedication, might generate a politically subversive tomb-cult. In 1118, a third royal tomb was added to those at Westminster, that of the first wife of Henry I, Queen (Edith) Matilda. Since she publicized her kinship to the old English royal line, she may have requested burial beside her kinsman, King Edward.[23]

The Norman Conquest had an impact upon the interests of Westminster, and some exchanges of land were enforced by William I. Overall these proved equitable, and occasionally favourable, but Edward's intentions as to certain endowments remained unfulfilled.[24] Abbot Edwin (*c.*1049–*c.*1068) had been appointed around the time that King Edward's decisive patronage for the abbey can first be traced. He would have been conversant with the King's intentions regarding the new role which the abbey was intended to fulfil.[25] Two forged writs in the name of William I, and a third which may contain genuine elements, depict Edwin successfully obtaining from this King confirmation of certain estates claimed by the abbey.[26] But Edwin's death shortly after the Conquest, followed successively by an abbatial vacancy and then by the unsatisfactory abbacy of Geoffrey (*c.*1072–*c.*1076), combined to produce a crisis of leadership, and hence to endanger the

20 *Vita Aedwardi Regis*, pp. 50, 73.

21 Emma Mason, '"*Pro statu et incolumnitate regni mei*": royal monastic patronage 1066–1154', *SCH*, 18 (1982), pp. 99–117.

22 *Vita Aedwardi Regis*, p. 100; *ASC*, ed. and tr. D. Whitelock (with D. C. Douglas and S. I. Tucker), *The Anglo-Saxon Chronicle, a Revised Translation* (London, 1961), D, E, *sa* 1075.

23 Ibid., E, *sa* 1118; see, however, *The Cartulary of Holy Trinity Aldgate*, ed. G. A. J. Hodgett, *London Record Society*, 7 (1971), nos 13, 997.

24 Harvey, *Westminster Abbey and its Estates*, pp. 27–8.

25 *The Heads of Religious Houses, England and Wales, 940–1216*, ed. D. Knowles, C. N. L. Brooke, and Vera C. M. London (Cambridge, 1972), p. 76; Gem, 'The Romanesque rebuilding of Westminster Abbey', p. 37; B. H. Scholz, 'Sulcard of Westminster: "Prologus de Construccione Westmonasterii" ', *Traditio*, 20 (1964), p. 60.

26 *Westminster Abbey Charters 1066–c.1214*, ed. Emma Mason, assisted by the late Jennifer Bray, continuing the work of the late D. J. Murphy, *London Record Society*, 25 (1988), nos 2–3, 13.

recently-won prestige of the abbey. Geoffrey's deposition cleared the way for the appointment of Vitalis (1076–*c.*1085).[27] A letter in the name of King William was addressed to John, Abbot of Fécamp, concerning this appointment. The King states that, after long thought on the matter, and on the advice of Archbishop Lanfranc and his barons, he has eventually compelled the unwilling Vitalis to accept this office, because he has greatly improved the condition of the monastery of Bernay. William asks Abbot John to approve this choice, and also that of Osbern, the brother of Vitalis, to succeed to the Abbey of Bernay.[28] After the demoralizing conclusion to Geoffrey's abbacy, the King and his advisers would want to ensure that the coronation church was managed by an abbot of proven ability, and Vitalis in return would make the conventional declaration that he was reluctant to accept this honour – whatever his private response to this major promotion.

But embedded in this letter are phrases which echo the propaganda which came to be generated at Westminster 'in which are buried King Edward of blessed memory, and Queen Edith of famous memory; in which, too, (King William) himself received the sceptre and crown of England.' In 1076, when this letter was apparently sent to the Abbot of Fécamp, there was as yet no recognition at William's court of King Edward's saintly merits, and Queen Edith is unlikely to have been described as 'of famous memory' in an official document. Once the fabrication of propaganda was under way at Westminster, the suspect phrases were probably added to a copy of a letter Abbot Vitalis acquired to serve as his record of appointment, and a transcript of the reworked version was forwarded to his former monastery.[29] Westminster had acquired its status as royal burial church and coronation church barely a decade before Vitalis's appointment, and what was so recently won might later be lost.

Abbot Vitalis commissioned the monk Sulcard to write his *Prologus de construccione Westmonasterii*.[30] Sulcard was probably of continental origin – perhaps from Lotharingia, or more likely Flanders, bearing in mind the hagiographical output of monks of St Bertin's.[31] His *Prologus* was a summarized history of Westminster, intended for the use of the new abbot, and to promote the cult of St Peter, the patron of Westminster.[32] The most striking feature of the *Prologus* is the motivation which it ascribes to King Edward in

27 *Heads of Religious Houses*, p. 76; Flete, *The History of Westminster Abbey*, p. 84.

28 *RR*, I, no. 91.

29 J. Mabillon, *Vetera Analecta*, ed. L. F. J. de la Barre, new edn (Paris, 1723, republished Farnborough, 1967), p. 450. I am grateful to Dr David Bates for his comments on this text, and for his information that it is transcribed from an early twelfth-century liturgical manuscript from Fécamp. The two letters written by Abbot John in response to that of the King are printed by Mabillon, ibid., pp. 450–1, and all three are also printed in *PL* 147, cols 463–6.

30 Scholz, 'Sulcard of Westminster', pp. 60, 80.

31 *Vita Aedwardi Regis*, pp. xiv and n. 3, xliv–xlv, lxi, 91–2; Antonia Gransden, *Historical Writing in England c.550 to c.1307* (London, 1974), pp. 56, 58, 63–4.

32 Scholz, 'Sulcard of Westminster', pp. 80–1.

rebuilding Westminster. Sulcard relates how Edward had planned to make a pilgrimage to Rome, but his magnates feared unrest in his absence and persuaded him to remain in his kingdom. Therefore, instead of making a pilgrimage, he restored a church consecrated to St Peter.[33] This story of Edward's motivation in founding Westminster contrasts with that in the first *Life* of King Edward. Sulcard does not portray Edward as a holy man, nor does he mention any of the miracle stories which were incorporated into this *Life*,[34] nor use his account as a basis for publishing any spurious claims to papal privileges. It may be that, at the instigation of the Norman Vitalis, he was simply reiterating Westminster's position as a protégé of St Peter and, by implication, playing down its role as the burial church of the late English King. With the royal palace virtually next door, it would not do to permit the abbey to become the potential focus of a native cult which might fuel a resistance movement. On the other hand, Sulcard's story about the magnates dissuading Edward from making his pilgrimage may reflect not the crises of Edward's day, but rather the monks' anxieties in the reign of William I. A monastic foundation adjacent to a major royal residence would be vulnerable to attack if dissidents took advantage of William's frequent absences from the realm in order to start a revolt.

The debate on the underlying intention of Sulcard's work in the more complex in that there are echoes of his narrative in some of the major Westminster forgeries. In particular the so-called First Charter of King Edward shares an entire sentence with Sulcard. In contrast, other forgeries enumerate privileges and possessions granted by Cenwulf of Mercia (d. 821) and Alfred (d. 899) which are not mentioned in the *Prologus*.[35] No Westminster forgeries can be ascribed to Sulcard on any grounds firmer that conjecture, even though the earliest such documents are almost contemporary with his *Prologus*. Since Sulcard justified his abbey's claims only by reference to St Peter, in a work composed on the orders of Abbot Vitalis, it is arguable that exploitation of the tomb of King Edward was still forbidden in the period 1076–*c*.1085. On the other hand, incoming Norman abbots defended the territorial interests of their houses against the new and predatory secular magnates, and utilized the cults of their local English saints in order to protect the lands and liberties of their monasteries.[36] Westminster's interests required the exploitation of such a cult, and one lay to hand in the tomb of King Edward.

The events of 1066 contributed indirectly to Edward's apotheosis into the saintly protector of Westminster, since the latter part of the panegyric on the

33 Ibid., pp. 69, 90–1.

34 Ibid., pp. 71–2. For Edward's lifetime healings and visionary experience, see *Vita Aedwardi Regis*, pp. 61–3, 75–6; and for early addenda, ibid., pp. 64–9.

35 Scholz, 'Sulcard of Westminster', pp. 64, 66.

36 Susan J. Ridyard, '*Condigna Veneratio*: Post-Conquest attitudes to the saints of the Anglo-Saxons', *Anglo-Norman Studies IX. Proceedings of the Battle Conference 1986*, ed. R. Allen Brown (Woodbridge, 1987), pp. 179–206.

house of Godwin, which Queen Edith commissioned, had then to be rewritten. For want of other suitable material, the revised version concluded with the hagiographical portrayal of Edward.[37] Sulcard had read the *Life* of King Edward, whom he (like the King's biographer, and also the composer of the spurious First Charter of Edward) likened to Solomon in respect of the peacefulness of his reign.[38] Yet Edward's appearance in Sulcard's *Prologus* was minimal compared to that of St Peter, who was said to have miraculously consecrated the first church on Thorn Island.[39]

But the abbey had no exclusive claim on St Peter. Its one potential focus for a unique cult was King Edward.[40] A few miracle stories had been included in Edward's first *Life*, and others were subsequently dated to his lifetime.[41] Abbot Gilbert Crispin (*c.*1085–*c.*1117/18) encouraged the cult, although the description of the opening of Edward's tomb in 1102 has been questioned.[42] In a series of three writs which Gilbert issued, he evoked the name of King Edward, jointly with those of Christ and St Peter, in order to defend the abbey's right to offer sanctuary. Two writs in series are in English, indicating a date early in Gilbert's abbacy, and the first can be dated to a period no later than *c.*1104.[43]

In the charter of liberties issued on 5 August 1100, following his coronation at Westminster, Henry I placed voluntary restraints on his use of the royal prerogative, citing in three clauses the laws of Edward's reign as standards of right conduct.[44] Henry, participating in a solemn ceremony at Westminster, was more likely inspired to cite Edward's laws as the norm of good government because of the pre-existing use of his cult to defend Westminster's rights, rather than that Gilbert derived the idea of Edward as guarantor of the abbey's sanctuary because of his previous citation by Henry I. But once the King exploited the political potential of Edward's cult, there was all the more reason for the monks of Westminster to encourage it. Politically-inspired royal cults had a long pedigree. In the late tenth century, minor cults centred on the tombs of Edith and Edward, the half-siblings of Edward's father, Æthelred II.[45] Despite, or perhaps because of, the underlying political tensions of Edward's own reign, he styled himself king *Dei gratia*, and the writer of his first *Life* repeatedly referred to him as the *Christus Dei*, God's anointed one. It is arguable, too, that Edward's continental advisers

37 *Vita Aedwardi Regis*, pp. xvi–xviii.

38 Scholz, 'Sulcard of Westminster', p. 90 and n. 3.

39 Ibid., pp. 61, 72–4, 82–5, 87–9.

40 *Vita Aedwardi Regis*, p. 113.

41 Ibid., pp. 61–74; F. Barlow, *Edward the Confessor* (London, 1970), pp. 257–63.

42 *Vita Aedwardi Regis*, pp. 113–15.

43 *Westminster Abbey Charters*, nos 238–40.

44 W. Stubbs, *Select Charters and other Illustrations of English Constitutional History*, 9th edn rev. H. W. C. Davis (Oxford, 1913), pp. 116–19, clauses 5, 9, 13.

45 Susan J. Ridyard, *The Royal Saints of Anglo-Saxon England* (Cambridge, 1988), pp. 140–75.

encouraged belief in his thaumaturgical powers by analogy with the Frankish kings.[46] The story in Edward's first *Life*, depicting him stretching out his hands to heal the woman suffering from the King's Evil, has been interpreted as a political allegory, to be equated with Christ reaching out in mercy to the beleaguered English after the Battle of Hastings,[47] a rather strained suggestion, which depends on a misconception as to the authorship and purpose of Edward's first *Life*. Yet the citation of his laws by Henry I ensured that Edward would indeed assume a protective role towards the harassed English.

Westminster was probably advised on the exploitation of the cult of King Edward by Baldwin, Abbot of Bury St Edmunds (1065–97), and formerly monk of St Denis. He has been identified as the originator of a series of major forgeries produced in the late eleventh century for Bury St Edmunds, and which have features in common with some made in the interests of other religious houses, notably Durham Cathedral Priory, but including also St Augustine's, Canterbury, Ramsey, St Peter's, Ghent – and Westminster Abbey.[48] It is likely that while Abbot Baldwin provided the models for these documents, they were actually composed by Guerno, a well-known forger active at St Augustine's. The resemblance between certain forgeries produced at St Augustine's and others made in Westminster's interests is significant, in view of the hagiographical portrayal of Edward as a bearded and venerable patriarch in scenes from the Bayeux Tapestry, the design of which is believed to have originated in St Augustine's.[49] The visual portrayal of Edward in his work echoes the connotations of his name in those Westminster forgeries influenced by St Augustine's. Particular significance may be discerned in the scene in the Tapestry where Edward's body is being conveyed towards the abbey, over the roof of which the Hand of God is stretched in blessing.[50] The designing of the Tapestry has been dated as early as the mid-1070s, but perhaps more convincingly to *c.*1081/2,[51] by which time, it may be inferred,

46 *Vita Aedwardi Regis*, pp. lxix–lxx; F. Barlow, *The Norman Conquest and Beyond* (London, 1983), pp. 23–47.

47 *Vita Aedwardi Regis*, pp. 61–2; T. J. Heffernan, *Sacred Biography: Saints and their Biographers in the Middle Ages* (Oxford, 1988), pp. 5–6.

48 Antonia Gransden, 'Baldwin, abbot of Bury St Edmunds, 1065–1097', *Proceedings of the Battle Conference on Anglo-Norman Studies IV. 1981*, ed. R. Allen Brown (Woodbridge, 1982), pp. 68–71.

49 The literary portrayal of Edward in the *Vita Aedwardi Regis*, p. 12, should be compared with his visual depiction in the Bayeux Tapestry: D. L. Bernstein, *The Mystery of the Bayeux Tapestry* (London, 1986), plates I, XXVIII, and XXX. But see also Barlow, *Edward the Confessor*, pp. 70, 71 and n. 1. On the likelihood that the Tapestry derived visual motifs from St Augustine's, see N. P. Brooks and H. E. Walker, 'The authority and interpretation of the Bayeux Tapestry', *Proceedings of the Battle Conference on Anglo-Norman Studies I. 1978*, ed. R. Allen Brown (Ipswich and Totava, 1979), pp. 13–15.

50 Bernstein, *The Mystery of the Bayeux Tapestry*, plate XXIX.

51 Shirley Ann Brown, 'The Bayeux Tapestry: why Eustace, Odo and William?', *Anglo-Norman Studies XII. Proceedings of the Battle Conference 1989*, ed. Majorie Chibnall (Woodbridge, 1990), pp. 25–6.

the cult of Edward had radiated from his court circle to that bastion of English culture, St Augustine's, Canterbury.

The influence of Abbot Baldwin of Bury St Edmunds, transmitted through the medium of a scribe of St Augustine's, has been traced in some of Westminster's major forgeries, which were modelled upon charters possessed by the Abbey of St Denis, including Westminster's Great Charter of Edgar; its Great Charter of Dunstan and the Second Charter of Edward. The two latter were designed to assist Westminster in its struggle to evade the control of the bishop of London.[52] Further Westminster forgeries in the names of Pope Nicholas II and Pope Paschal II included the abbey's claim to be both the permanent venue for the coronation (which had not been the case before 1066) and also the place where the royal insignia was kept. But while the texts of some early charters of St Denis were utilized at Westminster, the terminology of further charters, in which the abbey was variously styled *corona regni*; *caput* of the churches of England, or a place of *regalis excellencia*, is evocative of later French royal charters, and indicates that channels of communication remained open for generations between Westminster and St Denis. The texts of Westminster's charters were designed to maximize the abbey's claims to all manner of liberties, something which could most effectively be achieved by linking its twin roles as coronation church and as the resting place of King Edward, a point which is forcefully made in the Great Charter of King Henry. The holier a place which Westminster was seen to be, the better its chances of asserting its independence.[53]

Westminster had no rival for the role of coronation church, inaugurated in 1066, when both Harold II Godwinson and William I urgently needed to establish themselves as legitimate successors of King Edward, which each achieved by inaugurating his rule in the church which housed Edward's tomb. The precedents set in 1066 were normally followed. Down to 1154, each king had to struggle to assert his right to the throne, and consecration in the church of King Edward was a good guarantee of legitimacy. But the kings of England were buried individually, in churches which they had patronized in their lifetimes, and selected as their mausolea.[54] The separation of inauguration from that of royal burial paralleled developments in France. The earlier Capetians were buried in St Denis, gaining major advantages from their association with this powerful cult, but Rheims was retained as the coronation church, symbolizing continuity with the previous Carolingian rulers. There was perhaps also a wish to dissociate the ritual of king-making from the site of a predecessor's obsequies. In the period between 1066 and 1216, Westminster was less the English equivalent of St Denis than of Rheims. A closer continental parallel was Aachen, the burial church of

52 B. W. Scholz, 'Two forged charters from the Abbey of Westminster and their Relationship with St Denis', *EHR*, 76 (1961), pp. 466–7.

53 Ibid., pp. 468–78; *Westminster Abbey Charters*, no. 57.

54 Mason, ' "*Pro statu et incolumnitate regni mei*" ', pp. 99–117.

Charlemagne and coronation church of later German rulers descended from successive dynasties.[55]

The knowledge that St Denis housed the French royal insignia probably inspired Westminster's claim to be the depository of the English sceptre and crown, as claimed in the surviving – and suspicious – text of William I's letter to the Abbot of Fécamp.[56] This claim was repeated at Westminster, for instance in the bulls forged in the names of Pope Nicholas II and Pope Paschal II, and in a forged charter of William I, supposedly dating from 1067.[57] In the mid-fifteenth century, John Flete maintained that the regalia in the abbey was that bequeathed by King Edward. But this 'vulgar error' had already been refuted by another monk of the house, William of Sudbury, who stated that the regalia largely comprised items bestowed on King Alfred by Pope Leo at his 'coronation' in Rome, even though this collection was perhaps augmented by King Edward.[58] The unconfirmed account by Osbert de Clare of the opening of Edward's tomb in 1102 described the King as wearing a crown and a ring, with a sceptre at his side.[59] A papal bull, which Osbert forged in 1139, contains the allegations that the monks were considering the sale of the regalia.[60] The crown and sceptre were perhaps removed during the tomb opening in 1102, since only the ring remained on Edward's body when his tomb was next opened, in 1163. The ring was then removed, together with three cloths which were to be made into embroidered copes.[61] Yet whatever the nature of the regalia found in Edward's tomb on either occasion, it is likely that his 'effective' crown was taken for use by Harold II. William I is said to have had a new crown made, but he would not have left so powerful a symbol as Edward's chief crown in a place as vulnerable as Westminster Abbey.[62]

In the decades after the Norman Conquest, Westminster was one of the three churches where solemn crown-wearings were held at the major festivals of the Church's year. Henry I, in a writ dating from no later than 1107, ordered that Gloucester, Westminster, and Winchester were to have an ounce of gold on each festival when the King wore his crown in one of these churches, as Maurice, Bishop of London (1085–1107) testified was the case in the time of the King's *antecessors*.[63] There is evidence of such seasonal visits to Westminster only from the last years of Edward's reign, but the abbey

55 Emma Mason, 'Westminster Abbey and the monarchy between the reigns of William I and John (1066–1216)', *JEH*, 41 (1990), p. 201 and nn. 9–10.

56 *RR*, 1, no. 91.

57 Scholz, 'Two forged charters', p. 473; *Vita Aedwardi Regis*, p. 115 and nn. 3–4.

58 *Vita Aedwardi Regis*, pp. 115–16; Flete, *The History of Westminster Abbey*, pp. 71–2.

59 *Vita Aedwardi Regis*, p. 117.

60 *Westminster Abbey Charters*, no. 161; Barbara Harvey, 'Abbot Gervase de Blois and the Fee Farms of Westminster Abbey', *BIHR*, 40 (1967), pp. 128–9.

61 Flete, *The History of Westminster Abbey*, pp. 71–2.

62 *Vita Aedwardi Regis*, p. 93.

63 *Westminster Abbey Charters*, no. 58.

received occasional visits, either at Christmas or at Pentecost, by both William I and William II. Henry I usually celebrated Christmas there, and occasionally Pentecost, too, down to 1109, but subsequently Pentecost 1121 was the only major festival which he is known to have celebrated at Westminster.[64] Westminster's relationship with the Anglo-Norman and early Angevin kings can be determined only on the evidence of the royal charters granted to the abbey, of which a considerable proportion is suspect. While some of the dubious documents contain interpolations or addenda of minimal significance, the authenticity of other documents is highly questionable.[65] In these, extensive and unsubstantiated claims are made for Westminster's enjoyment of lands and liberties, and in some of the documents of this type sweeping statements are made or implied about the special relationship existing between the abbey and the monarchy. Prior Osbert de Clare was probably the mastermind who drafted this series of documents, which include the First Charter of Edgar, the First, Second, and Third Charters of Edward, and the First, Second, Third, and Fourth Charters of William I, and his so-called *Telligraphus*. Their texts in several instances are closely related to that of Prior Osbert's new version of the *Life* of Kind Edward, made in preparation for the petition for his canonization which was submitted in 1139.[66] The saintly King was depicted as guarantor of Westminster's rights, while Westminster promulgated the cult of the saintly King. The rights of Westminster and the cult of Edward were inextricably interwoven.

During the reign of Henry I an effort was also made to associate the King and members of his family with the cult of King Edward, in charters which confirmed the possessions, or purported possessions, of Westminster Abbey. The three genuine charters in which the connection was made all date from within a short period after the White Ship disaster, when the future of Henry's dynasty appeared uncertain. The most explicit of these grants was made 'pro statu regni mei, et pro salute anime mee, et Edwardi Regis, cognati mei, et Willelmi regis patris mei, et Willelmi regis fratris mei, et Willelmi filii mei, et Mathildis regine matris mei, et Mathilde regine uxoris mee, et antecessorum et successorum meorum.'[67] This charter survives in its original form, with the King's Fourth Great Seal attached. The other two grants, which survive only as cartulary copies, were made 'pro salute anime mee et

64 M. Biddle, 'Seasonal festivals and residence: Winchester, Westminster and Gloucester in the tenth to twelfth centuries', in *Anglo-Norman Studies VIII. Proceedings of the Battle Conference 1985*, ed. R. Allen Brown (Woodbridge, 1986), pp. 51–72.

65 *Westminster Abbey Charters*, pp. 10–12.

66 P. Chaplais, 'The Original Charters of Herbert and Gervase, abbots of Westminster (1121–1157)', in Patricia M. Barnes and C. F. Slade, eds, *A Medieval Miscellany for Doris Mary Stenton* = *Pipe Roll Society*, ns 36 (London, 1962), pp. 91–4; *Westminster Abbey Charters*, nos 1, 14–15, 33, 43, and pp. 321–2.

67 *Westminster Abbey Charters*, no. 77. The full text is most readily accessible in *MonAngl*, I, p. 308, no. 52.

Edwardi regis cognati mei et antecessorum et successorum meorum.'[68] At this time of crisis the King was willing to be associated with his 'kinsman', King Edward, although the concern for his predecessor's soul shows that Henry did not regard Edward as a saint. The wording of these charters provided models for several documents which were either outright fabrications or were at least interpolated, and in their present form include variants of the phrasing of the first of the three genuine charters cited above.[69] These make particular mention of Henry's wife, Queen (Edith) Matilda, who in two cases is named as witness,[70] but it is arguable that all date from after the Queen's death, at the time when attempts were made at Westminster to promote her cult. A genuine charter of the King, dating from *c.*1121–2, concerned provision to be made for a lamp to burn perpetuity at her tomb.[71] Texts were produced at Westminster of two documents purportedly issued in the summer of 1121 by the papal legate, Peter Pierleoni, granting an indulgence to those who visited the abbey on the major feast of St Peter.[72] In the first of these it was said that the indulgence was granted in commemoration of King Edward and Queen Matilda, who were buried in the abbey,[73] and a similar clause is found in the indulgence apparently issued in 1125 by the legate John of Crema.[74] In the light of these indulgences, it may be questioned whether the suspect text of the letter concerning the appointment of Abbot Vitalis actually received its present form in the 1120s, when the cult of Queen (Edith) Matilda was being fostered.

The supposed text of Henry's charter for Westminster issued on the day of his coronation, taking the abbey under his protection, and confirming its liberties, has been identified as a fabrication of the late twelfth century.[75] Nearly identical texts survive in the names of King Stephen, of Henry II, and of Richard I, with adjustments to the king's name and family relationships, attestations and dating clause. The language of these charters is monastic, and it might be argued that each newly-crowned king conceded the extensive liberties enumerated in a document placed before him after his coronation, but the texts have been exposed as forgeries on various grounds.[76] These texts embodied the claims of Westminster, as they were maintained in the late twelfth century, to be the coronation church, which housed the shrine of St

68 *Westminster Abbey Charters*, no. 76 (full text printed by J. Armitage Robinson, *Gilbert Crispin, Abbot of Westminster = Notes and Documents relating to Westminster Abbey*, no. 3 (Cambridge, 1911), pp. 163–4), and no. 87 (full text printed *MonAngl*, i, p. 307).

69 *Westminster Abbey Charters*, nos 62–3, 74.

70 Ibid., nos 62–3.

71 Ibid., no. 79.

72 Ibid., nos 187–8.

73 Ibid., no. 187.

74 Ibid., no. 189.

75 Ibid., no. 57.

76 Ibid., nos 110, 123, 140. For discussion of the grounds on which such charters might be presumed genuine, see R. Mortimer, 'The Charters of Henry II: what are the criteria for authenticity?', *Anglo-Norman Studies XII*, pp. 119–34.

Edward, and which uniquely guarded both the spiritual welfare of the king and his family, and also ensured the stability of the dynasty. The relevant phrases of Henry I's charter run:

> Sciatis communiter me pro redemptione anime mee et patris et matris mee, necnon et beate memorie Regis Edwardi, cognati mei, qui patrem meum liberosque illius in regnum suum adoptivos heredes instituerat, accepisse in mau mea et defensione totum honorem ecclesie Sancti Petri Westmonasterii. In qua ecclesia ego oleo sancte unctionis, sicut et ceteri ante me reges, perunctus, quia ille locus antiquitus regum consecrationis fuisse cognoscitur, et corona regni a Deo per pontificales manus celebriter coronatus sum, et in cuius etiam predicte ecclesie materno utero corpus domini ac predecessoris nostri et prefati Regis Eadwardi refotum sepulture requie ut cernimus requiescit per quem nempe me in regimen regni Anglie sublimatum fore cognosco . . . Privilegia itaque antiquorum regum . . . confirmo . . . (The king then confirms all quittances or dignities granted by ancient kings, and by King Edward, of blessed memory, and by his father [William I]. . . .)[77]

The cult of Queen (Edith) Matilda which was promoted in the years following her death soon afterwards faded away. She was a benefactor of the abbey,[78] and promoted good works in London which were both socially useful and also conductive to the increase of goodwill towards the monarchy in this politically sensitive city.[79] Whereas King Edward's cult was the more useful one from the viewpoint of the monks of Westminster, that of Queen (Edith) Matilda surely had more potential for the monarchy. Henry I's financial provision for her tomb light post-dated the death of their son in the White Ship disaster,[80] but there is not evidence that he continued to promote her cult. While she was the ancestress of a long line of kings, this would not be obvious to her husband in the years after her death. In the mid-1120s there would be the sustaining hope of a son by his second wife, and until the birth of Henry Plantagenet in 1133 there was no certainty that future kings of his line would trace their descent from (Edith) Matilda, and Henry's religious patronage focused on his new foundation of Reading Abbey during the latter part of his reign.[81] Queen (Edith) Matilda's cult survived tenuously at Westminster for some years longer. When Prior Osbert was at the Curia, to petition for the canonization of King Edward, he obtained from Pope Innocent II a batch of letters, including one addressed to David King of Scots, issued at the petition of Osbert, 'prior of the royal monastery of Westminster'. The Pope requested David confirm to Westminster the land which supported the anniversary of his sister, 'pro incolumitate regni tui

77 *RR*, 2, appendix I; cal. *Westminster Abbey Charters*, no. 57.

78 Ibid., no. 97.

79 C. N. L. Brooke and Gillian Keir, *London 800–1216: the Shaping of a City* (London, 1975), pp. 32, 99–100, 315–23, 334.

80 *Westminster Abbey Charters*, no. 79.

81 *Reading Abbey Cartularies*, I, ed. B. R. Kemp, *CSer*, 31 (1986), pp. 13–19, and nos 1–7.

heredumque tuorum, et pro redemptione eorum qui te genuerunt, et gloriose memorie sororis tue'.[82] A confirmation to Westminster of the endowment of Matilda's anniversary was expected to ensure the stability of David's realm, and that of his heirs; the salvation of his parents and that of his sister 'of glorious memory'. Yet there was apparently no petition to have (Edith) Matilda recognized as a saint. Since another of the papal bulls which Osbert brought back from his mission has been shown to be a forgery,[83] it may be that the text concerning the Queen's anniversary is not above suspicion. Westminster made strenuous and successful efforts to ensure that David and his descendants confirmed earlier endowments, while they, in turn, made it plain that the prayers of the monks were expected for their kindred, but these Scottish charters place no emphasis on (Edith) Matilda's cult.[84]

The test of sanctity became more stringent as the papacy assumed the sole right to acclaim new saints, while the cult of King Edward was backed by little suitable evidence to bring forward, and little popular support. In December 1139 Pope Innocent II declined Westminster's petition, on the grounds that a genuine cult needed to be supported by the whole realm. It was up to Westminster to seek out such testimony.[85] When the first petition was submitted, King Stephen's illegitimate son Gervase was Abbot of Westminster (1138–*c*.1157), and the project was supported both by Stephen and by his brother, Henry of Blois, Bishop of Winchester and papal legate.[86] But in June 1139 the King had arrested Bishop Roger of Salisbury and his episcopal nephews.[87] King Stephen's assertion of control over his realm by demoting his ecclesiastical ministers perhaps prompted the rejection of the petition for Edward's canonization. No royal saint could be proclaimed in the realm of a king who treated churchmen in this way. The rejection of the first petition for Edward's canonization was a blow to Westminster, but perhaps also to the King, who claimed to rule according to the good laws of King Edward.[88] If Edward the Confessor's cult was recognized, it would not only enhance the status of Westminster Abbey (the underlying aim of Prior Osbert in embarking on the project), but would also enhance Stephen's claim to rule, which was more tenuous than that of his immediate predecessors. When the

82 *The Acts of Malcolm IV King of Scots 1153–1165*, ed. G. W. S. Barrow, *Regesta Regum Scottorum*, I (Edinburgh, 1960), no. 319; calendared *Westminster Abbey Charters*, no. 160.

83 Harvey, 'Abbot Gervase de Blois and the Fee-Farms of Westminster Abbey', pp. 128–9.

84 *Westminster Abbey Charters*, nos 99–104.

85 Ibid., no. 158; B. W. Scholz, 'The Canonization of Edward the Confessor', *Speculum*, 36 (1961), pp. 38–49.

86 *The Letters of Osbert of Clare, Prior of Westminster*, ed. E. W. Williamson (London, 1929), pp. 17–18; Barlow, *Edward the Confessor*, pp. 275–6.

87 William of Malmesbury, *The Historia Novella*, ed. and tr. K. R. Potter (London, 1955), pp. 25–34.

88 Stubbs, *Select Charters*, p. 142.

petition was rejected, Stephen, like his Norman predecessors, commissioned a new burial church elsewhere in his realm.[89]

Stephen was aware of the mutually supportive relationship between the Abbey of St Denis and the French Crown. Writing to his 'dear friend' Abbot Suger of St Denis, Stephen thanked him for his recent mediation at the French court, and undertook to defend those lands of St Denis which lay in his territory, promising also to restore, so far as possible, those which were controlled by his enemies (that is, Geoffrey of Anjou and his supporters).[90] Nearer home, Stephen ordered his officers to protect the lands of his son, Abbot Gervase, as though they were royal demesne.[91] But only one other of his genuine charters for Westminster hints at a special relationship with the abbey. This dates from the early 1150s, when Stephen's hopes of establishing a dynasty on the English throne were fading.[92] He conceded quittance of geld and customary exactions on six and a half acres of land in the manor of Westminster, because his court and palace, and the infirmary of St Giles, were established there. The grant was made for his soul, and those of his wife and children, King Henry and his other predecessors as kings of England.[93] There also survive in Stephen's name several lengthy forgeries, purportedly issued at various dates throughout his reign, in which close links are stressed between Stephen and his family; the abbey in its capacity as coronation church, his 'kinsman' King Edward, and King Henry and his other predecessors as kings of England.[94] His supposed general charters of liberties, in particular, associates his benefactions to Westminster with the continued stability of his rule and that of his descendants after him.[95] Yet the real purpose of these forgeries was not to enhance Stephen's authority, but the possessions and liberties of Westminster. So little faith did the monks have in the King's authority that they secured from Archbishop Theobald, in his capacity as papal legate, a confirmation of lands and rights both actually, and allegedly, granted by Stephen.[96] Westminster's title might rest more securely in consequence, but Stephen's jurisdiction was undermined when his acts of government were ratified by the spiritual power.

It was precisely this undermining of the royal authority which Henry II was determined to stamp out, and he therefore supported Westminster's renewed petition for the canonization of King Edward, through whom he and his Norman predecessors traced their claim to the English throne. It was becoming usual for European rulers to claim a saint among their ancestors in order to counter the infiltration of the *sacerdotium* into the sphere of secular

89 Mason, '*Pro statu et incolumnitate regni mei*', pp. 111–17.

90 *RR*, 3, no. 751.

91 *Westminster Abbey Charters*, no. 109.

92 R. H. C. Davis, *King Stephen 1135–1154*, 3rd edn (Harlow, 1990), pp. 108–24.

93 *RR*, 3, no. 938; *Westminster Abbey Charters*, no. 118.

94 *Westminster Abbey Charters*, nos 110–11, 119–21.

95 *RR*, 3, no. 928; *Westminster Abbey Charters*, no. 110.

96 *Westminster Abbey Charters*, no. 197.

jurisdiction. The canonization of Edward would strengthen his authority in his struggle to restore Church-State relations to the state of affairs in the reign of his grandfather, Henry I. Henry had no sympathy for Westminster's claims. His letter in support of Edward's canonization is one of the few among all those written to Pope Alexander III for that purpose which does not mention either the abbey or its abbot. Just as Henry's support for Edward's canonization was designed to enhance his own sovereignty, so his participation in the splendid translation of the new saint, on 13 October 1163, was a diplomatic demonstration of religious zeal, and of loyalty to Pope Alexander III just when the dispute with Thomas Becket over the relationship between spiritual and secular jurisdiction was coming to a head.[97] Among the letters which were solicited by Westminster in support of Edward's canonization, several made the point that a favourable papal decision would enhance the *honor regni*. Reading between the lines both of Henry's own supporting letter and those of Ailred of Rievaulx's new version of the *Life* of King Edward, it is plain that Edward's acclamation as a saint was expected to enhance the charismatic character of kingly rule and the sacred nature of English kingship.[98] The acknowledged sanctity of Edward would both strengthen Henry's authority against secular critics and render him independent of clerical constraints incurred through his anointing.

Westminster's series of forged royal charters of liberties includes one in Henry's name,[99] but this was made at a time when hope of royal patronage had waned. One forgery confirming financial exemptions on lands of the almonry, and supposedly issued early in the reign, stressed Henry's kinship with previous kings, but only to emphasize the antiquity of Westminster's claims.[100] Another forged charter, from the last years of the reign, confirmed the manor of Denham, associating the King with the cult of his kinsman King Edward.[101] By the reign of Richard I hopes had most likely faded entirely of securing any special relationship with the Crown. The last of the series of spurious royal charters of liberty is in the name of Richard I, and, like the earlier ones, emphasizes both the association between the King and his kinsman, King Edward of blessed memory, who adopted the present line of kings as his heirs, and also the abbey's role as coronation church.[102] The whole series perhaps dates from the early years of Richard's reign. There would have been no point in continuing it later, given the new methods which were being inaugurated of recording royal grants. The few genuine charters of Richard for Westminster, like those of his brother John, were brisk

97 Scholz, 'The canonization of Edward the Confessor', pp. 53, 55–6.
98 Ibid., pp. 56–9.
99 *Westminster Abbey Charters*, no. 123.
100 Ibid., no. 126.
101 Ibid., no. 138.
102 Ibid., no. 140.

and businesslike, and bought at a substantial price.[103] Neither king showed interest in the cult of King Edward, although John read popular English history, and his patron saint was the newly-canonized Englishman, Wulfstan of Worcester.[104] John's son, Henry III, was reared in a world in which English royal saints were venerated – hence his choice of names for his own sons – and hence his enhancement of his sovereignty through his exploitation of the cult of King Edward and his patronage of the church of Westminster.[105]

These happy days were unforeseen when the Westminster forgeries attempted to defend the abbey's possessions by stressing its role in conferring sovereignty upon the ruler. The diligence with which the task was undertaken, and sustained from one generation to another, helped lend credence to the abbey's claims as understood by Henry III, a point which was echoed by an eighteenth-century historian of the abbey, Richard Widmore. He observed:

> But when persons give themselves leave to defend even a good Title by undue means, they seldom know where to stop, and the Success at first emboldens them to enlarge beyond all Reason. And tho' I do not think, that in this Practice the whole was Fiction and Invention, they only added what they imagined would more especially serve their Purposes; yet by this means they have destroyed the Certainty of History and left those who came after them no better help, in separating the Truth from fables, that Conjecture and not altogether improbable Supposition.[106]

'Fiction and Invention' played no small part in creating the image, and hence the political potential, of Westminster as perceived in turn by Henry III and Richard II, whose patronage ensured that their successors would continue to regard it as the 'locus regiae consecrationis, regum sepultura, caput Angliae merito diademque regni ab antiquo nominatur'.

103 Ibid., nos 141–51. See particularly the notes to nos 149 and 151.

104 Emma Mason, 'St Wulfstan's staff: a legend and its uses', *Medium Aevum*, 53 (1984), pp. 157–60, 162.

105 Ibid., p. 171. See also S. H. Wander, 'The Westminster Abbey Sanctuary Pavement', *Traditio*, 34 (1978), pp. 137–56.

106 R. Widmore, *An Enquiry into the Time of the First Foundation of Westminster Abbey* (London, 1743), p. 11.

Appendix 3

The Donors of Westminster Abbey Charters c.1066–1240[1]

This prosopography springs, not from a known relationship or social background, but rather from a common activity which can be studied in some detail. The charters of Westminster Abbey, along with other documents that refer to donation and benefaction between 1066 and about 1240, enable us to begin with individuals who were involved in a common activity and then to move outwards. Beyond the act of benefaction to a single religious house, what did the men, women, and families who so gave have in common? To what extent were they linked, either in personal, social, or vocational ways? The examination of the Westminster donors also gives an insight into the importance of such benefaction in terms of mobility and status, in terms of the definition of family, and in terms of the link – in the context of urban history – between the residential community and its institutions and religious houses. The rich collection of Westminster charters allow us to look at these questions in the years between the death of Edward the Confessor and the time when Henry III reclaimed the abbey as a royal foundation. We know relatively little about commonplace benefaction in Norman and Plantagenet England, and the abbey charters are a rich source of material.

The 'universe' examined in this paper is that which comprises the laity and lesser clerics whose common link was their role of donor and benefactor of Westminster Abbey within a defined chronological period. The majority were also bound together, in a series of overlapping groups, by ties of other kinds. Many were neighbors within the vill of Westminster, at that time an outlying suburb of the City of London.[2] The close geographical proximity of

1 Successive phases of my work on the charters of Westminster Abbey have been generously supported by the Leverhulme Trust, the Nuffield Foundation, and the British Academy. An edition of the charters for the period 1066–1214 has been accepted for publication by the London Record Society. I am grateful to Professor Joel T. Rosenthal for discussions on the construction of this paper, to Miss Barbara Harvey and Professor Bernard S. Bachrach for advice on specific points, and to the staff of the Westminster Abbey Library and Muniment Room for much patient assistance. In the following notes, the abbreviation WAM represents Westminster Abbey Muniment.

2 A.G. Rosser, 'Medieval Westminster: The Vill and the Urban Community 1200–1540'

First published in *Medieval Prosopography*, 8, no. 2 (Autumn 1987)

the Westminster donors to one another is demonstrated by their mutual attestation of one another's charters. Corroborative evidence occurs in many of the charters, which state the boundaries of the land being transferred and, in doing so, list the ownership of the adjacent plots in each direction.

A large proportion of those donors who lived in Westminster was further linked by professional ties. Some were employed by the Royal exchequer, which was more or less permanently based at Westminster from the later years of Henry II's reign.[3] Other donors resident in the vill derived their livelihood and their social status from their employment by the abbey, whether as craftsmen or as lay officials. The social and religious bonding formed by such ties is demonstrated by the existence of the guild which rang the great bells of the church on the anniversary of the *obit* of notable benefactors.[4]

The Londoners among the donors were sometimes neighbors, as is demonstrated by the recital of the ownership of adjacent plots. Charter attestations are more ambivalent, since transactions concerning City property were customarily attested by prominent suitors of the Husting Court or by leading residents of the relevant ward of the City. Correlation between such witnesses and benefactors of the abbey was generally fortuitous. Evidence of commercial or of interfamilial ties is not readily forthcoming in material of this early date. Several of the London donors, however, were linked through their participation in the government of the City, whether as sheriffs or as aldermen.[5]

Evidence for connections between the Londoners and the residents of Westminster is rarely available. Within each geographical group, though, it may be argued that pre-existing ties were further strengthened by a conscious decision to patronize the abbey. Further evidence that some degree of social bonding was perceived to derive from their common status as benefactors may be inferred from the request of the (minor aristocratic) Exchequer chamberlain, Robert Mauduit, and his wife, Isabel, that the names of *all*

(Ph.D. Thesis, London University, 1984), documents the gradual urbanization of the environs of the abbey. An abridged version of his findings is published as 'The Essence of Medieval Urban Communities: The Vill of Westminster 1200–1540', *Transactions of the Royal Historical Society*, 5th ser., 34 (1984), 91–112.

3 The author of the *Dialogus de Scaccario* commenced his exposition in the twenty-third regnal year of King Henry II (December 1176 – December 1177) as he sat at a turret window overlooking the Thames: Richard Fitz Nigel, *Dialogus de Scaccario*, trans. and ed. Charles Johnson, rev. F.E.L. Carter and Diana E. Greenway (Oxford, 1983), p. 5. The treasurer's house was probably in Endiff (now lost), located between Westminster and Charing (Cross): Rosser, 'Medieval Westminster', p. 21.

4 WAM 3456, printed by Emma Mason, 'The Mauduits and Their Chamberlainship of the Exchequer', *Bulletin of the Institute of Historical Research* 49 (1976), 3–23.

5 Susan Reynolds, 'The Rulers of London in the Twelfth Century', *History* 57 (1972), 337–57, documents the major City families for this period. Her Index of Londoners to 1200 (to which Gillian Keir also contributed) may be consulted by appointment at the Museum of London.

benefactors of the Lady Altar should be enrolled in the Westminster martyrology.[6] Those who are working on comparable social groups may wish to compare this corpus of Westminster Abbey donors with the subjects of their own research.

Monastic charters have long been recognized as an important source of prosopographical interest, although attention has frequently been focused on limited groups of documents relating to the patronal family and to its territorial successors. Westminster, however, lost one royal patron with the death of King Edward in 1066, and obtained the patronage of King Henry III only in the middle decades of his reign (ca. 1240s). In the interim, the abbots and monks enlisted the support of the local populace in order to consolidate their existing urban holdings and to attract further benefactions. One hundred thirty-six charters of the laity, and of clerics below the rank of bishop, date from the period 1066–1214, while a sample of thirty-seven charters represents a substantial proportion, perhaps 30%, of those surviving from the years ca. 1215–40.[7] Some analysis of this later group is included as a check on whether, as the thirteenth century progressed, earlier trends were continuing or were beginning to undergo modification.

Scribes employed by the donors rarely dated their charters, so that dating has normally been assigned on the internal evidence of each text or series of texts. Since Westminster donors and witnesses regularly interrelate, dates can, however, be assigned with some confidence. In all, perhaps 10% of those charters in the main chronological group predate 1180, with the remainder forming a cohesive archive for the purposes of social analysis.

Of the charters in the group predating 1214, a few administrative writs, together with grants by A to B (who subsequently, but within the same period, granted the property to the abbey), total sixty-eight – that is, 50%. Of the sample of thirty-seven later charters, fifteen (some 40%) are similar grants at one remove, and a further four are administrative writs. The analysis of family structure can as readily be undertaken by examining the grants at one remove as it can in those issued directly for the abbey, as will become apparent below.

Westminster had obtained generous landed endowments from King Edward and was to receive lavish support from Henry III in his middle years;[8]

6 WAM LIII, printed Mason, 'The Mauduits and Their Chamberlainship', 21–22. Enrollment in the martyrology was also requested by the Londoner Richard Blund, even though his benefaction was not made specifically to the Lady Altar (Westminster Abbey Muniment Book 11, commonly styled 'the Domesday', cited hereafter as WAD, fol. 602r).

7 The present writer's work is confined to a study of those muniments which directly relate to Westminster's interests in the period 1066–1214. Early muniments which accrued to Westminster as a result of late-medieval acquisitions, including the important collection relating to the London collegiate church of St Martin le Grand, are excluded, as is a wealth of material from the mid-thirteenth century and later.

8 Barbara Harvey, *Westminster Abbey and Its Estates in the Middle Ages* (Oxford, 1977), documents the build-up of the abbey's lands.

but, in the intervening period, the support of the rank and file laity was both desirable and readily available. Indeed, the inhabitants of the vill of Westminster apparently preferred to bestow their donations upon the abbey, rather than upon the adjoining parish church of St Margaret – until in 1245 Henry III assumed financial responsibility for the rebuilding of the abbey church in the gothic style; then the support of the laity was abruptly withdrawn.[9] Although some Exchequer officers made occasional grants to the abbey, chiefly in King John's reign, those of the general populace who did so would have had no sense of 'joining the team' by supporting a church which enjoyed royal patronage. These lay donors of moderate means could take civic – or, rather, urban – pride in seeing the effects of their support, because the church was in their midst.

Taking the direct and indirect grants together, urban properties in the growing vill of Westminster were the subject of fifty-five charters, approximately 40% of the total predating 1214, and the subject of twenty-one charters, approximately 55% of the thirteenth-century sample. Properties in the City of London were conveyed in forty-five of the charters, approximately 33% of those prior to 1214, but in only four, perhaps 11% of the group dating from 1215 onwards. Taking the direct grants alone, thirty-three dating from before 1214 (that is, some 46%) relate to properties in Westminster, while twenty-one (about 30%) concern land in London. Of the later sample, four each relate to Westminster and to London, representing 9% in each case.

In London itself, there were other prestigious churches,[10] such as St Paul's Cathedral (an establishment of secular canons) and the Augustinian houses of Holy Trinity, Aldgate, and St Bartholomew's, Smithfield; but Westminster had no immediate local rival to which potential benefactors might be diverted. The major Augustinian houses, together with that of St Mary Overy, Southwark, just across the Thames, were founded in the early years of the twelfth century,[11] while in its middle decades the cult of St Erkenwald attracted renewed interest in St Paul's.[12] Donations to Westminster increased markedly in the last decades of the twelfth century, at a time when the interest generated earlier in these major London churches was perhaps waning. Those of the laity who supported Westminster were rarely, if ever, prominent benefactors of other major churches.

The social homogeneity of the donors is a feature both of the main body of charters and also of the later sample. Since Westminster was a royal foundation, nobles had nothing to gain by becoming its benefactors, and they would

9 Rosser, 'Medieval Westminster', 276, 282.

10 For a full survey of the London monasteries and hospitals in this period, see Christopher N.L. Brooke and Gillian Keir, *London 800–1216: The Shaping of a City* (London, 1975), pp. 293–337.

11 David Knowles and R. Neville Hadcock, *Medieval Religious Houses: England and Wales* (London, 1971), pp. 165, 174.

12 Brooke and Keir, *London 800–1216*, pp. 137, 272, 356.

have preferred to enhance their territorial position by continuing to patronize their own foundations. The only noble family which demonstrated an intermittent interest in Westminster over several generations was that of the Mandevilles, the main features of whose charters are discussed below. Identifiable Exchequer officers feature as grantors of perhaps 6%–7% of the charters. The 'typical' donor was a resident of suburban Westminster or, less frequently, a citizen of London – and dependent for a livelihood upon commerce or upon the exercise of a trade or skill. This predominantly urban, and in a broad sense metropolitan, bias puts difficulties in the way of any serious comparison with donors of grants to royal foundations elsewhere. The difficulties exist even in the case of well-documented houses such as Reading, since the locations, hence the populations, are so dissimilar from those of Westminster.

The 'average' donation to Westminster was a grant of a messuage, or of a rent deriving from a specified tenement or tenements, so that the monks were, in the course of time, enabled to build up contiguous blocks of land in prime sites. In London itself, one center of interest was around Ludgate. Commercial sites in Cheapside and in the Fishmarket were sought after, as were sites fronting the Thames. In Westminster, the monks' property in Tothill Street was steadily consolidated; and further areas of interest were (1) that around the present-day St James's Park (at that time the environs of a leper hospital with this dedication) and (2) the Endiff district downriver from Westminster, merging with Charing (the later Charing Cross). Such a policy of acquiring contiguous sites was very much an urban phenomenon, in contrast to the random rural acquisitions of abbeys sited in the countryside.

Whereas the charters of rural houses often reveal networks of interest in the form of tenurial relationships, rather than, or in addition to, one of common preference for a particular religious order or cult, this is not easily discerned in urban charters such as those of Westminster. Since the vill of Westminster itself was a rapidly developing suburb, it is probable that many of the donors there were parvenus. The population of London was also expanding as a result of immigration from the surrounding counties, and only a few of the London donors represent major City families. It might be argued, therefore, that patronage of the abbey was perceived as a means of stabilizing a donor's recent social advance. Moreover, the privileges of confraternity, of burial, and of the celebration of the anniversary of a benefactor's *obit* might all be obtained, for a price, at Westminster. The land or rent obtained in return for such privileges contributed steadily to the abbey's income both in this period and in successive generations.[13] Although the social motivation of donors can be deduced, and an economic one often demonstrated in grants made in return for a *gersum* (a payment in return), the religious motivations should not be underestimated. Many of the grants, both in the main body of charters and in the later sample, were made 'in pure alms' or 'in free alms',

13 Harvey, *Westminster Abbey*, pp. 365–401.

occasionally to St Peter, to whom the abbey church was dedicated, but increasingly also to the Blessed Virgin. From the 1190s there was a steady flow of grants to the Lady Altar, while work on the gothic Lady Chapel dates from the 1220s.[14] Of the main group of charters, twenty-nine are grants for the benefit of the Lady Altar, with a further four made less specifically to the Blessed Virgin, all together representing some 24% of the total of direct grants. Of the later sample, one three (that is, some 8%) claimed this motivation.

The canonization of Edward the Confessor in 1161 did not contribute to any great spate of benefactions. He is named in only seven of the direct grants in the main collection (just over 10%); of these, in five cases the donors were men of some official status, who perhaps perceived an advantage in honoring the new royal saint. The laity in general were evidently not responsive to the royal associations of the abbey. On the evidence of the main group of charters, it appears that the laity were attracted by the cults of St Peter and of the Blessed Virgin, combined perhaps with the hope of sharing in the spiritual benefits of the house. Local patriotism probably motivated suburban residents, although those Londoners among the donors were consciously diverting their patronage outside the City. In view of London's growing civic pride, this diversion represents a major decision – perhaps to seek association with the nearest large Benedictine monastery, although the drawing power of the cults of the Blessed Virgin and of St Peter must have been major attractions in themselves.

Among the donors are several individuals representing major City families. Richard Blund listed (without identifying) categories of his kinsfolk whom he expected would enjoy the spiritual benefits of his donation, while his own name was to be enrolled in the martyrology.[15] Andrew Bucherel, about to embark on a pilgrimage to the Holy Sepulchre at Jerusalem, made a grant for his 'ancestors' and specified that the anniversary of his *obit* should be commemorated.[16] Henry Fitz Ailwin, London's first mayor, made a grant for his 'ancestors and successors'.[17] These men were attracted by Westminster's perceived spiritual drawing power, whereas William Fitz Alulf received a *gersum* in return for a transaction which was essentially a sale.[18] The spiritual merits of Westminster attracted three generations of the Haverhill family, each of which made a new grant, not simply a confirmation of a predecessor's benefaction. The particular interest of this group of charters is discussed below, in another context. Prominent Londoners are not conspicuous in the later sample of thirteenth-century charters.

The shift of the axis of government from Winchester to Westminster in

14 Rosser 'Medieval Westminster', 86–92.
15 WAD, fol. 602r.
16 WAD, fol. 493r–v.
17 WAD, fols. 485v–486r.
18 WAD, fol. 491r–v.

the latter part of Henry II's reign accounts for the donations of royal officials, many of whom acquired houses in the vill. Several charters concern Robert Mauduit, chamberlain of the Exchequer from 1194, and his wife, Isabel Basset, descendant of another, and rather grander, curial family. Robert initially remained aloof from the spiritual attractions of the abbey, obtaining license from the abbot to maintain a private chapel in his residence.[19] Isabel, however, bought up land in Westminster with the intention of donating it to the abbey for the Lady Altar. One of her grants, made exclusively for her own spiritual benefit, is sealed with her own seal bearing the Basset arms. The other, made for the ancestors and successors of her husband, as well as for her own, was attested by her husband Robert and 'her' son William Mauduit.[20] Although these grants were in Isabel's name, they had Robert's sanction, and he probably financed them, since he expected to share with Isabel in the spiritual returns.[21] The aura surrounding the abbey church evidently made an increasing impression upon Robert, who in his last years made a generous donation on his own account in return for the commemoration of his anniversary in the manner accorded to Westminster's more esteemed abbots.[22]

Evidence in the charters concerning family relationships is variable. Indirect grants from A to B (the subsequent donor) are most explicit, because the descent of land, and the existence of other interested parties, had to be recorded. Twenty-five of the sixty-eight indirect grants in the group predating 1214 (about 30%) contain evidence on family relationships, although in the thirteenth-century sample only three of the nineteen indirect grants (about 15%) contain comparable evidence.

In the case of direct grants 'in pure alms', although the existence of wives, parents, and, occasionally, children is indicated, named kinsfolk are the exception to the general rule. Of the sixty-eight direct grants predating 1214, eleven (15%) are made for the souls of the grantor's father and mother; one grant by a couple is for the souls of the father and mother of both spouses; one grant is for an unnamed mother only, and one is for a father. Both (unnamed) parents of the donor are included in three of the eighteen direct grants in the later sample.

Unspecified *antecessores* were expected to benefit from thirty-two grants (48%) of the main group, and nine (or 50%) of the later sample. *Parentes* (kinsfolk, rather than 'parents' in the modern sense) were to receive spiritual benefits as a result of nine donations in the main group, three in the later sample. The younger generation received a lower priority. The spiritual

19 WAD, fol. 352r–v, printed Mason, 'The Mauduits and Their Chamberlainship', 19.

20 WAM 17327; WAD, fol. 520v, both printed Mason, 'The Mauduits and Their Chamberlainship', 20–21. 'Hiis testibus, domino Roberto Mauduyt uiro meo, Willelmo Mauduyt filio meo . . .' (ibid., 21). The use of 'meo', rather than 'nostro', in describing the son of her marriage, is perhaps on a par with Isabel's retention of her distinctive seal.

21 WAM LIII, printed ibid., 21–22.

22 WAM 3456, printed ibid., 22–23.

welfare of unspecified *successores*, or occasionally of *posteriores*, was invoked in nine donations in the main group and one in the later sample, and the welfare of 'heirs' was invoked in four grants in the main group and three in the later sample. These general terms were usually preferred to the more specific 'sons' (employed in four charters), 'children' (in two), and 'daughters' (in one), all in the group predating 1214. Direct grants are particularly unspecific on familial relationships in which the donor received a *gersum* from the abbey, presumably because, in the case of *de facto* sales, spiritual returns to the grantor or his kindred would be minimal – although they were promised in rare cases.

In general, the evidence in the direct grants is not helpful in determining family size; however, two groups of donations stand out in contrast: those of Geoffrey de Mandeville I and his descendants, ranging in date from the late eleventh century to the mid-twelfth, and those of the Haverhill family, dating from the later twelfth to the early thirteenth century. Geoffrey named his two successive wives and specified that it was the former, Alice, who was the mother of his sons. He stated that he had daughters as well as sons, and that he had designated his son William as his heir. Further Mandevilles of unspecified kinship attested one of his charters.[23] A grant of Geoffrey's grandson and namesake distinguished his father and mother (unnamed) from other *antecessores*, and mentioned (without identifying) his wife and heirs.[24] The distinction noted above between the factual terms of indirect grants and the imprecise wording of direct grants 'in alms' is corroborated by two charters of the younger Geoffrey's successor, William. In a confirmation of land to one of his tenants, William identifies his brother, his father, and his (maternal) grandfather,[25] although a grant to the abbey refers only to his unnamed father and mother and to other *antecessores*.[26]

Concern by members of the City family of Haverhill to name those kinsfolk who were to benefit by their grants dwindled with the passing generations. Brichtmar of Haverhill, in a grant of ca. 1175–90, named his deceased wife (who was buried at Westminster), his son and heir William, and the latter's wife. The younger couple were recorded as having (unnamed) children, and Brichtmar's unnamed *antecessores* and *posteriores* were also to share in the spiritual benefits of his grant. The whole clan were admitted into

23 Geoffrey's charters are printed respectively by J. Armitage Robinson, *Gilbert Crispin, Abbot of Westminster* (Cambridge, 1911), p. 139, no. 15; and by Pierre Chaplais, 'The Original Charters of Herbert and Gervase, Abbots of Westminster (1121–1157)', A *Medieval Miscellany for Doris Mary Stenton*, ed. Patricia M. Barnes and C.F. Slade, Pipe Roll Society, n.s. 36 (London, 1962), pp. 105–108. William and Richard de Mandeville, who attest the latter charter, were in fact Geoffrey's sons: C. Warren Hollister, 'The Misfortunes of the Mandevilles', *History* 58 (1973), 19, 26.

24 WAD, fols. 492v–493r. On Geoffrey's family, see Hollister, 'The Misfortunes of the Mandevilles', 18–28.

25 WAM 1231.

26 British Library, Cotton Charter X.1.

confraternity.[27] William de Haverhill made, at some time between 1190 and 1212, a new donation for the souls of his unnamed father and mother, wife, children, and kinsfolk – both *antecessores* and *posteriores* – with the assent of his son and heir, Thomas.[28] Thomas himself made a further new grant, but did not name, let alone identify, a single member of his family. Perhaps he was simply continuing a family tradition in a perfunctory way.[29] Much of his attention was taken up by his overseeing of property transactions relating to the hospital of St Giles, Holborn, in the cartulary of which he features prominently.[30]

The Mandeville charters and the Haverhill group illustrate a point which is present by implication in many other of the direct grants: that spiritual benefits were enlisted chiefly for the nuclear, linear family, rather than for a kin-group extending laterally. Uncle-nephew relationships are rarely stated in charters of laymen. One exception occurs in a grant of Richard Blund of London, a married man with children of his own.[31] The status achieved by his nephew Robert may be relevant, since he can probably be identified with the Robert Blund who was sheriff in 1196–97.[32] Charters occasionally document the relationship between a clerical uncle and his nephew, or nephews, such as those grants which link William of Northolt (archdeacon of Gloucester, shortly to become bishop of Worcester), with Walter of Greenford and with Roger of Missenden.[33] The relationship between Richard of Ilchester, bishop of Winchester, and his (genuine) nephews, Richard and Thomas de Barentin, is explicit. The ubiquitous Adam 'of Westminster', who used the alias *nepos episcopi*, was another (genuine) nephew; but, in contrast, the bishop's son, Herbert le Poore, conspicuously failed to identify his father when he restored land which the latter had appropriated from the abbey.[34]

In a society in which property largely descended in the male line, it is not surprising that the majority of grants, direct or indirect, were made by men. Of the main group, only seven were made jointly by husband and wife; three were made with the assent of the (named) wife, and two were made with the assent of the donor's mother. In each case, it was presumably the woman's marriage portion or dower assignment which was being transferred. Interestingly, one such joint grant was made primarily for the soul of the (named)

27 WAD, fol. 367v.

28 WAD, fol. 368r–v.

29 WAD, fol. 483v.

30 British Library, Harleian MS 4015.

31 WAD, fol. 602r.

32 Reynolds, 'The Rulers of London', 356.

33 WAD, fol. 446r–v.

34 The Ilchester-Barentin relationship is stated in WAM 662. See WAM 661 for the parentage of Richard and Thomas. Adam of Westminster used the alias 'Fitz Henry': *The Beauchamp Cartulary*, ed. Emma Mason (Pipe Roll Society, n.s. 43, 1980), no. 183. *Nepos episcopi* was his usual cognomen (ibid., nos. 185–186; 191–92). His kinship to Richard of Ilchester is explicitly stated in WAD, fol. 342r–v. Herbert le Poore's reticent charter is WAM 16737.

mother of the wife.[35] In the later sample, there are two joint grants, plus one made with the wife's consent. In two more, a *gersum* rendered to the wife is sole evidence of her participation.[36]

There are two instances in the main chronological group in which a grant made jointly to the abbey by a man and woman omits mention of their marital status. In one instance, the man in question, Alexander, 'clerk of the Exchequer', can probably be identified with the distinguished royal clerk Alexander de Swereford, whose reticence was perhaps prompted by the hope of clerical preferment.[37] He and his partner Edith had obtained the land from her father, William Little of Temple Bar, who had empowered them to designate as heir whichever of their sons they pleased.[38] The man named in the other such joint grant, Ralph Mauduit, was certainly in the king's service ca. 1180, but is not readily identifiable as a clerk.[39]

Taking the direct and indirect grants together, we find that six women describing themselves as widows were grantors of charters in the main group; three widowed grantors occur in the later sample. Two women whose marital status is undefined were grantors of charters in the main group,[40] and one in the later sample.[41] These women describe themselves as 'daughter of', probably in order to indicate their titles to the land in question, rather than to specify unmarried status. Indeed, three widows in the main group[42] and one in the later sample[43] additionally describe themselves as 'daughter of'.

The property rights of children were occasionally acknowledged when land was being transferred. Consent may be assumed in those cases in which a son attested the relevant charter; more specifically, there are rare instances of the grantor's son[44] or daughter[45] receiving a *gersum*. One donor specified the assent of his two sons and heirs,[46] who were perhaps twins.

Cognomens are quite varied. Surnames in the modern sense, ranging from 'feudal' names such as Mandeville or De Vere through such City names as

35 WAM 17437.

36 WAD, fol. 475r; WAM 17141.

37 WAM 17416. This identification is reinforced by a contemporary charter of Abbot Ralph Arundel: WAD, fol. 561r.

38 WAM 17321.

39 WAM 17438. On Ralph Mauduit, see *Pipe Roll 34 Henry II*, 17.

40 Four charters were issued by Matilda 'de Paris': WAD, fols. 489v–490v; 502v, alias Matilda, daughter of Simon Fitz Osmar. Her final grant was made in return for food and clothing: WAD, fol. 502r–v.

41 Two charters were issued by Beatrice Fitz Brungar. One, which omits mention of her marital status, was a grant to her grandson, the son of her son: WAM 17109. In the other, in which no offspring are mentioned, Beatrice styled herself a widow: WAM 17110.

42 WAM 13900, 17413; WAD, fol. 487r.

43 WAD, fol. 442r.

44 WAD, fol. 491r.

45 WAM 17079.

46 WAM 17456. Only two seals survive, but the parchment was prepared to accommodate three.

Blund or Buccuinte, and Westminster names such as Testard, are borne by thirty-four donors in the main group (about 25% of direct and indirect grants combined) and eleven in the later sample (about 29%). Patronymics such as Fitz Osbert are borne by thirty-nine donors in the main group and by thirteen in the later sample (25% and 33% respectively).

Toponymics (not usually documented in these charters as descending to a second generation and thereby becoming a 'surname') account for twenty-five and five donors in the respective groups, while the remainder of donors are designated by occupation. (Again, their trade names cannot normally be demonstrated to descend from one generation to the next, in this collection.) Statistics become blurred when one individual employs a succession of names, of which a memorable illustration is Laurence of Stanstead, surnamed *diabolus*, son of William surnamed *diabolus*,[47] William of Northolt, the cleric mentioned earlier, uncle of Walter of Greenford and Roger of Missenden, evidently came from a family in which individual toponymics were probably assigned according to place of birth, or perhaps derived from the individual's major landholding. William himself named his grandfather as Hugh of Colham, whereas his uncle was styled Richard Fitz Hugh.[48]

Ethnic backgrounds are not readily distinguished because of the rapidity with which French and English assimilated in urban society.[49] The above-mentioned Haverhill family presumably had some English ancestors from whom Brichtmar was named. A family such as the Barentins are known from the internal evidence of their charters, quite apart from their surname, to have maintained a French connection down to the reign of John.[50]

Extensive family or professional connections are not usually documented, and the donations of any one family are insufficiently coherent to provide evidence of naming patterns. At this early date, surviving evidence for links such as that between godparents is virtually nonexistent. Attestations are often those of suitors of the court in which a given transaction was ratified, whether that of the abbot, or of the Husting Court of London; and, while members of a kin-group or a professional circle might be included, they attested in another capacity. The one regular exception is in the case of grants by Exchequer officers, who habitually attested one another's charters.

47 WAD, fol. 474r–v.

48 WAM 381. Colham, Greenford, and Northolt were neighboring vills in Middlesex. Missenden lies a few miles over the county border, in Buckinghamshire.

49 Cecily Clark, 'People and Languages in Post-Conquest Canterbury', *Journal of Medieval History* 2 (1976), 1–33; 'Women's Names in Post-Conquest England: Observations and Speculations', *Speculum* 53/2 (1978), 223–51. The much-quoted dictum of Richard Fitz Nigel on intermarriage is particularly apposite: 'But nowadays, when English and Normans live close together and marry and give in marriage to each other, the nations are so mixed that it can scarcely be decided (I am talking about freemen), who is of English birth and who of Norman, except, of course, the villeins . . .' (*Dialogus de Scaccario*, p. 53). Richard was a resident of Westminster in the later twelfth century: ibid., p. 5, and n. 3 above.

50 WAD, fol. 140v.

Inter-connections between the Westminster material and that in the cartularies of other London houses is rarely easy to discern. Leading citizens of London would naturally attest transactions relating to City properties, no matter to which religious house these pertained.

The prosopographical lacunae in the Westminster Abbey charters for this period could probably have been filled with the evidence which was formerly available in the martyrology. The importance of such source materials is illustrated by Cecily Clark's analysis of the twelfth-century *Liber Vitae* of Thorney Abbey.[51] The Westminster muniments and associated records have been utilized by Barbara Harvey in order to compile a list of burials of laity at Westminster,[52] a short list of grants of confraternity,[53] and a considerably longer list of perpetual anniversaries and chantries.[54] The habitual grant by charter of an endowment in return for the award of such spiritual benefits made her task feasible. The imbalance in surviving documentation ensures that her lists are inevitably more detailed for the later medieval centuries. The expectation of donors that they and their kindred would enjoy a spiritual return for their grants has ensured that the records of medieval religious foundations, even those beyond the confines of the Latin West,[55] provide, to a varying extent, evidence on family structure. In this respect, the Westminster Abbey muniments have much to offer the student of medieval history.

51 Cecily Clark, 'British Library Additional MS 40,000, ff.1v–12r', *Anglo-Norman Studies VII*, ed. R. Allen Brown (Woodbridge, 1985), pp. 50–65.

52 Harvey, *Westminster Abbey*, pp. 365–86.

53 Ibid., pp. 386–7.

54 Ibid., pp. 387–99. This section concludes with a short list of recipients of other forms of spiritual benefit; ibid., pp. 400–01.

55 Valerie Nunn, 'The Encheirion as Adjunct to the Icon in the Middle Byzantine Period', *Byzantine and Modern Greek Studies*, 10 (1986), 73, 75.

Appendix 4

Westminster Abbey and its Parish Churches c.1050–1216*

Westminster abbey was a rich monastery, thanks largely to the endowment of King Edward (1042–66), who intended that the church of St. Peter of Westminster should be his mausoleum.[1] It possessed considerable property in London and of course in Westminster itself; estates in all of the 'home counties', and outlying properties in the east and west Midlands, and in Sussex.[2] Appurtenant to many of these properties were parish churches which were in themselves sources of income. They also afforded the means of financing the abbey's expert secular clerks, and of offering an acceptable *quid pro quo* to those who mattered in high places. This present survey of Westminster's administration of its churches is confined to the century and a half between King Edward's endowment of the abbey and the end of King John's reign, a period which spanned developments in church history from the beginnings of the Gregorian reform movement down to the Fourth Lateran Council. Westminster's splendid collection of muniments includes more than 490 documents emanating from this period.[3] Some 144 of these concern churches and/or tithes, an indication that considerable attention was paid to parochial sources of income, and their administration. Much the same problems in dealing with these were faced by ecclesiastical proprietors throughout England, and to a large extent they responded in similar ways, although local circumstances also gave rise to some divergences.[4]

1 *Vita Aedwardi Regis qui apud Westmonasterium requiescit*, ed. and transl. Frank Barlow (London, 1962), pp. 44–6; Barbara Harvey, *Westminster Abbey and its Estates in the Middle Ages* (Oxford, 1977), pp. 24–5.

2 Harvey, *Westminster Abbey and its Estates*, pp. 335–64. For the abbey's property in the vill of Westminster itself, see also Gervase Rosser, *Medieval Westminster 1200–1540* (Oxford, 1989), pp. 12–16.

3 *Westminster Abbey Charters 1066–c.1214*, ed. Emma Mason, assisted by the late Jennifer Bray, continuing the work of the late Desmond J. Murphy (London Record Society, 25, 1988).

4 For the administration of parish churches and parochial sources of income in various regions of twelfth-century England, see Janet E. Burton, 'Monasteries and Parish Churches in Eleventh and Twelfth-Century Yorkshire', *Northern History*, 23 (1987), pp. 39–50; Christopher Harper-Bill, 'Bishop William Turbe and the Diocese of

First published in *Monastic Studies: the Continuity of Tradition*, II, ed. Judith Loades (Bangor, 1991)

Analysis of Westminster's charters relating to ecclesiastical property reveals that about twenty-five per cent are concerned solely with the tithe income. Conversely several of the abbey's parish churches may comprise the subject of any one document, while some individual churches, usually the richest and therefore the most contested, gave rise to repeated negotiation and hence to frequent documentation. In contrast, poor and remote churches, and small assignments of tithe income, earned a bare mention even in the most all-embracing confirmatory charters of this period. So far as the documentation allows, the present paper will examine the evidence for the geographical spread of parochial revenues; the uses to which they were assigned; the action taken to secure title to parochial income in confirmations obtained from kings, from popes and their agents, and from diocesan bishops; the evidence in charters of the abbots of Westminster, and in those of benefactors, for the administration of individual churches and, in a concluding section, several case-studies will be examined for evidence, on the one hand, of the impact of canon law on parochial administration, and of the growing efficiency of ecclesiastical jurisdiction in the reform era. On the other hand, these case-studies will also reveal the impact of royal intervention and persuasion; pressures from influential *curiales*, and the entrenched rights, or claims, of incumbents.

The reliability of this survey depends on the validity of the evidence. Westminster assiduously retained texts of the grants which it received, and of those charters which were issued by its abbots and chapter – but texts were also kept of those grants which the monks would like to have received – if only someone had granted them. The question of authenticity looms large over royal charters, and in particular those of King Edward, William I and Henry I, but forgers continued at work in the abbey long after these reigns. Many documents were elaborated in order to lend respectability to older grants by adding witness-lists and place-dates, so that the substance of many charters 'improved' in this way contains a strong factual base. Other suspect charters record genuine grants, but augment them with long lists of judicial and financial liberties which the chapter would like to have seen attached to its properties.[5] The churches and tithes recorded in both categories of document can generally be shown from later and genuine charters to be the possessions of Westminster. Only towards the end of the period under discussion can checks be made against royal records, while papal and episcopal records of the transactions under discussion are virtually non-existent, so

Norwich, 1147–1174', *Anglo-Norman Studies 7*, ed. R. Allen Brown (Woodbridge, 1985), pp. 142–60; and his 'The Struggle for Benefices in Twelfth-Century East-Anglia', *Anglo-Norman Studies 11*, ed. R. Allen Brown (Woodbridge, 1989), pp. 113–32; and B. R. Kemp. 'Monastic Possession of Parish Churches in England in the Twelfth Century', *Journal of Ecclesiastical History*, 31 (1980), pp. 133–60.

5 *Westminster Abbey Charters*, pp. 8–11.

that the evidence of the Westminster charters must be considered largely as it stands.

Most of Westminster's churches pertained to lands acquired either before the reign of King Edward or in consequence of his own endowment, but early charters rarely if ever mention the church when granting a manor or a vill. Usually the place was granted 'with everything pertaining to it'. The charters of William I are in general scarcely more explicit, while the grandiose forgeries in the names of both kings include sweeping confirmations of estates, 'with all churches, tithes, income for lights, dues . . .' etc. etc.[6] This may indicate that such documents were consciously designed to show the open-handed generosity which these kings displayed towards a privileged abbey. But there was another reason for the sparse documentation of parish churches in genuine charters of the eleventh century, namely that the movement was only then under way whereby each substantial vill was acquiring a parish church of its own, and assuming in its own locality the functions of the older minster churches.[7] In the transitional period, acrimonious disputes might arise over the revenues formerly due to the old church of the neighbourhood. This is demonstrated in a writ of Abbot Herbert (1121–*c.*1136), in which he ordered the French and English men of Pershore and its hundred to render all rights and customs which the church of Saints Mary and Edburg of Pershore (i.e. Pershore abbey), the mother church of Pershore hundred (Worcs.), was accustomed to receive in the time of Herbert's predecessors, in tithes, alms and all other services which the tenants owed the church. They were forbidden to contradict or harass any spiritual pastor set over them, nor act in any way which was detrimental to the rights of that mother church. Abbot Herbert's writ in effect confirmed an earlier concession of the major tithes due from the hundred, which had been made by Abbot Gilbert Crispin (*c.*1085–1117/8), and were later confirmed to Pershore by John of Pagham, bishop of Worcester, in 1151/7.[8]

Early royal grants or confirmations of vills to Westminster rarely mention a church, whereas these same places were normally provided with one by the early twelfth century. While the pre-existence of old 'mother churches' might impede Westminster's efforts to establish fully-fledged parish churches for its tenants on outlying manors, the abbey regarded several of its own churches as 'mother churches', including those at Benfleet (Essex), Bloxham (Oxon.),

6 For instance, the so-called Third Charter of William I: Westminster Abbey Domesday (Muniment Book 11), ff. 51r–52v.

7 J. Blair, 'From Minster to Parish Church', in *Minsters and Parish Churches: the Local Church in Transition 950–1200*, ed. J. Blair (Oxford University Committee for Archaeology, Monograph no. 17, 1988), pp. 1–19. See also J. Blair, 'Minster Churches in the Landscape', in *Anglo-Saxon Settlements*, ed. Della Hooke (Oxford, 1988), pp. 35–58.

8 Brian R. Kemp, 'The Mother Church of Thatcham', *Berkshire Archaeological Journal*, LXIII (1967–68), p. 21, note 32. On the dedication of Pershore abbey, see Alison Binns, *Dedications of Monastic Houses in England and Wales 1066–1216* (Woodbridge, 1989), pp. 81–2.

Hambledon, Oakham, Uppingham and Wardley (all in Rutland), but the term occurs only in suspect charters which are in the name of William I, although they date in fact from the early twelfth century.[9]

Some of Westminster's churches were acquired by the abbey when individuals – probably priests, but occasionally lay proprietors – were admitted as monks to the abbey and brought their churches with them. In Suffolk, the church of St. Bartholomew, Sudbury, was acquired when the royal moneyer Wulfric donated it on becoming a monk at Westminster. The abbey's subsequent right to it was challenged in the royal court, but upheld by the judges, and ratified by King Henry I.[10] This church later became the site of a small cell pertaining to Westminster, and one of its early inmates, Ivo, donated to it the greater tithe from his demesne at Torp when he became a monk of Sudbury.[11] In London, the church of St. Agnes was donated to Westminster by Godric Lobbe when he became a monk there,[12] while the advowson of St. Martin's Ludgate, was surrendered to the abbey by Laurence, surnamed 'the Devil', in return for confraternity in life and in death.[13]

But Westminster was not the goal of all those with a religious vocation. Ranulph the clerk of Feering (Essex) joined the Arroasian canons of Missenden (Bucks.), and unlawfully detained Westminster's church of Feering. As a brother of the late English pope, Adrian IV, and as father of a substantial tenant of St. Albans abbey, he perhaps felt able to act with impunity. But Abbot Walter of Westminster appealed to the papal *curia*, and Gilbert Foliot, bishop of London, was commissioned as a papal judge-delegate in the case. The outcome was that the church was resigned to the bishop, who restored it to the abbot. The bishop then instituted the abbot's clerk, Mr Maurice, to Feering, which he was to hold of the abbot of Westminster.[14] Occasionally a church might accrue to Westminster while its former possessor prevaricated about his religious vocation. By an agreement dated 1125, Abbot Herbert and the convent granted their manor of Ockenden (Essex) to Henry son of Wilfrid, to hold for life at an annual rent of £10. Henry gave the church of Ockenden to the abbey, but would continue to hold it at an annual rent of £1.

After his death, his heir would continue to render £1 for the church, but £11 for the manor. If Henry asked to be admitted as a monk, he would be

9 These churches are enumerated both in the 'First Charter of King William I', printed in *Calender of Charter Rolls IV*, pp. 330–6, and in the 'Telligraphus' or Land Book of William I (Westminster Abbey Muniment XXVI). On the spurious nature of these texts, see *Westminster Abbey Charters*, notes to nos. 1, 43.

10 *Westminster Abbey Charters*, no. 72.

11 Ivo's grant was confirmed by King Henry I, and later ratified by Henry II: *Westminster Abbey Charters*, no. 130.

12 *Westminster Abbey Charters*, no. 257.

13 *Ibid.*, no. 359.

14 *The Letters and Charters of Gilbert Foliot*, ed. Z. N. Brooke, A. Morey and C. N. L. Brooke (Cambridge, 1967), nos. 465–6.

received without the need to make a further agreement, and in that eventuality one heir of his would hold manor and church on the above-mentioned terms. And if Henry's heir wanted to become a monk, he would be received by the same agreement by which his father was admitted, and then both manor and church would revert to Westminster, unencumbered, and with all improvements.[15]

The dispersal pattern of Westminster's ecclesiastical sources of income and patronage can be learned from a few key documents, of which the most reliable were those issued by Pope Adrian IV (1154–9) and by two successive bishops of London, Gilbert Foliot (1163–87) and Richard Fitz Nigel (1189–98). In a confirmatory bull dated 1 June 1157, Pope Adrian enumerated the churches, chapels and tithes which pertained to Westminster: in Middlesex, churches and/or chapels in seven named places, with tithe income elsewhere, 'and all ecclesiastical possessions in London – including Newchurch' (to which we return later in this paper); in Surrey, four churches; in Kent, one church; two churches in Sussex; one in Wiltshire; five churches in Hertfordshire, of which one had an appurtenant chapel; six churches in Essex, of which one had appurtenant land, and another a chapel; only one church in Buckinghamshire, but this was Denham, clearly valuable in view of its subsequent history; two churches in Oxfordshire, of which one had a chapel; three churches in Northamptonshire, of which one had appurtenant chapels and another had substantial appurtenant tithes; five churches listed under Rutland, including one in Stamford, and unspecified quantities of appurtenant chapels, tithes, land and houses; one church in Lincolnshire with its chapels; one church in Staffordshire; two churches and one chapel in Gloucestershire; fourteen churches and seven chapels in Worcestershire, with tithes appurtenant to fourteen of the twenty-one, and tithe income in eleven other places.[16] But these Worcestershire churches and tithes have left little trace in Westminster's archives for the period under discussion. Perhaps there were amicable agreements with the abbey's tenants in that region, since many of the West Mercian properties were let at farm at the time. There was also the possibility that the income from any one of these churches was insufficient to tempt ambitious courtiers and the like to challenge Westminster's rights and thereby leave traces in the abbey's archives.

The churches in London, which received only a glancing reference in Pope Adrian's confirmation, were listed in a confirmation issued by Bishop Gilbert Foliot early in the 1180s. He named 13 churches in London and its suburbs, together with the pension due from each incumbent. Elsewhere in his diocese, he confirmed in Essex the churches of Ockenden, Kelvedon and Feering, the chapel of Little Tey and unspecified tithes in White Roding, but

15 *Westminster Abbey Charters*, no. 247.

16 *Papsturkunden in England*, ed. W. Holtzmann, 3 vols. (Abhandlungen der Gesellschaft der Wissenschaften in Göttingen phil. hist. Klasse, Berlin, Göttingen: I = neue Folge XXV, 1930–31; II = 3. Folge XIV–XV, 1935–6; III = 3 Folge XXXIII, 1952), I, no. 70.

omitted mention of the churches of Benfleet and *Bymton*, and the chapel of Moulsham, which were included in Pope Adrian's confirmatory bull. In Hertfordshire he confirmed the valuable church of Sawbridgeworth, with its pension of £15, but omitted to mention those of Wheathampstead, Aldenham, Stevenage, Datchworth and Ashwell, which were included in the papal confirmation. In Middlesex, he confirmed only the church of Hendon, omitting those of Staines, with its chapels; Shepperton, Sunbury, Hanwell, Chelsea, the chapel of Greenford and the tithes in *Edelinton*.[17] The confirmation by Richard Fitz Nigel recited these identical properties.[18] Some of the churches missing from the episcopal confirmations were mentioned in a bull dated 18 April 1177 addressed by Pope Alexander III to Abbot Walter and the convent. He confirmed the possessions of the abbey and its exemptions from the jurisdiction of the bishop of London, but prohibited the alienation of the churches of Oakham (Rutland), Staines (Middlesex), Aldenham, Ashwell and Wheathampstead (Herts.), with their chapels.[19] Evidently a petition had been sent to the *curia* in the course of the ongoing effort to evade the jurisdiction of the bishop of London and the opportunity was taken to counteract the alienation of the churches in question, but whether the initiative in this matter came from the monastic delegation, or from Abbot Walter himself, is conjectural. If the churches had been allocated to senior royal clerks on the king's instructions, Walter's only means of remedying this was perhaps to request the papacy for a mandate on the subject. On the other hand, the monastic delegation might have secured this on their own initiative, to counteract what they regarded as abbatial mismanagement of Westminster's properties. More likely the mandate concerning the churches had some direct link with the jurisdiction of the bishopric of London, since on 20 July 1189 Pope Clement III, in a bull in which he in turn confirmed the abbey's possessions and exempted it from jurisdiction of the bishop of London, pointedly confirmed Westminster's control over these same five churches, and any others which it might acquire.[20] Rival claims to the possession of these churches by the chapter of St. Paul's, perhaps resulting from their occupancy by royal clerks who were also canons of the cathedral, would account for the otherside unlikely combination of benefits conferred by these two papal bulls. Westminster would be eager to fortify its position before a new bishop was appointed in succession to Gilbert Foliot.[21]

In the period covered by this paper, few of Westminster's churches were formally appropriated. Exceptions include the rectories of Battersea and

17 *Letters and Charters of Gilbert Foliot*, no. 462.

18 *Westminster Abbey Domesday*, folio 627 r–v.

19 *Papsturkunden in England*, I, no. 144; on the date, see *Westminster Abbey Charters*, no. 176.

20 *Papsturkunden in England*, I, no. 262.

21 Gilbert Foliot died on 18 February 1187, and Richard Fitz Nigel was elected on 15 September 1189: John Le Neve, *Fasti Ecclesiae Anglicanae 1066–1300 I. St. Paul's London*, compiled Diana E. Greenway (London, 1968), p. 2.

Wandsworth (appropriated in 1185) and that of South Benfleet (appropriated in 1189–90). Most of Westminster's appropriations date from the mid-thirteenth century and later.[22] On the other hand, it is clear that Westminster was systematically utilizing its parochial income throughout much of the twelfth century. Evidence of formal appropriation from the latter part of the century onwards normally indicated only the date at which the situation was regularized in the eyes of the diocesan bishop concerned, when he ensured that adequate provision was made for a vicar.[23]

From the mid-twelfth century, the income from certain of Westminster's churches was increasingly earmarked for specific monastic offices. For instance, the Almonry received assignments of grants of tithes in Kensington; in Clakelose Hundred, Norfolk (lost to Shouldham nunnery in King John's reign), and in *Buchetuna* (Buckton, Hereford?).[24] In July 1189, Pope Clement III permitted the abbot and convent to appropriate the tithes of the churches of which they were patrons, when vacancies occurred, for the support of the brethren, their guests and the poor, provided that vicarages were ordained and synodals paid.[25] The ecclesiastical sources of income assigned to the abbey's chamber included revenues from the London churches of St. James, Garlickhithe, and from St. Margaret, Fish Street, together with a pension from the rector of the church of Sunbury, Middlesex.[26] The pittancer's assignments of parochial income included that from the church of South Benfleet.[27] In addition, the church of Easthampstead, in Berkshire, was confirmed by successive abbots to Westminster's cell at Hurley, to provide extra food on the feast of St. Edward.[28] One of the earliest documented assignments of parochial income is that made by Abbot Gervase (1138–*c.*1157) from St. Matthew, Friday Street, towards the monks' clothing.[29]

The proper adornment and furnishing of the great abbey church was an expensive business. Abbot Gervase assigned tithes from Roding (Essex) towards the repair of books, and a substantial pension from Bloxham church (Oxon.) to the sacristy.[30] Sawbridgeworth (Herts.) was another church from which revenues, of £15, were assigned to the sacristy early in the abbacy of

22 Harvey, *Westminster Abbey and its Estates*, pp. 402–12.

23 This point is reinforced by comparison with the dealings of the bishop and monks of Norwich in the twelfth century towards their churches: Harper-Bill, 'Bishop William Turbe and the Diocese of Norwich', pp. 154–5; and his 'Struggle for Benefices in Twelfth-Century East Anglia', pp. 117–19. See also Kemp, 'Monastic Possessions of Parish Churches', pp. 148–57.

24 *Westminster Abbey Charters*, nos. 456, 477–8.

25 *Ibid*., no. 178.

26 *Ibid*., nos. 217, 365, 369.

27 *Ibid*., nos. 214, 299, 317.

28 *Ibid*., nos. 285, 302.

29 *Ibid*., no. 255.

30 *Ibid*., nos. 251, 253.

Laurence (*c*.1158–1173),[31] an assignment which was confirmed by Popes Alexander III and Innocent III.[32] In the time of Abbot Herbert (1121–*c*.1136) St. Margaret's Westminster contributed £3 annually to the service of the high altar, and to other necessities of the church, both within and without. When Abbot William Postard (1191–1200) allowed the royal chamberlain Robert Mauduit to have a private chapel in this Westminster residence, he required an annual payment to two besants to the sacristy, in lieu of diverted parochial dues.[33] Two further churches in Middlesex, Hendon and Staines, also contributed income to the sacristy. The latter assignment, of £2 annually, was confirmed by the bishop of London in the 1190s, 'on account of the poverty of the sacristy . . . to improve the lighting in the church'.[34] Revenues from the Buckinghamshire church of Denham were assigned to the high altar in the time of Abbot Herbert, as were those of the 'lost' St. Mary Newchurch in London.[35] But the revenues of St. Mary's, and to some extent those of other churches assigned to the sacristy, were not forthcoming in practice. Given the high inflation rate of the late twelfth century, it was not to be expected that the sacristy could function adequately on a fraction of the assignments made some fifty or more years earlier – hence Bishop Richard Fitz Nigel's acceptance of the need to supplement the revenues required by the sacrist.

The monastic infirmary is documented from the latter part of the twelfth century, when the revenues of the Surrey churches of Battersea and Wandsworth were assigned to its support by Abbot Laurence, and confirmed by Popes Alexander III and Lucius III, and additional revenues were assigned from the Rutland churches of Hambleton and Oakham.[36] The hospital of St. James in Westminster received revenues assigned by Abbot Walter (1175–90) from the London church of St. Alban, Wood Street.[37]

Those of the abbey's churches named above are by no means the only ones for which the revenues are known in the twelfth century, but in the other cases, the purposes to which the income was put are uncertain, beyond the fact that an annual pension was due to the abbot from the clerk whom he had presented to the living. Similarly, those revenues which the various monastic offices derived from churches were only a fraction of what each received annually, because each office was also assigned estates and/or rent income.

Since many of the abbey's churches accrued with estates which were granted to Westminster, and were not separately enumerated, it became necessary to obtain royal confirmations when the use of written records grew more commonplace, and the developing canon law made it essential to

31 *Ibid*., nos. 211, 283–4.
32 *Ibid*., nos. 170, 185.
33 *Ibid*., nos. 244, 312.
34 *Ibid*., nos. 216, 459.
35 *Ibid*., no. 244.
36 *Ibid*., nos. 169, 177, 321, 336.
37 *Ibid*., no. 288.

define Westminster's legal rights and sources of income. Churches and/or tithes are granted or confirmed in thirteen of the 46 charters which survive in the name of William I.[38] Although this group includes several fabrications, it also includes useful evidence of individual donations at manorial level, which were then brought together in one or another of the spurious catch-all confirmations. And while the authenticity of the latter has usually been challenged on grounds of diplomatic or palaeography, a case has recently been made by Dr Richard Mortimer, Keeper of the abbey's Muniments, for the possibility that kings were on occasion prepared to ratify some confirmatory charters, unorthodox in wording and historically unsubstantiated, which had been composed by monastic petitioners rather than by royal clerks.[39]

Of the ten charters for Westminster surviving in the name of William II Rufus, four include confirmation of churches pertaining to the abbey.[40] A wider confirmation of Westminster's ecclesiastical possessions was probably included in the great *pancarte* which he is known – from sculptural evidence – to have issued for the abbey, but which does not now survive, or at least not in his name.[41] Of the 40 charters surviving in the name of Henry I for the abbey, 13 relate to particular churches or tithe income.[42] Most of these are concerned with the administration of individual churches, in contrast to the vaguely-worded confirmations of ecclesiastical property which occur in the spurious general charters of confirmation which survive in Stephen's name (two out of a total of seventeen charters issued for Westminster in his reign).[43] Since Stephen's reign was later regarded as a time of unlaw, the monks of Westminster were perhaps disinclined to preserve his charters, but this is unlikely, since his genuine grants of secular properties have survived. Charters from the reign of Henry II again related to individual churches or tithes, which are subjects of five of his seventeen charters for Westminster.[44] The abbey's churches are generally confirmed in the charter of liberties which survives in the name of Richard I, and which forbids the intrusion of ecclesiastical or secular officials into the churches of the lands of the abbey.[45] Individual churches pertaining to Westminster are the subject of two charters issued by King John.[46] Ecclesiastical sources of income comprised the subject of about thirty percent of Westminster's petitions to the crown. Successive

38 *Ibid.*, nos. 1, 15, 18–20, 28, 33, 35, 37–38, 40, 43, 45–46.

39 Richard Mortimer, 'The Charters of Henry II: What are the Criteria for Authenticity?', *Anglo-Norman Studies 12*, ed. Marjorie Chibnall (Woodbridge, 1990), pp. 119–34.

40 *Westminster Abbey Charters*, nos. 49, 54–56.

41 Frank Barlow, *William Rufus* (London, 1983), pp. 113–14.

42 *Westminster Abbey Charters*, nos. 67, 70, 72, 77–78, 81, 83–84, 86–87, 90, 92–93.

43 *Regesta Regum Anglo-Normannorum III. 1135–54*, ed. H. A. Cronne and R. H. C. Davis (Oxford, 1968), nos. 928–29.

44 *Westminster Abbey Charters*, nos. 123, 127–128, 130, 138.

45 *Ibid.*, no. 140.

46 *Rotuli Chartarum in Turri Londoniensi asservati 1199–1216*, ed. T. Duffus Hardy (Record Comm., London, 1837), ff. 139, col. b; f. 165, col. b.

kings were willing to confirm, at a price, the abbey's rights in its existing ecclesiastical properties, defended the parish churches against predators, and on occasion even increased Westminster's sources of parochial income. Their charters reveal what the abbey held, or aspired to hold, in this category, but only on rare occasions reveal anything about conditions in the parishes.

Papal and episcopal records are more helpful when considering the administration of the abbey's churches. Some eighteen papal documents are concerned with its churches and tithe income, including two spurious bulls in the names of Popes Leo IX and Paschal II, which both contain a generally-worded confirmation of churches, tithes, and other ecclesiastical income.[47] Papal bulls issued for the abbey from the pontificate of Innocent II onwards are more specific in their confirmation of individual churches and tithe revenues. This in turn suggests that the abbot and convent were increasingly aware of the economic potential of each item, now that the development of the English parochial structure was well under way. Ecclesiastical sources of income were more likely to be contested not only by neighbouring territorial lords but also by prominent clerks in the royal service, since kings habitually rewarded favoured clerks with grants of churches.[48] Churches, with their appurtenant lands and tithe income, were becoming more valuable in the twelfth century, as the expanding population not only generated growing numbers of those liable to pay tithe and render the customary oblations, but also triggered a rise in land values, and in the profits from the sale of agricultural produce. A parish church, with its glebe and its associated parochial income, was a prize well worth contesting. The pressures on Westminster to present thrusting royal clerks to its richer benefices were probably intensified by the abbey's proximity to the royal residence of Westminster Hall, and the inevitable close contact with royal officers. It is likely that, when the king was petitioned for favours, such as confirmation of particular estates, or the grant of financial or legal exemptions on specific property, the *quid pro quo* comprised not only the customary cash payment (rarely mentioned in the ensuing confirmatory charter), but also, on occasion, the appointment of a high-flying clerk to some lucrative Westminster living. Indeed, to obtain the king's ear at all, it would be as well to 'make friends with the mammon of unrighteousness', by proposing to a confidential clerk that, if he would expedite matters on behalf of the abbey, then a lucrative rectory would soon come his way. The snag with such arrangements was that the richer abbey churches would come to be regarded as the natural perks of office, and it would be progressively more difficult for the abbey to assert its title, a danger which

47 *Papsturkunden in England*, I, nos. 2, 9.

48 For instance, King Edward granted to his physician, Baldwin, the church of Deerhurst (Gloucs.), and probably also that of Taynton (Oxon.); F. E. Harmer, *Anglo-Saxon Writs*, 2nd edn. (Stamford 1989), pp. 244, 293.

was intensified in that royal courts were disposed to uphold hereditary succession to benefices throughout the twelfth century.[49]

Such curial expectations and pressures would increase when the abbot was the king's son. Prior Osbert de Clare, the reputed mastermind of many of Westminster's forgeries,[50] brought back from the papal court a bull reprimanding Abbot Gervase about alienations of lands and other properties made without the consent of the convent.[51] Barbara Harvey considers that this document was probably a forgery concocted by the prior in the wake of his mission to the papal court in 1139, when he failed to secure the canonization of King Edward.[52] But even if the document is forged, it demonstrates that Osbert's criticisms of Gervase included allegations of high-handed alienations of monastic property. Probably Osbert derived his inspiration from one of the genuine bulls issued by Innocent on behalf of Westminster in December that year. This was addressed to Henry of Blois, bishop of Winchester and papal legate, ordering him to hear the complaint of the monks (conveyed to the *curia* by Prior Osbert) about the wrongful seizure of their goods, which had been unjustly detained, and to render them justice.[53] This question of the unjust detention of Westminster's property was evidently a major preoccupation of Prior Osbert's – since even the papal letter conveying Innocent's decision not to canonize King Edward added that instructions were being sent to Bishop Henry to ensure restitution of misappropriated lands.[54] If genuinely violent misappropriation had taken place, then surely restitution would have been ordered by the abbot's father, King Stephen, but there are no surviving writs in his name to this effect. It is likely, therefore, that Osbert's real complaint was that Abbot Gervase had been too compliant in fact of pressures upon him to make grants to courtiers upon favourable terms. Barbara Harvey has carefully examined all of Gervase's leases which might support such allegations, which were later made against him. Her conclusion was that, while his judgement can still be challenged in a few cases, most of his leases were made on reasonable terms as regards Westminster's interests and most had the consent of the chapter.[55] Four charters of Gervase survive in which he is shown granting churches, in return for pension.[56] In three cases, those of Bloxham (Oxon.); St. Agnes, and St. Matthew, Friday Street,

49 Harper-Bill, 'The Struggle for Benefices in Twelfth-Century East Anglia', p. 126.

50 P. Chaplais, 'The Original Charters of Herbert and Gervase, abbots of Westminster (1121–1157)', in his *Essays in Medieval Diplomacy and Administration* (London, 1981), pp. XVIII, 89–110; see esp. pp. 91–95.

51 *Westminster Abbey Charters*, no. 161.

52 Barbara Harvey, 'Abbot Gervase de Blois and the Fee Farms of Westminster Abbey', *Bulletin of the Institute of Historical Research*, 40 (1967), pp. 128–9.

53 *The Letters of Osbert de Clare*, ed. E. W. Williamson (London, 1929), p. 88, no. 20, calendered *Westminster Abbey Charters*, no. 159.

54 *The Letters of Osbert de Clare*, pp. 87–8, no. 19; calendared *Westminster Abbey Charters*, no. 158.

55 Harvey, 'Abbot Gervase de Blois and the Fee Farms of Westminster', pp. 127–41.

56 *Westminster Abbey Charters*, nos. 253, 255, 257, and 270.

both in London, the amount of the pension was identical with that acceptable to the abbey later in the twelfth century.[57] Evidence is lacking on the pension then required from the church of Islip, but the amounts subsequently required from the other three suggest that Gervase fixed their pensions at a rate beneficial to Westminster. Gervase might occasionally oblige an influential clerk by granting him a church, as in the case of Robert de Chesney and Bloxham,[58] but he expected a proper return. Hints of maladministration appear to have subsided as rapidly as they arose, and were not revived when changing circumstances at the papal *curia* might have encouraged them. Pope Eugenius III was not well disposed towards King Stephen, thanks to intensive lobbying at the *curia* by Abbot Bernard of Clairvaux,[59] but he addressed to Abbot Gervase two generally-worded confirmations of Westminster's property, including its churches and tithe income, and did not hint that anything was amiss in the abbey's administration.[60]

On 1 June 1157, Pope Adrian IV issued two major charters of confirmation for Westminster. One of these confirmed its three monastic cells, of Great Malvern (Worcs.); Hurley (Berks.) and Sudbury (Suffolk), together with the long list of the abbey's churches, chapels and tithe income which is discussed above.[61] Its companion document confirmed the abbey in its dignities, privileges, and estates, and ordered that anything taken by violence from Westminster, or contrary to its interests, was to be restored.[62] Properties had undoubtedly been taken from the abbey's control during the unrest in Stephen's reign[63] so that this bull was not issued in response to revived allegations of mismanagement.

The increasing permeation of Canon Law into England in the decades after 1170, combined with the application of the decrees of the Third Lateran Council (1179), resulted in Westminster's having recourse to the papal *curia* on a widening range of matters concerning its parish churches. These were increasingly subject to demands made upon them by the growing numbers of expert royal clerks employed in the king's *curia*. From the long pontificate of Alexander III, four papal letters specifically relate to Westminster's churches. The delegation charged with the second, and successful, mission to secure the canonization of King Edward evidently included both Walter the sacrist and Roger the infirmarer. With the support of Abbot Laurence, they

57 *Westminster Abbey Charters*, no. 225; *Letters and Charters of Gilbert Foliot*, no. 462.

58 *Westminster Abbey Charters*, no. 253.

59 R. H. C. Davis, *King Stephen 1135–1154*, 3rd edn. (Harlow, 1990), pp. 96, 98–9, 101–3, 113–14. See, however, C. Holdsworth, 'St Bernard and England', *Anglo-Norman Studies VIII*, ed. R. Allen Brown (Woodbridge, 1986), pp. 151–2.

60 *Patrologiae Latina* 180, cols. 1115–17, no. XC; *Papsturkunden in England* I, pp. 286–8, no. 47; calendared *Westminster Abbey Charters*, nos. 162–3.

61 *Papsturkunden in England* I, no. 70.

62 *Ibid*., no. 69.

63 A. Saltman, *Theobald, archbishop of Canterbury* (London, 1956, reprinted New York, 1969), pp. 507–8, no. 277. See also *Westminster Abbey Charters*, note to no. 195.

took the opportunity to obtain papal confirmation of the more valuable, and also the more insecurely-held, of the churches pertaining to their respective offices. On 7 February 1161, the pope confirmed the church of Sawbridgeworth, to provide lights for the sacristy, and the churches of Battersea and Wandsworth for the benefit of the brethren of the infirmary.[64] The pope confirmed the abbey's three monastic cells in 1163,[65] but no further petition was made to him concerning Westminster's ecclesiastical properties until 1177. In April of that year he concluded a general confirmation of the abbey's properties and exempt status by prohibiting the alienation of five churches with their appurtenant chapels: Oakham (Rutland); Aldenham, Ashwell and Wheathampstead (Herts.); and Staines (Mddx.).[66] From the case study given below, it is plain that Oakham was insecurely held, because royal clerks clearly regarded it as a prize worth having. The same applies to Battersea and Wandsworth (discussed below), which were consequently confirmed by Pope Lucius III c.1185, while in the abbatial vacancy which followed the death of Abbot Laurence in 1173, King Henry II presented his clerk Walter Map to the church of Ashwell, which he held until his death in c.1208–10.[67] Notwithstanding the papal ruling, these five churches remained at risk, and Westminster obtained another confirmation of them from Pope Clement III on 20 July 1189. This is found in a bull covering the abbey's wider ecclesiastical interest, since the pope also prohibited archbishops or bishops from saying mass, or holding synods, in St. Margaret's, Westminster; exempted the abbey from the jurisdiction of the bishop of London (a long-standing aspiration of the monks), and confirmed all pensions from churches which the abbey held before the Third Lateran Council.[68] Individual pensions might well be endangered if powerful men developed entrenched claims to occupy particular churches, hence the confirmation of such income, but so far as can be gauged, once a pension had been set at a given rate, no attempt was made to raise it, despite the current inflation. It might be regarded by the incumbent as having the same status as would rent from land, which was fixed by custom. In an effort to mitigate such a consequence the monks also obtained from Pope Clement, on 5 July 1189, permission to appropriate the tithes of their churches, when vacancies occurred, so long as they appointed vicarages (i.e. established a guaranteed income for the resident priest), and paid the synodal dues. These appropriations were permitted by the pope in

64 *Papsturkunden in England*, I, nos. 85–6.

65 *Ibid.*, I, no. 101.

66 *Ibid.*, I, no. 144.

67 Pope Lucius's confirmation of Battersea and Wandsworth is printed in *Papsturkunden in England*, I, no. 232. For Walter Map and the church of Ashwell, see *Curia Regis Rolls*, VI, p. 93; Walter map, *De Nugis Curialium*, ed. and transl. M. R. James, revised by C. N. L. Brooke and R. A. B. Mynors (Oxford, 1983), pp. 496–7.

68 *Papsturkunden in England*, I, no. 262. For the impact of c.7 of the Third Lateran Council upon agreements concerning pensions, see for example *English Episcopal Acta VI, Norwich 1070–1214*, ed. C. Harper-Bill (Oxford, 1990), no. 332, note.

order to enable the balance of the income to sustain the monks, and to enable them to offer hospitality, and to provide for the poor.[69]

Apparently there was an interval of almost ten years before the monks of Westminster were again in communication with the papacy over the specific issue of ecclesiastical sources of income. Early in 1199, a group of aggrieved monks evidently complained that Abbot William Postard was acting solely in his own initiative in such matters. On 24 April 1199, Pope Innocent III wrote that he had heard that benefices intended for the use of the chapter, and for the poor, had occasionally been assigned, at the instance of certain magnates, to their clerks. He now specifically ordered that the church of Sawbridgeworth, assigned to the sacristy, was not to be diverted to other uses, and that the same applied to any churches which were assigned to hospitality or to other pious uses.[70] Evidently the monastic delegation was dissatisfied with the wording of this mandate, because they obtained another, issued on 30 April 1199, prohibiting Abbot William from alienating the churches or other possessions pertaining to the whole community, without the consent of the chapter, or of the greater and wiser part.[71] But Abbot William was in a dilemma. After the death of his predecessor, the chapter had fought hard against the justiciar, William Longchamp, in order to secure the free election which resulted in Prior William Postard becoming abbot. In return, a heavy fine was exacted by influential persons, and consequently all Postard's managerial skills were needed to enable him to raise the 1,500 marks which were demanded.[72] From the complaints of the monastic delegation to the papal *curia* in 1199, it seems that presentation of baronial nominees to certain churches had also formed part of the bargain, hence the grievance of the monastic *seniores*. The delegation had set off for Rome with the overt mission of obtaining from the pope a confirmation of Westminster's privileges and indulgences, something which was successfully accomplished on 23 April 1199.[73] The complaints of the *seniores* about the diversion to other uses of churches assigned to hospitality or to the infirmary revived from time to time,[74] but the abbey, like many major landholders at this period, was experiencing a prolonged financial crisis, which call for arbitrary solutions.

69 *Papsturkunden in England*, I, no. 261.

70 *Monasticon Anglicanum*, I, 312a, no. LXXIII. See also *Westminster Abbey Charters*, no. 185, note.

71 *The Letters of Pope Innocent III (1198–1216) concerning England and Wales: a calendar with an appendix of texts*, ed. C. R. Cheney and Mary Cheney (Oxford, 1967), p. 203, no. 113.

72 *Westminster Abbey Charters*, no. 186, note; Harvey, *Westminster Abbey and its Estates in the Middle Ages*, p. 64, note 2.

73 *Letters of Pope Innocent III*, p. 203, no. 105. For the chief privileges granted before that date, see *Westminster Abbey Charters*, nos. 155, 162–3, 165, 172–5, 179–80.

74 There is evidence that Innocent III responded in similar vein on 8 January, in some uncertain year of his pontificate. On this occasion, too, the monastic delegation was sent to secure confirmation of Westminster's privileges: *Letters of Pope Innocent III*, p. 189, nos. 1152–53; but cf. *Westminster Abbey Charters*, nos. 184–5, notes. Since these

In those Westminster documents which survive in the names of visiting papal legates *a latere*, there is no mention of the abbey's administration of its ecclesiastical property, whereas Archbishop Theobald, in his capacity as papal legate, restored to Westminster the disputed church of Ockendon (Essex).[75] Another charter which he issued for Westminster in his capacity as legate confirmed the substance of several charters, in the name of King Stephen, which were possessed by the abbey. These alleged royal grants included a virgate of land pertaining to the church of Hanwell (Mddx.). All of the purported royal charters carry Theobald's attestations, but only one is genuine.[76] Towards the end of Stephen's turbulent reign, the abbey would be glad to have his grants confirmed by someone in unchallenged authority, but it is remarkable that Theobald was prepared to ratify grants which bore his attestation when he must surely have recalled that he had not witnessed them.

Suits concerning the abbey's churches occasionally came before papal judges-delegate. Disputes over St. Margaret Eastcheap, in London; Doddington and Thorpe (Lincs.) and Bloxham (Oxon.) were all resolved by compromise,[77] whereas the contest over Feering (Essex) resulted in an outright verdict for Westminster.[78] The more prominent of these judges-delegate included both Gilbert Foliot, bishop of London,[79] and Hugh, bishop of Lincoln.[80]

The diocesan bishops with whom the abbot and monks of Westminster were most frequently in contact were those of London and Lincoln in which see the abbey held a considerable number of parish churches. In the diocese of London, successive bishops are recorded instituting to the abbey's churches the parsons presented by the abbot and monks: to the churches of Greenford and Hanwell (Mddx.); South Benfleet (Essex); and to the London churches of St. Martin, Ludgate, and St. Magnus the Martyr.[81] From the diocese of

bulls of 8 January survive only as brief memoranda in a late muniment book, it may be that scribal errors were made. The grantor was perhaps actually Pope Celestine III, since a Westminster delegation is known to have been at the papal *curia* on 13 January 1192 (*Westminster Abbey Charters*, nos. 180–82). The antecedent complaints would therefore have been directed against Abbot William Postard. But if Innocent III was indeed the grantor, then the bulls were probably obtained in the course of a Westminster mission later than 1199, in which case the abbot reprimanded would be Ralph Arundel (who was removed from office in 1214).

75 Saltman, *Theobald, archbishop of Canterbury*, p. 507, no. 276.

76 *Ibid.*, pp. 505–6, no. 275. See also *Westminster Abbey Charters*, no. 197, note. King Stephen's grants are printed in *Regesta Regum Anglo-Normannorum III. 1135–1154*, ed. H. A. Cronne and R. H. C. Davis (Oxford, 1968), nos. 938–41.

77 *Westminster Abbey Charters*, nos. 194, 209, 225.

78 *Ibid.*, nos. 207–8.

79 *The Letters and Charters of Gilbert Foliot*, nos. 465–7.

80 Jane Sayers, *Papal Judges-Delegate in the Province of Canterbury 1198–1254: a study in Ecclesiastical Administration* (Oxford, 1971), Appendix B, pp. 354–5, no. 5; *English Episcopal Acta IV: Lincoln 1186–1206*, ed. D. Smith (London, 1986), no. 211.

81 *Westminster Abbey Charters*, nos. 210, 215, 218, 220.

Lincoln, records survive of the institutions of Westminster's nominees to the churches of Datchworth (Herts.); Deene (Northants); Thorpe-on-the-Hill and Doddington (Lincs.) and Launton (Oxon.),[82] and from the diocese of Worcester an institution to the church of Todenham (Gloucs.),[83] one of the infrequent references in the Westminster archives of this period to its ecclesiastical property in the West Midlands. When making such presentations, care was taken to stipulate the pension payable to the abbey by the incumbent.[84] The abbey's main concern regarding its churches was therefore twofold: the preservation of its control over the advowson, and the guaranteed receipt of the annual pension due. Given that some presentations were in fact of compromise candidates, as much the choice of other interested parties as of the abbot and monks, the receipt of the pension was all that could be hoped for, along with a glancing recognition of the abbey's patronal rights.[85] Bishop Richard Fitz Nigel of London, and both Hugh (of Avallon), bishop of Lincoln, and his successor Hugh (of Wells), expressed care for the maintenance of the vicarages of the churches to which they made presentations, while Godfrey de Lucy, of Winchester, was concerned that perpetual vicars should observe their obligations.[86] Several charters also emphasised the due observance of the rights of the diocesan bishop.[87]

Westminster is known to have contested rights of advowson in the royal court from the time of Abbot Walter onwards. It was ordained in the Constitutions of Clarendon (1164), Clause 1, that disputes over advowson were reserved for the royal court, and there is evidence from 1184 of the amercement of those who took pleas concerning advowson to the church courts. Westminster's success in such lawsuits heard by the royal justices was variable.[88] Equal rights in the church of St. Magnus the Martyr were accorded to Westminster and to Bermondsey priory, whereas the advowson of Datchworth was lost in the time of Abbot William, although the abbey's entitlement to an annual pension was secured.[89] It proved necessary to defend the advowson of Parham (Sussex) both in the time of Abbot William and again during the abbacy of Ralph Arundel, in order to secure Westminster's title[90] and the abbey's claim to the advowson of Uppingham (Rutland) was also successfully upheld in Ralph's time.[91] This abbot was willing to offer rights of

82 *Ibid.*, nos. 222–4, 227.

83 *Ibid.*, no 233.

84 *Ibid.*, nos. 209, 217–18, 220, 222, 224, 226–27, 232.

85 *Ibid.*, nos. 209, 222–23, 315, 368.

86 *Ibid.*, nos. 214–15, 223, 227, 232.

87 *Ibid.*, nos. 198, 223–24, 227, 233.

88 *English Historical Documents II. 1042–1189*, ed. D. C. Douglas and G. W. Greenway, 2nd edn. (London, 1981), p. 767 no. 126. See also *The Treatise on the Laws and Customs of the Realm of England commonly called Glanvill*, ed. G. D. G. Hall (London, 1965), p. 4; Mary G. Cheney, *Roger, bishop of Worcester 1164–1179* (Oxford, 1980), p. 148.

89 *Westminster Abbey Charters*, nos. 287, 320.

90 *Ibid.*, nos. 325, 334.

91 *Ibid.*, no. 338.

confraternity to litigants who relinquished their claims.[92] When abbots leased land to tenants, or granted estates to monks, their charters carefully defined whether or not the advowson was being transferred. Increasingly, from the later twelfth century, it seems from final concords and from abbatial charters that there was an unwillingness to concede an advowson. In granting the Lincolnshire manor of Doddington to his knight William Picot, Abbot William excluded the advowson,[93] and he also reserved the advowson of Parham when granting the vill to the monks.[94] Abbot Ralph, on the other hand, included the advowson with his later confirmation to them.[95]

The men presented to the abbey's churches are rarely identified as clerks who were in the service of the abbot, but a few such identifications can be made from the time of Abbot Laurence onwards, since he presented his clerk, Mr. Maurice, to the church of Sawbridgeworth (Herts.), and his physician, Mr. Ralph de Beaumont (who also served King Henry II in this capacity) to the church of Bloxham (Oxon.).[96] Abbot Walter recompensed his clerk, Mr. Nicholas, with tithes in Bulby and Elsthorpe (Lincs.),[97] whereas Abbot Ralph and the convent granted houses in London to their clerk Alexander of Swerford, who can probably be identified with the Exchequer official of that name.[98] Any abbatial clerks who were appointed to Westminster's rural parish churches would be expected to be non-resident. They might have the cure of souls to a vicar, while they themselves continued to make their expertise available to the abbot. And yet the paucity of references to the presentation of the abbey's clerks to its living may have an explanation other than that they wished to avoid episcopal censure for non-residence. The careers of Ralph de Beaumont and Alexander of Swerford illustrate the point that the able and ambitious men who served the abbot were liable to enter the king's service. There was an ensuing risk that the abbey might lose the churches held by such men, as demonstrated in the case of Bloxham, discussed below. A grant of tithes, or better still, of City real-estate held at an annual rent, would be a safer recompense.

Naturally there is no documentation of the pressure which kings might put upon the abbots to present royal clerks to the abbey's livings, or which influential clerks might personally bring to bear. And conversely there is no record of the reasoning which might prompt the abbot and convent, on their own initiative, to present such men to the abbey's livings. Only the results of such pressures and thought-processes can be discerned on occasion. Since the king of England governed a cross-Channel *regnum*, his clerks might well pursue a cross-Channel career. Men who in their earlier years were incumbents of Westminster's churches might later be elected to Continental bishoprics. Froger, bishop of Seez, held the church of St. James, Garlickhithe,

92 *Ibid.*, nos. 334, 338.
93 *Ibid.*, no. 322.
94 *Ibid.*, no. 326.
95 *Ibid.*, no. 335.
96 *Ibid.*, nos. 284, 286.
97 *Ibid.*, no. 303.
98 *Ibid.*, no. 327 and note.

in London , but in the mid 1170s he granted it to John, the nephew of the recently-canonized Thomas Becket. John, for his part, undertook to render an annual pension to the chamber of Westminster abbey. The agreement was witnessed by several of the archbishop's other kinsfolk, including his sister Mary, abbess of Barking. Since the bishop had twice acted on behalf of Henry II in negotiations involving Becket, his concession to John was perhaps made by way of expiation for injuries which the Becket family perceived that Froger himself had committed against the new saint.[99]

On occasion, Continental clerics could be positively helpful to Westminster. When Abbot Walter had trouble in asserting the abbey's claim to Ockendon church against the tenant of the manor, he wrote to Bartholomew, archbishop of Tours, to enlist his help. Bartholomew obligingly sent a letter addressed jointly to Archbishop Richard and to the justiciar, Ranulf Glanville. In this he gave evidence on behalf of Westminster, stating that he was a former incumbent of Ockendon church, to which he had been presented by Abbot Laurence at the request of Queen Eleanor.[100]

Property rights, rather than parochial administration, form the contents of virtually all Westminster's charters concerning it churches. There are in the archives a few charters of archdeacons, of London and of Huntingdon, concerning the induction of clergy to churches held by the abbey, but there are fewer such documents that might be expected from the later twelfth century. These have evidently been preserved because in each case there had either been some prior dispute between claimants or else a pension to define.[101]

In King John's reign, Stephen, parson of Hendon (Mddx.), was nearing the end of the long incumbency, during which the abbey's right to the advowson had not been asserted. No doubt on the prompting of the abbot and monks, he issued a charter to safeguard Westminster's rights. This stated that his father Ralph possessed the church peacefully for several years, on the presentation of Abbot Laurence and the convent. When Ralph died, the abbot and monks, as true patrons, presented Stephen himself with that church, and he was instituted by Bishop Gilbert Foliot. Since then he had possessed the church of Hendon peacefully and prosperously for 43 years, rendering two marks annually to the sacristy of Westminster.[102] It is conjectural whether the bishop was aware that he was perpetuating a hereditary incumbency, but so far as the abbey was concerned, the security of its advowsons and parochial pensions was of more consequence that taking a stand on clerical celibacy among secular priests, or the ending of hereditary succession to benefices. Contemporaries elsewhere in England might share the abbey's financial priorities, although not all would have agreed that Westminster was pursuing its own best interests by relying on the old-style pension instead of

99 *Ibid.*, no. 365 and note.
100 *Ibid.*, no. 463.
101 *Ibid.*, nos. 368–9, 468.
102 *Ibid.*, no. 459.

appropriating the church and appointing a vicar.[103] A pension fixed some forty three years earlier could scarcely be bringing in a proper return, in view of the rate of inflation in King John's reign.

Many of Westminster's parish churches have left little trace in its twelfth-century records, but a few recur disproportionately often in the muniments of this period, usually because they were wealthy churches, prized by others beside the abbot and convent. A few brief case-studies will serve to illustrate the range of problems with which Westminster faced.

The church of Bloxham (Oxon.) was assigned by Abbot Gervase, at the petition, and with the assent, of the chapter, to provide lights and other necessities for the sacristy. The incumbent, Robert de Chesney, would pay a pension of five marks annually. If he died, or changed his matter of life (i.e. if he became a monk), of if he was promoted to a higher dignity, then the church at Bloxham would revert to the abbey.[104] In fact, Robert (already archdeacon of Leicester in 1145/6) was elected bishop of Lincoln in December 1148.[105] The church presumably reverted to Westminster, but Abbot Laurence granted it to his physician, Mr. Ralph de Beaumont. The pension due to the sacristy was set at the old rate of five marks, perhaps because Laurence felt bound by precedent, or because he wanted to oblige an influential man, or because Ralph himself insisted on preferential terms. It appears that Laurence had suspicions as to his intentions, because his charter stated that Ralph was not to give this church to anyone, not to alienate it in any way, except by permission of the abbot. If he died, or became a monk, or was promoted to the rank of bishop, then the church would revert to Westminster. In fact Ralph was drowned in the Channel in March 1170, when the royal entourage was crossing from Normandy. Bloxham should again have reverted to the abbey, and perhaps did so.[106] But some six years later, Henry II's mistress, Rosamund Clifford, was buried in the nunnery of Godstow (Oxon.). Wishing to make a donation to this house, the king granted it the church of Bloxham, a benefaction which was severally confirmed by the archdeacon of Oxford; by Hugh bishop of Lincoln; by Pope Celestine III and by King Richard I. When Westminster tried to challenge this alienation, in 1197, the case came before papal judges-delegate, headed by Bishop Hugh, who upheld the nuns' title, provided that the annual pension of five marks continued to be paid to the sacristy.[107] Abbot William had no choice but to concede the church on these terms, and Abbess Juliana through her

103 Harper-Bill, 'The struggle for benefices in twelfth-century East Anglia', pp. 126–8.

104 *Westminster Abbey Charters*, no. 253.

105 John Le Neve, *Fasti Ecclesiae Anglicanae 1066–1300 III. Lincoln*, compiled by Diana E. Greenway (London, 1977), pp. 2, 33.

106 *Westminster Abbey Charters*, no. 286 and note. Seffrid, archdeacon of Chichester (1176–8), and dean (1180) was rector of Bloxham, possibly in succession to Ralph de Beaumont. (R.A.R. Hartridge, *A History of Vicarages in the Middle Ages* (Cambridge, 1930), p. 209.)

107 *Westminster Abbey Charters*, no. 225 and note.

chaplain, solemnly undertook to pay the pension.[108] Senior royal servants had occupied the church for so long during the middle decades of the twelfth century, presumably in response to royal wishes, that Henry II would regard Bloxham as being at his own disposal.

Westminster's churches in Rutland also presented administrative problems. King Edward had intended that the whole geographical area which came to be known as Rutland would pass to the abbey on the death of his widow, but the land was retained by King William I.[109] He granted to Westminster only the tithes of Rutland, adding certain 'mother churches' with their appurtenant lands, which had previously been held by a royal clerk. This grant was confirmed by William Rufus.[110] The royal grant included tithes on the borders of Lincolnshire, in Bulby and Elsthorpe, which Abbot Walter granted to one of his clerks.[111] Abbot William granted twenty-one marks annually from two of the Rutland churches, Oakham and Hambleton, to sustain the monastic infirmary,[112] while in 1197/8, Hugh bishop of Lincoln confirmed both churches to the abbot and convent, so that the monks received annually from the incumbent a pension of thirty marks to maintain a hospital.[113] The pension, at the lower figure of twenty-one marks, was confirmed to the convent by Abbot Ralph, who was also granted to a secular tenant a hereditary lease of a two-virgate holding appurtenant to Oakham Church, at a rent of 2s.[114] Another of the Rutland churches, Uppingham, was claimed by a local landholder, but in 1210, following an assize of darrein presentment, Abbot Ralph was adjudged the lawful possessor. When the defendant surrendered the advowson, he and his heirs were admitted to confraternity.[115] Given the distance from Westminster, Uppingham church presented problems of effective oversight, but by securing the goodwill of the former litigant, a local notable, the abbey could maintain its hold over the advowson.

Oakham and Hambleton were the real plums among Westminster's Rutland churches, and naturally enough they were prized by royal clerks. In this instance the clerk was James le Salvage. Evidently he regarded his rights as entrenched, because in 1206 he fined three palfreys for a grant from King John that the tenants of Oakham church and its appurtenant chapels were to be quit in perpetuity of suits of shire and hundred courts, and of customary payments to sheriffs, and their officers and bailiffs.[116] James had earlier served Archbishop Hubert Walter, and it seems that he moved to the royal clerical

108 *Ibid.*, nos. 323, 481.

109 Harvey, *Westminster Abbey and its Estates in the Middle Ages*, p. 47.

110 *Westminster Abbey Charters*, nos. 45–6, 55–6.

111 *Ibid.*, no. 303.

112 *Ibid.*, no. 321.

113 *English Episcopal Acta IV*, no. 212.

114 *Westminster Abbey Charters*, nos. 336–7.

115 *Ibid.*, no. 338.

116 *Ibid.*, no. 150.

staff shortly after the archbishop's death in 1205.[117] Probably it was royal favour which prompted his institution to these rich churches, but Westminster asserted its financial claims and James swore in chapter at Westminster that he would render thirty marks annually to Westminster from Oakham church. He would try to obtain permission from the pope, and from the diocesan bishop (of Lincoln) to make this payment, but if they refused, he would grant in lieu thirty marks from his churches of Swanscombe and Stockbury (Kent).[118] These had presumably been acquired while he was in the service of the archbishop. He was also challenged over Hambleton church, and agreed to render twenty marks annually.[119] Westminster reinforced its control over Oakham church and its dependent chapels in the course of the thirteenth century, and also retained the advowson of Uppingham. But Rutland was remote from Westminster's main areas of interests, and it proved difficult to maintain its other ecclesiastical property there. Hambleton church and a dependent chapel were lost to the bishop of Lincoln; and following separate pleas in the royal court, the Norman priory of St. Fromond's won control of St. Peter's Stamford, which James le Salvage had held of Westminster; and the Augustinian priory of Launde (Leics.) gained control of Wardley church.[120]

Nearer home, St. Mary Newchurch in London was lost under rather different circumstances. It was initially donated to the abbey, together with its appurtenant properties, by Alward the clerk of London, and was successively confirmed to Westminster by William I, twice by William II and again by Henry I.[121] The latter confirmations were probably requested in response to the seizure of the church by a royal officer, Eudo *dapifer*. He held it in 1100, and granted it to St. John's abbey, Colchester, which supported its own claims by a series of blatant forgeries.[122] Despite subsequent confirmations of the church to Westminster by King Stephen and by Pope Adrian IV, it was not recovered.[123]

Royal officers might by the chief predators on Westminster's churches in the London area, but in the countryside there was an added menace from thugs. The church of Wennington, in Essex, granted by Eadser and his wife Ealvida, was confirmed by both King Edward and William I.[124] The wording

117 *Ibid.*, no. 483 note.

118 *Ibid.*, no. 482.

119 *Ibid.*, no. 483.

120 Emma Mason, 'Westminster Abbey's Rutland Churches', *Rutland Record*, 5 (1985), p. 165. For St. Fromond's other churches in Stamford, see D. Matthew, *The Norman Monasteries and their English Possessions* (Oxford, 1962, reprinted Westport CT. 1979), p. 99 and note 2.

121 *Westminster Abbey Charters*, nos. 40, 49, 54, 90.

122 J. Armitage Robinson, *Gilbert Crispin, abbot of Westminster* (Cambridge, 1911), pp. 158–66.

123 *Westminster Abbey Charters*, nos. 109, 166, 244.

124 Harmer, *Anglo-Saxon Writs*, no. 73; *Westminster Abbey Charters*, no. 35 and note.

of King William's writ indicated that unnamed persons – presumably rival claimants to the church – had tried to intrude into it, to the detriment of Westminster's interest. The problem recurred, and Henry I ordered the bishop of London to render justice on the armed men who broke into Wennington church by night.[125]

The complexities of feudal inheritance affected Westminster's control over Sawbridgeworth church in Hertfordshire, which lay on estates held by the family of de Mandeville. After the death of William I de Mandeville, his wife Margaret de Ria was married to the *curialis* Otwel Fitz Count, who thereby acquired Mandeville lands. Like many other notables, he was drowned in the wreck of the White Ship in November 1120, when his estates escheated to King Henry I. In consultation with the bishop of London, the king granted Sawbridgeworth church to Westminster abbey.[126] The king also ordered that all goods and supplies which the monks' officers at Sawbridgeworth could swear to be their demesne possessions should be quit of tolls – a privilege worth fining for, to bring it into line with the abbey's other properties, since Westminster had recently acquired a general exemption from toll on its lands overall.[127] The lands of the late Otwell Fitz Count were granted at farm by the king to the notable William d'Aubigny 'the Breton'. Evidently the monks of Westminster complained to him about harassment by his officers, since William issued a writ addressed to his French and English officials and tenants in Sawbridgeworth, reminding them that he was the custodian of Sawbridgeworth church and its property, and that the monks and their possessions there were to be left in peace. Any further dispute must be heard in his presence. His men must do right to the monks and their tenants, and render their tithes.[128] It is conjectural whether the monks at Sawbridgeworth simply constituted a small cell to administer the abbey's property there, or whether they also performed pastoral duties in the earlier twelfth century.[129]

125 *Westminster Abbey Charters*, no. 84. For an analogous situation concerning a church of the abbey of St. Benet of Holme in this period, see Harper-Bill, 'Bishop William Turbe and the Diocese of Norwich', pp. 151–2.

126 *Westminster Abbey Charters*, nos. 86, 203. On Otwel Fitz Count and the Mandeville inheritance, see also C. Warren Hollister, 'The Misfortunes of the Mandevilles', *History*, 58 (1973), pp. 18–28.

127 *Westminster Abbey Charters*, nos. 85, 87.

128 *Ibid.*, no. 469 and note.

129 For discussion of pastoral activities undertaken by monks at this period, see Marjorie Chibnall, 'Monks and Pastoral Work: a problem of Anglo-Norman History', *Journal of Ecclesiastical History*, 18 (1967), pp. 165–72; Kemp, 'Monastic Possession of Parish Churches in England in the Twelfth Century', pp. 144–5; Giles Constable, 'Monasteries, Rural Churches and the *Cura Animarum* in the Early Middle Ages', in his *Monks, Hermits and Crusaders in Medieval Europe* (London, 1988), pp. 349–89; see also his 'Monastic Possessions of Churches and "Spiritualia" in the Age of Reform', in *Il Monachesimo e la Riforma Ecclesiastica 1049–1122*, Universita Cattolica del Sacro Cuore (La Mendola 1968, Milan 1971), *Miscellanea del Centro di Studi Medievali*, no. 6, pp. 304–35; T. L. Amos, 'Monks and Pastoral Care in the Early Middle Ages', in T.

William de Mandeville II succeeded to his family lands in 1166, and evidently raised the question of Sawbridgeworth church, which had been granted to Westminster by the king without the consent of William's forebears. But this grant was of long standing, and had been ratified by the ecclesiastical authorities.[130] All that remained for William to do was to confirm the church to Westminster, for the souls of himself and his kindred, and that of King Henry II.[131] Its revenues were assigned to the sacristy,[132] and when Abbot Laurence presented his clerk Mr. Maurice as perpetual vicar, it was stipulated that Maurice must pay £15 annually to the sacristy, and render episcopalia and other dues, besides rendering accounts of the stock of the attached lands. After the death of Maurice, everything would revert to the abbey, together with all stock and improvements. But if Maurice died just after making an annual payment, then the abbot would either pay it back to Maurice's assign, or else grant him custody until the following Michaelmas.[133] Evidently Maurice could drive a bargain as well as any abbot – after all, that is what Laurence employed him to do.

While abbatial clerks could be kept in check, this was not the case with the grandest of the king's employees. Time and again, Henry II's powerful official Richard of Ilchester recurs in the Westminster charters. Like others of Henry's *curiales*, he gained posts on both sides of the Channel. During the abbacy of Laurence, Richard was both archdeacon of Poitiers and parson of Westminster's church of Datchworth (Herts.). Acting together with Abbot Laurence, he requested the bishop of Lincoln to present the clerk Elias to the perpetual vicarage of that church. Elias, who was apparently a clerk of the Bishop, Robert de Chesney, undertook to pay an annual pension of two besants to Richard, but if the latter relinquished that church, or died, then the pension would revert to Westminster.[134] The reversion presumably occurred when Richard of Ilchester was elected bishop of Winchester in May 1173,[135] but the advowson was claimed in the time of Abbot William by another *curialis*, Hugh of Buckland. In 1192, Westminster agreed to surrender the advowson, provided that any clerk presented to that church would solemnly swear in chapter at Westminster that he would pay a pension of £1 to the abbot and convent.[136]

Whether or not Richard of Ilchester had played a part in weakening Westminster's title to Datchworth church is conjectural, but he was certainly

F. X. Noble and J. J. Contreni, eds., *Religion, Culture and Society in the Early Middle Ages*, (Kalamazoo, 1987), pp. 165–80.

130 *Westminster Abbey Charters*, nos. 170, 203.

131 *Ibid.*, no. 470.

132 *Ibid.*, nos. 170, 185, 211, 283.

133 *Ibid.*, no. 284.

134 *Ibid.*, no. 468. On Elias, see also no. 222 and note.

135 John Le Neve, *Fasti Ecclesiae Anglicanae 1066–1300 II. Monastic Cathedrals*, compiled by Diana E. Greenway (London, 1971), p. 85.

136 *Westminster Abbey Charters*, no. 320.

up to no good as regards others of its properties. Westminster held land in Staines (Mddx.) by virtue of grants of King Edward and William I.[137] Probably in the reign of Henry II, some alienation occurred, because, between 1188 and 1194, Westminster obtained from Herbert le Poer, archdeacon of Canterbury, a charter by which he restored land at Staines which his (unnamed) father took from the abbey and treated as his own demesne, and which Herbert himself later held of the abbot at a rent of ten shillings per annum. Herbert was shortly to be elected to a bishopric, and naturally he chose to be discreet about the fact that he himself was the son of a bishop – the deceased Richard of Ilchester.[138]

The churches of Battersea and Wandsworth had long been held by the abbey, and their income assigned to the infirmary,[139] but they also lay on the northernmost fringe of the bishopric of Winchester. At some stage during Richard of Ilchester's episcopate he seems to have claimed them, and (probably in response to protests) effectively restored them under the guise of a grant to sustain the infirmary.[140] His donation, or restoration, was confirmed in July 1193 by his successor at Winchester, Bishop Godfrey de Lucy. Perpetual vicars were to be instituted to both churches by the bishop of Winchester, to whom they would render all proper oblations, and they would also render the monks six marks annually from Wandsworth, and two marks from Battersea.[141] Powerful men could manipulate the abbey's ecclesiastical property to a fairly late date in the twelfth century, but eventually even they had to move with the times, and make proper provision for parish churches by appointing perpetual vicarages.

The foregoing accounts represent only a selection of the problems which Westminster experienced in controlling its churches. This survey is inevitably biased in its portrayal of the management of Westminster's churches. Those which were contested, for their high income, have left a trail of documentation – one which was not generated by the poorer churches – or those less desirable for other reasons. As a result of this imbalance attention has focused on eastern England, while Mercia is barely mentioned. Royal intervention – and the intrusion of royal clerks – is a theme which runs through the surviving records – but these again probably did not affect every church. On one level we can discern acceptance on the part of Westminster of the need to compromise principles for the sake of a guaranteed income, a more relaxed attitude fostered by the awareness that an ever more pervasive canon law, and the activities of energetic archdeacons, would defend their parochial rights in far flung dioceses. Moreover – although *curiales* could be a

137 Harvey, *Westminster Abbey and its Estates in the Middle Ages*, p. 354; *Westminster Abbey Charters*, nos. 38, 53.

138 *Westminster Abbey Charters*, no. 457 and note.

139 *Ibid.*, no. 169, 177.

140 *Ibid.*, no. 231.

141 *Ibid.*, no. 232.

nuisance on some occasions, on others they – or their associates – could be exceptionally well placed to further the interests of Westminster – and might consider that their own status was enhanced by doing so. Many of the Westminster charters of John's reign are attested by the Exchequer staff – the very men who so often heard lawsuits such as those of darrein presentment.[142] But parallel with this growing recourse to the lawcourts, and to civilized compromise, Westminster reserved the right to deploy spiritual weapons whose power was still feared by transgressors – and down to the last years of John's reign, solemn grants issued by its abbots occasionally concluded by threatening transgressors with anathema.[143]

Westminster had been a privileged and highly favoured royal church in King Edward's reign – and was to become so again during the reign of Henry III. But intervening kings showed little positive enthusiasm for the abbey – reserving their generosity for the other churches which each individually chose to patronize. Westminster needed to husband its existing resources as best it could – not least its parochial churches.

* The Leverhulme Trust, the Nuffield Foundation and the British Academy generously funded successive phases of my work on the Westminster Abbey charters. I am grateful to the late Dr. Jennifer Bray for her assistance throughout this project; to Miss Barbara Harvey, Dr. Diana Greenway, Dr. Jane Sayers and Dr. David Bates for their views on the documents discussed here, and to the staff of Westminster Abbey library for much patient help. Miss Brenda Bolton, Dr. Janet Burton, Dr. Antonia Gransden, Dr. Brian R. Kemp and the Revd. Martin Dudley contributed bibliographical references, and Dr. Christopher Harper-Bill discussed with me the conclusions which he drew from his own work on the administration of parochial churches in East Anglia during the twelfth century, but I accept sole responsibility for any omission or misinterpretation.

142 *Ibid.*, pp. 18–19, and extensive references given there.
143 *Ibid.*, nos. 329, 335–6.

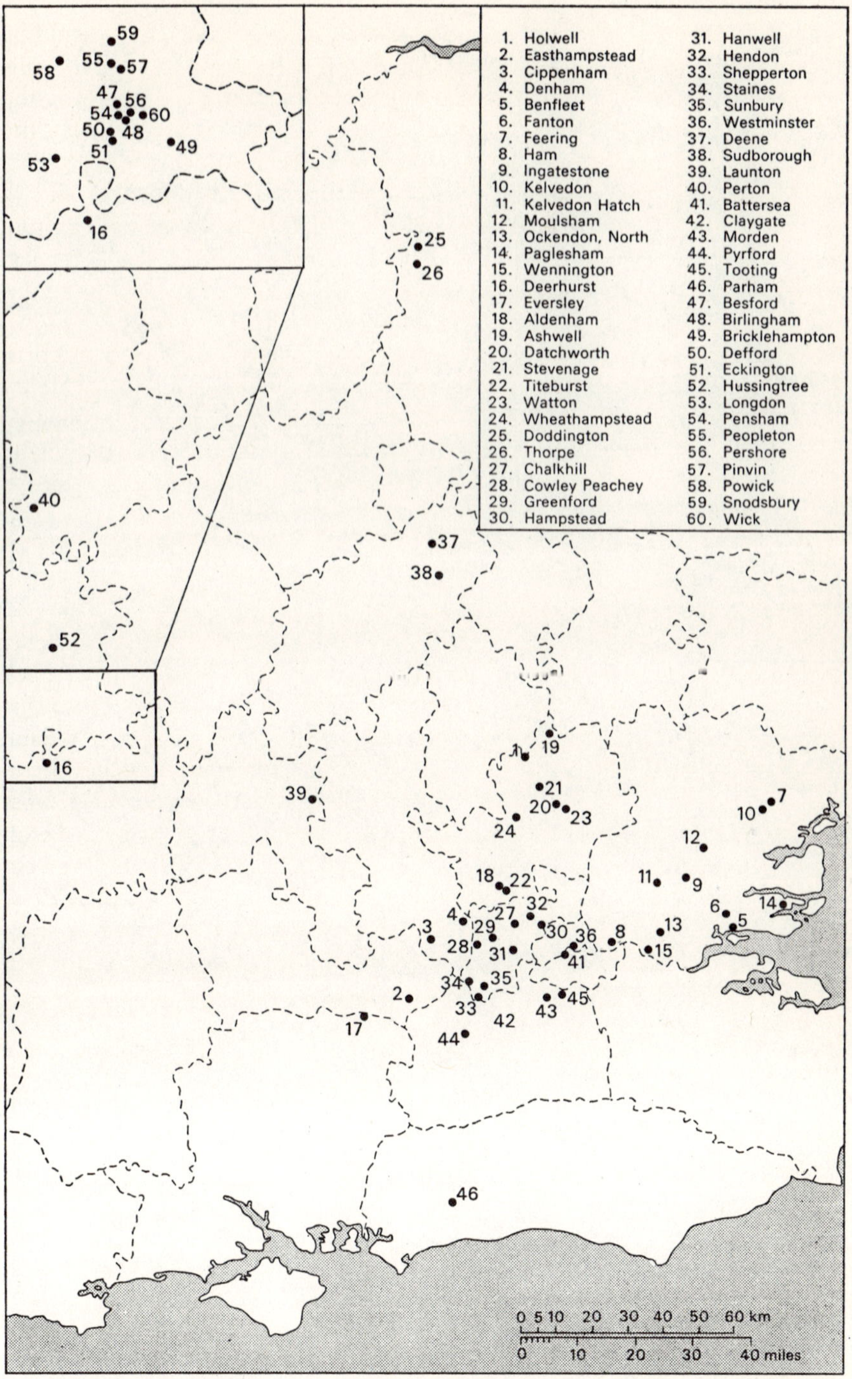

MAP I. THE DEMESNE MANORS OF WESTMINSTER ABBEY IN 1086

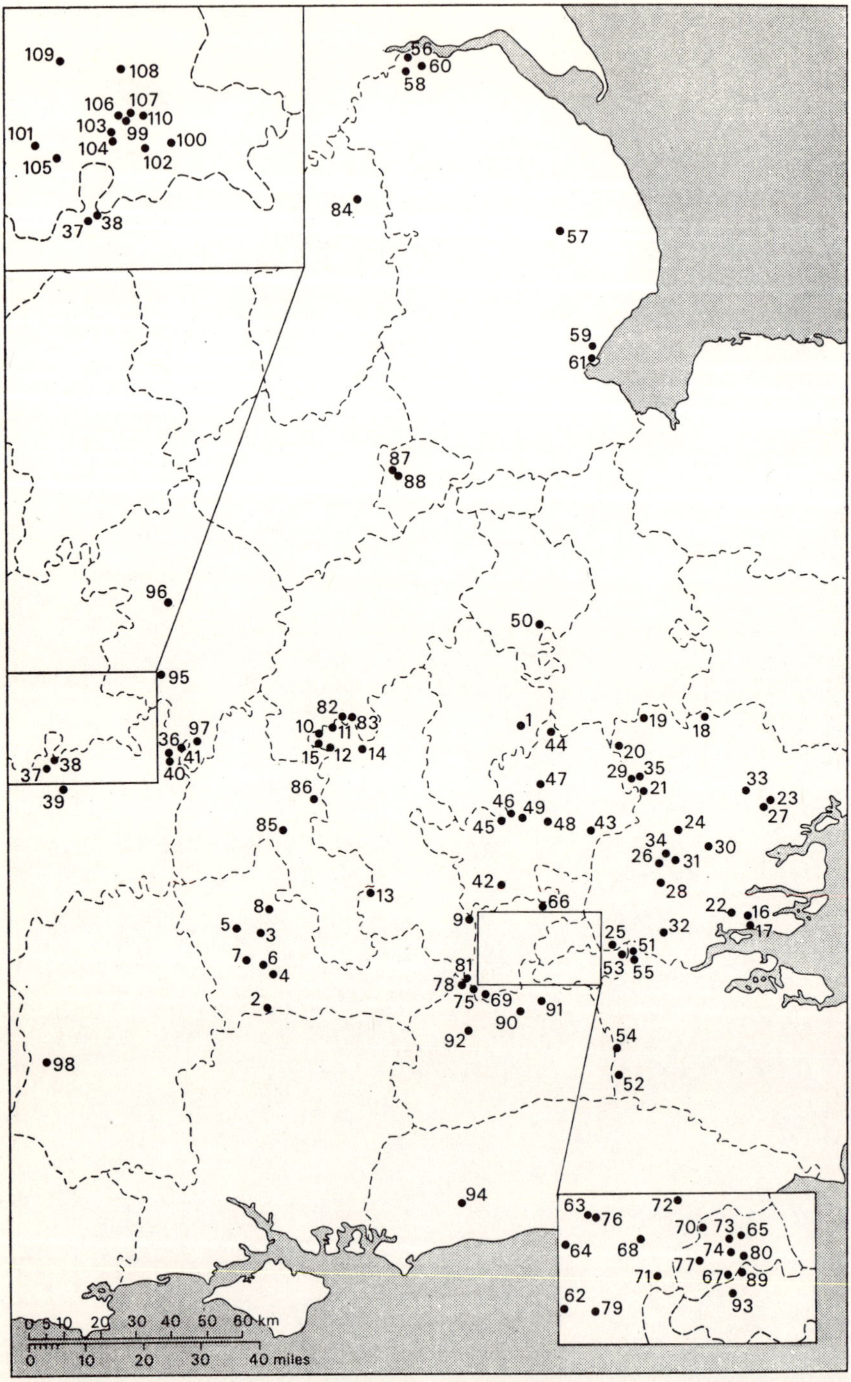

MAP II. THE PRINCIPAL ESTATES OF WESTMINSTER ABBEY IN 1535

Map 2 The Principal Estates of Westminster Abbey in 1535

Beds.
1. Holme with Langford

Berks.
2. Bagnor
3. Betterton
4. Curridge
5. Letcombe Regis
6. Peasemore
7. Poughley
8. Steventon

Bucks.
9. Denham
10. Evershaw
11. Luffield
12. Shalstone
13. Stokenchurch
14. Thornborough
15. Turweston

Essex
16. Benfleet, N.
17. Benfleet, S.
18. Birdbrook
19. Chesterford, Great
20. Clavering
21. Elsenham
22. Fanton
23. Feering
24. Good Easter
25. Ham
26. High Ongar
27. Kelvedon
28. Kelvedon Hatch
29. Manewden
30. Moulsham
31. Norton Mandeville
32. Ockendon, N.
33. Pattiswick
34. Shelley
35. Ugley

Glos.
36. Bourton-on-the-Hill
37. Chaceley
38. Deerhurst
39. Hardwicke
40. Moreton-in-Marsh
41. Todenham

Herts.
42. Aldenham
43. Amwell, Great
44. Ashwell
45. Harpenden
46. Kinsbourne
47. Stevenage
48. Tewin
49. Wheathampstead

Hunts.
50. Offord Cluny

Kent
51. Boarstall
52. Edenbridge
53. Plumstead
54. Westham
55. Wickham, E.

Lincs.
56. Alkborough
57. Belchford
58. Burton Stather
59. Fenne
60. Halton
61. Skreyne

Middx*
62. Ashford
63. Down
64. Drayton
65. Eye
66. Finchley
67. Fulham
68. Greenford
69. Halliford
70. Hampstead
71. Hanwell
72. Hendon
73. Hyde
74. Knightsbridge
75. Laleham
76. Northolt
77. Paddington
78. Paddington
78. Staines
79. Teddington
80. Westminster
81. Yeoveney

Northants
82. Silverstone
83. Whittlebury

Notts.
84. Oswald Beck Soke

Oxon.
85. Islip
86. Launton

Rutland
87. Barleythorpe
88. Oakham

Surrey*
89. Battersea
90. Claygate
91. Morden
92. Pyrford
93. Wandsworth

Sussex
94. Parham

Warwicks.
95. Grafton Minor
96. Knowle
97. Sutton-under-Brailes

Wilts.
98. Westbury

Worcs.
99. Birlingham
100. Bricklehampton
101. Castlemorton
102. Comberton
103. Defford
104. Eckington
105. Longdon
106. Pensham
107. Pershore
108. Pinvin
109. Powick
110. Wick

* Including estates now in London.

Table 1

Abbots of Westminster c.1049–1222

Edwin	c.1049–c.1068
Geoffrey	c.1072–c.1076
Vitalis	1076–1085 (?)
Gilbert Crispin	(?) 1085–1117/18
Herbert	1121–c.1136
Gervase	1138–c.1157/8
Lawrence	c.1158–1173
Walter	1175/6–1190
William Postard	1191–1200
Ralph Arundel	1200–1214
William de Humez	1214–1222

Table 2

Priors and Other Monastic Officers

This list largely depends upon attestations to charters which have chanced to survive and there are inevitable gaps. For this reason the obedientiaries are normally dated only to the time of a given abbot, or abbots.

Priors

Robert	temp. Abbot Gilbert Crispin
Edwy	temp. Abbot Herbert
Osbert de Clare	temp. Abbots Herbert and Gervase
Hugh	temp. Abbot Gervase
Elias	temp. and post. Abbot Gervase
Alquin	temp. Abbot Lawrence
Richard	temp. Abbot Walter
William Postard	temp. Abbot Walter
Robert of Moulsham	temp. Abbot Ralph
Richard of Barking	temp. Abbot William de Humez

Obedientiaries

ALMONERS	
Herbert	temp. Abbot Gilbert
Ralph	temp. Abbot Walter
Peter	temp. Abbot Ralph Arundel
CELLARERS	
Thomas	temp. Abbots Gervase and Lawrence
James	temp. Abbot William Postard
CHAMBERLAIN	
Stephen	temp. Abbots Walter and William Postard

INFIRMARER

Roger	temp. Abbot Lawrence

PRECENTOR

Robert of Moulsham	temp. Abbot Ralph Arundel

PROCTOR OF THE LADY ALTAR

Robert of Moulsham	temp. Abbot Ralph Arundel
Walter	? temp. Abbot Richard of Barking
Henry of Colchester	? temp. Abbot Richard of Barking

SACRIST

Walter	temp. Abbot Lawrence

Table 3

Individual Religious

The identification of these depends upon their appearance in witness lists or else in chance references in other sources. Consequently their chronological listing can be only approximate.

ELEVENTH CENTURY

Baldwin, godson of King Edward
Aelfnoth
Alfwold of St Botulph's Gate
[ ] son of Living
[ ] son of Aelfwin Faremann
Aegelwin son of Brihtmaer
Wlsi Lickescoppe, a hesitant postulant
Sulcard, author of the *Prologus de Construccione Westmonasterii*
Hubert
Reinald, chaplain of King William I
Herbert, possibly the future abbot
Nicholas
William, *alias* William the chaplain (?)

[ ] a converted Jew of London	temp. Abbot Gilbert
[ ] courier to Bec	temp. Abbot Gilbert

TWELFTH CENTURY

Maurice, formerly a subdeacon of Bishop Wulfstan, d.1115x1122.
Riculf, d. by end 1122
Turstin, d. by end 1122
William, d. by end 1122 (? *alias* William 'the chaplain')
Hugh, perambulated land in Worcestershire
Warner, perambulated, as above, and
witn. Translation of St Etheldreda at Ely
Wulfric, formerly a moneyer temp. William II and Henry I
Henry, son of Wilfrid, and his heir, hesitant postulants
Gregory, mission to St Pancras, Lewes
Godefrid, mission to St Pancras, Lewes
Godfrey (*alias* Godefrid, as above?) mission to Rome in 1133

Godric Lobbe	
Ansgod	temp. Abbot Gervase
Hugh	temp. Abbot Gervase
John	temp. Abbot Gervase
Richard de Bissea (? Bushey)	temp. Abbot Gervase
Richard de Hair	temp. Abbot Gervase
Roger Branc	temp. Abbot Gervase
W. Capes	temp. Abbot Gervase
Geoffrey	temp. Abbot Lawrence
Peter of Windsor	temp. Abbot Lawrence
[ ] mission to Durham and Finchale	temp. Abbot Lawrence
Alexander	temp. Abbot Walter
Martin	temp. Abbot Walter
Ralph (? Arundel)	temp. Abbot Walter
Adam, chaplain	temp. Abbot William Postard
Gilbert, chaplain	temp. Abbot William Postard
Philip, chaplain	temp. Abbot William Postard

THIRTEENTH CENTURY

Alexander, chaplain and priest	temp. Abbot Ralph Arundel
Richard, chaplain	temp. Abbot Ralph Arundel
Robert, chaplain	temp. Abbot Ralph Arundel
Roger, chaplain	temp. Abbot Ralph Arundel
Salomon, chaplain and priest	temp. Abbot Ralph Arundel
Simon, chaplain	temp. Abbot Ralph Arundel
William, chaplain	temp. Abbot Ralph Arundel

MONKS OF SUDBURY

Martin	late 12th cent.
Robert de Clara	late 12th cent.
Mr Robert son of Godric	late 12th cent.

WOMEN RELIGIOUS

Brihtgyva, wife of Aelnoth	11th cent.
Aelfwynn	11th cent.
Emma, Kilburn	temp. Abbot Herbert
Gunhild, Kilburn	temp. Abbot Herbert
Christina, Kilburn	temp. Abbot Herbert

Table 4

Identified Lay Officers of the Abbey and Vill

DAPIFER, LATER SENESCHAL	
Hugh of Colham	temp. Abbot Gilbert
Gregory	temp. Abbots Herbert and Gervase
Alan	temp. Abbot Lawrence
Geoffrey Picot	temp. Abbot Walter
Theobald of Feering	temp. Abbot William Postard
(Walter son of Thurstan of Colham)	quitclaimed hereditary right in office 27 August 1198
Richard de Dol	temp. Abbot William Postard (?)
	temp. Abbot Ralph Arundel
Julian Chenduit	temp. Abbot William de Humez
(DOMESTIC) CHAMBERLAINS	
Gerold	temp. Abbot Herbert
Geoffrey	temp. Abbot Ralph Arundel
MARSHALS	
Robert	temp. Abbot Gervase
Robert (presumably another)	temp. Abbot William Postard
SUMMONERS	
Nicholas son of Geoffrey	? – 24 June 1209
Robert of Croxley	24 June 1209 –
BUTLERS	
William of Hurley	temp. Abbot Walter
Thomas (son of William of Hurley)	temp. Abbot William Postard
John	temp. Abbot William Postard
USHERS	
William of Hurley	temp. Abbot Walter
Bartholomew	temp. Abbot Ralph Arundel
VESTIBULE AND BUTTERY	
Walter Stantus	early twelfth cent.

William and Adelaide of Wenden	temp. Abbot Gervase
Hereditary in the Wenden family	until temp. Abbot Walter de Wenlok (1283–1307)

SERGEANTS c.1190–c.1214

(a) POSTS NOT IDENTIFIED

Adam	
Alan	
Geoffrey	
Henry Sumer	temp. Abbot Walter (and living later)
John	
Ralph	
Randulf	
William	
William Stutel	

(b) SERGEANTS AND OTHERS IN IDENTIFIED OFFICES

Almonry
Gilbert of Claygate
Walkelin

Infirmary
William

Sacristy
Thomas, brother of Pancras
William, 'servant of the church'

Kitchen
Gerard the cook
Ivo of the Kitchen
Ralph the baker (?)
Roger the cook

Cellar
Nicholas
Richard

Major Works

Gerin the Engineer	temp. Abbot Gervase

Doorkeeper	
Richard	temp. Abbot Walter
Garden	
Edric	
Stone-masons	
Godwine Greatsyd	temp. King Edward
Leofsi Duddesunu *alias* Leofsi of London	temp. King Edward
Teinfrith the church-wright	temp. King Edward
Painters	
Richard	temp. Henry II
William	temp. Henry II
Burchard, son of William	active to late Henry II
Simon, son of William	Henry II to John
Eustace	temp. John, in post. 1209
REEVES OF THE VILL OF WESTMINSTER	
Richard	temp. (late) Abbot Herbert and Abbot Gervase
Edward	late 12th cent. to c.1194
Roger Enganet	1197x1198
Henry Sumer	c.1198x1212
Richard Testard	c.1198x1212
Odo the Goldsmith	temp. John

Bibliography

Manuscripts

London

College of Arms:	MS Young 72
British Library:	Cotton Charter VI.5
	Cotton Charter Aug. II, part 54
	Harleian Charter 85 A 11
	MS Cotton Faustina A II.
Public Record Office:	E315/61 (The Pershore Cartulary)
Westminster Abbey:	Westminster Abbey Domesday (Muniment Book 11)
	Muniment II
	Muniment III
	Muniment XXIII (2)
	Muniment XXVI (The *Telligraphus*)
	Muniment XXVII
	Muniment XLIII
	Muniment 12733
	Muniment 15684
	Muniment 16218
	Muniment 17317
	Muniment 17319
	Muniment 17439
	Muniment 22443
	Muniment 22486
	Muniment 22492
	Muniment 22495
	Muniment 22497
	Muniment 23638 (d.)
	Muniment 32354

Printed Sources

The Acta of the Bishops of Chichester 1075–1207, ed. H. Mayr-Harting, Canterbury and York Soc. (London, 1964).

Acta of Henry II and Richard I, ed. J.C. Holt and R. Mortimer, List and Index Society Special Series, 21 (1986).

The Acts of Malcolm IV, King of Scots 1153–1165, together with Scottish Royal Acts prior to 1153, ed. G.W.S. Barrow, Regesta Regum Scottorum, I (Edinburgh, 1960).

The Acts of William I, King of Scots 1165–1214, ed. G.W.S. Barrow with W.W. Scott, Regesta Regum Scottorum, II (Edinburgh, 1971).

Alfred the Great: Asser's Life of King Alfred and Other Contemporary Sources, ed. and transl. S. Keynes and M. Lapidge (Harmondsworth, 1983).
The Anglo-Saxon Chronicle, transl. and ed. Dorothy Whitelock, with D.C. Douglas and Susie I. Tucker (London, 1961).
Anglo-Saxon Writs, ed. Florence E. Harmer, 2nd edn (Stamford, 1989).
Annales Monastici, ed. H.R. Luard, 5 vols, Rolls Series (1864–69).
The Beauchamp Cartulary. Charters 1100–1268, ed. Emma Mason, Pipe Roll Society, new series, 43 (1980).
Bede's Ecclesiastical History of the English People, ed. B. Colgrave and R.A.B. Mynors, (Oxford: Clarendon Press, 1969).
Calendar of the Charter Rolls Preserved in the Public Record Office (1226–1516; appendix 1215–1288), 6 vols (London, 1903–1927).
A *Calendar of the Feet of Fines for London and Middlesex, I, Richard I to Richard III*, ed. W.J. Hardy and W. Page (London, 1892).
Calendar of the Patent Rolls preserved in the Public Record Office, Henry III – Henry VII (1232–1509), 52 vols (London, 1893–1966).
The Carmen de Hastingae Proelio of Guy, Bishop of Amiens, ed. Catherine Morton and Hope Muntz (Oxford, 1972).
Cartularium Saxonicum, ed. W. de Gray Birch, 3 vols and index (London, 1885–93).
The Cartulary of Holy Trinity Aldgate, ed. G.A.J. Hodgett, London Record Society, 7 (London, 1971).
Cartulary of St Mary Clerkenwell, ed. W.O. Hassall, Camden Third Series, LXXI (1949).
The Cartulary of Worcester Cathedral Priory (Register I), ed. R.R. Darlington, Pipe Roll Society, new series, XXXVIII (1968).
The Chartulary of the High Church of Chichester, ed. W.D. Peckham, Sussex Record Soc., XLVI (1961).
Chronica Roberti de Torigneio, in *Chronicles of the Reigns of Stephen, Henry II and Richard I*, IV, ed. R. Howlett, Rolls Series (1889).
Chronica Rogeri de Wendover liber qui dicitur Flores Historiarum, ed. H.G. Hewlett, 3 vols, Rolls Series (1886–89).
Chronicle of the Archbishops of York, in *Historians of the Church of York and its Archbishops*, ed. J. Raine, 3 vols, Rolls Series (1879, 1886, 1894), II.
The Chronicle of Battle Abbey, ed. and transl. Eleanor Searle (Oxford, 1980).
The Chronicle of Jocelin of Brakelond, transl. and ed. H.E. Butler (London, 1949).
The Chronicle of John of Hexham, in *Symeonis Monachi Opera Omnia*, ed. T. Arnold, Rolls Series (1882–85), II, pp. 284–332.
The Chronicle of John of Hexham, printed in *The Priory of Hexham, its Chroniclers, Endowments and Annals*, ed. J. Raine, Surtees Society, xliv, xlvi (1864–65), I, pp. 107–72.
The Chronicle of John of Worcester, II, 450–1066, ed. R.R. Darlington and P.M. McGurk, Oxford Medieval Texts (Oxford, 1995).
The Chronicle of John of Worcester, 1118–1140, ed. J.R.H. Weaver, Anecdota Oxoniensia, Medieval and Modern Series, XIII (Oxford, 1908).
The Chronicle of Richard of Devizes of the Time of King Richard the First, ed. J.T. Appleby (London, 1963).
Codex Diplomaticus Aevi Saxonici, ed. J.M. Kemble, 6 vols (London, 1839–48).
Concilia Magnae Brittaniae et Hiberniae, ed. D. Wilkins, 4 vols (London, 1737).

Councils and Synods, with Other Documents Relating to the English Church, I, A.D. 871–1204, ed. D. Whitelock, M. Brett and C.N.L. Brooke, 2 vols (Oxford, 1981).

Councils and Synods, with Other Documents Relating to the English Church, II, 1205–1313, ed. F.M. Powicke and C.R. Cheney, 2 parts (Oxford, 1964).

The Crawford Collection of Early Charters and Documents now in the Bodleian Library, ed. A.S. Napier and W.H. Stevenson (Oxford, 1895).

Curia Regis Rolls of the Reigns of Richard I, John and Henry III Preserved in the Public Record Office (c.1196–) (London, 1938–).

Customary of the Benedictine Monasteries of St Augustine, Canterbury, and St Peter, Westminster, ed. E. Maunde Thompson, Henry Bradshaw Society, XXIII and XXVIII (1902, 1904).

Dialogus de Scaccario, ed. and transl. C. Johnson with corrections by F.E.L. Carter and D.E. Greenway (Oxford, 1983).

Documents Illustrating the Rule of Walter de Wenlok, Abbot of Westminster 1283–1307, ed. Barbara F. Harvey, Camden Fourth Series, 2 (1965).

Domesday Book sive Liber Censualis, ed. A. Farley, 2 vols, Record Comm. (1783).

Durham Liber Vitae, ed. A.H. Thompson, in facsimile, Surtees Soc., 136 (1923).

Eadmer, *Historia Novorum in Anglia*, ed. M. Rule, Rolls Series (1884).

Eadmer, *The Life of St Anselm, Archbishop of Canterbury*, ed., introd. and transl. R.W. Southern (Oxford, 1962, reprinted, with corrections, Oxford, 1972).

The Ecclesiastical History of Orderic Vitalis, ed. Marjorie Chibnall, 6 vols (Oxford, 1969–80).

English Episcopal Acta, I, Lincoln 1067–1185, ed. D.M. Smith (Oxford, 1980).

English Episcopal Acta, II, Canterbury 1162–1190, ed. C.R. Cheney and B.E.A. Jones (Oxford, 1986).

English Episcopal Acta, III, Canterbury 1193–1205, ed. C.R. Cheney and E. John (Oxford, 1986).

English Episcopal Acta, IV, Lincoln 1186–1206, ed. D.M. Smith (London, 1986).

English Episcopal Acta, V, York 1070–1154, ed. Janet E. Burton (Oxford, 1988).

English Episcopal Acta, VIII, Winchester 1070–1204, ed. M.J. Franklin (Oxford, 1993).

English Historical Documents, I, c.500–1042, ed. Dorothy Whitelock, 2nd edn (London, 1979).

English Historical Documents, II, 1042–1189, ed. D.C. Douglas and G.W. Greenaway, 2nd edn (London, 1981).

Facsimiles of English Royal Writs to A.D. 1100 presented to Vivian Hunter Galbraith, ed. T.A.M. Bishop and P. Chaplais (Oxford, 1957).

Feet of Fines for Essex (1182–1326), ed. R.E.G. Kirk and E.F. Kirk, Essex Archaeological Society, 2 vols (Colchester, 1899–1928).

Flete, John, *The History of Westminster Abbey*, Notes and Documents Relating to Westminster Abbey, no. 2, ed. J. Armitage Robinson (Cambridge, 1909).

Florentii Wigorniensis monachi Chronicon ex Chronicis, ed. B. Thorpe, 2 vols, English Historical Society (London, 1848–49).

Foedera, conventiones, literae et cujuscunque generis acta publica, ed. T. Rymer, 20 vols (London, 1704–35).

Formulare Anglicanum, ed. T. Madox (London, 1702).

Geoffrey of Monmouth, *The History of the Kings of Britain*, transl. and introd. L. Thorpe (Harmondsworth: Penguin Books, 1966).

Gesta Abbatum Monasterii Sancti Albani, ed. H.T. Riley, 3 vols, Rolls Series (1867–69).
Gesta Regis Henrici Secundi Benedicti Abbatis, ed. W. Stubbs, 2 vols, Rolls Series (1867).
Gesta Stephani, ed. and transl. K.R. Potter, introd. R.H.C. Davis (Oxford, 1976).
The Great Roll of the Pipe for the Thirty-First Year of the Reign of Henry I (Michaelmas 1130), ed. J. Hunter, Record Comm. (1833).
The Great Rolls of the Pipe for the Second, Third and Fourth Years of the Reign of King Henry the Second A.D. 1155–1158, ed. J. Hunter (London, 1844).
The Great Rolls of the Pipe for the Fifth to Thirty-Fourth Years of the Reign of King Henry II 1158–1188, Pipe Roll Soc. (1884–1925).
The Great Roll of the Pipe 1 Richard I, ed. J. Hunter, Record Comm. (1844).
The Great Rolls of the Pipe 2–10 Richard I, ed. D.M. Stenton, Pipe Roll Soc. (1925–32).
The Great Rolls of the Pipe 1–14 John, ed. D.M. Stenton, S. Smith, H.M. Kirkus, C.F. Slade and P.M. Barnes, Pipe Roll Soc. (1933–55).
Guillaume de Poitiers, *Historie de Guillaume le Conquérant*, ed. and transl. R. Foreville (Paris, 1952).
Hemingi Chartularium Ecclesiae Wigorniensis, ed. T. Hearne, 2 vols (Oxford, 1723).
Henrici Huntendunensis Historia Anglorum, ed. T. Arnold, Rolls Series, (1879).
Historians of the Church of York and its Archbishops, ed. J. Raine, 3 vols, Rolls Series (1879, 1886, 1894).
Hugh the Chantor, *The History of the Church of York 1066–1177*, transl. and introd. C. Johnson (London, 1961).
John of Salisbury, *Memoirs of the Papal Court*, transl. and introd. Marjorie Chibnall (London, 1956).
L'estoire des Engleis by Geffrei Gaimar, ed. A. Bell, Anglo-Norman Text Society, 14–16 (Oxford, 1960).
The Letters and Charters of Gilbert Foliot, ed. Z.N. Brooke, A. Morey and C.N.L. Brooke (Cambridge, 1967).
The Letters of John of Salisbury, I, The Early Letters (1153–1161), ed. W.J. Millor and H.E. Butler, revised by C.N.L. Brooke (London, 1955).
The Letters of John of Salisbury, II (1163–1180), ed. W.J. Millor and C.N.L. Brooke (Oxford, 1979).
The Letters of Lanfranc Archbishop of Canterbury, ed. and transl. Helen Clover and Margaret Gibson (Oxford, 1979).
The Letters of Osbert de Clare, Prior of Westminster, ed. E.W. Williamson, introd. J. Armitage Robinson (London, 1929).
The Letters of Pope Innocent III (1198–1216), concerning England and Wales: a Calendar, with an Appendix of Texts, ed. C.R. Cheney and Mary Cheney (London, 1967).
Liber Eliensis, ed. E.O. Blake, Camden Third Series, XCII (1962).
Liber Niger Scaccarii, ed. T. Hearne (London, 1774).
The Life of Ailred of Rievaulx by Walter Daniel, transl. and introd. F.M. Powicke (London, 1950; reprinted Oxford, 1978).
The Life of King Edward who Rests at Westminster, attributed to a Monk of Saint-Bertin, ed. and transl. Frank Barlow, 2nd edn (Oxford, 1992).
London Assize of Nuisance 1301–1431: a Calendar, ed. Helena M. Chew and W. Kellaway, London Record Soc., 10 (1973).

Materials for the History of Thomas Becket, Archbishop of Canterbury, ed. J.C. Robertson and J.B. Sheppard, 7 vols, Rolls Series (1875–85).

Matthew Paris, *Chronica Majora*, ed. H.R. Luard, 7 vols, Rolls Series (1872–84).

Memorials of St Edmund's Abbey, ed. T. Arnold, 3 vols, Rolls Series (1890–96).

The Monastic Constitutions of Lanfranc, ed. and transl. D. Knowles (London, 1951).

The Northamptonshire Survey, *The Victoria History of the County of Northampton*, I, ed. W.R.D. Adkins and R.M. Serjeantson (London, 1902), pp. 357–92.

Papsturkunden in England, ed. W. Holtzmann, 3 vols, Abhandlungen der Gesellschaft der Wissenschaften in Göttingen, phil-hist. Klasse, Berlin, Göttingen (I = neue Folge XXV, 1930–31; II = 3 Folge XIV–XV, 1935–36; III = 3 Folge XXXIII, 1952).

Patrologiae cursus completus, series Latina, ed. J.P. Migne, 221 vols (Paris, 1844–64).

Pipe Rolls, see *The Great Rolls of the Pipe*.

Placita Anglo-Normannica, ed. M.M. Bigelow (London, 1879).

Les Proverbes de Salemon by Sanson de Nantuil, ed. C. Claire Isoz, III, Anglo-Norman Text Society (1994).

Ralph de Diceto, *Abbreviationes Chronicorum*, *Opera Historica*, ed. W. Stubbs, 2 vols, Rolls Series (1876).

Reading Abbey Cartularies, ed. B.R. Kemp, Camden Fourth Series, vols 31, 33 (1986–87).

Recueil des Actes de Henri II, ed. and introd. L. Delisle and E. Berger, 4 vols (Paris, 1906–27).

Regesta Pontificum Romanorum . . . ad annum 1198, ed. P. Jaffé, 2nd edn, 2 vols (Leipzig, 1885–1888).

Regesta Regum Anglo-Normannorum, I, 1066–1100, ed. H.W.C. Davis with the assistance of J. Whitwell (Oxford, 1913).

Regesta Regum Anglo-Normannorum, II, 1100–1135, ed. C. Johnson and H.A. Cronne (Oxford, 1956).

Regesta Regum Anglo-Normannorum, III, 1135–1154, ed. H.A. Cronne and R.H.C. Davis (Oxford, 1968).

Regesta Regum Anglo-Normannorum, IV, 1135–1154: Facsimiles, ed. H.A. Cronne and R.H.C. Davis (Oxford, 1969).

Reginald of Durham, *Libellus de vita et miraculis S. Godrici, heremitae de Finchale*, ed. J. Stevenson, Surtees Soc., 20 (1847).

Regularis Concordia: the Monastic Agreement, transl. and ed. T. Symons (London, 1953).

Richard of Cirencester, *Speculum Historiale de Gestis Regum Angliae*, ed. J.E.B. Mayor, Rolls Series, 2 vols (1863–69).

Rotuli Chartarum in Turri Londoniensi asservati, 1199–1216, ed. T. Duffus Hardy, Record Comm. (1837).

Rotuli Curiae Regis: Rolls and Records of the Court Held before the King's Justiciars or Justices, I, From the Sixth Year of King Richard I to the Accession of King John, ed. F. Palgrave, Record Comm. (1835).

Rotuli Hugonis de Welles, episcopi Lincolniensis, ed. W.P.W. Phillimore, Canterbury and York Soc., 3 vols (1907–9).

Rotuli Litterarum Clausarum in Turri Londiniensi asservati (1204–27), ed. T. Duffus Hardy, 2 vols, Record Comm. (1833–44).

Rotuli Litterarum Patentium in Turri Londiniensi asservati, ed. T. Duffus Hardy, Record Comm., I, i (1835).

Rotuli de Oblatis et Finibus in Turri Londiniensi asservati, tempore regis Johannis, ed. T. Duffus Hardy, Record Comm. (1835).

Rouleaux des Morts du IXe au XVe Siècle, ed. L. Delisle, Libraire de la Société de l'Histoire de France (Paris, 1866, reprinted Johnson Reprint Corporation, New York, 1968).

The Rule of St Benedict, ed. and transl. J. McCann (London, 1952).

Sacrorum Conciliorum Nova, et Amplissima Collectio, ed. J.D. Mansi *et al.* 54 vols in 59 (Graz, 1960–61).

Select Documents of the English Lands of the Abbey of Bec, ed. Marjorie Chibnall, Camden Third Series, LXXIII (1951).

Selected Letters of Pope Innocent III concerning England (1198–1216), ed. C.R. Cheney and W.H. Semple (London, 1953).

Textus Roffensis, ed. T. Hearne (Oxford, 1720).

Thomas of Walsingham, *Gesta Abbatum Monasterii Sancti Albani*, ed. H.T. Riley, I, Rolls Series (1867).

Three Coronation Orders, ed. J. Wickham Legg, Henry Bradshaw Society, XIX (1900).

Three Rolls of the King's Courts 1194–95, ed. F.W. Maitland, Pipe Roll Society, XIV (1891).

Vita Sancti Edwardi Regis, in *Patrologia Latina*, ed. J.P. Migne, CXCV, col. 746.

The Vita Wulfstani of William of Malmesbury, ed. R.R. Darlington, Camden Third Series, XL (1928).

Walter Map, De Nugis Curialium: Courtier's Trifles, ed. and transl. M.R. James, revised by C.N.L. Brooke and R.A.B. Mynors (Oxford, 1983).

Westminster Abbey Charters 1066–c.1214, ed. Emma Mason, assisted by the late Jennifer Bray, continuing the work of the late Desmond J. Murphy, London Record Society, 25 (1988).

William of Malmesbury, *De Gestis Regum Anglorum*, ed. W. Stubbs, 2 vols, Rolls Series (1887, 1889).

William of Malmesbury, *De Gestis Pontificum Anglorum*, ed. N.E.S.A. Hamilton, Rolls Series (1870).

Winchester Annals (519–1277), *Annales Monastici*, II, ed. H.R. Luard, Rolls Series (1865).

The Works of Gilbert Crispin, Abbot of Westminster, ed. A.S. Abulafia and G.R. Evans, *Auctores Britannici Medii Aevi*, VIII (1986).

Secondary Works

Anderson, Freda, 'The Westminster Abbots: a Problem of Identity', *Church Monuments*, IV (1989), pp. 3–15.

Appleby, J.T., *England without Richard 1189–1199* (London, 1965).

Ayton, Andrew, and Davis, Virginia, 'Ecclesiastical Wealth in England in 1086', in *The Church and Wealth*, ed. W.J. Sheils and Diana Wood, Studies in Church History, 24 (Oxford, 1987), pp. 47–60.

Baker, T., *Medieval London* (London, 1970).

Banton, N., 'Monastic Reform and the Unification of Tenth-Century England', in S. Mews, ed., *Religion and National Identity*, Studies in Church History, 18 (Oxford, 1982), pp. 71–85.

Barlow, Frank, *Edward the Confessor* (London, 1970).

Barlow, Frank, *The English Church 1000–1066*, 2nd edn (London, 1979).

Barlow, Frank, *The English Church 1066–1154* (London, 1979).

Barlow, Frank, 'The English, Norman and French Councils Called to Deal with the Papal Schism of 1159', reprinted from *English Historical Review*, 51 (1936), pp. 264–8, in F. Barlow, *The Norman Conquest and Beyond* (London, 1983), pp. 297–301.

Barlow, Frank, 'Two Notes: Cnut's Second Pilgrimage and Queen Emma's Disgrace in 1043', *English Historical Review*, 73 (1958), pp. 649–56; reprinted in F. Barlow, *The Norman Conquest and Beyond* (London, 1983), pp. 49–56.

Barlow, Frank, 'Leofric and his Times', in his *The Norman Conquest and Beyond* (London, 1983), pp. 113–28.

Barlow, Frank, *William Rufus* (London, 1983).

Barrow, Julia, 'How the Twelfth-Century Monks of Worcester Perceived their Past', in P. Magdalino, ed., *The Perception of the Past in Twelfth-Century Europe* (London, 1992), pp. 53–74.

Bassett, S., *The Origins of Anglo-Saxon Kingdoms* (Leicester: Leicester University Press, 1989).

Bates, David, *Bishop Remigius of Lincoln, 1067–92* (Lincoln, 1992).

Bates, David, 'The Earliest Norman Writs', *English Historical Review*, 100 (1985), pp. 266–84.

Bates, David, *Normandy before 1066* (London, 1982).

Biddle, Martin, 'Seasonal Festivals and Residence: Winchester, Westminster and Gloucester in the Tenth to Twelfth Centuries', *Anglo-Norman Studies, VIII, Proceedings of the Battle Conference 1985*, ed. R. Allen Brown (Woodbridge, 1986), pp. 51–72.

Binns, Alison, *Dedications of Monastic Houses in England and Wales 1066–1216*, Studies in the History of Medieval Religion, I (Woodbridge, 1989).

Bishop, T.A.M., *Scriptores Regis: Facsimiles to Identify and Illustrate the Hands of Royal Scribes in Original Charters of Henry I, Stephen and Henry II* (Oxford, 1961).

Blair, John, ed., *Minsters and Parish Churches: the Local Church in Transition 950–1200*, Oxford University Committee for Archaeology, Monograph no. 17 (1988).

Blair, John, 'From Minster to Parish Church', in John Blair, ed., *Minsters and Parish Churches: the Local Church in Transition 950–1200*, Oxford University Committee for Archaeology, Monograph no. 17 (1988), pp. 1–19.

Blair, John, 'Minsters in the Landscape', in D. Hooke, ed., *Anglo-Saxon Settlements* (Oxford, 1988), pp. 35–58.

Brand, Paul, ' "*Multis Vigiliis Excogitatem et Inventam*": Henry II and the Creation of the English Common Law', *The Haskins Society Journal*, II, ed. R.B. Patterson (1990), pp. 197–222.

Brett, M., 'The Annals of Bermondsey, Southwark and Merton', in D. Abulafia, M. Franklin and M. Rubin, eds, *Church and City 1000–1500. Essays in Honour of Christopher Brooke* (Cambridge, 1992), pp. 279–310.

Brett, M., *The English Church under Henry I* (Oxford, 1975).

Brooke, C.N.L., assisted by Keir, G., *London 800–1216: the Shaping of a City* (London, 1975).

Brown, R.A., Colvin, H.M. and Taylor, A.J., *The History of the King's Works*, I (London, 1963).

Cam, Helen, '*Manerium cum hundredo*: the Hundred and the Hundredal Manor', *English Historical Review*, 47 (1932), pp. 353–76.

Carpenter, Edward, *A House of Kings: the History of Westminster Abbey* (London, 1966).

Chaplais, P., 'The Original Charters of Herbert and Gervase, Abbots of Westminster (1121–1157)', in P.M. Barnes and C.F. Slade, eds, *A Medieval Miscellany for Doris Mary Stenton*, Pipe Roll Soc., new series, XXXVI (1960), pp. 89–110; reprinted in P. Chaplais, *Essays in Medieval Government and Administration* (London, 1981), pp. XVIII, 89–110.

Cheney, C.R., *Handbook of Dates for Students of English History*, Royal Historical Society Guides and Handbooks, 4 (London, 1948).

Cheney, Mary G., *Roger, Bishop of Worcester 1164–1179* (Oxford, 1980).

Clark, J. *Saxon and Norman London* (London: HMSO, 1989).

Clarke, P.E., *The English Nobility under Edward the Confessor* (Oxford, 1994).

Colvin, H.M., ed., *The History of the King's Works*, 6 vols (London: HMSO, 1963–82).

Cowdrey, H.E.J., 'The Anglo-Norman *Laudes Regiae*', reprinted from *Viator*, 12 (1981), pp. 37–78 in H.E.J. Cowdrey, *Popes, Monks and Crusaders* (London, 1984), pp. VIII, 37–78.

Cronne, H.A., *The Reign of Stephen 1135–1154: Anarchy in England* (London, 1970).

Crosby, Everett U., *Bishop and Chapter in Twelfth-Century England* (Cambridge, 1994).

Crouch, D., *William Marshal: Court, Career and Chivalry in the Angevin Empire 1147–1219* (Harlow, 1990).

Croydon, F.E., 'Abbot Lawrence of Westminster and Hugh of St Victor', *Medieval and Renaissance Studies*, II, ed. R. Hunt and R. Klibansky (London, 1950), pp. 169–171.

Dales, Douglas, *Dunstan: Saint and Statesman* (Cambridge, 1988).

Darlington, R.R., 'Æthelwig, Abbot of Evesham', *English Historical Review*, 48 (1933), pp. 1–22, 177–98.

Davies, R.R., *The Age of Conquest: Wales 1063–1415* (Oxford, 1991).

Davis, H.W.C., 'London Lands and Liberties of St Paul's 1066–1135', in A.G. Little and F.M. Powicke, eds, *Essays in Medieval History Presented to Thomas Frederick Tout* (Manchester, 1925), pp. 45–59.

Davis, R.H.C., 'The *Carmen de Hastingae Proelio*', in his *From Alfred the Great to Stephen* (London, 1991), pp. 79–100.

Davis, R.H.C., 'The College of St Martin-le-Grand and the Anarchy 1135–54', reprinted from *London Topographical Record*, 23 (1974), pp. 9–26, in R.H.C. Davis, *From Alfred the Great to Stephen* (London, 1991), pp. 237–54.

Davis, R.H.C., *King Stephen 1135–1154*, 3rd edn (Harlow, 1990).

Decaens, J. 'La datation de l'abbatiale de Bernay: quelques observations architecturales et résultats des fouilles récentes', in R. Allen Brown, ed., *Anglo-Norman Studies, V, Proceedings of the Battle Conference 1982* (Woodbridge, 1983), pp. 97–120.

Dugdale, W., *Monasticon Anglicanum*, revised H. Caley, H. Ellis and B. Bandinel, 6 vols in 8 (London, 1817–30).

Duggan, C., 'Richard of Ilchester, Royal Servant and Bishop', *Transactions of the Royal Historical Society*, 5th series, 16 (1966), pp. 1–21.

Dumville, David N., 'Ecclesiastical Lands and the Defence of Wessex in the First Viking Age', in D.N. Dumville, *Wessex and England from Alfred to Edgar* (Woodbridge, 1992) pp. 29–54.

Dumville, David N., *Wessex and England from Alfred to Edgar* (Woodbridge, 1992).

Edwards, G., 'The Royal Household and the Welsh Lawbooks', *Transactions of the Royal Historical Society*, fifth series, 13 (1963), pp. 163–176.

Evans, G.R., 'Gilbert Crispin, Abbot of Westminster: the Forming of a Monastic Scholar', *Studia Monastica*, XXII (1980).

Ewig, E., 'Résidence et capitale pendant le Haut Moyen Age', *Révue Historique*, 230 (1963), pp. 25–72.

Eyton, R.W., *Court, Household and Itinerary of King Henry II* (London, 1878).

Fleming, Robin, 'Monastic Lands and England's Defence in the Viking Age', *English Historical Review*, 100 (1985), pp. 241–65.

Franklin, M.J., 'The Identification of Minsters in the Midlands', in R. Allen Brown, ed., *Anglo-Norman Studies, VII, Proceedings of the Battle Conference 1984* (Woodbridge, 1985), pp. 69–88.

Fryde, E.B., Greenway, D.E., Porter, S., and Roy, I., eds, *Handbook of British Chronology*, 3rd edn (London, 1986).

Gameson, R., 'English Manuscript Art in the Mid-Eleventh Century: the Decorative Tradition', *The Antiquaries Journal*, 71 (1991), pp. 64–122.

Gem, R.D.H., 'The English Parish Church in the Eleventh and Early Twelfth Centuries: a Great Rebuilding?', in John Blair, ed., *Minsters and Parish Churches: the Local Church in Transition*, Oxford University Committee for Archaeology, Monograph No. 17 (1988), pp. 21–30.

Gem, R.D.H., 'The Romanesque Architecture of Old St Paul's Cathedral and its Late Eleventh-Century Context', in Lindy Grant, ed., *Medieval Art, Architecture and Archaeology in London*, The British Archaeological Association Conference Transactions for the Year 1984 (London, 1990), pp. 47–63.

Gem, R.D.H. 'The Romanesque Rebuilding of Westminster Abbey (with a reconstruction by W.T. Ball)', *Proceedings of the Battle Conference on Anglo-Norman Studies, III, 1980*, ed. R. Allen Brown (Woodbridge, 1981), pp. 33–60.

Gibson, Margaret, *Lanfranc of Bec* (Oxford, 1978).

Gillingham, J., 'The Context and Purposes of Geoffrey of Monmouth's *History of the Kings of Britain*', *Anglo-Norman Studies, XIII, Proceedings of the Battle Conference 1990*, ed. Marjorie Chibnall (Woodbridge, 1991), pp. 99–118.

Golding, B., *Conquest and Colonization: the Normans in Britain 1066–1100* (Basingstoke, 1994).

Gover, J.E.B., Mawer, A., and Stenton, F.M., with Madge, S.J., *The Place-Names of Middlesex*, English Place-Name Society, XVIII (1942).

Gover, J.E.B., Mawer, A., Stenton, F.M., with Bonner, A., *The Place-Names of Surrey*, English Place-Name Society, XI (reprinted 1982).

Gransden, A., 'Baldwin, Abbot of Bury St Edmunds 1065–1097', *Proceedings of the Battle Conference on Anglo-Norman Studies, IV, 1981*, ed. R. Allen Brown (Woodbridge, 1982) pp. 65–76, 187–95.

Gransden, Antonia, *Historical Writing in England c.550 to c.1307* (London, 1974).

Green, Judith A., *The Government of England under Henry I* (Cambridge, 1986).

Green, Judith A., 'The Sheriffs of William the Conqueror', *Anglo-Norman Studies, V, Proceedings of the Battle Conference 1982*, ed. R. Allen Brown (Woodbridge, 1983), pp. 129–45.

Habington, T., *A Survey of Worcestershire*, Worcestershire Historical Society, V, 2 vols (Oxford, 1893–99).

Hallam, Elizabeth M., 'Henry II as a Founder of Monasteries', *Journal of Ecclesiastical History*, 28 (1977), pp. 113–32.

Hallam, Elizabeth M., 'Royal Burial and the Cult of Kingship in France and England 1060–1330', *Journal of Medieval History*, 8 (1982), pp. 359–80.

Hart, Cyril, *The Danelaw* (London, 1992).

Harvey, Barbara F. 'Abbot Gervase de Blois and the Fee-Farms of Westminster Abbey', *Bulletin of the Institute of Historical Research*, 40 (1967), pp. 127–41.

Harvey, Barbara, *Living and Dying in England 1100–1540: the Monastic Experience* (Oxford, 1993).

Harvey, Barbara, *Westminster Abbey and its Estates in the Middle Ages* (Oxford, 1977).

Heiser, R., 'The Households of the Justiciars of Richard I: an Inquiry into the Second Level of Medieval English Government', *The Haskins Society Journal*, 2 (1990), pp. 223–35.

Hollister, C. Warren, 'The Misfortunes of the Mandevilles', *History*, 58 (1973), pp. 18–28.

Honeybourne, M.B., 'The Sanctuary Boundaries and Environs of Westminster Abbey and the College of St Martin-le-Grand', *Journal of the British Archaeological Association*, new series, 38 (1932), pp. 316–32.

Howell, Margaret, 'Abbatial Vacancies and the Divided Mensa in Medieval England', *Journal of Ecclesiastical History*, 33 (1982), pp. 173–92.

Jenkinson, H., 'William Cade, a Financier of the Twelfth Century', *English Historical Review*, 28 (1913), pp. 209–27.

John, E., *Orbis Britanniae and Other Studies* (Leicester, 1966).

Kealey, E.J., *Roger of Salisbury, Viceroy of England* (Berkeley, Los Angeles, London, 1972).

Keene, D., and Harding, V., *A Survey of Documentary Sources for Property-Holding in London before the Great Fire*, London Record Society, 22 (1985).

Kelly, J.N.D., *The Oxford Dictionary of Popes* (Oxford, 1986).

Kelly, Susan, 'Trading Privileges from Eighth-Century England', *Early Medieval Europe*, 1 (1992), pp. 3–28.

Kemp, B.R., 'The Mother-Church of Thatcham', *Berkshire Archaeological Journal*, LXIII (1967–68), pp. 117–21.

Keynes, Simon, 'The Æthelings in Normandy', *Anglo-Norman Studies, XIII, Proceedings of the Battle Conference 1990*, ed. Marjorie Chibnall (Woodbridge, 1991), pp. 173–205.

Keynes, Simon, 'Regenbald the Chancellor (*sic*)', *Anglo-Norman Studies, X, Proceedings of the Battle Conference 1987*, ed. R. Allen Brown (Woodbridge, 1988), pp. 185–222.

Kidson, P., 'The Cathedral of Speyer and the Salian Dynasty', paper delivered to the London Society for Medieval Studies, Institute of Historical Research (London, 12 November 1991).

King, Edmund, *The Anarchy of Stephen's Reign* (Oxford, 1994).

Knowles, D., Brooke, C.N.L., and London, V.C.M., *The Heads of Religious Houses England and Wales 940–1216* (Cambridge, 1972).

Knowles, D., and Hadcock, R.N., *Medieval Religious Houses England and Wales* (London, 1971).

Lancaster, R. Kent, 'Artists, Suppliers and Clerks: the Human Factors in the Court Patronage of King Henry III', *Journal of the Warburg and Courtauld Institutes*, 35 (1972), pp. 81–107.

Lawson, M.K., *Cnut: the Danes in England in the Early Eleventh Century* (Harlow, 1993).

Legg, J. Wickham, *English Coronation Records* (Westminster, 1901).

Le Neve, John, *Fasti Ecclesiae Anglicanae 1066–1300, I, St Paul's, London*, compiled Diana E. Greenway (London, 1968).

Le Neve, John, *Fasti Ecclesiae Anglicanae 1066–1300, II, Monastic Cathedrals*, compiled Diana E. Greenway (London, 1971).

Le Neve, John, *Fasti Ecclesiae Anglicanae 1066–1300, III, Lincoln*, compiled by Diana E. Greenway (London, 1977).

Le Neve, John, *Fasti Ecclesiae Anglicanae 1066–1300, IV, Salisbury*, compiled Diana Greenway (London, 1991).

Leyser, K.J. 'Frederick Barbarossa, Henry II and the Hand of St James', reprinted from *English Historical Review*, 90 (1975), pp. 481–506, in K. Leyser, *Medieval Germany and its Neighbours 950–1250* (London, 1982) pp. 215–40.

Madox, T., *Baronia Anglica* (London, 1736).

Mason, Emma, 'The King, the Chamberlain and Southwick Priory', *Bulletin of the Institute of Historical Research*, 53 (1980), pp. 1–10.

Mason, Emma, 'The Mauduits and their Chamberlainship of the Exchequer', *Bulletin of the Institute of Historical Research*, 49 (1976), pp. 1–23.

Mason, Emma, '*Pro Statu et Incolumnitate Regni Mei*: Royal Monastic Patronage 1066–1154', in S. Mews, ed., *Religion and National Identity*, Studies in Church History, 18 (Oxford, 1982), pp. 99–117.

Mason, Emma, *St Wulfstan of Worcester c.1008–1095* (Oxford, 1990).

Mason, Emma, 'Westminster Abbey's Rutland Churches', *Rutland Record*, 5 (1985), pp. 163–6.

Matthew, D., *The Norman Monasteries and their English Possessions* (Oxford, 1962; reprinted Westport, CT, 1979).

Meale, Carol M., ed., *Women and Literature in Britain 1150–1500* (Cambridge, 1993).

Mercati, Angelo, 'La prima Relazione de Cardinale Nicolò Romanis sulla Legazione in Inghilterra (1213)', in *Essays Presented to R.L. Poole*, ed. H.W.C. Davis (Oxford, 1927), pp. 274–89.

Merrifield, Ralph, 'The Contribution of Archaeology to our Understanding of pre-Norman London 1973–1988', in Lindy Grant, ed., *Medieval Art, Architecture and Archaeology in London*, The British Archaeological Association Conference Transactions, X, for the year 1984 (London, 1990), pp. 1–15.

Moore, N., *History of St Bartholomew's Hospital*, I (London, 1918).

Morey, A., and Brooke, C.N.L., 'The Cerne Letters of Gilbert Foliot and the Legation of Imar of Tusculum', *English Historical Review*, 63 (1948), pp. 523–7.

Morey, A., and Brooke, C.N.L. *Gilbert Foliot and his Letters* (Cambridge, 1965).
Morgan, Marjorie, *The English Lands of the Abbey of Bec* (London, 1946).
Morris, C., *The Papal Monarchy: the Western Church from 1050 to 1250* (Oxford, 1991).
Mortimer, Richard, *Angevin England 1154–1258* (Oxford, 1994).
Mortimer, R., 'The Charters of Henry II: What are the Criteria for Authenticity?', *Anglo-Norman Studies, XII, Proceedings of the Battle Conference 1989*, ed. Marjorie Chibnall (Woodbridge, 1990), pp. 119–34.
Nelson, Janet L., 'The Rites of the Conqueror', reprinted from *Proceedings of the Fourth Battle Conference on Anglo-Norman Studies*, ed. R. Allen Brown (Woodbridge, 1982), pp. 117–32, 210–21, in Janet L. Nelson, *Politics and Ritual in Early Medieval Europe* (London, 1986), pp. 375–401.
Nightingale, Pamela, 'The Origin of the Court of the Husting and Danish Influence on London's Development into a Capital City', *English Historical Review*, 102 (1987), pp. 559–78.
Ortenberg, Veronica, *The English Church and the Continent in the Tenth and Eleventh Centuries: Cultural, Spiritual and Artistic Exchanges* (Oxford, 1992).
Pearce, E.H., *The Monks of Westminster*, Notes and Documents Relating to Westminster Abbey, no. 5 (Cambridge, 1916).
Perring, Dominic, *Roman London* (London, 1991).
Powicke, F.M., *King Henry III and the Lord Edward* (Oxford, 1947).
Renoux, Annie, *Fécamp: du palais ducal au palais de Dieu* (Paris, 1991).
Renoux, Annie, 'Fouilles sur le site du château ducal de Fécamp (Xe–XIIe siècle). bilan provisoire', *Proceedings of the Battle Conference on Anglo-Norman Studies, IV, 1981*, ed. R. Allen Brown (Woodbridge, 1982), pp. 133–52 and 221–3.
Reynolds, Susan, 'The Rulers of London in the Twelfth Century', *History*, 57 (1972), pp. 337–53.
Richardson, H.G., 'The Coronation in Medieval England', *Traditio*, 16 (1960), pp. 111–202.
Richardson, H.G. and Sayles, G.O., *The Governance of Medieval England from the Conquest to Magna Carta* (Edinburgh, 1963).
Richardson, H.G., 'William of Ely, the King's Treasurer', *Transactions of the Royal Historical Society*, fourth series, 15 (1932), pp. 45–90.
Robinson, I.S., *The Papacy 1073–1198: Continuity and Innovation* (Cambridge, 1990).
Robinson, J. Armitage, *Gilbert Crispin Abbot of Westminster: a Study of the Abbey under Norman Rule*, Notes and Documents Relating to Westminster Abbey, no. 3 (Cambridge, 1911).
Rosser, Gervase, *Medieval Westminster 1200–1540* (Oxford, 1989).
Roth, C., *The History of the Jews in England*, 3rd edn (1964; reprinted Oxford, 1979).
Round, J.H., *Feudal England*, 2nd edn (New York, 1964).
Saltman, A., *Theobald, Archbishop of Canterbury* (London, 1956; reprinted New York, 1969).
Sanders, I.J., *English Baronies: a Study of their Origin and Descent 1086–1327* (Oxford, 1960).
Sawyer, P.H., *Anglo-Saxon Charters: an Annotated List and Bibliography* (London, 1968).
Sayers, Jane, 'Monastic Archdeacons', in Brooke, C.N.L., Luscombe, D., Martin,

G.H., and Owen, D., eds, *Church and Government in the Middle Ages: Essays presented to C.R. Cheney on his 70th Birthday* (Cambridge, 1976), pp. 177–203.

Sayers, Jane, *Papal Judges-Delegate in the Province of Canterbury 1198–1254: a Study in Ecclesiastical Administration* (Oxford, 1971).

Scholz, B.W., 'The Canonization of Edward the Confessor', *Speculum*, 26 (1961), pp. 38–60.

Scholz, B.W, 'Sulcard of Westminster: "*Prologus de Construccione Westmonasterii*" ', *Traditio*, 20 (1964), pp. 59–91.

Scholz, B.W., 'Two Forged Charters from the Abbey of Westminster and their Relationship with St Denis', *English Historical Review*, 76 (1961), pp. 466–78.

Searle, Eleanor, 'Possible History', *Speculum*, 61 (1986), pp. 779–86.

Short, Ian, 'Gaimar's Epilogue and Geoffrey of Monmouth's *Liber Vetustissimus*', *Speculum*, 69 (1994), pp. 323–43.

Short, Ian, 'Patrons and Polyglots: French Literature in Twelfth-Century England', *Anglo-Norman Studies, XIV, Proceedings of the Battle Conference 1991*, ed. Marjorie Chibnall (Woodbridge, 1992), pp. 229–49.

Smalley, Beryl, 'Gilbert the Universal', *Recherches de Théologie Ancienne et Médiévale*, VII (1935), pp. 254–7.

Southern, R.W., *Saint Anselm and his Biographer* (Cambridge, 1966).

Southern, R.W., *Saint Anselm: a Portrait in a Landscape* (Cambridge, 1990).

Southern, R.W., 'St Anselm and Gilbert Crispin, Abbot of Westminster', *Medieval and Renaissance Studies*, ed. R.W. Hunt and R. Klibansky, III (1954), pp. 78–115.

Spiegel, Gabrielle M., 'The Cult of St Denis and Capetian Kingship', *Journal of Medieval History* 1 (1975), pp. 43–69.

Squire, A., 'Aelred and King David', *Collectanea Sacri Ordinis Cisterciensium Reformatorum*, XXII (1960), pp. 356–77.

Stacey, R.C., *Politics, Policy and Finance under Henry III 1216–1245* (Oxford, 1987).

Stenton, Doris Mary, *English Justice between the Conquest and the Great Charter 1066–1215* (London, 1965).

Stenton, F.M. *The First Century of English Feudalism 1066–1166*, 2nd edn (Oxford, 1961).

Sullivan, David, *The Westminster Corridor* (London, 1994).

Taylor, Pamela, 'The Endowment and Military Obligations of the See of London: a Reassessment of Three Sources', *Anglo-Norman Studies, XIV. Proceedings of the Battle Conference 1991*, ed. Marjorie Chibnall (Woodbridge, 1992), pp. 287–312.

Thompson, Kathleen, 'Robert of Bellême Reconsidered', *Anglo-Norman Studies, XIII, Proceedings of the Battle Conference 1990*, ed. Marjorie Chibnall (Woodbridge, 1991), pp. 263–86.

Thompson, Sally, *Women Religious: the Founding of English Nunneries after the Norman Conquest* (Oxford, 1991).

Thomson, R., 'Twelfth-Century Documents from Bury St Edmunds Abbey', *English Historical Review*, 92 (1977), pp. 806–19.

Turner, R.V., *The English Judiciary in the Age of Glanvill and Bracton c.1176–1239* (Cambridge, 1985).

Turner, R.V., *The King and his Courts: the Roll of John and Henry III in the Administration of Justice 1199–1240* (Ithaca, N.Y., 1968).

Van Engen, John, 'The "Crisis of Cenobitism" Reconsidered: Benedictine Monasticism in the Years 1050–1150', *Speculum*, 61 (1986), pp. 269–304.

Wander, S.H., 'The Westminster Abbey Sanctuary Pavement', *Traditio*, 34 (1978), pp. 137–56.

Warren, W.L., *Henry II* (London, 1973).

West, F., *The Justiciarship in England 1066–1232* (Cambridge, 1966).

White, Graham, 'Continuity in Government', in E. King, ed., *The Anarchy of Stephen's Reign* (Oxford, 1994), pp. 117–143.

Widmore, R., *A History of the Church of St Peter of Westminster* (London, 1751).

Williams, Ann, 'Some Notes and Considerations on Problems Connected with the English Royal Succession 866–1066', in *Proceedings of the Battle Conference on Anglo-Norman Studies, 1, 1978*, ed. R. Allen Brown (Woodbridge, 1979), pp. 144–67.

Wogan-Brown, Jocelin, '"Clerc u lai muine u dame": Women and Anglo-Norman Hagiography in the Twelfth and Thirteenth Centuries', in Carol M. Meale, ed., *Women and Literature in Britain 1150–1500* (Cambridge, 1993), pp. 62–83.

Wormald, F., 'Paintings in Westminster Abbey and Contemporary Paintings', *Proceedings of the British Academy*, XXXV (1949), pp. 161–76.

Wormald, P., 'Oswaldslow: an "immunity"?', in N. Brooks and C. Cubitt, eds, *St Oswald of Worcester, Life and influence* (London, 1996), pp. 117–28.

Yorke, Barbara, 'The Kingdom of the East Saxons', *Anglo-Saxon England*, 14 (1985), pp. 1–36.

Zarnecki, G., Holt, J., and Holland, T., eds, *English Romanesque Art 1066–1200* (London, 1984).

Index